Heritage Signature® Auction
U.S. Coins
March 28-31, 2009 | Baltimore, Maryland

D1621744

Featuring: THE BELLE COLLECTION OF CARSON CITY COINAGE • THE BURNING TREE COLLECTION, PART ONE
THE MARIO ELLER COLLECTION, PART FOUR • THE ED LEPORDO COLLECTION, PART TWO • THE PASADENA COLLECTION, PART TWO

LOT VIEWING
Baltimore Convention Center
One West Pratt Street • Halls A, B, C; Booth 1758
Baltimore, Maryland 21201

Thursday, March 26 • 10:00 AM - 7:00 PM ET
Friday, March 27 • 9:00 AM - 7:00 PM ET
Saturday, March 28 • 9:00 AM - 5:00 PM ET

*View Lots and Video Lot Descriptions
Online at HA.com/Coins*

LIVE FLOOR BIDDING
Bid in person during the floor sessions.

LIVE TELEPHONE BIDDING *(floor sessions only)*
Phone bidding must be arranged on or before
Friday, March 27, 2009, by 12:00 PM CT.
Client Service: 866-835-3243.

HERITAGE Live!™ BIDDING
Bid live from your location, anywhere in the world,
during the Auction using our HERITAGE Live!™ program
at HA.com/Live

INTERNET BIDDING
Internet absentee bidding ends at 10:00 PM CT
the evening before each session. HA.com/Coins

FAX BIDDING
Fax bids must be received on or before Friday,
March 27, 2009, by 12:00 PM CT. Fax: 214-409-1425

MAIL BIDDING
Mail bids must be received on or before
Friday, March 27, 2009.

*Please see "Choose Your Bidding Method" in the back of this
catalog for specific details about each of these bidding methods.*

Participating auctioneer: Cindy Isennock of Isennock Auctions.

LIVE AUCTION
SIGNATURE® FLOOR SESSIONS 1-4
(Floor, Telephone, HERITAGE Live!,™ Internet, Fax, and Mail)
Sheraton Inner Harbor
300 South Charles Street; Severn 1
Baltimore, Maryland 21201

SESSION 1
Saturday, March 28, 2009 • 6:00 PM ET • Lots 1–1206

SESSION 2
Sunday, March 29, 2009 • 9:00 AM ET • Lots 1207–1888

SESSION 3
Sunday, March 29, 2009 • 1:30 PM ET • Lots 1889–2462

SESSION 4
Sunday, March 29, 2009 • 5:00 PM ET • Lots 2463–3494

NON FLOOR/NON PHONE BIDDING SESSIONS 5-6
(HERITAGE Live!,™ Internet, Fax, and Mail only)

SESSION 5 *See separate catalog*
Monday, March 30, 2009 • 9:00 AM CT • Lots 7001-9140

SESSION 6 *See separate catalog*
Tuesday, March 31, 2009 • 9:00 AM CT • Lots 9141-11476

AUCTION RESULTS
Immediately available at HA.com/Coins

LOT SETTLEMENT AND PICK-UP
Available weekdays 9:00 AM – 5:00 PM CT
by appointment only.

Extended Payment Terms available. See details in the back of this catalog.

*Lots are sold at an approximate rate of 200 lots per hour, but it
is not uncommon to sell 150 lots or 300 lots in any given hour.*

This auction is subject to a 15% Buyer's Premium.

THIS AUCTION IS PRESENTED AND CATALOGED BY HERITAGE NUMISMATIC AUCTIONS, INC.

Heritage World Headquarters

HERITAGE HA.com
Auction Galleries

Home Office • 3500 Maple Avenue, 17th Floor • Dallas, Texas 75219
Design District Annex • 1518 Slocum Street • Dallas, Texas 75207
214.528.3500 | 800.872.6467 | 214.409.1425 (fax)
Direct Client Service Line: Toll Free 1.866.835.3243 • Email: Bid@HA.com

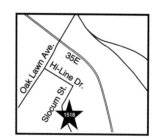

Heritage Design District Annex

16522

U.S. Coin Specialists

Steve Ivy
CEO
Co-Chairman
of the Board

Todd Imhof
Vice President

Leo Frese
Vice President

Jim Halperin
Co-Chairman
of the Board

David Mayfield
Vice President,
Numismatics

Jim Stoutjesdyk
Vice President,
Numismatics

Greg Rohan
President

Paul Minshull
Chief Operating
Officer

3500 Maple Avenue, 17th Floor • Dallas, Texas 75219
Phone 214-528-3500 • 800-872-6467
HA.com/Coins

DIRECTORY FOR DEPARTMENT SPECIALISTS AND SERVICES

COINS & CURRENCY

COINS – UNITED STATES
HA.com/Coins
U.S. Coins

Leo Frese, Ext. 1294
Leo@HA.com
Sam Foose, Ext. 1227
SamF@HA.com
Jim Jelinski, Ext. 1257
JimJ@HA.com
Katherine Kurachek, Ext. 1389
KKurachek@HA.com
David Lisot, Ext. 1303
DavidL@HA.com
Bob Marino, Ext. 1374
BobMarino@HA.com
David Mayfield, Ext. 1277
DavidM@HA.com
Mike Sadler, Ext. 1332
MikeS@HA.com
Doug Nyholm, Ext. 1598
DNyholm@HA.com
Dave Lindvall, Ext. 1231
David@HA.com
Jason Friedman, Ext. 1582
JasonF@HA.com
Darrill Batté, Ext. 1715
DarrillB@HA.com
Chris Dykstra, Ext. 1380
ChrisD@HA.com
Shaunda Fry, Ext. 1159
ShaundaF@HA.com
Dennis Nowicki, Ext. 1121
DennisN@HA.com

COINS – WORLD
HA.com/WorldCoins
World Coins & Currencies

Warren Tucker, Ext. 1287
WTucker@HA.com
Scott Cordry, Ext. 1369
ScottC@HA.com
Cristiano Bierrenbach, Ext. 1661
CrisB@HA.com

CURRENCY
HA.com/Currency
Paper Money

Len Glazer, Ext. 1390
Len@HA.com
Allen Mincho, Ext. 1327
Allen@HA.com
Dustin Johnston, Ext. 1302
Dustin@HA.com
Jim Fitzgerald, Ext. 1348
JimF@HA.com
Michael Moczalla, Ext. 1481
MichaelM@HA.com

UNITED STATES COINS PRIVATE TREATY SALES
HA.com/Coins

Todd Imhof, Ext. 1313
Todd@HA.com

UNITED STATES COINS PURCHASED
HA.com/Coins

Jim Stoutjesdyk, Ext. 1310
JimS@HA.com

COMICS
HA.com/Comics
Comics, Original Comic Art and Related Memorabilia

Ed Jaster, Ext. 1288
EdJ@HA.com
Lon Allen, Ext. 1261
LonA@HA.com
Barry Sandoval, Ext. 1377
BarryS@HA.com

FINE ART

ART OF THE AMERICAS
HA.com/FineArt

Michael Duty, Ext. 1712
MichaelD@HA.com
Atlee Phillips, Ext. 1786
AtleeP@HA.com
Courtney Case, Ext. 1293
CourtneyC@HA.com

DECORATIVE ARTS
HA.com/FineArt

Meredith Meuwly, Ext. 1631
MeredithM@HA.com

EUROPEAN & RUSSIAN ART
HA.com/FineArt

Edmund P. Pillsbury, Ph.D., Ext. 1533
EPP@HA.com
Courtney Case, Ext. 1293
CourtneyC@HA.com
Douglass Brown, Ext. 1165
DouglassB@HA.com

ILLUSTRATION ART
HA.com/Illustration

Ed Jaster, Ext. 1288
EdJ@HA.com
Todd Hignite, Ext. 1790
ToddH@HA.com

PHOTOGRAPHY
HA.com/ArtPhotography

Lorraine Anne Davis, Ext. 1714
LorraineD@HA.com

SILVER & VERTU
HA.com/FineArt

Tim Rigdon, Ext. 1119
TimR@HA.com

20TH-CENTURY ART & DESIGN
HA.com/FineArt

Christina Japp, Ext. 1247
CJapp@HA.com
Courtney Case, Ext. 1293
CourtneyC@HA.com

HISTORICAL

AMERICAN INDIAN ART
HA.com/AmericanIndian

Delia Sullivan, Ext. 1343
DeliaS@HA.com

AMERICANA & POLITICAL
HA.com/Historical
Historical & Pop Culture Americana, Vintage Toys, Presidential & Political Memorabilia, Buttons & Medals, Books & Manuscripts, First Editions and Collectible Autographs

Tom Slater, Ext. 1441
TomS@HA.com
Marsha Dixey, Ext. 1455
MarshaD@HA.com
John Hickey, Ext. 1264
JohnH@HA.com
Michael Riley, Ext. 1467
MichaelR@HA.com

CIVIL WAR AND ARMS & MILITARIA
HA.com/CivilWar
Artifacts, Documents and Memorabilia Related to the American Civil War

Dennis Lowe, Ext. 1182
DennisL@HA.com

RARE BOOKS
HA.com/Books

James Gannon, Ext. 1609
JamesG@HA.com

HISTORICAL MANUSCRIPTS
HA.com/Manuscripts

Sandra Palomino, Ext. 1107
SandraP@HA.com

TEXANA
HA.com/Historical

Sandra Palomino, Ext. 1107
SandraP@HA.com

JEWELRY & TIMEPIECES

JEWELRY
HA.com/Jewelry

Jill Burgum, Ext. 1697
JillB@HA.com

TIMEPIECES
HA.com/Timepieces

Jim Wolf, Ext. 1659
JWolf@HA.com

MOVIE POSTERS
HA.com/MoviePosters
Posters, Lobby Cards, and Hollywood Ephemera

Grey Smith, Ext. 1367
GreySm@HA.com
Bruce Carteron, Ext. 1551
BruceC@HA.com
Isaiah Evans, Ext. 1201
IsaiahE@HA.com

MUSIC & ENTERTAINMENT MEMORABILIA
HA.com/Entertainment
Autographs, Stage-worn Costumes, Film and Television-used Props and Wardrobe, Celebrity-played Instruments, Pop-Culture Memorabilia, Rare Records and Acetates

Doug Norwine, Ext. 1452
DougN@HA.com
John Hickey, Ext. 1264
JohnH@HA.com
Garry Shrum, Ext. 1585
GarryS@HA.com
Jim Steele, Ext. 1328
JimSt@HA.com

NATURAL HISTORY
HA.com/NaturalHistory

David Herskowitz, Ext. 1610
DavidH@HA.com

SPORTS COLLECTIBLES
HA.com/Sports
Sports Cards, Artifacts, Game-Used Jerseys & Equipment

Chris Ivy, Ext. 1319
CIvy@HA.com
Stephen Carlisle, Ext. 1292
StephenC@HA.com
Mike Gutierrez, Ext. 1183
MikeG@HA.com
Lee Iskowitz, Ext. 1601
LeeI@HA.com
Mark Jordan, Ext. 1187
MarkJ@HA.com
Jonathan Scheier, Ext. 1314
JonathanS@HA.com
Peter Calderon, Ext. 1789
PeterC@HA.com

STAMPS
HA.com/Stamps

Steven Crippe, Ext. 1777
StevenC@HA.com
Brian Degen, Ext. 1767
BrianD@HA.com

CORPORATE & INSTITUTIONAL COLLECTIONS/VENTURES
Jared Green, Ext. 1279
Jared@HA.com

AUCTION OPERATIONS
Norma Gonzalez, Ext. 1242
V.P. Auction Operations
Norma@HA.com

CREDIT DEPARTMENT
Marti Korver, Ext. 1248
Marti@HA.com
Eric Thomas, Ext. 1241
EricT@HA.com

MARKETING
Debbie Rexing, Ext. 1356
DebbieR@HA.com

MEDIA & PUBLIC RELATIONS
Kelley Norwine, Ext. 1583
KelleyN@HA.com

CORPORATE OFFICERS
R. Steven Ivy, Co-Chairman
James L. Halperin, Co-Chairman
Gregory J. Rohan, President
Paul Minshull, Chief Operating Officer
Todd Imhof, Executive Vice President
Leo Frese, Executive Vice President

WIRING INSTRUCTIONS
Bank Information:
JP Morgan Chase Bank, N.A.
270 Park Avenue, New York, NY 10017
Account Name:
Heritage Numismatic Auctions
Master Account
ABA Number: 021000021
Account Number: 1884827674
Swift Code: CHASUS33

Dear Bidder,

On behalf of more than 260 consignors who have entrusted their numismatic treasures to Heritage's Baltimore Signature® auction, we welcome you to this catalog and auction. For your bidding pleasure, you have thousands of high-quality rare coins from which to choose, including hundreds and hundreds of Registry-level rarities. We are proud to be such an important part of our consignors' collecting activities, including the dispersal of these wonderful coins to thousands of new bidders and collectors. I invite you to read about our fascinating anchor consignors and their stories – those both familiar and unfamiliar. In spite of the love of history that we share, there are as many differences in collecting goals and strategies as there are collectors!

The Belle Collection of Carson City Coinage

The Belle Collection was started some eight years ago by a doctor who was looking for enjoyment, relaxation from the pressures of his medical practice, preservation of capital, and a diversified investment. Having collected coins modestly in his childhood, he easily recalled the early pleasures pursuing these fascinating pieces of history. Now a more sophisticated investor, he quickly realized that for maximum knowledge and enjoyment he needed to focus on one area in numismatics. Influenced by his history readings and early dreams of owning great rarities, he chose the exciting coinage of the Carson City Mint.

He then further focused on higher-end examples, following a very logical strategy – seeking one of the top fifty coins (in that grade and higher) in the combined (NGC and PCGS) populations. Since resubmissions could never be excluded, he assumed for the most part that he was often buying one of the top two-dozen finest-known examples. He couldn't always adhere to this approach, as exceptional eye-appealing coins made a habit of appearing, and some population profiles didn't allow for a strict application. Still, of the 111 coins he began to pursue, he was able to locate and procure more than half over the years, and we are proud to offer them here. Along the way, he received coins and advice for many specialists in the series, "a neat mix of experts and friends." Additional selections from other series in the Belle Collection will be offered in our Central States auction. We invite you to look at the Video Lot Descriptions at HA.com for his 1876-CC twenty cent piece and his 1870-CC double eagle offered in Baltimore.

The Burning Tree Collection, Part One

The collector behind the Burning Tree Collection started collecting wheat cents from circulation, as have many young collectors. He made his first purchases of 'rare' coins from Jim Halperin's New England Rare Coin Gallery in 1972, when, as a recent college graduate, the collecting bug resurfaced and a few dollars were available to invest. Those first two rarities were submitted for certification shortly after PCGS was formed, and those same coins – in their original holders – will be offered in our upcoming auctions: the 1883 Trade dollar, graded PR63 by PCGS, will be sold in this Baltimore auction, and the second, an 1800 half cent, PCGS MS62 RB will be offered in Central States.

Trade dollars became more of a fascination, and culminated in the assembly of a set of Mint State and proof examples, including many varieties. Over the years, many coins were added to the collection, most of them purchased through Heritage, which was the single largest source of quality coins in the collection. Included in the collection are the beginning efforts in a set of Mint State Barber dimes, an assortment of wonderfully toned coins, especially proof Seated and Barber half dollars, a number of which were purchased from the Benson Collection. Another series of interest was Mint State and proof Indian cents. The consignor's love of coins has not departed, and he anticipates buying additional items in the future. He also enjoyed spending time with like-minded people, enjoying the camaraderie, and making lasting friendships.

The Mario Eller Collection, Part Four

Heritage presented Part Three of the Mario Eller Collection in our May 2008 Long Signature® Auction, Part Two in FUN 2008, and Part One in September 2007 Long Beach. Mr. Eller started seriously collecting rare coins about a decade ago – although he had been fascinated by them since childhood. A change in his circumstances gave him the freedom to pursue what he had desired when young, but simply couldn't afford then. This belated opportunity resulted in enthusiastic buying across many denominations, and his completion of several significant series. After ten-plus years of pure fun, Mr. Eller decided the time was right to sell, and he sincerely wishes that the new owners of his coins enjoy the chase and pride of ownership as much as he has.

The Ed Lepordo Collection, Part Two

Heritage offered Part One of the Ed Lepordo Collection in our February 2009 Long Beach Signature® Auction. Ed Lepordo started collecting coins when he was nine, but unlike most youthful collectors, he never stopped – there was no break in high school or college resulting from the discovery of girls, cars, or rock and roll! He immediately loved collecting coins, and always has, and in 1977, he began even more serious numismatic pursuits. The results were most impressive, with a complete type set (1793 to date), an impressive collection of large cents (1834-1857, with varieties, and many among the finest known), Mercury dimes (mostly FB), and Franklin halves (all FBL). Despite his wide-ranging collecting interests, many of his collections arose from expanding narrower collecting goals; his interest in all of the varieties of 1839 large cents (his 1839/6 is the 4th finest known) expanded to other years, and his collection of 1796 coinage has been completed and upgraded. He has listed around two dozen NGC Registry sets, and is still collecting – and he intends to do so at least until his retirement, and perhaps beyond. A history buff his entire life, Mr. Lepordo especially enjoyed learning about the changes in coin design, technology, and politics over the sweep of American coinage. He especially enjoys error coins and overdates. His wish for a new generation of collectors would be to interest youth in real pieces of history instead of computerized fantasies. We are pleased to offer Part Two of this fascinating collection.

The Pasadena Collection, Part Two

The consignor of the Pasadena Collection has been collecting off and on for more than half a century (since the age of ten), but this collection really is the culmination of four generations of family interest. His start in rare coins was equal parts timing (the interest created when the Lincoln Memorial was placed on the cent reverse) and magic (he inherited a box of old and curious coins set aside by his great-grandfather and grandfather). His great-grandfather had emigrated from Sweden in 1880, and through hard work, eventually became the sole owner of the general store in Houtzdale, a small coal burg in Pennsylvania, where he first found employment; the Scandinavian Store and additional local businesses would stay in the family until 1941. The spool box became a repository for old and unusual coins received from customers – an accumulation including early half cents, assorted Bust half dollars, some Uncirculated 20th century coins, and a 1774 British ha'penny.

The consignor's father shared the box's contents and began to take him to meetings of the Lancaster Coin Club as his interest deepened. Plus, as he relates: "My paternal grandfather was a director of the First National Bank of Houtzdale, and saved some large size currency, including a Series 1902 National Bank Note bearing the signature of my maternal grandfather (the bank's cashier). My mother was born in the apartment on the second floor of the bank!" As his interest grew, he found other collectors among family and friends, and formed a coin club at school. An uncle, who had a substantial collection of his own, contributed a partially-filled Whitman Lincoln cent album, and an aunt gave him a proof set. "My pediatrician, a close friend of my parents, gave me a well-worn 1909-S VDB!"

Over time, the consignor attended UCLA and set up a successful legal practice in Southern California. In 1988, after his uncle passed away, the consignor was able to purchase additional family items, which immediately revived his interest in coins and currency. "Over the past two decades, my passion for collecting has blossomed to become an irresistible challenge. My book shelves are filled with coin references. An attorney friend and I attend every Long Beach show and purchase new treasures, faithfully exceeding our budgets. Fortunately I know my passion is also a wonderful long-term investment."

The consignor started the process of auctioning his coins now for several reasons: "The accumulation has become a challenge to store. Many series have been completed, and upgrading would be prohibitively expensive. My wife tolerates my collecting, but such a large collection would be a burden to my family. It is time to let other enthusiastic collectors enjoy these little works of art. Still, I plan to continue collecting." Not coincidentally, he is also keeping the old box of curious coins from the Scandinavian Store: "What my storekeeper great-grandfather started to accumulate in the 1880s will stay in the family as an heirloom for future generations; perhaps one of those folks may someday become a collector!"

The consignor especially enjoyed working with Bob Merrill, and notes that "Having the leading numismatic auction firm in the country team with me to sell the coins has provided me with at least as much enjoyment as I had in building the collection in the first place." Part One of the Pasadena Collection sold in our February 2009 Long Beach Signature® Auction, and we are pleased to offer additional coins in Baltimore.

Heritage is offering an incredible array of important coins at Baltimore, so you will want to start your research today in our free Permanent Auction Archives at HA.com. Focusing on your favorites may be difficult when so many neat coins are being offered, but our interactive systems maximize your chances of buying and adding to your important collection. In the Archives are amazing images, lot descriptions, and prices realized data from more than 1.4 million numismatic items sold over more than a decade of auctions! Using our free tools, you can be as fully informed as the most active dealer or other collector.

We look forward to your bids, and wish you much bidding success. We expect between one thousand and two thousand bidders to be successful in Baltimore, whether they are participating via our Interactive Internet™ or our HERITAGE Live! bidding systems. Incidentally, you will love HERITAGE Live! ™ the first time you try it – and you will be amazed at just how easy it is to bid at the floor session via the Internet. It may even be better than being there! And if you can join us, please stop by and say "Hello" at the Heritage tables.

Sincerely,

Greg Rohan
President

Denomination Index

SESSION ONE

Floor, Telephone, Heritage Live!™, Internet, Fax, and Mail Signature® Auction #1126
Saturday, March 28, 2009, 6:00 PM ET, Lots 1-1206
Baltimore, Maryland

A 15% Buyer's Premium ($9 minimum) Will Be Added To All Lots

Visit HA.com to view full-color images and bid.

COLONIALS

1 **1652 Pine Tree Shilling, Large Planchet—Holed, Scratched—NCS. Genuine.** Crosby 12-I, Noe-1, R.2. This authentic Pine Tree shilling is not assigned a details grade, though the details remain bold. From the reverse, the hole runs through the O in DOM, and light scratches appear in the silver-gray and slate field to the right of the tree. Listed on page 37 of the 2009 *Guide Book*.(#23)

2 **1652 Pine Tree Shilling, Small Planchet VG10 PCGS.** Crosby 20-L, Noe-19, R.5. 65.3 grains. A vertical bend is evident on the obverse of this medium gray shilling. the surfaces are pleasing, and all of the legends are complete. Slight surface irregularity is noted on the reverse. Listed on page 37 of the 2009 *Guide Book*. (#24)

1652 Pine Tree Shilling, Noe-29
Small Planchet, VF Details

3 **1652 Pine Tree Shilling, Small Planchet—Environmental Damage—NCS. VF Details.** Crosby 14-R, Noe-29, R.3. 69.1 grains. This is the so-called Heavy R variety. The planchet is noticeably clipped on the lower obverse near 6 o'clock. A typically wavy example with an accumulation of dark verdigris on both sides, which NCS refers to as environmental damage. Listed on page 37 of the 2009 *Guide Book*.(#24)

Desirable 1652 Pine Tree Shilling, Small Planchet
Crosby 22-L, Noe-17, VF25

4 **1652 Pine Tree Shilling, Small Planchet VF25 PCGS.** Crosby 22-L, Noe-17, R.3. 69.0 grains. This example is softly struck on the tops of the pine tree, on the E in MASATHVSETS; and on 1652 XII and W on the reverse. The flan is typically wavy, and there is normal wear for the grade, along with a few random pinscratches. A nice VF example of this scarce type. Listed on page 37 of the 2009 *Guide Book*.(#24)

Rare Saint Patrick Farthing, VF30, Breen-216

5 **(1670-75) St. Patrick Farthing VF30 PCGS. CAC.** Breen-216. A rarely encountered variety that features a large 8 below the king. Generally chestnut-brown in color, with a porous, somewhat darker purple-rose and greenish area on the upper obverse. The reverse is quite sharp for the grade, especially on the church building and the peripheral legends. Listed on page 39 of the 2009 *Guide Book*. (#42)

Very Rare VF Details
LON DON Elephant Token

6 **(1694) London Elephant Token, LON DON—Damaged—NCS. VF Details.** Breen-190, Hodder 2-D. Breen's "Godless" London variety, which he listed as "very rare." Hodder 2-B is the usually encountered Elephant token. A golden-brown piece with pleasing definition on the pachyderm. DON is absent, perhaps due to failure of the reverse die. Each side has a few of what appear to be toned-over planchet flaws, but the two on the shield accompany bends in the flan. Listed on page 44 of the 2009 *Guide Book*.(#67)

7 **1722 Rosa Americana Penny, UTILE AU50 PCGS.** Rosette after 1722, Breen-115. Light but distinct wear crosses the high points. Luminous teak-brown surfaces show splashes of cinnamon. Listed on page 40 of the 2009 *Guide Book*.(#113)

1722 Rosa Americana Penny, UTILE
MS62 Brown, Breen-115, Ex: Ford

8   **1722 Rosa Americana Penny, UTILE MS62 Brown PCGS.**
Ex: Ford. Breen-115. Rosette before, but not after, ROSA
AMERICANA. Short ribbons. The fields are toned mahogany-
brown, although brassy olive-gold fills the legends and recessed
devices. Well struck and void of distractions. Listed on page 40 of
the 2009 *Guide Book*. Population: 5 in 62, 5 finer (2/09).
*Ex: Henry Chapman, 6/1911, lot 527; F.C.C. Boyd; John J. Ford, Jr.
Collection, Part IX (Stack's, 5/2005), lot 114.*(#113)

Famous 'Rocks' 1722 Hibernia Halfpenny
Martin 1.1-A.1, VG Details

9   **1722 Hibernia Pattern Halfpenny, Rocks—Corroded—NCS.
VG Details.** Breen-143, Martin 1.1-A.1, High R.7. A famous and
desirable rarity within the Hibernia series. This dark circulated
example has aqua and red corrosion on the obverse field and in front
of the face on the reverse. A few wispy old pinscratches are found
on the reverse. Moderately off center toward 7 o'clock. Except for
Ford VII:19, the Rocks halfpenny is always found in circulated
grades, which implies that it might not have been a pattern despite
its alternative design. Listed on page 42 of the 2009 *Guide Book*.
*Ex: Oak Collection of American Colonial Coinage (Heritage, 9/2005),
lot 41, which realized $5,175.*(#164)

10   **1723 Hibernia Farthing, DEI GRATIA MS63 Brown PCGS.**
Martin 2.1-Bc.1, R.5. The first G in GEORGIUS always has a
small die break in the middle, and the E in HIBERNIA has the
upper and lower serifs joined to the middle. There is also the usual
die crack through the NIA in HIBERNIA that ends at the 1 in the
date. These die flaws can typically identify this variety. Pleasing
mahogany patina covers each side of the present piece, with a few
patches of darker toning at the perimeter. The strike is sharp, and
there are no marks visible to the unaided eye. A couple of slight
blemishes are noted at the top of the reverse, but they do not affect
the central design elements. Listed on page 42 of the 2009 *Guide
Book*.(#176)

11   **1723 Hibernia Farthing, DEI GRATIA MS64 Brown PCGS.**
Martin 2.1-Bc.4, R.4. The fine details of the portrait's hair are
swirling and delightful. Deep chocolate-brown surfaces are
minimally marked with occasional reddish overtones. Listed on
page 42 of the 2009 *Guide Book*.(#176)

12   **1723 Hibernia Farthing, DEI GRATIA MS64 Brown PCGS.**
Martin 2.1-Bc.4, R.4. Each side is well-defined with glossy surfaces,
teak-brown with elements of violet and blue. Population: 18 in 64
Brown, 0 finer (1/09). Listed on page 42 of the 2009 *Guide Book*.
(#176)

13   **1723 Hibernia Farthing, DEI GRATIA MS64 Brown PCGS.**
Martin 3.3-Bc.2, R.4. D in DEI joined to hair. A beautiful golden-
brown near-Gem that has a crisp strike and a smooth reverse. The
obverse has a couple of slender planchet marks on the neck and
the R in GEORGIUS; these were uneffaced by the strike. Listed
on page 42 of the 2009 *Guide Book*. Population: 18 in 64 Brown, 0
finer (1/09).(#176)

14   **1723 Hibernia Halfpenny MS64 Brown PCGS. CAC.** Martin
4.34-Gb.3, R.2. Beaded Cincture. A distinctive variety with beads
at waist. This smooth chocolate-brown piece shows occasional
glimpses of mahogany. Listed on page 43 of the 2009 *Guide Book*.
(#180)

Eliasberg's MS66 1723 Hibernia Halfpenny

15   **1723 Hibernia Halfpenny MS66 Brown NGC.** Martin 4.14-Fb.2,
R.4. This mildly prooflike Premium Gem is predominantly light
golden-brown, but has glimpses of mint red within the legends.
Beautifully preserved, and the strike is crisp aside from a hint of
incompleteness in the centers. Listed on page 43 of the 2009 *Guide
Book*.
*Ex: Louis E. Eliasberg, Sr. Collection (Bowers and Merena, 5/1996),
lot 38.*(#180)

Excellent 1723 Hibernia Halfpenny
MS65 Red and Brown

16   **1723 Hibernia Halfpenny MS65 Red and Brown NGC.** Martin
8.2-Gb.12, R.5. An impressive Gem that exhibits about 30%
original color on each side. The remaining surfaces are medium
brown with minor splashes of pale blue. An excellent coin for
a type or variety set. Listed on page 43 of the 2009 *Guide Book*.
(#181)

17 1670-A French Colonies 5 Sols—Bent—NCS. XF Details. Deep slate-blue patina with hints of rose and gold. The flan shows two diagonal, roughly parallel bends that have been straightened out. Listed on page 50 of the 2009 *Guide Book*.(#158627)

18 1711-AA French Colonies 30 Deniers AU53 PCGS. Lightly circulated and well struck with modest granularity to the planchet. Silver-gray surfaces show scattered blue and gold elements. The single finest example of the issue known to PCGS (1/09). Listed on page 51 of the 2009 *Guide Book*.(#158606)

19 1762-BB French Colonies Sou Marque MS62 PCGS. Breen-634. Vlack-276. A highly lustrous pearl-gray representative with strong olive accents near the peripheries. Essentially blemish-free on both sides. Struck near the end of the billon sou marqué series, which was produced between 1738 and 1764.(#158657)

20 1773 Virginia Halfpenny, Period MS63 Brown PCGS. CAC. Newman 24-K. Rich, glossy chocolate-brown surfaces show undercurrents of gold. Minimally marked for the grade with strong eye appeal. Listed on page 43 of the 2009 *Guide Book*. (#240)

21 1773 Virginia Halfpenny, Period MS63 Brown PCGS. CAC. Newman 27-J. Seven harp strings. This Select deep brown Virginia halfpenny has pleasing surfaces and a bold strike. Listed on page 43 of the 2009 *Guide Book*.(#240)

22 1773 Virginia Halfpenny, Period MS64 Brown PCGS. Newman 25-M. Rich chocolate-brown surfaces show occasional glimpses of copper-orange. Smooth and elegant eye appeal. Listed on page 43 of the 2009 *Guide Book*.(#240)

23 1773 Virginia Halfpenny, Period MS64 Brown PCGS. Newman 27-J. On the reverse, the A of VIRGINIA is repunched. Smooth chocolate-brown surfaces and pleasing detail combine for strong eye appeal on this Choice example. Listed on page 43 of the 2009 *Guide Book*. PCGS has graded only four finer Brown examples (2/09).(#240)

24 1773 Virginia Halfpenny, Period MS64 Red and Brown PCGS. Newman 24-K. Orange luster illuminates GEORGIVS and the shield, while the open fields are chocolate-brown and the king's cheek is deep brown. A problem-free example of this late pre-Revolutionary War issue. Listed on page 43 of the 2009 *Guide Book*. (#241)

Near-Gem Red 1773 Virginia Halfpenny
With Period, Newman 26-Y

25 1773 Virginia Halfpenny, Period MS64 Red PCGS. CAC. Newman 26-Y. A solid near-Gem Red of this delightfully high-quality and available issue. The lovely orange-red of the fields would do justice to a Lincoln cent from the early 20th century, much less the third quarter of the 18th century. Minor mellowing appears, still within the Red context, only on King George's cheek and the raised design outlines on the reverse. Listed on page 43 of the 2009 *Guide Book*. For all Periods varieties, Population: 29 in 64, 1 finer (2/09).
From The Burning Tree Collection.(#242)

Superb Gem Red and Brown Newman 7-D
No Period 1773 Virginia Halfpenny

26 1773 Virginia Halfpenny, No Period MS67 Red and Brown NGC. Newman 7-D. Orange-red luster dominates the reverse, and fills the obverse legends as well as King George's hair. Steel-blue toning consumes the obverse field and portrait, in addition to the cross section of the shield. This is a remarkable coin with no indication of carbon or contact. The strike is complete, and the eye appeal is exemplary. Anyone in search of the ultimate quality No Period Virginia halfpenny need look no further. Neither NGC nor PCGS has certified any other Virginia halfpenny finer than this piece. Listed on page 43 of the 2009 *Guide Book*.
Ex: Houston Signature (Heritage, 11/2007), lot 60008, which realized $13,800.(#244)

27 1760 Hibernia-Voce Populi Halfpenny AU50 PCGS. Z. 6-C, N.9, R.1. The "Stern Bust" variety, familiar to the dedicated collectors of this Irish import type. A medium brown copper that lacks the small marks often seen on lightly circulated pieces. Listed on page 47 of the 2009 *Guide Book*.(#262)

28 1760 Hibernia-Voce Populi Halfpenny AU53 PCGS. Z. 2-A, N-4, R.1. Briefly circulated with heavy die crumbling at the periphery of the obverse. Pleasing olive-brown patina covers each side, with a few areas of darker color to the left of the bust. The obverse is well-centered but the last few letters of HIBERNIA are partially obscured at the edge. Listed on page 47 of the 2009 *Guide Book*.(#262)

29 1785 Connecticut Copper, Bust Right AU50 NGC. M. 4.4-C, R.3. A mahogany-brown piece with pleasing sharpness on the major devices. Well centered, with all legends intact aside from the very bottom of the date. The strike is soft on the lower left obverse and opposite on the upper right reverse. A minor rim bruise at 4 o'clock is noted, and the seated effigy has a number of small pits. Listed on page 58 of the 2009 *Guide Book*.(#316)

30 **1786 Connecticut Copper, Small Head Right, ETLIB INDE— Bent—NCS. VF Details.** M. 2.1-A, R.3. A nick on the shield of the seated effigy causes a mild bend. The medium brown surfaces are slightly bright, and hints of russet verdigris accompany protected regions. All legends are bold. Listed on page 59 of the 2009 *Guide Book*.(#325)

31 **1786 Connecticut Copper, Hercules Head VF20 PCGS.** M. 5.3-N, R.2. An appealing midrange representative of this widely popularized die pair. Lightly abraded walnut-brown surfaces are surprisingly glossy. Listed on page 59 of the 2009 *Guide Book*. Population: 3 in 20, 7 finer (2/09).(#334)

32 **1786 Connecticut Copper, Hercules Head—Obverse Planchet Flaw—NCS. VF Details.** M. 5.3-N, R.2. A mildly granular walnut-brown example that has an intermittent planchet flaw on the upper right obverse quadrant. The reverse also has a couple of slender but noticeable flaws. A late die state with severe clashes and buckling on the reverse, as made. Listed on page 59 of the 2009 *Guide Book*. (#334)

33 **1787 Connecticut Copper, Mailed Bust Left XF45 PCGS.** M. 14-H, R.3. An attractive piece with rich chocolate-brown coloration and unabraded surfaces. Two or three tiny planchet laminations are noted. Lightly worn on the high points, with soft striking definition on the peripheral design elements. Listed on page 59 of the 2009 *Guide Book*.(#349)

34 **1787 Connecticut Copper, AUCIORI Good 6 NGC.** M. 38-GG, R.4. Only a single obverse die bears the blundered AUCIORI legend. Perhaps the T punch was broken or misplaced when the die was made. This is a well centered light brown example with good eye appeal. The date is bold, as are half of the remaining legends. Listed on page 60 of the 2009 *Guide Book*.(#373)

35 **1787 Connecticut Copper, AUCTOPI—Damaged—NCS. VG Details.** M. 42-kk.2, High R.5. Apparently the "R" punch was unavailable at the time the obverse die was made. A moderately granular tan-brown copper with myriad fine pinscratches on the seated effigy and a couple of scratches near the left obverse border. A cluster of small digs or flaws are noted on the obverse near 6 o'clock. Listed on page 60 of the 2009 *Guide Book*.(#376)

36 **1787 Connecticut Copper, AUCTOPI XF40 NGC.** M. 42-kk.2, High R.5. A rare variant with blundered ET IIB on reverse in addition to the AUCTOPI blunder on the obverse. Deep walnut-brown surfaces are minimally marked with walnut and mahogany accents. Listed on page 60 of the 2009 *Guide Book*.(#376)

AU53 ETLIR 1787 Connecticut Copper
Rare Miller 33.43-hh.2

37 **1787 Connecticut Copper, ETLIR AU53 PCGS.** M. 33.43-hh.2, High R.5. A partly lustrous medium brown example of this much better Miller variety. The usual ETLIR dies are 30-hh.1 or 31.1-gg.1. Due to slight die misalignment, the strike shows some softness near the obverse nose and opposite behind the head on the reverse. Otherwise well struck, and the lightly circulated surfaces are pleasantly free from marks or verdigris. Listed on page 60 of the 2009 *Guide Book*. Listed on page 67 of the 2009 *Guide Book*.(#391)

---

38 **1788 Connecticut Copper, Mailed Bust Right AU50 PCGS.** M. 2.-D, R.1. The usual die state with a prominent obverse cud at 7 o'clock. The centers are slightly soft and show the texture of the planchet, but the remainder of the designs are well brought up. Mildly granular here and there, but void of abrasions. LIB displays a few specks of aqua debris. Listed on page 60 of the 2009 *Guide Book*. Population: 4 in 50, 2 finer (1/09).(#397)

39 **1788 Connecticut Copper, Draped Bust Left XF40 PCGS.** M. 16.1-H, R.4. A close ET LIB helps identify the reverse, while the obverse has several diagnostics including a period after AUCTORI. Lovely medium brown patina drapes the surfaces, which have moderate porosity and a few minor marks. The lower left of the obverse is soft and INDE is partly obscured, but the rest of the details are crisp. Listed on page 60 of the 2009 *Guide Book*. (#409)

40 **1788 Connecticut Copper, Draped Bust Left AU55 PCGS.** M. 16.3-N, R.2. A chestnut-brown state copper with impressive sharpness and unmarked surfaces. Nicely centered with a full date and complete obverse legends. A desirable example. Listed on page 60 of the 2009 *Guide Book*. Population: 4 in 55, 0 finer (1/09). (#409)

41 **1747 Machin's Mills Halfpenny—Corroded—NCS. VF Details.** Vlack 1-47A, R.5, impressively detailed but somewhat granular from environmental exposure, dark lavender-brown toning; and a **1772 GEORGIVS Machin's Mills Halfpenny—Scratched—NCS, VG Details,** Vlack 5-72A, R.6, dark brown toning, legends are sharp and the types are well outlined, both sides are tooled with myriad fine to moderate pinscratches from verdigris removal. Listed on page 64 of the 2009 *Guide Book*.(Total: 2 coins)

42 **1771 Machin's Mills Halfpenny VF30 PCGS.** Vlack 2-71A, R.4. The single finest of five examples certified by PCGS. Most survivors are likely too corroded, cleaned, or damaged to make it into a PCGS holder. This medium brown piece has the usual strike with a softly brought up head of Britannia. Smooth aside from a concealed vertical mark on the shield. Listed on page 64 of the 2009 *Guide Book*.(#448)

43 **1776 Machin's Mills Halfpenny VF25 PCGS.** Vlack 6-76A, R.4. Deep brown overall with occasional hints of cinnamon. This moderately worn example is characteristically weak in the centers. Listed on page 64 of the 2009 *Guide Book*. Population: 5 in 25, 6 finer (1/09).(#460)

44 **1778 Machin's Mills Halfpenny VF35 PCGS.** Vlack 11-78A, R.3. All major device details are clear on this New York imitation British halfpenny. Abrasions are absent across the lightly striated chocolate-brown and deep gray surfaces. Listed on page 64 of the 2009 *Guide Book*. Population: 2 in 35, 4 finer (2/09).(#466)

45 **1786 New Jersey Copper, Narrow Shield AU58 PCGS.** Maris 14-J, R.1. Dusky walnut-brown surfaces show central striking softness, but neither side shows more than a trace of wear. Appealing with few marks. Listed on page 66 of the 2009 *Guide Book*.(#496)

46 **1787 New Jersey Copper, Outlined Shield AU53 PCGS.** Maris 48-g, R.1. A lightly worn example of this relatively available die pair, chocolate-brown with the telltale die crack across the lower part of the shield. Minimally marked and interesting. Listed on page 66 of the 2009 *Guide Book*.(#503)

47 **1787 New Jersey Copper, Camel Head XF40 PCGS.** Maris 56-n, R.1. This distinctive die pair, notable for its oddly shaped horse's head on the obverse, has its own *Guide Book* listing. This lightly worn example is glossy and pleasing with generally teak-brown surfaces. Listed on page 67 of the 2009 *Guide Book*.(#515)

48 **1787 New Jersey Copper, Camel Head XF45 PCGS.** Maris 56-n, R.1. Pleasing semigloss light brown surfaces exhibit well struck devices, save for weakness in the central part of the shield. Devoid of significant marks. Listed on page 67 of the 2009 *Guide Book*. (#515)

49   1786 Vermont Copper, VERMONTENSIUM VF30 NGC.
RR-7, Bressett 5-E, R.3. An unabraded medium brown Republic
copper with pleasing definition on the landscape, including the
face of the rising sun. Slightly misaligned dies cause softness on the
lower left obverse and opposite on the upper left reverse. A small
planchet defect is noted left of the plow. Listed on page 68 of the
2009 *Guide Book*.(#545)

Double Struck 1786 RR-10 Vermont Copper, VF30

50   1786 Vermont Copper, Bust Left VF30 PCGS. RR-10, Bressett
8-G, R.4. Boldly double struck with the second strike about 25%
off-center. In addition to the double strike, this piece is important
for its overall quality. Typical examples of RR-10 and RR-11 are
horrible-looking affairs from extremely poor quality planchets.
In *The Copper Coins of Vermont*, Tony Carlotto writes: "Metal
for the bust lefts probably came from the melting of a previously
made object. I use the word metal because very few of these coins
resemble pure copper." Although the surfaces of this example have
a few planchet fissures and some traces of reddish and greenish
corrosion, the overall appearance is that of a medium brown
example that was probably produced on a copper planchet. Listed
on page 68 of the 2009 *Guide Book*.(#551)

51   1787 Vermont Copper, BRITANNIA AU50 NGC. RR-13,
Bressett 17-V, R.1. Medium brown with glimpses of cherry-wine
on the reverse effigy. The portrait has a wealth of detail, while the
reverse legends are fragmented, as always due to a worn-out reverse
die. A small mint-made clip is noted on the reverse at 3 o'clock.
Listed on page 68 of the 2009 *Guide Book*.(#554)

52   1787 Fugio Cent, STATES UNITED, 4 Cinquefoils, Pointed
Rays AU50 PCGS. CAC. Newman 8-X, R.3. An advanced die
state with a break across the central portion of MIND YOUR
BUSINESS. This walnut-brown Fugio copper is clashed along the
obverse border but is free from any planchet or surface detractions.
Listed on page 83 of the 2009 *Guide Book*.(#883)

53   1787 Fugio Cent, STATES UNITED, 4 Cinquefoils, Pointed
Rays MS61 Brown NGC. Newman 8-X, R.3. From a later die
state with prominent die break across the motto MIND YOUR
BUSINESS. Glossy chocolate-brown surfaces are minimally
marked for the grade. Listed on page 83 of the 2009 *Guide Book*.
(#883)

1787 Fugio Cent, Newman 13-X
MS62 Brown

54   1787 Fugio Cent, STATES UNITED, 4 Cinquefoils, Pointed
Rays MS62 Brown NGC. Newman 13-X, R.2. A pleasing,
lustrous example, struck from a clashed obverse die. The dentils
are incomplete, and SS in BUSINESS is weak. A few tiny planchet
laminations and scattered copper specks are noted on each side, but
there are no distracting marks to be found. Listed on page 83 of the
2009 *Guide Book*.(#883)

AU Club Rays 1787 Fugio Cent
Rounded Ends, Newman 4-E

55   1787 Fugio Cent, Club Rays, Rounded Ends AU50 PCGS. CAC.
Newman 4-E, R.3. This chocolate-brown example is evenly struck
and minimally abraded. Consequential planchet flaws are absent
aside from the right reverse border. One of only two Rounded
Ends varieties. Much scarcer than its Pointed Rays counterpart,
particularly in better grades. Listed on page 84 of the 2009 *Guide
Book*.(#904)

56   1789 Mott Token, Thick Planchet, Plain Edge MS61 Brown
PCGS. Breen-1020. Considerable blue overtones enliven generally
mocha-brown surfaces. Well struck save for the often-weak eagle.
Eye appeal is strong for the grade. Listed on page 70 of the 2009
Guide Book.(#603)

Unique White Metal '1789' Mott Token
Breen-1027, Rulau-NY-613A, Ex: Ford

1794 Talbot, Allum & Lee/John Howard Mule
MS63 Brown, Single Finest at PCGS

60 **1794 Talbot, Allum & Lee/John Howard Mule MS63 Brown PCGS.** Breen-1049. British philanthropist John Howard is featured on the portrait side of this interesting Talbot, Allum & Lee mule. The strike is typically deficient in certain areas of the design, but the surfaces exhibit a pleasing glossy brown sheen that is only interrupted by diagnostic die lumps in the obverse fields. The single finest among 11 pieces certified by PCGS (1/09).(#976)

61 **1783 Washington & Independence Cent, Large Military Bust AU58 PCGS.** Baker-4, R.1. The Large Bust with the W in WASHINGTON close to the truncation. Blue-accented violet-brown surfaces are minimally marked, and the well-defined devices show only a trace of friction. Listed on page 75 of the 2009 *Guide Book*.(#667)

62 **1783 Washington & Independence Cent, Small Military Bust, Engrailed Edge AU55 PCGS.** Baker-4A. The scarcer edge variety of the Small Military Bust type, which is in turn more elusive than the Large Military Bust. A sharp Washington piece with rich golden-brown patina, accompanied in areas by a deeper and finely granular surface. A couple of short, unimportant marks are beneath the ampersand. There are several heavy die cracks along the obverse margin, as produced. Listed on page 75 of the 2009 *Guide Book*.(#673)

63 **1783 Washington & Independence Cent, Draped Bust, No Button, Copper Restrike, Engrailed Edge PR65 Brown PCGS.** Baker-3, the W.S. Lincoln restrike with Large 3 in date. Despite the Brown designation, this well-defined Gem proof shows considerable orange overtones to the otherwise chocolate-brown surfaces. Listed on page 76 of the 2009 *Guide Book*.(#685)

Wonderful PR67 Brown Copper Restrike
1783 Draped Bust Washington Cent
Engrailed Edge, Baker-3

57 **1789 Mott Token, White Metal MS60 PCGS.** Breen-1027, Rulau-NY-613A, R.9. 99.2 gm, 25.3 mm, 1.8 mm thick, per its Ford appearance. This is the pewter, tin, or white metal Mott token listed in the Breen *Complete Encyclopedia*. Presumably unique, although it is possible that one or two others exist in pewter. This example has lustrous light gray surfaces. It is an early die state with no evidence of the often-seen die break from the upper left clock corner. Struck on a slightly undersized flan, from dies a few degrees out of alignment. As a result, the reverse legend is absent between 4 and 7 o'clock. The early die state gives credence to the theory that this is a trial piece. Mildly and evenly granular, as made. One or two moderate obverse marks need no further elaboration. The type is listed on page 70 of the 2009 *Guide Book*.
Ex: Jascha Heifetz Collection (J.C. Morgenthau, 3/1938); F.C.C. Boyd Estate; John Ford, Jr. Collection, Part II (Stack's, 5/2004), lot 326, where it brought $6,500; Palm Beach Signature (Heritage, 3/2005), lot 5017, which realized $12,075.(#608)

58 **(1792-94) Kentucky Token, Engrailed Edge AU58 PCGS.** Breen-1162. Described by Breen as "very rare." An attractive coin for both the type and the grade. The glossy surfaces display only a single mark of note, near the S in STRENGTH. Medium golden-brown toning yields to sea-green and lavender peripheral shades. Population: 7 in 58, 7 finer (2/09). Listed on page 71 of the 2009 *Guide Book*.(#617)

59 **1794 Franklin Press Token MS64 Brown NGC.** A middle die state with a single break on the right side of the press. The obverse is a glossy medium-brown with traces of blue toning through the obverse lettering, while the reverse is more chocolate-brown. Lustrous throughout and sharply struck with smooth surfaces for the grade. Listed on page 72 of the 2009 *Guide Book*.(#630)

64 **1783 Washington & Independence Cent, Draped Bust, Copper Restrike, Engrailed Edge PR67 Brown PCGS.** Baker-3. An early die state that lacks the reverse peripheral crack between 2 and 5 o'clock. The popularity of Washingtonia in the mid-19th century encouraged British entrepreneur W.S. Lincoln to produce his own well-made copy of Baker-2. Precisely struck and virtually flawless. Brick-red with subtle blue-violet and lime-green tints. Listed on page 76 of the 2009 *Guide Book*. Population: 4 in 67 Brown, 0 finer (1/09).(#685)

65   1783 Washington & Independence Cent, Draped Bust, No Button, Silver Restrike PR55 PCGS. Baker-3A. The Silver Restrike with Engrailed Edge. Despite rub on the high points, considerable reflectivity remains in the gold-gray fields. Wispy hairlines are present on each side. Listed on page 76 of the 2009 *Guide Book*. (#688)

Superb Gem Proof Silver Restrike Baker-3A
1783 Washington Draped Bust 'Cent'
Single Finest Certified by PCGS

66   1783 Washington & Independence Cent, Draped Bust, Silver Restrike PR67 PCGS. Baker-3A, Breen-1195. The W.S. Lincoln "No Button, Large 3" restrike in silver, produced during the mid-19th century from copy dies with thick legends. These well-made restrikes are collectible in copper, but examples struck in silver are very scarce. They are often confused with the W.J. Taylor restrikes (Baker-3C) of the same era, identified by slender lettering and a Small 3 in the date.

The present piece is the single finest certified by PCGS by a margin of two grades, as it has been for several years. The pearl-gray devices show moderate contrast with the nearly untoned fields. Fully struck and virtually perfect. Listed on page 76 of the 2009 *Guide Book*. *Ex: Fairchild Family Trust Collection (Ira & Larry Goldberg, 5/2001), lot 74.* (#688)

67   1783 Washington Unity States Cent AU55 NGC. Baker-1. Medium brown with glimpses of lighter tan toning. The peripheral roller marks peculiar to this issue are also seen on the present piece, although mostly confined to the left borders. Listed on page 76 of the 2009 *Guide Book*. (#689)

68   Undated Washington Double Head Cent AU58 PCGS. Baker-6. Well struck with varying shades of dusky brown on each side. A minimally marked piece that shows just a trace of friction on the high points. Listed on page 76 of the 2009 *Guide Book*. (#692)

Rare XF 1792 Washington Cent
Born Virginia, Inscribed Reverse, Baker-60

69   1792 Washington Born Virginia Cent, Inscribed Reverse XF40 PCGS. Baker-60, R.6. Breen-1239. Copper. This rare variety is part of a series of copper Washington pieces struck between 1791 and 1792 by the Westwood Mint in Birmingham, England. The 1791 issues were private patterns for Federal coinage, the latter issues were simply produced for export and circulation in the United States. There are two die varieties of the Born Virginia, Inscribed Reverse. The first (Breen-1238) is extremely rare, and has the 1 in 1789 centered between the TE in UNITED. Breen-1239 is collectible, but rare in all grades, and usually found in VF. This mahogany-brown example is evenly struck and has the expected number of moderate field marks. Listed on page 78 of the 2009 *Guide Book*. Population: 2 in 40, 7 finer (2/09). (#723)

Gem 1795 Washington Grate Halfpenny
Large Buttons, Reeded Edge, Baker-29AA

70   1795 Washington Grate Halfpenny, Large Buttons, Reeded Edge MS65 Brown PCGS. Baker-29AA. This impressive Gem has semiprooflike fields and beautiful tan-brown and gunmetal-blue toning. The strike is exquisite, and even the aid of a loupe locates only trivial imperfections. A middle die state with a small break through the F in FIRM. Listed on page 79 of the 2009 *Guide Book*. Population: 4 in 65 Brown, 0 finer (1/09). (#746)

71   1795 Washington Grate Halfpenny, Small Buttons, Reeded Edge AU58 PCGS. Baker-29D. The scarcer of the two button varieties. A deep brown representative with light wear on Washington's hair and shoulder. A good strike save for the usual blending on the OND in LONDON. Listed on page 79 of the 2009 *Guide Book*. Population: 9 in 58, 5 finer (2/09). (#749)

72   1795 Washington Liberty & Security Halfpenny, BIRMINGHAM Edge AU58 NGC. Baker-31B. Luminous olive-brown surfaces show only slight traces of friction. A minimally marked piece with smooth luster and eye appeal. Listed on page 80 of the 2009 *Guide Book*. (#758)

Uncirculated Washington Liberty & Security Penny
Baker-30, ASYLUM EDGE

73   **Undated Washington Liberty & Security Penny MS60 Brown NGC.** Baker-30, Bust Left, Plain rims. The "Plain Rims" variety lacks the tooth-like texture seen on the scarce Baker-30E. A dark brown example with a crisp strike, a few faint field marks, and a hint of granularity on the reverse field. Listed on page 80 of the 2009 *Guide Book*.(#767)

Important Choice Fine 1795 North Wales Halfpenny
Two Stars on Each Harp Side, Baker-35

74   **1795 Washington North Wales Halfpenny, Two Stars at Each Side of Harp Fine 15 PCGS.** Baker-35, Breen-1298, R.7. This great rarity is not to be confused with the comparatively plentiful Baker-34 variety with one star on each side of the harp. Diagnostic for Baker-35, the obverse has prominent die cracks, and the arc-shaped crack above Washington's head presumably developed into a large die break shortly later and ceased the production of this variety. A dark brown example with softly impressed devices and worn but partly readable peripheral legends. A different Fine 15 PCGS example of this very rare variety appeared in our 2008 Baltimore ANA Signature (lot 1489), and despite some surface pitting, realized $12,650. Listed on page 80 of the 2009 *Guide Book*. Population: 3 in 15, 2 finer (2/09).(#776)

Famous Libertas Americana Medal
Uncirculated, Struck in Bronze, Betts-615

75   **1781 Libertas Americana Medal MS61 Brown NGC.** Betts-615. Bronze. 47.78mm. The most famous of all Betts medals, and perhaps the most historically significant, since the obverse motif inspired the Liberty Cap design of the 1793 half cent. Benjamin Franklin commissioned the Libertas Americana medal while conducting diplomacy in France.

The Paris Mint struck the medal from dies engraved by Alexander Dupre. The obverse features a youthful bust of Liberty facing left. Her hair flows freely. A Liberty cap, supported by a pole, ascends behind her. On the reverse, France as Athena defends the infant America from an aggressive English lion. This leaves America able to vanquish two snakes, which represent the military victories of Saratoga and Yorktown.

The present satiny chocolate-brown representative has an exemplary strike and no indication of wear. Inspection beneath a loupe reveals a few unimportant field marks. The die break on the obverse rim near 7 o'clock is diagnostic for the issue. An important addition to a collection of Early Americana. Listed on page 86 of the 2009 *Guide Book*.

HALF CENTS

Popular 1793 C-1 Half Cent, VF Details

76   1793—Corroded—NCS. VF Details. C-1, B-1, R.3. The dark surfaces of this piece show mostly even corrosion on both sides with only a few local areas of heavier porosity. Quite a bit of detail remains on both sides, and the overall appearance of this example is far finer than the description suggests. EAC 12.(#1000)

Well Defined 1793 Half Cent
C-2, B-2, VF Details

77   1793—Corroded—NCS. VF Details. C-2, B-2, R.3. A defect in the form of a spur is visible on the top left of the 9, each wreath branch has 15 leaves, and a large center dot is between HALF and CENT. Glossy medium brown surfaces exhibit uniform light porosity, but this does not significantly interfere with the design detail. The reverse is rotated about 15 degrees clockwise. EAC 10.
Ex: Steven Ellsworth (2/2003).
From The Pasadena Collection, Part Two.(#1000)

Elusive VF 1793 Half Cent, C-3, B-3

78   1793 VF20 PCGS. C-3, B-3, R.3. Golden-brown with lilac highpoints. The types and legends are clear, although Liberty's curls show expected wear. Reverse rim dings are seen at 5 o'clock and 10:30, and a few abrasions neighbor the B in LIBERTY. Encased in a green label holder. EAC 8.
Ex: Tide Collection (Heritage, 10/2006), lot 35, which realized $9,200.
From The Burning Tree Collection.(#1000)

Bold AU53 1793 Half Cent, C-3, B-3

79   1793 AU53 PCGS. C-3, B-3, R.3. A magnificently detailed chocolate-brown representative of this single year type, struck during the first year of operations at the Philadelphia Mint. There is not even a hint of verdigris, and the planchet is ideal. A few thin marks are noted above the date, on the neck, and near the H in HALF.

The Liberty Cap design is undoubtedly based upon the influential Libertas Americana medal, which features a bust of Liberty facing left. Although Liberty Cap half cents were struck through 1797, and cents of that type were produced through 1796, Liberty faces right on all of those dates except for the 1793 half cent. EAC 30.(#1001)

Choice VF C-4a 1794 Half Cent

80 **1794 VF35 PCGS.** C-4a, B-6b, R.3. Manley Die State 2.0, "rare." An attractive medium brown Choice VF first year Bust Right half cent. One hair-thin mark above the date, but the surfaces are otherwise unusually unabraded. EAC 25.
Ex: Tom Reynolds (6/2001).
From The Pasadena Collection, Part Two.(#1003)

Choice VF 1794 Half Cent, C-2a

81 **1794 VF35 PCGS.** C-2a, B-2b, High R.2. Manley Die State 3.0. The usual Small Letters Edge subvariety is presumed. A medium brown half cent with an unabraded reverse and a few tiny marks on the right obverse. The portrait is well detailed. What appears to be a retained die break on the reverse near 8 o'clock is more likely a rim burr struck into the coin. EAC 20.
From The Burning Tree Collection.(#1003)

82 **1795 Lettered Edge—Damaged—NCS. VF Details.** C-1, B-1, R.2. The Lettered Edge paired with a non-Punctuated Date obverse. This moderately worn chocolate-brown example shows slight rim damage at 3 o'clock, but the surfaces themselves are minimally marked. EAC 15.
Ex: Steve Estes (4/2001).
From The Pasadena Collection, Part Two.(#1009)

Reflective 1795 C-1 Half Cent, MS62 Brown Lettered Edge Type

83 **1795 Lettered Edge MS62 Brown NGC.** C-1, B-1, R.2. Manley Die State 2.0 with a bulge through AME. The second year of the Liberty Cap type, but with an entirely different head than appeared in 1794. The basic design is the same, but engraving differences are enough that the 1795 to 1797 half cents should be considered an entirely new design.

Lustrous mahogany surfaces exhibit the usual scattered marks that often accompany high grade pieces, and they are generally attributed to planchet roughness before the coins were struck. The fields are faintly reflective, and retain remnants of original mint red near some devices. This extraordinary piece will be a nice addition to the cabinet of a specialist or a type collector. EAC 50.(#1009)

84 **1795 Plain Edge, Punctuated Date VF20 PCGS.** C-4, B-4, R.3. The Punctuated Date obverse paired with a reverse that shows a leaf pair below the C in AMERICA. Plain edge. A luminous midrange example with varying degrees of chocolate-brown and teak color. Striking weakness in the centers is typical. A number of faint lines appear on the obverse. EAC 8.(#1012)

Elusive 1795 C-5 Half Cent, AU50

85   **1795 Plain Edge AU50 PCGS.** C-5, B-5, R.3. Our consignor identifies this piece as C-5b but there is no weight on the holder, so we are uncertain of that attribution. If it is a C-5b, it ranks among the top five or six known examples. However, if it is a C-5a, it ranks among the dozen finest pieces. Pleasing golden-olive surfaces are smooth, with only a few trivial lines and abrasions on each side. EAC 35.(#1018)

Choice AU 1795 Half Cent
Plain Edge, Thin Planchet, C-6a

86   **1795 Plain Edge AU55 PCGS.** C-6a, B-6a, R.2. The absence of the weight on the PCGS holder means that the identity of this piece as C-6a is presumed, although C-6b is a remote possibility. There is no sign of a Talbot, Allum & Lee undertype. An unabraded chocolate-brown example that has a sharp strike and excellent eye appeal. Struck a few degrees off center toward 9:30, affecting only the width of the denticles. EAC 45.(#1018)

Desirable 1796 C-2 Half Cent, Good Details
The Eliasberg Specimen

87   **1796 With Pole—Environmental Damage—NCS. Good Details.** C-2, B-2, R.4. The 1796 half cents are the rarities of the denomination, with only about 150 examples of both varieties known to exist. Mint records indicate a total mintage of just 1,390 pieces for the No Pole and With Pole varieties combined, and the current population is consistent with such a production. The dark brown surfaces have minor corrosion, described as "Environmental Damage" by NCS. However, the overall appearance is much finer than one might expect for the grade. A tiny obverse rim nick is evident at 2 o'clock, clearly identifying this piece as the Clapp-Eliasberg specimen. EAC 4.
Ex: Charles Morris Collection (S.H. and H. Chapman, 4/1905); J.M. Clapp; John H. Clapp; Clapp Estate (1942); Louis E. Eliasberg, Sr.; Eliasberg Estate (Bowers and Merena, 5/1996), lot 408. From The Pasadena Collection, Part Two.(#1027)

88   **1800 AU50 PCGS.** C-1, B-1, R.1. Manley Die State 4.0, the usual die state. Lone variety for the year: A second obverse die was made but remained unused until 1802, when it was overdated. A pleasingly detailed coin with elegant eye appeal, medium-brown with delicate lilac and blue overtones. EAC 45.(#1051)

Late State 1800 C-1 Half Cent, MS62 Red and Brown

89   **1800 MS62 Red and Brown PCGS. CAC.** C-1, B-1, R.1. Manley Die State 3.0, with a diagonal die scratch from the left top of F in HALF. Housed in a first generation PCGS holder, this impressive half cent bluish-brown surfaces with quite a bit of mint red remaining, especially on the reverse. Most of the high grade 1800 half cents are in the later die state from a Boston hoard discovered in the middle 1930s, or an earlier hoard found circa 1910. EAC 63. Population: 4 in 62 Red and Brown, 7 finer (2/09). *From The Burning Tree Collection.*(#1052)

Scarce 1802/0 Reverse of 1802 Half Cent C-2, B-2, Fine 15 Details

90   **1802/0 Reverse of 1802—Cleaned—ICG. Fine 15 Details.** C-2, B-2, R.3. The more available of the two varieties this year, though still scarce in an absolute sense. The chocolate-brown surfaces of this piece show light hairlines and are altogether too glossy for the amount of wear present, though the coin remains readily collectible. An abrasion is noted at Liberty's lower cheek. EAC 8. *Ex: Northeast Numismatics (1/2007).*
From The Pasadena Collection, Part Two. (#1057)

Remarkable 1806 C-4 Half Cent, MS63 Red

91   **1806 Large 6, Stems MS63 Red PCGS. CAC.** C-4, B-4, R.1. The plentiful Large 6, Stems variety is the most frequently encountered 1806 half cent, although it is seldom seen with full original red color. This lovely piece has bright orange luster that has only slightly mellowed on the high points, with a few abrasions and spots that limit the grade. It is almost certainly an example from the circa 1906 Chapman hoard. EAC 64. Population: 2 in 63 Red, 0 finer (2/09). *From The Burning Tree Collection.*(#1101)

92   **1810 AU55 ICG.** C-1, B-1, R.2. Elusive as a whole and easily scarce at this level, the 1810 half cent issue has a strong representative in the present piece. Deep chocolate-brown surfaces offer warm luster. Softly struck at the margins as usual, but with few marks. EAC 50. *Ex: Tom Reynolds (2/2006).*
From The Pasadena Collection, Part Two.(#1132)

Sharply Defined 1811 C-2 Half Cent, XF40

93   **1811 XF40 ICG.** C-2, B-2, R.2. Splashes of deep steel toning appear over the medium to dark brown surfaces of this pleasing half cent. As a key date, 1811 half cents are normally encountered in lower grades, and they are seldom seen with the amount of detail and the excellent quality of this example. EAC 30. *Ex: Doug Bird (2/2007).*
From The Pasadena Collection, Part Two. (#1135)

Wonderful 1828 C-3 Half Cent, MS63 Red

94   **1828 13 Stars MS63 Red PCGS.** C-3, B-2, R.1. The highest leaf point is below the right side of the final S, an instant attribution point for this 13 Star variety. Housed in a green label PCGS holder, the present piece retains virtually all of its original orange mint luster with only slight mellowing on the highest design points. Minor spots and abrasions limit the numerical grade. EAC 63. Population: 9 in 63 Red, 7 finer (2/09). *From The Burning Tree Collection.*(#1149)

95   **1849 Large Date MS64 Brown NGC.** C-1, B-1, R.1. Dusky violet-brown on the obverse with slight lightening of color on the reverse. Well-defined and modestly abraded, an attractive near-Gem. EAC 60.(#1218)

96   **1855 MS63 Red PCGS.** C-1, B-1, R.1. The 1855 half cent is the most plentiful Braided Hair issue with original red mint color, yet even this date is becoming more elusive with time. The present examples is housed in a first generation PCGS holder with pinkish-orange mint luster, some minor mellowing, and a few insignificant spots on each side. EAC 63. *From The Burning Tree Collection.*(#1235)

97   **1855 MS64 Red PCGS. CAC.** C-1, B-1, R.1. As an important hoard issue in the Braided Hair half cent series, examples of this date are routinely encountered with most or all of their original orange mint luster intact. The present piece is just such a coin with brilliant pinkish-orange luster, frosty surfaces, and few carbon spots of any significance. EAC 65. PCGS has only certified 24 finer Red examples of this date (2/09). *From The Burning Tree Collection.*(#1235)

PROOF CLASSIC HEAD HALF CENTS

Desirable PR63 Brown 1833 Half Cent, C-1

98   **1833 PR63 Brown PCGS.** C-1, B-1, R.5 as a proof. Walter Breen suggests that the proof half cents of 1833 may have been made as part of the celebration surrounding the new Mint Building of that year. The surfaces of the present coin are generally deep brown, though rotation under a light reveals surprising overtones, including olive, blue, and even fire-orange. EAC PR60. Population: 3 in 63 Brown, 4 finer (1/09).(#1198)

Rich 1834 C-1 Half Cent, PR64 Red and Brown

99   **1834 PR64 Red and Brown PCGS. CAC.** C-1, B-1, R.6 as a proof. The bold strikes on Liberty's curls and the wreath bring out a level of detail rarely seen on business strikes, and the warm copper-gold and mahogany shadings that grace each side greatly enhance the eye appeal. Only a few trivial hairlines are noted in the fields. EAC PR63. Population: 4 in 64 Red and Brown, 4 finer (2/09). (#1202)

PROOF BRAIDED HAIR HALF CENT

Charming B-3 1856 Half Cent, PR64 Brown

100   **1856 PR64 Brown PCGS.** B-3, R.4. The doubling on HALF CENT and the ribbon below is diagnostic for the variety. Excellent strike with rich mocha-brown color and only occasional flecks of deeper toning. The reverse assumes a subtle blue cast. Aside from a handful of hairlines, a carefully preserved piece. EAC PR60. Population: 9 in 64 Brown, 4 finer (2/09).(#1329)

LARGE CENTS

Coveted 1793 Chain Cent VG10 AMERICA, Sheldon-3

101   **1793 Chain AMERICA VG10 PCGS.** S-3, B-4, Low R.3. The most familiar Chain cent variety, quickly identified by the high and leaning R in LIBERTY. This dark brown representative has full legends, although the bottom of the 3 in the date and the ST in STATES are faint. Liberty possesses some hair detail, and the moderately granular surfaces are surprisingly unabraded save for a minor reverse rim nick at 1 o'clock. The majority of surviving Chain cents are well worn and corroded, but this comparatively sharp example clearly demonstrates the type. Certified in a green label holder. EAC 7.(#1341)

102   **1793 Chain Periods—Corroded, Damaged—ANACS. VG Details, Net AG3.** S-4, B-5, R.3. A period is visible after the date. Both sides show extensive corrosion, and the lower left reverse shows a substantial depression. The chain and ONE CENT remain intact and bold, however. EAC 2.(#91341)

Sharp 1793 Chain AMERICA Cent
S-4, VF Details

103 **1793 Chain AMERICA—Damaged—NCS. VF Details.** S-4, High R.3. The Periods variety, so-called because of the periods that follow both the word LIBERTY and the date; the fraction bar is high and relatively distant from the denominator. Medium brown surfaces reveal several shallow digs. Despite this, the design elements exhibit relatively sharp definition. EAC 12. *Ex: River Hollow Coins (10/2000). From The Pasadena Collection, Part Two.*(#91341)

VF Details S-9 1793 Wreath Cent

104 **1793 Wreath Cent, Vine and Bars—Environmental Damage—NCS. VF Details.** S-9, B-12, R.2. Despite the NCS designation, this deep brown example is evenly and only moderately granular. Marks are few and far between, and in the days before third party certification, the present Wreath cent would often have traded hands as problem-free. All legends are sharp, and the portrait has abundant detail. EAC 12.(#1347)

Interesting 1793 Wreath Cent, XF Details
Vine and Bars Edge, S-11a

105 **1793 Wreath Cent, Vine and Bars Edge—Scratched—NCS. XF Details.** S-11a, B-16a, High R.4. Incorrectly described as a Lettered Edge piece on the insert, though the holder permits ready viewing of the Vine and Bars edge. Though the blue-brown fields of this modestly worn Wreath cent shows a number of ancient pinscratches, it is still an appealing example at first glance. EAC 25.(#1347)

Noble XF 1793 Wreath Cent
Vine and Bars Edge, S-6

106 **1793 Wreath Cent, Vine and Bars XF40 PCGS.** S-6, B-7, R.3. A charming chocolate-brown representative with medium brown toning on the highpoints. Unlike so many Wreath cents, this piece is devoid of rim dings, corrosion, or consequential abrasions. A minute tick on the cheek is mentioned solely as an identifier. Moderate laminations (as produced) are located near the T in CENT and within the hair curls. An original and attractive example of a conditionally rare and highly coveted first year, single year type. S-6 is the sole appearance of the obverse die, but the reverse die also coined S-5 and S-7. Encased in a green label holder. EAC 30.(#1347)

Lovely AU 1793 Wreath Cent
S-8, B-13, Vine and Bars Edge

107 1793 Wreath Cent, Vine and Bars AU50 PCGS. S-8, B-13, R.3. The diagonal die crack across the reverse provides immediate variety identification. A splendidly detailed Wreath cent with even deep brown toning. The hair and wreath shimmer with luster. The leaves display light wear but many exhibit central veins. Impressively smooth overall, although minor retained laminations are encountered on the obverse near 4 o'clock, and the reverse has a subtle rim knock at 8 o'clock. An important example that would highlight an early copper type collection. Encapsulated in a green label holder. EAC 40.(#1347)

108 1794 Head of 1794—Environmental Damage—NCS. XF Details. S-46, B-36, R.3. The Crossed E variety, always with a heavy die chip or break crossing the E in CENT. Dark brown surfaces show faint corrosion and minor old scratches that are now mostly blended with the surrounding surface. EAC 20.
Ex: Tom Reynolds (10/2000).
From The Pasadena Collection, Part Two.(#901374)

109 1794 Head of 1794—Corroded—ANACS. AU Details, Net XF40. S-22, B-6, R.1. The "Bent Lock" on the obverse is diagnostic. The teak-brown surfaces of this lightly worn piece are glossy, which mitigates the degree of peripheral corrosion present at the margins. EAC 15.(#901374)

110 1794 Head of 1794—Environmental Damage—NCS. AU Details. S-55, B-47, R.2. For this relatively available issue, a well-defined example with little actual wear. The ebony surfaces show environmental effects that suggest time spent underground. EAC 35.(#901374)

Exquisite Choice AU 1794 Cent
Head of 1794, S-28

111 1794 Head of 1794 AU55 PCGS. S-28, B-10, R.2. This olive-brown Liberty Cap cent is refreshingly devoid of abrasions, and the devices glimmer with luster. The hair shows only moderate wear near the ear. Struck from a prominently clashed reverse die, and encased in a green label holder. EAC 45. Population: 25 in 55, 44 finer (2/09).(#901374)

S-72 1794 Head of 1795 Cent VF30

112 1794 Head of 1795 VF30 PCGS. CAC. S-72, B-65, R.2. A chocolate-brown representative that displays an even strike and has a minimally abraded reverse. A few faint thin marks are noted near the chin and ear. Traces of luster emerge from the hair and wreath. Most 1794 cents exhibit the head of 1794 subtype. S-72 is believed to be the final 1794-dated variety struck, and is the sole *exact* 1794 Head of 1795 variety, distinguished by the lowest curl pointing straight down. EAC 20.(#1365)

Legendary Starred Reverse 1794 Cent
S-48, Collectible Fair 2 Grade

113 1794 Starred Reverse Fair 2 PCGS. S-48, B-38, R.5. Among the most famous of all Sheldon varieties, S-48 is the "Starred Reverse" with 94 tiny stars entered near the dentils. The purpose behind these stars is unknown, and it may just have been "an idle hour at the Mint" one day in 1794. Some 70 examples are known, and the number of early copper collectors seeking specimens is substantially higher. This example has surprising obverse detail, including a clear date and LIBERTY. The reverse is heavily worn, but several stars are plainly visible (with magnification) between 6 and 8 o'clock. EAC 3.(#1374)

114 1795 Plain Edge—Corroded—NCS. VF Details. S-76b, B-4b, R.1. A midrange example of this relatively accessible Plain Edge variety. Both sides of this deep brown piece show moderate corrosion at the margins, with a lesser degree of the same at the centers. EAC 12.(#1380)

115 **1795 Plain Edge VF25 NGC.** S-78, B-8, R.1. An attractive example of this popular *Guide Book* class of large cents. Moderately worn mahogany-brown surfaces show light pink accents near the rims. EAC 15.(#1380)

116 **1795 Plain Edge—Scratched—NCS. XF Details.** S-76b, B-4b, R.1. A thin straight scratch journeys in a diagonal direction from the E in ONE to the F in OF, and a lesser pinscratch is noted near the base of the cap. Otherwise, this medium brown cent is impressive, since traces of luster cling to Liberty's lower hair curls. EAC 30. *Ex: Denis W. Loring; Robinson S. Brown, Jr. (Superior, 9/1986), lot 101; later, Steven Ellsworth (10/2001). From The Pasadena Collection, Part Two.*(#1380)

1795 Plain Edge Cent AU50, S-78

117 **1795 Plain Edge AU50 NGC.** S-78, B-8, R.1. The top of the 5 barely touches the bust, and the full curve of the upper stroke is visible; there are three berries on the right branch and four on the left. This softly struck example has smooth violet-brown and cherrywood surfaces. Some shallow, relatively inoffensive pinscratches are visible in the lower left obverse field. EAC 30.(#1380)

118 **1796 Liberty Cap Fine 12 ANACS.** S-81, B-2, R.3. Deep brown with aqua undertones. CENT is softly impressed, but the other legends are crisp. Granular near the F in OF. The final year of the Liberty Cap motif. EAC 8.(#1392)

119 **1796 Liberty Cap—Corroded—NCS. XF Details.** S-91, B-1, R.3. The obverse has light tan with splashes of deep steel toning, while the reverse is darker and approaches an ebony appearance. Both sides show modest corrosion with a couple of thin reverse scratches. EAC 20. *Ex: Bowers and Merena (3/1998), lot 139; Steven Ellsworth (10/2001). From The Pasadena Collection, Part Two.*(#1392)

120 **1798 Second Hair Style—Corroded—NCS. XF Details.** S-169, B-28, R.3. This medium brown cent is richly detailed and only mildly granular. The right obverse field has a few faint parallel lines. Evenly struck and free from visual impairments. EAC 30. *Ex: Tom Reynolds (6/2001) From The Pasadena Collection, Part Two.*(#1434)

121 **1798 Second Hair Style XF45 NGC.** S-166, B-32, R.1. Die State VI, late dies with a heavy reverse crack and reverse breaks at 10:30 and on the C in CENT. A bold dark brown piece. Only the first A in AMERICA is unevenly struck. A few moderate obverse marks are unworthy of further elaboration. EAC 25.(#1434)

Imposing Choice AU 1798 Cent Second Hair Style, S-187

122 **1798 Second Hair Style AU55 NGC.** S-187, B-40, R.1. Breen Die State IV-V. Arc-shaped die cracks on the right obverse and a rim die break at 3 o'clock promptly identify the Sheldon marriage. This handsome Draped Bust cent has exemplary definition and consistent deep brown patina. The evenly microgranular surfaces are free from abrasions. EAC 40.(#1434)

1799/8 Cent, S-188, VG8

123 **1799/8 VG8 PCGS.** S-188, B-2, R.4. Breen's large cent *Encyclopedia* comments that this is the rarest large cent date and certainly the most famous, repeating the old—and possibly apocryphal—chestnut about Joseph J. Mickley beginning his celebrated career as a numismatist in a vain search for a cent from his birth year. The present piece shows smooth, even wear over dark-brown surfaces that are otherwise untroubled. The closed loop of the last 9 that characterizes the overdate is distinguishable, if not bold, and all major devices and legends are well brought up. A nice opportunity to fill that missing slot in an advanced large cent collection. EAC 6.(#1446)

124 **1800/79 Fine 15 NGC.** S-196, B-10, R.1. Medium brown surfaces exhibit splashes of deeper steel toning on both sides of this overdate cent. The obverse has a few faint, old scratches and other minor imperfections, while the reverse is wholesome. A pleasing example of the commonest 1800 overdate cent variety. EAC 10. *Ex: Tom Reynolds (2/2002). From The Pasadena Collection, Part Two.*(#1455)

125 **1801 100/000—Burnished—NCS. VF Details.** S-221, B-5, R.2. A scarce *Guide Book* variety, one of several blundered fraction issues dated between 1801 and 1803. Deep gray-brown and steel patina has a subdued or matte appearance, rather than the usual glossy surfaces normally associated with burnished large cents. EAC 15. *Ex: Tom Reynolds (10/2001). From The Pasadena Collection, Part Two.*(#1467)

Desirable 1802 S-229 Cent, AU50

126 **1802 AU50 PCGS.** S-229, B-6, Low R.3. Glossy steel-brown surfaces with faint iridescence, and smooth surfaces despite a few small marks on each side. This excellent representative is housed in a green-label PCGS holder, and probably qualifies at the low end of the Condition Census. EAC 40.(#1470)

Worthy Choice AU S-237 1802 Cent

127 **1802 AU55 PCGS.** S-237, B-10, R.2. Numerous slender die cracks throughout the reverse attribute the Sheldon die pairing. Medium brown overall with mahogany patina on the O in ONE and the CE in CENT. Crisply struck save for softness on the O in OF. The obverse field has a few faint marks, while the reverse is splendidly unabraded. EAC 40.(#1470)

AU Blundered Fraction
1/000 S-228 1802 Cent

128 **1802 1/000 AU50 PCGS.** S-228, R.2. The only blundered fraction variety among 1802 die pairings and a popular issue as such. The surfaces are a deep chestnut-brown color with an attractive glossy finish, accompanied by an essentially mark-free appearance. This unusually high grade example appears to have originated from an early state of the dies as there are no singularly mentionable flaws or cracks. About 15 degrees of clockwise die rotation is also noted. While researching the current population data on the S-228 variety, this is the single AU50 thus far certified by PCGS, and just four pieces are graded finer (2/09). EAC 30.
Ex: FUN Signature (Heritage, 1/2005), lot 7038, which realized $3,220.(#1473)

129 **1803 Small Date, Large Fraction—Improperly Cleaned—NCS. XF Details.** S-258, B-17, R.1. An arc-shaped die crack beneath the hair ribbons helps attribute this Draped Bust Sheldon variety. The obverse is pale olive-green, and the reverse is walnut-brown. The obverse field is slightly cloudy, but this bold example will please many collectors. EAC 25.
Ex: Jim Long (3/2002).
From The Pasadena Collection, Part Two.(#1485)

Bold MS63 Brown 1803 Cent
S-258, Large Fraction, Large Date

130 **1803 Small Date, Large Fraction MS63 Brown NGC.** S-258, B-17, R.1. A curved die crack beneath the hair ribbon and a die line above the D in UNITED confirm the Sheldon marriage. This nicely struck chocolate-brown cent has impressive eye appeal when viewed without magnification. A loupe reveals faded thin marks near the nose, the bust tip, and at 9 o'clock on both borders. EAC 60.(#1485)

131 **1803 100/000 VF30 PCGS. CAC.** S-249, B-7, R.2. Medium brown surfaces exhibit hints of orange-brown and faint bluish-green patina. The surfaces are generally hard and smooth, with a few minor abrasions that are consistent with the grade. A tiny obverse rim bruise can be seen at about 8 o'clock. EAC 15.(#911501)

132 **1804—Scratched, Burnished—NCS. Fine 12 Details.** S-266, B-1, R.2. Despite considerable wear, this piece retains moderate detail. Several scratches are noted within the reverse wreath, and the chocolate-brown surfaces have been burnished, giving each side an unnatural gloss. Still, a readily collectible representative of this challenging issue. EAC 6.(#1504)

Pleasing VF Details S-266 1804 Cent

133 **1804—Corroded—NCS. VF Details.** S-266, B-1, R.2. Lone variety for this famous year. The intermediate or "B" die state. An intriguing example that retains moderate detail. Surfaces are generally chocolate-brown with the usual assorted abrasions. Though both sides show appreciable corrosion, most noticeably at the margins, this piece remains pleasing and readily collectible. EAC 12.
Ex: Doug Bird (9/2007).
From The Pasadena Collection, Part Two.(#1504)

Interesting 1804 Restrike Cent
MS66 Red and Brown

134 **1804 Restrike MS66 Red and Brown PCGS.** One of the few out-of-mint restrikes to achieve a measure of collectability in its own right, the "1804" cent is an incongruous fantasy struck from rusted-out dies. This example is well-preserved by the standards of the limited production run, generally bright copper-orange with only occasional glimpses of mahogany and violet. EAC 64.(#45344)

135 **1806—Environmental Damage—NCS. XF Details.** S-270, B-1, R.1. The sole variety for this later Draped Bust date. Moderately granular near the UN in UNITED, but the glossy brown surfaces have only one discernible mark, on the base of the neck. EAC 30. *Ex: Stack's (10/1978), lot 869; 1985 EAC, lot 263; later, Steven Ellsworth (9/2002).*
From The Pasadena Collection, Part Two.(#1513)

136 **1807/6 Large 7—Obverse Damage, Burnished—NCS. AU Details.** S-273, B-3, R.1. An incuse mark is present near the Y in LIBERTY and opposite near the C in AMERICA. The fields appear smoothed, and portions of LIBERTY and AMERICA are blurry. The portrait displays substantial hair definition. EAC 30. *Ex: Steven Ellsworth (2/2003).*
From The Pasadena Collection, Part Two.(#1528)

Mint State Brown 1807/6 Cent, S-273

137 **1807/6 Large 7 MS61 Brown NGC.** S-273, B-3, R.1. Die State IV. The 80 are closely spaced, more so than the remaining digits, and the large 7 is "heavily repunched" over a 6. On the reverse a leaf point is directly beneath the upright of the D in UNITED. Both sides show numerous clashes, die breaks, and bulging in this late state. The surfaces are glossy dark brown, with considerable weakness on some the letter tops (likely due both to die fatigue and misalignment) and a small planchet void at about 10:30. EAC 50.(#1528)

Appealing MS62 Brown 1812 Cent
Small Date, S-290, B-2

138 **1812 Small Date MS62 Brown NGC.** S-290, B-2, R.1. The dramatic die anomaly above STATES on the reverse is diagnostic. Blue and violet overtones enliven deep walnut-brown surfaces. Unusually well-defined for a Classic Head cent, though a handful of wispy abrasions scattered in the fields preclude a finer designation. EAC 60. Census: 9 in 62 Brown, 14 finer (2/09).(#1561)

Lovely 1813 Cent
XF45, S-292

139 **1813 XF45 PCGS. CAC.** S-292, R.2. A lovely walnut-brown large cent, minimally marked and verdigris-free. Lighter brown color outlines some of the reverse elements. Struck from late stage dies, the stars are drawn to the borders, and no reverse dentils are present. The design elements are well defined, though the star centers are weak. In a green label holder. EAC 40.(#1570)

140 **1814 Plain 4 AU55 ICG.** S-295, B-2, R.1. Liberty has a prominent die break beneath the chin, and an arc crack extends from the bottom of star 11 through the lower curl and 8 to the rim. Pleasing semigloss brown surfaces exhibit well defined design elements, and are free of significant contact marks other than slight old reverse corrosion. Some rim crumbling is visible on both sides. EAC 45. *Ex: Jim Long (7/2003).*
From The Pasadena Collection, Part Two.(#1576)

Uncirculated 1814 Plain 4 Cent, S-295

141 **1814 Plain 4 MS61 Brown NGC.** S-295, B-2, R.1. A splendid medium brown representative of this conditionally rare design. Satin luster dominates the reverse and fills the stars, hair, and obverse legends. Free from marks or carbon. A die break beneath the chin gives Liberty a bearded appearance. EAC 55.(#1576)

142 **1817 13 Stars—Improperly Cleaned—NCS. AU Details.** N-9, R.2. Deep brown surfaces show blue accents as well as a handful of pinkish overtones. Modestly hairlined from a past cleaning but still an interesting and desirable piece. EAC 45.(#1594)

143 **1817 13 Stars—Improperly Cleaned—NCS. Unc Details.** N-9, R.2. A later state with the stars drawn to the rim. This mahogany-accented chocolate-brown coin shows no trace of wear, though the luster is subdued from a past cleaning. EAC 40.(#1594)

144 **1817 15 Stars AU58 NGC.** N-16, High R.1. This popular die pair has its own *Guide Book* listing. Aside from slight striking softness, this deep brown example is pleasing. Just a touch of rub crosses the high points. EAC 45.(#1597)

145 **1818 MS64 Brown NGC.** N-10, R.1. The cartwheel luster is magnificent, and comprehensively covers this Choice Matron cent. The deep brown toning has turquoise-green and lilac undertones. The portrait has minor contact, but the fields are smooth and the eye appeal is obvious. EAC 60.(#1600)

146 **1820 Large Date MS64 Red and Brown PCGS.** N-13, R.1. The often encountered Randall Hoard variety with the heavy obverse die cracks and a multiply punched L in LIBERTY. Ample orange luster outlines the legend and portrait, and the strike is bold aside from a couple of stars. EAC 60+.(#1616)

147 **1821 XF45 NGC.** N-2, R.1. The second S in STATES is distant from the nearest leaf. A lightly circulated chocolate-brown example with pleasing detail on the portrait but slight striking softness elsewhere. EAC 40.
Ex: Doug Bird (3/2008).
From The Pasadena Collection, Part Two.(#1621)

Near Census Level 1823/2 N-1 Cent, AU50

148 **1823/2 AU50 ICG.** N-1, Low R.2. This piece was previously NGC certified AU53. Although faint hairlines are evident in the left obverse field, with other patches of trivial corrosion, it is an exceptional example of the elusive 1823 overdate cent. Mottled tan and dark brown surfaces on both sides present a pleasing appearance. EAC 45.
Ex: Steven Ellsworth (9/2005).
From The Pasadena Collection, Part Two.(#1630)

149 **1830 Large Letters MS63 Brown PCGS.** N-4, Low R.3. Heavy die cracks across both borders facilitate the attribution. A walnut-brown representative with glimpses of faded red in protected areas. Pleasing surfaces and bold device detail ensure the eye appeal. EAC 55.(#1672)

150 **1831 Large Letters—Undertype for Haiti 100 Centimes, Corroded—NCS. XF Details.** N-1, R.1. The large cent served as a "planchet" for a Republic of Haiti 100 centimes, An 27 (1830), KM-A23. However, the 100 centimes was a silver issue, and pieces in copper or brass are believed to be "well executed counterfeits" according to the Krause World Coin catalog.(#1678)

151 **1837 Plain Cords, Medium Letters MS66 Brown NGC.** N-4, R.2. Significant cracks at left and upper obverse as well as the upper right reverse. Generally teak-brown surfaces show ample blue overtones on the obverse and mahogany-rose tints on the reverse. EAC 63.(#1735)

152 **1838 MS65 Brown PCGS. CAC.** N-1, R.1. The peak of the 1 in the date is recut, as are the I in UNITED and E in AMERICA. Hints of orange luster peek through the light to medium brown patina. Well struck, except for central weakness on most of the star centers. A small greenish spot is visible within the U of UNITED. EAC 60. Population: 33 in 65 Brown, 10 finer (2/09). (#1741)

Desirable N-1 1839/6 Cent, VF30

153 **1839/6 VF30 NGC.** N-1, High R.3. Grellman Die State b with the die crack in front of Liberty's head but not the one behind. A midrange example of this popular and unusual overdate variety, rich chocolate and olive-brown with parallel stripes of slightly deeper patina visible on the obverse. Slight striking softness is as expected, and marks are few. EAC 12.
From The Ed Lepordo Collection, Part Two.(#1756)

Exquisite 1840 N-8 Cent, MS64 Red

154 **1840 Large Date MS64 Red PCGS.** N-8, R.1. A lustrous and exquisitely struck near-Gem that has magnificent orange-gold color. A tiny toning fleck in the field below the chin, and another above the northwest corner of the N in ONE, take nothing away from the impressive eye appeal of this coin. A late die state with heavy die cuds on the obverse rim between 1 and 6 o'clock. EAC 64. Population: 1 in 64 Red, 2 finer (2/09).
From The Burning Tree Collection.(#1822)

155 **1840 Small/Large Date—Reverse Planchet Flaw—NCS. Unc Details.** N-2, R.2. Grellman state a. The 18 in the date is dramatically recut. A lamination, mostly retained, on the CA in AMERICA, is apparently referred to by the NCS designation. The obverse also has a small retained lamination on the second star. Well struck save for some left side stars. Primarily red-brown in color, although steel-blues hues on the portrait and OF A on the upper right reverse suggest a long-ago cleaning. EAC 45.
Ex: George Ramont (5/1971); Jules Reiver (Heritage, 1/2006), lot 20142.
From The Ed Lepordo Collection, Part Two. (#1826)

156 **1846 Small Date MS62 Brown NGC.** N-18, R.1. Incorrectly described as a Medium Date on the holder, but without the low extension of the crosslet. A deep chocolate-brown example with a mark-free appearance and no shortage of glistening luster. The strike is precise aside from minor blending on the left-side stars. EAC 55.(#1865)

157 **1847/1847 Horizontal MS63 Brown NGC.** N-1, R.2. Grellman state b. The date is triple punched, with vestiges of prior logotypes both above and to the lower right of the prominent date. The date logotype was too large to readily fit in the space between the bust and the dentils, which led to the date recuttings. This attractive chocolate-brown piece is quite pleasing despite trivial mahogany spots in front of the nose and coronet edge, a trace of granular surface near the final star, and a small mark in the field between the chin and the second star. EAC 50.
Ex: George Ramont (8/1971); Jules Reiver (Heritage, 1/2006), lot 20262.
From The Ed Lepordo Collection, Part Two.(#1874)

158 **1847 MS66 Brown NGC.** N-35, High R.3. Die State C, die crack through base of date. A crisply struck and lovingly preserved golden-brown Premium Gem. NGC has certified just four pieces as Newcomb-35, only one of which (the present coin) is certified as Mint State. EAC 60+.(#1877)

159 **1847 MS65 Red and Brown PCGS. CAC.** N-24, R.1. Newcomb varieties N-9 and N-25 are later die states of the same die pair. This example is Grellman State d that was originally called N-9. It is an outstanding example with pleasing olive surfaces and considerable original mint red. There are several similar quality examples known but few that are finer. EAC 63.(#1878)

160 **1848 MS66 ★ Brown NGC.** N-12, R.1. Glossy medium brown surfaces display considerable orange luster on the reverse. Sharply struck, and impeccably preserved. A highly appealing large cent. EAC 63. Census: 2 in 66 ★ Brown, 0 finer (2/09).(#1883)

161 **1850 MS65 Red and Brown PCGS.** N-7, R.2. Grellman Die State b. This unabraded Mature Head Gem boasts considerable brick-red luster, although the wreath and open fields are brown. Sharply impressed aside from a few stars. Encased in a green label holder. EAC 63.(#1890)

162 **1851 MS64 Red and Brown PCGS. CAC.** N-2, R.1. This late state example has the top of the 8 extremely thin, and dull reverse clash marks that are nearly invisible. It is a hoard coin in the late die state. The present example has nearly full orange mint color with slight mellowing that is more prevalent on the obverse. EAC 63. *From The Burning Tree Collection.*(#1893)

163 **1851/81 MS64 Brown NGC.** N-3, R.1. The date was initially entered inverted, although perhaps a two digit logotype was used since only the 51 digits reveal the prior logotype. Heavy die lines (as made) are noted behind Liberty's head. A lovely near-Gem with an especially undisturbed reverse. EAC 55. *From The Ed Leopordo Collection, Part Two.*(#1895)

164 **1853 MS65 Red and Brown PCGS. CAC.** N-3, R.1. The tiny die lump in the field below the ball of the 5 provides identification of the variety in earlier die states. The blurry lump indicates that this piece is actually a middle die state, Grellman State b. Both sides are virtually full red with mellowing on the high points, and olive-brown on the rims. It is a lovely Gem with exceptional eye appeal. EAC 64. Population: 83 in 65 Red, 4 finer (2/09). *From The Burning Tree Collection.*(#1902)

165 **1853 MS65 Red NGC.** N-3, R.1. Intensely lustrous, with fiery mint-red color across each side. Seemingly untouched and blemish-free, with a few scattered carbon flecks that keep it from an even loftier grade. A lovely, well preserved Gem. EAC 64. Census: 3 in 65 Red, 0 finer (2/09).(#1903)

166 **1854 MS66 Red and Brown ICG.** N-6, R.1. Grellman Die State b. Rich reddish-orange and violet-brown colors blend on this carefully preserved example. Warmly lustrous and eminently appealing. EAC 63.(#1905)

Full Red 1855 Large Cent, MS65 Red, N-4

167 **1855 Upright 5s MS65 Red PCGS.** N-4, R.1. A wonderfully original, full red example of this popular date in the Braided Hair series. Full, glowing mint red covers each side and the striking details are sharply defined throughout. The only noticeable flaws are a bit of carbon spotting and marks around OF on the reverse, and tiny flyspecks that are scattered over each side. EAC 64.(#1909)

FLYING EAGLE CENTS

168 **1857 MS64 NGC.** Flaming cherry-red and vibrant golden-tan coloration adorns the satiny, well preserved surfaces of this near-Gem Flying Eagle cent. A high-end example for the grade, with no noticeable surface disturbances on either side. Census: 21 in 64, 16 finer (1/09).(#2016)

Elusive 1857 Flying Eagle Cent, MS64 Prooflike

169 **1857 MS64 Prooflike NGC.** A highly popular three-year type, the Flying Eagle cents were the first so-called "small cents" produced in the United States and were made between 1856 and 1858. The second-year 1857 issue is readily available in Mint State, but Prooflike examples are extremely rare. This piece is sharply struck and well preserved, with nary a distracting mark on either side. Essentially untoned, with highly reflective fields and lightly frosted devices. Census: 4 in 64 Prooflike, 0 finer (2/09).(#2016)

170 **1858 Large Letters MS64 PCGS.** Low Leaves Reverse. Vibrant reddish-orange color only slightly tempered by mahogany. Well-defined and highly desirable, a great example of this final Flying Eagle cent issue.(#2019)

171 **1858 Large Letters MS64 PCGS.** High Leaves, Closed E in ONE. Well struck and lustrous, with golden-brown coloration. The satiny surfaces are blemish-free, with a handful of scattered flyspecks that are minimally disturbing.(#2019)

172 **1858 Small Letters MS64 NGC.** Low Leaves, Closed E in ONE. A lovely, Choice Mint State representative of this popular issue. Rich golden-brown coloration covers the satiny, highly lustrous surfaces. Well struck and unmarked, with just a couple of small carbon flecks on each side.(#2020)

PROOF FLYING EAGLE CENTS

Fully Mirrored 1856 Flyer, PR63

173 **1856 PR63 PCGS. CAC.** Snow-9, the usual proof-only variety. This gorgeous, deeply toned proof has fully mirrored fields and it is clearly a proof, unlike some others that are proofs but more closely resemble business strikes. Both sides exhibit intermingled brown, tan, pale blue, light green, and lilac toning, with sharp devices that stand boldly against the background. A few tiny surface marks are evident on each side, with a planchet defect at the center of the reverse, certainly present before the coin was struck. Such imperfections should have little or no effect on the grade. An exceptional example of the popular 1856 Flying Eagle cent.(#2037)

Important PR64 1858 Small Letters Flying Eagle Cent

174 **1858 Small Letters PR64 PCGS. CAC.** As Rick Snow enthuses in his *A Guide Book of Flying Eagle and Indian Head Cents*: "Proof Flying Eagle cents are some of the most attractive coins in numismatics!" They are also some of the most elusive, as there are actually many more proof 1856 pattern Flying Eagle cents than there are proof 1858 Small Letters pieces, which have an estimated original mintage of only 200 pieces, per Snow. This near-Gem offers sharp devices and associated squared rims, and the pleasing surfaces are light chocolate-brown with occasional hints of olive. Modest hairlines in the fields have little effect on the overall eye appeal. PCGS has graded just seven finer specimens (2/09). (#2043)

INDIAN CENTS

175 **1859 MS64 NGC.** The surfaces are immediately suggestive of an even finer grade, with glowing tan-orange coloration on both sides, but it is probable that the minor carbon flecks on the reverse around the denomination are the determinant. Nonetheless sharply struck and pleasing overall.(#2052)

Desirable Gem 1859 Indian Cent

176 **1859 MS65 NGC.** This is a lovely Gem example, with impressive striking definition and smooth, seemingly pristine surfaces on both sides. Soft, satiny luster and pleasing gold-tan and amber coloration ensure the outstanding eye appeal of the piece. An important type coin, both as a first year of issue coin and as a one-year reverse design variation. Census: 2 in 65, 0 finer (1/09).(#2052)

Single Year Type 1859 Cent MS65

177 **1859 MS65 NGC.** Golden-tan patina bathes both sides of this copper-nickel Gem, and a well executed strike imparts sharp definition to the design features, save for minor weakness on the feather tips. All four diamonds are crisp. Light granularity is visible at 3 o'clock on the obverse rim. NGC has certified 11 pieces finer (2/09).(#2052)

Appealing MS66 1860 Cent

178 **1860 MS66 NGC.** Tan and mushroom-brown surfaces offer strong, pleasing luster. The tips of the feathers show some pillowy detail, but the four diamonds on the ribbon are plain. Overall, a highly desirable representative of this first Oak Wreath Reverse Indian cent. Census: 3 in 66, 0 finer (2/09).(#2058)

Exquisite MS66 1861 Cent

179 **1861 MS66 NGC.** Decisively struck with uncommonly vibrant surfaces. Occasional pink accents grace otherwise mahogany-orange surfaces. Marvelous eye appeal. 1861 was the first year of the Civil War and the final year of the Pony Express. Cents were commonplace in circulation in 1861, but would vanish within two years. Census: 41 in 66, 2 finer (1/09).(#2061)

Marvelous MS66 1861 Cent

180 **1861 MS66 PCGS.** This early Civil War cent is extraordinary, with its brilliant orange and tan luster and sharp details, all except the extreme feather tips. A few minuscule spots appear on each side, but otherwise the surfaces are virtually perfect. Only a few exist in higher grades than this Premium Gem. Population: 54 in 66, 10 finer (2/09).(#2061)

Crisply Struck MS66 1861 Cent

181 **1861 MS66 PCGS.** A crisply struck and marvelously preserved Premium Gem representative of this early copper-nickel date. Clean and lustrous surfaces display slightly greenish copper-tan coloration. Fewer than 100 pieces are graded as MS66 by NGC and PCGS combined as of (2/09), despite the mintage exceeding 10 million coins.(#2061)

Nearly 'White' 1862 Copper-Nickel Cent, MS66

182 **1862 MS66 PCGS. CAC.** The 1862 is the date usually used for type purposes in the copper-nickel series. More than 28 million pieces were struck, and even with Civil War hoarding a sufficient number of higher grade examples still exist today. What sets this piece apart from many other copper-nickel type coins are the nearly unmellowed "white" surfaces of the high-nickel alloy. Well, but not fully struck, each side is remarkably free from abrasions. Population: 58 in 66, 7 finer (2/09).(#2064)

183 **1864 Copper-Nickel MS65 PCGS.** Impressively lustrous and strongly struck for this final copper-nickel cent issue. Salmon surfaces are bright with occasional mint-green accents. PCGS has graded just 10 finer pieces (2/09).(#2070)

184 **1864 L On Ribbon MS64 Red and Brown PCGS.** An appealing example of this variant struck later in the year. Each side offers a blend of original copper-orange and olive-brown.(#2080)

Important 1864 L on Ribbon Cent, MS65 Red and Brown Repunched Date, Snow-3

185   **1864 L On Ribbon MS65 Red and Brown NGC.** FS-2302, Snow-3. A prominent repunched date with tripling on the 18 and doubling on the rest of the digits. Surfaces range from copper-pink to salmon and olive-blue. A well-defined Gem that is minimally marked and offers considerable variety in its eye appeal. A condition census for the variety is necessarily speculative, but it is hard to imagine this coin being near the top, if not at the summit.(#2080)

Extraordinary 1864-L Cent, MS66 Red

186   **1864 L On Ribbon MS66 Red NGC.** Compared with its Bronze, No L counterpart, the 1864 L On Ribbon business strike cent is elusive, though in most grades it is available for a price. Coins above the Gem level are rarities, particularly with full Red surfaces. Warm peach and orange shadings prevail on this well-defined and attractive Premium Gem, and a tiny spot at the lower obverse margin is the only appreciable flaw. One of just seven MS66 Red coins in the combined certified population, four at NGC and three at PCGS, with none numerically finer at either service (2/09).(#2081)

Sharp 1866 Cent, MS65 Red

187   **1866 MS65 Red NGC.** Although this early bronze cent boasts a respectable (for the era) mintage of 9.8 million-plus pieces, fully lustrous Gems are few and far between in today's market, as one might expect from the available population figures. Softly frosted in texture, this lustrous representative displays even red-bronze color over crisply defined devices. Essentially distraction-free. Struck from slightly rotated dies. Census: 12 in 65 Red, 1 finer (2/09).(#2087)

188   **1869 MS65 Red and Brown NGC.** This better date Gem cent displays considerable copper-gold luster, and is sharply struck, save for the usual softness on some of the feather tips. Pleasing surfaces are devoid of mentionable marks or spotting.(#2095)

189   **1869 MS66 Red and Brown NGC.** Well-defined with warm luster. Both sides show an inviting blend of copper-orange, rosewood, violet, and maple-brown patina. Census: 10 in 66 Red and Brown, 0 finer (2/09).(#2095)

190   **1870 MS64 Red and Brown NGC.** Light copper-orange and pumpkin surfaces show only slight elements of mahogany, making this piece more Red than Brown. Pleasingly preserved for the grade with an above-average strike.(#2098)

191   **1871 MS65 Brown NGC.** Deep ebony surfaces show olive and blue undercurrents. A smooth Gem that is boldly detailed and surprisingly mark-free. Housed in a prior-generation holder. (#2100)

192   **1871 MS64 Red and Brown NGC.** Well struck for this highly collectible date. The obverse is deep reddish-gold, while the reverse is more golden-tan. Slight muting on each side accounts for the Red and Brown designation.
From The Burning Tree Collection.(#2101)

Well Struck 1872 One Cent MS65 Red and Brown

193   **1872 MS65 Red and Brown NGC.** The copper-gold reverse displays hints of tan, and cedes to a mix of crimson, light green, and greenish-tan on the reverse. The design elements are well struck—much better so than usually seen, for as Richard Snow (2006) writes: "Most are poorly struck, or are struck through machine oil." Both sides are devoid of mentionable contacts or spots. Census: 73 in 65 Red and Brown, 8 finer (2/09).(#2104)

194   **1873 Open 3 MS65 Red and Brown PCGS. CAC.** Golden-tan patina is imbued with traces of lavender, and a well executed strike leaves strong definition on the design elements. Both sides are free of mentionable contacts or spots. Population: 46 in 65 Red and Brown, 3 finer (2/09).(#2107)

195   **1874 MS64 Red NGC.** Peach and rose colors intermingle on this intricately struck and lustrous representative. A strike-through on the reverse border at 10 o'clock and a faint pinscratch east of the date are noted. Census: 20 in 64 Red, 22 finer (1/09).(#2120)

196 **1877 Good 4 ANACS.** Shallow N. This medium brown key issue cent has a bold date and only a few weak letters in OF AMERICA. A loupe locates a couple of minor marks. A nice collector-grade example.(#2127)

197 **1877 Fine 12 ICG.** This chocolate-brown key date cent displays the L, R, and T in LIBERTY, although each of the three letters is faint. Minor buildup is noted within protected areas of the reverse. (#2127)

198 **1877 VF20 PCGS.** A desirable midrange example that is minimally marked for the grade. Primarily walnut-brown surfaces show elements of cinnamon at the rims.(#2127)

199 **1877—Obverse Strike-Through—VF35 NGC.** The obverse is indistinct relative to the reverse's level of detail, indicative of a strike-through, possibly of grease. That aspect aside, this is a solid Choice VF example of its ever-popular key Indian cent issue. (#2127)

200 **1877 VF35 PCGS.** Semi-glossy medium brown surfaces reveal a few circulation marks, the most noticeable being a pinscratch in the lower left obverse field. The letters LI of LIBERTY show, as do the tops of the next two or three letters.(#2127)

201 **1877—Improperly Cleaned—NCS. XF Details.** Chocolate-brown surfaces have subdued luster and faint hairlines from a past cleaning. The detail is crisp, however, and the piece remains readily collectible. (#2127)

202 **1877—Environmental Damage—NCS. XF Details.** Each side of this modestly worn example offers deep brown color. The obverse shows olive-rose tints, while the reverse is darker violet-blue with indicators of environmental damage. Still, this piece displays attractively. *From The Pasadena Collection, Part Two.*(#2127)

Coveted Near-Mint 1877 Cent

203 **1877 AU58 ICG.** From 1875 to 1877, a curious pattern of cent coinage emerges: after a redemption program for worn cents slowed but before commercial demand for the denomination picked up, production of the cent plunged from 13.5 million examples in 1875 to just 852,500 pieces a mere two years later. This well-defined representative shows just a trace of friction on each side. The obverse is primarily violet-brown, while the reverse show a mixture of olive, walnut, and cinnamon.(#2127)

Series Key 1877 Cent, MS65 Red and Brown

204 **1877 MS65 Red and Brown NGC.** Shallow N in ONE. This crisply struck key date Gem features variegated jade-green and apricot-gold. Satin luster sweeps minimally abraded surfaces. Lightly clashed above the O in ONE. A small planchet flake on the lower neck will identify this desirable example. Census: 74 in 65 Red and Brown, 8 finer (2/09).(#2128)

205 **1881 MS65 Red PCGS.** Yellow-gold luster is imbued with traces of red. A nicely struck coin, with the reverse rotated about 20 degrees counterclockwise. There are no mentionable abrasions. Housed in a green-label holder. Population: 71 in 65 Red, 26 finer (2/09).(#2141)

206 **1886 Type Two MS64 Red and Brown PCGS.** Deep rose and orange shadings prevail, though areas of mahogany also show. A well struck example with few superiors in the color category. (#92155)

Appealing MS67 Red 1898 Cent

207 **1898 MS67 Red NGC.** This eye-catching Superb Gem has vibrant reddish-orange surfaces that show only two small areas of discoloration at the upper obverse rims. Overall detail is pleasing, and the surfaces are carefully preserved with only a handful of tiny marks discernible to the unaided eye. Tied for numerically finest among Red examples known to NGC or PCGS (2/09). (#2201)

208 **1899 MS66 Red NGC.** The obverse and part of the reverse are glowing brick-red, with the remainder almond-tan and pleasingly well struck. Thoroughly appealing, with no visible carbon. (#2204)

Exquisite 1899 Cent, MS67 Red

209 **1899 MS67 Red NGC.** A coin of extraordinary beauty and fire. Rich copper-orange surfaces offer twinkling, lively luster. The fields and the boldly impressed devices are equally well-preserved with none but the most imperceptible flaws. A gorgeous representative for the dedicated collector. Census: 9 in 67 Red, 1 finer (2/09). (#2204)

210 **1905 MS66 Red NGC.** Well-defined and brightly lustrous. The obverse shows rich sun-orange color, while the reverse displays noticeable olive overtones. Census: 56 in 66 Red, 4 finer (1/09). (#2222)

211 **1908-S MS66 Red and Brown NGC.** A superior, carbon-free example of this much-needed branch mint Indian cent. The surfaces have mellowed only slightly from the full red of 1908. Pleasing and problem-free, among the finest examples we have offered. Census: 10 in 66 Red and Brown, 0 finer (1/09).(#2233)

PROOF INDIAN CENTS

Extraordinary 1859 Cent, PR65 Ultra Cameo
The Only Certified Ultra Cameo Proof

212 **1859 PR65 Ultra Cameo NGC.** Splashes of orange-gold toning grace the light tan surfaces of this glittering Gem proof. Both sides exhibit amazing contrast with bold design definition that is completely delineated. This is one of the finest, most eye-appealing examples of the 1859 Indian cent that we have ever handled. While we have offered several higher numerical grade proofs, this is the only Ultra Cameo proof 1859 cent we have ever offered. In fact, it is the only Ultra Cameo proof 1859 cent that has ever been certified by NGC or PCGS, regardless of grade. As the first year of issue, it is in great demand from type and date collectors, and this piece ranks as one of the most important Indian cents ever to cross the auction block.(#92247)

Sharp 1860 Cent, PR66 ★

213 **1860 PR66 ★ NGC.** Proof 1860 cents are rare in Gem and finer levels of preservation (Richard Snow, 2006). Copper-gold, crimson, and sky-blue patina adorn the well cared-for surfaces of this Premium Gem awarded the coveted Star designation. The design elements are sharply struck, except for the usual softness on the feather tips. Census: 1 in 66 ★, 2 finer (2/09).(#2253)

214 **1862 PR64 PCGS.** The 1862 is one of just five years of Variety Two (Copper-Nickel with Shield) Indian cents issued, and it boasts a diminutive mintage of approximately 550 proofs. Bright red and orange intermingle on the surfaces of this resplendent specimen. A few tiny flecks and abrasions are noted.(#2259)

215 **1862 PR65 NGC.** Rich copper-orange color in the fields with a more pink hue to the portrait. Carefully preserved for a proof copper-nickel cent and appealing.(#2259)

216 **1862 PR65 NGC.** Copper-orange at its base with ample salmon-pink overtones. An appealing Gem proof representative of this popular copper-nickel cent issue.(#2259)

217 **1862 PR65 Cameo NGC.** Each side of this pink-accented copper-gold Gem offers light, yet distinct contrast. A pleasingly preserved representative of this mid-date copper-nickel Indian cent issue. Census: 19 in 65 Cameo, 24 finer (2/09).(#82259)

Fully Struck 1862 Cent, PR66 ★ Cameo

218 **1862 PR66 ★ Cameo NGC.** The *Guide Book of Flying Eagle and Indian Cents* notes that the 1862 is the most common proof date among the copper-nickel issues, possibly because the original mintage was saved and resold to collectors later, probably after the end of the Civil War. However, examples in Premium Gem or finer grades are still remarkably elusive. This piece sports wonderful cerise fields with lilac tints around the peripheral lettering on the obverse, and deep contrast. The reverse has more-typical sandalwood patina. Thoroughly appealing, fully struck, and justly meriting the Star designation. NGC has certified five numerically finer Cameo pieces (2/09).(#82259)

Amazing 1864 Copper-Nickel Indian Cent
PR67 ★ Cameo

219   1864 Copper Nickel PR67 ★ Cameo NGC. In 1864, most proof sets included the copper-nickel cent, as they were the first coins made that year. Only a few additional sets and singles sold in the middle months had bronze proofs, and those sold at the end of the year included proofs with the designer's initial, L.

  Copper-nickel Indian cents with cameo contrast are few and far between, especially in Superb Gem quality. This amazing piece has frosty light tan devices with deeply mirrored fields. Both sides have rose and gold toning that becomes more vibrant near the border. Census: 2 in 67 Cameo, 0 finer (2/09).(#82265)

Stunning PR65 Ultra Cameo 1864 Copper-Nickel Cent

220   1864 Copper Nickel PR65 Ultra Cameo NGC. An eye-catching specimen in every sense, this Ultra Cameo Gem proof is decisively struck with ample mint frost stretching across the central devices. Even the letters are frosted and share in the contrast with the gleaming copper-black mirrors. Well-preserved and absolutely memorable.(#92265)

221   1864 Bronze No L PR64 Red and Brown PCGS. Bronze composition proof 1864 Indian cents are quite rare with relatively few survivors from a small but unknown mintage. This boldly detailed Choice proof has virtually full red on the obverse and mostly olive and iridescent brown on the reverse.(#2277)

Elegant PR65 Red 1864 Cent
Bronze, No L

222   1864 Bronze No L PR65 Red NGC. Each side shows a number of vertical die striations, and several circular die striations are noted on the portrait, with a planchet flake to the left, below E. Post-striking flaws, however, are just these few, and the bright copper-gold surfaces are immensely appealing. A great example of this challenging transitional issue. Census: 2 in 65 Red, 0 finer (2/09). (#2278)

223   1866 PR65 Red and Brown NGC. One of an estimated 725 pieces struck in proof format in 1866. Coppery-gold patina displays accents of light green in the central obverse, and speckles of lavender in the central reverse. The reflective fields offer a nice contrast with the motifs. The design features are exquisitely struck, and there are no mentionable abrasions or spots to report. Census: 34 in 65 Red and Brown, 8 finer (2/09).(#2286)

Stirring PR66 ★ Red and Brown Cameo 1866 Cent

224   1866 PR66 ★ Red and Brown Cameo NGC. Beyond the historic worth of this popular post-Civil War issue, this astonishing Premium Gem offers overwhelming eye appeal. Rich copper-gold and rose-mahogany shadings mingle on each side, and the fields are virtually distraction-free. Beautifully contrasted and memorable in all possible respects.(#82286)

225   1867 PR65 Red and Brown NGC. The obverse is generally copper-orange with only subtle violet overtones, though the reverse has a more mahogany-amethyst appearance. Pleasingly preserved and crisply detailed.(#2289)

Flashy PR66 Red 1869 Cent

226   1869 PR66 Red NGC. In contrast to this issue's comparatively small proof mintage of 600 coins, production surged to a four-figure level the following year. This crisply struck, carefully preserved example offers bold, bright orange surfaces with a hint of olive and rose on each side. Census: 5 in 66 Red, 0 finer (1/09).(#2296)

227   1870 PR66 Red and Brown NGC. The margins are reddish-orange or copper-gold, while the centers are violet-brown and mahogany. Carefully preserved and appealing. Census: 11 in 66 Red and Brown, 0 finer (2/09).(#2298)

Gorgeous 1870 Indian Cent, PR66 Red

228 **1870 PR66 Red NGC.** The fields show the usually seen die polishing marks on each side. Bright and highly reflective, each side shows deep cherry-red color that lightens around the denticles. The devices are fully struck, and the surfaces overall are problem-free. Census: 6 in 66 Red, 0 finer (2/09).(#2299)

Brilliant 1870 Indian Cent, PR66 Red

229 **1870 PR66 Red NGC.** Fully brilliant red proof surfaces and sharp design features ensure that this example ranks among the finest proof 1870 Indian cents ever certified. Just 10 similar examples have been graded by NGC and PCGS with none finer. Census: 6 in 66, 0 finer (2/09).(#2299)

230 **1870 PR63 Red Cameo PCGS.** A few small spots and minor lilac toning splashes interrupt the brilliant red proof surfaces of this Cameo proof. Population: 1 in 63 Red Cameo, 8 finer (1/09). (#82299)

231 **1875 PR65 Red and Brown NGC.** Nicely toned with hints of gold and lavender. An impressively preserved Gem proof with a razor sharp strike. Census: 40 in 65 Red and Brown, 7 finer (2/09). (#2313)

232 **1875 PR64 Red NGC.** This near-Gem is boldly defined with amazing orange mint color on both sides. The fields are moderately mirrored but still provide excellent contrast to the lustrous devices. Census: 10 in 64 Red, 7 finer (2/09).(#2314)

Captivating PR66 Red 1875 Cent

233 **1875 PR66 Red PCGS.** The proof production of 1875 cents was only 950 coins, a typical figure for the era. This piece offers spot-free surfaces with reddish orange field color and deeper orange-tan high points. There is much field-device contrast, although uncredited by PCGS. The strike is sharp as expected. This Premium Gem proof is one of only two Red coins in PR66 at PCGS, and there are none finer (2/09).(#2314)

Exquisite 1877 Cent
PR65 Red and Brown

234 **1877 PR65 Red and Brown PCGS.** The 1877 proof cent mintage is controversial. Walter Breen (1989) estimates 510+ pieces, while the 2009 *Guide Book* gives a figure of 900 coins. Richard Snow (2006) suggests that "... at least 1,500 coins were produced, with the remaining unsold pieces being destroyed or released into circulation." In any event, Gem and finer coins in all color categories are challenging. This exquisitely struck Red and Brown PR65 displays noticeable field-motif contrast at certain angles. Whispers of purple and sky-blue patina visit nicely preserved surfaces. Population: 60 in 65 Red and Brown, 5 finer (1/09). (#2319)

235 **1878 PR65 Red and Brown Cameo NGC.** Violet-brown and blue-brown centers yield to glimmers of untoned copper-orange near the rims. Distinctly contrasted and sharply detailed.(#82323)

236 **1878 PR65 Cameo PCGS.** Stunning cameo contrast greets the viewer of this Gem proof, and exquisitely struck devices enhance this variance. Copper-orange surfaces are imbued with traces of lilac and ice-blue, and are devoid of significant contacts or spots. Population: 7 in 65 Red Cameo, 5 finer (2/09).(#82323)

237 **1881 PR66 Red and Brown PCGS. CAC.** Exquisitely detailed with abundant eye appeal. The obverse is straight lemon-orange, while the reverse has similar peripheral color and olive-mint in the center. Population: 10 in 66 Red and Brown, 3 finer (1/09). (#2331)

238 **1881 PR66 Red and Brown PCGS.** Orange, rose-red, and apple-green shadings enliven this intricately struck and unabraded specimen. Exemplary despite a pinpoint fleck near the chin, and housed in a green label holder. Population: 10 in 66 Red and Brown, 3 finer (1/09).(#2331)

239 **1883 PR65 Red PCGS.** Crisply struck with excellent reflectivity and eye appeal. The copper-orange surfaces are bright and free of all but the most trivial distractions. Population: 16 in 65 Red, 6 finer (2/09).(#2338)

240 **1884 PR66 Red and Brown NGC.** Sharply struck and carefully preserved with electric coloration. Joining the dominant reddish-orange are elements of magenta and violet-blue.(#2340)

Wonderful PR67 Red 1884 Cent

241 **1884 PR67 Red PCGS.** Wonderful tinges of almond, sage, and sunset-orange grace both sides of this delightful Superb Gem, with the considerable field-device contrast noted a further enhancement. There is some strike softness noted on the ribbon feather, but the eye appeal is over the top. Among the finest Red coins certified at either service. Population: 10 in 67, 0 finer (2/09).(#2341)

242 **1885 PR65 Red NGC.** Vivid red and orange patina covers the intricately detailed surfaces. This well preserved and fully struck Gem shows only a couple of tiny lint marks under magnification. One of just 3,790 proofs minted. Census: 4 in 65 Red, 4 finer (1/09).(#2344)

1886 Type Two Cent, PR65 Red and Brown
Scarce With This Much Red

243 **1886 Type Two PR65 Red and Brown PCGS.** By far the scarcer of the two types from this year. There are few full Red coins known, making this Red and Brown piece a good buy for the collector. This piece displays deep cherry-red surfaces and a dash of iridescence on the upper rim of the reverse and corresponding area of the reverse. Nicely mirrored with no mentionable flaws on either side. Population: 9 in 65 Red and Brown, 1 finer (2/09).(#92346)

Near-Gem Proof Red 1886 Type Two Indian Cent

244 **1886 Type Two PR64 Red PCGS.** Bowers' *Guide Book of Flying Eagle and Indian Cents* estimates that perhaps 40% of the total proofs for this year were of the new Type Two hub variety, introduced this year and lasting through the end of the series. Only in 1954 did collectors begin discriminating between the two variants. This piece displays plenty of dusky orange-red coloration, with some waves of light olive toning in the left obverse field. Seldom seen finer. Population: 10 in 64 Red, 3 finer (1/09).(#92347)

245 **1892 PR66 Red PCGS.** Bright reddish-orange surfaces are essentially unturned. A crisply detailed and gorgeous Premium Gem that offers stirring eye appeal. Population: 12 in 66 Red, 2 finer (1/09).(#2365)

246 **1897 PR65 Red NGC.** Sharply detailed with excellent eye appeal. The surfaces have satiny, reflective luster that resembles Mint State coins, although this piece has all other earmarks of a brilliant Gem proof.(#2380)

247 **1902 PR66 Red and Brown PCGS.** Sea-green, gold, orange, and fire-red shades embrace this intricately struck Premium Gem. A colorful and carefully preserved matte proof specimen for the toning enthusiast. Housed in a green label holder.(#2394)

LINCOLN CENTS

248 **1909 VDB Doubled Die Obverse MS63 Brown NGC.** FS-1101. A substantial spread is noted on LIBERTY and the date. Deep brown surfaces offer vibrant blue and violet-rose overtones. Amazing eye appeal.(#82423)

249 **1909-S VDB Fine 15 ICG.** Lush blue overtones grace the otherwise chocolate-brown surfaces of this minimally marked example. An excellent piece for the grade that would fit well in an otherwise Very Fine to Extremely Fine set.(#2426)

250 **1909-S VDB VF25 PCGS.** This midgrade piece is medium brown with darker toning and a few moderate marks near the rims. A readily collectible example of this sought-after issue.(#2426)

251 **1909-S VDB XF40 PCGS.** Deep brown surfaces show violet overtones. The strike is crisp, and the surfaces are surprisingly mark-free save for a graze on Lincoln's jawline.(#2426)

252 **1909-S VDB—Improperly Cleaned—NCS. AU Details.** Chocolate-brown surfaces are oddly glossy. This minimally worn example offers an affordable opportunity to acquire this key issue at its level of detail.
From The Pasadena Collection, Part Two.(#2426)

253 **1909-S VDB—Scratched—ICG. AU53 Details.** Light to medium brown patina displays subtle maroon undertones. Relatively strong design detail is evident, and semiglossy surfaces are quite clean, except for a shallow, toned-over scratch on the upper part of Lincoln's head. Prospective bidders should not be intimidated, as the scratch is not that bad.(#2426)

254 **1909-S VDB AU58 PCGS.** Only slightly worn and entirely mark-free, this is a marvelous near-Mint example of the premier Lincoln cent key date. Even mahogany-brown coloration covers both sides. (#2426)

255 **1909-S VDB AU58 PCGS.** An intriguing piece with dusky tan and darker brown on both sides, the obverse showing streaks of both colors, the reverse with additional iridescence.(#2426)

256 **1909-S VDB AU58 PCGS.** This key date Lincoln cent must have spent only the briefest amount of time in circulation. A trace amount of wear is seen on Lincoln's beard and hair, and a handful of nicks are noted on the collar and in the right obverse field. The reverse is virtually untouched.(#2426)

257 **1909-S VDB MS62 Brown NGC.** This issue was almost immediately guaranteed to become a Lincoln cent key date, as soon as the design was changed to remove the designer's initials VDB from the lower reverse, before the end of 1909. This is a pleasing Mint State specimen with bold design details and few surface marks.
From The Ed Lepordo Collection, Part Two.(#2426)

258 **1909-S VDB MS63 Brown PCGS.** Well struck with clear definition on Lincoln's beard, the wheat ears, and Victor D. Brenner's initials. Mostly brown, with traces of red-gold luster on each side. Free of blemishes, with a few copper flecks on the upper reverse that limit the grade of this Select key date specimen. (#2426)

259 **1909-S VDB MS63 Red and Brown ANACS.** Largely violet-brown, though considerable copper-orange clings to the margins of this Select piece. Well-defined and minimally marked for the grade, a desirable key-date Lincoln cent housed in a small-format holder. (#2427)

Famous 1909-S VDB Cent, MS64 Red and Brown

260 **1909-S VDB MS64 Red and Brown PCGS. CAC.** A boldly defined SVDB cent, this example exhibits brilliant orange mint luster that has just begun to fade to light brown on the high points. This famous variety is far the most popular Lincoln cent, and ranks among the best known of all 20th century varieties, regardless of denomination.(#2427)

Sharp 1909-S VDB Cent MS64 Red and Brown

261 **1909-S VDB MS64 Red and Brown PCGS.** Whispers of grayish-tan patina visit the copper-gold lustrous surfaces of this near-Gem key date Lincoln, and a superior strike endows the design elements, including crisp definition on the date, mintmark, and VDB. No significant contact marks or spots are noted on either side. (#2427)

Desirable 1909-S VDB Cent, MS64 Red and Brown

262 **1909-S VDB MS64 Red and Brown NGC.** Some purple-brown toning on each side prevents this piece from being designated as a fully Red coin by NGC, but other attributes guarantee its desirability, not the least of which is its key date status. Well struck with clean surfaces that are virtually blemish-free. A few scattered carbon flecks are found on both sides.(#2427)

Choice Key Date 1909-S VDB Cent, Red and Brown

263 **1909-S VDB MS64 Red and Brown NGC.** Zones of tan and reddish-orange alternate on this near-Gem example, with enough dots of olive-brown to preclude a fully Red designation. Attractive and well-defined. Of all numismatic issues, the 1909-S VDB cent is probably on the greatest number of want lists.(#2427)

Pretty 1909-S VDB Cent, MS64 Red and Brown

264 **1909-S VDB MS64 Red and Brown PCGS.** As with many examples of this perennially popular issue, the strike is well executed throughout, extending here even to the sometimes-weak designer's initials and the intervening periods. Pretty cherry and mint-green coloration abounds and the eye appeal is otherwise high, but a largish carbon spot atop Lincoln's hair requires singular mention.(#2427)

Popular 1909-S VDB Cent, MS65 Red and Brown

265 **1909-S VDB MS65 Red and Brown PCGS. CAC.** The highly popular 1909-S VDB cent is desirable in all grades, and it is especially popular in Mint State grades. This Gem has light olive patina over substantial portions of original orange mint frost. A couple of tiny spots appear on the obverse.(#2427)

Lovely 1909-S VDB Cent, MS65 Red and Brown

266 **1909-S VDB MS65 Red and Brown PCGS. CAC.** Although PCGS gave this piece a Red and Brown designation, it has full red luster that has mellowed slightly over the years. It is also sharply struck and has limited flecks that prevent a higher numerical grade. A highly desirable example.(#2427)

Opulent MS66 Red and Brown 1909-S VDB Cent

267 **1909-S VDB MS66 Red and Brown NGC.** Both sides of this gorgeous Premium Gem retain ample crimson-red luster with only hints of mellowing. This is a sharply impressed representative with no surface blemishes to report. As attractive an example of this key Lincoln cent as can be imagined without fully Red coloration. (#2427)

MS66 Red and Brown, Key 1909-S VDB Cent

268 **1909-S VDB MS66 Red and Brown NGC.** Whispers of tan patination visit both sides of this key-date Lincoln cent representative, but copper-gold luster still dominates. An attentive strike imparts sharp definition to the design elements, including the grains and lines in the wheat stalks. The designer's initials, while plain, are somewhat softly struck. Splendidly preserved surfaces appear mark-free and display only negligible carbon. Protected within an early NGC holder.(#2427)

Famous 1909-S VDB Cent, MS66 Red and Brown

269 **1909-S VDB MS66 Red and Brown PCGS.** A thoroughly lustrous key date Premium Gem that boasts unabraded, carbon-free surfaces. Wheat-gold and orange with glimpses of yellow. The strike is precise aside from the VDB initials, which are nonetheless distinct. Certified in a prior generation holder.(#2427)

Pleasing MS63 Red 1909-S VDB Cent

270 **1909-S VDB MS63 Red PCGS.** A beautiful sun-gold cent that possesses ebullient luster, bright color, minimal marks, and only a faint indication of carbon. The strike is needle-sharp, especially on the all-important initials. Although the 1909-S VDB cent was set aside by alert collectors from its initial release, the demand for this low mintage key issue remains voracious.(#2428)

Appealing 1909-S VDB Cent, MS64 Red

271 **1909-S VDB MS64 Red PCGS.** Luminous copper-orange surfaces show a hint of blue at the right obverse. Well struck with considerable eye appeal for the Choice designation and few flaws. As the key to the most widely collected issue in American numismatics, the 1909-S VDB cent experiences particularly heavy demand.(#2428)

Vibrant MS64 Red 1909-S VDB Cent

272 **1909-S VDB MS64 Red PCGS.** Bright lemon and orange shadings dominate the eye appeal of this shining near-Gem, crisply detailed with surprisingly few marks. For the grade, it is difficult to see how even a discerning Lincoln cent aficionado could do better. This key-date coin is housed in a green label holder.(#2428)

Sharp 1909-S VDB Cent, MS65 Red

273 **1909-S VDB MS65 Red PCGS.** Lustrous surfaces exhibit uniform copper-gold color laced with hints of light green, and a well directed strike impresses sharp definition onto the design features, including a crisp date, mintmark, and VDB. A hair-thin mark on Lincoln's shoulder is mentioned for complete accuracy. Encapsulated in a green label holder.(#2428)

274 **1909-S MS65 Red NGC.** Remarkable satiny luster with a combination of copper-orange and pink surfaces. Crisply detailed and carefully preserved, a notable first-year beauty.(#2434)

275 **1909-S MS65 Red PCGS.** Peach and yellow-olive colors endow this satiny Gem. Needle-sharp aside from the right border of the east wheat ear. A small obverse spot at 3 o'clock does not distract. Certified in an older generation PCGS holder.(#2434)

Luminous MS66 Red 1909-S Cent

276 **1909-S MS66 Red PCGS.** A luminous and magnificent Premium Gem representative of this first-year issue, not as famous as its VDB counterpart but genuinely elusive in its own right. Excellent detail with vibrant orange, copper-gold, and peach surfaces. PCGS has certified only four finer Red representatives (1/09).(#2434)

277 **1910-S MS65 Red PCGS.** A beautifully preserved Gem displaying lovely tan color across subtly textured surfaces. Well-defined with a few specks of olive noted in the fields.(#2440)

Red Gem Semi-Key 1911-S Cent

278 **1911-S MS65 Red NGC.** This beautiful pumpkin-gold Gem is mark-free, and strong magnification is required to locate its trivial carbon. The strike is crisp overall despite slight softness on the mintmark and the L in LIBERTY. The 1911-S is a popular low mintage semi-key. Housed in a former generation holder. Census: 26 in 65 Red, 4 finer (2/09).(#2449)

279 **1912 MS66 Red PCGS.** The obverse has pleasing copper-orange color, while the reverse is paler lemon-gold. A well struck Premium Gem that offers impressive eye appeal. PCGS has graded seven finer Red examples (1/09).(#2452)

280 **1912 MS66 Red PCGS.** From pumpkin to rose and copper-orange, this early Lincoln cent shows a wide variety of colors without crossing into Red and Brown territory. Crisply detailed and carefully preserved.(#2452)

281 **1912-D MS65 Red PCGS.** Vibrant copper-orange color overall with a hint of violet at the right reverse. The obverse also shows evidence of a fingerprint. A well-defined example, minimally abraded. PCGS has graded nine finer Red pieces (2/09). (#2455)

282 **1914-D AU50 PCGS.** Rich violet-brown color with occasional glimpses of orange. A well-defined example of this popular Lincoln cent key, minimally worn for the grade with few abrasions. (#2471)

283 **1914-D MS60 Brown ANACS.** Deep walnut-brown surfaces are glossy with blue overtones. No trace of wear, though each side shows wispy abrasions and a few small digs.(#2471)

Smooth MS62 Brown 1914-D Cent

284 **1914-D MS62 Brown NGC.** An exactly struck example of this key date cent. Toned deep golden-brown overall with plum-red and cobalt-blue undertones on the reverse. Satiny and unmarked. Only two issues have lower mintages, the 1909-S VDB and the 1931-S. Unlike those two dates, the 1914-D was little considered upon release and Uncirculated pieces are rare.
From The Ed Lepordo Collection, Part Two.(#2471)

Charming MS63 Red and Brown 1914-D Cent

285 **1914-D MS63 Red and Brown PCGS.** Violet-brown, mahogany, and copper-orange shadings mingle on each side of this Select key-date coin. The strike is solid for the issue, with only a few wispy abrasions determining the numeric grade. Powerfully appealing and a readily collectible example of this famous Lincoln cent key. (#2472)

Commendable 1914-D Cent, MS64 Red and Brown

286 **1914-D MS64 Red and Brown PCGS.** There is much to commend this coin, aside from its obvious status as a near-Gem of one of the most-desired keys to the Lincoln cent classic collection. The surfaces glow softly with orange-red coloration that seems just barely over the border of full Red appellation. The strike is boldly executed for the issue, and the few tiny flecks that appear under a loupe are neither distracting nor prevalent.(#2472)

Choice Red and Brown 1914-D Cent

287 **1914-D MS64 Red and Brown NGC.** A nicely impressed and satiny key date near-Gem with ample dusky fire-red iridescence. Smooth aside from a solitary inconspicuous thin mark on the reverse exergue. Among business strike issues, only the 1931-S and the 1909-S VDB have lower mintages.(#2472)

288 **1914-S MS64 Red and Brown NGC.** An attractive near-Gem cent, with slight browning in the upper right obverse quadrant that keeps it from receiving a Red color designation from NGC. Boldly struck, lustrous, and nicely preserved. Census: 41 in 64 Red and Brown, 28 finer (2/09).
From The Ed Lepordo Collection, Part Two.(#2475)

Gem Red and Brown 1914-S Cent

289 **1914-S MS65 Red and Brown NGC.** Like many mintmarked issues from the teens, the 1914-S has a low mintage. Only 4.137 million pieces were struck, and most examples set aside by West Coast collectors are in circulated grades. This is a smooth, satiny, glossy, and unblemished Gem with lovely chestnut-gold color. The obverse provides additional rose and lime undertones. (#2475)

290 **1915 MS65 Red PCGS.** A well struck Gem that has flashy luster and bright red-gold color. A few minuscule carbon flecks reside near the left wheat ear. PCGS has accidentally encapsulated a hair on the reverse at 10 o'clock, but it rests harmlessly away from the coin.(#2479)

Splendid 1915-S Cent, MS64 Red and Brown

291 **1915-S MS64 Red and Brown PCGS.** A splendid example of this semikey Lincoln cent, one likely to appeal to the many collectors assembling non-Red cents of this elusive series. The obverse is brick-red and lavender, with some pretty bluish-brown tints on the reverse. Sharply struck and appealing. PCGS has certified only 14 Red and Brown coins finer (2/09).(#2484)

292 **1916-D MS64 Red PCGS.** Sharp and lustrous. A Choice example that has a few small carbon flecks and a couple of tiny abrasions on the reverse, but no individually mentionable flaws. PCGS has graded 43 finer Red representatives (2/09).(#2491)

Lustrous Red Gem 1916-D Cent

293   **1916-D MS65 Red ANACS.** The 1916-D is an underappreciated issue in Gem full Red. Both PCGS and NGC have certified more examples of the 1914-D in MS65 Red and finer, yet, when available, the 1916-D can be secured at a fraction of the price of its key date predecessor. This is a lustrous orange-gold example with an exemplary strike. Carbon is limited to the reverse exergue. (#2491)

294   **1917 MS66 Red PCGS.** Both sides of this Premium Gem cent are awash in dazzling orange-gold luster, and a solid strike leaves excellent definition on the design elements. Devoid of mentionable contacts. Faint traces of a fingerprint in the right obverse field are mentioned for complete accuracy. Housed in a first-generation holder.(#2497)

295   **1919-D MS65 Red and Brown PCGS.** This is a marvelous Gem specimen that displays remarkable striking definition and highly lustrous champagne-tan surfaces. Mark-free on both sides, with a handful of scattered flyspecks that are hardly noticeable. In an old green label PCGS holder. Population: 25 in 65 Red and Brown, 2 finer (1/09).(#2517)

Razor-Sharp 1919-D Cent, MS65 Red

296   **1919-D MS65 Red PCGS.** Examples of this postwar issue are generally poorly struck, with mediocre color and surface qualities. Not so the present razor-sharp Gem with medium rose-gold color, full cartwheel luster, and a seemingly immaculate obverse, clearly an early strike from fresh dies. While not as elusive as its sibling the 1919-S, Gem Red 1919-D Lincolns are still incredibly difficult to find in such good shape. Population: 57 in 65 Red, 12 finer (2/09). (#2518)

297   **1919-S MS65 Red and Brown NGC.** An attractive early Lincoln cent from the San Francisco Mint, with satin luster and hints of red still visible on both sides. This issue is common in low grades but extremely scarce in Gem condition, with any color designation. Census: 23 in 65 Red and Brown, 0 finer (2/09).(#2520)

298   **1919-S MS64 Red PCGS.** Rich copper-orange color with glimpses of gold and minimal carbon. This near-Gem is well struck with few abrasions. PCGS has graded 22 finer Red examples (2/09). (#2521)

299   **1920-S MS65 Red and Brown NGC.** A conditionally challenging early Lincoln cent issue at the Gem grade level. This example is boldly struck overall, if slightly weak on Lincoln's temple area and on AME in AMERICA. The lustrous red-brown surfaces are impressively preserved and nearly pristine. Census: 19 in 65 Red and Brown, 0 finer (2/09).(#2529)

300   **1921 MS66 Red PCGS.** Bright wheat-gold and honey-orange surfaces teem with luster. The cheek has a blush of rose-red. Excellent strike and eye appeal. PCGS has graded only 11 finer Red representatives (2/09).(#2533)

301   **1921-S MS65 Red and Brown NGC.** The lustrous surfaces show an amalgam of deep, variegated red-gold and purple-rose patina, with occasional glints of lime-green color also noted on each side. Well struck throughout and carefully preserved, with mark-free surfaces that display minimal carbon. Census: 33 in 65 Red and Brown, 0 finer (2/09).(#2535)

302   **1922 No D Strong Reverse VF30 PCGS.** FS-013.2. Die Pair 2. Even on a midrange example such as the present red-brown piece, the lines of the wheat ears remain bold. Minimally marked and attractive.(#3285)

1922 No D Strong Reverse Cent, AU Details

303   **1922 No D Strong Reverse—Improperly Cleaned—NCS. AU Details.** FS-401, formerly FS-013.2. Die Pair 2. The obverse details are quite mushy, while the reverse details were produced from a fresh die, and are quite sharp. This piece displays some surface granularity and minor discoloration from improper cleaning. An affordable example of the most valuable of the three 1922 No D varieties.(#3285)

Luminous AU53 1922 No D, Strong Reverse Cent

304   **1922 No D Strong Reverse AU53 PCGS.** FS-401, formerly FS-013.2. Die Pair 2. Grading by the reverse (as is traditional for the variety), this is a lovely violet-brown survivor with only a touch of wear across the devices. A handful of small marks are visible on each side, but none of these is particularly distracting. *From The Ed Lepordo Collection, Part Two.*(#3285)

Scarce 1922 No D Cent, Strong Reverse, AU55

305   **1922 No D Strong Reverse AU55 PCGS.** FS-401 (formerly FS-013.2). Die Pair 2. The so-called Strong Reverse type is the most popular of the three 1922 No D Lincoln cent varieties. This variety is rare in Mint State and scarce in AU condition. The current example is well struck and displays variegated violet-brown and deep purple toning over both sides. Lightly worn and minimally marked for a briefly circulated coin.(#3285)

Appealing AU55 1922 No D Cent, Strong Reverse

306   **1922 No D Strong Reverse AU55 PCGS. CAC.** FS-401, formerly FS-013.2. Die Pair 2. Rich brown color overall with glimpses of caramel close to the rims. The obverse is characteristically ill-defined, but the wheat ears on the reverse show their signature bold lines. This example was saved early, with only a touch of rub visible on the high points.(#3285)

Condition Rarity 1924 Cent, MS67 Red

307   **1924 MS67 Red PCGS.** Ex: Jack Lee Collection. The 1924 Lincoln cent, sporting a mintage of 75,178,000 pieces, is readily available, even in comparatively high Mint State grades. Various commentators have noted this availability, including Q. David Bowers (2008), who described it as "common in all grades, including Mint State," and David Lange (1996), who notes that "... gems should not be considered rare." Indeed, at the MS65 Red level, there are sufficient extant survivors to meet current demand, and even Premium Gems can be acquired with a little patience and searching. MS67 examples, however, are elusive, and higher-grade specimens are virtually nonexistent

The surfaces of this remarkable Superb Gem are bright and primarily copper-orange. Strongly lustrous with hints of frostiness throughout. The strike is slightly above-average for the date, though Lincoln's hair and beard exhibit the usual weakness. On the reverse, the wheat ears are sharp and crisp and all lettering is clear, despite die clashing. At this lofty level, the combined certified population shows just five MS67 Red examples, one graded by NGC and four by PCGS, with none numerically finer (2/09).(#2551)

308   **1924-D MS64 Red PCGS.** Rich reddish-orange color mingles with pale copper-gold. Modestly abraded but undeniably appealing. PCGS has graded 39 finer Red examples (2/09).(#2554)

309   **1925-D MS64 Red PCGS.** This satiny red-orange near-Gem is well struck on the reverse, and only shows minor weakness on the obverse. Fully Red pieces are scarce, but MS64 Red is the most available level for such coins. Well-preserved and free of noticeable surface distractions.(#2563)

Challenging Gem Red and Brown 1925-S Cent

310 **1925-S MS65 Red and Brown PCGS.** The 1925-S is among the rarest dates in the series in full Red. The present Gem does have some mellowing of color on the portrait, but the remainder of the surfaces are orange-red. Lustrous, crisply struck, spot-free, and unabraded. Housed in a green label holder. *From The Burning Tree Collection.* (#2565)

Difficult MS65 1925-S Cent, Red and Brown

311 **1925-S MS65 Red and Brown NGC.** Olive-green, rose-red, walnut-tan, and sky-blue confirm the originality of this lustrous and pleasing Gem. The 1925-S is among the most difficult issues to secure at the MS65 level, and only one example (an MS66 Brown NGC) has been certified above that grade. (#2565)

312 **1926 MS67 Red PCGS.** Sharply struck with a beautifully pristine appearance and full mint-red color highlighted by intense, satiny mint luster. Expertly preserved and nearly immaculate, save for a tiny nick near the lower end of the left wheat stalk. Population: 57 in 67, 0 finer (2/09). (#2569)

Elusive 1926-S Cent, MS64 Red and Brown

313 **1926-S MS64 Red and Brown PCGS.** The lustrous surfaces are still mostly red on this piece, and while visible contact is minor, it is the generally soft strike that keeps the piece from the Gem category. This coin is a nice compromise between quality and price, as there is only a single Gem Red specimen of this issue certified at PCGS, as series aficionados are well aware, a coin that has sold recently for well into the six figures. PCGS has certified only 12 1926-S coins in MS65 Red and Brown (2/09). (#2574)

Well Struck 1926-S Cent
MS64 Red and Brown

314 **1926-S MS64 Red and Brown PCGS.** Whispers of light green and crimson visit the copper-gold lustrous surfaces of this near-Gem S-mint representative. A well executed strike leaves strong definition on the design elements, including completeness in the lines and grains of the wheat stalks. Minute brownish freckles are scattered over each side. (#2574)

Conditionally Rare Choice 1926-S Cent, Red and Brown

315 **1926-S MS64 Red and Brown NGC.** Struck better than the typical San Francisco Mint issues of the 1920s. The mint-red coloration is slightly faded to reddish-brown. This is a very pleasing near-Gem specimen of this noted conditional rarity. The 1926-S is the single most difficult issue to locate in MS65 Red. *From The Ed Lepordo Collection, Part Two.* (#2574)

Gem Red and Brown 1926-S Cent

316 **1926-S MS65 Red and Brown NGC.** Since NGC has certified exactly one 1926-S cent as MS65 Red, even the most determined collector must settle for a Red and Brown example if the MS65 grade is desired. Apparently West Coast collectors were too busy chasing the new 1926-S Oregon half to set aside cents. This is a satiny and well struck Gem with smooth and slightly mellowed orange-gold surfaces. The reverse displays hints of aqua and rose. (#2574)

317 **1927-S MS64 Red PCGS.** Slight striking softness at the portrait, though this Choice coin has many other redeeming features, chief among them well-preserved reddish-orange fields. The upper left obverse shows a fingerprint fragment. *From The Burning Tree Collection.* (#2584)

318 **1928 MS67 Red NGC.** This is a blazing-red coin with a rich, frosted texture. There are no noticeable abrasions, but a small carbon spot between the ST in STATES is noted for accuracy. Census: 14 in 67 Red, 0 finer (1/09). (#2587)

319 **1928 MS67 Red ANACS.** Crisply detailed with fresh and vibrant luster that ranges from copper-gold to fiery orange. Amazing eye appeal with no singularly mentionable flaws. (#2587)

Sharp Gem Red 1928-D Cent

320 **1928-D MS65 Red PCGS.** While not quite in the same echelon as the 1928-S, 1927-D, or 1927-S, the 1928-D is still quite scarce in Gem Red condition: PCGS has graded 72 pieces so far, with 11 pieces finer (2/09). This attractive piece offers appealing, lustrous, and pristine brick-red surfaces on both obverse and reverse, with a razor-sharp strike. Glints of ice-blue appear on the high points, and there are minimal carbon flecks. (#2590)

321 **1930-D MS66 Red PCGS.** Vibrant copper-orange color and a pleasing strike for the issue. This D-mint cent has few superiors in the color category; PCGS acknowledges just seven such pieces (1/09). (#2608)

322 **1931-D MS65 Red PCGS.** For an issue seldom seen with such bright, lustrous surfaces, this is an unusually attractive and important example. A few light flecks are noted on each side. PCGS has certified only 30 Red coins finer (2/09). (#2617)

Top-Flight 1943 Cent, MS68

323 **1943 MS68 PCGS.** The surfaces are nearly flawless and show no traces of oxidation. One tiny fleck is noted on Lincoln's cheek, this perhaps the only bar to an even finer designation. This coin's virtually unimprovable quality is reflected in the combined certified population, which shows none better (1/09). (#2711)

324 **1947-D MS67 Red PCGS.** Fresh copper-orange color with a sharp strike and vibrant eye appeal. This D-mint Superb Gem is tied for the finest Red example known to PCGS (2/09). (#2755)

325 **1952-D MS67 Red PCGS.** Ex: Ron Bozarth Collection. A superlative example with deep cherry-red surfaces and booming luster. Excellent eye appeal. Population: 48 in 67 Red, 0 finer (2/09). (#2800)

326 **1955 Doubled Die Obverse XF45 NGC.** FS-101, formerly FS-021.8. Generally violet-brown surfaces show glimpses of original reddish-orange and tinges of gloss on this briefly circulated piece. Well struck and pleasing, a minimally marked example of this popular doubled die. (#2825)

327 **1955 Doubled Die Obverse AU55 PCGS.** FS-101, formerly FS-021.8. Evenly worn across the obverse high points, with rich chocolate-tan coloration and minimal surface marks. One of the most famous and popular Doubled Dies in all of U.S. numismatics. Housed in a PCGS holder with a light-green label. (#2825)

Exciting Select Brown Doubled Die 1955 Cent

328 **1955 Doubled Die Obverse MS63 Brown NGC.** FS-101, formerly FS-021.8. A lustrous example of this spectacular *Guide Book* variety. Predominantly golden-brown with glimpses of blue-green on the highpoints. Marks are minimal, and the eye appeal is imposing. Perhaps the best known doubled die in all numismatics. *From The Ed Lepordo Collection, Part Two.* (#2825)

Popular 1955 Doubled Die Obverse Lincoln Cent MS62 Red and Brown

329 **1955 Doubled Die Obverse MS62 Red and Brown PCGS.** FS-101, formerly FS-021.8. One of the most important and popular overdate varieties in all of U.S. numismatics, the 1955 Doubled Die obverse shows dramatic doubling on all of the obverse lettering, and on the date. This example is boldly struck and lustrous, with minimal surface marks and a few scattered carbon specks on each side. (#2826)

Desirable 1955 Doubled Die Cent, MS63 Red

330 **1955 Doubled Die Obverse MS63 Red PCGS.** FS-101, formerly
FS-021.8. Rich reddish-orange color overall with occasional
glimpses of tan. This Red Select piece shows plainly the doubling
on the peripheral elements of the obverse. Minimally marked for
the grade, if a trifle softly struck on the portrait. Excellent eye
appeal for the variety that sparked widespread interest in doubled
dies, and a tough issue with the Red certification from PCGS.
(#2827)

Bright MS63 Red 1955 Doubled Die Cent

331 **1955 Doubled Die Obverse MS63 Red PCGS.** FS-101, formerly
FS-021.8. The first known and most dramatic of all the doubled die
Lincoln cent varieties. No loupe is needed to see the wide spread
throughout the obverse legends. Most Uncirculated survivors are
toned brown, but the present piece retains its bright initial orange-
red color, and is only limited in grade by a minor aqua streak on the
right obverse field.
From The Burning Tree Collection.(#2827)

Impressive 1955 Doubled Die Obverse Cent
MS64 Red, FS-101

332 **1955 Doubled Die Obverse MS64 Red PCGS.** FS-101, formerly
FS-021.8. This is an especially impressive and desirable Doubled
Die cent. The mint luster is unfaded from the original bright
orange-red color when the coin was new. The MS64 grade is
accounted for by the presence of several tiny obverse specks and
a streak of navy-blue near the forehead. An important full Red
example of this popular Lincoln cent rarity. PCGS has certified
only 18 Red pieces finer (02/09).(#2827)

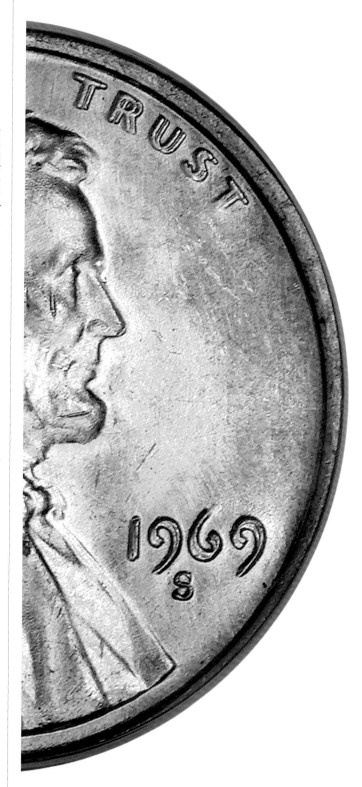

333   **1969-S Doubled Die Obverse MS63 Red PCGS.** FS-101 (formerly FS-028). The recently released fifth edition of Bill Fivaz and J.T. Stanton's popular *Cherrypickers' Guide* records the rarity of this variety as "URS-6," which means that between 17 and 32 examples are believed to exist. That is an extremely small number of coins for a collecting specialty as popular as Lincoln cents. (In fact, that is a small number of coins for nearly any collecting specialty.)

In addition to its rarity, Fivaz and Stanton have estimated its "Interest Factor" and "Liquidity Factor" as I-5 and L-5, respectively. Both ratings are the highest they give. An I-5 Interest Factor means "very high interest (most general collectors interested)" and an L-5 Liquidity Factor means it "will sell easily, and often above listed value." They further comment that "the publicity this coin has received over its lifetime has been enormous, hence the very high values, which are well deserved. This is a very rare, strong doubled die."

This beautiful cent has fully brilliant orange luster with satiny, slightly reflective surfaces and bold design features. A few tiny surface marks and a minor obverse spot are all that prevent a higher numerical grade. The date, LIBERTY, and IN GOD WE TRUST are all boldly doubled, sharply enough that the doubling can be seen without a magnifying glass. That is part of what makes this doubled die variety so popular. Machine doubled 1969-S cents are very common and have no premium value. Those machine-doubled pieces have a doubled mintmark in addition to other doubling. As always on genuine examples, the mintmark is normal with no doubling. That is the case because the die doubling occurred before the mintmark was punched into the die. This piece is one of only three Red Mint State coins at PCGS, and among the finest certified. There are two MS64 Red pieces and one MS64 Red and Brown numerically finer (1/09).(#2923)

Superlative 2008-D Cent, MS68 Red
The 100th Annual Lincoln Cent Issue

334   **2008-D MS68 Red PCGS.** With all the celebrations taking place this year to honor Abraham Lincoln on the 200th anniversary of his birth, and the 100th anniversary of the Lincoln cent, it is important to remember that 2008, not 2009, is the 100th year of Lincoln cent production. This example was struck at the Denver Mint, a facility that had its start at the very end of Lincoln's Presidency, although it would be many more years before actual coinage operations started.

     This example is certified as a normal circulation strike 2008-D Lincoln cent, and it has a PCGS population of just four examples in MS68 Red, with none finer (1/09). Another variety is the Satin Finish 2008-D cent that was produced specially for collectors. More than 400 of those have been certified at this same grade level, with 42 more in MS69 Red. It is highly important to distinguish between the two different issues. The advanced PCGS Registry Set collector will want to be successful bidding on this coin to gain that extra little advantage over other Lincoln cent collectors. There are currently 80 individual collectors of PCGS-certified Lincoln Memorial cents, including major varieties.

     An incredible, superlative Superb Gem, this unsurpassable example has a bold strike that shows every feature from the die. The surfaces have fully brilliant and highly lustrous satin gloss with blazing pink color and traces of copper-orange toning. The number of tiny imperfections that prevent an even higher grade can almost literally be counted on one hand. This coin was struck early in the life of the individual coinage dies, showing no evidence of clash marks, die cracks, or other signs of die wear on either side. (#394905)

PROOF LINCOLN CENTS

Red and Iridescently Toned 1909 VDB Cent
PR63 Red and Brown

335   **1909 VDB PR63 Red and Brown ANACS.** Mostly red with a faint accent of light iridescent gold, lime-green, and violet colors. An exquisitely struck and beautifully preserved matte proof. Much scarcer than the variety without the reverse initials and the key to the series with only 1,194 proofs struck. Few of the remaining recognizable proofs will show as much red as is present on this example. (#3301)

336   **1910 PR65 Red and Brown NGC.** A well-defined example of this popular matte proof issue. The obverse has a rich blend of violet and pumpkin shadings, while the reverse mostly shows the latter color. (#3307)

337   **1910 PR65 Red and Brown NGC. CAC.** Both sides of this boldly defined matte proof have deep orange surfaces with splashes of pale gold and iridescent toning. Heavy die polishing lines along the upper obverse border are characteristic of the matte proof 1910 cents, and they are clearly visible on this Gem. *From The Burning Tree Collection.* (#3307)

338   **1911 PR64 Red and Brown PCGS.** This well struck near-Gem displays soft maroon patina through which glints of copper-orange luster show. Both sides are devoid of significant contact marks. (#3310)

Elusive PR64 Red 1912 Lincoln Cent

339   **1912 PR64 Red PCGS.** Instantly identifiable as a proof specimen by virtue of razor-sharp definition on all of the familiar design elements. Essentially red on both sides, with intermingled accents of mint-green and copper-gold. A conditionally scarce near-Gem, from a low mintage of 2,172 pieces. Population: 32 in 64 Red, 17 finer (1/09). (#3314)

340   **1913 PR64 Red and Brown PCGS.** Purple and orange coloration bathes each side of this near-Gem proof, and an exacting strike imparts sharp definition to the design features. Several flecks are scattered about the obverse. (#3316)

341   **1914 PR64 Brown PCGS.** Crisp definition on the design elements is the hallmark of this proof cent, which is especially evident on Lincoln's hair and bow tie, and on the lines and grains of the wheat stalks. Uniform, medium brown surfaces are nicely preserved. A tiny light fleck is visible left of the 1 in the date. (#3318)

Attractive PR65 Red 1915 Cent

342   **1915 PR65 Red NGC.** Only 15% of the mintage of 1,150 proof 1915 cents is known today with full Red color. Undoubtedly this is because the coins were wrapped in tissue paper at the Mint, and the sulphur in the paper caused the coins to tone. This piece has lovely red surfaces, and the only variation is seen on the right side of the obverse, where slight iridescence is noted. A few flecks of carbon keep this lovely piece from an even higher grade. Census: 5 in 65 Red, 0 finer (1/09). (#3323)

Razor-Sharp 1936 Satin Finish Cent
PR66 Red and Brown

343 **1936 Type One—Satin Finish PR66 Red and Brown PCGS. CAC.** Ruby-red and peach colors enrich this razor-sharp and virtually immaculate Premium Gem. Satin Finish proof Lincoln cents were only struck in 1936, and serve as a transitional finish between the matte proofs of earlier years and the brilliant proofs that are still produced today. Population: 4 in 66 Red and Brown, 0 finer (2/09).(#3331)

344 **1936 Type One—Satin Finish PR64 Red NGC.** A bright piece, generally pale copper-gold with orange accents and a ring of violet around the obverse rim. Faint hairlines preclude a finer designation. (#3332)

345 **1936 Type One—Satin Finish PR65 Red NGC.** Generous salmon-pink overtones invigorate the smooth surfaces. A crisply detailed example of this popular issue, the beginning of the modern proof Lincoln cent series.(#3332)

Lovely 1936 Type Two—Brilliant Finish Cent, PR65 Red

346 **1936 Type Two—Brilliant Finish PR65 Red PCGS.** The first year of issue for modern proofs and highly popular as a result. Sharply struck, with brilliant gold surfaces occasionally splashed with cherry-red , and hints of pale green near the reverse peripheries. Both sides seem pristine, or essentially so. A lovely Gem proof Lincoln cent.(#3335)

1936 Type Two Lincoln Cent, PR66 Red

347 **1936 Type Two—Brilliant Finish—PR66 Red NGC.** This is a gorgeous Premium Gem specimen from the second proof type produced in 1936: the so-called Brilliant Finish. This example demonstrates razor-sharp striking on all of the Lincoln cent's familiar features, including Lincoln's beard, hair, and ear. Vivid orange-red toning dominates on both sides, but areas of bright silver-blue also occur, especially on Lincoln's cheek, neck, and collar. Census: 18 in 66 Red, 2 finer (1/09).(#3335)

Splendid PR67 Red 1937 Cent

348 **1937 PR67 Red NGC.** Splendid brick-red surfaces show absolutely no imperfections or carbon of even the remotest sort. The second year of proof coinage saw a limited mintage of only 9,320 cents, in a period when the various components of the proof set could be each ordered individually. Census: 14 in 67 Red, 0 finer (2/09). (#3338)

349 **1937 PR66 Red Cameo NGC.** Luminous copper-gold surfaces display splashes of orange and crimson on the obverse, and well struck design elements exhibit modest contrast with the reflective fields. A hair-thin mark is visible in the field above the N in ONE. (#83338)

350 **1938 PR66 Red Cameo NGC.** A sparkling, unmellowed Premium Gem with impressive contrast for the issue. Excellent visual appeal with strong reflectivity. Census: 11 in 66 Red Cameo, 2 finer (2/09).(#83341)

351 **1939 PR67 Red NGC.** It would be difficult to overstate the quality of this impressive proof Lincoln cent. Fully struck with utterly immense reflectivity in the fields, and immaculate surfaces. A mere 13,520 pieces were produced, and Superb Gem survivors are rare. Census: 27 in 67 Red, 0 finer (2/09).(#3344)

TWO CENT PIECES

Luminous MS64 Red 1864 Small Motto Two Cent

352 **1864 Small Motto MS64 Red NGC.** FS-401, formerly FS-000.5. The Small Motto has been one of the most treasured varieties for the two cent series since collectors first tackled it in earnest. The present coin is pale copper-gold overall with minor carbon at the upper right obverse and a degree of spotting at the lower and central reverse.(#3581)

Sharp 1864 Small Motto, MS65 Red and Brown

353 **1864 Small Motto MS65 Red and Brown NGC. CAC.** The stem to the leaf beneath WE shows plainly, and the first T in TRUST nearly touches the scroll crease. Whispers of light tan visit the copper-orange surfaces of this key-date two cent piece, and a well executed strike imparts strong detail to the design elements. Nicely preserved. Some thin peripheral cracks are visible on both sides. Census: 52 in 65 Red and Brown, 14 finer (2/09).(#3580)

Pleasing Gem 1864 Small Motto Two Cent, Red and Brown

354 **1864 Small Motto MS65 Red and Brown NGC.** The 1864 Large Motto two cent may be common, but the same cannot be said for its Small Motto counterpart, which is rare in Mint State. This boldly struck and unabraded Gem has slightly mellowed brick-red surfaces and a solitary tiny fleck at the obverse center. Certified in a former generation holder.
Ex: Summer FUN Signature (Heritage, 6/2008), lot 302, which realized $3,737.50.
From The Ed Lepordo Collection, Part Two.(#3580)

Splendid 1864 Large Motto, MS66 Red

355 **1864 Large Motto MS66 Red PCGS. CAC.** A highly lustrous peach-gold Premium Gem. This piece is impressively devoid of abrasions, and the type is practically unobtainable any finer. The obverse is essentially as made, and we note just a couple of tiny flecks on the reverse periphery. Population: 46 in 66 Red, 1 finer (2/09).(#3578)

356 **1865 MS65 Red NGC.** Plain 5. The obverse is generally pale copper-gold, though more muted orange shadings are present on the reverse. A well struck Gem from the second year of issue. Certified in a former generation holder.(#3584)

357 **1865 MS65 Red PCGS.** Plain 5. The 865 in the date is repunched, most noticeably within the lower loop of the 6. Well struck except for NIT in UNITED. A lustrous Gem that has bright gold color and immaculate surfaces. A small carbon fleck left of the prominent 2 is of little importance.(#3584)

358 **1866 MS65 Red PCGS.** Vivid red-gold color dominates, although a whisper of apple-green is also present. The strike is good, and marks are virtually absent. Population: 35 in 65 Red, 7 finer (1/09).(#3590)

359 **1868 MS64 Red PCGS.** Sharply struck with rich red-gold coloration and minimal surface disturbances for the grade. Interesting, wispy die lines reside beneath the date. Population: 28 in 64 Red, 14 finer (2/09).(#3599)

PROOF TWO CENT PIECES

Glorious 1864 Large Motto Two Cent
PR66 ★ Brown

360 **1864 Large Motto PR66 ★ Brown NGC.** The mintage of this issue is unknown, although the most often used guess is in the range of 100-200 pieces. Either extreme makes this a rare and underrated issue. It is known that 100 proof sets were made at the end of July 1864, but other pieces were probably made earlier in the year, in April, to celebrate the passage of the Act of Congress authorizing the bronze cents and the new two cent denomination.
This piece is the fourth of the various die varieties Breen describes in his 1989 edition of the *Proof Encyclopedia:* minute die chip left of W(E), left base of 1 right of center of denticle. Glorious ocean-blue highlights appear under a light, with pinkish-tan remaining in protected areas near the devices. Inordinately attractive, with no visible carbon. NGC has certified one Brown coin numerically finer (2/09).(#3621)

PR66 Brown 1864 Large Motto Two Cent

361 **1864 Large Motto PR66 Brown NGC.** Although hardly as famous as its nearly noncollectible Small Motto counterpart, the proof 1864 Large Motto is also a rarity. The *Guide Book* reports a proof mintage of only 100+ pieces, few of which can compare to the present Premium Gem. This is an incisively struck specimen that displays rose-red and jade-green when it is rotated beneath a light. Unabraded and carbon-free.(#3621)

362 **1864 Large Motto PR65 Red and Brown Cameo NGC.** A strongly reflective specimen, largely reddish-gold with mottled brown overtones and a distinct cameo effect. Sharp overall; there are no mentionable spots or marks. Strong eye appeal.(#3622)

Lovely PR66 Red and Brown 1866 Two Cent

363 **1866 PR66 Red and Brown PCGS.** The fields are still fully within the Red designation, actually a lovely sunset-orange color, but the raised devices and a small portion of the reverse fields inside the wreath are Brown, creating a lovely cameo effect. Sharply struck and pleasing. Population: 8 in 66 Red and Brown, 0 finer (2/09). (#3631)

364 **1867 PR65 Red and Brown PCGS. CAC.** This gorgeous Gem proof has deep orange color on both sides with hints of iridescence, especially on the reverse. It is a boldly struck representative with exceptional eye appeal.
From The Burning Tree Collection.(#3634)

365 **1867 PR66 Red and Brown NGC.** This alluring two-toned specimen exhibits lime-green color in the fields and reddish-copper patina on the high points of the design. Sharply struck, well preserved, and free of distractions. Census: 18 in 66 Red and Brown, 1 finer (2/09).(#3634)

Cameo Red Gem Proof 1867 Two Cent

366 **1867 PR65 Red Cameo NGC.** A prominently mirrored and decisively struck Gem with noticeable contrast and only minor carbon. Generally yellow-gold with hints of peach-red in design crevices. NGC has certified only three proofs as Red Cameo, a PR64 piece and two that grade PR65 (2/09). Just 625 proofs were struck.
From The Burning Tree Collection.(#83635)

367 **1869 PR66 Red and Brown PCGS. CAC.** Mirrored fields nicely highlight the boldly struck design features of this Premium Gem proof. Whispers of purple-tan visit the orange-gold surfaces, which are devoid of mentionable contacts or spots. Population: 9 in 66 Red and Brown, 2 finer (2/09).(#3640)

368 **1869 PR66 Red and Brown NGC.** Whispers of sky-blue, crimson, and golden-orange toning adorn both ides of this Premium Gem proof. Sharply struck design elements are highlighted against reflective fields when the coin is rotated slightly under a light source. Free of mentionable contacts or spots. Census: 24 in 66 Red and Brown, 1 finer (2/09).(#3640)

369 **1870 PR65 Red and Brown NGC.** The design elements are produced with razor-sharp precision, which is not always true for proof two cent pieces. The glassy surfaces are well preserved and free of distractions. Census: 51 in 65 Red and Brown, 16 finer (2/09).(#3643)

370 **1872 PR65 Red and Brown PCGS. CAC.** Boldly impressed with electrifying patina. The violet and blue hues present on the otherwise copper-orange obverse give only a hint of the similar but more striking colors that dominate the reverse.(#3649)

Rich Red Gem Proof 1872 Two Cent

371 **1872 PR65 Red NGC.** Crisply detailed with rich copper-orange color that takes on an olive tinge within the reverse wreath. The fields are carefully preserved, and the overall eye appeal is grand. A great specimen from the last of the proof two cent issues to have an accompanying circulation striking. Census: 20 in 65 Red, 5 finer (2/09).(#3650)

Gem Red and Brown Proof-Only 1873 Two Cent Piece
Closed 3, Original Striking

372 **1873 Closed 3 PR65 Red and Brown NGC. CAC.** Precisely struck and flashy with an unabraded appearance. Generally sungold with glimpses of plum-red. Carbon-free save for a solitary fleck on the reverse at 1 o'clock. A scant 600 proofs were struck for the Closed 3 variety of this proof-only date.(#3652)

Choice Proof 1873 Open 3 Two Cent Piece

373 **1873 Open 3 PR64 Brown PCGS.** A gently shimmering near-Gem that has a good strike and a nearly carbon-free appearance. Although designated as Brown, orange-red luster persists within the shield and about the reverse legend. A popular proof-only date, limited to 600 Closed 3 originals and 500 Open 3 restrikes. (#3654)

Premium Gem 1873 Open 3 Two Cent

374 **1873 Open 3 PR66 Brown NGC.** 1873 was a landmark year in American numismatic history. Several denominations, including the two cent piece, ended production that year. Like its three cent silver counterpart, the 1873 two cent piece is proof only. Two varieties are known, Open 3 and Closed 3, and they are of comparable scarcity. This is a boldly struck Premium Gem with undisturbed deep brown surfaces. Glimpses of lighter gold persist near design recesses.(#3654)

THREE CENT SILVER

375 **1851 MS65 PCGS. CAC.** Splashes of tan-orange peripheral toning surround silver-gray centers. A pleasing Gem example of this first-year issue, well-defined with strong eye appeal.(#3664)

376 **1851 MS65 PCGS.** Ivory surfaces have underlying frosty luster with few marks of any kind. A few small splashes of darker patina are present on the obverse. The reverse has a short die crack through the star just shy of 12 o'clock.(#3664)

377 **1851 MS66 NGC.** Glowing luster is evident beneath the layer of attractive bluish-gray and beige-gold patina. An unobtrusive hair-thin reverse mark is noted on otherwise impeccably preserved surfaces. We mention some localized design softness, typical of Type One three cent silver pieces.(#3664)

378 **1851 MS66 PCGS. CAC.** A nearly immaculate pearl-gray Premium Gem that has freckled pale tan toning and blazing cartwheel sheen. A good strike with only subtle incompleteness on the peripheral stars and on the center of the shield.(#3664)

379 **1851 MS66 PCGS. CAC.** Well-defined with soft, pillowy luster lending grand eye appeal to each side of this Premium Gem. Delicate silver-blue and green-gold shadings converge on each side. (#3664)

380 **1852 MS65 PCGS.** Despite a rather weak impression, this Gem, housed in a first generation PCGS holder, has highly lustrous and frosty silver surfaces. It is a lovely piece suitable for a high quality date or type collection.(#3666)

Wonderful 1852 Three Cent Silver, MS67

381 **1852 MS67 PCGS.** This gorgeous Superb Gem is fully lustrous with faint champagne toning over frosty silver surfaces. Fine reverse roller marks are evident at the center. The dies are late, but they were still serviceable for additional strikes. Population: 11 in 67, 2 finer (2/09).(#3666)

Late State 1852 Three Cent Silver, MS67

382 **1852 MS67 NGC.** Highly lustrous silver surfaces exhibit faint traces of champagne toning. The strike is typically weak for the issue, and the reverse shows fine parallel roller marks. Struck from an extremely late state of the obverse die with cracks, clash marks, and peripheral flow lines. An amazing Superb Gem for the die state enthusiast. Census: 12 in 67, 0 finer (2/09).(#3666)

383 **1853 MS65 PCGS.** Bright luster with dabs of green-gold and silver-blue patina over much of the centers. This pleasingly detailed Gem is housed in a green label holder.(#3667)

384 1853 MS66 PCGS. Faint tan toning visits this lustrous and beautifully preserved Premium Gem. Well struck on the shield, with incompleteness limited to a few peripheral stars. A magnificent type coin from early in the series. Population: 45 in 66, 5 finer (1/09).(#3667)

Exceptional 1855 Three Cent Silver, MS65

385 1855 MS65 NGC. Repunched 855. Breen wrote in his *Encyclopedia* that all proofs and nearly all business strikes were from the same obverse die with the date repunched. He also noted that the proofs were coined first, and the business strikes were produced later with only traces of the repunching visible beneath the 55. However, the present piece shows clear repunching of the 855 and is in the same die state as the proofs. The present example is fully brilliant with frosty mint luster, bold design definition, and heavy reverse clash marks. Census: 10 in 65, 6 finer (2/09).(#3671)

Lustrous 1862 Three Cent Silver, MS67

386 1862 MS67 PCGS. This boldly detailed three cent piece has frosty silver surfaces with exceptional aesthetic appeal. The surfaces are brilliant and highly lustrous with subtle evidence of champagne toning. Both sides have light clash marks. There are no evident abrasions or other imperfections on this Superb Gem. Population: 11 in 67, 0 finer (2/09).(#3680)

387 1862/1 MS66 PCGS. CAC. An incredible Premium Gem with amazing eye appeal that is created through a combination of sharp design motifs and frosty mint luster. Population: 63 in 66, 12 finer (1/09).(#3681)

Captivating MS66 1864 Three Cent Silver

388 1864 MS66 PCGS. Gorgeously toned in autumn-gold, lime-green, and fire-red. The borders exhibit the deeper colors. Well struck and shimmering with an immaculate appearance. The obverse is boldly clashed. A mere 12,000 pieces were struck for this heavily melted Civil War-era issue. Population: 16 in 66, 12 finer (2/09). (#3684)

389 1868 MS63 PCGS. A brilliant Mint State example, this lovely piece has fully mirrored fields around lustrous devices. Typical grade-consistent abrasions are evident on both sides. Mint State silver three cent pieces from the post-Civil War era are especially elusive. A tiny raised die artifact above the 1 suggests that the date may have been repunched. Population: 4 in 63, 11 finer (2/09). *From The Ed Lepordo Collection, Part Two.*(#3688)

Low Mintage 1868 Three Cent Silver, MS64

390 1868 MS64 NGC. A mere 3,500 circulation strike three cent silvers were coined in 1868. Despite heavy mauve, cobalt-blue, lavender, and gold toning, partially prooflike fields are still somewhat discernible when the coin is tilted beneath a light source. The surfaces are sharply struck, and devoid of mentionable marks. Census: 7 in 64, 6 finer (2/09).(#3688)

Desirable MS66 1871 Three Cent Silver

391 1871 MS66 PCGS. Characteristically reflective, though the rims are not so squared-off as is the norm on proofs, confirming its business strike status. Richly toned lavender-silver on the obverse with a less patinated reverse. A great example of this issue which experienced mass melting in 1873. Population: 15 in 66, 11 finer (2/09).(#3692)

Superb Gem 1871 Three Cent Silver

392 1871 MS67 NGC. An extraordinary 1871 trime with typically reflective surfaces that are overlaid in attractive coppery-gold and steel-blue iridescence. Just 3,400 business strikes were issued and the bulk of high grade survivors traces back to a single well preserved hoard. Census: 17 in 67, 3 finer (2/09).(#3692)

Extremely Rare 1872 Three Cent Silver, MS65

393 **1872 MS65 NGC.** An impressive Gem, and extremely rare in business strike format. In fact this is one of few instances where the business strike and proof mintages were nearly the same. Mint records report that 1,000 business strikes and 950 proofs were minted. Today proofs are common but business strikes are almost unheard of. This piece has deep blue-green and iridescent toning with reflective fields and sharp design elements. Census: 8 in 65, 4 finer (2/09).(#3693)

PROOF THREE CENT SILVER

Desirable 1855 Three Cent Silver, PR65

394 **1855 PR65 NGC.** Repunched date with the 855 showing clear doubling as always on the proof examples and virtually all of the business strikes also. Breen claimed that the proofs were struck first, and the business strikes came later with less of the repunching visible, although a business strike in the present sale seems to suggest otherwise. This wonderful Gem proof has exquisite gold, blue-green, lilac, and iridescent toning with fully mirrored fields and frosty devices. Census: 8 in 65, 5 finer (2/09).(#3702)

395 **1862 PR63 Cameo PCGS.** Sharply struck with watery, pearl-gray fields and mildly frosted silver devices. A pleasing cameo effect is achieved on both sides. Faint hairlines occur on the obverse, and the reverse reveals slight die rust. Population: 2 in 63 Cameo, 7 finer (1/09).(#83711)

396 **1864 PR64 Cameo PCGS.** Stark contrast is evident on each side between sharply frosted devices and watery fields. Crisply struck with minor clash marks noted on the obverse. An attractively toned near-Gem specimen with champagne-tan and golden-brown patina. Population: 9 in 64 Cameo, 19 finer (2/09).(#83714)

397 **1866 PR66 NGC. CAC.** This is a lavishly toned Premium Gem proof with shades of deep electric-green and coral toning gracing highly reflective surfaces. Sharply struck and well-preserved with contact-free surfaces that show none of the frequently-seen die clash marks of this brief denomination. Census: 19 in 66, 1 finer (2/09).(#3716)

398 **1866 PR64 Deep Cameo PCGS.** The contrast on this example is extraordinary, with fully brilliant silver surfaces and impeccable mirrored fields. This interesting study piece has a small planchet lamination that crosses from the field to the star at three o'clock. The tiny laminated piece apparently fell away prior to the planchet polishing process, as the interior surface of the lamination has a polished appearance. Population: 5 in 64 Deep Cameo, 3 finer (2/09).(#93716)

399 **1867 PR64 PCGS.** A beautiful near-Gem proof, this example exhibits lovely blue-green, gold, and iridescent toning on both sides, with full underlying mirrored fields and subdued devices. It is an outstanding example for the date, type, or proof coin collector. (#3717)

Impressive 1867 Three Cent Silver, PR66

400 **1867 PR66 PCGS. CAC.** This is an impressive Premium Gem proof survivor from a scant mintage of just 625 pieces. The lightly frosted design elements and deeply mirrored fields are attractively toned in shades of deep gold, coral-red, and sea-green. A corresponding business strike production of only 4,000 pieces increases the demand for this proof issue. Population: 21 in 66, 1 finer (2/09).(#3717)

Gorgeous 1867 Three Cent Silver, PR66

401 **1867 PR66 PCGS. CAC.** An impressive Premium Gem proof, displaying rich azure and aqua on the obverse, with hints of plum toning at the center, and intermingled aqua, azure, russet, and gold on the reverse. The devices are lightly frosted with deeply mirrored fields beneath the toning. Population: 21 in 66, 1 finer (2/09). (#3717)

402 **1868 PR64 PCGS.** Lovely turquoise-green, gold, and salmon toning adorns the clean, well preserved surfaces of this near-Gem proof. Sharply struck and free of hairlines or contact marks. (#3718)

403 **1868 PR65 NGC.** Excellent contrast for a piece not awarded a Cameo designation, though each side also shows a measure of cloud-white patina. Well-preserved beneath the toning. Census: 45 in 65, 18 finer (2/09).(#3718)

Wonderfully Toned 1868 Three Cent Silver, PR66 Cameo

404 **1868 PR66 Cameo PCGS. CAC.** This sensational Premium Gem has a perfect blend of cameo contrast, deeply mirrored fields, lustrous devices, and gorgeous toning. Both sides have light emerald at the center with peripheral blue, violet, and iridescent toning. Population: 6 in 66 Cameo, 0 finer (2/09).(#83718)

405 **1870 PR65 NGC.** Exquisitely struck, with splashes of lavender, cobalt-blue, and reddish-gold. Bright surfaces are nicely preserved. Census: 36 in 65, 33 finer (2/09).(#3721)

406 **1871 PR66 PCGS. CAC.** Attractive silver-blue and green-gold patina embraces each side of this sharply struck Premium Gem proof. Carefully preserved and housed in a green label holder. Population: 22 in 66, 4 finer (2/09).(#3722)

407 **1871 PR64 Cameo PCGS.** Light champagne toning enhances the eye appeal of this glittering, sharply struck near-Gem Cameo proof. Splashes of golden-brown and sky-blue are evident on the obverse. A few light marks deny Gem classification. Population: 13 in 64 Cameo, 7 finer (2/09).(#83722)

Sharply Struck 1872 Three Cent Silver, PR66 ★

408 **1872 PR66 ★ NGC.** The luminous surfaces of this Premium Gem proof displays electric-blue, purple, and gold-orange patina in the obverse right center area and margins, and along the reverse periphery. The strike is uniformly sharp throughout, and both sides are nicely preserved. Census: 2 in 66 ★, 3 finer (2/09). (#3723)

Marvelous 1872 Three Cent Silver, PR68 ★

409 **1872 PR68 ★ NGC.** The 1872 proof three cent silver, with a mintage of 950 pieces, has a relatively high demand from date collectors, as only 1,000 circulation strikes were coined, which are seen infrequently. Proof specimens are available through the Gem level of preservation, after which the certified population tapers off.

A mere five 1872 proofs have been awarded the coveted Star designation, including the present PR68 specimen. Splashes of aqua-blue, purple, and yellow-gold mingle throughout both sides, and each offers modest field-motif variance. An exacting strike leaves crisp definition on the design features, and both faces are immaculately preserved. Census: 3 in 68 ★, 0 finer (2/09). (#3723)

410 **1872 PR64 Cameo PCGS.** Brilliant silver surfaces are enhanced by pale gold toning along the obverse and reverse borders. The contrast is excellent with fully mirrored fields and attractively lustrous devices. Population: 8 in 64 Cameo, 9 finer (2/09). (#83723)

411 **1873 PR64 PCGS.** Sharply struck and free of clash marks or contact marks. A deep layer of dusky purple-gray and forest-green patina coats each side.(#3724)

Lovely PR65 Cameo 1873 Three Cent Silver

412   **1873 PR65 Cameo NGC.** A gleaming, richly toned specimen from the final year of the denomination in silver. Blue-green, golden-tan, and violet zones prevail on each side, though the central reverse shows an area of minimal patina that lets this coin's essential contrast shine through. Census: 13 in 65 Cameo, 13 finer (2/09).(#83724)

THREE CENT NICKELS

413   **1865 MS66 PCGS.** Swirling luster with light nickel-blue patina overall. This attractive Premium Gem is well struck for its first-year issue. A dot of deeper toning is noted on the rim between OF and AMERICA. Population: 35 in 66, 2 finer (1/09).(#3731)

Remarkable MS67 1865 Three Cent Nickel

414   **1865 MS67 PCGS. CAC.** Ex: Bruce Scher Collection. Delicate chestnut and cream-gray colors grace this shimmering and magnificently preserved Superb Gem. A boldly struck piece, the A in STATES and the pillars of the denomination are not completely brought up, but nonetheless have excellent definition for a commercial strike. The Three Cent nickel was introduced in 1865, and was important to commerce during its initial years since silver coins were hoarded, driven from circulation by paper money without specie backing. Although more than 11 million pieces were struck, and Uncirculated pieces are not rare, most have indifferent strikes or are abraded from improper storage. Virtually immaculate examples, such as the present piece, are of the highest rarity. Population: 2 in 67, none finer (2/09).
Ex: Bruce Scher Collection (Heritage, 2/2005), lot 4001, which realized $13,368.75.(#3731)

Exceptional MS67 1866 Three Cent Nickel

415   **1866 MS67 PCGS. CAC.** Ex: Bruce Scher Collection. Boldly struck with bright, satiny fields and an extensively striated reverse. Only a handful of comparable quality examples are known to exist despite heavy production in the denomination's second year. Struck from prominently clashed dies. Population: 2 in 67, 0 finer (2/09).
Ex: Bruce Scher Collection (Heritage, 2/2005), lot 4002, which realized $12,218.75.(#3732)

416   **1867 MS66 PCGS. CAC.** Light golden-pink patina drapes each side of this lustrous Premium Gem. Well-defined for the issue and attractive. Population: 11 in 66, 0 finer (2/09).(#3733)

417   **1867 MS66 PCGS. CAC.** Ex: Bruce Scher. A bold striking accompanied by delicate golden patina and outstanding luster for the type. Die clashing is fairly pronounced and a few peripheral die cracks indicate early pressure on the dies. Grand eye appeal. Despite a mintage of over 3.9 million pieces, this coin is tied for finest certified by PCGS (2/09).(#3733)

418   **1868 MS66 NGC.** The design elements are sharply defined for a business strike of this series. Attractive luster radiates from nickel-gray surfaces that are devoid of significant marks. Strong clash marks are visible on each side, as are a scattering of light flecks. Census: 13 in 66, 2 finer (1/09).(#3734)

419   **1869 MS66 PCGS. CAC.** Ex: Bruce Scher. Subtle golden overtones grace surfaces that are pale nickel-blue otherwise. Smoothly lustrous and well struck, an appealing Premium Gem. Population: 16 in 66, 0 finer (2/09).(#3735)

420   **1871 Tripled Die Obverse MS66 ANACS.** FS-101. TDO-001. The obverse die is tripled, most prominently on the right side of the final A in AMERICA. UNITED appears widely die-doubled. Likely among the nicest examples of this unheralded *Cherrypickers'* variety. Lustrous and close to brilliant with prominent clashing on both fields.(#3737)

Impeccable MS66 1872 Three Cent Nickel

421   **1872 MS66 PCGS. CAC.** Ex: Bruce Scher Collection. Radiant and sharp, with pale lilac accents. Only a paper-thin blemish to the left of the portrait keeps this satiny Premium Gem from attaining an even higher grade. Extremely challenging this nice. Population: 12 in 66, 0 finer (2/09).
Ex: Bruce Scher Collection (Heritage, 2/2005), lot 4008, which realized $7,618.75.(#3738)

422   **1872 MS66 PCGS. CAC.** Luminous reddish-gold toning drapes much of the obverse, though the reverse shows only a faint echo of the patina. Lustrous and desirable. Population: 12 in 66, 0 finer (2/09).(#3738)

Dazzling MS66 Closed 3
1873 Three Cent Nickel

423 **1873 Closed 3 MS66 PCGS. CAC.** Ex: Bruce Scher Collection. Unlike the 1873 logotypes on the cent and double eagle, one can use the naked eye to distinguish between the Open 3 and Closed 3 subtypes of the Three Cent nickel. The Closed 3 is similar to an 8 when viewed without magnification, hence the complaint by the Chief Coiner on January 18 to led to a change of the logotype. Since the modification was early in the year, the Closed 3 is the scarcer subtype for business strikes. This sharply struck piece has battleship-gray color and vibrant cartwheel luster. The surfaces are unabraded, although faint clash marks (as produced) are noted on each side. Population: 8 in 67, 0 finer (2/09).
Ex: Bruce Scher Collection (Heritage, 2/2005), lot 4009, which realized $6,468.75.(#3739)

Crisp Gem 1873 Open 3 Three Cent Nickel

424 **1873 Open 3 MS65 PCGS. CAC.** The Open 3 1873 is a true sleeper. The *Guide Book* reports a mintage of 783,000 pieces and prices the issue as only a slightly better date. Yet both NGC and PCGS have certified relatively few pieces in Mint State. Gems are unquestionably rare. Presumably, the published mintage is incorrect and includes a large delivery of Close 3 pieces. No Open 3 proofs were struck. This is a lustrous and lightly golden-toned Gem with pleasing surfaces and a crisp strike. Population: 11 in 65, 0 finer (2/09).(#3740)

425 **1874 MS66 PCGS. CAC.** Well struck for this business strike issue with strong, swirling luster. Pale nickel-white surfaces are virtually untouched. Population: 9 in 66, 1 finer (2/09).(#3742)

426 **1875 MS66 PCGS. CAC.** Strong, swirling luster graces this charming Premium Gem, a minimally toned beauty. A trifle softly struck at the centers, though the eye appeal is redeeming. Population: 16 in 66, 2 finer (2/09).(#3743)

427 **1880 MS66 NGC.** This piece displays flashy luster, and attractive silver-gray surfaces with pale sky-blue undertones. Nicely struck, with sharp detail showing on the inner lines of the III. A couple of small ticks are noted on Liberty's cheek and chin. Census: 25 in 66, 4 finer (1/09).(#3748)

MS67 1880 Three Cent Nickel

428 **1880 MS67 PCGS. CAC.** Ex: Bruce Scher. Unusually well struck and undisturbed for a business strike, although the potent cartwheel luster confirms the designation as a Mint State piece. A pair of tiny strike throughs (as made) southwest of the F in OF identify this superlative Superb Gem, which displays light gold color. Just 21,000 business strikes were struck, and unlike proofs of the same date, not many pieces were set aside by contemporary numismatists. Population: 32 in 67, 0 finer (2/09).
Ex: Bruce Scher Collection (Heritage, 2/2005), lot 4015, which realized $7,618.75.(#3748)

Outstanding Superb Gem Mint State
1881 Three Cent Nickel

429 **1881 MS67 PCGS. CAC.** Ex: Bruce Scher Collection. A decision was made in 1881 to dramatically increase the production of Three Cent Nickels, but despite a mintage of over one million pieces, relatively few Gems survive and Superb Gem pieces are almost never seen. This delicately tinted example displays luxuriant luster and excellent highpoint definition. Bruce Scher's PCGS Registry Set of proof three cent nickels is ranked #2 all-time. Population: 7 in 67, 0 finer (2/09).(#3749)

Pleasing MS66 1882 Three Cent Nickel

430 **1882 MS66 PCGS.** Pale pink and lavender accents enliven the otherwise nickel-blue surfaces of this charming Premium Gem. Well struck, subtly lustrous, and carefully preserved with great eye appeal for this later issue, a low-production date that came on the heels of the denomination's last great mintage in 1881. Population: 15 in 66, 3 finer (2/09).(#3750)

431 **1883 AU55 NGC.** One of the late-series keys, with a mintage of only 4,000 business strikes. Crisp nickel-gray surfaces with light wear and a pleasing aspect.(#3751)

Seldom-Seen Gem 1885
Business Strike Three Cent

432 **1885 MS65 PCGS. CAC.** With a business-strike emission of 1,000 coins versus the proof total of nearly 4,000 pieces, the 1885 three cent nickel is one of those curious upside-down productions that occasionally happened in the 19th century Mint. Business strikes are rare in all grades (witness the current *Guide Book* price of $400 in Good 4), and in Gem condition this piece is one of 12 so certified at PCGS, with 10 coins finer (2/09). The surfaces are golden-gray, with good overall appeal and a minimum of distractions for the grade. Although the present coin is clearly a business strike, the denticulation is full on this piece.(#3753)

Elusive Business Strike 1885
Three Cent Nickel, MS66

433 **1885 MS66 PCGS.** The proof and business-strike emissions are topsy-turvy on this issue, with 3,790 proofs measuring up against only 1,000 business strikes. So it comes as no surprise that business strikes are much more desired than proofs of this date, and are also incredibly rare in high grades. The present coin more than fits the bill. It is unquestionably a business strike, as the nonexistent denticles from 9 o'clock to 1:30 attest. Most of the reverse denticulation is also absent, and yet the surfaces are pleasingly well struck in the centers. The surface texture is frosty, with glimpses of mint-green, gold, and lavender. Only faint evidence of contact is seen. Population: 8 in 66, 2 finer (2/09).(#3753)

434 **1887 MS65 PCGS. CAC.** Sensationally preserved with surfaces that show light golden color and incandescent luster. Slight striking softness along the rims is perhaps the only barrier to an even higher grade. Population: 26 in 65, 9 finer (2/09).(#3755)

435 **1888 MS67 NGC.** Strong, swirling luster and uncommon eye appeal for this penultimate three cent nickel issue. The obverse has suggestions of pink-gold toning, while the reverse remains straight nickel-gray.(#3757)

Wonderful 1889 Three Cent Nickel MS67

436 **1889 MS67 PCGS. CAC.** Ex: Bruce Scher Collection. Extraordinary quality for this final year issue. The liberally frosted surfaces have a soft golden and lilac tint over both sides and are well defined on the major devices. Both sides are free from abrasions, although the reverse border has two radial die cracks at 3 and 11 o'clock. Population: 10 in 67, 0 finer (2/09).
Ex: Bruce Scher Collection (Heritage, 2/2005), lot 4024, which realized $8,193.75.(#3758)

PROOF THREE CENT NICKELS

Deeply Reflective 1865 Three Cent Nickel PR66 Cameo

437 **1865 PR66 Cameo PCGS.** This first-year proof is the key to the series with a low percentage of survivors, especially in high grade. Few are seen with the cameo contrast present on this coin, and the fields are unusually deep for this date. Each side shows light golden-rose toning. Population: 23 in 66 Cameo, 1 finer (2/09). (#83761)

438 **1866 PR66 PCGS.** The obverse shows hints of champagne toning, while the reverse remains essentially nickel-white. Gleaming mirrors reflect this coin's gorgeous eye appeal. Population: 24 in 66, 1 finer (2/09).(#3762)

439 **1866 PR66 Cameo PCGS. CAC.** A lovely specimen from the second year of three cent nickel production, strongly mirrored with subtle golden overtones across the fields and the essentially ivory-white devices. Strongly detailed with considerable contrast for a three cent nickel proof. Population: 13 in 66 Cameo, 1 finer (1/09). (#83762)

440 **1866 PR66 Cameo PCGS. CAC.** Save for glimpses of gold, this Cameo coin shows little patina, though the contrast on each side is readily apparent. A pleasingly preserved Premium Gem. Population: 13 in 66 Cameo, 1 finer (2/09).(#83762)

441 **1866 PR66 Cameo PCGS. CAC.** Three cent nickel proofs do not ordinarily show the stark white-on-black contrast exhibited on both sides of this outstanding specimen. Fully struck and near-pristine; a great Premium Gem example. Population: 13 in 66 Cameo, 1 finer (2/09).(#83762)

442 **1867 PR65 PCGS. CAC.** The avid collector of three cent pieces will realize that high quality examples of the earlier dates in the series are elusive, whether business strikes or proofs. This glittering Gem probably deserves the Cameo designation, although such quality went unnoticed by the grading service. Population: 55 in 65, 8 finer (2/09).(#3763)

443 **1867 PR66 Cameo PCGS.** Thin gold-orange patina embraces each side of this charmingly contrasted Premium Gem. Eye-catching reflectivity is its greatest attribute. Population: 18 in 66 Cameo, 0 finer (2/09).(#83763)

444 **1867 PR66 Cameo PCGS. CAC.** Crisply detailed and gleaming with suggestions of golden toning in the fields. Strongly contrasted and carefully preserved, a delightful specimen. Population: 18 in 66 Cameo, 0 finer (2/09).(#83763)

Impressive 1867 Three Cent Nickel PR65 Deep Cameo

445 **1867 PR65 Deep Cameo PCGS.** A brilliant specimen that displays strong contrast between the fields and the devices. Early proof three cent nickels produced with this much care are quite unusual. This is reflected in the population figures, which in this case closely correlates to the low mintage for this year. Population: 1 in 65 Deep Cameo, 3 finer (2/09).(#93763)

446 **1868 PR66 PCGS. CAC.** Delicate nickel-blue and pastel-yellow tints invigorate each side of this gleaming Premium Gem. A well struck proof that is carefully preserved. Population: 7 in 66, 0 finer (2/09).(#3764)

447 **1868 PR66 Cameo PCGS. CAC.** Occasional whispers of green-gold supply the only color on this otherwise black-and-white Premium Gem. Carefully preserved and immensely appealing. Population: 11 in 66 Cameo, 0 finer (2/09).(#83764)

Gorgeous PR65 Deep Cameo 1868 Three Cent Nickel

448 **1868 PR65 Deep Cameo PCGS. CAC.** The bold contrast on each side of this Gem is its most noteworthy feature. Profoundly mirrored fields show a slight golden cast, and the well-defined central devices are thickly frosted. Outstanding visual appeal for this earlier proof issue. Population: 7 in 65 Deep Cameo, 0 finer (2/09).(#93764)

449 **1869 PR66 PCGS. CAC.** Intermingled gold and periwinkle-blue shadings grace each side of this strongly reflective proof. Well-defined with powerful eye appeal. Population: 12 in 66, 1 finer (2/09).(#3765)

450 **1869 PR65 Cameo PCGS.** Strongly contrasted on each side, almost to the Deep Cameo level. The obverse shows faint golden toning, while the reverse is essentially unpatinated. Population: 32 in 65 Cameo, 9 finer (2/09).(#83765)

451 **1869 PR66 Cameo PCGS.** The present sale has a nice offering of high quality proof three cent nickel pieces, including the present Premium Gem Cameo proof with its pleasing lilac and gold toning over deeply mirrored fields and frosty devices. The earlier dates in the series are quite hard to locate so fine. Population: 6 in 66 Cameo, 3 finer (2/09).(#83765)

452 **1869 PR65 Deep Cameo PCGS.** This reflective Gem offers lovely champagne-gold iridescence. The underlying surfaces are fully appreciable at all angles, each side by turns smooth, sharp, and boldly contrasted. Population: 14 in 65 Deep Cameo, 2 finer (2/09).(#93765)

453 **1870 PR65 Cameo PCGS. CAC.** This nickel-gold example is every bit the Gem. There are no distracting post-production features, nor are there any as struck anomalies. The reverse shows slight rotation counterclockwise. Population: 23 in 65 Cameo, 7 finer (2/09).(#83766)

454 **1870 PR65 Cameo PCGS. CAC.** Richly frosted over Liberty's portrait, and the fields are dramatically reflective. A handful of tiny contact marks contribute to the grade. Population: 23 in 65 Cameo, 7 finer (2/09).(#83766)

Beautifully Toned PR66 1870 Three Cent Nickel

455 **1870 PR66 Cameo PCGS. CAC.** The early years of the three cent nickel series all had low mintages in proof format. In 1870 the mintage "spiked" to 1000 pieces. However, this larger mintage did not translate into a significantly larger number of high grade proofs that were saved. Only six other PCGS PR66 Cameo pieces have been certified with none finer (2/09). This is a beautiful example whose vibrant blue surfaces have a touch of pale rose color here and there. A trifle softly struck on the high points of the obverse but fully defined on the reverse.(#83766)

Marvelous 1870 Three Cent Nickel
PR65 Ultra Cameo

456 **1870 PR65 Ultra Cameo NGC.** This is the *only* Ultra Cameo specimen certified by NGC (2/09), and a single glance at this outstanding Gem proves that the designation is richly deserved. Delicate blue and canary-yellow shadings grace the gleaming, powerful mirrors, and the boldly impressed devices offer exquisite frost. Two or three tiny contact marks to the left of Liberty's portrait preclude an even finer designation.(#93766)

457 **1871 PR66 PCGS. CAC.** Ex: Bruce Scher-R. Iskowitz. Champagne-orange shadings drape much of each side. Profoundly reflective through the patina and carefully preserved. Population: 23 in 66, 0 finer (2/09).(#3767)

458 **1871 PR66 PCGS. CAC.** Rich caramel-gold color dominates the eye appeal of this lovely Premium Gem. Moderately reflective fields are carefully preserved beneath the patina. Population: 23 in 66, 0 finer (2/09).(#3767)

459 **1872 PR66 PCGS.** Delicately toned gold and nickel-gray. This carefully preserved Premium Gem has well-defined central devices for the issue. Population: 16 in 66, 0 finer (2/09).(#3768)

460 **1872 PR66 Cameo PCGS. CAC.** Faint gray-gold speckles grace both sides of this lovely cameo, whose surfaces are virtually free of distracting marks. The design features are generally well struck, save for minor weakness in the central lines of the first upright of the III. Population: 7 in 66 Cameo, 0 finer (2/09).(#83768)

461 **1873 Closed 3 PR66 PCGS. CAC.** The Closed 3 logotype is common to all proofs and to some business strikes of this date, and the present Premium Gem proof is an exquisite representative. It has light nickel-gray surfaces with pale champagne toning. The design motifs are boldly detailed. Population: 10 in 66, 0 finer (2/09).(#3769)

462 **1873 Closed 3 PR66 Cameo PCGS. CAC.** Strongly struck with great mirrors and excellent quality for the grade. While many three cent nickel pieces show little contrast, this piece sports a great cameo effect. Population: 10 in 66 Cameo, 1 finer (2/09). (#83769)

463 **1874 PR65 PCGS.** A handsome example delicately toned in hues of pale rose and pewter-gray. The mirror brilliance of the fields is somewhat subdued, as is typical of many nickel proofs coined during the era. Although the proof mintage for the date is not known with certainty, the figure most often reported is 700 pieces. PCGS has graded 20 finer specimens (1/09).(#3770)

464 **1874 PR66 Cameo PCGS. CAC.** With the recent advances in the numismatic marketplace over the past few years, coins such as this low population three cent nickel seem to represent excellent value. This lovely nickel-gray Premium Gem has gorgeous cameo contrast with brilliant surfaces. The fields are nicely mirrored around lustrous devices. Population: 13 in 66 Cameo, 0 finer (2/09).(#83770)

465 **1875 PR66 PCGS. CAC.** Nickel-white overall with delicate golden tints noted inside the wreath on the reverse. Crisply struck with a modicum of contrast. Population: 13 in 66, 0 finer (2/09). (#3771)

466 **1875 PR66 PCGS. CAC.** Strongly reflective with crisp detail. Minimally toned save for occasional glimpses of green-gold. Carefully preserved and delightful. Population: 13 in 66, 0 finer (2/09).(#3771)

467 **1876 PR66 Cameo PCGS. CAC.** In Premium Gem Cameo proof quality, this low population three cent nickel piece is sure to be hotly contested in the present sale. It is a lovely piece with light champagne toning over brilliant gray surfaces. The design elements are boldly detailed. Population: 12 in 66 Cameo, 0 finer (2/09).(#83772)

Starkly Contrasted 1876 Three Cent Nickel PR65 Deep Cameo

468   1876 PR65 Deep Cameo PCGS. Even though 1,150 proofs were struck in this year, there is a pronounced lack of cameo coinage. PCGS has certified only four Deep Cameos at this grade level, and none higher. Brilliant throughout, the fields are deeply mirrored and the devices display thick mint frost that gives the coin its sharp two-toned contrast.(#93772)

Lovely Cameo Gem Proof-Only 1877 Three Cent Nickel

469   1877 PR65 Cameo PCGS. CAC. Variegated light golden toning visits this flashy and intricately brought up Gem. Cameo contrast is obvious for both the portrait and wreath. The proof-only 1877 is the key date of this completable 19th century series. Population: 22 in 65 Cameo, 42 finer (2/09).
From The Burning Tree Collection.(#83773)

Brilliant 1877 Three Cent Nickel PR66 Cameo

470   1877 PR66 Cameo PCGS. CAC. This is an immensely popular date inasmuch as it boasts the lowest total mintage in the series. At least 510 pieces were produced, all in proof format. There is no toning on either side—a feature that allows full appreciation of the glowing fields and their degree of contrast with the frosty textured devices. The strike is sharp throughout, and there are no singularly distracting carbon or hairlines to report. (#83773)

Series-Key 1877 Three Cent Nickel, PR66 Cameo

471   1877 PR66 Cameo PCGS. CAC. Always a popular and highly sought-after issue in the three cent nickel series, approximately 510 proofs were struck with no business strikes produced. This is a thoroughly brilliant coin that has thick mint frost over the devices and deeply reflective mirrors in the fields. A problem-free, splendid example of this key issue. Population: 34 in 66 Cameo, 8 finer (2/09).(#83773)

Impressive PR67 Cameo 1877 Three Cent Nickel

472   1877 PR67 Cameo PCGS. CAC. A Superb specimen that is truly delight to behold. There is no toning on either side—a feature that allows full appreciation of the glowing fields and their degree of contrast against the frosty textured devices. The 1877 is a popular date that boasts the lowest total mintage in the 1865-1889 three cent nickel series. At least 510 pieces were produced, all proofs. Population: 8 in 67 Cameo, 0 finer (2/09).(#83773)

473   1878 PR67 PCGS. CAC. The luster is thick and satiny, the strike is bold, and the surfaces are virtually untoned. The lower beads in the coronet show doubling and the second 8 in the date is filled, as struck. Population: 14 in 67, 1 finer (2/09).(#3774)

474   1878 PR66 Cameo PCGS. Light green-gold overtones enliven the obverse, while the reverse shows little patina. Strongly mirrored with pleasing contrast and interesting eye appeal. Population: 63 in 66 Cameo, 8 finer (2/09).(#83774)

1878 Three Cent Nickel, PR67 Cameo

475   1878 PR67 Cameo PCGS. CAC. The last 8 in the date shows both loop frosted, as usual for this proof-only issue of 2,350 pieces, along with the 1877 and 1886 the proof-only keys to the series. This is a stunning silver-white piece that lacks even the faintest distraction. Essentially unimprovable, both judging from the obvious aesthetic considerations and the certified population data. (One PR68 non-Cameo at PCGS is technically finer.) Population: 8 in 67 Cameo, 0 finer (2/09).(#83774)

Pristine 1878 Three Cent, PR67 Cameo

476 **1878 PR67 Cameo NGC.** The second proof-only issue of the series. The present piece sports untroubled steel-gray surfaces with bold contrast on both sides. Among the finest-certified Cameo/Deep-Ultra Cameo examples at NGC or PCGS, although one non-Cameo at PCGS is numerically finer (2/09). A tiny strikethrough appears beneath the last 8, which also shows frosty, filled-in loops, while the first 8 is prooflike. Otherwise essentially mark-free. Some minor strike weakness appears at the upper denticles on the reverse. Census: 22 in 67 Cameo, 0 finer (2/09).(#83774)

477 **1880 PR67 NGC. CAC.** The outstanding quality of this piece is readily evident, at first glance. Razor-sharp striking details and pristine surfaces are combined with glassy fields and pleasingly frosted devices. Census: 39 in 67, 2 finer (2/09).(#3776)

478 **1881 PR67 PCGS. CAC.** This lovely coin displays golden iridescence over silky-smooth surfaces. Sharply struck with modest, yet appreciable brightness in the fields. A perfect coin for inclusion in a Superb Gem type set. Population: 59 in 67, 3 finer (2/09). (#3777)

Spectacular PR68 1881 Three Cent Nickel

479 **1881 PR68 NGC.** While it is does not rank in the top five highest-mintage proof three cent nickel issues, the 1881 is underrated due to its association with the high-mintage business strike of the same year, creating an opportunity for the clever collector. This exquisitely preserved example is sharply struck and profoundly reflective. Pastel blue, pink, and yellow shadings enrich each side. Census: 9 in 68, 0 finer (2/09).(#3777)

Remarkable 1881 Three Cent Piece, PR68

480 **1881 PR68 NGC.** A scintillating Superb Gem proof, this remarkable piece has deeply mirrored nickel-gray surfaces with exceptionally sharp design details on both sides. The devices have a hint of mint frost, although insufficient to garner a Cameo designation. While proofs of this date are relatively plentiful, few can match the quality of this specimen. Census: 9 in 68, 0 finer (2/09).(#3777)

481 **1881 PR67 Cameo NGC.** Frosty white devices stand out amidst mirrored fields. This is a sharply struck and well preserved Superb Gem. Census: 32 in 67 Cameo, 8 finer (2/09).(#83777)

482 **1881 PR67 Cameo PCGS. CAC.** In the present rare coin market place, proof three cent nickel pieces have failed to keep pace with most other series, and now provide a prime buying opportunity. This exquisitely detailed Superb Gem Cameo proof has deeply mirrored fields surrounding the lustrous devices, all beneath light gold toning. Population: 18 in 67 Cameo, 3 finer (2/09). (#83777)

483 **1882 PR65 PCGS.** Aside from occasional glimpses of sky-blue and pastel-yellow, this Gem proof is devoid of color. Pleasingly lustrous with interesting eye appeal, a desirable specimen.(#3778)

Splendid 1882 Three Cent Nickel, PR68

484 **1882 PR68 PCGS. CAC.** Splendid mint-green and saffron fields complement pristine powder-gray high points on this wonderful Superb Gem coin. As expected for the grade, even the most remote distractions are essentially nonexistent. From a proof mintage of 3,100 pieces. Population: 7 in 68, 0 finer (2/09).(#3778)

485 **1882 PR67 Cameo PCGS. CAC.** Wispy champagne toning accents the light gray surfaces of this incredible Superb Gem Cameo proof three cent piece. Both sides are boldly detailed. With only a few finer Cameo proofs certified, this example should prove to be highly popular with bidders. Population: 55 in 67 Cameo, 4 finer (2/09).(#83778)

486 **1882 PR67 Cameo PCGS. CAC.** A gleaming and needle-sharp Superb Gem with impressive cameo contrast and immaculate surfaces. A short die crack (as made) is on the reverse at 9 o'clock. Virtually untoned. Population: 55 in 67 Cameo, 4 finer (2/09). (#83778)

487 **1882 PR67 Cameo PCGS.** Essentially untoned with stark cameo contrast. A tiny mark at the center of the obverse is the only flaw of any note. Both the fields and devices are free of spots and hairlines, and the overall effect is impressive. PCGS has graded just four finer Cameo proofs (2/09).(#83778)

488 **1883 PR67 PCGS.** Sharply impressed on all of the design motifs. The surfaces are mostly steel-blue, but an arc of red-brown toning resides on the the lower right obverse quadrant. Immaculately preserved and virtually pristine. Population: 63 in 67, 4 finer (2/09).(#3779)

489 **1883 PR67 PCGS. CAC.** Only a small number of higher grade 1883 proof three cent pieces have been certified. This example has bold design motifs with reflective fields. It is an excellent example for the grade. Population: 63 in 67, 4 finer (2/09).(#3779)

490 **1883 PR67 Cameo PCGS.** Occasional canary-yellow accents appear in the fields of this exquisite Superb Gem. Moderate contrast between the mildly frosted devices and the profoundly reflective, watery fields. Population: 32 in 67 Cameo, 0 finer (2/09). (#83779)

491 **1883 PR67 Cameo PCGS. CAC.** Crisply detailed with gorgeous mirrors. Hints of canary-yellow patina visit parts of the fields, leaving the rest of the coin bright nickel-white. Population: 32 in 67 Cameo, 0 finer (2/09).(#83779)

492 **1884 PR67 PCGS.** Delicate green-gold overtones add to the eye appeal of this sharply struck Superb Gem proof. Exquisitely preserved with only one numerically finer example known to PCGS (2/09).(#3780)

493 **1884 PR67 PCGS.** Sun-gold and ocean-blue endow this satiny Superb Gem. Meticulously struck and devoid of contact. A low mintage date. Population: 38 in 67, 1 finer (1/09).
Ex: Hill Country Collection (Heritage, 1/2007), lot 2036. (#3780)

494 **1884 PR67 PCGS. CAC.** An outstanding Superb Gem proof, this example has light gray surfaces with a hint of contrast between the reflective fields and lightly frosted devices. Population: 38 in 67, 1 finer (2/09).(#3780)

495 **1884 PR67 Cameo PCGS. CAC.** Rarely does PCGS hand out the Cameo designation to examples of this date in Superb Gem proof preservation. This one has lovely light gold toning over the contrasting light gray fields and devices. Population: 21 in 67 Cameo, 2 finer (2/09).(#83780)

496 **1885 PR67 PCGS. CAC.** An amazing Superb Gem proof, this light blue toned piece has accents of pale yellow on each side. It is a boldly defined piece with incredible mirrored fields and lustrous devices.(#3781)

497 **1885 PR67 Cameo NGC. CAC.** Outstanding contrast for the issue with richly frosted, if softly struck devices and profound nickel-white mirrors. Amazing preservation and eye appeal. Census: 9 in 67 Cameo, 0 finer (2/09).(#83781)

498 **1885 PR67 Cameo PCGS. CAC.** Pale gold and pink overtones grace the smooth surfaces of this delightful Superb Gem. Lightly frosted central devices supply pleasing contrast. Population: 8 in 67 Cameo, 0 finer (2/09).(#83781)

499 **1886 PR67 PCGS. CAC.** A medium gray Superb Gem proof, this three cent nickel has a dusting of iridescent toning on both sides to enhance its aesthetic appeal. Population: 43 in 67, 3 finer (2/09). (#3782)

500 **1886 PR67 Cameo PCGS. CAC.** An astounding Superb Gem with blindingly reflective fields that are exquisitely preserved. Well struck devices show coats of elegant nickel-white frost. Population: 17 in 67 Cameo, 0 finer (2/09).(#83782)

501 **1887 PR66 Cameo PCGS. CAC.** Strongly reflective with only faint suggestions of golden toning that bring out the nickel-white present elsewhere. Gorgeously contrasted with notable eye appeal. Population: 9 in 66 Cameo, 0 finer (2/09).(#83783)

Splendid 1887/6 Three Cent, PR67

502 **1887/6 PR67 PCGS. CAC.** Ex: Bruce Scher-Ron Iskowitz. The remains of the 6 underdigit are blatantly obvious, even on the top flag of the 7 overdate. This splendid Superb Gem appears near to a Cameo designation, and lovely mint-green and blue tinges in the fields are a definite bonus. Population: 4 in 67, 0 finer (2/09). (#3784)

503 **1887/6 PR66 Cameo PCGS. CAC.** Bold remnants of the underdigit are clearly evident even without magnification. The nickel-gray surfaces combine bright fields with frosty textured devices to create powerful contrast. Population: 25 in 66 Cameo, 4 finer (2/09).(#83784)

Exceptional PR67 Cameo 1887/6 Three Cent Nickel

504 **1887/6 PR67 Cameo PCGS.** The striking details are full and the fields are highly reflective. Each side is notably contrasted, and the lightly toned surfaces appear pristine. One of only four Superb Gems, as designated by PCGS, with two pieces graded higher (both by NGC). Population: 4 in 67 Cameo, 0 finer (2/09). (#83784)

505 **1888 PR66 NGC. CAC.** The proof mintage is recorded as 4,582 coins, although one wonders how the numismatic marketplace of the late 19th century would have absorbed so large a number— or, indeed, if it did. This pretty Premium Gem has grayish-gold surfaces with good eye appeal and the expectedly sharp strike. NGC has certified 18 pieces finer (2/09).(#3785)

506 **1888 PR67 PCGS. CAC.** A green label PCGS holder holds this Superb Gem proof with its satiny and reflective nickel-gray surfaces. Bold design definition establishes its status as a proof strike. Population: 20 in 67, 1 finer (2/09).(#3785)

507 **1888 PR67 PCGS.** At first glance, this satiny proof is reminiscent of business strikes, but one look at the intricate detail will prove its true proof status. The surfaces are light gray with delicate champagne toning. Population: 20 in 67, 1 finer (2/09).(#3785)

1888 Three Cent Nickel, PR67 Cameo

508 **1888 PR67 Cameo PCGS. CAC.** The silver-white surfaces are highly reflective and contrast well against the grayish-white, well-frosted device high points. An appealing coin, albeit showing some minor crumbling in the denticulation, as made, above the last S in STATES. The next-to-last proof mintage of the issue, recorded as more than 4,500 coins. Population: 7 in 67 Cameo, 0 finer (2/09). (#83785)

509 **1889 PR67 Cameo NGC.** This sharply struck Superb Gem proof is devoid of toning, and reveals no post-strike impairments. A minor planchet defect is visible in the upper left obverse, and another at the left reverse rim. Census: 8 in 67 Cameo, 0 finer (2/09).(#83786)

510 **1889 PR67 Cameo PCGS. CAC.** This is a lovely, seemingly unimprovable Superb Gem from the final year of issue. Sharply struck and nearly pristine with a tiny nick near the upper obverse rim as the only possible pedigree marker. The fields are deeply reflective and the devices are fully frosted, creating splendid contrast. Population: 18 in 67 Cameo, 1 finer (2/09).(#83786)

SHIELD NICKELS

511   1866 Rays MS65 NGC. Light golden overtones grace each side. A trifle softly struck on the stars with a small fleck above the M in AMERICA on the reverse, but highly appealing nonetheless. NGC has graded 25 numerically finer pieces (2/09).(#3790)

Desirable 1866 Rays Nickel, MS66

512   1866 Rays MS66 NGC. Despite a mintage of over 14.7 million pieces for the issue, this Premium Gem is tied for numerically finest graded by either NGC or PCGS (2/09). Gold-kissed nickel-white surfaces are brightly lustrous and carefully preserved. Slight striking softness on the reverse stars has little effect on the eye appeal. (#3790)

Impressive PR66 1866 Rays Nickel

513   1866 Rays MS66 PCGS. CAC. A brilliant and lustrous Gem with a bold strike and impressive preservation. The upper and lower obverse rims display multiple die cracks, as struck, while the reverse has wispy die cracks throughout the peripheral legends. Slender die striations (as made) are seen beneath the left vertical shield lines and bisect the reverse. This first-year issue was plagued by striking problems, leading to the removal of the rays between the stars, on the reverse. Some striking irregularity in this region is seen on the current example, but, along with the previously mentioned "as struck" features, this does not affect the coin's technical grade. Therefore, we rely on luster (excellent), surface preservation (nearly flawless), and overall eye appeal (splendid), to determine the premium quality status of this conditionally scarce example. Population: 27 in 66, 0 finer (2/09).(#3790)

Popular Gem 1867 Rays Shield Nickel

514   1867 Rays MS65 NGC. A popular type coin, the 1867 Rays saw a plentiful mintage in excess of 2 million pieces. Gem or finer examples are nonetheless elusive and in demand today: NGC has certified 50 MS65 coins, and 10 finer (2/09). This Gem offers silver-gold and mauve-accented surfaces with some interesting lathe lines on either side of the obverse cross ornament.(#3791)

515   1870 MS65 PCGS. CAC. The die state enthusiast will love this piece, struck from a shattered obverse die and a cracked reverse die. It is a fully brilliant and lustrous Gem with splendid light gray surfaces and bold design details. The date is seldom seen any finer than this example. Population: 25 in 65, 7 finer (2/09). (#3797)

516   1873 Open 3 MS65 PCGS. Well struck and satiny, with unmarked surfaces that display unusually light, champagne-beige toning. A conditionally scarce issue at the Gem level of preservation, as noted by Dave Bowers. Population: 27 in 65, 6 finer (2/09). (#3800)

517   1875 MS65 NGC. David Bowers (2006), writing about the 1875 nickel, indicates that "quality is elusive for this date" because of poor planchet preparation. The Gem offered here deviates from this profile. Its light gray surfaces yield soft luster and nicely impressed design features. A couple of light obverse flecks are noted for complete accuracy. Census: 26 in 65, 5 finer (1/09). (#3804)

518   1876 MS65 PCGS. Light golden overtones grace the pillowy nickel-gray surfaces of this Gem. Slight striking softness as usual on the obverse stars, though the eye appeal remains high. Population: 31 in 65, 8 finer (2/09).(#3805)

Splendid 1881 Shield Nickel, MS67

519   1881 MS67 PCGS. CAC. The business-strike mintage of the 1881 Shield nickel was a modest 68,800 pieces before the series gave one last great gasp the following year, more than 11 million coins. This splendid Superb Gem shows nickel-gray surfaces tinged with gold and cinnamon, and numerous die cracks appear throughout the obverse. Population: 5 in 67, 0 finer (2/09).(#3811)

Phenomenal 1882 Nickel, MS67

520   1882 MS67 PCGS. Most of the enormous mintage of 1882 Shield nickels—11.5 million coins—show careless production standards that keep them from the highest Mint State levels. Not so this phenomenal Superb Gem, with noteworthy surfaces in hues of gray and gold, with excellent luster and equal eye appeal. (#3812)

521   1883 MS66 PCGS. Well-defined, particularly on the reverse stars, with strong luster for this final Shield nickel issue. Subtle blue accents visit otherwise minimally toned surfaces. PCGS has graded just nine finer pieces (2/09).(#3813)

Sensational 1883 Shield Nickel, MS67

522   1883 MS67 PCGS. CAC. Typical of so many Shield nickels of all different issues, this example has several prominent obverse and reverse die cracks. Despite its status as a common date, few 1883 Shield nickels survive in Superb Gem quality, and none have been certified finer than MS67. This sharply defined piece has delightful light gray surfaces with wisps of pale gold toning. Population: 9 in 67, 0 finer (2/09).(#3813)

PROOF SHIELD NICKELS

523   1867 No Rays PR64 Cameo PCGS. Sharply struck and essentially untoned, with intense cameo contrast noted between the watery, deep mirror fields and the richly frosted devices. The 1867 No Rays is the third-scarcest proof in the Shield nickel series, although nowhere near as scarce as its 1867 With Rays counterpart. Population: 20 in 64 Cameo, 35 finer (1/09).(#83821)

524   1868 PR65 Cameo PCGS. CAC. An amazing Gem proof, this example has excellent cameo contrast that was created through a combination of satiny devices and fully mirrored fields. Both sides are light nickel-gray with splashes of iridescence. Population: 20 in 65 Cameo, 9 finer (2/09).(#83822)

525   1869 PR66 NGC. A radiant silver-white beauty from this proof mintage of only 600 coins, and the obverse on its own would undoubtedly rate a Cameo designation. The contrast is insufficient on the central reverse, however. Nonetheless highly appealing, and with little contact evident.(#3823)

526   1870 PR65 Cameo NGC. Light golden overtones with potent mirrors and crisply struck devices. Moderate contrast assures the Cameo designation. Census: 8 in 65 Cameo, 13 finer (1/09).(#83824)

Eliasberg's 1870 Shield Nickel
PR66 Cameo

527   1870 PR66 Cameo PCGS. CAC. Ex: Eliasberg. Graded PR67 in its Eliasberg auction appearance, and the piece appears essentially as made even when after prolonged study beneath a loupe. Precisely struck and nearly untoned. Population: 14 in 66 Cameo, 0 finer (2/09).
Ex: Edouard Frossard, 3/1894; J.M. Clapp; Clapp estate, 1942; Louis E. Eliasberg Collection (Bowers and Merena, 5/1996), lot 757. (#83824)

528   1872 PR66 NGC. CAC. An impressive Premium Gem proof with bold design elements and reflective light gray surfaces. Both sides have subtle champagne toning that gathers near the borders. Slight doubling is visible at the upper obverse, especially at the annulet below the cross, and through some of the letters in the motto. Census: 43 in 66, 5 finer (1/09).(#3826)

529   1872 PR66 Cameo NGC. Stunning field-device contrast is apparent at all angles. The color free obverse cedes to a veneer of nearly imperceptible gold-tan on the reverse. Wonderfully preserved surfaces exhibit boldly struck design elements. Census: 13 in 66 Cameo, 4 finer (2/09).(#83826)

530   1872 PR66 ★ Cameo NGC. CAC. An extraordinary Premium Gem Cameo proof example of this Shield nickel issue, with all the appeal that the Star appellation implies. The surfaces are entirely brilliant, with light gray devices and fully mirrored fields. Census: 2 in 66 ★ Cameo, 4 finer (2/09).(#83826)

531   1872 PR66 Cameo PCGS. CAC. This boldly detailed Shield nickel has excellent contrast between the fields and devices. Such pieces are elusive, as the nature of the coinage composition tended to diminish the contrast of these coins. Population: 17 in 66 Cameo, 2 finer (2/09).(#83826)

PR66 Cameo 1873 Closed 3 Nickel
From the Legendary Eliasberg Collection

532   1873 Closed 3 PR66 Cameo PCGS. CAC. Ex: Eliasberg. In its appearance within the second catalog for the famously complete Eliasberg collection, the present piece was succinctly described as "brilliant with blushes of pale gold. Outstanding quality." To this we can only add that the strike is excellent. Population: 15 in 66 Cameo, 0 finer (2/09).
Ex: Louis E. Eliasberg, Sr. Collection (Bowers and Merena, 5/1996), lot 760.(#83827)

533   1873 Closed 3 PR66 Cameo PCGS. CAC. Strongly struck with impressive eye appeal for this Closed 3 proof issue. Minimally toned save for occasional whispers of green-gold near the rims. Population: 15 in 66 Cameo, 0 finer (2/09).(#83827)

Marvelous 1874 Shield Nickel, PR67

534   1874 PR67 PCGS. CAC. The mintage is estimated but undocumented at 700+ pieces, according to the 2009 *Guide Book*. The present marvelous coin offers yellow and lilac-tinged surfaces that reveal scant evidence of contact. Considerable die-polishing lines are in evidence in the upper obverse, which of course must not be confused with hairlines. Certified in a green-label holder, this Superb Gem is among the finest of the issue at either service, and one of only seven pieces so graded at PCGS; there are none finer (2/09).(#3828)

Scarce Premium Gem Proof 1875 Shield Nickel

535   **1875 PR66 NGC. CAC.** Fully struck and well preserved, with just a bit of haze noted in the fields. Variegated reddish-gold and sea-green patina decorates the reverse; the obverse shows uniform green-gray toning. A scarcer date among proof Shield nickels, especially in such lofty condition. Census: 20 in 66, 1 finer (1/09). (#3829)

536   **1876 PR66 Cameo PCGS.** Freckles of faint gold, russet, and violet patina graces this Premium Gem proof, and boldly struck devices stand out against the mirrored fields. Impeccably preserved throughout. Population: 18 in 66 Cameo, 3 finer (2/09). (#83830)

Gleaming 1877 Shield Nickel, PR66 Cameo

537   **1877 PR66 Cameo NGC.** Delicate hints of ice-blue patina drape the gleaming mirrors of this strongly contrasted Premium Gem. The strike is crisp on the mildly frosted central devices. Impressive eye appeal for this noted and popular proof-only Shield nickel issue. Census: 28 in 66 Cameo, 4 finer (2/09). (#83831)

Impressive PR66 Cameo 1877 Shield Nickel
Key to the Series

538   **1877 PR66 Cameo PCGS. CAC.** The proof-only 1877 has long enjoyed a place of honor in the Shield nickel series. Its original mintage is the lowest in the entire series, and many examples were carelessly produced with dull surfaces and/or distracting planchet flaws. This is a fully struck and lightly toned Gem that is seemingly pristine aside from a few trivial contact marks near the reverse center. The fields are deeply mirrored and warm golden overtones dominate the outward appearance of both sides. One should not, however, overlook the powerfully impressed, frosty textured devices. Population: 24 in 66 Cameo, 5 finer (2/09). (#83831)

539   **1879 PR67 PCGS. CAC.** Not an overly flashy specimen, but the moderately mirrored and virtually untoned surfaces display a technical superiority that is found on only a small percentage of Shield nickel proofs. Great eye appeal. Population: 15 in 67, 0 finer (2/09).(#3833)

Splendid 1879 Shield Nickel, PR67 Cameo

540   **1879 PR67 Cameo NGC.** Clear doubling shows on the date, as Breen documents in his *Proof Encyclopedia*. This variety is different from the overdate, which shows a small spike upward from the right side of the ball ornament above the date. Nifty shelf or strike doubling shows on some of the other areas of the obverse. The silver-white surfaces show splendid eye appeal. Census: 6 in 67 Cameo, 0 finer (2/09).(#83833)

541   **1879/8 PR66 PCGS. CAC.** This extraordinary Premium Gem is housed in an older green-label PCGS holder. The surfaces are pristine with reflective fields and frosty devices. Lovely gold, rose, and iridescent toning accompanies the light nickel-gray surfaces. (#3834)

542   **1879/8 PR67 PCGS. CAC.** Outstanding preservation and eye appeal. The most winning facet of this Superb Gem is its patina, pale nickel-blue at the margins with peach centers. Population: 24 in 67, 7 finer (2/09).(#3834)

543   **1879/8 PR66 Cameo NGC.** A shimmering, near-flawless example of this popular overdate variety. Untoned with sharply struck features and immaculate preservation.(#83834)

544   **1879/8 PR66 Cameo PCGS.** Even gold toning adds a touch of luxury to both sides of this flashy Premium Gem. The fields are deeply reflective and the devices are frosty and boldly defined. To find a more attractive example would prove to be a challenge. Population: 28 in 66 Cameo, 7 finer (2/09).(#83834)

545   **1880 PR67 Cameo NGC.** Fields are largely brilliant with just a touch of green-gold patina at the margins. Pleasingly frosted devices create considerable contrast with the mirrors. Great eye appeal. Census: 19 in 67 Cameo, 1 finer (2/09).(#83835)

546   **1880 PR67 Cameo PCGS.** Profound contrast pierces through the thin peach-gold patina that drapes each side. The obverse in particular exhibits an outstanding cameo effect, with strong mirrors and richly frosted devices. Population: 14 in 67 Cameo, 0 finer (2/09).(#83835)

547   **1881 PR66 NGC. CAC.** Much more available than the business strike of the same date, the proof 1881 Shield nickel is nonetheless conditionally elusive only one grade point finer. This silver-white piece appears to verge on a Cameo designation, although NGC has not given one. Well struck and pleasing. A tiny reverse lint mark below the denomination fails to detract.(#3836)

Appealing PR67 Cameo 1881 Nickel

548 **1881 PR67 Cameo NGC.** Delicate gold and nickel-blue accents invigorate this moderately contrasted Superb Gem. A few tiny planchet flaws are noted in the area of the shield, but these do not affect the technical grade and the eye appeal is unhindered. With just one finer Cameo example known to NGC (2/09), this is a top-flight survivor.
From The Mario Eller Collection, Part Four.(#83836)

549 **1882 PR67 PCGS. CAC.** Crisply detailed with a hint of orange patina over the shield on the obverse. Beautifully preserved and flashy, a Superb Gem sure to delight. Population: 39 in 67, 0 finer (2/09).(#3837)

550 **1883 PR66 PCGS. CAC.** A striking Premium Gem specimen of this final proof Shield nickel issue, surprisingly well-contrasted for a coin not awarded the Cameo designation. Rich nickel-blue patina drapes the delightfully preserved fields.(#3838)

Outstanding 1883 Shield Nickel, PR67 Cameo

551 **1883 PR67 Cameo PCGS. CAC.** Always popular as the final year of issue, and coincidentally one of the best-produced dates in the series. This is a splendid example that shows noticeable contrast between the fields and devices. Each side is virtually flawless and there is just a slight accent of golden patina present. Population: 5 in 67, 0 finer (2/09).(#83838)

LIBERTY NICKELS

552 **1883 With Cents MS66 PCGS.** A subtle mix of apple-green, orange-gold, nickel-gray, and ice-blue resides on the lustrous surfaces of this Premium Gem. A sharply struck piece, except for the usual softness in the corn ear and leaves left of the bow knot. Both sides are well cared for. Population: 49 in 66, 1 finer (2/09). (#3844)

553 **1885 XF45 NGC.** A fine, evenly worn example of this key date Liberty nickel. Natural khaki-gray toning covers each side, and there are no disturbing marks. An appealing Choice XF example that will be of great interest to collectors.(#3846)

Key 1885 Liberty Nickel, MS62

554 **1885 MS62 PCGS.** The perennially popular key issue to the Liberty nickel series, the 1885 is usually the last "hole" remaining to complete a set, despite the many caveats to make the key coins the first obtained. This piece is lustrous and well struck, save for the lower left ear of corn on the reverse. Pretty lilac-champagne coloration adds to the appeal, but some planchet roughness, most notable on Liberty's face and neck, prevents an even finer grade. (#3846)

Lustrous Key Date 1885 Nickel MS62

555 **1885 MS62 NGC.** This key date nickel exhibits vibrant luster and is essentially devoid of marks. The strike is meticulous, even on the often-troublesome left ear of corn. Distributed minute gray toning flecks are all that limit the grade.
Ex: Beau Clerc Collection (Heritage, 9/2007), lot 595, which realized $2,875.
From The Ed Lepordo Collection, Part Two.(#3846)

Pleasing 1885 Five Cent, MS64

556   **1885 MS64 PCGS.** A lovely near-Gem representative of this most prized of circulation-strike Philadelphia Liberty nickels. Warm gold and orange patina of varying degrees drapes lustrous surfaces. The strike is substantially above-average, with only faint evidence of weakness on the reverse wreath. There are no marks of consequence on either side. Population: 85 in 64, 53 finer (2/09). (#3846)

557   **1886 MS63 NGC.** The 1886 is one of the keys to the Liberty Head five cent series. Soft golden-gray patina bathes both sides of this lustrous Select example. Well struck, except for weakness in the first two stars and in the elements immediately left of the bowknot. Some faint peripheral cracks are visible, as are a few minute obverse handling marks.(#3847)

558   **1886 MS63 PCGS.** Lustrous and boldly struck, with typical softness on the reverse left ear of corn, and on some of the obverse stars. The pearl-gray surfaces are mark-free but exhibit numerous charcoal specks on each side, limiting the grade.(#3847)

559   **1890 MS65 PCGS.** Solidly detailed for the issue with soft, pleasing luster. Splashes of peach patina visit otherwise light nickel-gray surfaces. A lovely Gem. Population: 47 in 65, 11 finer (2/09). (#3851)

560   **1890 MS66 NGC.** Dusky golden-gray and sky-blue patination runs over both sides of this Premium Gem nickel. The design elements are well impressed, except for weakness in the leaves left of the bow knot. Well preserved lustrous surfaces reveal no significant marks or spots. Census: 11 in 66, 1 finer (2/09).(#3851)

Well Struck 1894 Five Cent, MS67

561   **1894 MS67 ICG.** Substantially above-average detail for this mid-date issue; while the margins, such as the centers of a couple of stars, show trifling softness, the central definition is impressive. Luminous violet-gray and nickel-blue shadings consume each side of this carefully preserved Superb Gem.(#3855)

562   **1896 MS65 PCGS.** Sharply struck for the issue with crisp definition on the often-weak wreath. Strong luster with subtle nickel-blue and rose accents. Population: 65 in 65, 7 finer (1/09). (#3857)

563   **1898 MS66 NGC.** Delicate pastel shades of lilac and ice-blue coat each side of this stunning Premium Gem. Neither side shows any significant contact, and the overall eye appeal is most impressive. Sharply struck throughout, save for stars 1 and 2. Census: 16 in 66, 1 finer (2/09).(#3859)

Vibrant 1906 Five Cent, MS66

564   **1906 MS66 PCGS.** Splashes of gold toning add color to the mostly silver-gray surfaces. The design elements are well brought up, though the corn ear and leaves left of the bow reveal the often-seen softness. There are no mentionable marks on either side. Vibrant luster enhances the wonderful eye appeal. Population: 12 in 66, 0 finer (2/09).(#3867)

565   **1912 MS66 ★ NGC.** Highly lustrous light gray surfaces serve as the canvas to display amazing gold, blue, and rainbow toning. This piece ranks among the very finest surviving 1912 nickels. Neither NGC nor PCGS has graded a numerically finer example (2/09). (#3873)

566   **1912-D MS65 PCGS.** Along with its S-mint counterpart, the 1912-D was the first branch mint five cent nickel issue. The present Gem representative offers strong, pleasing luster beneath luminous green-gold and peach patina. Though the peripheral design elements are softly struck, the well-preserved central devices are comparatively sharp. PCGS has graded 27 finer examples (2/09). (#3874)

PROOF LIBERTY NICKELS

567   **1883 No Cents PR66 NGC. CAC.** Impressively lustrous with subtle champagne overtones across much of each side. Crisply detailed and gleaming with elegant eye appeal. Although a plentiful issue, even in proof, NGC has only certified 19 finer examples (2/09).(#3878)

568   **1883 No Cents PR66 Cameo PCGS.** Splendid silver-white surfaces display enormous contrast and equal eye appeal. A sharp strike is as expected for the grade, and significant contact is virtually nonexistent. A premier candidate for a first-year type set. (#83878)

Stunning 1883 No Cents Nickel
PR67 Cameo

569   **1883 No Cents PR67 Cameo PCGS. CAC.** Between the No Cents and With Cents Liberty nickels, almost 12,000 proofs were produced of the year. However, both varieties are rare at the Superb Gem level of preservation. This stunning piece fully merits the Cameo label, with excellent field-device contrast over the lightly gold-kissed surfaces. Population: 11 in 67 Cameo, 0 finer (2/09). (#83878)

570 **1884 PR67 Cameo NGC.** Both sides show distinct contrast between the deep nickel-gray reflectivity of the mirrors and the lighter, mildly frosted effect on the sharply struck central devices. Carefully preserved with noteworthy eye appeal for this second-year proof Liberty nickel issue. Census: 15 in 67 Cameo, 2 finer (1/09).(#83882)

Noteworthy Ultra Cameo 1884 Nickel PR66

571 **1884 PR66 Ultra Cameo NGC.** Unfathomably deep mirrors in the fields with obvious cameo contrast and delicate golden toning. One slender mark is noted under Liberty's chin. A lovely proof type coin and the single finest example thus far certified as Ultra Cameo by NGC (2/09).
Ex: Long Beach Signature (Heritage, 9/2006), lot 895, which realized $3,881.25.(#93882)

572 **1885 PR64 PCGS.** Sharply struck on all design elements, including the reverse left ear of corn. A light coating of milky tan-gray patina keeps the piece from grading higher, in the absence of contact marks or hairlines. Housed in a first-generation PCGS holder.(#3883)

573 **1885 PR66 PCGS.** Light golden shadings drape the fields, while the sharply struck central devices remain nickel-gray. An elegantly reflective example of this most popular regular-issue proof Liberty nickel. Encapsulated in a green label holder.(#3883)

574 **1885 PR66 NGC.** A splendid Premium Gem proof with glassy fields and vibrant rainbow toning. Green, gold, rose-gray and lilac colors are seen on each side. The right side stars are somewhat weak, but this mint-made defect seems very minor on such a beautiful specimen.(#3883)

Charming PR67 1885 Nickel

575 **1885 PR67 PCGS. CAC.** Crisply detailed with only trifling softness at a few of the obverse stars. The luster is more satiny than reflective, but the green-gold and sky-blue patina draping each side is redeeming. A carefully preserved example of what is arguably the most popular regular-issue proof Liberty nickel, owing to its associated business strike. Population: 15 in 67, 1 finer (2/09). (#3883)

Marvelous 1885 Five Cent, PR66 Cameo

576 **1885 PR66 Cameo NGC.** Frosty motifs appear to float over the deep watery fields of this marvelous Premium Gem cameo. Wisps of localized light gold are the only color evident on each side. A decisive strike emboldens the design features, and impeccable preservation is seen throughout. Census: 28 in 66 Cameo, 14 finer (2/09).(#83883)

Cameo PR66 Key 1885 Nickel

577 **1885 PR66 Cameo PCGS.** Sharply struck with light green-gold toning across parts of the otherwise nickel-white obverse. The mirrors are powerful, and the eye appeal is spectacular. The proofs of 1885 are popular as business-strike substitutes, though with this specimen's strong contrast and bold detail, there is no mistaking it for a circulation coin. Population: 32 in 66 Cameo, 5 finer (2/09). (#83883)

Exceptional 1885 Nickel, PR67 Cameo

578 **1885 PR67 Cameo NGC. CAC.** The fields on each side are deeply mirrored with light gold toning and sharply contrasting design elements. The 1885 is an always-popular issue in proof format because of the well-known scarcity of Uncirculated 1885 nickels, the key date in the series. The reverse exhibits a tiny strike-through near the base of the V that is only visible with magnification. Census: 14 in 67 Cameo, 0 finer (2/09).
Ex: Milwaukee ANA Signature (Heritage, 8/2007), lot 376, which realized $4,312.50.(#83883)

579 **1888 PR67 PCGS. CAC.** Soft nickel-blue toning drapes each side of this well-defined Superb Gem. Pleasingly lustrous and delightfully well-preserved. Population: 5 in 67, 0 finer (2/09). (#3886)

Stunning 1891 Five Cent
PR66 Ultra Cameo

580 **1891 PR66 Ultra Cameo NGC.** Frosty motifs appear to glide over the deep watery fields of this stunning Premium Gem Cameo. Exquisite definition on the design elements adds to the appeal, as do impeccably preserved surfaces. Just an occasional glint of faint gold color shows up under high magnification. Census: 2 in 66 Ultra Cameo, 2 finer (2/09).(#93889)

581 **1892 PR66 Cameo PCGS.** Light gold and pink overtones invigorate the mirrors on this well-defined Premium Gem. A small depression at Liberty's lower neck is a planchet flaw, not a contact mark. Population: 16 in 66 Cameo, 0 finer (2/09).(#83890)

582 **1898 PR66 Cameo PCGS. CAC.** Pinpoint striking definition is nearly universal. The shimmering features reveal scattered blushes of pale lilac and tan iridescence. Population: 13 in 66 Cameo, 3 finer (2/09).(#83896)

583 **1900 PR67 NGC.** Rich green-gold patina dominates the centers, while lighter nickel-gray is present at the margins. A gorgeous, sharply struck Superb Gem. Census: 26 in 67, 1 finer (1/09). (#3898)

584 **1900 PR67 PCGS. CAC.** Light golden overtones with a touch of tan on the portrait. This virtually undisturbed Superb Gem is strongly reflective with exquisite visual appeal. Population: 13 in 67, 1 finer (2/09).(#3898)

PR66 ★ Ultra Cameo 1901 Nickel
White on Black Beauty

585 **1901 PR66 ★ Ultra Cameo NGC.** The single finest Ultra Cameo example of this issue certified by NGC (3/09), with or without a Star designation. The contrast is virtually black-and-white, and the glassy fields are beautifully preserved. Surprisingly strong frost invigorates the devices.(#93899)

586 **1902 PR66 PCGS. CAC.** Crisply detailed and gleaming, a largely untoned proof of obvious quality. A bold strike complements the exquisite mirrors. Population: 60 in 66, 12 finer (2/09). (#3900)

587 **1906 PR66 ★ Cameo NGC.** Spectacular cameo contrast is apparent between the frosted devices and the highly reflective surfaces. The reverse has a lovely hazel center, and a few streaks of light toning accent the otherwise brilliant obverse. Sharply struck with virtually no marks. One of just 1,725 proofs struck. NGC has certified only two in 66 Star Cameo, with none finer (1/09). (#83904)

Rich PR67 Cameo 1906 Nickel

588 **1906 PR67 Cameo PCGS. CAC.** Contrast is unusual for most 20th century proof Liberty nickel issues, but this coin has a pleasing cameo effect despite a dearth of frost on the devices. Light blue patina graces the fields, while the portrait shows subtle mint-green tints. Population: 12 in 67 Cameo, 1 finer (2/09).(#83904)

589 **1908 PR67 PCGS. CAC.** An exquisite jewel, this Liberty nickel has incredible iridescence over its light gray surfaces. The strike is powerful with every detail fully defined. Population: 9 in 67, 0 finer (2/09).(#3906)

590 **1909 PR67 NGC.** Moderately mirrored and virtually untoned with traces of lilac haze on each nearly immaculate side. An exquisite Superb Gem specimen that soon will venture into antique territory. NGC has graded just seven finer pieces (2/09).(#3907)

591 **1909 PR67 PCGS. CAC.** This Superb Gem proof is boldly detailed with exceptional aesthetic appeal. The fields are fully mirrored, and just enough mint frost graces the central devices to suggest the possibility of a Cameo designation. Both sides are light champagne and gray with splashes of rich gold toning. Population: 34 in 67, 2 finer (2/09).(#3907)

592 **1910 PR67 Cameo PCGS.** An outstanding Superb Gem Cameo proof with light gray surfaces that are accented by traces and splashes of ice blue, lemon, and iridescent toning. Population: 11 in 67 Cameo, 2 finer (2/09).(#83908)

Pleasing PR67 Cameo 1911 Nickel

593 **1911 PR67 Cameo PCGS.** With 1,733 specimens struck, the 1911 is among the lower-mintage proof Liberty nickel issues, and it rarely comes so fine as this PR67 Cameo example. Excellent field-to-device contrast persists through rich patina, zones of aquamarine and peach. Carefully preserved and gorgeous. Population: 7 in 67 Cameo, 0 finer (2/09).(#83909)

594 **1912 PR66 Cameo NGC.** Highly contrasted for this final proof Liberty nickel issue with bold detail and powerful mirrors. Minimally toned and gorgeous. Census: 15 in 66 Cameo, 5 finer (1/09).(#83910)

595 **1912 PR66 Cameo NGC. CAC.** A gleaming and strongly contrasted representative of this final regular-issue proof Liberty nickel, sage-tinted in the fields with virtually untoned devices. Census: 15 in 66 Cameo, 5 finer (2/09).(#83910)

BUFFALO NICKELS

596 **1913 Type One MS67 ★ NGC.** Magnificent swirls of rose-red, lemon-gold, powder-blue, and sea-green embrace this intricately struck and scintillating Superb Gem. A prize for the connoisseur of patinated coinage. Census: 34 in 67 ★, two finer with a Star designation (1/09).(#3915)

Fantastic MS68 1913 Type One Buffalo Nickel

597 **1913 Type One MS68 NGC.** A top-flight example of this popular one-year type, strongly lustrous with the sharp and rugged detail that makes the variety so prized. Pale nickel-blue patina drapes the centers, while the margins show varying degrees of green-gold and olive toning. Census: 11 in 68, 0 finer (2/09).(#3915)

598 **1913 Type Two MS66 PCGS.** Delicate peach and gold patina graces much of each side, leaving brilliant nickel-white at the remainder. A crisply struck and attractive Premium Gem from this less-saved first-year variety.(#3921)

599 **1913-D Type Two MS65 PCGS.** Delicate nickel-blue patina overall with undercurrents of green-gold and pink. A softly struck Gem that is carefully preserved. PCGS has graded 60 finer pieces (1/09).(#3922)

Sharp 1913-D Type Two Five Cent, MS67

600 **1913-D Type Two MS67 NGC.** A melange of sky-blue, lilac, orange-gold, violet, and mint-green patina resides on the lustrous surfaces. The design features are in receipt of an exacting strike, resulting in sharp definition on the braid, horn, and tail. A scattering of light flecks on well preserved surfaces do not disturb. Census: 7 in 67, 1 finer (2/09).(#3922)

Worthy Gem Type Two 1913-S Nickel

601 **1913-S Type Two MS65 NGC.** A shimmering Gem with exquisite preservation and attractive pastel lilac, chestnut, and olive toning. The strike is crisp save for the curve of the tail and the hair above the braid. Clashed beneath the chin and opposite on the motto. This low mintage issue is avidly pursued in all grades, but provides better value in Mint State. Census: 67 in 65, 21 finer (2/09).(#3923)

Remarkable 1913-S Type Two Nickel, MS66

602 **1913-S Type Two MS66 NGC.** Well struck with just a hint of softness noted on the bison's head and shoulder, and on the word LIBERTY along the upper right obverse border. Lovely mint-green and silver toning adorns the softly lustrous surfaces. This Type Two example is from the first year of the series, and represents a minor design change that altered the original mound beneath the bison's feet, changing it to a thin border that was easier to strike up. Census: 15 in 66, 6 finer (1/09).(#3923)

Superlative 1913-S Type Two Nickel, MS66

603 **1913-S Type Two MS66 PCGS.** The surfaces are superlative on this Premium Gem key-date example. The quicksilver luster is tempered with glints of gold and carmine. From an early stage of the die, and lacking the "beard" die clash that many specimens show. The strike is nearly definitive, and the eye appeal is over the top. Population: 30 in 66, 1 finer (2/09).(#3923)

Splendid 1913-S Type Two Buffalo Nickel, MS67

604 **1913-S Type Two MS67 NGC.** The 1913-S Type Two Buffalo nickel, showing the bison standing on a thinner mound of grass with a straight line at the base, is the first acknowledged series key, one that is popular and available in all grades, albeit for a price.

In MS67, however, this piece is tied with a half-dozen other examples at NGC and PCGS combined as the finest certified (and likely the finest known, as it is unlikely that there are any uncertified Superb Gem examples remaining undiscovered, ungraded, and unauthenticated of this elusive issue). Splendid lilac and hazel low points accent the golden high points on the obverse, and the reverse offers lilac and golden coloration throughout. The coin appears to be an early die state, as it lacks the "beard" die clash that so many later examples show. Both sides are expectedly free of distractions, and the strike is excellent for the issue. Census: 6 in 67, 0 finer (2/09).(#3923)

605 **1914-D MS65 PCGS. CAC.** Nickel-blue, golden-orange, and yellow-green shadings embrace most of each side. Well-defined and attractive for the grade. Housed in a green label holder. (#3925)

606 **1914-D MS65 PCGS.** Excellent detail on the central devices. Both sides show luminous rose-gray patina over quicksilver luster. A minimally marked Gem.(#3925)

607 **1914-D MS65 PCGS. CAC.** A green-label PCGS holder houses this Gem 1914-D nickel. Deep gold and iridescent patina drapes frosty fields and well-defined devices. Although both sides have myriad tiny spots, none are evident without magnification. (#3925)

608 **1914-D MS66 NGC. CAC.** Excellent design definition with lovely luster. Luminous gold-orange and powder-blue toning embraces each side. Census: 15 in 66, 1 finer (2/09).(#3925)

Beautiful MS66 1914-S Nickel

609 **1914-S MS66 PCGS.** Iridescently toned in pastel butter-gold, jade-green, and rose-red. A loupe fails to locate any marks, and the lustrous fields and devices offer a superior strike. A small retained lamination is noted between the back legs. An early branch mint issue, little-saved in Mint State despite an enticingly low mintage. Population: 32 in 66, 0 finer (2/09).(#3926)

610 **1914/3-S AU55 ANACS.** FS-101, formerly FS-014.89. In *The Complete Guide to Buffalo Nickels*, David Lange writes that the 1914/3 overdate from the San Francisco Mint is extremely difficult to identify, and this piece it no exception. It does, however, feature the characteristic faint die crack beneath the denomination, and has a faint trace of the top of the 3. Medium gray patina covers both sides of this briefly circulated piece, which Lange states is significantly less available than its P-mint counterpart. A small spot to the left of the bison's head is noted.(#93926)

Elusive Gem 1915-S Buffalo Nickel

611 **1915-S MS65 PCGS. CAC.** Well struck with smooth, unmarked surfaces that exhibit a lovely mixture of sea-green, steel-blue, coral, and gold toning. The surfaces are impressively preserved and virtually pristine, save for a single faint mark on the bison's flank. A conditionally elusive Gem example; PCGS has only certified 30 pieces finer (2/09).(#3929)

612 **1916-D MS65 PCGS.** Subtle gold and pink tints visit each side of this luminous Gem. A well-defined example with few superiors; PCGS has graded only 11 such pieces (2/09).(#3932)

613 **1916-S MS65 ★ NGC.** Unlike so many weakly struck, indifferently lustrous examples of this issue, the present Gem is bold in both respects. The gold-orange and mauve patina that makes each side furthers the already impressive eye appeal. A top-notch coin that is entirely deserving of the Star designation. NGC has certified just 14 numerically finer pieces (2/09).(#3933)

Very Rare 3 1/2 Leg 1917-D Nickel MS63

614 **1917-D 3 1/2 Leg MS63 PCGS.** FS-901, formerly FS-016.42. Die abrasion has removed much of the bison's front foreleg, reminiscent of the well known 1937-D Three Legged variety. The 1917-D version is far more rare, listed in *Cherrypickers'* as URS-5 while the 1937-D variety is URS-14. Lustrous and unabraded with an above-average strike. FS-901 Population: 2 in 63, none finer (2/09).

615 **1917-D MS64 PCGS.** Despite typical softness on the bison's head and shoulder, this near-Gem example from the Denver Mint is generally well detailed. The surfaces are mostly untoned and steel-gray, but some bluish-gray color occurs near the peripheries. Surface blemishes are virtually absent, other than a small mark across the lower parts of 19 in the date.(#3935)

Delightful 1917-D Gem Nickel

616 **1917-D MS65 PCGS.** Although the 1917-D is not quite as elusive in Gem condition as some of the later-series S-mint condition rarities, it is seldom seen finer than MS65; PCGS has certified only 13 examples finer, and NGC six specimens higher. This example boasts quicksilver surfaces that are largely gold-tinged silver, save for an interesting swath of ice-blue down the buffalo's midsection. A well-struck and thoroughly delightful coin.(#3935)

617 **1917-S MS64 PCGS.** Lustrous and typically softly struck for the issue. A light golden glow occurs over both sides. A shallow, curving line across the left side of the Indian's face limits the grade. (#3936)

618 **1918 MS65 PCGS.** Whispers of soft brown toning adorn the radiantly lustrous surfaces of this lovely Gem, and a decisive strike leaves strong design impressions. A few minute grade-consistent marks are not worth individual mention.(#3937)

619 **1918-D MS64 PCGS.** Pink and orange toning drapes the fields, while the luminous devices remain medium nickel-gray. A well struck example for the issue with a crisp horn.(#3938)

Pleasing 1918/7-D Nickel
Fine 12, FS-101

620 **1918/7-D Fine 12 PCGS.** FS-101, formerly FS-016.5. The crossbar and downstroke of the underdigit 7 is apparent despite 48 points of wear. Light nickel-gray surfaces retain a good amount of detail, and are quite clean for a coin that saw moderate circulation. The Fifth Edition of the *Cherrypickers' Guide* call this issue "a very rare overdate."(#3939)

1918/7-D Nickel, XF Details

621 **1918/7-D—Obverse Scratched, Improperly Cleaned—NCS. XF Details.** FS-101, formerly FS-016.5. While not problem-free, this coin would fit nicely in an XF set of Buffalo nickels. This dual-hubbing error is generally not found finer than XF, as this variant remained undetected until 20 years after it was minted; most examples had slipped into circulation. A shallow diagonal scratch on the obverse accounts for one of the problems. The cleaning was lightly done and has lightly toned over since. Actually an attractive coin, especially at arm's length.(#3939)

Elusive Choice 1918-S Nickel

622 **1918-S MS64 PCGS.** This low mintage near-Gem has coruscating luster and a splendidly smooth appearance. Dove-gray with peripheral hints of almond-gold. The strike is impressive, since the mintmark and the bison's hair and tail all have intricate detail. Only the hair above the ear shows any softness.(#3940)

623 **1919-S MS62 NGC.** The smooth surfaces are very clean, and have a somewhat mattelike texture in the fields. Light silver-gray and antique-gold patina covers each side.(#3943)

Lovely 1919-S Buffalo, MS64

624 **1919-S MS64 NGC.** The 1919-S is a well-known strike rarity along with most other early S-mints in the Buffalo nickel series. This piece has the usual softness on the reverse, but that is compensated for by the lovely mint frost over each side. Attractively toned as well, with rich reddish-golden color that is evenly matched on both obverse and reverse.(#3943)

Appealing 1919-S Gem Five Cent

625 **1919-S MS65 PCGS.** Enormously appealing, with a light bluish-gray patina on the obverse, accented by tinges of gold at the rim, and a light gold cast on the reverse. The obverse strike is pleasingly bold, with good details on the Indian's hair and LIBERTY. The reverse shows the usual weak impression, although die erosion is also suspected, as numerous heavy die flow lines are visible in the fields. The horn is sharp, but much of the hair detail on the bison's back and head is soft. The reverse luster is radiant, while that on the obverse is somewhat diffuse because of the toning. Despite the technical issues, this piece nonetheless has abundant eye appeal, and is decidedly rare in Gem grade. Population: 31 in 65, 2 finer (2/09).(#3943)

626 **1920-D MS64 NGC.** Soft golden-gray patina accented with powder-blue adheres to the lustrous surfaces of this near-Gem D-mint coin. Generally well struck, except for localized weakness on the bison. Both sides are devoid of mentionable marks. (#3945)

Scarce 1920-D Gem Five Cent

627 **1920-D MS65 PCGS.** Fully lustrous surfaces display soft variegated shades of violet and golden-brown. A bit better struck than ordinarily seen, though the hair on the bison's head is weak. The few minute marks visible are within the parameters of the designated grade. Scarce in Mint State. Population: 47 in 65, 1 finer (2/09).(#3945)

Exemplary Choice 1921-S Nickel

628 **1921-S MS64 ANACS.** The 1921-S is among the most difficult Buffalo nickel issues. It is a strike rarity, as with many other mintmarked Nickels from 1917-26. The challenge of finding a pleasing piece is often compounded by surface problems such as planchet flaws, die cracks, grease stains, and heavy metal flow—all the result of hurried planchet preparation in the Mint. This coin is refreshingly free from any of those planchet problems. It is also better struck than other examples we have seen of this issue. Both sides are toned a pleasing lilac-rose coloration with bright underlying mint frost. A very attractive example of this scarce issue. In an old ANA cache holder.
Ex: Jim Joyner Collection (Heritage, 9/2002), which realized $2,875. (#3948)

629 **1923-S MS64 PCGS.** Well struck and luminous with quicksilver surfaces. Green-gold toning covers parts of the fields, while the rest of this minimally marked piece is nickel-gray.(#3950)

630 **1923-S MS64 NGC.** Though the usual striking softness is noted on the high points, the effect is slight save at the bison's shoulder. Gold-orange patina of varying intensity drapes quicksilver surfaces. (#3950)

Sharply Struck 1923-S Gem Five Cent

631 **1923-S MS65 PCGS.** An uncommonly sharp strike for a San Francisco nickel from the 1920s. The hair above the braid, the feathertips, the date, the mintmark, and the bison's hair and shoulder all have superior definition. Minor softness is present on LIBERTY and the curve of the tail. This shimmering and mark-free Gem is toned apricot, light blue, and olive. Population: 32 in 65, 2 finer (2/09).(#3950)

Attractive Gem 1924-D Nickel

632   **1924-D MS65 PCGS.** The 1924-D does not get the same level of recognition as some other mintmarked Buffalo nickel issues, but it is elusive nonetheless, scarce at the Gem level and exceedingly rare any finer. The present example is well struck for the issue with soft nickel-gray luster that shows delicate reddish-orange elements. (#3952)

Desirable MS64 1924-S Nickel

633   **1924-S MS64 NGC.** This Choice example shows this issue's typical quicksilver luster, and characteristic softness is noted on the highest design elements. The horn is intact, however, and the gold-orange and violet patina that drapes each side offers considerable redemptive eye appeal. NGC has graded just 22 numerically finer pieces (1/09).(#3953)

634   **1925 MS66 PCGS.** Exquisite gold and rose overtones drape each side of this Premium Gem. Vibrant, swirling luster dominates the eye appeal. PCGS has graded six finer pieces (1/09).(#3954)

635   **1925 MS66 PCGS.** Impressive, swirling luster and vibrant color are the chief attributes of this Premium Gem. Nickel-blue surfaces show elements of violet and green-gold. PCGS has graded six finer examples (1/09).(#3954)

636   **1925 MS66 PCGS.** While the obverse shows some weakness, the reverse is sharp, and the surfaces are sensational. Both sides have light gray frost with splashes of gold and iridescent toning. PCGS has only certified six finer examples.(#3954)

637   **1925-S MS63 NGC.** The '25-S is one of the noteworthy strike and condition rarities in the Buffalo nickel series. This appealing Select Mint State example displays terrific luster and lovely amber, olive-gold, and steel-gray toning. Minimally abraded for the grade. (#3956)

638   **1925-S MS63 NGC.** The lustrous surfaces of this Select S-mint display whispers of purple and sky-blue patina on the obverse, ceding to more extensive and deeper hues of the same palette on the reverse. Localized softness shows on the design features, which is typical for the issue. Nicely preserved for the grade designation. (#3956)

Near-Gem 1925-S Buffalo Nickel

639   **1925-S MS64 PCGS.** The 1925-S Buffalo nickel is a well-known strike rarity in the series, and the present piece does show softness on the first two digits of the date, which are completely present but far from bold. The high points of each side are also softly struck, although there is a full horn. Die erosion produces some orange-peel effect, more prominent on the reverse. However, the surfaces are relatively unmarked, and generous luster is present. Conditionally elusive any finer, as PCGS has certified only 19 coins in higher grade (2/09).(#3956)

Series Key 1926-S Buffalo Nickel, MS64

640   **1926-S MS64 PCGS. CAC.** Golden-brown streaks cross this lustrous and unabraded near-Gem. The mintmark is sharp, and the grade is only limited by the strike, which is nonetheless relatively strong for this characteristically softly defined issue. The 1926-S is famous for its mintage of 970,000 pieces, the lowest of any regular issue Buffalo nickel. The scarcity of the 1926-S in Mint State ensures its status as the regular issue series key. As of (2/09) PCGS and NGC combined have certified just 17 pieces in MS65, and two coins finer. The overall eye appeal confirms the CAC green label. (#3959)

641   **1927 MS66 PCGS. CAC.** Delicate gold and champagne overtones drape otherwise nickel-gray surfaces. A well-defined and elegant Premium Gem example of this popular Philadelphia issue. (#3960)

Gorgeous 1927 Buffalo, MS67

642   **1927 MS67 NGC.** Iridescent caramel-gold and powder-blue consume the obverse, while the reverse exhibits tan, sky-blue, and honey patina. A wonderfully preserved Superb Gem that has scintillating luster and an above average strike. Only the hair near the braid lacks intricate detail. Census: 9 in 67, 0 finer (2/09). (#3960)

643   1927-S MS62 PCGS. Luminous with quicksilver luster beneath the gold-gray and nickel-blue shadings that envelop each side. A well struck example that is just a few abrasions shy of Select status. (#3962)

Appealing MS64 1927-S Nickel

644   **1927-S MS64 PCGS.** Most 1927-S nickels show light striking. The present near-Gem offering, while not fully struck, exhibits better definition than most, though the tops of LIBERTY and the hair on the bison's head are soft. Both sides are lightly patinated, and show a couple of typical toning streaks on the reverse. Pleasingly preserved for the grade.(#3962)

645   **1928-S MS64 PCGS.** Though the central reverse is softly struck, the piece is well-defined elsewhere. Luminous quicksilver surfaces are largely nickel-gray with splashes of yellow at the margins. (#3965)

646   **1931-S MS66 PCGS.** Boldly struck overall, if a tad weak above the knot in the hair braid, and on the bison's head and shoulder areas. A luminous, impressively preserved specimen with surfaces that are nearly blemish-free.(#3971)

Choice XF 1935 Doubled Die Reverse Nickel

647   **1935 Doubled Die Reverse XF45 PCGS.** FS-801, formerly FS-018. Several of the letters in UNITED STATES OF AMERICA and FIVE show obvious die doubling, although perhaps the most prominent pickup point for this rare die variety is NUM, which shows blatant doubling almost directly east to west. *Cherrypickers'* fifth edition says that "this variety is extremely rare in any grade above Very Fine. About 10 are known in Mint State."

The present piece shows light, grade-consistent wear over the nickel-gray surfaces, but there are no singularly mentionable abrasions or other distractions present. Population: 8 in 45, 26 finer (2/09).(#93974)

1935 Doubled Die Reverse Nickel Rarity
AU55, FS-801

648   **1935 Doubled Die Reverse AU55 PCGS.** FS-801, formerly FS-018. FIVE CENTS is blatantly die doubled, and UNITED is also nicely doubled. A briefly circulated piece that has streaky slate-gray and walnut-tan toning. The devices conceal a couple of moderate marks. The Fifth Edition *Cherrypickers' Guide* says: "This variety is extremely rare in any grade above Very Fine. About 10 are known in Mint State."(#93974)

649   **1935-D MS66 PCGS.** Warm gold-orange toning visits parts of each side, while the rest remains nickel-gray. A well struck Premium Gem with great eye appeal. PCGS has graded five finer examples (1/09).(#3975)

Rare Variety 1936-D 3 1/2 Legs Nickel
XF45 Details, FS-901

650   **1936-D 3 1/2 Legs—Scratched—ICG. XF45 Details.** FS-901, formerly FS-019. The Fifth Edition of *Cherrypickers' Guide* says: "This is an extremely rare variety, with fewer than 40 known in any grade." The front leg of the bison has been partially polished off the die. The light to medium gray surfaces of this XF45 Details coin reveal well defined design elements. A thin, shallow scratch travels from below the bison's eye to the hip.(#93978)

651   **1936-S MS67 PCGS.** Tobacco-brown borders encompass the forest-green and pale plum-mauve centers. A splendidly smooth and lustrous San Francisco Superb Gem. Population: 61 in 67, 0 finer (1/09).(#3979)

652   **1937-D Three-Legged VF20 ICG.** A moderately worn example of this popular variant, one that became widely known almost as soon as it was released. Gold and nickel-gray patina dominates the present coin.(#3982)

653   **1937-D Three-Legged VF30 PCGS.** Moderately worn with hints of olive patina over parts of the otherwise nickel-gray surfaces. An interesting midrange piece that shows the missing foreleg clearly. (#3982)

654   **1937-D Three-Legged VF30 PCGS.** FS-901 (formerly FS-020.2). A greenish and pearl-gray example of this perennially popular variety. The Indian's cheekbone is slightly worn, while most of the bison's horn remains evident.(#3982)

655   **1937-D Three-Legged XF45 ICG.** FS-901 (formerly FS-020.2). A well detailed key date nickel, slate-gray overall with hints of chestnut-brown. The bison's hip and hair show wear, but most of the horn is present, and the portrait has only a couple of marks. (#3982)

656 **1937-D Three-Legged AU50 NGC.** FS-020.2. A satiny AU survivor, with smooth surfaces that are entirely free of blemishes. Evenly worn across the high points, and lightly toned in shades of ochre and light-gray.(#3982)

657 **1937-D Three-Legged AU53 PCGS.** FS-901 (formerly FS-020.2). The high bidder will love this coin, with pleasing nickel-gray surfaces throughout. A couple of minor scrapes are noted through the Indian's cheek and eye.(#3982)

658 **1937-D Three-Legged AU55 NGC.** FS-020.2. Fortunately, there is a relatively ample number of survivors from this famous Buffalo nickel variety, which is well known even outside of the numismatic world. Even so, the demand for this aptly named type is relentless at all grade levels. This Choice AU example exhibits deep green-gray toning. The surfaces display slight diagnostic die rust, but lack even the smallest abrasion on either side.(#3982)

659 **1937-D Three-Legged AU55 PCGS.** Rich rose and orange peripheral color gives way to deep nickel-gray at the centers. Only a touch of wear is noted on the highest design elements. (#3982)

660 **1937-D Three-Legged AU58 NGC.** Pink-orange elements are largely at the peripheries, and the centers are generally nickel-gray. Only a trace of friction crosses the high points. The bison's head is crisply struck.(#3982)

661 **1937-D Three-Legged AU58 NGC. CAC.** FS-901 (formerly FS-020.2). Well struck for the issue with quicksilver luster and only modest friction on the high points. Deep violet-gray and dusty rose patina embraces each side.(#3982)

662 **1937-D Three-Legged AU58 PCGS.** Well struck for the die state with just a touch of friction across the high points. Luminous pink-orange color drapes quicksilver surfaces.(#3982)

663 **1937-D Three-Legged AU58 NGC. CAC.** FS-901 (formerly FS-020.2). Tinges of gold and mint-green occur on both sides of this splendid near-Mint State Three-Legged Buffalo. The softly glowing luster on this example is much better than usually seen, although its peculiar creation is responsible for the said luster being somewhat diffused in the first place.(#3982)

664 **1937-D Three-Legged AU58 NGC.** Pink and peach shadings drape otherwise nickel-gray surfaces, the color on the reverse being more intense. Softly struck as usual but with only a trace of wear. (#3982)

Attractive 1937-D Three-Legged Select Nickel

665 **1937-D Three-Legged MS63 PCGS. CAC.** FS-901, formerly FS-020.2. This is a colorfully toned representative of this popular variety. A medley of soft yellow-green, lilac, violet, and ice-blue patina adorns lustrous surfaces. There are a few areas of localized weakness, but the braid and horn are quite sharp. Nicely preserved, with great overall appeal.(#3982)

Select Mint State 1937-D Three-Legged Nickel

666 **1937-D Three-Legged MS63 NGC.** FS-901 (formerly FS-020.2). Bathed in satiny luster, the surfaces of this unusually high-grade example display lovely champagne-gray toning. Well struck and conspicuously free of distracting marks. There will never be a sufficient number of Three-Legged Buffalo nickels to completely satisfy the demand from collectors.(#3982)

Imposing 1937-D Three-Legged Nickel MS64, FS-901

667 **1937-D Three-Legged MS64 NGC.** FS-901, formerly FS-020.2. Caramel-gold and steel-blue embrace this lustrous and minimally abraded near-Gem. The strike is sharp, and the eye appeal is imposing. All diagnostics are present, such as the attenuated back leg and the diagonal series of die dots beneath the flank. A perennially collected key date.(#3982)

671 **1915 PR66 PCGS. CAC.** Second scarcest date in the matte proof series. Only 1,050 pieces were produced of the 1915, and it is likely that some were melted as unsold in the following year. This particular piece shows the arcing die crack Breen mentions as diagnostic of proofs, one that traverses the bison's shoulder and chest. (This die crack, however, is inconclusive evidence of a proof striking.) This is a splendid proof with no carbon in evidence on either side. The surfaces are light gray overall, with a tinge of rose and lilac interspersed throughout.(#3992)

672 **1936 Type One—Satin Finish PR66 PCGS.** Though it lacks the mirrors of a Brilliant Finish piece, this Satin example nonetheless has a greater gleam than most. Sharply struck and essentially untoned.(#3994)

673 **1936 Type One—Satin Finish PR66 NGC.** Beautifully detailed with a touch of golden toning over the obverse. Wonderful satiny texture and eye appeal for this issue that marked the return of Buffalo nickel proofs.(#3994)

674 **1936 Type One—Satin Finish PR66 NGC.** Dusky reddish-orange patina embraces each side of this Satin Finish example. Strongly executed details and great eye appeal for this return to proof coinage.(#3994)

675 **1936 Type One—Satin Finish PR67 PCGS.** With the impeccable detail of a proof but swirling satin luster in place of mirrors, the Type One proofs of 1936 were not well-received and were replaced with the Brilliant Finish type later the same year. This Superb Gem, however, is readily appreciable today. Hints of golden-tan toning drape beautifully preserved surfaces.(#3994)

676 **1936 Type Two—Brilliant Finish PR66 ICG.** Fully struck with impressive depths of mirrored reflectivity in the fields. Free of hairlines and contact marks, with faint iridescence noted in the reverse fields.(#3995)

677 **1937 PR65 PCGS.** Luminous goldenrod and nickel-gray shadings drape each side of this carefully struck Gem proof. Pleasingly preserved with strong visual appeal.(#3996)

678 **1937 PR65 PCGS.** This brilliant Gem proof yields mild field-motif variance at certain angles, and is exquisitely struck. Some tiny, light toning flecks in the fields are visible under magnification. (#3996)

679 **1937 PR66 PCGS.** Brilliant in finish, as are all proof Buffalo Nickels of this date, this coin possesses glassy fields that form a splendid backdrop to the fully brought up devices. There is some light milky toning on either side, and the surfaces are free of mentionable blemishes. A final-year proof issue that would fit nicely into a Gem quality type set.
Ex: Central States Signature (Heritage, 5/2004), lot 6424, which realized $1,610.(#3996)

680 **1937 PR67 NGC.** Minimally toned with gleaming mirrors and razor-sharp definition on the devices. A beautifully preserved Superb Gem example of this final proof Buffalo nickel issue. (#3996)

668 **1937-D Three-Legged MS65 NGC.** FS-901 (formerly FS-020.2). This coin is an interesting and instructive example of the Three-Legged Buffalo, combining as it does Gem quality with a late state of dies that already advanced when the error was created. On the reverse there is more die erosion present than normal, creating an extra dose of the orange-peel effect in the field before the buffalo's head. The tiny plant on the mound before the missing leg is smaller than usual, and the various areas of the obverse show advanced die markers as well. On the other hand, the strike is as well delivered as ever on this issue, the luster is head-and-shoulders superior to most examples, and evidence of post-strike contact is minuscule. Census: 48 in 65, 18 finer (2/09).(#3982)

PROOF BUFFALO NICKELS

669 **1914 PR66 NGC.** A crisply detailed, elegantly textured matte proof that offers great eye appeal. Subtly gold-tinged on the obverse with deeper green-gold and sage shadings present on the reverse. (#3991)

670 **1915 PR62 PCGS.** This remarkably bold matte proof Buffalo nickel has full details on both sides with deep gold toning on the obverse and lighter gold on the reverse. Both sides have myriad spots that prevent a higher grade.(#3992)

JEFFERSON NICKELS

681 **1939-D Reverse of 1940 MS66 Full Steps PCGS.** The "Straight Steps" reverse subtype introduced in 1939. Lustrous and unmarked with light tan-gold toning. The key date of the series if die varieties are excluded. Population: 26 in 66 Full Steps, 2 finer (2/09). (#894005)

682 **1943/2-P MS65 Full Steps PCGS.** FS-101, formerly FS-028. Another of the dual-hubbing errors that seemed to pop up during both World Wars at the Mint, this is technically a Doubled Die Obverse as well as an overdate. The lower curve of the underdigit 2 is readily apparent under a glass, and doubling is visible on LIBERTY and IN GOD WE TRUST. According to Fivaz and Stanton, the reverse is also a tripled die. A medley of soft violet, ice-blue, and lilac patina resides on highly lustrous surfaces. This sharply and uniformly struck Gem is nicely preserved. Population: 40 in 65 Full Steps, 23 finer (2/09).(#84019)

683 **1943/2-P MS65 Full Steps PCGS.** FS-101, formerly FS-028. A fully brilliant and highly lustrous example of this popular *Guide Book* overdate, the only such variety in the Jefferson nickel series. The steps on the reverse are unusually well-defined. Population: 40 in 65 Full Steps, 23 finer (2/09).(#84019)

684 **1944-S MS67 Full Steps PCGS.** Ex: Omaha Bank Hoard. Well-defined for the issue with powerful, swirling luster. Glimpses of golden toning appear close to the rims. Population: 27 in 67 Full Steps, 0 finer (1/09).(#84024)

685 **1950-D MS67 PCGS.** The low-mintage 1950-D nickel was perhaps most responsible for the roll craze that swept the numismatic hobby during the early 1960s. Most rolls have long since been broken up to provide singles for complete collections. Lustrous and nearly immaculate with medium almond-gold toning. Population: 10 in 67, 0 finer (1/09).(#4042)

Popular MS67 Full Steps 1950-D Nickel

686 **1950-D MS67 Full Steps PCGS.** Ex: Compradore Collection. This issue's low mintage of slightly over 2.6 million pieces spurred mass saving among speculators, and while the 1950-D is desirable, across most grades, it is not a rarity. Full Steps coins are elusive, however, and at the MS67 level, the 1950-D is just as much a condition rarity as its peers. The present Superb Gem example is a remarkable piece with frosty luster and sharp design details. The obverse has vivid gold and iridescent toning, and the reverse is essentially brilliant nickel-white with just a touch of champagne. Population: 6 in 67 Full Steps, 0 finer (2/09).(#84042)

PROOF JEFFERSON NICKEL

687 **1938 PR68 NGC.** Pale green toning at the bottom of the bust lends a touch of color to this specimen, an early modern proof with immaculate surfaces. The old-style steps of the Reverse of 1938 are wavy and incomplete, though the other design elements are sharply struck. Census: 10 in 68, 0 finer (2/09).(#4175)

EARLY HALF DIMES

Impressive 1794 V-2, LM-2 Half Dime, MS60 The Logan-McCloskey Plate Coin

688 **1794 MS60 NGC.** V-2, LM-2, R.5. Ex: Price. **The Logan-McCloskey plate coin.** Last August, we were privileged to offer the remarkable early dime and quarter eagle collections assembled by Ed Price. Similarly remarkable was the Price Collection of half dimes, which was sold privately several years ago. This Mint State 1794 is just one of those coins with gorgeous original gold, russet, blue, and iridescent toning over reflective fields. Slight weakness is noted on the lower hair tips of the obverse and the eagle's breast on the reverse, but the impression is well centered with bold borders around the entire circumference on both sides. A strict Mint State coin; the grade is limited only by a few minor surface marks on each side. NGC has only certified 44 Mint State 1794 half dimes, including all four different varieties, and most of those are probably LM-4. We would be surprised if more than half a dozen Mint State examples of LM-2 survive.
Ex: American Numismatic Rarities (6/2004), lot 2609.(#4250)

Appealing Near-Mint 1795 Half Dime, V-5, LM-8
The Logan-McCloskey Plate Coin, Ex: Ed Price

689 **1795 AU58 NGC.** V-5, LM-8, R.3. Though Logan-McCloskey describes this issue as being "available in all grades through mint state," their plate coin, from the collection of Ed Price, is perhaps the nicest AU58 example imaginable. Rich blue, pink, and green-gold overtones drape strongly lustrous surfaces that show just a touch of friction. As shown in the plate, the reverse displays a number of adjustment marks that add charm to the coin. (#4251)

Desirable Near-Mint 1795 Half Dime, V-4, LM-10

690 **1795 AU58 NGC.** V-4, LM-10, R.3. Although the LM-10 die combination is considered one of the most common varieties of the Flowing Hair half dimes, examples are elusive in higher grades. This piece has pewter-gray surfaces with excellent luster beneath lovely gold and pale blue toning that is especially vibrant on the reverse. *From The Ed Lepordo Collection, Part Two.*(#4251)

Lofty Gem 1795 Half Dime, V-5, LM-8

691 **1795 MS65 NGC.** V-5, LM-8, R.3. The familiar variety with a lengthy die crack that traverses the obverse between the Y in LIBERTY and the 7 in the date, causing a "Scarface" appearance (as made) on Liberty. Both sides are attractively toned yellow-gold, cherry-red, and lime-green. Sharply struck throughout aside from minor blending on the eagle's wings and breast. The fields are magnificently smooth, luster shimmers across the fields and devices, and the eye appeal is blatant. The Flowing Hair type was only coined in 1794 and 1795. Census: 6 in 65, 13 finer (2/09). (#4251)

Popular V-1, LM-1 LIKERTY 1796 Half Dime, AU Details

692 **1796 LIKERTY—Improperly Cleaned—NCS. AU Details.** V-1, LM-1, R.3. Although only two die varieties are known, the *Guide Book* continues to list three different entries for the date, including the Normal Date, the Overdate, and the LIKERTY variety. This latter issue is merely a die state of the Normal Date variety; Logan-McCloskey makes no mention of the LIKERTY die state. This example shows several obverse and reverse die cracks. The sharpness is exceptional, and is virtually Mint State. Rose-gray surfaces display a few ancient pinscratches and slight glossiness from a past cleaning, but the overall eye appeal holds up.(#94254)

Desirable Near-Mint 1797 Half Dime
15 Stars, V-2, LM-1

693　**1797 15 Stars AU58 PCGS.** V-2, LM-1, R.3. The three different obverse dies used to coin four varieties of 1797 half dimes are quickly identified by the number of stars. In this case, 15 stars are arranged with eight to the left and seven to the right. This darkly toned near-Mint specimen has a lovely combination of steel-blue and deep gold, with nearly complete underlying luster. The central obverse and reverse design motifs are quite weak, as always, while the remaining detail is bold. The obverse die is lightly lapped and the reverse die is moderately clash marked. A splendid example of this important design type. Population: 11 in 58, 16 finer (2/09). (#4258)

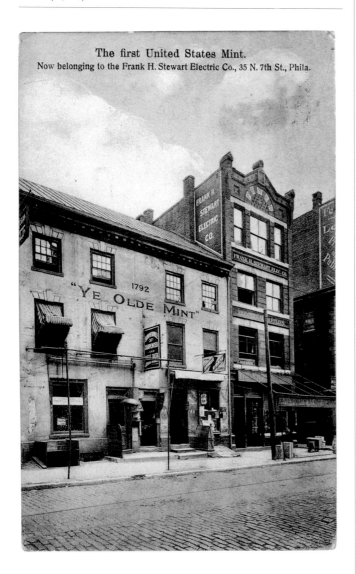

The first United States Mint.
Now belonging to the Frank H. Stewart Electric Co., 35 N. 7th St., Phila.

Impressive 1797 V-4, LM-2
16 Stars Half Dime, MS62
Logan-McCloskey Plate Coin

694　**1797 16 Stars MS62 NGC.** V-4, LM-2, R.4. Ex: Price. **The Logan-McCloskey plate coin.** A late die state with extensive cracks and clash marks, especially on the reverse. The center of the obverse and most of the eagle's detail on the reverse are bluntly struck as always for the 1797 16 Stars half dimes, and most other varieties of this design combination. The eagle's head, breast, and leg were cut a little too deep in the die, and as the coin was struck, metal attempted to fill those recesses in the reverse die, and at the same time diminishing the amount of metal available for the obverse. The result was that both sides had extreme weakness at opposing points, as seen on this coin. Examination of the remaining bold detail on both sides confirms that the problem was more the original dies, and less the striking pressure. Both sides of this wonderful piece have light gold toning over frosty silver luster. Census: 10 in 62, 24 finer, including all four different varieties (2/09).(#4259)

Rare V-3, LM-3 1797 Half Dime, MS64

695 **1797 16 Stars MS64 NGC.** V-3, LM-3, R.5. The more elusive of two die pairs to share the 16 Stars obverse for the 1797 dime, this one distinguished by a wreath kept well away from the word STATES on the reverse. The Logan-McCloskey reference describes this variant as "very rare in Mint State," a profound understatement. The present example is wonderfully detailed for the issue with a degree of watery reflectivity to the fields. The margins show a degree of golden-brown patina that fades out into the silver-white that is dominant at the centers. Incredible visual appeal.(#4259)

Original 1800 Half Dime, V-1, LM-1, VF30

696 **1800 VF30 ICG.** V-1, LM-1, R.3. A moderately worn example of this most common die marriage from 1800. A number of small to midsized abrasions are seen on each side, and the coin has overall light gray-lilac coloration with deeper hues around the margins and within the device recesses.(#4264)

Wonderful 1800 V-2, LM-3 LIBEKTY Half Dime, AU58
Logan McCloskey Plate Coin

697 **1800 LIBEKTY AU58 NGC.** V-2, LM-3, R.4. Ex: Price. **The Logan-McCloskey plate coin.** Each of the two major types, the Normal LIBERTY and the LIBEKTY, have two individual die marriages, and in each case one variety is common, and the other rare. The V-2, LM-3 die marriage is the common variety of the LIBEKTY type. A small crack is evident to the left of the date, with a raised area at the border that is probably a result of the minor field bruise at the opposing point on the reverse. Still a remarkable example with nearly full luster beneath lilac, gold, and steel-blue toning. Census: 22 in 58, 50 finer (2/09), including all four die varieties of the year.(#4265)

Important 1803 Large 8 Half Dime, MS61
V-1, LM-2, Ex: Ed Price

698   **1803 Large 8 MS61 NGC.** V-1, LM-2, R.4. The scarcer of the two Large 8 varieties this year. For an issue that often comes weakly struck in the centers, this is an unusually well-defined coin, particularly on the strands of Liberty's hair. Each side offers lively luster beneath a blend of attractive gold-gray and orange-brown patina. Aside from wispy abrasions, the only marks on this appealing coin are a handful of small digs in the fields. Excellent preservation and eye appeal, a most desirable early half dime.
Ex: Ed Price; Superior (5-6/2004), lot 1233 (erroneously described as the Logan-McCloskey plate coin at this appearance).(#4269)

BUST HALF DIMES

699   **1829 MS64 NGC.** V-2, LM-3, R.2. A gorgeous display of turquoise-blue and antique-gold toning adorns each side, highlighted by full satiny luster. Well struck, minimally marked, and conservatively graded by NGC.(#4276)

Marvelous Prooflike 1829 Half Dime
V-7, LM-1, MS67

700   **1829 MS67 NGC.** V-7, LM-1, R.2. A marvelous example in an early die state for the pairing, with no visible clash marks on either side and much prooflikeness in evidence, clearly an early strike from the fresh dies. Although there is no Prooflike designation forthcoming from NGC, this piece is a serious contender for such an appellation. Light roller marks appear on the central obverse under a loupe, but otherwise the eye appeal is over the top. The highly contrasting surfaces are most silver-white, with a hint of pink-champagne at the centers. The fields are blinding white mirrors. Essentially unimprovable. Census: 5 in 67, 0 finer (2/09). (#4276)

701   **1830 MS64 NGC.** V-1, LM-14, R.3. A somewhat scarcer variety attributable by the location of the T in STATES over the left half of the second U in PLURIBUS. The present near-Gem is well struck, and displays a mix of sea-green, pearl-gray, and pale tan-gold patination.
Ex: FUN Signature (Heritage, 1/2006), lot 1637.(#4277)

Dusky Gem 1830 Half Dime, V-7, LM-7

702   **1830 MS65 PCGS.** V-7, LM-7, R.2. The 8 in the date is lightly repunched. This satiny and exquisitely struck Gem displays rich tobacco-brown and slate-gray patina. Post-strike contact is inconsequential, and the originality and eye appeal are unchallenged. Population: 35 in 65, 27 finer (2/09).(#4277)

703   **1831 MS64 PCGS.** V-2, LM-3, R.4. A brightly lustrous example of this elusive variant. Light golden-brown and pink peripheral shadings surround pale silver-white centers. Elegant eye appeal. (#4278)

MS66 1831 Half Dime, V-4, LM-4
Early Die State, Possible Proof Strike

704 **1831 MS66 PCGS.** V-4, LM-4, R.2, R.7 if proof. Star 2 is repunched, and star 1 nearly touches the denticles. On the reverse MERI touch, and the right edge of E2 is centered over the S in PLURIBUS. The O in OF is repunched.

Our consignor believes this coin to be a proof. We feel the piece is possibly—even probably—a proof as well, but it is certified as a business strike. The following arguments weigh in favor of this piece's proof status:

—The strike is sharp to nearly full, including broad, square rims and pinpoint definition of the denticles. The only area of weakness is the left juncture of the eagle's wing with the shield, the same area that is weak on the Eliasberg proof (see below).

—The coin is struck from the same apparent die state as the Eliasberg Collection coin (Bowers and Merena, 5/1996, lot 916), which was cataloged as a proof. Specifically, it is in an earlier die state than the business strikes as documented in Logan-McCloskey, which normally show a die crack from the eagle's right (facing) wing tip downward through the arrow shafts. It also lacks the normally seen weakness of the obverse denticles between star 13 and the date.

—The mirror-finish fields extend even to the areas between the denticles.

—Faint diagonal die striations in the obverse field, extending from northwest to southeast, indicate the dies were polished shortly before this coin was struck. The same die-polishing striae appear on the obverse of the Eliasberg proof. Die polishing is also visible, albeit more faintly, on the reverse, unmentioned in Eliasberg.

—The Breen *Proof Encyclopedia* and Logan-McCloskey half dime references both acknowledge proof 1831 half dimes struck from this die pairing.

The possibility remains that this piece could be a prooflike business strike, from an earlier die state than generally acknowledged or known for the variety. One minor factor—the only one we see—that mitigates against its proof status is some tiny planchet laminations that appear under a loupe in the central obverse, on Liberty's cheek and neck. However, we do not believe the Mint would have rejected this planchet for those barely seen surface irregularities.

In either case, this is simply a splendid coin, with original pinkish-gold patina in the centers radiating outward to iridescent steel-blue at the rims on both sides. Considerable cameo contrast is evident, and the superlative eye appeal is obvious. We recommend that prospective bidders make a personal inspection of this coin and decide its status for themselves.(#4278)

Stunning MS67 1831 Half Dime, V-1, LM-6

705　1831 MS67 NGC. V-1, LM-6, R.1. Both 1s in the date are centered over dentils, and delicate repunching shows on star 3. On the reverse the right edge of the C in is just below the tip of the stem. Although this is a common variety, this piece would certainly be near the top of the Condition Census, regardless of variety. Stunning steel-blue and coral-pink patina graces both sides. Although there is some localized planchet roughness around the portrait, as made, there is essentially no bothersome post-strike contact. The sharp strike is every bit as pleasing as are the overall aesthetics. For the date, Census: 13 in 67, 2 finer (2/09). (#4278)

Notable Gem 1832 Half Dime, V-8, LM-5

706　1832 MS65 NGC. V-8, LM-5, R.1. An early die state, with the top of the final S and the lower part of the F filled, but no other die cracks, chips, or clash marks. An impressive and fully brilliant Gem with white-silver surfaces. The fields are reflective and the devices frosty, imparting noticeable contrast.(#4279)

707　1833 MS64 PCGS. V-1, LM-10, R.1. Dappled sea-green, plum-red, and orange-gold endow this satiny and intricately struck Choice half dime. A pleasing Capped Bust type coin. Population: 62 in 64, 63 finer (2/09).(#4280)

708　1833 MS64 NGC. V-6, LM-9, R.2. Original medium golden-brown and forest-green toning graces this shimmering and unmarked near-Gem. Blending of detail along the left shield border appears to be all that limits the grade.(#4280)

Brilliant 1833 V-1, LM-10 Half Dime, MS65

709　1833 MS65 PCGS. CAC. V-1, LM-10, R.1. This Gem half dime exhibits brilliant silver luster with delicate peach toning on the high points. Slight weakness is evident at the center of the obverse but all other design features are sharp. The obverse has a vertical die crack from the drapery to the neck, cheek, and cap. This die combination represents the fourth use of the reverse die, with several chips and cracks.(#4280)

Late State 1833 V-1, LM-10 Dime, MS66

710　1833 MS66 PCGS. CAC. V-1, LM-10, R.1. An absolutely gorgeous Premium Gem, this beauty has highly lustrous silver surfaces with brilliant mint frost and exceptional design definition. Both sides have impeccable surfaces that are void of any contact marks or other unsightly distractions. A late die state with a vertical die crack on the obverse. Population: 19 in 66, 7 finer (2/09).(#4280)

711　1834 MS64 NGC. CAC. V-1, LM-2, R.1. Both sides of this pleasing near-Gem are deeply toned with steel-blue and iridescent surfaces. Excellent preservation overall with only trivial flaws. (#4281)

Prized Gem 1834 Half Dime, V-1, LM-2

712　1834 MS65 PCGS. V-1, LM-2, R.1. A relatively available variety for the year, though at the Gem level, any die pair becomes a rarity. This beautifully detailed piece is brightly lustrous and generally pale silver-gray, though the rims show a few glimpses of gold. For all Normal Date varieties, Population: 29 in 65, 29 finer (2/09). (#4281)

Exceptional MS66 1834 Half Dime
V-1, LM-2

713   1834 MS66 PCGS. CAC. V-1, LM-2, R.1. The F in OF is punched too low, and a die crack across the portrait descends beneath Liberty's nose. A sharply struck and lustrous Premium Gem with light to medium autumn-gold toning. Essentially immaculate, and many would consider this piece to be worthy of the next higher grade. Population: 19 in 66, 10 finer (2/09).(#4281)

Marvelous 1834 Half Dime, MS67 ★
V-4, LM-4

714   1834 MS67 ★ NGC. V-4, LM-4, R.1. Simply put, one of the most marvelously appealing Bust half dimes imaginable. The strike is crisp and the luster vibrant. Light silver-gray centers yield to deep, yet translucent golden-tan, peach, and violet-blue shadings. Beautifully preserved and notable in all respects. The only NGC-certified Superb Gem 1834 half dime to have earned the Star designation, with none numerically finer (2/09).(#4281)

Worthy MS66 1834 Half Dime
V-5, LM-1

715   1834 3 Over Inverted 3 MS66 PCGS. CAC. V-5, LM-1, R.2. A small obverse die break at 12 o'clock identifies this available Valentine variety. Satiny and meticulously struck with faint chestnut patina. Remarkably bereft of contact, and the eye appeal is superlative. Population: 19 in 66, 10 finer (2/09).(#94281)

Outstanding Gem 1835 Half Dime, V-11, LM-4

716   1835 Large Date, Large 5C MS65 NGC. V-11, LM-4, R.3. A beautifully preserved half dime with lovely antique toning in deep shades of pewter-gray, rose-gray and sea-green. The design elements are crisply struck, and the coin's surfaces reveal outstanding preservation, in the absence of any noticeable surface marks on either side.(#4282)

Popular 1836 Half Dime, MS64
V-4, LM-3, '3 Over Inverted 3'

717   1836 3/Inverted 3 MS64 NGC. V-4, LM-3, R.1. The single most available die pair for the year, though its status as a standalone *Guide Book* variety makes it more valuable than some of its rarer peers. Deep silver-blue central toning gives way to russet and reddish-orange patina closer to the margins. Highly desirable. (#94288)

718   1837 Large 5C PCGS Genuine. V-5, LM-3, R.6. Our grade VG details, bent. The 3 Low obverse paired with a Large Denomination reverse, which combine for the year's rarest Capped Bust half dime variety. Midnight-blue, violet, gold, and silver-gray color enriches each side, with the toning deeper on the reverse.(#4289)

Choice 1837 Capped Bust Half Dime
Large 5C, V-1, LM-5

719   1837 Large 5C MS64 PCGS. V-1, LM-5, R.1. An exquisite final-year Capped Bust half dime. A precise strike, shimmering luster, and dappled tan-gold and aqua toning ensure the quality of this unmarked near-Gem. A desirable contribution to an early silver type set. Population: 17 in 64, 10 finer (2/09).(#4289)

SEATED HALF DIMES

Lovely Gem 1837 No Stars, Small Date Half Dime With Large Die Break, V-6

720 **1837 No Stars, Small Date (Flat Top 1) MS65 PCGS.** V-6. Mislabeled on the holder as a No Stars, Large Date. A beautifully toned example of this coveted type coin, one that never fails to appeal with its open cameo obverse fields. Deep lilac and lavender patina covers both sides to splendid effect, and as a further lagniappe, this documented Valentine variety has, in his words, "... a bad flaw to right of arm holding Liberty cap, and continuing downward from the knee."(#4311)

Appealing 1837 Large Date Half Dime, MS65

721 **1837 No Stars, Large Date (Curl Top 1) MS65 NGC.** Incorrectly described as a Small Date on the holder, though the curled top of the 1 and the script 8 in the date attest to the piece's Large Date status. Both sides are strongly lustrous beneath rich patina, rose-violet and gold-gray colors dominant. Well-defined and pleasingly preserved.(#4311)

Delightful 1837 Half Dime, No Stars, Large Date, MS66

722 **1837 No Stars, Large Date (Curl Top 1) MS66 NGC.** A delightfully preserved example of this first-year issue, of approximately equal rarity to its Small Date counterpart until the upper circulated grades, when the Large Date becomes more available. This well-defined piece is largely silver-gray with glimmers of golden-tan at the margins. NGC has graded just 18 finer examples (02/09).(#4311)

Sharply Struck 1837 No Stars, Large Date Half Dime, MS66

723 **1837 No Stars, Large Date (Curl Top 1) MS66 NGC.** Light gold toning enriches the borders of this highly lustrous and decisively struck Premium Gem. Essentially pristine aside from a delicate mark beneath the E in STATES. The sole date without stars, aside from a very scarce emission in 1838 at New Orleans.(#4311)

1837 Large Date Half Dime, MS66 A Sought-After, Short-Lived Type Coin

724 **1837 No Stars, Large Date (Curl Top 1) MS66 PCGS. CAC.** Distinguished from the "Small Date" by the pointed top in the 1, rather than any actual difference in size between the two date punches. This is an early die state that shows pronounced triple punching below the 8. The design elements are fully struck throughout, and the surfaces are bright and heavily frosted with no trace of toning on either side. Just a splendid example of this minimalist design, that in some ways is more suggestive of a medal than a regular production coin. Population: 30 in 66, 3 finer (2/09). (#4311)

725 **1838 Large Stars, No Drapery MS64 PCGS.** Rich green-gold and orange patina surrounds small silver-pink centers. A lustrous near-Gem that offers interesting and elegant eye appeal.(#4317)

726 **1838 Large Stars, No Drapery MS64 PCGS.** The obverse is pale silver-blue, while the reverse shows slightly deeper toning in the same vein. Shining luster enlivens the patina. Highly appealing. (#4317)

Impressive 1838 Half Dime, MS66 ★ Large Stars, No Drapery

727 **1838 Large Stars, No Drapery MS66 ★ NGC.** Exotic rose-red, aquamarine, straw-gold, and plum-mauve endow this shimmering and penetratingly struck Premium Gem. An attractively toned and minimally abraded representative of the briefly made No Drapery subtype. Well struck and impressively preserved. Census: 2 in 66 ★, 6 finer with a ★ designation (2/09).(#4317)

Lustrous 1838 Large Stars, No Drapery Half Dime, MS66

728 **1838 Large Stars, No Drapery MS66 NGC.** The obverse is evenly divided between forest-green and rose-gold. The reverse is sun-gold with glimpses of ocean-blue and plum-red across the periphery. This lustrous and exactingly struck Premium Gem is delightfully devoid of mentionable marks. Census: 47 in 66, 26 finer (2/09).(#4317)

Splendid 1838 Large Stars, No Drapery Half Dime MS67 ★

729 **1838 Large Stars, No Drapery MS67 ★ NGC.** Gorgeous, variegated patina is the key to this coin's special visual allure. Rich shades of sunset-orange and purple-red adorn the obverse, while the reverse displays lighter notes of gold-tan, champagne, and cerulean-blue. Sharply struck and expectedly free of surface distractions. Census: 4 in 67 ★, 2 finer with the ★ (2/09).(#4317)

Important MS67 1838 Half Dime No Drapery, Large Stars

730 **1838 Large Stars, No Drapery MS67 PCGS. CAC.** A gorgeous Superb Gem that exhibits sweeping luster and an unimprovable strike. The fields are nearly bereft of even the faintest grazes, and the delicate golden-brown toning further ensures the eye appeal. The Stars, No Drapery type was only struck between 1838 and 1840. Encapsulated in a green label holder. Population: 4 in 67, 1 finer (2/09).(#4317)

731 **1839 No Drapery MS64 NGC.** Dappled blue-violet and silver-white colors enhance each side of this near-Gem. Well-defined and bright, a gorgeous survivor. NGC has graded 61 finer pieces (1/09). (#4319)

732 **1839 No Drapery MS64 PCGS.** Softly lustrous beneath ample burgundy and reddish-silver patina. This minimally marked near-Gem offers great eye appeal and a sharp strike. Population: 41 in 64, 43 finer (2/09).(#4319)

Elusive 1839 No Drapery Half Dime, MS66

733 **1839 No Drapery MS66 NGC.** Impressively struck with crisp definition on Liberty's head and all of the obverse stars. Flashy with only a hint of champagne patina along the lower left obverse rim. The otherwise silver-white surfaces are carefully preserved and exhibit sharply struck devices. Census: 20 in 66, 7 finer (2/09). (#4319)

Appealing 1839 No Drapery Half Dime, MS66

734 **1839 No Drapery MS66 PCGS. CAC.** An amazing Premium Gem, and seldom found any finer, this brilliant silver piece has light champagne toning on both surfaces. All of the design elements are bold and fully defined. The reverse has curious raised spines in the area of the terminal leaves, extending up to the legend. Population: 19 in 66, 5 finer (2/09).(#4319)

735 **1841 MS65 PCGS.** A lustrous Gem beneath the rich patina that is this coin's hallmark. Dappled cerulean, violet, and blue-gray shadings embrace each side. Population: 10 in 65, 13 finer (1/09). (#4328)

Superb Gem 1841-O Half Dime Single Finest Certified by NGC

736 **1841-O MS67 NGC.** Medium O. Those in search of the single finest NGC-graded 1841-O half dime need look no further, because that piece is the present lot. Despite a seemingly plentiful mintage of 815,000 pieces, the 1841-O is rare in Mint State, with only 12 pieces certified by NGC in such condition. Only one piece each has been graded by NGC as MS65 and MS66, followed by the currently offered MS67 at the summit of the Condition Census.

This immaculate Superb Gem provides vibrant cartwheel sheen and original dappled almond-gold and stone-gray toning. The strike is consistently bold throughout. Relatively late dies with numerous spindly die cracks along the reverse periphery.(#4329)

Sharply Struck 1842 Half Dime, MS66

737 **1842 MS66 PCGS.** Powder-blue, apple-green, and lavender patination slightly more vivid on the reverse, runs over the lustrous surfaces of this Premium Gem half dime. A solid strike leaves sharp, uniform definition on the design elements. Impeccable preservation adds to the appeal. Population: 4 in 66, 0 finer (2/09). (#4330)

738 **1844 MS65 PCGS.** Faint purple toning gravitates to the margins on this Gem half dime, and all of the design features are clear. An elegant example offering grand eye appeal. Population: 18 in 65, 29 finer (2/09).(#4333)

739 **1844 MS66 PCGS.** Elegantly toned and softly lustrous. The obverse shows subtle sky-blue toning, while more electric shadings drape the sage-accented reverse. Population: 20 in 66, 9 finer (2/09).(#4333)

Charming Superb Gem 1844 Half Dime

740 **1844 MS67 PCGS.** An exactingly struck and nicely lustrous Superb Gem. The dappled apple-green and tan-gold surfaces are devoid of contact. The mintage of 430,000 pieces is low for a Philadelphia issue of the era. An unimprovable representative of the Stars, No Arrows subtype. Population: 9 in 67, 0 finer (2/09). (#4333)

Appealing VF25 1846 Half Dime

741 **1846 VF25 ANACS.** A moderately worn example that shows primarily silver-gray surfaces with startling dabs of enamel-blue over parts of the fields. Minimally marked with pleasing remaining detail for the midrange grade. The 1846 half dime has a mintage of 27,000 pieces, with precious few of them surviving to the present day.(#4336)

Scarce 1848-O Medium O Half Dime, MS66

742 **1848-O MS66 PCGS.** V-2, Medium O. The date is bold, with all numerals touching the base. Stars 4 through 6 are recut, and the Medium O mintmark is high and centered. Splashes of yellow-green, forest-green, violet, and purple toning visit lustrous surfaces, and a sharp strike brings out good definition on the design elements, except for the usual weakness in the upper left part of the wreath. Both sides are devoid of significant contact marks. Scarce in Mint State. Population: 8 in 66, 4 finer (1/09).(#4340)

743 **1850 MS65 PCGS. CAC.** Occasional hints of periwinkle-blue patina visit otherwise bright silver-white surfaces. A well-defined and minimally marked Gem. Population: 19 in 65, 24 finer (2/09). (#4345)

Coveted 1851 Half Dime, MS67

744 **1851 MS67 NGC.** Light silver-gray overall with strong, swirling luster and above-average detail. What is most impressive about this Superb Gem is that its surfaces are essentially pristine, a rare state for any Seated half dime, much less a Stars on Obverse example. Census: 4 in 67, 1 finer (2/09).(#4347)

745 **1852 MS66 NGC.** A razor-sharp, satiny, and mark-free Premium Gem with original russet, almond-gold, and lime-green toning. Encased in a prior generation holder. Census: 10 in 66, 5 finer (2/09).(#4349)

Pleasing 1853 Arrows Half Dime, MS66

746 **1853 Arrows MS66 PCGS.** The 1853 Arrows half dime can be located through the MS64 level. Gems become more difficult, and Premium Gems are challenging. Higher-grade pieces are elusive. Electric-blue and lavender concentrates at the margins, ceding to yellow-green in the centers. The design elements are well brought up, and both sides are nicely preserved. Clash marks are visible on the reverse. Housed in a green label holder. Population: 31 in 66, 6 finer (2/09).(#4356)

Resplendent 1853 Arrows Half Dime, MS66

747   1853 Arrows MS66 PCGS. CAC. Faint traces of lilac and gold iridescence are evident over the frosty silver surfaces of this brilliant Premium Gem. Both sides are remarkable for their bold strike. The surfaces have a scaly appearance from well worn coinage dies. Population: 31 in 66, 6 finer (2/09).(#4356)

Outstanding 1855 Arrows Half Dime, MS66

748   1855 Arrows MS66 PCGS. CAC. An amazing Premium Gem with hints of pale gold toning over highly lustrous and frosty silver surfaces. Some fine roller lines remain from the original planchet. Minor clash marks are also visible. The strike is bold everywhere except along parts of the borders. Population: 3 in 66, 0 finer (2/09).(#4360)

749   1856 MS66 NGC. The ivory-gray surfaces are lustrous and distraction-free. Light gold peripheral toning enhances the eye appeal of this conditionally elusive Premium Gem. Census: 39 in 66, 6 finer (1/09).(#4363)

750   1856 MS66 NGC. Soft orange, blue-green, and violet patina drapes the lustrous surfaces of this Premium Gem. Well struck except for the denticles, and clean aside from a shallow mark above the HA in HALF. Census: 39 in 66, 6 finer (2/09).(#4363)

751   1857 MS65 NGC. Strongly lustrous and interestingly toned. The obverse is largely silver-gray with cerulean crescents to the left and right, while the reverse shows blue-green, violet, mustard-gold, and sage concentric circles.(#4365)

752   1857 MS66 NGC. Light golden overtones visit pale silver-gray surfaces. An appealing Premium Gem, well struck and carefully preserved. Census: 39 in 66, 6 finer (2/09).(#4365)

753   1858 MS66 NGC. A stunning beauty with frosty mint luster and gorgeous rainbow toning on both sides. Heavy clash marks add to the overall desirability of this Seated half dime. Census: 57 in 66, 21 finer (2/09).(#4367)

754   1858 MS66 PCGS. This precisely struck Premium Gem is patinated sky-blue and autumn-gold. Satiny and undisturbed. Struck from prominently clashed dies. Population: 41 in 66, 13 finer (1/09).(#4367)

755   1859 MS65 NGC. Soft champagne-gold patina dominates both sides of this Gem, accented with lavender and electric-blue. The design elements are well impressed, and stand above partially prooflike fields that display light die polish lines. Nicely preserved throughout.(#4371)

756   1859 MS66 PCGS. CAC. V-2. An impressive Premium Gem with vibrant luster and lovely original toning. Both sides are well preserved and virtually flawless. An important date in the half dime series, now recognized as a one-year type, with hollow centers in the stars. Population: 10 in 66, 11 finer (2/09).(#4371)

757   1860 MS66 NGC. First year of the Legend Obverse design modification for the Seated half dimes. This Premium Gem has exquisite ivory surfaces with enticing blue, russet, lilac, and gold toning splashes across both surfaces. Census: 58 in 66, 37 finer (2/09).(#4377)

758   1860 MS66 PCGS. Strong, swirling luster with a pleasing strike and careful preservation. The obverse has midnight-blue and green-gold peripheral tints around a silver-gray center, while deep cerulean patina drapes the reverse. Population: 49 in 66, 34 finer (1/09).(#4377)

Stunning 1860 Half Dime, MS67

759   1860 MS67 PCGS. CAC. This stunning Superb Gem has variegated gold, violet, russet, and blue-green toning over reflective obverse and reverse surfaces. The strike is bold and the aesthetic appeal is exceptional, truly a coin for the connoisseur. Population: 32 in 67, 2 finer (2/09).(#4377)

Beautiful MS67 1863 Half Dime

760   1863 MS67 PCGS. CAC. A bright, essentially brilliant example of this low-mintage Civil War-era half dime issue, crisply detailed and nearly flawless to the unaided eye. Though close to three dozen such exemplary survivors appear in the combined certified population, there are only six known finer coins (1/09).(#4382)

761   1864—Improperly Cleaned—NCS. Unc Details. No trace of wear, though each side shows subdued luster. Orange, rose, blue, violet, and gray shadings mingle over the lightly hairlined surfaces. (#4384)

Beautiful Superb Gem 1864 Half Dime
Tied for Finest Graded

762 **1864 MS67 NGC.** A lightly toned and pristine Superb Gem with minor incompleteness on the wreath opposite the left corner of Liberty's rock. Struck from prominently clashed dies. Because silver coins were widely hoarded during the Civil War, the Philadelphia Mint issued only 48,000 pieces in 1864. Census: 4 in 67, 0 finer at either service (2/09).(#4384)

763 **1865 MS65 NGC.** Subtle pink and navy toning embraces each side of this charming Gem. Well-defined and carefully preserved, a half dime enthusiast's delight. Census: 6 in 65, 14 finer (2/09). (#4386)

764 **1868 MS65 NGC.** Brightly lustrous with modest reflectivity to the untoned fields. Frosted devices are snow-white with strong definition. Census: 11 in 65, 10 finer (2/09).(#4392)

Splendid MS66 1868-S Half Dime

765 **1868-S MS66 NGC.** This forest-green and stone-gray Premium Gem has dynamic luster, an intricate strike, and magnificent eye appeal. Among the nicest examples to survive from this relatively low mintage issue. Certified in a prior generation holder. Census: 5 in 66, 0 finer (2/09).(#4393)

766 **1869 MS65 PCGS. CAC.** Strongly lustrous with light golden-tan tints over much of the centers. The peripheries are nearly brilliant, and the strike is bold. Population: 9 in 65, 12 finer (1/09). (#4394)

767 **1869-S MS64 PCGS.** Although a relatively common coin in circulated grades, the 1869-S is very scarce in Mint State. This is a well struck piece (except for parts of the wreath), with slightly muted luster under light lilac-gray toning. Population: 12 in 64, 3 finer (2/09).(#4395)

768 **1870 MS66 PCGS. CAC.** Both sides of this Premium Gem display a medley of low to medium intensity cobalt-blue, purple, gold-beige, and gray toning, and each projects a degree of field-motif contrast. Impeccably preserved surfaces exhibit well struck design elements. This coin generates considerable eye appeal, aptly recognized by the CAC label. Population: 8 in 66, 4 finer (2/09). (#4396)

769 **1870 MS66 PCGS.** Semiprooflike fields create mild contrast with motifs. Well struck, and devoid of mentionable contact. Some minute spots are visible on the lower obverse. Population: 8 in 66, 4 finer (1/09).(#4396)

770 **1872-S Mintmark Below Bow MS65 PCGS.** A delightful Gem, this piece exhibits frosty mint luster beneath deep gold, blue, and iridescent toning on both sides. Boldly struck and well preserved, with no noticeable surface flaws.(#4401)

771 **1872-S Mintmark Above Bow MS65 PCGS. CAC.** Pale silver-blue color with glimpses of peach. Excellent strike and luster, an all-around appealing Gem survivor. Population: 23 in 65, 14 finer (1/09).(#4402)

PROOF SEATED HALF DIMES

772 **1859 PR63 PCGS.** The reflective fields display even lilac-gray toning, while the high points exhibit steel-gray color. A one-year type coin, redesigned by Paquet, with hollow stars and a slightly altered figure of Liberty. This is a lovely, sharply struck, nicely preserved specimen.
From The Burning Tree Collection.(#4438)

Charming PR66 1859 Half Dime

773 **1859 PR66 NGC.** The last official Legend on Reverse proof half dime issue, offered here as an exquisite Premium Gem. Each side offers excellent detail and reflectivity. Surfaces range from gold-orange at the left to pale cloud-gray at the right, with the latter color more dominant on the reverse. Census: 17 in 66, 8 finer (2/09).(#4438)

774 **1862 PR65 NGC.** This is an immensely appealing Gem specimen with amazingly deep, lovely rainbow toning near the obverse and reverse peripheries. Sharply struck and well preserved, with highly reflective fields and a few wispy hairlines that prevent an even finer grade. A desirable, low-mintage Civil War issue of just 550 pieces. Census: 18 in 65, 24 finer (2/09).(#4445)

775 **1862 PR63 Cameo NGC.** The cameo contrast is obvious on both sides of this conditionally scarce specimen. Well struck and essentially untoned, with glassy fields and lightly frosted devices. A few hairline scratches are evident in the obverse and reverse fields. Census: 2 in 63 Cameo, 28 finer (1/09).(#84445)

776 **1864 PR64 Cameo NGC.** A mere 470 proof half dimes were struck in 1864, and survivors are very scarce with the Cameo designation. This untoned near-Gem displays an impressive shimmer across both sides, and appealing contrast between fields and devices. Census: 3 in 64 Cameo, 11 finer (1/09).(#84447)

777 **1867 PR65 Cameo NGC.** A gorgeous Cameo proof, this Gem has fully mirrored fields and lustrous devices beneath delightful lilac, gold, and blue toning on both sides. Census: 11 in 65 Cameo, 11 finer (2/09).(#84450)

778 **1867 PR66 Cameo NGC.** Peripheral electric-blue and purple toning is more extensive and deeper on the reverse, ceding to light golden-brown in the centers of both sides. This is a well struck and nicely preserved piece. Census: 9 in 66 Cameo, 2 finer (2/09). (#84450)

779 **1868 PR66 NGC.** Well-defined and carefully preserved with winning eye appeal. Mirrors are strong beneath dappled blue-green and violet patina. Census: 15 in 66, 5 finer (1/09).(#4451)

780 **1870 PR66 NGC.** Deep blue and amber toning covers the fields of the obverse, which contrasts nicely against the dramatic lilac, gold, and orange on the reverse. The figure of Liberty is essentially untoned and frosted, and is particularly eye-catching next to the dark toning around it. A loupe reveals only a couple of light hairlines. One of just 1,000 proofs struck.(#4453)

781 **1870 PR66 PCGS.** Light champagne and steel-gray toning are intermingled over both sides. Sharply struck and free of any obvious defects. The original patina reduces the reflectivity in the fields slightly. Population: 11 in 66, 1 finer (2/09).(#4453)

782 **1870 PR65 Cameo PCGS.** This lightly frosted, richly toned Gem offers pleasing contrast and strong overall visual appeal. Crisply struck and free of distractions. Although 1,000 proofs were struck in 1870, few have received the Cameo designation. Population: 2 in 65 Cameo, 6 finer (2/09).(#84453)

783 **1872 PR65 NGC.** Subtly gold-tinged with a pleasing strike. An attractive and carefully struck survivor that offers a hint of contrast on each side. Census: 26 in 65, 14 finer (1/09).(#4455)

Spectacular 1873 Half Dime, PR67

784 **1873 PR67 NGC.** Final year of the half dime denomination. This is a spectacular proof example that is deeply mirrored. The surfaces display rich blue-violet centers with rose and yellow color around the margins. An essentially perfect example of this popular type coin. Census: 8 in 67, 0 finer (2/09).(#4456)

EARLY DIMES

Good 1796 Dime, JR-6

785 **1796 Good 4 PCGS.** JR-6, R.3. This first year dime displays deep blue-green and cream-gray toning. The date is sharp, and the only reportable marks are two minor ones on the upper reverse. There is a heavy die crack that raises the reverse field between 6 and 10 o'clock and affects the sharpness in that region.(#4461)

Rare JR-5 1796 Dime, AU55
The Reiver Plate Coin

786 **1796 AU55 PCGS.** JR-5, R.5. JR-5 is one of the two 1796 dime varieties to carry an R.5 rarity rating, and it is unusual in anything approaching the quality of the current coin. This piece, then graded AU50, was cited in the 1984 JR reference (where it served as the plate coin) as the finest the authors had seen, and it remains perhaps the finest example of the variety available.

It is interesting to note that this is both a relatively late die state, as evidenced by the vertical die crack that bisects the obverse between 1 o'clock and 5 o'clock, and a substantially prooflike coin, quite possibly also one of the earlier strikes from this die pair. In retrospect, the scarcity of the variety is quite understandable due to the obviously short die life. This is a well-struck coin, with only a small area of bluntness on the highest points of the eagle's chest and leg, as always. A good deal of both luster and reflectivity remain under deep, iridescent toning. Wear is at an absolute minimum, and a few small pinscratches do not detract from the abundant appeal. *Ex: An unknown late 1930s Wayte Raymond Sale, Lot 395; Harold Bareford Collection (Stack's, 10/81, lot 132); Allen F. Lovejoy Collection (Stack's, 10/90, lot 6); private collection; American Numismatic Rarities (7/05, lot 977).*(#4461)

Unworn JR-6 1796 Dime

787   **1796—Cleaned—ICG. MS60 Details.** JR-6, R.3. One of the more available die pairs in the context of the variety, though still scarce in all grades. Neither side of this crisply detailed first-year dime shows any trace of wear. Though the fields are glossy and lightly hairlined from a past cleaning, the surfaces have retoned silver-blue and violet-gold. An interesting piece.

    The 1796 to 1797 dimes bear the Draped Bust, Small Eagle type introduced on the silver dollar of late 1795. This type only lasted two years on the dime, although the Heraldic Eagle reverse appears crowded on the small diameter of the half dime.(#4461)

Luminous AU Details 1797 16 Stars Dime, JR-1

788   **1797 16 Stars—Improperly Cleaned—NCS. AU Details.** JR-1, R.4. The only appearance of this year's 16 Stars obverse. Strongly struck with only light wear on the high points, particularly the eagle's breast. Light hairlines indicate that this piece was cleaned in the past, though the surfaces have since retoned silver-gray, violet, and gold.(#4462)

Late State 1807 JR-1 Dime, AU50

789   **1807 AU50 PCGS.** JR-1, R.2. An extraordinary late die state specimen with sharp central details but considerable peripheral weakness. Both dies were used well beyond their normal life expectancy, exhibiting heavy clash marks and several prominent die bulges. Surprisingly, there are no die cracks apparent on either side. Both sides have light silver-gray surfaces with wispy gold toning.(#4480)

Late Die State 1807 JR-1 Dime, MS63

790   **1807 MS63 PCGS.** JR-1, R.2. The only known die pair for the date and easily the most plentiful die variety of the Draped Bust type, from a mintage of 165,000 coins. The heavy obverse clash marks and peripheral design weakness indicate that this piece is a late die state, although later state examples do exist. Population: 30 in 63, 28 finer (2/09).(#4480)

BUST DIMES

Toned Large Date 1814 JR-3 Dime, MS64

791   **1814 Large Date MS64 PCGS.** JR-3, R.2. The obverse has normal stars without repunching on stars 3, 4, and 5, and the reverse has no period following 10 C. Somewhat bluntly struck on the hair curls and stars to the right as usual; additional weakness appears on the eagle's neck and claws. The surfaces are fully lustrous beneath deep lilac and iridescent toning. A relatively common variety, with a number of Choice or Gem Mint State pieces known, and ideal for the type collector. Population: 25 in 64, 6 finer (2/09). (#4488)

Stunning Gem 1814 Large Date Dime
JR-3, Late Die State

792   **1814 Large Date MS65 NGC.** JR-3, R.2. The date is large, and the lowest hair curl extends to the right edge of the second 1 in the date. On the reverse there is no period after 10 C, confirming the attribution. Both dies are in advanced states, with numerous clash marks around Liberty in several areas, and the several die breaks noted in the JR dime reference all clearly visible on the reverse. The surfaces are unimpaired by any post-strike distraction, however, with pretty silver-gray centers complementing tinges of lavender and cerise near the margins. A stunning Gem of this interesting die variety and state.(#4488)

Gem 1814 STATESOF Dime, JR-5

793   **1814 STATESOF MS65 NGC.** JR-5, R.3. The popular *Guide Book* STATESOF variety with only letter spacing before and after OF. A lustrous Gem with lovely golden-russet patina that deepens slightly toward the rims. No marks are readily apparent, and the strike is good despite some blending on Liberty's forehead curls and opposite near the fletchings.(#4490)

Popular 1820 Dime, MS64
Small 0, JR-3

794   **1820 Small 0 MS64 NGC.** JR-3, R.4. An enchanting example, richly lustrous with deep gold-orange and rose-gray patina draping each side. Well struck devices are minimally marked. Placing this JR-3 piece in any sort of condition census is necessarily speculative, but it almost assuredly ranks highly.(#4493)

Elegant Gem 1829 Dime
Large Denomination, JR-2

795   **1829 Large MS65 NGC.** JR-2, R.2. The reverse is notable for the large size of the denomination and the defective right foot of the 1 therein. This Gem offers excellent central detail and gorgeous luster beneath rich patina, largely forest-green with glimpses of gold, emerald, and sage. A marvelous survivor.(#94511)

796   **1830 Medium 10C MS63 PCGS.** JR-6, R.2. Low 3 in date, and the top arrow shaft is detached. Light golden-gray toning is accented with splashes of deep mauve on the obverse. Soft luster resides on minimally marked surfaces that exhibit well struck design elements.(#4516)

Magnificent MS66 1831 Dime

797   **1831 MS66 PCGS. CAC.** JR-6, R.3. This beautiful Premium Gem has dazzling luster and a pinpoint strike. Glimpses of caramel-gold visit the margins. A magnificent Capped Bust type coin. JR-6 is identified by die crumbling near the arrowheads and a die crack through the first three stars. Population: 6 in 66, 5 finer (2/09). (#4520)

Elusive Gem 1833 Bust Dime, JR-9

798   **1833 MS65 NGC.** JR-9, R.2. Well struck with intense satiny mint luster on both sides, and a slight degree of champagne and speckled russet-red patina on the obverse. The reverse is brilliant. A rather elaborate latticework of die cracks and clash marks exists on the reverse, particularly noticeable near STATES. A conditionally scarce Gem example.(#4522)

Exceptional MS65 1833 Bust Dime, JR-6

799   **1833 MS65 NGC.** JR-6, R.1. The second S in STATES is directly above the second U in PLURIBUS. A highly impressive Gem with gorgeous variegated toning that completely covers each side in shades of gold, purple, turquoise-green, and rose. The surfaces are exceptionally well preserved and blemish-free.(#4522)

Unperturbed Gem 1837 Dime, JR-4

800   **1837 MS65 PCGS. CAC.** JR-4, R.1. A bold die crack nearly bisects the obverse between 11:30 and 5 o'clock. A lightly toned and satiny Gem. The strike is powerful, and there is little evidence of post-strike contact. An outstanding final year silver type coin. Population: 5 in 65, 3 finer (2/09).(#4529)

SEATED DIMES

Popular 1837 No Stars Dime, MS64

801   **1837 No Stars, Large Date MS64 PCGS. CAC.** The date is tall and sits high in the field, closer to the base of Liberty than the border. The final digit is doubled at its bottom curve. Both sides are boldly defined with full details in Liberty's head, foot, the shield, and the wreath. This fully lustrous piece has speckled gold and blue toning over ivory surfaces. Population: 53 in 64, 30 finer (2/09). (#4561)

Gem 1837 No Stars, Large Date Dime

802   **1837 No Stars, Large Date MS65 NGC. CAC.** Elegant pearl-gray and champagne toning adorns the immaculate surfaces of this conditionally elusive Gem example. Well struck with bold, satiny luster. The No Stars dime type was only produced in 1837 and 1838, making it an important design subtype for collectors. Census: 22 in 65, 28 finer (2/09).(#4561)

Exemplary 1837 No Stars Dime, MS66

803   **1837 No Stars, Large Date MS66 NGC.** Large Date. Repunched 7. Greer-102. A first-year issue that is always in demand among type collectors, the present lot offers a conditionally scarce Premium Gem. Both sides are fully lustrous and bright with essentially untoned, brilliant-white features. The sharply impressed devices are equally as blemish-free as the smooth, placid fields. Both major grading services report a combined MS66 population of 26 coins, and there are only nine pieces finer (2/09).(#4561)

804   **1838-O No Stars—Cleaned—ANACS. AU55 Details.** A well struck and interesting dime from the first year of production for the New Orleans Mint. Partly retoned violet and tan-orange from a past cleaning.(#4564)

805   **1838 No Drapery, Large Stars MS65 PCGS. CAC.** Delicate green-gold peripheral tints frame light silver-gray centers. A sharply struck Gem that offers stirring eye appeal. Population: 26 in 65, 16 finer (1/09).(#4568)

Lovely Gem 1839 No Drapery Dime

806 **1839 No Drapery MS65 NGC.** A definite wire rim is noted on each side of this lovely Gem example. The design elements are sharply struck, including Liberty's hair and the obverse stars. A shimmering, untoned, impressively preserved example of the short-lived No Drapery dime type. Census: 26 in 65, 34 finer (2/09). (#4571)

Fabulous MS67 1839-O No Drapery Dime

807 **1839-O No Drapery MS67 NGC.** Large O. This early New Orleans dime issue of over 1.3 million pieces is relatively available in the circulated grades, though Mint State examples are elusive and only a handful of Superb Gem pieces have survived to the present day. This is one such example, an immensely lustrous MS67 beauty that offers exacting detail, unusual for an O-mint minor silver coin. Glimpses of peach and rose patina grace otherwise silver-white surfaces that are exquisitely preserved. A noteworthy and memorable representative that should find a home in an exclusive cabinet.(#4572)

808 **1844—Damaged—ANACS. XF Details, Net VF20.** A small but deep mark between the wreath ends flattens a small portion of the design opposite, above the first 4 in the date. The central obverse has a faint circular impression. The obverse is deeply toned, the reverse is tobacco-brown. A key date.(#4585)

809 **1844 VF25 ANACS.** LIBERTY is bold on this collector grade key date dime. Toned iridescent apricot and powder-blue. A few concealed abrasions are seen near star 13.(#4585)

810 **1844 VF35 ANACS.** This cream-gray key date dime has ample detail and attractive eye appeal. The so-called "Little Orphan Annie" dime, coveted for its low mintage and fanciful history. (#4585)

811 **1844 VF35 ANACS.** Rich forest-green and orange-russet patina accompanies this midgrade key date Seated dime. No marks merit individual mention.(#4585)

812 **1844 VF35 ANACS.** Deep steel-blue and plum-mauve toning embraces this Choice VF key date example. Only 72,500 pieces were struck, and most were presumably melted or lost during the 19th century.(#4585)

813 **1844—Whizzed—ANACS. AU Details, Net XF40.** The surfaces appear microgranular from whizzing, but the borders have attractively retoned golden-brown and ocean-blue. A well defined example of this famous key date.(#4585)

814 **1844—Obverse Tooled—ANACS. AU Details, Net XF40.** The left obverse field has a patch of hair-thin marks, and more consequential ticks are noted near stars 4 and 8. Tan and aquamarine toning aids the eye appeal of this key date dime. (#4585)

815 **1844 XF45 PCGS.** Attractively toned in peripheral bands of lemon-gold and apple-green. Minor field marks are present near star 1 and DIME. A partly lustrous Choice XF key date dime. Encapsulated in an old green label holder. Population: 8 in 45, 17 finer (1/09).(#4585)

Highly Regarded Gem 1844 Dime
'Little Orphan Annie'

816   **1844 MS65 PCGS.** Deep ocean-blue patina bathes this sharply defined and gently shimmering Gem. The fame of the 1844 dime begins with its enticingly low mintage of 72,500 pieces. The tiny production led Frank C. Ross to hoard examples and promote the issue as the "Little Orphan Annie" variety. Various implausible scenarios were generated to explain the rarity of the 1844 dime, such as pirate seizures of ships and the like. While nothing so dramatic likely occurred, examples may have been melted after the 1848 discovery of gold in California, an event that removed most silver from circulation until the silver content in new coinage was reduced in 1853. Population: 5 in 65, 0 finer (2/09).(#4585)

Richly Toned MS61 1846 Dime

817   **1846 MS61 NGC.** Among early Philadelphia Seated dimes, the date that has received the most publicity by far is the 1844, nicknamed the "Little Orphan Annie" for decades. By comparison, the 1846 dime has played "Sandy" to the 1844, lower in mintage and far more elusive, yet accorded second billing at best. Recent years, however, have been more kind to the 1846. This MS61 example is the single finest piece certified by NGC (2/09). Dappled rose-gold and blue-green shadings drape surfaces that show surprisingly few abrasions for the grade assigned. Well struck and attractive.(#4588)

818   **1848 MS64 PCGS.** A satiny near-Gem with exquisite surfaces and excellent design details. Both sides have ivory or russet toning at the centers, framed by vivid blue toning. Only the slightest surface marks are evident, and they are consistent with the grade. Population: 9 in 64, 3 finer (2/09).(#4590)

819   **1853 Arrows MS65 PCGS.** An appealing Gem example of this brief three-year design variant. Well struck and satiny with light gold-gray toning and speckled russet patina near the borders. Carefully preserved and essentially unmarked, a great example for the type enthusiast. Population: 74 in 65, 56 finer (2/09). (#4603)

Vibrant 1853 Arrows Dime, MS66

820 **1853 Arrows MS66 PCGS. CAC.** Vibrant gold toning enhances the brilliant mint frost of this Premium Gem. Both sides have bold design elements and pristine, nearly unmarked surfaces. The large arrowheads merge into the border and the base of Liberty, dwarfing the individual date elements. Population: 38 in 66, 18 finer (2/09). (#4603)

Fabulous MS67 1853 Arrows Dime

821 **1853 Arrows MS67 NGC.** This Superb Gem features an exemplary strike and a frosty finish that yields pleasing luster. An occasional wisp of tan-gold color is visible under magnification, and both sides are impeccably preserved. This is an excellent coin for a high grade type collection. Census: 8 in 67, 5 finer (2/09). (#4603)

Frosty Silver-White 1853 Arrows Dime, MS67

822 **1853 Arrows MS67 NGC.** A wonderful type coin, this frosty silver-white Superb Gem offers a bold strike and equally bold eye appeal. Light clash marks are noted on each side. Despite the prodigious mintage exceeding 12 million pieces, NGC has certified less than a dozen examples in this grade or higher (2/09). (#4603)

823 **1854 Arrows MS64 PCGS.** Softly lustrous with silver-gray centers and ample peripheral toning. Deep violet, green-gold, and ruby patina dominates the rims. Population: 30 in 64, 29 finer (1/09). (#4605)

824 **1854 Arrows MS65 NGC.** A sharply struck example of this Arrows issue, subtly lustrous beneath blue-tinged silver-gray patina. Housed in an older-generation holder. Census: 17 in 65, 15 finer (2/09).(#4605)

825 **1857 MS65 NGC.** Fortin-103. The 1 in the date is lightly repunched south. An essentially brilliant Gem that has bountiful luster, clean surfaces, and an intricate strike. Census: 34 in 65, 13 finer (1/09).(#4614)

Sumptuous Superb Gem 1857-O Dime

826 **1857-O MS67 NGC.** Large O. The 1857-O dime issue was a workhorse, with a considerable mintage in excess of 1.5 million pieces. While scattered Mint State examples survive to the present day, Superb Gems such as the present coin are nearly unfathomable treasures. Elegant gold-orange central patina yields to peach and blue shadings close to the margins. Sharply struck and immensely lustrous. Census: 7 in 67, 1 finer (1/09).(#4615)

827 **1858 MS65 NGC.** Though the obverse of this minimally toned Gem shows pillowy detail, the reverse is sharp. The luster is soft and highly appealing. Census: 16 in 65, 11 finer (1/09).(#4616)

Elusive 1859 Seated Dime, MS66

828 **1859 MS66 NGC.** The 1859 dime, despite a generous mintage of 430,000 pieces, is challenging above VF levels of preservation. For Uncirculated examples, Brian Greer (1992) assigns a rarity value of low R.4. Electric-blue, lavender, and golden-brown toning rings the margins of this Premium Gem specimen, and a well executed strike accounts for above-average definition on the design features. This is significant, as Greer indicates that: "Soft strikes make this date challenging for the fussy collector." Highly lustrous surfaces are impeccably preserved. Census: 10 in 66, 17 finer (1/09). (#4619)

829 **1859-S XF40 PCGS.** A well detailed and unmarked stone-gray piece. The 1859-S is a challenging issue due to its low mintage of 60,000 pieces. The inadequate facility for the First San Francisco Mint caused it to concentrate on the half dollar and double eagle denominations. Population: 5 in 40, 10 finer (2/09). (#4621)

Scarce Fortin-102b 1866 Seated Dime, MS65 ★

830 **1866 MS65 ★ NGC.** Fortin-102b, R.6. The small postbellum emission of only 8,000 business strikes for the issue nearly guarantees that high-grade survivors will show prooflikeness, as is the case here. The minuscule mintage nonetheless failed to prevent the dies from colliding, as bold clash marks appear on both sides. Tinges of gold and cinnamon accompany a couple of minor ticks that fail to diminish the significant appeal. A bold, raised die line connects the inner upper wreath tips. A nice choice for a date set, and quite a rare variety for the Seated dime specialists. Census: 8 in 65, 9 finer (2/09).(#4643)

Incredible MS66 1871 Dime

831 **1871 MS66 PCGS. CAC.** Swirling, frosty luster with a hint of gray-gold patina. This Premium Gem is well-defined and carefully preserved. With a mintage of under a million pieces, this is an elusive Seated dime issue that is underrated by many of today's collectors. Population: 7 in 66, 0 finer (2/09).(#4653)

Desirable 1872-CC Dime, VF30

832 **1872-CC VF30 NGC.** The first four Carson City dime issues minted from 1871 to 1874 are all elusive, low mintage issues. In 1872 the total production was a mere 35,480 coins, and few have survived. This original example has medium gold toning with hints of lilac and specks of steel. It is moderately worn but still desirable.
From The Belle Collection of Carson City Coinage.(#4657)

Condition Census 1872-CC Seated Dime, AU55
Tied for Third Finest Certified

833 **1872-CC AU55 NGC.** The 1872-CC is arguably the key issue to the Seated dime series in grades above XF. This was stated in Brian Greer's reference to the series in 1992, and it still holds true today. Only 35,480 pieces were struck, and apparently almost all of the production run entered the channels of commerce and stayed there. NGC and PCGS combined have recorded a total of 80 submission events (2/09). Less resubmissions, a realistic estimate of survivors in all grades is in the range of 50-60 pieces.

Breen states that two dies were shipped to the Carson City Mint in 1872 and then questions whether both were used. There is only evidence that one set of dies was used this year. Interestingly, all Carson City dimes from 1871 through 1874 are struck from the same reverse die, showing widely spaced reeding. A die crack is seen on the later dates and on some of the 1872-CC dimes, although it is absent here. 1872-CC dimes are usually irregularly struck and often show softness on the head and foot of Liberty, as seen here.

This is one of the finest examples of this date and mintmark known. The finest known is a miracle of preservation at the MS63 level. One AU58 coin has been certified, followed by this and another AU55. The surfaces of this piece are somewhat rough and have the appearance of the unalloyed Comstock silver seen on some 1871-CC dimes. Each side has variegated medium and darker gray patina. A small planchet flaw in the right field appears under a loupe, but post-strike contact is insignificant. Census: 2 in 55, 0 finer (2/09).
From The Belle Collection of Carson City Coinage.(#4657)

Significant VF25 1873-CC Arrows Dime

834 **1873-CC Arrows VF25 PCGS.** The 1873-CC Arrows dime has long been considered a series key, and ownership of any example is a mark of distinction among Seated dime collectors. Its stated mintage of nearly 19,000 pieces must be taken with a grain of salt, since this issue has one of the lowest survival rates of any Carson City issue. The present mid-range example, though it would miss most Condition Census lists, offers solid eye appeal for the grade. All letters in LIBERTY are bold and the aquamarine and stone-gray surfaces are smooth and largely mark-free. Population: 3 in 25, 15 finer (2/09).
Ex: Houston Signature (Heritage, 12/2008), lot 1098, which realized $9,200.
From The Belle Collection of Carson City Coinage.(#4666)

Charming 1874 Arrows Dime, MS66

835 **1874 Arrows MS66 PCGS.** Much luster radiates from the silver-white surfaces of this charming Premium Gem type coin. Some bold clashing, visible under Liberty's right (facing) breast from the bifurcated leaf tip below (DIM)E on the reverse, adds some extra panache to an already flashy coin. Well but not fully struck, and certified in a green-label holder.(#4668)

Rare XF Details 1874-CC Arrows Dime

836 **1874-CC Arrows—Improperly Cleaned—NCS. XF Details.** The fourth charter member of what Rusty Goe memorably termed the "Fearsome Foursome" of Carson City dimes in his *The Mint on Carson Street*, the 1874-CC is the only Arrows issue in that esteemed company. With its tiny mintage of 10,817 pieces and a pitiful survival rate, it is little wonder that the 1874-CC Arrows dime is a major prize in any grade. The present example is minutely granular from a past cleaning, and is retoned in deep ice-blue and golden-brown shades. A solitary pinscratch crosses the waist. A sharply detailed example of this Old West rarity.
From The Belle Collection of Carson City Coinage.(#4669)

Impressive 1874-S Arrows Dime, MS66

837 **1874-S Arrows MS66 NGC.** Greer 101, Micro S, the more common of the two mintmark varieties of the year. This is a later die state with the mintmark resembling a blob (or perhaps a late 1970s S mintmark). Impressively lustrous under light golden-brown color, with a bare minimum of notable surface contact. Decently, if not quite fully struck, with some weakness visible on the left arrow and wreath end.(#4670)

838 **1875 MS66 NGC.** Minimally toned with strong, swirling luster. A well-defined Premium Gem example from this higher-mintage issue, ideal for a type set. Census: 42 in 66, 7 finer (1/09).(#4672)

839 **1875-CC Mintmark Above Bow MS64 PCGS.** An appealing near-Gem example of the Mintmark Above Bow variety of the 1875-CC dime. Light champagne-gray toning adorns satiny, lustrous surfaces. A couple of minute marks on the lower reverse seemingly limit the grade. Population: 42 in 64, 28 finer (2/09). *From The Belle Collection of Carson City Coinage.*(#4673)

Desirable 1875-CC Dime, MS65

840 **1875-CC Mintmark Above Bow MS65 NGC.** The scarcer mintmark location variety for this Carson City issue. This moderately prooflike Gem has light lemon patina and bright, unmarked surfaces. Well struck aside from the upper portion of the wreath. Census: 32 in 65, 13 finer (2/09). *From The Belle Collection of Carson City Coinage.*(#4673)

Colorful 1875-CC Mintmark Above Bow Dime, MS66

841 **1875-CC Mintmark Above Bow MS66 NGC.** The slightly more available of the mintmark-placement varieties for the year, though at the Premium Gem level both qualify as conditionally rare. This highly lustrous piece shows deep butter-yellow and green-gold toning across each side. Carefully preserved and immensely desirable. Census: 9 in 66, 4 finer (2/09).(#4673)

842 **1875-S Mintmark Below Bow MS65 PCGS. CAC.** Soft greenish-gold patina is a touch deeper in hue on the obverse of this lovely Gem. Better struck than usually seen, except for softness on Liberty's head, the mintmark, and bowknot. A nicely preserved piece. Population: 17 in 65, 3 finer (2/09).(#4676)

843 **1877 MS66 PCGS. CAC.** An older green-label holder houses this Premium Gem, a lovely piece that has fully mirrored fields and lustrous devices beneath outstanding gold and electric-blue obverse toning, and deep blue and rose reverse toning. Population: 9 in 66, 4 finer (1/09).(#4682)

844 **1877-CC MS65 PCGS.** Splashes of brownish-gold and steel-blue patina visit the highly lustrous surfaces of this nicely struck Gem, and are slightly more extensive and deeper on the obverse. A handful of grade-consistent marks are not bothersome. Population: 49 in 65, 26 finer (2/09).(#4683)

845 **1877-CC MS65 NGC.** A fully lustrous steel-blue Gem, this example shows traces of pink and iridescent toning. Seldom is a finer example of this popular issue seen in the market place. Census: 71 in 65, 48 finer (2/09). *From The Burning Tree Collection.*(#4683)

Curious 1878-CC Dime, MS66

846 **1878-CC MS66 NGC.** This Carson City product is an incredible Premium Gem with highly lustrous, satiny silver surfaces that are virtually unmarked with traces of champagne toning. An amazing coin for the die state enthusiast who must study the reverse. The obverse has some curious raised die lines within Liberty's gown and the shield, as well as faint die cracks and clash marks. But the reverse is astounding. The left ribbon end and many of the leaves have been lapped away, and in there place are heavy die cracks the encircle much of the die. There are die cracks hidden in the right branch that blend in to the design in such a way that they could be easily missed. A truly remarkable coin struck from a die that could have struck few additional pieces. Census: 8 in 66, 3 finer (2/09). *From The Belle Collection of Carson City Coinage.*(#4686)

847 **1879 MS66 ★ NGC. CAC.** Flashy fields offer considerable reflectivity, and the crisply detailed devices are richly frosted. A carefully preserved and gorgeous example from this lower-mintage issue.(#4687)

Low Mintage 1879 MS67 Dime

848 **1879 MS67 NGC.** Brian Greer (1992) suggests that Mint State 1879 dimes are more plentiful than what would be expected considering their low business strike mintage of 14,000 pieces. That said, Superb Gems such as the present offering are elusive. Snow-white surfaces exhibit semiprooflike fields that highlight the devices. Well struck, save for the usual weakness on the head. Both sides are impeccably preserved. Census: 25 in 67, 3 finer (2/09). (#4687)

Elusive 1880 Seated Dime, MS67

849 **1880 MS67 PCGS. CAC.** Dazzling luster and light golden-brown toning endow this pinpoint-sharp Superb Gem. Even a loupe fails to locate more than negligible contact. Only 36,000 business strike dimes were coined in 1880, undoubtedly due to ceaseless production of silver dollars at the four mints. Certified in a green label holder. Population: 12 in 67, 0 finer (2/09).(#4688)

Splendid White 1881 Dime, MS66

850 **1881 MS66 NGC.** The 1881 business strike dimes saw a mintage of only 24,000 coins, exceedingly small by any standards of the series. This splendid Premium Gem is clearly among the finest survivors of the issue, both numerically and aesthetically. The surfaces are uniformly powder-white, with essentially no hint of toning. Well struck, if a trifle short of full. Census: 7 in 66, 3 finer (2/09).(#4689)

851 **1883 MS66 PCGS. CAC.** The bottom of the 3 in the date is broken, as made. Vivid sea-green, violet, and cobalt-blue toning enriches the obverse of this impressive Premium Gem dime. Boldly struck with minimal surface marks. Population: 46 in 66, 11 finer (2/09).(#4691)

852 **1883 MS67 NGC.** The brilliance and overall reflectivity of this piece lend it a flashy, alluring appearance. The design elements are crisply reproduced, and the surfaces are impeccably preserved. Curiously, the lower half of the 3 in the date shows dark color, but this is not a grade-limiting factor. Census: 20 in 67, 1 finer (1/09). (#4691)

853 **1885-S VF20 NGC.** A mix of silver-gray, violet, and heather toning drapes each side of this midrange example. All letters of LIBERTY are clear on the obverse. Great eye appeal for the grade and issue with only a few disturbances in the fields. Census: 2 in 20, 36 finer (2/09).(#4695)

854 **1886 MS65 PCGS. CAC.** This highly lustrous Gem in its first generation PCGS holder is deeply toned with underlying mint frost. Both sides have deep brownish-gray with iridescent highlights. Population: 62 in 65, 33 finer (2/09).
From The Burning Tree Collection.(#4696)

Lustrous MS65 1886-S Dime

855 **1886-S MS65 NGC.** An awe-inspiring example of this difficult San Francisco dime issue; one that does not receive the attention of lower mintage issues such as the 1879-1881. Both sides offer sensational luster and are partially framed on the obverse in delicate golden patina. Census: 6 in 65, 13 finer (2/09).(#4697)

856 **1887 MS66 NGC.** A lustrous and brilliant Premium Gem. This lovely type coin is well preserved. A small planchet flaw (as made) is noted before the upright of the E in ONE. Struck from lightly clashed dies. Census: 44 in 66, 5 finer (1/09).(#4698)

857 **1890 MS66 PCGS.** Iridescent cobalt-blue, light-gray, and gold toning visits shimmering, exquisitely preserved surfaces. With a mintage approaching 10 million pieces, this issue is popular with type collectors. PCGS has only graded three coins finer (1/09). (#4704)

858 **1890 MS66 NGC.** A lovely Premium Gem, well made with delicate rose, green, and gold toning on each side, and no surface marks worth mentioning. Census: 33 in 66, 8 finer (1/09). (#4704)

859 **1891-O MS65 PCGS. CAC.** Shades of cobalt-blue, lilac, apple-green, and gold bathe the lustrous surfaces of this wonderful Gem. A decisive strike lends strong definition to the design features, save for softness in the hair atop Liberty's head. Nicely preserved, and housed in a green label holder. Population: 15 in 65, 9 finer (2/09). (#4707)

PROOF SEATED DIMES

Historic PR61 1845 Dime

860 **1845 PR61 PCGS. CAC.** Amply patinated blue-green with watery fields beneath. Though scattered hairlines and contact preclude a finer designation, such flaws have no effect on this coin's remarkable and historic nature. Not listed conclusively in our prior census of survivors, published in the January 2008 FUN catalog and accompanying the Pittman-Kaufman specimen. Population: 1 in 61, 0 finer (2/09).(#4732)

Delightful 1856 Small Date Dime, PR64

861 **1856 Small Date PR64 NGC.** Ex: Richmond Collection. Clear evidence of obverse die doubling is visible on the shield and lower skirt lines, and it is believed that all of the 35 to 50 survivors are from this obverse die, indicating that it was the only obverse die used for all 1856 proof dimes. The reverse die is well made with no unusual characteristics. A vibrant near-Gem, this beauty has a hint of cameo contrast with lovely blue and lilac toning over deeply mirrored fields. Census: 9 in 64, 6 finer (2/09).
Ex: Richmond Collection (David Lawrence, 3/2005), lot 1248. (#4745)

Rare Gem Proof 1857 Dime

862   **1857 PR65 NGC. CAC.** A well struck Gem with glossy rose-gold and olive-green surfaces. The proof mintage is unknown, but undoubtedly low given the paucity of survivors. In an early pre-hologram holder. The most recent appearance of any NGC PR65 at auction was in Superior's Feb. 2008 sale, and that coin realized $6,325. Census: 8 in 65, 7 finer (2/09).(#4746)

Exquisite 1857 Dime, PR66 Cameo

863   **1857 PR66 Cameo NGC.** A sensational proof with amazing silver-white surfaces. The fields are deeply mirrored and essentially free of marks, other than a few mint-caused planchet flakes and lint marks. Both sides have frosty devices with intense silver luster and exquisite design details. The connoisseur will appreciate the remarkable quality of this Premium Gem. Census: 1 in 66 Cameo, 2 finer (1/09).(#84746)

Elusive 1859 Seated Dime, PR66 ★ Cameo

864   **1859 PR66 ★ Cameo NGC.** Stark field-to-device contrast is apparent on each side of this sharply struck, impressively preserved Premium Gem proof specimen. The surfaces are free of contact marks, with only microscopic hairlines noted on either side. An important date among type collectors, the 1859 is the final proof issue in the Stars Obverse Seated dime series. Census: 3 in 66 ★ Cameo, 0 finer with the ★ (2/09).(#84748)

1859 Ultra Cameo PR66 Dime
A Significant With Stars Proof Type Coin

865   **1859 PR66 Ultra Cameo NGC.** This amazing proof has the deepest mirrored fields and highly lustrous devices that can be imagined. Both sides are fully brilliant-white and possess amazing aesthetic appeal. Ultra Cameo proofs are truly rare. NGC has certified 214 proof 1859 dimes, and only two are designated as Ultra Cameo. Census: 1 in 66 Ultra Cameo, 1 finer (2/09). (#94748)

866   **1862 PR64 PCGS. CAC.** Pale bluish-gray surfaces have brilliant green and gold accents along the borders. An important Civil War issue, the 1862 dime is scarce, even in the present moderate grade. Population: 30 in 64, 5 finer (2/09).
From The Burning Tree Collection.(#4755)

867   **1862 PR64 Cameo PCGS.** An attractive, conditionally scarce Cameo proof with highly reflective fields and mildly frosted devices. A curved lint mark extends from Liberty's ankle to the left base of the second A in AMERICA. Close to Gem quality, save for a few faint hairlines on the obverse. Population: 4 in 64 Cameo, 2 finer (1/09).(#84755)

868   **1863 PR65 Cameo NGC.** The regal design is crisply reproduced on each side; even Liberty's upper hair detail is sharply struck. Wispy die striations inhabit the fields and increase the flashy reflectivity. Scarce with the Gem Cameo grade at both major services. Census: 8 in 65 Cameo, 7 finer (1/09).(#84756)

Superb Gem Proof 1864 Dime

869   **1864 PR67 NGC.** Caramel-gold, plum-red, and lime-green toning enriches this flashy and intricately struck Superb Gem. This Civil War date has a proof mintage of only 470 pieces, and the associated business strikes were limited to 11,000 pieces. Census: 6 in 67, 0 finer (2/09).(#4757)

Fascinating PR66 Cameo 1864 Dime

870 **1864 PR66 Cameo NGC.** Largely untoned with moderate field-to-device contrast. The mirrors are strong, and the effigy of Liberty offers excellent frost. A few tiny imperfections in the fields on each side are planchet flakes and not post-striking flaws. Strong eye appeal for this Civil War-era proof issue. Census: 5 in 66 Cameo, 4 finer (2/09).(#84757)

Gorgeous 1866 Seated Dime, PR67 ★

871 **1866 PR67 ★ NGC.** Attractively patinated in rose-red, emerald-green, and sun-gold. Intricately struck and devoid of lint marks or abrasions. The date is lightly repunched near the first and final digits. A meager 625 proofs were struck. Census: 2 in 67 ★, 1 finer with a ★ designation (2/09).(#4759)

872 **1867 PR65 NGC.** Deep green-gold, violet, and ocean-blue shadings embrace each side of this Gem. Boldly detailed with flashy reflectivity where it peeks through the toning. Census: 17 in 65, 7 finer (2/09).(#4760)

Interesting 1867 Dime, PR66 ★

873 **1867 PR66 ★ NGC.** Greer-102. The Breen *Proof Encyclopedia* entry is worth quoting in its entirety: "B-1. Double punching shows on bases of 1 and 7 and sometimes also just within bottom of lower loop of 8; rev. ribbon ends touch. Always available at a price although under considerable pressure from date collectors as business strikes are very seldom available. It is not impossible that the normal date die used on uncirculated coins (struck January 29) might also have been used on the earliest proofs."

The 1867 business strikes have the lowest mintage of any regular-issue Seated dime, at 6,625 pieces. This appears to be the Greer-102, with 1 and 8 in the date centered over denticles and stripe 8 centered over the left edge of the 1. Greer writes, "Ahwash listed these as business strikes, but those I have seen have had proof characteristics." The present piece shows absolutely no repunching, and the lower loops of reverse ribbon do not touch the wreath above. Yet it is unquestionably a proof, both in its creation and preservation. Stunning original iridescent toning includes steel-blue at the rims and glowing pinkish-gold in the centers. Likely worth a substantial premium, if not liable to incite an outright bidding war.(#4760)

874 **1869 PR64 Cameo PCGS.** The central obverse and reverse are brilliant, with excellent contrast, and both sides have a delightful frame of cobalt-blue, violet, and iridescent toning. Population: 7 in 64 Cameo, 6 finer (2/09).(#84762)

Magnificent 1869 Dime, PR67 ★ Cameo

875 **1869 PR67 ★ Cameo NGC.** In terms of sheer visual splendor, it would be difficult to envision a more impressive example. This magnificent Superb Gem shows radiant, frosty-white central devices surrounded by deeply watery, dark proof fields and magical golden-brown and electric-blue peripheral toning. Immaculately preserved, with several wispy lint marks on the obverse (including one in the field area near Liberty's elbow) that should not be mistaken for contact marks. The single finest-graded Cameo specimen at either of the major grading services, as of (2/09). (#84762)

Significant 1873 Arrows Ten Cent, PR65

876 **1873 Arrows PR65 NGC.** Colorful and captivating, a delightful Gem of an 1873 Arrows dime proof. The crisply detailed devices and powerful mirrors are carefully preserved beneath rich violet, blue-green, and rose patina. A great representative of this short-lived subtype. Census: 14 in 65, 11 finer (2/09).(#4769)

Superlative 1874 Arrows Dime, PR66 Cameo

877 **1874 Arrows PR66 Cameo NGC.** High quality examples of the short-lived 1873 to 1874 Arrows type are always in demand. This Premium Gem Cameo proof is just such a coin with brilliant silver surfaces and excellent contrast between the fields and devices. Census: 3 in 66 Cameo, 0 finer (2/09).(#84770)

878 **1875 PR66 Cameo NGC.** A flashy and boldly struck Premium Gem with faint golden toning near the rims. Only 700 proofs were produced. A lovely high quality proof silver type coin. Census: 11 in 66 Cameo, 4 finer (2/09).(#84772)

Amazing 1875 Seated Dime, PR66 Ultra Cameo
Single Finest Graded by NGC

879 **1875 PR66 Ultra Cameo NGC.** The field-device contrast is absolutely amazing, with stunning white devices and deeply mirrored fields. A few tiny ticks prevent a Superb Gem grade. Both sides have subtle champagne accents to enhance the coin's overall eye appeal. Census: 1 in 66 Ultra Cameo, 0 finer (2/09). (#94772)

880 **1876 PR65 Cameo PCGS.** Light golden overtones with grand, watery reflectivity. The rich frost across the sharply struck devices supplies excellent contrast. Population: 4 in 65 Cameo, 0 finer (2/09).(#84773)

Delightful PR67 Cameo 1879 Dime

881 **1879 PR67 Cameo NGC.** A crisply struck and exquisitely preserved Superb Gem proof, from a reasonably low mintage of 1,100 pieces. The devices are sharply frosted, while the fields are deeply watery, and the result is the much-coveted Cameo effect that is so prominently favored by collectors. Census: 13 in 67 Cameo, 0 finer (2/09).(#84776)

Impressive 1879 Seated Dime, PR67 Cameo

882 **1879 PR67 Cameo NGC. CAC.** Every intricate detail of this Superb Gem Cameo proof is bold and fully defined. The surfaces are entirely brilliant with no evidence of toning. Doubling on the reverse is a result of a slight mechanical deficiency when this piece was struck. Census: 13 in 67 Cameo, 0 finer (2/09). (#84776)

883 **1880 PR65 PCGS. CAC.** Lacking a Cameo designation, this Gem proof may be a review candidate, for it has brilliant silver surfaces, deeply mirrored fields, and fully lustrous devices. Population: 44 in 65, 34 finer (2/09).
From The Burning Tree Collection.(#4777)

Sparkling 1880 Dime, PR65 Ultra Cameo

884   **1880 PR65 Ultra Cameo NGC.** A low-mintage date with 1,355 proofs struck out of a total mintage for the year of only 37,355 pieces. This is a spectacular, starkly contrasted example that displays deeply reflective mirrors and noticeably frosted devices. Only the slightest contact marks can be made out with the aid of a loupe. Brilliant throughout. Census: 1 in 65 Ultra Cameo, 1 finer (1/09).(#94777)

Glorious 1881 Dime, PR67 ★ Cameo

885   **1881 PR67 ★ Cameo NGC. CAC.** This Superb Gem Cameo proof is a delightful exception to the rule that toned coins usually fail to receive a Cameo designation. Both sides have gorgeous rainbow toning that covers the entire obverse and the reverse periphery. Census: 2 in 67 ★ Cameo, 0 finer (2/09).(#84778)

886   **1884 PR66 PCGS. CAC.** Splashes of cobalt-blue, lavender, and golden-brown toning enrich the well preserved surfaces of this Premium Gem proof. Nicely struck, save for portions of Liberty's hair. Population: 32 in 66, 15 finer (2/09).(#4781)

887   **1884 PR65 Cameo NGC.** Though the frost across the central devices is light, the contrast between those devices and the gleaming silver-white fields is not. Great eye appeal. Census: 10 in 65 Cameo, 30 finer (2/09).(#84781)

Captivating 1884 Seated Dime, PR67 Cameo

888   **1884 PR67 Cameo NGC. CAC.** This Superb Gem Cameo proof has brilliant silver centers with peripheral toning that gradually changes from vivid gold to deep violet and cobalt-blue. The toning remains outside the primary devices, accentuating the exceptional contrast. Census: 17 in 67 Cameo, 3 finer (2/09).(#84781)

Gorgeous 1884 Seated Dime, PR67 Cameo

889   **1884 PR67 Cameo NGC. CAC.** The fully brilliant fields and centers are surrounded by thick bands of deep electric-blue, red-brown, and gold peripheral iridescence. The design features are sharply struck, with just a bit of the usual softness on Liberty's head. A tiny planchet void (as struck) is located on the upper left reverse field, very near to the upper left shaft of the wreath, and should not be mistaken for a contact mark. A great, conditionally scarce example of this Seated dime proof issue. Census: 17 in 67 Cameo, 3 finer (2/09).(#84781)

Flashy 1885 PR67 Dime

890   **1885 PR67 PCGS.** Peach, sky-blue, cherry-red, and straw-gold enrich this exactingly struck and flashy Superb Gem. Even the aid of a loupe fails to locate any imperfections. A scant 930 proofs were struck. Encapsulated in a green label holder. Population: 7 in 67, 1 finer (2/09).(#4782)

891   **1886 PR64 Cameo NGC.** An essentially untoned example of this later proof Seated dime issue. Powerful mirrors contrast with the frostiness of the crisply struck devices. Census: 11 in 64 Cameo, 27 finer (1/09).(#84783)

892   **1888 PR66 PCGS. CAC.** This amazing Premium Gem proof possibly deserves a Cameo designation as it has exquisite contrast with fully mirrored fields and lustrous devices. Amazing peripheral blue and russet toning is insufficient to mask the contrast of this remarkable piece. Population: 13 in 66, 4 finer (2/09). *From The Burning Tree Collection.*(#4785)

893   **1891 PR65 PCGS. CAC.** A deeply mirrored Gem, each side is rather heavily toned with variegated golden-brown and ultramarine toning. Final year of issue for the long-lived Seated series. Population: 33 in 65, 26 finer (2/09). *From The Burning Tree Collection.*(#4788)

BARBER DIMES

Sensational 1892-S Barber Dime, MS65

894 **1892-S MS65 NGC.** A highly lustrous and frosty Gem, this 1892-S dime has vivid gold, violet, blue, and iridescent toning on both sides. It is boldly defined with exceptional obverse and reverse design details. Faint parallel roller lines are visible on both sides. EAC 64. Census: 4 in 65, 2 finer (2/09).
From The Burning Tree Collection.(#4798)

895 **1893-O MS64 PCGS.** Strong, swirling luster with a hint of satin. Patina ranges from subtle off-white to more overt silver-blue. Gorgeous visual appeal. Population: 32 in 64, 18 finer (2/09).
From The Burning Tree Collection.(#4801)

896 **1893-O MS64 PCGS. CAC.** A remarkable Barber dime with frosty devices and fully prooflike fields that provide pleasing cameo contrast on this Choice example. The surfaces are brilliant and the design elements are sharp. Population: 32 in 64, 18 finer (2/09).
From The Burning Tree Collection.(#4801)

897 **1894 MS65 PCGS. CAC.** Glowing luster exudes from surfaces delicately toned in pastels of powder-blue, beige-gold, and lavender. Sharply struck, and revealing just a few minor marks that likely preclude an even higher grade. Population: 21 in 65, 7 finer (2/09). (#4803)

898 **1895-S MS63 PCGS.** Delicate rose and iridescent toning enhances the aesthetic desirability of this Select Mint State piece. The 1895-S is a scarce date despite a mintage that exceeded 1 million coins. Population: 19 in 63, 30 finer (2/09).
From The Burning Tree Collection.(#4808)

899 **1895-S MS64 PCGS.** Precisely struck and lustrous with only a hint of caramel-gold toning. Refreshingly free from grade-limiting contact, and certain to elicit interest from Barber specialists. Few finer examples of this semikey date have been certified by PCGS. Population: 24 in 64, 6 finer (1/09).(#4808)

900 **1897-S MS63 NGC.** Rich reddish-orange peripheral color with paler sea-green in the fields. Well-defined with impressive luster and eye appeal. Census: 11 in 63, 23 finer (2/09).
From The Burning Tree Collection.(#4814)

Attractive 1900-O Dime, MS67
The Highest-Graded Example

901 **1900-O MS67 NGC.** The present piece is the single highest-graded 1900-O dime. The 1900-O is a significantly better date, partly due to a lower mintage (2.010 million pieces), but also because of a shortage of contemporary Southern dealers setting aside high grade examples. The 1900-O is rare in Mint State, and nearly unobtainable above Gem. This lustrous Superb Gem is beautifully toned in medium golden-brown and aquamarine. The strike is bold aside from the uppermost portion of the wreath, and the reverse appears immaculate. The obverse is also uncommonly smooth, as careful rotation reveals only a few faint grazes on the portrait. A fleeting opportunity for the Barber specialist. Census: 1 in 67, 0 finer (02/09).(#4822)

902 **1900-S MS65 PCGS.** Rich cerulean, sage, and silver-blue shadings embrace each side of this lustrous Gem. Well-defined and carefully preserved. Population: 19 in 65, 7 finer (2/09).(#4823)

903 **1903 MS65 PCGS.** RPD-002. Powder-blue and honey hues enrich this shimmering and unblemished Gem. A high mintage date, but few contemporary collectors set pieces aside, and the issue is scarce in higher Mint State grades. The 1 in the date is nicely repunched. Certified in a green label holder. Population: 20 in 65, 11 finer (1/09).(#4830)

904 **1903-O MS64 PCGS.** The obverse shows golden peripheral toning around a silver-gray center, while on the reverse, the former color has more even coverage. A pleasingly lustrous and well struck O-mint near-Gem. Population: 25 in 64, 13 finer (1/09). (#4831)

905 **1903-O MS64 PCGS.** This boldly detailed near-Gem is fully brilliant beneath wispy champagne toning. The surfaces are satiny and attractive. Despite a mintage of more than 8 million coins, this date is elusive in higher grades as the population data indicates. Population: 25 in 64, 13 finer (2/09).
From The Burning Tree Collection.(#4831)

906 **1905-O MS65 NGC.** The frosty surfaces have desirable ivory toning with traces of slightly deeper color on the high points. The strike is blunt from obviously worn dies that are cracked and rusted. Census: 14 in 65, 9 finer (2/09).
From The Burning Tree Collection.(#4836)

907 **1906-S MS64 PCGS.** A remarkable example with highly lustrous and brilliant silver surfaces. The design definition is exceptional. Population: 20 in 64, 42 finer (2/09).
From The Burning Tree Collection.(#4841)

Exceptional 1907-D Gem Ten Cent

908 **1907-D MS65 NGC.** As early D-mint Barber dime issues were not well preserved, it is not surprising that this second-year example represents an important bidding opportunity for the Gem date collector. Lustrous and clean, the surfaces are enhanced by mottled russet-gold, sea-green, and golden-brown rim accents. The striking softness that plagues many branch mint examples is not a factor in this coin's final eye appeal assessment. Census: 12 in 65, 10 finer (2/09).(#4843)

909 **1910 MS67 PCGS. CAC.** Considered common in lower grades, the 1910 is rarely seen as a Superb Gem. This example is heavily frosted and presents a blazing, snow-white color overall. A fully struck coin for the connoisseur who requires the finest quality. Population: 9 in 67, 1 finer (2/09).(#4854)

910 **1910-D MS65 PCGS.** An impressive Gem example of this Denver Mint production. The coin is entirely white and untoned, with well struck design features and expertly preserved surfaces that are blemish-free on both obverse and reverse. Population: 10 in 65, 8 finer (2/09).
From The Burning Tree Collection.(#4855)

Elusive 1910-S Barber Dime, MS66

911 **1910-S MS66 PCGS.** Between the low mintage of 1.24 million pieces and the heightened commercial activity of San Francisco in the early 20th century, it is little surprise that this issue is a condition rarity at such a lofty level. Well defined with vibrant luster beneath warm reddish-orange and plum peripheral toning that fades to golden-gray at the centers. Population: 8 in 66, 2 finer (1/09).(#4856)

Superlative 1911 Barber Dime, MS67

912 **1911 MS67 NGC.** This beautiful high grade Barber dime features booming luster and attractive preservation. Wisps of gold deny full brilliance. The 1911 trades as a type coin and is available in middle Mint State grades, but is conditionally rare as a Superb Gem. Census: 11 in 67, 2 finer (2/09).(#4857)

913 **1914-D MS66 PCGS.** Well-defined for this later issue with grand luster. Each side shows dramatic contrast between the silver-white that is in the majority on each side and the arcs of lemon-gold and burgundy-wine visible to the left. Population: 19 in 66, 2 finer (1/09).(#4866)

914 **1914-S MS65 PCGS.** Lovely, light golden-green toning covers each side of this bright, highly lustrous Gem. Well struck and virtually pristine. Population: 16 in 65, 12 finer (2/09). (#4867)

PROOF BARBER DIMES

915 **1892 PR66 PCGS. CAC.** Low to medium intensity multicolored toning embraces this Premium Gem, and reflective fields highlight crisply impressed design elements. Impeccably preserved throughout. Population: 30 in 66, 11 finer (2/09).(#4875)

916 **1892 PR66 Cameo NGC.** A strongly contrasted silver-white survivor, crisply detailed with beautifully preserved mirrors. Though this first-year Barber dime issue has the highest mintage among proofs of the design, high-end Cameo specimens remain particularly elusive. Census: 7 in 66 Cameo, 13 finer (1/09). (#84875)

917 **1893 PR64 Cameo NGC.** Strongly contrasted through a thin layer of silver-gray patina. A tiny contact mark is noted on Liberty's frosted cheek, and a few faint hairlines are present in the fields. Census: 6 in 64 Cameo, 39 finer (2/09).(#84877)

918 **1893 PR66 Cameo PCGS.** Despite the rich silver-blue patina that embraces a majority of each side, this Premium Gem also shows immense contrast, as shown by the snow-white cheek of Liberty. Population: 20 in 66 Cameo, 8 finer (1/09).(#84877)

919 **1893 PR66 Cameo NGC.** Stunning cameo contrast jumps out at the observer of this Premium Gem. Untoned surfaces exhibit exquisitely struck design elements, and are impeccably preserved. Census: 13 in 66 Cameo, 18 finer (2/09).(#84877)

920 **1898 PR65 PCGS.** Sharply struck with deep electric-blue and purple-rose toning. A swath of amber color resides on Liberty's lower cheek, just above the jawline. A lovely Gem proof specimen. Population: 33 in 65, 44 finer (2/09).(#4882)

Pleasing 1898 Barber Dime, PR66

921 **1898 PR66 PCGS.** Bold cameo contrast is visible through the lovely deep iridescence of this Premium Gem proof, although it lacks the Cameo designation. Generally the grading services will only provide a Cameo or Deep/Ultra Cameo label to those coins that are brilliant, or nearly so. Population: 31 in 66, 13 finer (2/09). (#4882)

Elusive 1898 Dime
PR66 Deep Cameo

922 **1898 PR66 Deep Cameo PCGS. CAC.** 1898 dimes are relatively available in the better proof grades. Deep Cameo pieces are elusive, however. PCGS has graded only nine examples in this finish, and NGC 11 specimens. Magnificent field-motif contrast shows on this exquisitely struck coin that has just an occasional hint of light tan-gold color. Impeccable preservation adds to the eye appeal. Population: 4 in 66 Deep Cameo, 2 finer (2/09).(#94882)

923 **1899 PR66 NGC.** Light golden toning over the centers with veins of pink throughout and blue peripheral patina. This lively Premium Gem offers powerful reflectivity and eye appeal in spades. Census: 29 in 66, 30 finer (2/09).(#4883)

Eliasberg's Remarkable PR68 1899 Dime
Single Highest Graded by PCGS

924 **1899 PR68 PCGS. CAC.** Ex: Eliasberg. As of (2/09), the present Barber dime is the sole proof 1899 to achieve the lofty grade of PR68 at PCGS, with none finer. The strike is full aside from the left peak of the wreath, and the flashy surfaces are attractively toned in golden-brown, lime-green, ocean-blue, and cherry-red. *Ex: J.M. Clapp, from the Philadelphia Mint in 12/1899; Clapp estate, 1942; Louis E. Eliasberg, Sr. Collection (Bowers and Merena, 5/1996), lot 1263.*(#4883)

Scintillating 1900 Barber Dime, PR67 Cameo

925 **1900 PR67 Cameo NGC.** An unimpeachable Superb Gem that will serve as the highlight of any Barber dime collection, type collection, or early proof collection. Both sides are brilliant aside from faint champagne toning. The fields have seemingly unending mirrors that surround the lustrous and boldly detailed devices. Census: 8 in 67 Cameo, 3 finer (2/09).(#84884)

926 **1901 PR65 PCGS. CAC.** Ex: Benson. An impressive Gem with light silver centers and peripheral rainbows, this example is highly desirable for both date collectors and type collectors. Population: 32 in 65, 29 finer (2/09). *From The Burning Tree Collection.*(#4885)

927 **1901 PR66 NGC.** This outstanding Premium Gem proof is fully brilliant with excellent cameo contrast, although it lacks a Cameo designation on the holder. Early 20th century proofs with any degree of contrast are quite rare. Census: 44 in 66, 16 finer (2/09). (#4885)

Exquisite, Deeply Toned 1905 Dime, PR67

928 **1905 PR67 PCGS.** The coloration is unusual but attractive on this Superb Gem specimen, with deep cinnamon, russet, and cerulean on the obverse and similar colors prevailing on the reverse. Exquisitely struck, and with absolutely impeccable surfaces that appear free of any contact whatsoever. Population: 14 in 67, 0 finer (2/09).(#4889)

Glassy PR67 Cameo 1905 Barber Dime

929 **1905 PR67 Cameo NGC. CAC.** The glassy surfaces are brilliant silver-white and essentially as struck, further endowed with stark contrast between the fields and the devices. The quality of this impeccable proof is second to none. From a proof mintage of 2,152 coins originally. Population: 3 in 67, 0 finer (2/09). (#84889)

930 **1910 PR66 PCGS. CAC.** Ex: Benson. If the toning on this amazing Premium Gem was somewhat lighter, we expect it would have received a Cameo designation, as the contrast is clearly apparent. Population: 10 in 66, 9 finer (2/09). *From The Burning Tree Collection.*(#4894)

Deeply Reflective PR67 1913 Dime

931 **1913 PR67 NGC.** A superlative proof striking that displays deeply reflective fields on each side. The obverse and reverse are quite different in appearance with the obverse showing light to medium golden-rose color while the reverse is mostly bright blue. The striking details are complete, as one would expect from a proof, and there are no contact marks, as one would expect from a PR67. Census: 12 in 67, 2 finer (2/09).(#4897)

932 **1913 PR65 Cameo NGC.** This lightly toned Gem displays obvious contrast between the frosty portrait and the glassy obverse field. A needle-sharp strike contributes further to the eye appeal. Just 622 proofs were struck. Census: 5 in 65 Cameo, 6 finer (1/09). *From The Mario Eller Collection, Part Four.*(#84897)

933 **1914 PR66 PCGS.** Hints of green-gold and sage peripheral toning yield to virtual brilliance in the centers. Crisply struck and carefully preserved. Population: 15 in 66, 6 finer (2/09).(#4898)

934 **1915 PR65 NGC.** Excellent strike and reflectivity, the latter shining through thin, milky patina. Pleasingly preserved with ample eye appeal. Census: 30 in 65, 25 finer (1/09).(#4899)

MERCURY DIMES

935 **1916-D Good 4 NGC.** Warm orange and pink overtones lend color to this otherwise silver-gray piece. Heavily circulated yet unquestionably authentic, an appealing example of this key date. (#4906)

936 **1916-D VG10 PCGS.** The date, mintmark, and all other legends are clear. The pearl-gray surfaces are smooth aside from a faded mark or two on the cheek. The lowest mintage issue, usually found in low grades.(#4906)

Remarkable 1916-D Ten Cent, Fine 15

937 **1916-D Fine 15 PCGS.** The key date 1916-D is especially scarce in the Fine to Extremely Fine grade range, which David Lange (2005) says is "... forever on dealers' want lists." The degree of smooth, honest wear evidenced by this problem-free, rose-gray Choice Fine example would seem to support the assigned grade. Its remarkably clean surfaces generate considerable eye appeal for a coin that saw moderate circulation.(#4906)

Popular XF 1916-D Mercury Dime

938 **1916-D XF40 PCGS. CAC.** A problem-free pearl-gray representative of this famous key date. Even casual Mercury dime collectors can recite the 1916-D mintage of 264,000 pieces. A majority of survivors are in Fair to VG grades, and XF examples with bold fasces lines are subject to strong demand.(#4906)

Key Date 1916-D Mercury Dime, XF Details

939 **1916-D—Improperly Cleaned—NCS. XF Details.** This key date specimen exhibits strong design definition, even if a touch of weakness is evident in the centers. Steel-gray toning covers both sides. Highpoint wear is slight, and surface blemishes are barely evident on either side. Improper cleaning has left the piece with a rather subdued appearance. *From The Pasadena Collection, Part Two.*(#4906)

940 **1916-S MS66 Full Bands PCGS.** Dramatically toned in fire-red, sun-gold, mauve, and apple-green. The borders are well struck, and the shimmering surfaces are undisturbed. Population: 59 in 66 Full Bands, 17 finer (2/09).(#4909)

941 **1917-D MS64 Full Bands PCGS.** A colorfully toned example, this Choice Mint State 1917-D exhibits a veritable palette of toning on the obverse, with golden-brown and iridescent toning on the reverse. The underlying surfaces have pleasing frosty luster. (#4913)

942 **1919-D MS65 PCGS.** Deep rose-gray and straw-gold patina visits lustrous surfaces that have been well cared for. Boldly struck, save for softness on the central and lower diagonal reverse fasces. Population: 17 in 65, 4 finer (1/09).(#4924)

Desirable MS65 Full Bands 1920-D Dime

943 **1920-D MS65 Full Bands PCGS.** Mauve patination dominates the obverse of this Gem, but cedes to yellow-green and soft violet on the reverse. The design features are well brought up, culminating in Full Bands. The diagonal bands are also bold. Lustrous surfaces reveal a few grade-consistent reverse marks. Population: 43 in 65 Full Bands, 18 finer (2/09).(#4931)

944 **1920-S MS64 Full Bands PCGS. CAC.** Scarce in AU and better grades, since attrition thinned the ranks of the 1920-S considerably. As a result, high grade Mint State pieces are elusive. This particular coin shows prominent die polishing at Liberty's nose. This is an especially lustrous coin that has a slight overlay of golden patina on each side. PCGS has graded 35 finer Full Bands pieces (2/09). (#4933)

945 **1924 MS67 Full Bands NGC.** Exuberant mint frost radiates from the surfaces of this utterly brilliant, snow-white Superb Gem. The striking details are nearly flawless, and both sides of the piece are impeccably preserved. Census: 12 in 67 Full Bands, 1 finer (1/09). (#4943)

Exceptional 1924-S Dime
MS64 Full Bands

946 **1924-S MS64 Full Bands PCGS.** The 1924-S is one of the best known strike rarities in the Mercury dime series, and population data has also proven this to be one of the most difficult issues in Mint State. The current example is an intensely lustrous piece that shows substantially above-average detail. Splashes of purple and sky-blue toning visit the obverse, and golden-brown toning is apparent at the reverse periphery. A couple of trivial grade-defining marks are noted on each side. A planchet lamination is present at 8 o'clock on the reverse border. PCGS has graded only 16 finer Full Bands pieces (2/09). (#4947)

947 **1926-D MS65 Full Bands PCGS.** Both sides are primarily silver-white, but tinges of russet and lavender appear on both sides near the rim. The bold strike encompasses not only the all-important split bands, but most of the devices throughout, save for a hint of softness on the E of ONE. (#4957)

948 **1926-D MS65 Full Bands PCGS.** Crisply detailed with delicate blue, gold, pink, and charcoal-violet patina across parts of each side. The immensely lustrous surfaces are carefully preserved. PCGS has graded 20 finer Full Bands coins (2/09). (#4957)

Impressive 1926-S Mercury Dime
MS65 Full Bands

949 **1926-S MS65 Full Bands PCGS.** The placid, essentially undisturbed surfaces display a slight greenish hue across both sides. Faint reddish toning streaks are also noted on the obverse, but only upon close inspection. A lustrous, well struck Gem with full definition of the central reverse bands. Population: 21 in 65 Full Bands, 16 finer (2/09).(#4959)

Brilliant 1926-S Dime, MS65 Full Bands

950 **1926-S MS65 Full Bands PCGS.** This brilliant, lustrous, and penetratingly struck Gem has exemplary preservation and outstanding eye appeal. A halo of prooflike surface outlines the portrait. An exceptional example of this low mintage issue. Certified in a green-label holder. Population: 21 in 65 Full Bands, 16 finer (2/09).(#4959)

951 **1927-D MS66 PCGS.** Brightly lustrous with pleasing overall detail, though the bands fall just shy of full separation. Virtually brilliant and assuredly beautiful. Population: 13 in 66, 0 finer (2/09).(#4962)

Splendid 1938 Dime, MS68 Full Bands

952 **1938 MS68 Full Bands PCGS.** It is seldom indeed that the happy combination of Full Bands definition coincides with the MS68 Superb Gem level of preservation, but when it does the results are extraordinary. Of the nearly 180,000 Mercury dimes certified at PCGS thus far, only 436 pieces are certified MS68 Full Bands, less duplicates. For the 1938 issue, this piece is one of eight MS68 Full Bands coins (2/09). The surfaces show delightful ice-blue, olive, and lilac shadings, with generous luster and essentially flawless surfaces, as expected. The strike is uniformly sharp throughout. A wonderful coin for a type or Registry Set.(#5011)

953 **1942/1 AU50 PCGS.** Pale silver-blue color overall. This modestly marked example passed from hand to hand only briefly before it was saved. An appealing coin for the circulated dime collector. (#5036)

954 **1942/1 AU55 NGC.** A gorgeous example of this signature Mercury dime overdate, modestly worn but with pleasing luster beneath the sky-blue and green-gold patina that drapes each side. Minimally marked and desirable.(#5036)

955 **1942/1 AU55 ANACS.** Champagne and periwinkle shadings grace parts of each side. This impressively lustrous overdate dime shows just a touch of wear on the highest design elements. (#5036)

956 **1942/1—Rim Damaged—ICG. AU58 Details.** The overdate feature is obvious to the naked eye. The natural, light-gray surfaces are unmarked and show a few small charcoal specks. The rim is damaged near 2 o'clock on the obverse. An affordable example of this Mercury dime key date.(#5036)

957 **1942/1-D AU58 PCGS. CAC.** Just a touch of rub is noted on the high points. This luminous example has generally pale silver-gray surfaces with glimpses of gold and charcoal close to the devices. Population: 42 in 58, 4 finer (2/09).(#5040)

958 **1942-S MS67 Full Bands PCGS.** A splendiferous Superb Gem, with blazing silver-white surfaces that are completely untoned and essentially pristine. Fully struck with excellent definition on the central reverse bands. PCGS has only certified one finer example (2/09).(#5043)

959 **1945-S Micro S MS66 Full Bands NGC.** A brilliant, intensely lustrous Premium Gem. The design motifs are crisply reproduced, and the central reverse bands are fully defined. Surface marks are minimal, as expected for the grade. Census: 23 in 66 Full Bands, 1 finer (2/09).(#5063)

PROOF MERCURY DIMES

Lovely PR67 1936 Mercury Dime

960 **1936 PR67 NGC.** After 20 years of not producing any proof coinage, since the early years of World War I, the Philadelphia Mint finally resumed proof production in 1936. Seven years later, alas, another World War would again freeze this type of special coin manufacture. This lovely Mercury dime is fully struck, brilliant, and immaculately preserved. Census: 78 in 67, 2 finer (2/09). (#5071)

Admirable PR67 1936 Dime

961 **1936 PR67 NGC.** The quicksilver surfaces of this admirable Superb Gem are entirely devoid of distractions of even the smallest sort. Careful perusal under a loupe provides confirmation, both of the quality and the overall beauty. A wonderful type coin. Census: 78 in 67, 2 finer (2/09).(#5071)

Coveted Superb Gem Proof 1936 Dime

962 **1936 PR67 NGC.** Speckled apple-green and fire-red invigorates the obverse, although the reverse is only minimally toned. The strike is needle-sharp. Proof Mercury dimes were only struck between 1936 and 1942, and the 1936 has the lowest mintage of the proof type. Census: 78 in 67, 2 finer (2/09).(#5071)

Magnificent PR68 ★ 1936 Mercury Dime

963 **1936 PR68 ★ NGC.** Examples of this issue are always in demand due both to their low mintage and to their status as the first year of the proof emissions. (Although Walter Breen's *Complete Encyclopedia* has made some claims concerning the existence of early [1916-17] proofs, no such examples have ever been certified at either service.)

The present piece, in addition to its pristine preservation, justly merits the Star designation awarded by NGC for exceptional eye appeal. Here the award-winner is the stunning peripheral patina in shades of emerald, amber, and cerise, with the occasional dollop of violet. This piece is the only PR68 ★ certified at NGC, and there are none finer (11/08).(#5071)

Subtly Toned 1937 Dime, PR68

964 **1937 PR68 NGC.** David Lange (2005) writes of 1937 proof dimes that "Their survival rate in gem condition seems to be higher as a percentage of total mintage." NGC/PCGS census/population data do indeed indicate a plentiful supply of this issue through the Premium Gem level. The numbers drop off in PR67, and the lofty grade of PR68 is rare. Wisps of iridescent cobalt-blue, lavender, and olive-tan are seen over both sides of this exquisitely struck specimen. Impeccably preserved surfaces. Census: 32 in 68, 0 finer (2/09).(#5072)

Exquisite 1938 Dime, PR68

965 **1938 PR68 NGC.** The seven-year span of proof coinage from 1936 to 1942 resulted in a number of issues that have tiny mintages by modern standards. The 1938 dime offered here, for example, is one of just 8,728 specimens struck, and quite the specimen at that. Rainbow iridescence covers the obverse, while the reverse offers subtle tinges of olive and ice-blue. The strike is equally exquisite. (#5073)

Marvelous Superb Gem 1939 Mercury Dime

966 **1939 PR68 NGC.** A marvelous specimen with absolutely razor-sharp striking definition on all design elements, as always expected but not always achieved on a proof coin. There is a faint layer of milkiness across the obverse and reverse fields, but it does little to obscure the glassy reflectivity in the fields. A slight degree of coral-gold toning near the peripheries improves the overall eye appeal. Census: 64 in 68, 0 finer (2/09).(#5074)

Luminous 1939 Mercury Dime, PR68

967 **1939 PR68 PCGS.** The luminous surfaces of this Superb Gem proof display splashes of deep green, crimson, orange-gold, and brown at the left obverse border, ceding to streaks of purple and deep brown throughout the remaining surfaces. Immaculate preservation and boldly struck motifs characterize each side. Population: 31 in 68, 0 finer (2/09).(#5074)

Crisp PR68 1939 Dime

968 **1939 PR68 PCGS.** Ex: Tom Mershon Collection. The 1939 is of medium rarity among proof Mercury dimes, but precious few examples grade so well as the present Superb Gem. This seemingly flawless representative is smooth from rim to rim, with just a hint of powder-gray iridescence. The needle-sharp strike is all that one would expect of a proof specimen. Population: 31 in 68, 0 finer (2/09).(#5074)

Brilliant 1939 Dime, PR68

969 **1939 PR68 NGC.** Both sides of this exquisite proof display fully brilliant surfaces, and an exacting strike leaves strong delineation on the design features. Close examination with a loupe reveals no imperfections on the immaculately preserved surfaces. Census: 64 in 68, 0 finer (2/09).(#5074)

970 **1941 PR68 NGC.** Decisively struck with gleaming, seemingly flawless mirrors that show only the slightest traces of patina. Marvelously preserved with spectacular eye appeal. Tied for the finest graded by either NGC or PCGS (1/09).(#5076)

971 **1942 PR68 NGC. CAC.** The untoned reverse of this Superb Gem proof dime cedes to reddish-gold and mint-green peripheral toning on the obverse. An exacting strike leaves complete delineation on the design elements. Both sides are immaculately preserved. (#5077)

Gorgeous PR68 1942 Dime

972 **1942 PR68 PCGS.** Ex: Tom Mershon Collection. Essentially a flawless coin to the unaided eye. Glimpses of pale rose-gray toning are the only evidence of color on this gleaming and otherwise brilliant Superb Gem specimen. Razor-sharp striking definition and crisp eye appeal. Population: 37 in 68, 0 finer (2/09). (#5077)

ROOSEVELT DIME

973 **1946 MS67 Full Bands PCGS.** Crisply detailed for this first-year issue. A Superb Gem that is essentially untoned save for a hint of golden patina in the fields. Population: 22 in 67 Full Bands, 1 finer (1/09). (#85082)

PROOF ROOSEVELT DIMES

Rare PR68 Ultra Cameo 1950 Dime

974 **1950 PR68 Ultra Cameo NGC.** The issues of 1950 marked the beginning of the modern frosted proof era, but few pieces in that earliest year have the same striking contrast found on the present piece. The coin is decisively struck, with nicely iced devices that emerge from untoned, highly reflective fields. NGC has graded just four pieces as PR68 with the Ultra Cameo designation, and none finer (2/09).
Ex: Milwaukee ANA Signature (Heritage, 8/2007), lot 1032, which realized $5,175. (#95225)

975 **1951 PR69 Cameo NGC.** Brilliant with seemingly perfect surfaces, the contrast between the fields and devices is moderate but noticeable. Very scarce as such. Census: 7 in 69 Cameo, 0 finer in Cameo (2/09). (#85226)

TWENTY CENT PIECES

976 **1875 MS63 NGC.** Richly toned in shades of violet and electric-blue. The design elements are boldly struck and there are few marks on either side. Highly lustrous, with a few spots and hairlines that limit the grade. (#5296)

977 **1875-CC MS61 ANACS. Breen-3876.** Light gold-orange and violet overtones grace lustrous surfaces. Though each side shows scattered marks and a few wispy abrasions, there is no trace of wear. (#5297)

Splendid Gem 1875-CC Twenty Cent

978 **1875-CC MS65 NGC.** This fully original Gem 1875-CC twenty cent piece, the only collectible Carson City Mint issue of the denomination, has frosty silver luster beneath light ivory toning with iridescent highlights. The obverse is nicely defined while the reverse is also sharp aside from the often-seen flat area at the top of the eagle's left (facing) wing. Seldom is this important Carson City issue found finer than the present Gem. Census: 32 in 65, 6 finer (2/09).
From The Belle Collection of Carson City Coinage. (#5297)

979 **1875-S MS63 PCGS. CAC.** Well struck with strong luster beneath rich, dappled patina. Violet, crimson, reddish-orange, and silver-gray shadings mingle on each side. (#5298)

980 **1875-S MS64 PCGS.** Shimmering luster over the silver-white surfaces is the most noteworthy attribute of this near-Gem. Boldly struck, save for a hint of weakness on Liberty's head, and on the top of the eagle's left (facing) wing. A few trivial field marks prevent an even finer grade. (#5298)

981 **1875-S MS64 NGC.** Splashes of electric-blue, magenta, and golden-orange patina rest on the lustrous surfaces of this well struck near-Gem. A few minute abrasions limit the grade, and light roller marks are visible on the central devices. (#5298)

982 **1875-S MS64 PCGS.** The obverse is bright and shining with crisp detail. Though that side is minimally toned, the reverse exhibits ample cloud-white toning. (#5298)

983   **1876-CC MS64 NGC.** The introduction of the ill-fated twenty cent piece occurred at the nexus of partisan politics and poor planning. Thomas Jefferson's original coinage recommendation from the mid-1780s envisioned denominations of a half dollar, fifth of a dollar, tenth dollar, 20th dollar, and 100th dollar or cent. There was no quarter dollar in the Jefferson scheme. However, as adopted per the recommendation of Robert Morris, superintendent of finance for the Continental Congress, the quarter dollar was introduced instead of the fifth dollar.

According to Rusty Goe's *The Mint on Carson Street*, "For over 80 years, quarter dollars were one of the nation's primary subsidiary coins. They served their purpose well—until a shortage of 1/20th dollars (or half dimes) in the West and parts of the South caused chronic problems in the nation's retail markets. Customers using quarters to pay for items priced at ten cents often received only a dime in return. Merchants claimed to be out of smaller denominations. In saloons all throughout the western states, a glass of beer cost five cents, and well drinks were commonly priced at 12-1/2 cents. Beer drinkers had no problem, but customers imbibing in shots of liquor faced the annoyance of being shortchanged when paying for a drink with a quarter, as bartenders only tendered a dime in change. Obviously many tavern patrons would order two drinks at a time, either being accompanied by a friend or simply accelerating their own inebriation."

On the political front, although earlier attempts to expand domestic uses for silver had met with failure, Western silver mining interests had grown increasingly powerful. They also had a new champion in the form of new Nevada Senator John Percival Jones. A successful silver mine owner, Jones succeeded in 1875 in overseeing passage of a Congressional bill authorizing production of the twenty cent denomination. Production began in 1875, only to cease altogether by 1878.

From the start, the denomination was flawed in concept and execution. It was too close in size to the quarter, and both denominations shared (basically) the same obverse, with similar reverses. Mint officials, sensing the dangers, produced the coin with a plain edge rather than the quarter's reeded edge, a subtlety that—like the raised LIBERTY on the twenty cent—was lost on the public at large. (Fast forward: In 1979 the Mint introduces the Susan B. Anthony dollar, slightly larger than a quarter and with an 11-sided inner rim to aid in distinguishing it. It lasts three years in "circulation," despite a final whimper 20 years afterward.)

The Carson City Mint personnel raced to beat San Francisco to produce the first mintmarked coinage of the denomination in 1875, barely beating their California cousins. Senator Jones received the first 1875-CC twenty cent piece off the presses, and the net mintage for the year totaled an impressive 133,290 coins.

Although the mintage of 1876-CC twenty cent pieces was recorded as 10,000 coins, nearly the entire production was melted in 1877 on order of Mint Director Henry Linderman. Goe notes besides the probable survivors from specimens sent to the Assay Commission, various Mint personnel in Carson City or Philadelphia, including Linderman himself, could have obtained specimens.

The current estimate of surviving examples, including the "Maryland Hoard" of seven to nine pieces discovered in the 1950s, is 16 to 18 coins. The 1876-CC twenty cent piece was known as a special and incredibly rare coin as early as 1893, when Augustus Heaton published his famous *Mint Marks* pamphlet that changed American numismatics forever.

All known examples, including the present piece, show prominent doubling of the raised LIBERTY on the shield, as well as several of the left-side stars (specifically, stars 2-8 here). We also note the presence of errant parts of a second 8 and 7 buried in the denticles at 6 o'clock, also diagnostic. Generous luster prevails on both sides. The satiny surfaces are lightly kissed with tinges of gold and champagne. For pedigree purposes we mention a small scrape from Liberty's left (facing) arm into the left field nearby. Other contact is unworthy of mention.

Although we have handled specimens of this legendary rarity twice before, it has been nearly a decade since we last offered an example. Coins of this ilk rarely come onto the market, and the present piece may mark the last such appearance for many years to come. In MS64 this piece is one of three so certified at NGC, with four finer. PCGS has graded five MS64 coins, with five finer—although resubmissions and duplications are a distinct possibility in all those figures (2/09).

Although some other issues from the Carson City Mint are now known to be rarer in an absolute sense, the 1876-CC twenty cent has a long-lasting cachet unmatched by any other issue from that fabled and legendary institution.
From The Belle Collection of Carson City Coinage. (#5300)

🎥 See: Video Lot Description

PROOF TWENTY CENT PIECES

984   1875 PR62 PCGS. Crisply detailed with strong mirrors that shine through rich blue and violet toning. Though hairlines preclude Select status, this remains a desirable specimen from the first year of the denomination.(#5303)

Excellent 1875 Twenty Cent Piece, PR64

985   1875 PR64 PCGS. This beautiful near-Gem proof has exquisite old-time toning gray-gold and pale lilac on the obverse, and rich grayish-brown, blue, and rose on the reverse. Beneath the toning is excellent cameo contrast with lustrous devices and deeply mirrored fields. Population: 61 in 64, 30 finer (2/09).(#5303)

Beautiful 1875 Twenty Cent, PR64 Cameo

986   1875 PR64 Cameo NGC. This flashy cameo displays a beautiful color scheme. The obverse periphery has a cobalt-blue, golden-brown, lavender, and light blue pattern, while the same color palette is evenly distributed over the reverse. The design elements are sharply defined and frosted, yielding evident contrast against the reflective fields. Census: 14 in 64 Cameo, 22 finer (1/09). (#85303)

Appealing 1876 Twenty Cent, PR65

987   1876 PR65 PCGS. This is a colorful Gem proof, toned in gold-mauve on the obverse, and in swaths of gold, burgundy, and blue emanating out from the reverse center. A well executed strike results in strong definition on the design features, and close inspection reveals nicely preserved surfaces. This piece generates great overall eye appeal. Population: 19 in 65, 10 finer (2/09). (#5304)

988   1878 PR60 PCGS. While the mirrors show numerous light hairlines, the overall eye appeal of this lightly toned silver-gray specimen is better than the PR60 designation might suggest. Housed in a green label holder.(#5306)

EARLY QUARTERS

Challenging 1796 Quarter, B-2, VG10

989   1796 VG10 PCGS. B-2, R.3. The second rarest silver type, trailing only the half dollars of 1796 to 1797, which also combine the Draped Bust and Small Eagle designs. Two die varieties are known for the 1796 quarter, commonly referred to as the Low 6 (B-1) and the High 6 (B-2). B-2 is moderately more available than B-1, although both varieties are subjected to remarkable demand from early type collectors. The present piece is a cream-gray example with glimpses of deeper russet throughout the borders. Undisturbed by marks aside from a few wispy hairlines and a faint thin line through the R in AMERICA.(#5310)

1796 B-2 Quarter, Fine 12

990 **1796 Fine 12 PCGS.** B-2, R.3. On this variety, the 6 in the date is high and very near the bust; in LIBERTY, T and Y do not touch at the top; and the lower right star is spaced farther from the bust than star 1 is from the curl.

Light to medium gray patination bathes both sides of this Fine 12 example and shows occasional splashes of bluish-purple color. The obverse dentilation is bold, as always on the 1796, while that on the reverse is weak in the upper right quadrant. The remaining design elements are nicely defined for the grade. The surfaces are remarkably clean for a coin that has seen moderate circulation. (#5310)

Rare B-2 1804 Quarter, Fine 12

991 **1804 Fine 12 ICG.** B-2, R.5. The scarcer of the two varieties for the year and a rarity in all grades, distinguished by the 4 in the date being high relative to the portrait and distant from the rest of the digits. Rich rose and slate-gray patina drapes surfaces that are significantly worn yet minimally marked overall.(#5312)

Elusive 1804 Quarter, B-2, Fine 15

992 **1804 Fine 15 PCGS.** B-2, R.5. A rare variety, B-2 is distinguished by the high 4 in the date and a final star that is further from the bust truncation. This variety is seldom encountered in grades above the VG level. Of course, the low mintage 1804 (just 6,738 pieces struck) is one of the key dates of the entire denomination. The issue has always been prized by collectors, and auction appearances go back at least as far as the A.C. Kline Sale (M. Thomas & Sons, 6/1855), when an example was included as lot 277. The present coin is an attractive specimen, with rich mauve and gold colors bathing the nicely detailed surfaces. Abrasions are minimal for the grade. Listed in the condition census in the Steve Tompkins reference *Early United States Quarters 1796-1838.*(#5312)

993 **1806/5 Fine 15 ANACS.** B-1, R.2. A widely recognized overdate that has its own *Guide Book* variety. Deep blue and gold patina dominates the fields, while the worn zones of the devices are lighter silver-gray.(#5315)

994 **1806/5 VF35 PCGS.** B-1, R.2. The lone instance of this overdated obverse, enshrined as its own *Guide Book* variety. The present example is a pleasing Choice VF number, luminous gold-gray overall with deep rose and blue overtones at the margins. Population: 11 in 35, 37 finer (1/09).(#5315)

Early Stage 1806 B-9 Quarter, AU Sharpness

995   **1806—Improperly Cleaned—NCS. AU Details.** B-9, R.1 for the variety, which is attributed by: the missing lower left serif of 1, the flag of which touches the hair curl; the tip of the flag of the 5 embedded in the arrow feathers; and five large berries, two inside and three outside of the olive branch. This piece hails from an unusual early die state.

    The silver-colored surfaces retain traces of luster in the recesses, and reveal occasional fine hairlines under magnification. A few brownish toning streaks are visible on the obverse. The design elements are sharply defined, except for softness in the eagle's breast feathers and adjacent shield stripes. A few light adjustment marks are located on the central reverse, but significant abrasions are absent.(#5314)

Attractive 1806 Quarter, B-9, Unc Details

996   **1806—Improperly Cleaned—NCS. Unc Details.** B-9, R.1. A thick die crack bisects the obverse, extending from the rim just below 1 to the L in LIBERTY. Moderate clash marks are observed on both sides. The centers are a lovely ivory-white color, while russet toning adorns the peripheries. There are minimal effects noticeable from any improper cleaning.(#5314)

997   **1807 Fine 12 PCGS.** B-2, R.3. The design elements are well centered on the planchet, and there are only a few faint adjustment marks on each side. A nice, evenly worn example for the grade, from the final year of the Draped Bust type. Browning-2 is much scarcer than the single other B-1 die variety for the year.(#5316)

Select Mint State 1807 Quarter, B-2

998   **1807 MS63 PCGS.** B-2, R.3. The first S in STATES is centered over the cloud before, diagnostic for the reverse and thus the variety. Both the B-1 and B-2 variants are scarce in an absolute sense, and this is a top-flight example of the latter. The fields offer considerable reflectivity beneath silver-gray and gold patina that shows occasional rose accents. Despite grade-defining shallow flaws to the right of the portrait, the overall preservation is impressive, and the eye appeal is excellent. For both 1807 quarter varieties, Population: 17 in 63, 14 finer (2/09).(#5316)

BUST QUARTERS

999   **1818/5 VF35 PCGS. CAC.** B-1, R.2. Not described as an overdate by PCGS, though the reverse diagnostics confirm this coin's overdate status. A pleasing Choice VF piece with charcoal and pale silver-gray shadings across each side, attractive and desirable.(#5323)

Charming B-1 1818/5 Quarter, MS64

1000   **1818/5 MS64 PCGS.** B-1, R.2. This is a singular overdate, diagnostic for the variety with its own listing in the *Guide Book*. Though the present piece is a trifle softly struck across the central devices, its wonderfully frosty luster is redeeming. Violet and rose-gold peripheral shadings yield to subtle silver-gray at the centers. Population: 20 in 64, 9 finer (2/09).(#5323)

1001   **1818 XF45 NGC. CAC.** B-10, R.3. This example has shimmering peripheral luster and a wisp of golden toning. Nearly unabraded aside from a cluster of faded marks beneath the right scroll end. Struck from moderately clashed dies.(#5322)

Pleasing 1818 Quarter, AU58, B-8

1002   **1818 AU58 NGC.** B-8, R.3. Three crowded dentils below first 1, a die scratch from inner side of star 2 into the field, and I of PLURIBUS slightly left of center of second T in STATES confirms the variety. This later die state shows obverse clash marks, and a die crack from the rim through the rightmost leaf into the eagle's left (facing) foot. Deep bluish-gray and lavender toning covers surfaces that display traces of luster in the protected areas. The design elements are well defined, though the star centers are somewhat soft. A few light circulation marks are not bothersome. (#5322)

Gorgeous 1818 Quarter, B-4, MS66
Top of the Condition Census

1003   **1818 MS66 PCGS.** B-4, R.2. Tompkins Die State 2, die crack from star 13-bust. This is one of the more easily obtainable varieties of this Capped Bust quarter delivery, but the awesome technical quality of this coin certainly sets it apart from most, if not all other representatives of this die marriage. This is a simply gorgeous Premium Gem with richly toned lavender-charcoal surfaces that display a ring of electric-blue peripheral iridescence. Both sides are frosty in texture with well centered, sharply defined features and only the lightest striking softness over the high points of Liberty's hair curls and the eagle's talons. With no mentionable abrasions, this coin is worthy of a fine reference collection. Housed in a green-label holder. For all 1818 varieties, Population: 3 in 66, 1 finer (2/09). At the top of the Condition Census for the variety, per Tompkins. *Ex: FUN Signature (Heritage, 1/2001), lot 6871, which realized $17,365; Dallas Signature (Heritage, 12/2005), lot 581, which realized $23,000.*(#5322)

1004   **1821 AU53 NGC.** B-4, R.3. A well detailed and only lightly abraded representative. The deep dove-gray surfaces display emerald-green and sun-gold undertones upon rotation beneath a light.(#5331)

1005   **1825/4 VF35 PCGS.** B-2, R.2. PCGS refers to the overdate as 1825/4/(2), although the Guide Book (as well as Heritage) simply call it an 1825/4. A luminous Choice VF piece, minimally marked save for a slight disturbance at the upper obverse rim. Rose and tan shadings suffuse otherwise silver-gray surfaces.(#5336)

1006   **1825/4/3 XF40 NGC.** B-2, R.2. An interesting variety created by multiple overdates on the same die. This piece is evenly worn and shows attractive champagne-gray coloration. There are no distracting abrasions on either side.(#5336)

Select Mint State B-2 1825/4/3 Quarter

1007 **1825/4/3 MS63 PCGS.** B-2, R.2. Powder-blue and steel-gray dominates the obverse, while the reverse is consistently chestnut-tan and pale apple-green. A well struck Capped Bust quarter with satin luster and relatively few marks. Specialists have long debated whether B-2 is an 1825/4/3 or an 1825/4/2. The *Guide Book* merely refers to it as an 1825/4. Population: 18 in 63, 25 finer (2/09). (#5336)

Rare 1825/2 B-1 Quarter, AU55

1008 **1825/2 AU55 NGC.** B-1, R.5. Tompkins Die Stage 1. The B-1 variety is the rarest of the three 1825 die marriages, and it is extremely difficult to locate in higher grades. This example is a tad below the Reiver coin for overall quality. In his revision of Browning, Walter Breen recorded two die states, either perfect or with die crumbling inside the digit 5. More recently, Steve Tompkins has described it as an 1825/4/2 overdate, putting forth the theory that the original die was produced by Robert Scot, then overdated by Christian Gobrecht, and finally resurrected and overdated again by William Kneass in late 1825. Little die crumbling is evident on the present piece; in fact, the die stage appears remarkably similar to that in the Tompkins reference. The surfaces have a blend of pewter, pale gold, and grayish-lilac color. The surfaces are reasonably problem-free, with evidence of underlying luster.(#5337)

Exceptional 1828 Quarter AU58, B-1

1009 **1828 AU58 NGC.** B-1, R.1. The 2 in the date has a curl base, and the two 8s are "fancy." On the reverse, there is a defect on the underside of the scroll under S. The light silver-gray surfaces display traces of luster in the recessed areas, and are devoid of mentionable marks. Sharply struck, except for weakness on the right (facing) claw. An exceptional piece overall.(#5342)

Desirable 1831 Small Letters Quarter, B-2, MS65

1010 **1831 Small Letters MS65 ICG.** B-2, R.2. The last die state identified by Tompkins, with the reverse die crack between UNITED and STATES developing a series of tiny cuds. Inexplicably described as a Small Letters piece by ICG, though simple visual inspection shows that the lettering on the reverse is indeed small.

Overall quality and eye appeal are excellent. The strike is solid overall, including at the often-weak denomination, and the luster is vibrant. Reddish-orange and violet peripheral toning graces each side, while the centers remain largely unpatinated. A noteworthy Gem, arguably of Condition Census quality.(#5348)

1011 **1831 Large Letters AU58 NGC. CAC.** B-6, R.3. An appealing example of the scarcest die pair of the year, vibrantly lustrous with just a trace of friction separating it from a Mint State designation. Tan-orange peripheral shadings yield to pale silver-gray in the centers.(#5349)

Near-Gem 1832 B-1 Quarter

1012 **1832 MS64 PCGS.** B-1, R.1. The "Large Arrowheads" variety, which readily distinguishes B-1 from the only other 1832 marriage. This is a beautifully toned Choice Bust quarter, fully patinated in golden-brown, yellow-gold, and forest-green. Satin luster encompasses pleasantly unperturbed fields and devices. Population: 11 in 64, 2 finer (2/09).(#5351)

Appealing MS64 1833 Quarter, B-1

1013 **1833 MS64 NGC.** B-1, R.2. The die marriage with a period after 25 C, which distinguishes it from the only other variety, B-2. This faintly toned Choice Capped Bust half has good luster, and abrasions are refreshingly absent. Struck from boldly clashed and notably rusted dies, all as made. Census: 15 in 64, 1 finer (2/09). (#5352)

Pleasing Select B-1 1834 Quarter

1014 **1834 MS63 NGC.** B-1, R.1. The "O/F" obverse, in which the O in OF is punched over an erroneous F. The most readily available of the 1834 quarter varieties, though at the Select level, even this "common" issue becomes scarce. Pleasingly detailed with varying degrees of purple and lilac-gray toning across each side. Lustrous surfaces show wispy abrasions.(#5353)

Gorgeous 1834 B-1 Quarter, MS65

1015 **1834 MS65 NGC.** B-1, R.1. An intermediate die stage, per Steve Tompkins, with a perfect obverse die and A1 and A2 both filled. The 1834 quarter has a reported mintage of 286,000 pieces. Engraver William Kneass prepared the quarter dies for the year, with a possible assist from Christian Gobrecht. Two obverse and four reverse dies were combined to strike the five known varieties of this issue. The present coin is an example of the B-1 variety, characterized by the use of only two lines in the stripes of the shield. The B-1 type is the most available variety for this date, and probably comes second in the die emission sequence.

The present specimen features a sharp strike, with fine detail on all design elements. Attractive gray and lilac toning enhances the fields, with much original color and luster remaining in areas near the devices. This coin is an attractive example of an early quarter and would serve admirably in an advanced type set. Census: 10 in 65, 5 finer (2/09).(#5353)

1835 B-1 Quarter, MS64

1016   **1835 MS64 ICG.** B-1, R.1. The 3 in the date is high, and star 13 is quite close to the hair. On the reverse the eagle has no tongue, 25 C is high with 2 and 5 widely spaced, and there is a period after the denomination. This piece shows powder-gray patina on each side, with the fields showing good reflectivity under a strong light, along with some light hairlines and golden-amber accents.(#5354)

Desirable MS62 ★ 1836 Bust Quarter, B-3

1017   **1836 MS62 ★ NGC.** B-3, R.1. Lengthy die cracks on both sides make attribution a cinch. This attractive example has a window of brilliance at the centers, bounded by bands of russet-brown, navy-blue, and jade-green. Minimally abraded, satiny, and a desirable type coin in such quality.(#5355)

SEATED QUARTERS

1018   **1838 No Drapery AU58 NGC.** Only a trace of friction visits the high points of this solidly struck Seated quarter. Dusky blue-gray peripheral toning lightens to rose-orange and steel at the centers. Census: 29 in 58, 66 finer (1/09).(#5391)

1019   **1838 No Drapery MS61 NGC.** Lustrous surfaces reveal hints of tan-gray under magnification, and show a few minor handling marks. Well struck in the centers, but star centers and rims are weak.(#5391)

1020   **1839 No Drapery MS61 NGC.** A bright and minimally toned example with modestly reflective surfaces. Light hairlines are noted in the fields, and Liberty's head is softly struck. A few tiny field marks are noted on each side. Census: 4 in 61, 25 finer (1/09). (#5392)

Condition Rarity 1841 Near-Gem Quarter

1021   **1841 MS64 PCGS. CAC.** The 1841 quarter has a mintage of 120,000 business strikes. It is obtainable in the lower circulated grades, but difficult to acquire in the better levels of preservation. Larry Briggs, in his *Comprehensive Encyclopedia of United States Liberty Seated Quarters* (1991), assigns the following rarity ratings for this issue: G/VG, R.3; F/VF, R.4; XF/AU, R.5; Unc, R-6.

This near-Gem displays pleasing luster emanating from essentially untoned surfaces, and a well executed strike manifests itself in strong definition on the design features. A few minute contact marks prevent Gem classification. Population: 5 in 64, 2 finer (2/09).(#5399)

Appealing 1842 Large Date Quarter, MS62

1022   **1842 Large Date MS62 PCGS.** The date with a flat top to the 1. Though the mintage for this earlier Seated quarter issue is only in the high five figures, it does not become a rarity until the Mint State levels, though even dedicated collectors can go through years of searching without encountering an example so fine as the present piece. Each side of this well-defined coin is strongly lustrous beneath ample blue and violet toning. Great eye appeal for the grade. Population: 6 in 62, 5 finer (2/09).(#5401)

Elusive Gem 1843 Seated Quarter

1023 **1843 MS65 NGC.** An impressive Gem example with sharp definition on all of the design elements, except for partial incompleteness on the first three obverse stars. The silver-gray centers yield to wisps of charcoal-gray and forest-green near the borders. The 1843 is known as a common date in circulated grades, but it becomes scarce in Uncirculated condition and rare as a Gem. Census: 3 in 65, 1 finer (12/08).(#5404)

1024 **1843-O—Cleaned—ICG. MS60 Details.** Well-defined with no trace of wear. Moderately dulled, lightly hairlined surfaces have retoned silver-gray with dots of reddish-tan.(#5405)

1025 **1845 MS63 NGC.** Briggs-3c. 1845/45. An appealing Select Mint State example of the 1845/45 overdate variety. The coin shows mottled toning, with russet-red, antique-gold, and orange-tan as the dominant colors. An attractive example that should be of great interest to the specialist.(#5408)

Near-Gem 1853 Arrows and Rays Quarter
Scarce One-Year Type

1026 **1853 Arrows and Rays MS64 PCGS. CAC.** In 1853, the weight of the U.S. quarter dollar coin was reduced from 6.68 grams to 6.22 grams. This change was signified by the addition of arrows to the obverse design near the date, and rays to the reverse around the eagle. The rays were omitted in 1854, however, making this a scarce and important one-year type. This example is well struck and essentially untoned, save for a faint golden cast. Surface marks are absolutely minimal for the grade.(#5426)

1027 **1853/4 Arrows and Rays AU58 PCGS.** While the overdate is a time-honored tradition in early American numismatics, usually a later date is applied over an earlier one. The 1853/4 Arrows and Rays quarter is the rare case when the rule apparently works in reverse. This near-Mint piece is strongly lustrous beneath blue and violet central toning with light sea-green peripheral bands. Just a trace of friction visits the high points. Population: 4 in 58, 12 finer (1/09).(#5427)

Smooth 1854 Arrows Quarter, MS64

1028 **1854 Arrows MS64 PCGS. CAC.** A pleasingly detailed example of this popular type issue, softly lustrous and well-preserved beneath rich patina. Pale silver-blue centers give way to green-gold, orange, and olive shadings near the rims. Excellent eye appeal. PCGS has certified just 21 finer examples (1/09).(#5432)

Well Struck 1854 Arrows Quarter, MS64

1029 **1854 Arrows MS64 PCGS.** Dappled cobalt-blue, purple, and golden-brown patina makes occasional visits to the peripheries of this near-Gem, more extensively and deeper on the reverse. Lustrous surfaces exhibit uniformly well struck design features. A few trivial marks prevent a Gem grade. Population: 64 in 64, 21 finer (2/09).(#5432)

Challenging Near-Gem 1854 Arrows Quarter

1030 **1854 Arrows MS64 NGC.** This near-Gem is well struck, with speckled russet, gold, and forest-green patina over most of the obverse. The reverse only shows slight tan toning, mostly near the peripheries. Well preserved with just one or two tiny contact marks on each side. NGC has graded just 24 pieces finer (2/09). (#5432)

Charming MS65 1857 Quarter

1031   **1857 MS65 NGC.** While the 1857 quarter is readily available in most grades, thanks to a mintage of over 9.6 million pieces, Gem and better survivors are elusive. This MS65 piece is well-defined in the centers, if a trifle softly struck at the margins, with strongly lustrous, minimally toned surfaces. Pleasingly preserved and attractive.(#5442)

Richly Toned 1857 Quarter, MS67 ★

1032   **1857 MS67 ★ NGC.** Splashes of electric-blue and orange-gold color dominate this shimmering and carefully preserved Superb Gem. The stars and dentils are needle-sharp, although the arrow fletchings and Liberty's chest shows moderate incompleteness of strike. Both sides show considerable reflectivity in the fields. Struck from clashed dies. Even though the 1857 quarter dollar is considered available, Superb Gems are seldom encountered. Only two MS67 ★ pieces have been certified by NGC (2/09) with only one (non-Star) graded finer.
Ex: Central States Signature (Heritage, 5/2005), lot 6861, which realized $8,050.(#5442)

1033   **1857-O AU58 NGC.** A very scarce grade level for this New Orleans Mint quarter issue. This example is boldly struck and seems unworn, with a soft, satiny appearance and even, pearl-gray coloration imbued with occasional golden undertones. A few tiny hairlines exist in the obverse fields. Census: 12 in 58, 17 finer (1/09).(#5443)

Enchanting Gem 1858 Quarter

1034   **1858 MS65 NGC. CAC.** One of several high-mintage No Motto quarter issues, the 1858 is a frequent choice for type collectors, though at the Gem level even this "common" issue becomes a rarity. The present MS65 piece is well-defined, with strong luster that shines through gold-orange and silver-blue patina that is thicker on the obverse. Census: 28 in 65, 17 finer (2/09).(#5445)

Conditionally Rare 1858-O Quarter, MS62

1035   **1858-O MS62 NGC.** While not generally recognized as an O-mint rarity, the 1858-O quarter is seldom encountered in mint condition. Breen (1988) said it most succinctly: "Ex. rare UNC." Only 11 coins have been graded in all Uncirculated grades, further underscoring the difficulty of this issue in mint condition. This is a sharply defined example that is brilliant throughout. A few obverse field marks limit the grade. Census: 4 in 62, 2 finer (2/09). (#5446)

1036   **1861 MS64 NGC.** Strongly lustrous beneath beautiful patina. Sharply struck centers are gold-orange and silver-gray, while the rest of the piece is deep blue.(#5454)

Vibrant Gem 1861 Quarter

1037   **1861 MS65 PCGS.** Boldly impressed with vibrant luster and delightful patina. Peripheral shadings are largely blue-green and violet, giving way to rich peach and reddish-orange closer to the centers. The 1861 is a popular choice for type collections that need an example of a No Motto Seated quarter, and this coin would make a marvelous addition. Population: 33 in 65, 13 finer (2/09). (#5454)

Elusive 1866 With Motto Seated Quarter, MS64

1038   **1866 Motto MS64 PCGS.** The surfaces show a combination of light silver-gray and pale gold-tan color. Faint diagonal die striations are noted across the obverse. Boldly struck and nicely preserved, with just a few trivial marks. This is a low mintage issue of 16,800 pieces, and the first U.S. quarter to display the motto IN GOD WE TRUST. Population: 5 in 64, 6 finer (2/09). (#5468)

Difficult Choice VF 1870-CC Quarter

1039 **1870-CC VF35 PCGS. CAC.** While the mintage figure of 8,340 pieces already suggests that the 1870-CC quarter is a rarity, that number alone may not tell the whole story, since several numismatic writers (among them Walter Breen and Rusty Goe) have questioned whether part or nearly all of that production was withheld from circulation. It is known that of those pieces which escaped the Mint, most circulated heavily. The present coin, though moderately worn, is actually upper-end for the issue. LIBERTY is bold, and the deep gray surfaces have only one mentionable mark, a pinscratch above Liberty's left (facing) leg. Population: 4 in 35, 7 finer (2/09).
From The Belle Collection of Carson City Coinage. (#5477)

Challenging 1873-CC Arrows Quarter VF25

1040 **1873-CC Arrows VF25 PCGS.** The mintage of 12,462 pieces tells the story of this rarity. Not only were very few quarters struck of the 1873-CC, but even fewer survived their stint in circulation in the West. Pre-1875 Carson City coinage was extensively used in the channels of commerce, and problem-free pieces are difficult to locate in nice collector grades. Demand for the 1873-CC Arrows is particularly strong, since it is the only Carson City Arrows issue of the denomination.

This is a completely problem-free piece with a bold LIBERTY and ample plumage detail. Gunmetal-gray overall with darker toning near the rims. Population: 1 in 25, 7 finer (2/09).
From The Belle Collection of Carson City Coinage. (#5492)

Popular 1874-S Arrows Quarter, MS66

1041 **1874-S Arrows MS66 NGC.** The 1874-S is the most available of the Arrows quarter dollar issues. As such, it is always of interest to type collectors, as Arrows quarters are such a popular and widely collected two-year issue. As with all examples we have seen of the 1874-S, this piece shows exceptionally bright and vibrant mint luster. The surfaces are covered with light, variegated patina on each side, and the striking details are fully brought up in all areas. Census: 16 in 66, 3 finer (2/09). (#5495)

Lovely MS66 1874-S Arrows Quarter

1042 **1874-S Arrows MS66 PCGS.** Despite a meager mintage of 392,000 pieces, a number of high-end survivors for this issue have come down to the present day, though Premium Gem and better coins remain elusive. This well struck piece has a generally silver-white obverse with only suggestions of the gold and tan toning that dominates the reverse. PCGS has graded only one finer example for the issue (2/09).(#5495)

Amazing 1874-S Arrows Quarter, MS66

1043 **1874-S Arrows MS66 PCGS. CAC.** A scarce issue, the 1874-S is pursued by both date and type collectors. Only 392,000 of these coins were struck, and few have survived in any Mint State grades. This piece is highly lustrous and brilliant, with bold design elements and entirely untoned silver surfaces. Population: 29 in 66, 1 finer (2/09).(#5495)

Challenging Choice 1875-CC Quarter

1044 **1875-CC MS64 PCGS.** A better Carson City issue, since the mintage of 140,000 pieces is only a fraction of the multi-million piece production of the 1876-CC and 1877-CC. The satiny surfaces of the present near-Gem display light silver-gray color and pleasing luster. A well executed strike leaves strong definition on the design features, except for the centers of the lower stars. Population: 6 in 64, 2 finer (2/09).
From The Belle Collection of Carson City Coinage.(#5499)

1045 **1875-S MS64 PCGS.** This highly lustrous near-Gem has all the eye appeal of a higher grade coin. The surfaces have satiny silver luster with light gold toning on each side. Struck from cracked and flowlined dies. Population: 20 in 64, 8 finer (2/09).
From The Burning Tree Collection.(#5500)

1046 **1876 MS65 PCGS.** A gorgeously toned offering with subtle shades of champagne-gray, sea-green, and antique-gold over well preserved surfaces. Boldly struck overall, even if a little weak on Liberty's head and some of the obverse stars. Nearly blemish-free. Population: 38 in 65, 25 finer (2/09).(#5501)

1047 **1876-CC MS64 NGC.** Type Two Reverse. Blended ivory and tan tints adorn this satiny and sharply struck Carson City type coin. A splendidly undisturbed reverse, and the obverse has only minor contact on the right field. Census: 46 in 64, 27 finer (2/09).
From The Belle Collection of Carson City Coinage.(#5502)

Meritorious Gem 1876-CC Quarter

1048 **1876-CC MS65 PCGS.** Type One Reverse. A "triple threat" combination, with the ever-popular Centennial date, the coveted CC mintmark, and certified Gem condition, this marvelous Seated quarter should make some type or date collector's set sparkle all the more. Light powder-gray patina is graced by tinges of ice-blue and copper-gold on both sides. Population: 10 in 65, 5 finer (2/09).
Ex: Dallas Signature (Heritage, 10/2008), lot 662, which realized $4,600.
From The Belle Collection of Carson City Coinage.(#5502)

1049 **1877-CC MS64 PCGS.** A splendid near-Gem with fully brilliant and lustrous surfaces that exhibit wonderful mint frost. Heavy die rust is evident on the central obverse motif. PCGS has only certified 47 finer examples (2/09).
From The Belle Collection of Carson City Coinage.(#5505)

Superb Gem 1877-CC Quarter

1050 1877-CC MS67 PCGS. CAC. In 1877, the fabled Carson City Mint produced a near-record 4.2 million quarters, second in quantity only to the 4.9 million pieces for the Centennial-year issue. Accordingly, collectors desiring a CC-mint quarter for type sets usually select either the 1876-CC or 1877-CC quarters to fulfill that purpose. The 1877-CC quarter production would be the last million-plus-coin quarter emission, as the introduction of the Morgan or "Bland" silver dollar in the following year would reduce the manufacture of other silver coins to token levels in order to accommodate the flood of the new cartwheels.

This splendid Superb Gem offers stunning, original amber-gold and cinnamon coloration on the obverse, with the reverse offering peripheral tinges of ice-blue and lilac centers. Despite the moderate intensity of the colors, there is much luster radiating forth, producing a visual treat and a coin of exceptional beauty. Housed in an old green label holder. Population: 6 in 67, 0 finer (2/09). *From The Belle Collection of Carson City Coinage.* (#5505)

Desirable MS66 1879 Quarter

1051 1879 MS66 NGC. Starting with the 1879 quarter issue, the denomination went nearly a decade with nothing but a token mintage at Philadelphia. This Premium Gem from the beginning of that drought has vibrant eye appeal and shining luster. Delicate golden peripheral tints give way to silver-pink at the centers. Census: 33 in 66, 32 finer (2/09). (#5511)

Gorgeous MS66 Prooflike 1879 Quarter

1052 1879 MS66 Prooflike NGC. As with many other low-mintage issues of the late 19th century, the 1879 quarter has a significant percentage of reflective survivors. Few of those coins, though, can boast the mirrors on this Prooflike Premium Gem. Sharply struck devices offer contrasting silver-white frost. A minimally toned beauty. (#5511)

1053 1880 MS65 PCGS. Well struck with dappled, variegated coloration in shades of electric-blue, copper-red, turquoise-green, and golden-tan. Rich satiny mint frost shimmers across each side, highlighting the lovely toning. From a scarce, low-mintage issue of just 13,600 coins. Population: 41 in 65, 41 finer (2/09). (#5512)

Lovely 1880 Seated Quarter, MS67

1054 1880 MS66 PCGS. CAC. A lovely, elegant Premium Gem example of this low-mintage Seated quarter issue. Softly frosted luster accompanies the subtly variegated toning in shades of champagne and greenish-gray. The carefully preserved surfaces are nearly pristine, as confirmed after close inspection with a loupe. Population: 33 in 66, 8 finer (2/09). (#5512)

Delightful MS66 1880 Quarter

1055 1880 MS66 NGC. Crisply detailed with a measure of reflectivity to the fields. Subtle gold and pink shadings grace the fields. Marvelous eye appeal for this low-mintage issue. The Mint was obligated to coin massive quantities of silver dollars during the 1880s, which sharply reduced mintages of quarters. Census: 35 in 66, 13 finer (2/09).(#5512)

Rare Superb Gem 1880 Seated Quarter

1056 1880 MS67 NGC. The entirely brilliant, snow-white surfaces display a layer of intense mint frost over each side. The striking definition is crisp and nearly full on both obverse and reverse. Immaculate surface preservation is, however, perhaps the single most impressive feature of this conditionally rare Superb Gem. Census: 9 in 67, 4 finer (2/09).(#5512)

1057 1881 MS62 PCGS. Well struck aside from a few obverse stars. A prooflike representative that has lovely peripheral golden-brown and electric-blue patina. The fields have a few wispy handling marks, as expected for the grade. A mere 12,000 pieces were issued. (#5513)

1058 1882 MS64 NGC. From a low-mintage issue of 15,200 pieces emerges this delightful near-Gem example. Untoned and well struck, with semireflective fields and a beautiful satin sheen over both sides. If not for a single small mark in the right obverse field, this example would likely have been graded as a Gem. Census: 16 in 64, 31 finer (1/09).(#5514)

Highly Attractive 1884 Quarter, MS67

1059 1884 MS67 PCGS. CAC. This low mintage issue (8,000 pieces) is scarce in all grades, and Superb Gems such as the current coin are seen only infrequently. Additionally, CAC has seen fit to affix the green label to this sharply struck, immaculately preserved specimen. Golden-tan patina on the obverse center is accented by sky-blue and purple at the borders. The reverse features a delicate blend of cobalt-blue and beige-gold. Population: 9 in 67, 0 finer (2/09).(#5516)

1060 1887 MS64 PCGS. Both sides of this enticing low-mintage quarter offer powerful, almost flashy luster. The boldly impressed eagle sports delightful frost as well. Pleasingly preserved. Population: 22 in 64, 44 finer (1/09).(#5519)

1061 1887 MS64 Prooflike NGC. Excellent contrast with minimal patina. The fields are watery and reflective. Only a lack of sharpness on the obverse stars signals that this piece is not, in fact, a proof. (#5519)

1062 1888-S MS64 PCGS. Rich rose, violet, and magenta patina embraces each side of this lustrous near-Gem. Strongly detailed with no singularly mentionable flaws. Population: 21 in 64, 8 finer (2/09).(#5521)

1063 1890 MS65 PCGS. A frosty Gem Mint State example, this 1890 quarter has pleasing ivory and golden-brown surfaces with mostly sharp design elements. Population: 33 in 65, 43 finer (2/09). *From The Burning Tree Collection.*(#5523)

Desirable 1891 Quarter, MS67

1064 1891 MS67 NGC. Forest-green, rose-red, and caramel-gold compete for territory across this lustrous and exquisitely struck Superb Gem. The 1891 was the first Philadelphia issue to exceed 100,000 pieces since 1878, but colorfully toned high grade pieces are desirable. Census: 14 in 67, 1 finer (02/09).(#5524)

Shining Superb Gem 1891 Quarter

1065 1891 MS67 NGC. From the final year of the Seated quarter design comes this shining beauty, minimally toned with only the faintest hints of gold and pink visible at the margins. Crisply struck and easily appreciated with no individually mentionable quibbles. A wispy die crack connects stars 8 and 9 with the Liberty cap. Census: 14 in 67, 1 finer (12/08).(#5524)

1066 1891-S MS62 Prooflike NGC. The fully mirrored obverse and reverse fields around lustrous devices suggest that this piece was struck from resurfaced dies. Several die cracks on the obverse indicate that it was a well used die pair, rather than a fresh set of dies. This brilliant silver representative has minor abrasions but excellent aesthetic appeal for the grade.(#5526)

PROOF SEATED QUARTERS

Important 1847 Seated Quarter, PR64

1067 **1847 PR64 ICG.** Larry Briggs estimates the number of proofs of this issue at five to 10, while Walter Breen provides no guess. This example has deep iridescent steel-blue and salmon coloration, with moderate reflectivity remaining when viewed under a strong lamp. The concise strike and squared-off rims are conclusive. (#5541)

Rare 1857 PR64 Seated Quarter

1068 **1857 PR64 PCGS. CAC.** The date slopes upward from left to right so that the bottom of the 7 is visibly further from the rim than the bottom of the 1. The left base of the 1 is right of the center of a dentil. Breen's 1989 *Proof Encyclopedia* estimated that "under 15, perhaps under 12 survive." That estimate appears to be on the low side even when duplicates are accounted for, but examples are nonetheless quite rare. This piece has considerable luster emanating from under mint-green, cinnamon, and ice-blue shadings on both sides. A few trivial contact marks in the obverse right field appear to preclude an even finer grade, but the eye appeal is generous. Population: 11 in 64, 2 finer (2/09).(#5553)

Sharp 1857 Quarter, PR64

1069 **1857 PR64 PCGS.** Light gray patination with a slight golden cast resides on both sides of this near-Gem proof, and a modest amount of field-motif contrast appears at certain angles. A solid strike leaves strong delineation on the design elements. Nicely preserved throughout. Population: 10 in 64, 2 finer (2/09).(#5553)

Elegant 1860 Gem Proof Quarter

1070 **1860 PR65 NGC.** Larry Briggs (1991) writes that 458 of the 1,000 1860 proof quarters minted were melted. Inspection of NGC and PCGS population data reveals that relatively few pieces in the Gem and higher levels of preservation are extant. Medium intensity cobalt-blue, purple, and beige-gold patina bathes both sides of the present Gem. The design elements are sharply struck, except for minor softness on the radials of the stars along the left border. Nicely preserved surfaces exhibit modest field-motif contrast. Census: 15 in 65, 7 finer (2/09).(#5556)

Attractive 1862 Quarter, PR64

1071 **1862 PR64 PCGS.** Splashes of deep purple, orange, yellow-gold, and sky-blue toning adorn the obverse of this near-Gem proof, ceding to much lighter hues on the reverse. The design elements are well struck, except for softness in the stars near Liberty's head. A few minute reverse marks preclude Gem status. Population: 35 in 64, 19 finer (2/09).(#5558)

Gleaming PR64 Cameo 1862 Quarter

1072 **1862 PR64 Cameo PCGS.** Strongly mirrored with excellent contrast. The centers are virtually untoned, though whispers of champagne-tan patina visit the margins. Only a few minor hairlines in the reverse fields preclude an even finer designation; the flaw below Liberty's foot is from a planchet flake and not contact. Population: 4 in 64 Cameo, 5 finer (2/09).(#85558)

Sumptuous PR65 Cameo 1864 Quarter

1073 1864 PR65 Cameo PCGS. A richly toned specimen that retains substantial contrast, aided by the strong frost on the sharply struck devices. The mirrors also offer penetrating reflectivity. On the obverse, the toning is light gold-gray with an arc of blue-green at the right rim, while the reverse shows a more even blend between the two colors. Population: 3 in 65 Cameo, 0 finer (2/09). (#85560)

1074 1865 PR64 PCGS. Swirling iridescent shades of golden-brown, honey-gold, and powder-blue embrace this boldly struck near-Gem. A small toning spot is noted between the eagle's right wing and the S of STATES. A mere 500 proofs were struck. A popular Civil War date. Population: 35 in 64, 18 finer (1/09).
Ex: New York Signature (Heritage, 6/2005), lot 5522.(#5561)

Gleaming Gem Proof 1865 Quarter

1075 1865 PR65 PCGS. This gorgeous Gem is sharply struck, carefully preserved, and strongly mirrored. The prime attraction, however, is its rich patina. The obverse has subdued gold-orange and mauve shadings with a touch of peripheral violet, while the reverse shows pale blue-green over much of the fields. Population: 5 in 65, 13 finer (2/09).(#5561)

Enchanting Gem Cameo Proof 1866 Quarter

1076 1866 Motto PR65 Cameo PCGS. The first official proof Motto quarter issue, represented here by a boldly contrasted and eminently appealing Gem. Carefully preserved fields show subtle cloud-white peripheral toning, but the fields closest to the frosted devices show pure silvery reflectivity. Population: 2 in 65 Cameo, 2 finer (2/09). (#85565)

1077 1869 PR65 NGC. Decisively struck with tantalizing glimpses of reflectivity at the margins. Deep blue-green and violet shadings dominate each side. Census: 14 in 65, 12 finer (2/09). (#5568)

1078 1869 PR65 NGC. With business strike 1869 quarters so elusive, demand for the proofs of that year is elevated beyond the norm for the issue's peers. This Gem is gleaming with mild contrast beneath a thin veil of cloud-white patina. Census: 14 in 65, 12 finer (2/09). (#5568)

1079 1869 PR65 PCGS. A deeply mirrored proof, this Gem is wonderfully toned with cobalt-blue, violet, rose, and gold on each side. It is boldly struck with a trace of contrast. Population: 9 in 65, 3 finer (2/09).
From The Burning Tree Collection.(#5568)

Cameo Gem Proof 1870 Quarter

1080 1870 PR65 Cameo NGC. An exactingly struck Gem with dazzling field reflectivity and attractive peach-gold toning. The right obverse field displays only a few faint hairlines. Although 1,000 proofs were struck, many went unsold and were eventually melted by the Mint. Census: 8 in 65 Cameo, 3 finer (2/09).(#85569)

1873 No Arrows Quarter, PR66

1081 1873 No Arrows PR66 NGC. Dense purple-blue and rose patina blankets the sharply struck, undisturbed surfaces. The striking detail shows only the faintest bit of weakness on Liberty's topmost hair detail; all of the other design features are crisply produced. One of just 600 No Arrows proofs struck, along with a mere 40,000 No Arrows business strikes. Census: 12 in 66, 5 finer (2/09). (#5572)

1082 1874 Arrows PR63 PCGS. This faintly toned Select proof is exactingly struck and has a well preserved reverse. Careful evaluation locates a few trivial obverse field hairlines. A very scarce proof subtype.
From The Mario Eller Collection, Part Four.(#5575)

Near-Gem Proof 1874 Arrows Quarter

1083 **1874 Arrows PR64 NGC.** Light multicolored toning on the reverse of this near-Gem proof cedes to deeper hues of the same color palette on the obverse. Consequently, the reflectivity of the obverse fields is subdued, while that of the reverse nicely accentuates the devices. This is a well struck piece, with just a few minor marks.(#5575)

Notable PR66 1874 Arrows Quarter

1084 **1874 Arrows PR66 PCGS. CAC.** Delicate gold and periwinkle-blue shadings drape each side of this charming Premium Gem proof. Strongly reflective and carefully preserved fields are visible through the ample toning, and the eye appeal is grand. PCGS has graded only three finer examples of this Arrows proof issue (2/09). (#5575)

1085 **1876 PR65 Cameo NGC.** Type Two Reverse. Flashy fields and delicate gold toning grace this lovely proof Gem. Intricately struck, and the devices display even, unmistakable frost. Census: 5 in 65 Cameo, 11 finer (1/09).
From The Mario Eller Collection, Part Four.(#85577)

1086 **1878 PR64 PCGS.** This richly toned Choice proof is housed in an early-generation holder. Deep blue-green, violet, cerulean, and rose-orange shadings help to conceal a handful of trivial hairlines. Population: 43 in 64, 21 finer (2/09).(#5579)

1087 **1878 PR65 NGC.** Both sides of this Gem proof are essentially untoned, and a well directed strike leaves good definition on the design features. A small toning spot is visible in the right obverse field, and die polish lines mingle with fine hairlines, again most evident in the right obverse field.(#5579)

Crisply Struck 1879 Quarter, PR66

1088 **1879 PR66 PCGS.** Profoundly mirrored, though the devices supply only subtle contrast. This crisply struck example shows glimpses of champagne patina on the well-preserved surfaces. A great specimen from this popular higher-mintage issue of 1,100 proofs. Population: 15 in 66, 1 finer (2/09).(#5580)

Attractive 1880 Quarter, PR67

1089 **1880 PR67 NGC.** Type Two Reverse. This Superb Gem exhibits deep electric-blue, rose-red, yellow, apple-green, and golden-brown toning on both sides, and a solid strike brings about strong definition on the design features that are highlighted by powerful reflectivity in the fields. Well preserved throughout. Census: 16 in 67, 4 finer (2/09).(#5581)

Impressive PR67 ★ 1880 Quarter

1090 **1880 PR67 ★ NGC.** Type One Reverse. The peripheral reddish-copper patina yields to brilliant, untoned centers on each side. The surfaces are fully brought up in all areas and reveal not a single blemish that would call into question the PR67 grade. A lovely, original representative of this, the second low-mintage issue at the end of the Seated quarter series. Census: 3 in PR67 ★, only four finer (all PR68 non-Star coins).(#5581)

1091 **1881 PR66 PCGS.** Luminous cherry-wine, gold, and sky-blue toning fails to diminish the reflectivity of the fields. A sharply struck and undisturbed Premium Gem. The date is lightly repunched within the loops of the 8s. Another post-1878 low mintage date, with 12,000 business strikes and 975 proofs produced. Population: 17 in 66, 8 finer (1/09).(#5582)

Near-Perfect, Beautifully Toned
PR68 1881 Quarter

1092   1881 PR68 NGC. The 1881 Seated quarter issue is always of interest because of the low total mintage: Only 975 proofs were struck, in addition to a mere 12,000 circulation strikes. The presents Superb Gem example offers sheer delight for the toning enthusiast and high-grade aficionado. The central obverse shows rich rose coloration, while the center of the reverse is bright green-gold. The peripheries display rich sapphire-blue and pale emerald bands as the eye moves closer to the rim. The piece overall is virtually pristine and eminently appealing. None are graded finer at either major service. Census: 5 in 68, 0 finer (2/09).(#5582)

Gorgeous PR66 Cameo 1881 Quarter

1093   1881 PR66 Cameo NGC. The mintage of 975 proofs is under pressure because of the small mintage of only 12,000 business strikes. The present coin is a virtually flawless example, with liquid-reflective fields and crisp detail on all the design elements. The contrast effect is strong enough to secure the vaunted Cameo designation from NGC. Census: 11 in 66 Cameo, 9 finer (2/09). (#85582)

Superb Ultra Cameo Proof 1881 Quarter
One of the Finest Known

1094   1881 PR67 Ultra Cameo NGC. As with all proofs of this issue, both 8s in the date show repunching. This is one of the finest examples known of this low-mintage date, with only 975 proofs out of a total mintage of 12,975 pieces. The surfaces are brilliant throughout, and the fields are deeply reflective with heavily frosted devices that provide the Ultra Cameo effect. Census: 4 in 67 Ultra Cameo, 0 finer (1/09).(#95582)

1095   1882 PR64 PCGS. A colorful and captivating near-Gem specimen. The obverse shows light silver-blue color, while the reverse exhibits patches of golden-brown, periwinkle, and champagne. A planchet flaw is noted to the right of the date.(#5583)

1096   1883 PR64 PCGS. Sharply struck throughout, with watery fields and well preserved surfaces. This near-Gem proof is from an original mintage of just 1,039 pieces. Plum-gray toning is seen on the obverse, while the reverse displays a colorful rainbow of deep crimson, electric-blue, and sunset-orange iridescence near the right border.(#5584)

1097   1884 PR63 Cameo PCGS. Outstanding contrast through considerable patina. The lightly hairlined surfaces show pale gold-orange central color framed by blue-green peripheral elements. Population: 6 in 63 Cameo, 34 finer (2/09).(#85585)

1098   1885 PR65 Cameo PCGS. The frosted silver-white devices seem to float above the watery, charcoal-gray fields. Sharply struck and well preserved, with no distracting features on either side. Population: 7 in 65 Cameo, 15 finer (1/09).(#85586)

Marvelous 1885 Quarter, PR67 Cameo

1099   1885 PR67 Cameo PCGS. Mauve-red and electric-blue dominate the peripheries, while the centers remain brilliant. This intricately struck Superb Gem Cameo proof possesses seamless mirrored fields and icy devices. Only a couple of minute, inoffensive contacts on the seated Liberty deny perfection. Population: 6 in 67 Cameo, 0 finer (02/09).(#85586)

1100   1886 PR64 Cameo NGC. Profoundly mirrored with strong contrast. Subtle tan-gold elements visit the rims. If not for a few stray hairlines and minor contact in the fields, this coin would have been a Gem candidate. Census: 11 in 64 Cameo, 41 finer (1/09).(#85587)

Gem Proof 1887 Seated Quarter

1101 **1887 PR65 PCGS.** This splendid late-series proof has silver-white, reflective centers with a touch of rose noted at the margins on each side. Several of the stars on the obverse periphery lack centril details, but the centers of each side are pleasingly bold. Population: 36 in 65, 23 finer (2/09).(#5588)

1102 **1888 PR63 PCGS. CAC.** Delicate sea-green peripheral shadings with richer blue patina over the centers. Strong eye appeal from the toning, though the fields show a handful of grade-defining hairlines.
From The Burning Tree Collection.(#5589)

The Finest Certified 1888 Quarter, PR67 ★ Cameo

1103 **1888 PR67 ★ Cameo NGC.** This stunning beauty has remarkable rainbow iridescence at the peripheries, surrounding light gold centers. Both sides have excellent contrast with boldly defined devices. NGC has certified six PR67 Cameo examples of this date but the present specimen is the only one that has been awarded the star designation.(#85589)

Lovely 1889 Quarter
PR67 ★ Cameo

1104 **1889 PR67 ★ Cameo NGC.** While the cameo contrast is not quite there to merit an Ultra Cameo appellation, the lovely original toning is more than sufficient to merit the Star designation. The obverse shows pastel jade at the extreme rims, moving toward ice-blue, ocean-blue, and finally lilac in the center. The reverse offers more-pastel shades: light gold, mint, and ice-blue predominate. Essential contact is absent, as expected. NGC has certified two examples in this grade, with one Cameo coin numerically finer (2/09).(#85590)

Radiant 1889 Seated Quarter
PR66 ★ Ultra Cameo

1105 **1889 PR66 ★ Ultra Cameo NGC.** A happy marriage for those who like both Ultra/Deep Cameo coinage and toning, as the bright silver centers are radiantly mirrored, with thickly frosted devices, while the margins on each side show original, fairly deep patina in shades of steel-blue and cinnamon. The over-the-top eye appeal is further enhanced by the relative absence of mentionable contact, well deserving of the Star designation. Census: 1 in 66 ★ Ultra Cameo, 2 numerically finer (2/09).(#95590)

Sharply Contrasted 1890 Quarter, PR68 ★

1106 **1890 PR68 ★ Cameo NGC.** Ice-white devices and mirrored fields appear to merit an Ultra Cameo designation, although NGC has instead bestowed a Star. This was likely awarded because the specimen is fully brilliant. The strike is precise aside from the star centers, and extensive evaluation is required to locate even trivial surface imperfections. A scant 590 proofs were struck, in addition to a mere 80,000 business strikes. Mintages were low since the Mint was busy producing millions of silver dollars that then sat unwanted in Treasury vaults. Census: 1 in 68 ★ Cameo, 1 finer (2/09).(#85591)

1107 **1891 PR65 Cameo NGC.** This splendid silver-white Cameo specimen looks every bit the Gem, with no distractions visible to the naked eye and overwhelming eye appeal. A great piece from the final year of the design. Census: 12 in 65 Cameo, 30 finer (2/09).(#85592)

1108 **1891 PR65 Cameo NGC.** A brilliant Gem with frosty devices that exhibit strong contrast with the smooth, mirrored fields. A sharply struck representative of the final proof issue of the long-running series. A mere 600 pieces were struck. Census: 12 in 65 Cameo, 30 finer (1/09).(#85592)

BARBER QUARTERS

1109 **1892 MS65 ★ NGC.** Type Two Reverse. Semiprooflike fields show beneath low intensity cobalt-blue, lavender, and golden-brown patina, and exhibit modest variance with the sharply struck, light gray, frosty devices. Impeccably preserved, and well deserving of the Star designation. Census: 4 in 65 ★, 4 finer (2/09).(#5601)

1110 **1892 MS66 NGC.** Type Two Reverse. An impressive Premium Gem with deep golden-brown and iridescent toning over frosty surfaces and bold design motifs. NGC has only certified 24 finer examples (2/09). (#5601)

1111 **1892-O MS65 PCGS.** A frosty and brilliant obverse exhibits light gold and iridescent toning, with deep bluish-green on the reverse. Few finer examples of this O-Mint quarter have been certified. Population: 33 in 65, 8 finer (2/09). *From The Burning Tree Collection.*(#5602)

Appealing MS64 1893-S Quarter

1112 **1893-S MS64 NGC.** Well-defined overall and shining. Each side is minimally toned. Aside from a single abrasion at Liberty's upper cheek, the surfaces show few marks. Overall, an interesting example of this second-year Barber quarter issue, a rarity even at the near-Gem level. Census: 17 in 64, 4 finer (2/09).(#5606)

1113 **1899 MS65 PCGS.** This Barber quarter issue is surprisingly scarce in upper Mint State grades, despite an original mintage in excess of 12.6 million pieces. This Gem example is highly lustrous and well preserved, except for a tiny luster graze on Liberty's cheek. Essentially untoned in the centers, with hints of golden color near the peripheries. Population: 20 in 65, 12 finer (1/09).(#5622)

1114 **1899 MS65 PCGS.** Glimpses of peach and rose peripheral patina enhance each side, while the centers remain lustrous silver-gray. This Gem offers excellent detail for the issue, down to the talons. Population: 20 in 65, 12 finer (2/09).(#5622)

Frosty 1900 Quarter, MS66

1115 **1900 MS66 PCGS.** Type One Obverse. Type Two Reverse. Frosty silver-gray surfaces give off a lustrous glow on both sides, and there are only a couple of tiny contact marks near Liberty's headband that apparently separate this coin from an even finer grade. The strike is full, even on the often-weak right shield corner. For a mintage exceeding 10 million coins, Premium Gems of this issue are far scarcer than believed. Population: 12 in 66, 3 finer (2/09). (#5625)

Desirable 1901-S Quarter, VG8

1116 **1901-S VG8 PCGS. CAC.** The chief rarity among Barber quarters, with examples in any grade selling for thousands of dollars. The present piece is an appealing VG, with two full and two partial letters visible in LIBERTY. Light abrasions at the portrait and right obverse field, as expected for a coin with substantial wear. Pale silver-gray centers give way to deeper slate-brown at the peripheries.(#5630)

1117 **1907-D MS64 PCGS. CAC.** Generally silver-gray in the centers, though the margins show rich blue and violet shadings intermittently. Subtly lustrous with delightful eye appeal. Population: 30 in 64, 12 finer (1/09).(#5646)

1118 **1907-O MS65 PCGS.** Dapples of reddish-gold and sky-blue run over the lustrous surfaces of this O-mint Gem, somewhat more extensively on the obverse. Sharply struck, save for minor weakness in the upper right corner of the shield. A few grade-consistent marks do not disturb. Population: 20 in 65, 13 finer (2/09).(#5647)

1119 **1907-O MS65 NGC.** Gold-orange at the margins with slight variation in the pale silver-gray found at the centers. The obverse is clean, though a small horizontal abrasion is noted at the lower shield on the reverse. Census: 17 in 65, 11 finer (2/09). *From The Burning Tree Collection.*(#5647)

Gorgeous MS67 1907-O Quarter

1120 **1907-O MS66 PCGS.** Highly lustrous with dramatic sunset-orange, electric-blue, purple, and crimson iridescence observed on both sides. Well preserved and boldly struck, with only the faintest weakness noted on the hair detail just above Liberty's forehead. A scarce Barber quarter in high grades, the 1907-O is seldom found with well defined design elements. Population: 8 in 66, 5 finer (2/09).(#5647)

1121 **1908-D MS65 PCGS.** A sharply struck example of an issue rarely encountered so fine. Gold-green and russet shadings surround a silver-gray center on the obverse, while the reverse has a melange of reddish-orange and violet.(#5650)

1122 **1909 MS65 NGC.** Lustrous surfaces exhibit well struck devices, and are free of all but a few inoffensive, grade-consistent marks. Freckles of light brownish-gray race over both sides. Census: 32 in 65, 14 finer (2/09).(#5653)

Elusive Premium Gem 1909-D Quarter

1123 **1909-D MS66 PCGS.** Beautiful light freckles of golden-brown toning cover the dove-gray surfaces of this lustrous Premium Gem. A few stars and the fletchings are incompletely brought up, but the strike is otherwise bold throughout the major devices. Lovingly preserved, and among the finest known examples of the issue. Population: 15 in 66, 3 finer (1/09).(#5654)

Splendid 1911 Quarter, MS67

1124 **1911 MS67 PCGS.** Light yellow-green, rich golden, and lilac patina covers the obverse. The opposite side is brilliant, snow-white, and highly lustrous. A sharp strike shows on virtually all of the smallest details, and the surfaces exhibit a satiny appearance, typical of the date. A couple of tiny abrasions appear at the base of Liberty's neck, mentioned as future identifiers on this beautiful coin. Although 3.7 million quarters were struck, few remain as Gems. This sole, splendid Superb Gem rests atop the pile as the single finest certified example at either service (2/09).(#5659)

1125 **1911-S MS65 NGC. CAC.** A remarkable Gem, this 1911-S quarter has frosty luster beneath pale gold, lilac, and blue toning. The '11-S is a scarce date with a sub-million coin mintage. Census: 23 in 65, 19 finer (2/09).
From The Burning Tree Collection.(#5661)

1126 **1912 MS66 PCGS.** The date set collector would be hard-pressed to pass up this pleasing Premium Gem. Hints of dappled rose-gold and violet-russet patina grace the shining surfaces and solidly struck devices. Marvelously well-preserved and nearly impossible to find any finer. Population: 14 in 66, 1 finer (1/09).(#5662)

1127 **1912-S MS64 PCGS.** Bright satiny luster shimmers across each side. The design elements are boldly impressed and surface marks are minor for the grade. A pale silver-gold cast improves the eye appeal of the piece. Population: 32 in 64, 30 finer (2/09). (#5663)

1128 **1913-S AG3 ICG.** This key date representative shows a considerable amount of detail for the AG designation. The L and Y of LIBERTY are visible, as are significant parts of the ear, eye, and several leaves in the head wreath. The jawline is also clear, as are the right obverse and left reverse rims. The date and mintmark are strong, as is most of the lettering on both sides. Medium gray patina in the fields and recessed areas highlights the lighter gray devices. A short, toned over shallow scratch on the lower reverse rim is the only mentionable mark, and in the context of a heavily circulated coin, it is quite inoffensive. In sum, this piece will fit comfortably in a low to medium grade Barber quarter collection, and is certain to please the new owner.(#5666)

Low Mintage 1913-S Quarter, Fine 12

1129 **1913-S Fine 12 PCGS.** Semibright surfaces display light gray patination, and are generally well defined. Most of the letters in E PLURIBUS UNUM are visible, as are the LI TY of LIBERTY; B and R are partial. Light hairlines appear under magnification. The 1913-S is one of the three keys to the Barber quarter series, and has its lowest mintage (40,000 pieces).(#5666)

1130 **1914 MS65 NGC.** Deep brown, steel-blue, and magenta patination resides in the fields of this Gem, leaving the central devices mostly silver-gray. The obverse exudes radiant luster, while that on the reverse is somewhat subdued by the toning. Well struck, except for weakness in the upper right shield corner. Census: 53 in 65, 13 finer (2/09).(#5667)

1131 **1915-D MS66 PCGS.** Strongly lustrous with pleasing overall detail. Light silver-gray centers yield to richer reddish-orange toning close to the rims. Population: 31 in 66, 2 finer (1/09). (#5671)

1132 **1916-D MS65 NGC.** This is a flashy, brilliant Gem with bright white surfaces and light golden rim toning on both sides. Sharply struck overall, if just a bit weak on the eagle's arrows and right (facing) talons. Surface marks are minimal.(#5674)

Stone-White Superb Gem 1916-D Quarter

1133 **1916-D MS67 NGC.** A fully brilliant Superb Gem that boasts blazing cartwheel sheen and possesses a precise strike. The fields are pristine, and even the portrait has only the faintest grazes. An outstanding silver type coin from the final year of the Barber design. Census: 10 in 67, 0 finer (2/09).(#5674)

PROOF BARBER QUARTERS

1134 1892 PR65 PCGS. Type Two Reverse. A magnificent first-year representative with lightly frosted devices and deeply mirrored fields. A few near-imperceptible contact marks in the fields limit the grade, but the strike is full. A patch of russet on the reverse rim is the only area of color on this otherwise brilliant Gem, one of only 1,245 proofs struck. Population: 33 in 65, 46 finer (2/09). (#5678)

Gorgeous PR67 Cameo 1892 Quarter

1135 1892 PR67 Cameo NGC. Type Two Reverse. A faint glimmer of golden toning at the margins lends color to this otherwise black-and-white Cameo Superb Gem. The strike is bold on the moderately frosted devices, and the mirrors are delightfully deep. A great example of this initial proof Barber quarter issue. Census: 20 in 67 Cameo, 4 finer (2/09).(#85678)

Elusive 1895 Barber Quarter, PR67 ★

1136 1895 PR67 ★ NGC. Razor-sharp striking detail and rich, variegated toning are hallmarks of this conditionally elusive proof Barber quarter. Beneath the deep patina the fields remain glassy and highly reflective. Only 880 pieces were produced, and Superb Gems are very scarce. Census: 4 in 67 ★, 0 finer (2/09). (#5681)

Splendid 1895 Barber Quarter, PR67 Cameo

1137 1895 PR67 Cameo NGC. This Superb Gem Cameo proof has exceptionally deep mirrored fields and brilliant devices with thick mint frost. Both sides are entirely brilliant with only a few minuscule toning spots on each side. It is a truly splendid representative of the Barber quarter series, and a popular date due to its association with the similarly dated Morgan dollar. Census: 11 in 67 Cameo, 13 finer (2/09).(#85681)

Glorious 1895 Barber Quarter, PR67 Deep Cameo

1138 1895 PR67 Deep Cameo PCGS. A most remarkable 1895 proof Barber quarter, this example has deeply mirrored fields and highly lustrous devices with brilliant silver surfaces and accents of pale gold along the borders. It is hard to imagine that any finer coins could exist, although PCGS has certified one higher numerical grade example. Population: 2 in 67 Deep Cameo, 1 finer (2/09). (#95681)

Marvelous 1897 Quarter, PR66 Cameo

1139 1897 PR66 Cameo NGC. The silver-white surfaces of this early proof Barber quarter show not the slightest hint of patina, for those who prefer their coins untoned, although there is a suggestion of powder-gray in the obverse field. The field-device contrast is marvelous on both sides, particularly deep on the reverse. Census: 13 in 66 Cameo, 14 finer (2/09).(#85683)

Wonderful 1898 Quarter, PR66 Cameo

1140 1898 PR66 Cameo PCGS. The surfaces are primarily untoned silver-white, although there mere suggestions of lilac on both sides. The surfaces are brilliantly mirrored, with thick mint frost on the devices and wonderful eye appeal. Essential contact is nonexistent. Population: 10 in 66 Cameo, 11 finer (2/09).
From The Burning Tree Collection.(#85684)

1141 1900 PR64 PCGS. Pale gold overtones drape the centers, while the margins show glimpses of deeper blue-green toning. Aside from a few faint hairlines in the fields, a well-preserved specimen. (#5686)

Outstanding 1900 Barber Quarter, PR67 ★

1142 1900 PR67 ★ NGC. The aficionado of deep, original toning will love this outstanding Superb Gem proof from the turn of the last century. A mere 912 pieces were struck, an adequate number in those earlier times when a quarter dollar was a fairly substantial sum of money to the average American. Fully struck and layered across both sides in rich shades of purple-red and navy-blue. A well preserved and conditionally scarce specimen. Census: 2 in 67 ★, 2 finer with the ★ (2/09).(#5686)

Lovely PR66 1902 Quarter

1143 1902 PR66 NGC. Both sides show hints of contrast, though only the reverse could be called Cameo if taken in isolation. The obverse shows a thin veil of cloud-white patina across each side. Crisply detailed and carefully preserved, a lovely example from the brilliant proof era for silver that began in the early 20th century. Census: 36 in 66, 14 finer (2/09).
From The Mario Eller Collection, Part Four.(#5688)

Colorful 1904 Quarter PR66

1144 1904 PR66 PCGS. CAC. Unusual but attractive dappled jade, olive, orange-gold, and ice-blue toning is more intense on the obverse of this exquisitely struck Premium Gem proof. Impeccably preserved surfaces add to the appeal. Housed in a green label holder. Population: 27 in 66, 10 finer (2/09).(#5690)

Exceptional PR66 ★ 1904 Quarter

1145 1904 PR66 ★ NGC. Lovely honey-gold and electric-blue colors encircle the peripheries. The devices exhibit moderate cameo contrast when viewed from selected angles. A needle-sharp and attractive specimen. A scant 670 pieces were struck. As of (1/09), NGC has only awarded five 1904 proof quarters in all grades with a Star designation for superior eye appeal.(#5690)

1146 1905 PR64 PCGS. Both sides exhibit rich patina. The blue-green, gold, and violet toning of the obverse blankets that side, while the reverse shows only a crescent centered at 9 o'clock on the rim. (#5691)

Brilliant 1905 Barber Quarter, PR67

1147 1905 PR67 NGC. The bold design elements have satin luster and present a light cameo appearance compared to the fully brilliant, mirrored fields. The contrast is just shy of that necessary to garner a Cameo designation from the grading service. Both sides are brilliant and untoned with pristine surfaces. Census: 22 in 67, 3 finer (2/09).(#5691)

Impressive PR66 Cameo 1910 Quarter

1148 1910 PR66 Cameo PCGS. CAC. This 1910 quarter is an extraordinary Premium Gem with amazing contrast; the surfaces are mostly brilliant with splashes of light gold toning. Seldom do finer examples of this issue appear in the market place. Population: 8 in 66 Cameo, 5 finer (2/09).(#85696)

Superior 1911 Quarter, PR66 Cameo

1149 1911 PR66 Cameo PCGS. The silver-white surfaces are highly contrasted, with just a glint of gold but ample superior eye appeal. The strike is expectedly full, and essential contact is lacking on both sides. By this late in the series, the 1911 proof mintage for the never-popular Barber quarter had dwindled to 543 pieces. Population: 12 in 66 Cameo, 8 finer (2/09).
From The Burning Tree Collection.(#85697)

1150 1915 PR64 PCGS. Considerable mirrors shine through rich aqua, green-gold, and sage patina. A well-defined Choice proof that has just a few minor hairlines hidden by the toning. Population: 39 in 64, 29 finer (1/09).(#5701)

STANDING LIBERTY QUARTERS

Desirable 1916 Quarter, AU55

1151 1916 AU55 PCGS. Silver-gray surfaces retain luster in the recessed areas, along with whispers of olive-green around the reverse periphery. The design elements are well defined, including a strong impression on the date. Both sides are quite clean for a coin that has seen some circulation. All in all, a nice Choice AU representative of this desirable issue.(#5704)

Well-Defined 1916 Quarter, Unc Details

1152 1916—Improperly Cleaned—NCS. Unc Details. Bright surfaces reveal an occasional hairline under magnification, along with wisps of light tan color, more so on the reverse. The design features exhibit better detail than typically seen, including most of the horizontal shield lines, and all of the rivets. A few unobtrusive marks are noted on the reverse.(#5704)

Key Date 1916 Standing Liberty Quarter, Unc Details

1153 1916—Improperly Cleaned—NCS. Unc Details. This first-year Standing Liberty quarter issue had a tiny mintage of just 52,000 pieces, permanently ensuring its key date status. Improper cleaning has had a minimal effect on the coin overall, although it does possess a somewhat muted appearance. Plenty of design detail remains evident, however, and surface abrasions are essentially nonexistent on both sides.
From The Pasadena Collection, Part Two.(#5704)

Popular 1916 Standing Liberty Quarter
MS62 Full Head

1154 **1916 MS62 Full Head NGC.** Problems in striking the new quarter design from Hermon MacNeil led to delays in its introduction. Barber quarters were struck for most of the year. The late 1916 mintage of 52,000 pieces was not issued until 1917, and was soon masked by large emissions of 1917 quarters. Those prone to save the first coin of the new design they came across generally set aside the 1917. Thus, 1916 Standing Liberty quarters are certified in grades as low as Fair 2. A number of pieces exist in Mint State, but similar to the 1916-D dime and the 1909-S VDB cent, demand is enormous for the low mintage keys. The present key date quarter has medium tan-gray toning that deepens near the rims. Lustrous, nicely struck, and well preserved aside from a faint diagonal line on the waist.(#5705)

1155 **1917 Type One MS65 PCGS.** Light gold-orange patina enriches each side of this immensely lustrous Type One Gem. Though the obverse falls just shy of Full Head status, the details are strong elsewhere.(#5706)

1156 **1917 Type One MS65 Full Head PCGS.** Dappled silver-blue and gray shadings embrace each side of this solidly struck Gem. A beautiful piece that would make an excellent addition to a similarly graded 20th century type set.(#5707)

1157 **1917 Type One MS65 Full Head NGC.** Excellent strike and luster. This lovely type coin is minimally toned save for a splash of peach-orange visible at the upper reverse.(#5707)

1158 **1917 Type One MS65 Full Head NGC.** This brilliant and bold Gem has frosty silver luster with outstanding peripheral gold and iridescent toning. An exciting coin destined for a fine U.S. type set. (#5707)

1159 **1917 Type One MS65 Full Head PCGS.** Vibrant luster, a meticulous strike, and original chestnut-gold toning confirm the quality of this beautifully preserved Gem. A popular and briefly issued silver type.
From The Mario Eller Collection, Part Four.(#5707)

1160 **1917-D Type One MS65 Full Head PCGS.** Pink-orange and claret patina of varying intensity drapes each side, with the reverse showing slightly deeper color. A well-defined example of this one-off Denver type.(#5709)

Scarce 1917-S Type One Quarter, MS67

1161 **1917-S Type One MS67 PCGS.** The Hermon MacNeil Type One Standing Liberty quarter is among the small group of milestone coin issues from the early 20th century renaissance in U.S. coin design. This Superb Gem example is an opportunity to own a near-flawless example of MacNeil's original concept for the coin. NGC and PCGS have certified only four pieces in MS67, with none finer among non-Full Head examples (1/09). Appealing champagne-gold and silver-gray patina adorns the obverse; much of the reverse is brilliant, save for a dark crescent of reddish-brown on the left side. Crisply struck overall, as expected for this Type One issue, with a hint of satin on the obverse and powerful luster on the reverse.(#5710)

Stunning 1917-S Type One Quarter
MS65 Full Head

1162 **1917-S Type One MS65 Full Head PCGS. CAC.** A stunning mintmarked example of this premier Standing Liberty design. Liberty's face and hairline are separated all along the length of her brow, and all of the shield rivets are full. The satiny surfaces are powder-gray with glints of amber-gold near the rims. Certified in a green-label holder.
From The Burning Tree Collection.(#5711)

1163 **1917 Type Two MS65 Full Head PCGS.** Pale silver-gray over the centers with olive and green-gold at the margins. Attractively detailed overall, not only on Liberty's head. PCGS has graded 68 finer Full Head coins (1/09).(#5715)

1164 **1917 Type Two MS65 Full Head PCGS.** Boldly defined and fully lustrous with rich gold, lilac, and iridescent toning over frosty mint surfaces. Darker speckled toning is evident on both sides. NGC has only certified 51 finer Full Head examples.(#5715)

1165 **1917-D Type Two MS66 PCGS. CAC.** Strong, swirling luster and powerful detail. This interesting Premium Gem shows occasional hints of golden-tan toning on the reverse.(#5716)

1166 **1917-D Type Two MS64 Full Head PCGS.** Crisply detailed, an unusual state for this Type Two issue, with soft luster beneath rich patina. Dappled silver-gray, reddish-orange, and slate-blue shadings dominate each side.(#5717)

Thickly Frosted MS66 1917-S Type Two Quarter

1167 **1917-S Type Two MS66 NGC.** Only one finer non-Full Head example of this issue has been certified by NGC, which has also graded 12 Full Head pieces in MS66 or finer. Notably weak on the design elements, this piece displays exceptional frosty silver luster with just a touch of light rose and lilac toning. Census: 20 in 66, 1 finer (2/09).(#5718)

1168 **1918 MS66 PCGS.** Light silver-blue toning prevails in the centers, while dots of deeper tan and claret toning are present at the margins. Impressively lustrous with great eye appeal for a Premium Gem. Population: 22 in 66, 1 finer (1/09).(#5720)

Desirable MS66 Full Head 1918 Quarter

1169 **1918 MS66 Full Head NGC.** Brightly lustrous and essentially untoned. On Liberty's head, the details are not merely full, but crisp. Outstanding eye appeal, even by the standards of a Premium Gem. Despite a mintage of over 14 million pieces, this Philadelphia issue is elusive at this level with Full Head detail. Census: 35 in 66 Full Head, 3 finer (2/09).(#5721)

1170 **1918-D MS64 Full Head PCGS. CAC.** Strongly struck with powerful luster and interesting patina. Gold-orange and silver-gray central patina yields to dots of deep crimson near the rims. (#5723)

Formidable VF 1918/7-S Quarter

1171 **1918/7-S VF20 PCGS.** FS-101, formerly FS-008.5. The 1918/7-S is the rarest *Guide Book* variety of the popular Standing Liberty series, and although the low mintage 1916 is the key date in circulated grades, the 1918/7-S ranks a close second. This is a cream-gray piece with glimpses of sea-green near the margins. The reverse periphery has a few blushes of deeper russet toning. The thickness of the downstroke and crossbar of the 7 is obvious on the present VF example.(#5726)

Glowing Premium Gem 1920-S Quarter

1172 **1920-S MS66 PCGS.** The 1920-S is an issue that is notorious for being among the most weakly struck in the entire Standing Liberty quarter series, a trait that also appears on the other S-mint minor coins for the year. This piece shows weakness on the head, some of the shield rivets and stripes, on Liberty's left (facing) arm, and on the eagle's lower breast. On the other hand, the lustrous silver-gray surfaces are virtually free of other distractions, and the softly glowing luster adds to the overall appeal. A small die crack runs through the upper portions of the date digits, with a second reverse crack from the rim through the right upright of the U in UNITED and to a feather tip. Certified in a green label holder. Population: 14 in 66, 1 finer (2/09).(#5738)

Elusive 1920-S Quarter, MS64 Full Head

1173 **1920-S MS64 Full Head PCGS.** Standing Liberty quarter specialist Jay Cline calls the 1920-S the "classic underrated coin in the whole series, especially in MS63 and up, and Full Head." This piece offers no-questions Full Head detail, although a couple of the shield rivets are weak, as usual for the issue. Glints of amber and gold peek from the obverse recesses, and the reverse shows a couple of areas of dark-brown and charcoal-gray color. Population: 30 in 64 Full Head, 22 finer (2/09).(#5739)

1174 **1921 MS64 PCGS.** An attentive strike imparts strong definition to the design elements, including Liberty's features, which fall just shy of Full Head status. Medium gray patination reveals soft golden undertones, and lustrous surfaces are only lightly marked. All factors considered, a fantastic coin for the grade.(#5740)

1175 **1923 MS67 NGC.** Brilliant and virtually pristine, with dazzling silver-white surfaces. Boldly struck, even if not quite full on Liberty's head detail. Census: 45 in 67, 0 finer (1/09).(#5742)

1176 **1923-S AU50 PCGS. CAC.** Whispers of champagne-gray and violet show up under magnification on the obverse, while the same color palette is somewhat deeper on the reverse. The surfaces are remarkably clean, retain a good amount of luster, and exhibit well defined design features. This is a pleasing example of this key date. (#5744)

Attractive Gem 1923-S Quarter

1177 **1923-S MS65 PCGS.** Though not as well-known as a low-mintage issue as some of its later counterparts, particularly the 1927-S, the 1923-S is highly popular in all grades. This Gem is well struck for the issue, though the head shows slight softness. Hints of reddish-gold peripheral toning visit otherwise unpatinated surfaces. PCGS has graded 28 finer examples (2/09).(#5744)

Beautiful Gem Full Head 1923-S Quarter

1178 **1923-S MS65 Full Head NGC.** Golden-brown and lime-green enrich the margins of this otherwise untoned Gem. Only the two shield rivets near the waist lack pinpoint definition. A mere 1.36 million pieces were struck, undoubtedly due to the heavy silver dollar production of the year. Census: 22 in 65 Full Head, 30 finer (2/09).(#5745)

1179 **1924-S MS64 PCGS.** We have seen many Full Head Standing Liberty quarters that actually have less head detail than the present coin has. In fact, this coin, with about 90% of its head details visible, is a borderline major rarity. Both sides are fully lustrous with exceptional eye appeal for the grade.(#5750)

Outstanding MS68 1926 Quarter

1180 **1926 MS68 NGC.** A just-miss Full Head coin, lacking that designation only because not much of the ear hole is visible, and only two of the three olive sprigs. Even close scrutiny with a loupe fails to reveal any mentionable abrasions, large or small. All of the shield rivets are present, but none of the shield lines are visible. Bold luster emanates from each side of this beautiful and seemingly unimprovable specimen. One of two MS68 pieces known to NGC, with none graded by PCGS (2/09).(#5754)

Rarely Seen 1926-S Quarter, MS66 Full Head

1181 1926-S MS66 Full Head NGC. The 1926-S quarter, sporting a mintage of 2.7 million pieces, is among the most weakly struck of all San Francisco coins in the 1920s. Indeed, J.H. Cline, in his fourth edition of *Standing Liberty Quarters*, estimates that 1% or less were struck with Full Heads.

Weak strikes are not the only problem with 1926-S quarters—there simply are not that many Mint State pieces available. Paul Green, in an August 12, 2003 *Numismatic News* article titled "1926-S Standing Liberty Quarter Attractive," presents a tentative explanation for this paucity:

"... quarters (were) a good deal of money for collectors of the day. Back in 1926, there were not that many people collecting quarters each year, and if some did save nice new quarters each year, just a few years after the 1926-S was released the stock market crashed and the Great Depression began. A lot of nice coins almost certainly were returned to circulation by financially strapped owners during the tough years that followed, and a date like the 1926-S would have been a leading candidate."

This Premium Gem is one of the few coins struck with a Full Head. Strong definition is apparent on the chain mail and stars as well, though two or three of the lower rivets reveal the usual weakness. Vibrant luster invigorates both sides, each of which is color-free and impeccably preserved. Die polish lines are visible in the fields, especially those on the reverse. In summary, this piece exhibits great technical quality and aesthetic appeal. Census: 4 in 66 Full Head, 0 finer (2/09).(#5759)

Brilliant 1927-D Quarter, MS65 Full Head

1182 1927-D MS65 Full Head NGC. This fully brilliant silver Gem has excellent design details, including full head details and nearly complete shield details. The surfaces are satiny and highly lustrous. The 1927-D is a scarce issue when fully struck, and the present piece will be a nice addition to the specialist's cabinet. Census: 40 in 65 Full Head, 7 finer (2/09).(#5763)

1183 1928 MS65 Full Head PCGS. Softly lustrous and attractive, a well-defined Gem. Lustrous surfaces are silver-gray save for deep violet-blue and gold crescents found at the left obverse and right reverse. Population: 70 in 65 Full Head, 29 finer (2/09). (#5767)

1184 1928-S MS66 Full Head NGC. The obverse is crisply detailed with little toning to interfere with the bright luster. On the reverse, the fields shine through rich, dappled blue-green and reddish-gold toning.(#5771)

Highly Lustrous MS67 1928-S Quarter
Small S Variant

1185 1928-S MS67 Full Head NGC. The Small S variety, a mintmark variant scarcer than the usually seen Large S, with the mintmark placed further from the adjacent star. Superb overall quality, the surfaces are brilliant, lustrous, and immaculate throughout. The strike is full aside from the usual two incomplete shield rivets. Census: 29 in 67, 1 finer (2/09).(#5771)

1186 1929-S MS66 NGC. Strongly lustrous with pleasing detail aside from the often-weak head and shield. The obverse is minimally toned, though the reverse shows pale golden patina.(#5776)

1187 1930 MS66 Full Head PCGS. Impressively lustrous and essentially silver-white with just a touch of golden toning. The strike is strong. Housed in a green label holder.(#5779)

1188 1930 MS66 Full Head PCGS. A hint of green-gold graces this lustrous Premium Gem. The design elements are sharply struck, save for the two rivets near the waist. Both sides are impeccably preserved. *Ex: Long Beach Signature (Heritage, 5/2006), lot 1486.* (#5779)

Appealing MS67 Full Head 1930 Quarter

1189 **1930 MS67 Full Head NGC.** From the final year of the Standing Liberty design, this Superb Gem shows impressive detail on the head and only slight weakness on the shield. Immense luster percolates beneath thin veils of gold-gray, tan, and orange patina. Tied for the finest Full Head example known to NGC or PCGS (1/09).(#5779)

Desirable MS67 Full Head 1930 Quarter

1190 **1930 MS67 Full Head NGC.** This so-called "common" date becomes conditionally highly elusive in this Superb Gem, Full Head category. The present coin shows light amber, gold, and smoke-gray peripheral toning, while the centers are untoned and extremely brilliant. The head details are bold, as are the strike details of the chain-mail bodice and the shield, excepting a stray rivet or two. Census: 26 in 67 Full Head, 0 finer (2/09).(#5779)

Gorgeous MS67 Full Head 1930 Quarter

1191 **1930 MS67 Full Head NGC.** Brightly lustrous and essentially untoned, a radiant Superb Gem example with plainly Full Head detail and only slight softness on the rivets of the shield. Only a handful of tiny flaws are visible under magnification. Tied for numerically finest among Full Head examples graded by NGC or PCGS (2/09).(#5779)

WASHINGTON QUARTERS

1192 **1932-D MS63 PCGS.** An originally toned example of this first-year key date. A full layer of bluish-gray patina covers each side. Well struck with vibrant satiny luster and lacking any noticeable surface marks. Just 436,800 pieces were coined, and Select Mint State survivors are relatively few.(#5791)

1193 **1932-D MS63 PCGS.** Whispers of light tan-gold are slightly more evident on the reverse of this Select key date specimen. Lustrous surfaces exhibit strongly impressed design elements, and a couple of minute contact marks on each side limit the grade. This piece will fit nicely in a high-grade Washington quarter collection. (#5791)

1194 **1932-S MS63 PCGS.** Vibrantly lustrous and essentially untoned. This desirable Select key offers impressive eye appeal despite wispy abrasions.(#5792)

1195 **1932-S MS64 PCGS.** A satiny near-Gem with heather and iridescent toning over fully lustrous surfaces. PCGS has graded 96 finer examples of this popular key-date Washington quarter (1/09). (#5792)

1196 **1936-D MS66 PCGS.** Fully struck with lovely pink and gray coloration over strong, satiny luster. Elegant eye appeal with no individually mentionable flaws. Considered a scarce Washington quarter emission. PCGS has graded nine coins finer (2/09). (#5801)

Shining MS67 1936-S Quarter

1197 **1936-S MS67 PCGS.** Brightly lustrous with delicate, elegant patina. This sharply struck coin shows pale silver-gray toning overall, with a blush of honey visiting the left obverse fields. This Superb Gem is tied for the finest example certified by NGC or PCGS (1/09) and a Registry Set collector essential as such. (#5802)

1198 **1938 MS67 NGC.** A lustrous and solidly struck piece with luminous silver-gray toning and a streak of cherry-red near the date. An elusive issue in the top grades. NGC has graded just one numerically finer example (1/09).(#5806)

1199 **1939-D MS67 PCGS.** A shining Superb Gem, minimally toned save for a hint of gold-gray at the margins. A powerfully lustrous piece, tied for finest known to PCGS (2/09).(#5809)

1200 **1940-D MS67 NGC.** Gleaming and carefully preserved. This remarkable Superb Gem offers grand eye appeal with minimal patina. Census: 37 in 67, 1 finer (2/09).(#5812)

1201 **1942-D MS67 PCGS.** Boldly struck and seemingly pristine, this Superb Gem quarter displays mottled iridescent patina in the fields and near the periphery, on the obverse. The reverse shows a complete layer of similar copper-red, orange, and lime-green toning. Population: 31 in 67, 0 finer (2/09).(#5818)

1202 **1942-S MS67 NGC.** Trumpet Tail S. Shining silver-white with strong definition and impressive preservation. This lovely S-mint Superb Gem quarter is tied for the finest graded by NGC (1/09). (#5819)

1203 **1942-S MS67 NGC.** Trumpet tail S. Subtle rose, orange, and lavender peripheral shadings embrace each side, while the centers approach brilliance. A fantastically lustrous S-mint Washington quarter. Census: 54 in 67, 0 finer (2/09).(#5819)

PROOF WASHINGTON QUARTERS

Challenging PR66 1936 Quarter

1204 1936 PR66 PCGS. CAC. Sharply struck and undisturbed with light green-gold and rose-red toning. 1936 is the introductory (and lowest mintage) proof date of the Washington quarter series. Collectors of the day focused on the myriad new commemorative issues, while proofs of the circulating designs were comparatively ignored.(#5975)

1938 Quarter, PR68
Superbly Preserved and Beautifully Toned

1205 1938 PR68 NGC. Beautifully toned with green, red, yellow, and gold iridescence near the upper and lower peripheries. The fields are as smooth as glass on the obverse, while a coating of opaque beige patina blankets the reverse. Fully struck and pristine. Census: 12 in 68, 0 finer (2/09).(#5977)

Pristine 1942 Quarter, PR68

1206 1942 PR68 NGC. Both sides yield whispers of soft yellow-gold, violet, powder-blue, and olive-green patination. The strike is well executed, and manifests itself in strong definition on the design elements. Close inspection reveals immaculately preserved surfaces. This is a super proof quarter. Census: 18 in 68, 1 finer (2/09). (#5981)

End of Session One

SESSION TWO

Floor, Telephone, Heritage Live!™, Internet, Fax, and Mail Signature® Auction #1126
Sunday, March 29, 2009, 9:00 AM ET, Lots 1207-1888
Baltimore, Maryland

A 15% Buyer's Premium ($9 minimum) Will Be Added To All Lots

Visit HA.com to view full-color images and bid.

DOLLARS

Excellent 1878 8 Tailfeathers Dollar, MS66

1207 **1878 8TF MS66 NGC.** A one-sided prooflike piece with fully mirrored obverse fields and frosty reverse fields. Both sides are nicely detailed with satiny luster on the central obverse motif, providing excellent cameo contrast. An important opportunity for the advanced Morgan collector. Census: 22 in 66, 0 finer (2/09). (#7072)

1208 **1878 7/8TF Strong, Tripled Blossoms—Cleaned—ICG. VF25 Details.** VAM-44. A Top 100 Variety. A midrange representative of the now-legendary Tripled Blossoms variant, pleasing despite a past cleaning. Moderately worn, lightly abraded surfaces show layers of tan and pink toning.(#7078)

1209 **1878 7/8TF Strong MS63 PCGS.** VAM-42, R.5. A stone-white representative of this scarce Strong 7/8TF variety. Sharply struck and lightly abraded with slightly subdued luster.(#7078)

1210 **1878 7/8TF Weak MS65 PCGS.** VAM-33. The legs of the eagle are die doubled, as are the two stars to the right of the date. This decisively struck Gem has pleasing surfaces and delicate caramel-gold toning.(#7070)

1211 **1878 7TF Reverse of 1878 MS65 PCGS. CAC.** Sharply struck with the Reverse of 1878. This minimally toned example has attractive luster and considerable frostiness across the devices. (#7074)

1212 **1878 7TF Reverse of 1878 MS65 PCGS.** A gorgeously toned, immensely lustrous survivor. The obverse has deep orange central shadings surrounded by blue, while the reverse shows the two colors intermixed and more balanced.(#7074)

1213 **1878 7TF Reverse of 1878 MS65 NGC.** VAM-84. A Top 100 Variety. The "Line Under 8," named for the near-horizontal dash appearing below the first 8 in the date. An interesting Gem, toned olive-blue over the central obverse with green-gold and orange peripheral shadings; the reverse has the same colors, but inverted. (#134044)

Exceptional Gem 1878 7 Tailfeathers Reverse of 1879 Dollar

1214 **1878 7TF Reverse of 1879 MS65 PCGS.** The 7 Tailfeathers "Reverse of 1879," with the uppermost arrow fletchings on the reverse at a slant, rather than parallel as on the so-called "Reverse of 1878." This piece is conditionally scarce as a Gem, and boasts exceptional eye appeal due to its gorgeous deep, variegated coloration. Amber, electric-blue, and purple-red hues prevail over the obverse, while the reverse shows mostly lighter golden-tan toning. Surface disturbances are minimal, as expected. PCGS has graded just six finer examples (2/09).(#7076)

1215 **1878-CC MS64 PCGS.** Impressively lustrous and strikingly toned. Bands of gold, orange, violet, ocean-blue, and aqua grace each side, across the upper right half of the obverse and at the reverse margins.(#7080)

1216 **1878-CC MS65 PCGS.** Fantastically mirrored for a coin not awarded a Prooflike designation. The devices are immensely frosty with razor-sharp striking definition.(#7080)

1217 **1878-CC MS65 NGC.** The obverse of this shining Carson City Gem is a treat for the toning lover, with bands of green-gold, ocean-blue, and magenta around an orange center. This last color shows up in crescents at the margins of the reverse, which is unpatinated otherwise.(#7080)

Lustrous 1878-CC Dollar, MS66

1218 **1878-CC MS66 NGC.** This 1878-CC Morgan dollar is a brilliant, frosty, and highly lustrous Premium Gem with extraordinary aesthetic appeal. Although NGC has certified nine finer examples of the date (2/09), it is hard to envision that any could be more attractive than this one.(#7080)

Untoned MS66 1878-CC Dollar

1219 **1878-CC MS66 NGC.** The year 1878 was a year of contrasts, between the enormous mintages of the shiny new Morgan silver dollars at three mints, for example, and the minuscule 12,000 examples of the Seated half in San Francisco. The present piece show untoned silver-white surfaces with radiant cartwheel luster, few abrasions, and considerable eye appeal. NGC has certified only nine pieces finer (2/09).(#7080)

1220 **1878-CC MS64 Deep Mirror Prooflike NGC.** Honey-gold and cherry-red toning invigorates the margins of this flashy and boldly impressed near-Gem. A few wispy hairlines on the reverse field and faint contact on the cheek are all that limit the grade. Encased in a former generation holder. NGC has certified 32 Deep Prooflike coins finer (2/09).(#97081)

1221 **1879-CC AU50 PCGS.** An appealing AU example with pearl-gray coloration and champagne-rose accents. The central highpoints are noticeably worn on both sides, but there are no distracting abrasions to report.(#7086)

Delightful 1879-CC Morgan Dollar, MS62

1222 **1879-CC MS62 PCGS.** Normal Mintmark. Silver-gray surfaces show only minor marks on Liberty's cheek and a small scrape on the reverse below S OF that likely determine the grade, but elsewhere there is plenty of appeal, with generous cartwheel luster radiating from both sides. A well struck and attractive example of this popular issue.(#7086)

Attractive MS63 1879-CC Morgan

1223 **1879-CC MS63 PCGS.** Normal Mintmark. The silver-white surfaces are moderately abraded, although those abrasions, aside from two on the lower cheek that do require singular mention, are neither overly numerous nor overly severe. The strike is sharply executed, and the overall appeal is high. An attractive example of this key CC-mint issue.(#7086)

Desirable 1879-CC Dollar, MS64

1224 **1879-CC MS64 PCGS. CAC.** The 1879-CC is highly desired in any grade, and rates second only to the 1889-CC in terms of rarity among Carson City issues. This near-Gem exhibits well struck devices, including the central areas. Semiprooflike fields highlight the motifs, and each side is essentially color-free and minimally marked.(#7086)

Appealing 1879-CC Morgan Dollar, MS64

1225 **1879-CC MS64 PCGS. CAC.** Although it falls just short of Gem status, this piece has aesthetic desirability that rivals the finest certified examples. Both sides are fully brilliant silvery-white with bold design elements and frosty high point luster. The fields around the devices on each side are satiny with a soft reflective appearance.(#7086)

Marvelous Near-Gem 1879-CC Morgan

1226 **1879-CC MS64 PCGS.** Normal Mintmark. "The prooflikeness trumps the marks." So several catalogers here concurred when viewing this marvelous near-Gem 1879-CC dollar. While there might be a few more abrasions than expected for the near-Gem level, both sides exhibit a startling amount of prooflikeness, even though it falls somewhat short of the actual designation from PCGS. The brightness of the fields on this silver-white coin perhaps overly accentuates the abrasions, which are mostly minor with the sole exception of a single nick on Liberty's cheek. A nice example of this key date that would fit into an otherwise Gem set with absolutely no apology.(#7086)

Mint State 1879-CC Morgan Dollar
Capped Die, VAM-3, Top 100

1227 **1879-CC Capped Die MS60 ANACS.** VAM-3. A Top 100 Variety. Attractive autumn-gold toning visits this lustrous and nicely struck key date Carson City dollar. The cheek has its share of small marks, but the fields are uncommonly smooth for the MS60 grade. The so-called "Capped Die" variety is scarcer than its Clear CC counterpart.
From The Mario Eller Collection, Part Four.(#7088)

Pleasing MS65 1879-O Morgan Dollar

1228 **1879-O MS65 NGC.** With just eight numerically finer examples known to NGC (1/09), this Gem ranks highly among today's survivors. Each side is minimally toned and immensely lustrous with unusually strong central detail for the issue. A few shallow luster grazes in the fields scarcely affect the eye appeal.(#7090)

Impressive, Sharply Struck MS65 1879-O Dollar

1229 **1879-O MS65 PCGS.** The 1879-O is available in lower grades, but in the context of Morgan dollars, this issue is rare at the Gem level. The present coin is sharply struck, with impressive mint luster and a minimum of handling marks. Excellent eye appeal makes this coin an appropriate choice for any high grade collection of Morgan dollars.(#7090)

1230 **1879-S MS67 NGC.** A beautiful layer of shimmering mint frost covers each side of this brilliant, snow-white Superb Gem. Fully struck with near-pristine surfaces and tremendous overall eye appeal.(#7092)

Remarkable 1879-S Dollar, MS68

1231 **1879-S MS68 PCGS. CAC.** The slanting top arrow feather confirms the Third Reverse. The fields show some prooflike tendencies, especially on the reverse, and a well executed strike lends sharp delineation to the design features, including the hair at Liberty's ear and the breast feathers. Immaculately preserved surfaces display whispers of reddish-gold at the margins. Population: 75 in 68, 0 finer (2/09).(#7092)

Breathtaking 1879-S Dollar, MS68

1232 **1879-S MS68 PCGS.** Perusal of the certified population figures indicates tens of thousands of this date are available through MS66, and even MS67 pieces are not that difficult to obtain. The population declines dramatically in the lofty grade of MS68, however, which is that of the current coin. The silvery surfaces are impeccably preserved, untoned, and radiate intense luster. All of the design elements are crisply impressed. Population: 75 in 68, 0 finer (2/09).(#7092)

Magical 1879-S Morgan Dollar, MS68 ★

1233 **1879-S MS68 ★ NGC.** Beautiful, swirling mint luster illuminates the snow-white surfaces of this conditionally rare example. Fully struck with impeccable preservation that seems almost magical. There is a distinct cameo effect noted on both sides, as the richly frosted devices are contrasted against glassy reflectivity in the fields. Only four examples have been graded as MS68 ★ by NGC, and none are finer with the ★ designation (1/09).(#7092)

Brilliant 1880 Morgan, MS66

1234 **1880 MS66 PCGS.** A scarce issue in Gem quality, and rare any finer. In fact, this piece is tied for the finest that either NGC or PCGS has certified. It is boldly detailed with strong hair details and full eagle details. The surfaces are entirely brilliant with frosty luster and exceptional aesthetic appeal. Population: 80 in 66, 0 finer (2/09).(#7096)

1235 **1880-CC MS65 PCGS.** Reverse of 1879. A frosty silver-gray Gem with some light die clashing visible on the reverse. Not uncommon in this grade, but always appealing due to its excellent production values.(#7100)

1236 **1880-CC MS65 PCGS.** A beautiful silver-white Gem with the Slanted Arrow Feather Reverse of 1879. Brilliant with cartwheel luster throughout and premium appeal. Only a couple of small marks on the neck from an even finer grade.(#7100)

1237 **1880-CC MS66 NGC.** The silver-gray surfaces of this Premium Gem display semiprooflike fields that yield mild variance with the motifs. Each side displays a few grade-consistent marks, and faint roller marks are located in the hair near the ear.(#7100)

1238 **1880-CC MS66 PCGS.** Crisply detailed with fine, satiny luster over the central devices that spills into the fields. Lightly toned cloud-white with carefully preserved surfaces. PCGS has graded 23 finer pieces (2/09).(#7100)

1239 **1880-CC MS66 PCGS.** Golden-tan shadings visit the margins, while the centers remain pale silver-gray. Lightly frosted on the softly struck devices. PCGS has graded 23 finer examples (2/09).(#7100)

1240 **1880-CC MS66 PCGS.** Well struck overall with luminous cloud-white and silver-gray patina across much of each side. A small dot of deeper patina is noted above Liberty's eye.(#7100)

1241 **1880-CC MS66 PCGS.** Luster sweeps across this silver-gray and almond-gold Carson City Morgan. Essentially unabraded save for a solitary shallow mark on the eagle's belly.(#7100)

1242 **1880-CC MS66 PCGS.** Ex: David S. Emery Collection. Gold, rose-red, and aqua-blue toning endows the right obverse margin. The reverse has numerous tiny autumn-brown freckles. Potent luster illuminates this attractively preserved Premium Gem. The obverse field is particularly clean, and the strike is good, although the hair above the ear has minor blurring of detail.(#7100)

1243 **1880-CC MS65 Prooflike PCGS.** This flashy Carson City Gem has medium chestnut toning and an above-average strike. The reverse is gorgeously smooth, and the portrait has only wispy grazes. Difficult to locate any finer.(#7101)

1244 **1880/79-CC Reverse of 1878 MS65 PCGS.** This precisely struck Carson City dollar possesses pleasing luster and has a whisper of golden-brown toning on each side. The fields are splendidly smooth, and the cheek has only moderate grazes.(#7108)

1245 **1880-CC 8/7 Reverse of 1878 MS65 PCGS.** VAM-7. Not the Top 100 variety (the VAM-4), but an interesting overdate nonetheless with the tip of a 7 visible below the second 8 in the date. Pleasingly lustrous with just a hint of gold-gray toning over each side.(#7110)

1246 **1880-O MS64 PCGS. CAC.** Sharply struck with bright luster and impressive eye appeal. Though a handful of stray marks affect the portrait, none of them jeopardize the Choice designation. PCGS has graded just 20 finer pieces (1/09).(#7114)

1247 **1880-O MS64 PCGS.** Well struck overall with bright luster. This minimally toned near-Gem offers interesting eye appeal. PCGS has graded only 20 finer examples (2/09).(#7114)

1248 **1880-O MS64 PCGS.** Strongly lustrous with subtle golden tints across the obverse. A well-defined O-mint near-Gem from an issue that is rare any finer. PCGS has graded just 20 such pieces (2/09).(#7114)

Rarely Seen Gem 1880-O Dollar

1249 **1880-O MS65 NGC. CAC.** Shining surfaces are essentially silver-white with only the faintest hints of patina or color. The strike is excellent by almost any standard, and whispers of delightful frost add interest to the well-preserved central devices. Excellent eye appeal does justice to the grade. Despite an ample mintage of over 5.3 million pieces, the 1880-O dollar is unknown for the reflectivity category above MS65 (2/09); surprisingly, save for brief comments about a lack of availability in MS64 and finer grades, this passes without mention in most numismatic references.(#7114)

Near-Gem 1880-O Morgan Dollar
Doubled Ear, VAM-43, Top 100
Single Finest PCGS-Certified

1250 **1880-O Doubled Ear MS64 PCGS.** VAM-43. A Top 100 Variety. The border of Liberty's ear is nicely die doubled. A satiny example that has a good strike and medium honey-gold toning. The single finest graded at PCGS, and tied for finest known with a solitary NGC MS64 example (1/09).(#7114)

1251 **1880-O MS63 Deep Mirror Prooflike NGC.** Aside from occasional glimpses of champagne patina at the centers and rims, this marvelously mirrored piece is essentially untoned. Well struck for the issue with a scattering of abrasions, as expected for the grade. *From The Burning Tree Collection.*(#97115)

Gorgeous 1880-S Morgan Dollar, MS67 ★

1252 **1880-S MS67 ★ NGC.** The 1880-S Morgan dollar is not a scarce date, even in MS67 condition, where well over 4,000 pieces have been certified by NGC and PCGS combined (2/09). However, fewer than 5% of those Superb Gems have also received the coveted Star designation from NGC (the Star denotes exceptional eye appeal). This example is well struck, and the obverse is adorned in a vivid rainbow of olive-gold, purple-red, and cobalt-blue. The reverse is largely untoned, save for slight peripheral tan-gold patina. (#7118)

Highly Attractive 1880-S Dollar, MS67 ★

1253 **1880-S MS67 ★ NGC.** Soft gold patina occupies most of the obverse, yielding to aqua-blue and lavender on the lower border, while the reverse displays wisps of light gold under magnification. Semiprooflike fields highlight the devices, and both sides are minimally marked. The design elements are generally well struck, except for some incompleteness in the centers. This is a nice looking coin, well deserving of the Star designation.(#7118)

1254 **1880-S MS67 PCGS.** Shining and essentially untoned, a strongly cartwheeled Superb Gem that offers this popular type issue's "classic" look. Great all-around eye appeal.(#7118)

Dazzling MS68 1880-S Dollar

1255 **1880-S MS68 PCGS.** An amazingly clean and highly attractive Morgan dollar, with dazzling cartwheel luster in the fields and light champagne-ivory toning over both sides. Fully struck and nearly pristine, with just a couple of nicks on the obverse, including one in Liberty's hair detail below RTY.(#7118)

Fresh 1880-S Dollar, MS68

1256 **1880-S MS68 NGC.** A coin that surpasses even the masses of MS67 survivors available in the marketplace. Sharply struck devices are carefully preserved with a dusting of mint frost, and the silver-white fields offer shining cartwheels. Amazing eye appeal, as demanded of the grade. NGC has certified just four finer pieces (1/09).(#7118)

Shining MS68 1880-S Dollar

1257 **1880-S MS68 NGC.** A fantastic choice for the high-end date collector, this Superb Gem goes above and beyond with its eye appeal. The strike showcases this issue's trademark excellence, and the strong cartwheel luster of the fields pierces thin veils of silver-gray toning. Nearly pristine to the unaided eye. NGC has graded a mere four numerically finer pieces (2/09).(#7118)

Amazing 1880-S Morgan, MS68

1258 **1880-S MS68 NGC.** An absolutely stunning Superb Gem with intense silver luster and pristine surfaces. Typical of the early San Francisco Mint Morgan dollars, all of the design features are boldly detailed. This is a wonderful example for the connoisseur who is working on a high quality type or date set. NGC has only certified four finer pieces (2/09).(#7118)

1259 **1880-S MS66 Prooflike NGC.** Fantastic flash and considerable reflectivity grace the essentially brilliant fields. Sharply struck central devices exhibit characteristically thick mint frost. (#7119)

1260 **1880-S MS66 Deep Mirror Prooflike PCGS.** Profoundly reflective with razor-sharp striking definition on thickly frosted devices. Modest cloud-white patina visits the rims. Housed in a first-generation holder.(#97119)

1261 **1881-CC MS65 PCGS.** Excellent strike and luster. Slight silver-gray patina visits each side, but this Carson City dollar retains its like-new vibrancy. A gorgeous Gem.(#7126)

1262 **1881-CC MS66 PCGS.** Morgan dollars are seldom seen with the intense mint frost and razor-sharp striking details of this Premium Gem. When these attributes are combined with excellent surface preservation, the result is a stunning display of technical merit and splendid visual appeal. This brilliant, snow-white piece would make a great example for a Carson City type collection.(#7126)

1263 **1881-CC MS66 ★ NGC.** Each side offers powerful, frosty luster with light silver-gray patina the norm. The exception is at the lower left obverse, which shows rich crescents of blue, violet, and gold.(#7126)

1264 **1881-CC MS66 PCGS.** Pearl-gray with infrequent hints of tan patina. A well struck and lustrous Premium Gem that has nearly pristine fields. The popularity of this low mintage Carson City issue remains a constant within the hobby.(#7126)

1265 **1881-CC MS66 NGC.** Shining cartwheels in the fields with considerable frostiness across the sharply struck central devices. Grand eye appeal with a silver-gray obverse and a gold-tinged reverse.(#7126)

1266 **1881-CC MS66 NGC.** Brilliant throughout with thick, frosted mint luster. The surfaces are virtually unaffected by luster grazes or abrasions, unlike most CC dollars. A splendid Carson City type coin.(#7126)

1267 **1881-CC MS66 PCGS.** A sharply struck and shining coin with hints of frostiness on the highest design elements. Minimally marked and highly desirable with only faint hints of patina. (#7126)

1268 **1881-CC MS66 PCGS.** Solidly struck with fresh luster. Whispers of cloud-white patina drape parts of the surfaces, but the cartwheels shine through elsewhere. A great Carson City Morgan dollar. (#7126)

Superior 1881-CC Dollar, MS67 ★

1269 **1881-CC MS67 ★ NGC.** A swath of medium intensity multicolored toning resides on the right obverse border, while that on the right reverse displays a narrow zone of purple and golden-tan color. A superior strike imparts sharp definition to the design features, and lustrous surfaces have been well cared for. Census: 9 in 67 ★, 1 finer (2/09).(#7126)

Appealing 1881-CC Morgan, MS67

1270 **1881-CC MS67 PCGS.** The stone-white surfaces are entirely untoned but offer premium eye appeal. Liberty's cheek is exceptionally clean, and indeed both sides reveal no singular abrasions. Some wispy die cracks encircle much of the reverse periphery. Nearly the finest obtainable, as PCGS has certified only three coins in higher grade (2/09).(#7126)

Exceptional MS67 1881-CC Morgan Dollar

1271 **1881-CC MS67 PCGS. CAC.** The surfaces are expectedly clean on this Superb Gem, but it is the exceptional cartwheel luster that gives it the extra boost. Only tiny luster grazes appear on the cheek, but there are no outright abrasions, and the silver-white surfaces reveal few distractions of any size. Faint roller marks appear on the ear and extending upward into the hair. PCGS has graded only three finer (2/09).(#7126)

Low-Mintage 1881-CC Dollar
MS65 Deep Mirror Prooflike

1272 1881-CC MS65 Deep Mirror Prooflike PCGS. Flashy mirrors and frosty devices combine for imposing eye appeal. A lustrous and well preserved Gem example of this low-mintage Carson City issue. Scarce at all grade levels, and especially so at MS65. Surprisingly, there are more Gems certified with Deep Mirror Prooflike surfaces than there are as plain Prooflikes at both services.(#97127)

1273 1881-O MS65 PCGS. Minimally toned with potent cartwheel luster. This well-defined Gem is near the top of the list among survivors; PCGS has graded just 12 finer pieces (1/09). (#7128)

1274 1881-O MS65 PCGS. CAC. A gleaming Gem with prominent cartwheel luster that enhances silver-white surfaces. Well-defined with powerful eye appeal. PCGS has graded just 12 finer examples (2/09).(#7128)

1275 1881-O MS65 PCGS. Slight striking softness in the centers is no obstacle to eye appeal, as the brightly lustrous silver-white surfaces of this Gem prove. PCGS has graded 12 finer pieces (2/09). (#7128)

Remarkable Gem Prooflike 1881-O Dollar

1276 1881-O MS65 Prooflike PCGS. Although Prooflike examples of the 1881-O are occasionally encountered, most of them show heavy bagmarks, making Gem Prooflike coins a true rarity. This piece has remarkable clean silver-white surfaces that are well mirrored and highly attractive. The stark field-device contrast is noteworthy. Population: 5 in 65 Prooflike, 0 finer (2/09).(#7129)

Breathtaking 1881-S Dollar, MS67 ★

1277 1881-S MS67 ★ NGC. CAC. The 1881-S is one of the commonest Morgan dollars in Mint State, as inspection of NGC/PCGS population data readily shows. Locating a specimen such as that in this lot, however, is another story. First, waves of cobalt-blue, purple, and yellow-gold reside on half of the obverse, and cling to the reverse rims. The remaining surfaces are brilliant. Second, an exacting strike emboldens the design elements, including the hair over Liberty's ear and the eagle's breast feathers. Finally, both sides are immaculately preserved. These attributes synergistically result in breathtaking technical quality and eye appeal, aptly confirmed by the Star designation and CAC green label.(#7130)

Marvelous 1881-S Dollar, MS68

1278 1881-S MS68 NGC. CAC. The 1881-S is one of the better produced issues in the Morgan dollar series, prompting David Bowers (2006) to write: "Specimens nearly always are sharply struck and beautiful." This MS68 example is one such product, with shimmering cartwheel luster, satin-smooth surfaces, and a bold strike, further enhanced by loving post-strike preservation. Liberty's cheek is virtually pristine, and the light gold, plum, and blue rim toning completes a marvelous package. Certified in an old-style NGC holder.(#7130)

Great 1881-S Morgan Dollar, MS68

1279 1881-S MS68 PCGS. The 1881-S is famous for being one of the most common issues in the Morgan dollar series, if not *the* most common. At the lofty MS68 grade tier, however, even the '81-S becomes conditionally scarce. This example boasts great technical merit as well as splendid eye appeal. The obverse is blanketed by lovely champagne and turquoise patina, while the reverse shows similar coloration, but only near the periphery. Fully struck, intensely lustrous, and virtually pristine, this is simply a great Morgan dollar in every respect. Population: 87 in 68, 2 finer (2/09).(#7130)

Marvelous 1881-S Morgan Dollar, MS68

1280 **1881-S MS68 NGC.** This brilliant Superb Gem displays snow-white surfaces that exhibit coruscating luster in the fields and a wonderfully clean appearance on both sides. The design elements are crisply and fully reproduced, as usual for this San Francisco Mint issue. The 1881-S is famous for being a common date, but the current offering represents an uncommon coin in such a lofty state of preservation.(#7130)

Amazing MS68 1881-S Dollar

1281 **1881-S MS68 PCGS.** For the type collector for whom a "mere" MS67 would not do, this MS68 survivor is impressively lustrous with only a hint of silver-gray patina on each side and a glimpse of champagne on the reverse. Aside from a handful of trifling grazes, the surfaces are virtually untouched. Population: 86 in 68, 2 finer (2/09).(#7130)

1282 **1882 MS66 PCGS.** Dappled peach and violet patina embraces each side of this shining Premium Gem. Well struck overall, though the hair over the ear shows slight softness. PCGS has graded six finer pieces (2/09).(#7132)

1283 **1882-CC MS66 PCGS.** Impressively lustrous with considerable flashiness to the fields. This is a minimally toned Carson City dollar with a pleasing strike on the highest parts of the devices. (#7134)

1284 **1882-CC MS66 ★ NGC. CAC.** Powder-blue, ruby-red, olive-gold, and sea-green endow the obverse. The rich patination undoubtedly inspired the Star designation from NGC. The reverse is only lightly toned. Well struck and lustrous.(#7134)

1285 **1882-CC MS65 Deep Mirror Prooflike PCGS.** Minimally toned with outstanding mirrors. The razor-sharp definition of the frosty devices is particularly pleasing. Housed in a first-generation holder. (#97135)

1286 **1882-O MS65 PCGS. CAC.** VAM-22. A meticulously struck and highly lustrous Gem, only gently toned in golden tints. The reverse is nicely die doubled, strongest on AMERICA.(#7136)

1287 **1882-O MS65 Prooflike NGC.** Blue and golden peripheral toning is noted on both sides of this Gem issue, which is housed is an early-generation NGC holder. A lovely piece with tremendous reflectivity in the fields. Conditionally scarce, with only a single Prooflikes graded higher at PCGS. Census: 20 in 65 Prooflike, 0 finer (2/09).(#7137)

1288 **1882-O MS65 Prooflike PCGS.** Though the mirrors are more flashy than deep, each side easily qualifies for Prooflike status. The devices are crisply struck and frosted, the obverse showing subtle rose overtones. Population: 32 in 65 Prooflike, 1 finer (2/09). (#7137)

VAM-4 1882-O/S Morgan, MS64

1289 **1882-O/S MS64 PCGS.** VAM-4. A Top 100 Variety. Identified by parallel die polish lines within the confines of Liberty's ear. Silvery surfaces at the center, with a tinge of gold around the rims. The overmintmark is prominent on this Top 100 example. A long scrape is noted on Liberty's lower chin, but elsewhere there are few mentionable distractions.(#7138)

Elusive Superb Gem 1883-CC Morgan Dollar

1290 **1883-CC MS67 NGC.** This is a beautiful, brilliant Superb Gem with intense mint luster across the icy silver-white surfaces. Fully struck and impressively preserved, with nearly immaculate fields and devices on each side. This is a common Carson City issue that is readily available at Mint State grade levels through MS66. At MS67 it suddenly becomes scarce, if not actually rare. Census: 92 in 67, 0 finer (2/09).(#7144)

Attractive 1883-CC Dollar, MS67

1291 **1883-CC MS67 PCGS. CAC.** The untoned obverse of this Superb Gem cedes to a melange of cobalt-blue, lavender, and golden-brown on the reverse, and partially prooflike fields nicely highlight the well impressed design features. Impeccable preservation characterizes both sides. The coin's attractiveness is attested to by the CAC green label.(#7144)

Amazing Superb Gem 1883-CC Dollar

1292 **1883-CC MS67 NGC.** Flashy cartwheel luster in the fields with a degree of reflectivity on each side. The solidly struck obverse offers dappled blue-green and gold toning, while the reverse is nearly brilliant. A carefully preserved and undeniably appealing survivor, tied for numerically finest graded by NGC (2/09).(#7144)

Marvelous MS67 1883-CC Dollar

1293 **1883-CC MS67 PCGS.** A shining and sharply struck piece with only hints of silver-gray patina over parts of the silver-white fields. Only a handful of utterly trivial faults are present on this coin, which is every bit the Superb Gem. As for finer examples, PCGS has certified just three and NGC has graded none (2/09). (#7144)

1294 **1883-S MS62 PCGS.** Glimpses of reddish-orange and violet toning visit the margins. Though this well struck piece shows numerous scattered marks, the luster of the fields remains intact. (#7148)

1295 **1883-S MS63 ★ NGC.** A flashy coin that falls just shy of Prooflike reflectivity. Minimally marked for the grade with considerable frost on the sharply struck portrait and eagle.(#7148)

1296 **1883-S MS63 PCGS.** Pleasingly detailed for this issue, which shows weak strikes more frequently than earlier S-mint dates. Gold and silver-gray shadings across the obverse yield to deeper reddish-orange hues on the reverse. Minute marks limit the grade. (#7148)

1297 **1883-S MS63 PCGS.** Sharply struck and essentially untoned with powerful cartwheel luster. While the portrait and fields show a number of wispy abrasions and light marks, the overall eye appeal remains strong.(#7148)

1298 **1883-S MS63 PCGS.** Hints of golden toning visit the obverse, as does a dot of russet to the left of the first U in UNUM, while the reverse is minimally toned. A strongly lustrous, lightly abraded Select coin.(#7148)

Sharp 1883-S Near-Gem Dollar

1299 **1883-S MS64 PCGS. CAC.** A medium-intensity mix of cobalt-blue, purple, orange, and purple toning runs over the lustrous surfaces of this near-Gem S-mint. Sharp detail characterizes the design features, including the hair over Liberty's ear and the eagle's breast feathers. A few stray marks preclude Gem status. The 1883-S is difficult to locate any finer.(#7148)

Pleasingly Preserved 1883-S Dollar, MS65

1300 **1883-S MS65 PCGS.** A fantastically lustrous, crisply detailed, and colorful Gem representative of this San Francisco issue, the first challenging date from that Mint after a string of popular type coins. Pleasingly preserved surfaces give off powerful cartwheels beneath ample orange, peach, silver-gray, and violet patina, with the first two colors dominant on the obverse and the last prevailing on the reverse. Described by Bowers as "very difficult to find, especially at higher Mint State levels." Examination of the certified population data reveals the extent of its condition rarity. Population: 15 in 65, 3 finer (2/09).(#7148)

1301 1884-CC MS67 PCGS. A large number of 1884-CC dollars are extant in Mint State grades, evident from the thousands certified by PCGS and NGC. The population declines precipitously in MS67, the condition of the present offering. Lustrous surfaces display various shades of olive-green on the obverse, while the reverse shows lighter hues of this color. Well preserved throughout. Population: 54 in 67, 3 finer (2/09).(#7152)

1302 1884-CC MS66 Deep Mirror Prooflike PCGS. Intense silver-white coloration and spectacularly deep mirror contrast between fields and devices are the hallmarks of this coin. There are expectedly few signs of contact, and the design elements are crisply impressed. Freckles of cinnamon toning appear on Liberty's cheek and the coronet above. This issue is all but unobtainable in Deep Mirror Prooflike only one grade point finer, where PCGS has certified only three pieces (2/09).(#97153)

Outstanding 1884-O Dollar
MS67 Deep Mirror Prooflike
Finest NGC Certified

1303 1884-O MS67 Deep Mirror Prooflike NGC. VAM-6. A Top 100 Variety. There are strong remnants of a second O mintmark both inside and at the lower left outside of the mintmark. The VAM number is not designated on the holder. The 1884-O was minted in quantity (9.73 million pieces), and is readily available through MS67. Even Prooflike and Deep Mirror Prooflike coins are readily located, as hundreds have been graded by NGC and PCGS right through the MS65 level.

Superb Gem DMPL specimens, such as this piece, are another matter altogether. Indeed, this example is the single finest graded by NGC. PCGS has certified one MS68, but no MS67s. The untoned surfaces present a near white-on-black cameo appearance and are impeccably preserved. The strike is complete and brings out all the design features, including the hair over Liberty's ear and the eagle's breast feathers. Both sides offer outstanding technical quality and aesthetic appeal.
From The Jack Lee Estate Collection.(#97155)

1304 1884-S AU55 NGC. VAM-8, R.5. This VAM has perhaps the most prominent misplaced date of the entire Morgan dollar series. The tops of an 18 are clearly evident within the obverse denticles near 6 o'clock. The 1884-S is also conditionally scarce in Choice AU. Lightly toned and partly lustrous with a good strike. (#7156)

1305 1884-S AU58 PCGS. A desirable near-Mint example from this little-saved issue of 3.2 million pieces. Light, scattered marks, including several on Liberty's cheek, and modest friction are present on the silver-gray surfaces.(#7156)

1306 **1884-S AU58 PCGS.** Strong remaining luster with just a trace of friction evident on the high points. Largely pale silver-gray though with subdued magenta elements at the lower and left reverse periphery.(#7156)

1307 **1885 MS66 PCGS.** VAM-1A. A Hot 50 Variety. The "Pitted Reverse," with rusted and clashed reverse die, the pits most noticeable around the denomination. Strongly lustrous with blue and orange peripheral shadings appearing intermittently around a silver-white center.(#7158)

1308 **1885 MS67 PCGS. CAC.** This nearly immaculate silver dollar is meticulously struck and offers coruscating luster. Light apple-green and stone-gray toning deepens slightly near the profile. Housed in a first generation holder. PCGS has graded just one finer example (1/09).(#7158)

1309 **1885 MS67 NGC. CAC.** Golden-brown and lilac-blue bands grace the obverse border. The portrait and the reverse are close to brilliant. Exactingly struck, even on the eagle's breast and the hair above the ear. The fields are practically pristine, and Liberty's cheek has only trivial grazes.(#7158)

1310 **1885-CC MS65 PCGS.** Sweeping luster and a precise strike ensure the originality of this lightly toned Carson City Gem. The reverse is exceptionally void of marks. Housed in a green label holder.(#7160)

1311 **1885-CC MS66 PCGS.** Well struck with impressive luster beneath rich, dappled patina. Rose, orange, blue-green, emerald, and sapphire shadings enrich each side.(#7160)

1312 **1885-CC MS66 PCGS.** Flashy with strong cartwheel luster and minimal patina. The razor-sharp striking definition complements the already-considerable eye appeal of this Premium Gem. (#7160)

1313 **1885-CC MS66 PCGS.** Slight central softness on the hair over the ear, though the reverse is crisply detailed throughout. Impressively lustrous and largely brilliant save for dabs of gold and rose patina in the centers.(#7160)

1314 **1885-CC MS66 PCGS.** Excellent strike with whispers of frostiness on the devices. Smooth fields are minimally toned and carefully preserved. In sum, a gorgeous coin.(#7160)

1315 **1885-CC MS66 NGC.** Slight frostiness is noted on the well-defined devices. An immensely lustrous and minimally toned Carson City dollar that offers grand eye appeal.(#7160)

1316 **1885-CC MS66 NGC.** Silver-gray surfaces radiate intense luster, and sharp definition shows on the design elements. A nicely preserved Premium Gem. NGC has only certified 62 finer examples.(#7160)

1317 **1885-CC MS66 PCGS.** Intense mint frost illuminates both sides of this lustrous and unabraded Carson City silver dollar. Sharply struck except for two wheat leaves near the coronet tip. (#7160)

Dazzling 1885-CC Dollar, MS67

1318 **1885-CC MS67 NGC.** Dazzling luster emanates from the silver-white surfaces of this wonderful Superb Gem, and a solid strike leaves strong detail on the design features, including the hair at Liberty's ear and the eagle's breast feathers. Satiny surfaces reveal just a few inoffensive, grade-consistent marks. Census: 57 in 67, 5 finer (2/09).(#7160)

1319 **1885-CC MS64 Deep Mirror Prooflike NGC. CAC.** Profoundly reflective with amazing contrast, thanks to potent and minimally toned mirrors and the icy-white devices that emerge from them. Light, scattered marks contribute to the grade.(#97161)

Delightful 1885-CC Dollar MS65 Deep Mirror Prooflike

1320 **1885-CC MS65 Deep Mirror Prooflike PCGS.** The vast majority of 1885-CC survivors still exist in Uncirculated grades. This Deep Mirror Prooflike Gem gives of a near white-on-black appearance when viewed from a direct angle. Its frosty motifs exhibit crisp definition, and both sides are essentially untoned. A scattering of minuscule grazes precludes an even higher grade. This delightful coin is sure to please the new owner.(#97161)

1321 **1885-O MS67 NGC.** Peripheral golden-orange patina is slightly more extensive and deeper on the obverse of this well preserved Superb Gem. Lustrous surfaces exhibit boldly struck design elements.(#7162)

1322 **1885-O MS67 NGC.** An impressively lustrous Superb Gem that shows occasional gold and pink elements over otherwise pale silver-gray surfaces. Well-defined with eye appeal that is equally solid. NGC has graded just nine numerically finer pieces (1/09). (#7162)

1323 **1885-O MS66 Deep Mirror Prooflike NGC.** This high-mintage issue was well produced, and tens of thousands of examples have been certified at the Gem and Premium Gem grade levels by NGC and PCGS. In Deep Mirror Prooflike condition, by contrast, there are only a few hundred graded at MS65 and MS66. This Premium Gem exhibits amazingly deep reflectivity in the fields. Well struck and nicely preserved, it only shows a few small marks on either side. Hints of yellow-gold patina cling to the obverse margins. Census: 17 in 66 Deep Mirror Prooflike, 1 finer (2/09).(#97163)

1324 **1885-S MS65 PCGS.** Fantastically lustrous and sharply struck. Centers are largely untoned, while the margins show orange patina. The reverse adds a dose of magenta-violet as well. PCGS has graded 27 finer examples (1/09).(#7164)

1325 **1885-S MS65 PCGS.** Boldly impressed and immensely lustrous with hints of frost on the well-defined portrait. The gold-orange toning that graces parts of the obverse is all but nonexistent on the reverse.(#7164)

1326 **1885-S MS65 PCGS.** Brightly lustrous with strong flashiness to the fields. Lightly frosted across the sharply struck high points. Delightfully appealing with only 27 finer examples known to PCGS (2/09).(#7164)

Uncommonly Nice 1886 Morgan Dollar, MS67

1327 **1886 MS67 PCGS.** This Superb Gem is a remarkable beauty with soft, frosty silver luster on both sides, framed by splendid peripheral gold and lilac toning. Both sides are pristine and virtually mark free. A common date in an uncommon condition. PCGS has only certified three finer examples (2/09).(#7166)

1328 **1886 MS67 NGC.** VAM-1C, "3+2" Clash. A Hot 50 Variety. Fully struck and essentially untoned, with bright silver-white surfaces and impressive, coruscating luster across each side. Expertly preserved and virtually blemish-free; a great Superb Gem. NGC Census (for VAM-1C): 4 in 67, 0 finer (2/09).(#7166)

1329 **1886-O MS62 PCGS. CAC.** Strongly lustrous with subtle golden tints on the obverse. The lightly abraded reverse is minimally toned. Slight striking softness at the hair over Liberty's ear is typical.(#7168)

1330 **1886-O MS62 PCGS.** This untoned piece is nicely struck and shows surprisingly few marks for the grade. An even, satiny sheen flows across both sides.(#7168)

1331 **1886-O MS62 NGC.** Morgan aficionados are well acquainted with the rarity of this issue in Mint State. The present coin offers silver-gray surfaces accented with golden glints. The luster is a trifle subdued by field haze, and a couple of reeding marks on Liberty's cheek help determine the grade, but this is a lot of coin for the assigned level.(#7168)

1332 **1886-O MS62 PCGS.** A fine Mint State representative, this piece shows bold striking definition, even in the centers, and satiny silver-gray surfaces imbued with slight accents of pale rose color. Small, scattered marks limit the grade.(#7168)

1333 **1886-O MS62 PCGS.** Hints of peripheral lavender and lilac offset the pale silver-gray found at the centers. Softly struck as usual but with slightly better-than-average definition and few marks for a coin not given a Select grade.(#7168)

Elusive 1886-O Morgan, MS63

1334 **1886-O MS63 PCGS.** The obverse of this Select Mint State 1886-O dollar has thick gold and iridescent toning, with some lighter silver shining through. The reverse is brighter, with champagne and pale blue patina. A pleasing piece with excellent surfaces for the grade. The 1886-O Morgan is an elusive issue in Mint State grades, often found on collectors' want lists.(#7168)

Lustrous 1886-O Morgan, MS63

1335 **1886-O MS63 NGC.** Blushes of autumn-gold and ocean-blue enrich the margins. Characteristic of the issue, the centers are lightly impressed. Lustrous and only minimally abraded. The 1886-O is common in VF, but confoundingly scarce in Select Mint State. Housed in a prior generation holder.(#7168)

Scarce Select 1886-O Dollar

1336 **1886-O MS63 NGC.** Strongly lustrous with just a touch of orange toning against otherwise silver-white surfaces. Great eye appeal for a "merely" Select coin. The 1886-O is perhaps the greatest conditional rarity of the Morgan series, common in VF but extremely rare as a Gem.(#7168)

1337 **1886-O MS65 PCGS. CAC.** Ex: Jack Lee 2. Some issues, such as the 1921-D half dollar, are celebrated for having the lowest mintage in a series, while others like the 1921 Peace dollar are distinguished as being a first-year issue. Sometimes it is the physical characteristics of a coin that make it special, as with 1820 N-13 large cents, which are relatively more available in high grades than other cents of that era, thanks wholly to the Randall hoard of cents found in the 1860s. The 1886-O dollar stands out as being the rarest New Orleans issue in MS65 or better condition as fewer than five Gem specimens are known to exist. The current offering belongs to that small fraternity of high-end 1886-O dollars. After more than 20 years of third-party grading, only five coins are currently documented at the MS65 level or above at both major services. NGC documents only one such coin—a lone MS66. The PCGS *Population Report* shows a total of four examples; three MS65 pieces and the famous MS67 Deep Mirror Prooflike coin that was considered by Wayne Miller in his 1982 reference to be "the most spectacular Morgan dollar now known." That piece sold for $231,000 in Bowers and Merena's November 1990 sale of the Chris Schenkel collection.

But why is this seemingly common issue so rare in high grade? The mintage of over 10 million coins makes it hard to believe that so few 1886-O dollars exist in Gem condition. The 1881-S issue saw a comparable output of coins, yet *well over 100,000 examples* of that date are known in MS65 or better condition. David Bowers speculates in his *Silver Dollars and Trade Dollars of the United States* (1993): "At or near the time of striking in the nineteenth century, probably a few million coins, say two to four million, were placed into circulation and saw commercial use. Probably, millions of other coins, perhaps as many as six to eight million pieces, went to the melting pot under the terms of the 1918 Pittman Act." Bowers continues by stating that "in MS64 grade it is extremely difficult to locate; probably somewhere between 125 and 250 remain. In MS65 preservation the 1886-O is the rarest New Orleans Mint Morgan dollar; at least one exists, but possibly no more than three." The steep drop of survivors between MS64 and MS65 is reflected in various price guides. For example the current *Coin Dealer Newsletter* indicates a staggering 21-fold increase in price for the 1886-O between MS64 and MS65 condition—more than any other issue in the entire Morgan dollar series.

The Gem offered here represents the only certified 1886-O dollar grading above MS64 to ever cross the auction block at Heritage. And, as to be expected with such a great condition rarity, the statistics are similar with other auction companies. John Dannreuther and Jeff Garrett's compilation of silver dollars sold at auction between 1995 and 2004 records not a single showing of an MS65 1886-O dollar. The landmark offering of the current example may represent one of the few appearances of this rare Gem issue in our lifetime.

Predominately white surfaces abound with intense cartwheel luster. Although known to be notoriously weekly struck, this 1886-O dollar boasts an unusually strong strike. The negligible scattered abrasions number fewer than the most conservative of graders would allow for a Gem Morgan dollar. A memorable specimen that was one of the prides of a great collector's cabinet. Population: 3 in 65, 0 finer (2/09).
See: Video Lot Description(#7168)

1338 1887 MS67 NGC. An impressive piece with brilliant surfaces and uniformly crisp striking definition on both sides. Under low magnification, some tiny marks are detected on Liberty's eyebrow and neck. Some milky specks on Liberty's lower cheek appear to be wispy planchet laminations. NGC has graded only two finer examples (2/09).(#7172)

1339 1887 MS67 PCGS. CAC. This outstanding silver type coin appears to be fully brilliant upon first glance, but both sides have a hint of golden toning. Sharply struck and clean-cheeked. Population: 60 in 67, 1 finer (1/09).(#7172)

1340 1887/6 MS65 PCGS. CAC. VAM-2. A Top 100 Variety. The remnants of a previous 6 are evident near the bottom of the 7 in the date. Well struck and impressively preserved, with only the most minor "chatter" marks evident on Liberty's cheek, and in the left obverse field. An arc of aquamarine and gold-tan iridescence resides along the upper right obverse border, with additional gold-tan toning a little lower down. A lovely Gem example of this popular overdate variety.(#7174)

1341 1887/6 MS65 PCGS. CAC. VAM-2. A Top 100 Variety. This popular overdate Gem displays well impressed design features, including the hair detail above Liberty's ear. Bright luster cascades over both sides, each of which is minimally marked. Color-free except for hints of light-gold along the rims.(#7174)

1342 1887/6 MS65 PCGS. VAM-2. A Top 100 Variety. The bottom loop of the 6 underdigit shows beneath the lower part of the 7. Bright silvery surfaces exhibit nicely struck design features, including partial detail in the hair over Liberty's ear and on the eagle's breast feathers. A few minor grade-consistent marks do not detract.(#7174)

1343 1887/6 MS65 NGC. VAM-2. A Top 100 Variety. The curve of the base of the underdigit 6 is visible on both sides of the bottom of the 7. A brilliant and mildly prooflike Gem. The strike is above average, and marks are surprisingly absent. An exemplary example of this *Guide Book* VAM. Census: 58 in 65, 5 finer (2/09). (#7174)

1344 1887-O MS65 PCGS. Bright silver-white luster is the prime attraction for this elegant piece. Aside from slight striking softness at the hair over the ear, this Gem is well-defined. PCGS has graded eight finer examples (2/09).(#7176)

1345 1887-O MS65 PCGS. Well-defined for this New Orleans issue, though some minor softness occurs in the central areas. Both sides exhibit pleasing luster, again unusual for an issue that is deficient in this attribute (David Bowers, 2006). Housed in a green-label holder.(#7176)

1346 1887-O MS65 PCGS. Slight striking softness as usual at the high points, but this Gem is strongly lustrous with high eye appeal. A hint of peripheral tan offsets the silver-gray of the centers. PCGS has graded eight finer examples (1/09).(#7176)

Scarce 1887-S/S VAM-2 Dollar, MS65

1347 1887-S/S MS65 PCGS. CAC. VAM-2. A Top 100 Variety. The upper serif of an additional S is obvious within the curve of the prominent S. This memorable VAM comprises a reasonable percentage of Uncirculated 1887-S dollars, but any Gem of the issue is both scarce and desirable. Lustrous and lightly toned with a precise strike and mark-free fields.(#133915)

Lustrous MS67 1888 Morgan Dollar

1348 1888 MS67 NGC. Highly lustrous surfaces show a sliver of medium intensity golden-tan and cobalt-blue toning at the lower left obverse margins, and whispers of light gold color at the upper left reverse rim. The design features exhibit sharp definition for an issue that sometimes can be weakly struck. Impeccably preserved surfaces occur on both sides. Census: 41 in 67, 1 finer (2/09). *From The Burning Tree Collection.*(#7182)

Extraordinary 1888 Morgan, MS67
Deep Mirror Prooflike

1349 1888 MS67 Deep Mirror Prooflike NGC. Among Philadelphia issues, the 1888 ranks among those with the most inconsistent striking characteristics. As Q. David Bowers writes in his *Guide Book of Morgan Silver Dollars*, "The 1888 rates as a common date in the Morgan series, although the quality of individual specimens can vary dramatically. Extended die use caused granularity and metal flow lines on some. On the other hand, more than just a few 1888 dollars are attractive and prooflike."

This outstandingly reflective Superb Gem is one of the latter, minimally toned in the deeply mirrored fields. Subtle rose tints accent the sharply struck central devices. A beautifully preserved coin that could win over even the fussiest numismatic aesthete. Census: 1 in 67 Deep Prooflike, 0 finer (2/09).(#97183)

1350 1888-O Doubled Die Obverse AU50 NGC. VAM-4. A Top 100 Variety. The famous "Hot Lips" VAM with prominent die doubling along Liberty's profile. Listed with a photograph in the *Guide Book*. A lightly toned and problem-free piece that retains hints of its initial luster. Census: 31 in 50, 67 finer (2/09).(#7308)

1351 1888-S MS64 NGC. VAM-12A, R.5. The mintmark is nicely repunched, but the key VAM feature is the die rust (or "pitting," as made) on the area near Morgan's designer initial on the reverse. A number of "Pitted Reverse" dies are listed in the Top 100, although the rare VAM-12A was omitted. Highly lustrous with peripheral sun-gold and sea-green toning.(#7186)

Bright 1888-S Dollar, MS65

1352 1888-S MS65 NGC. Bright luster emanates from both sides of this Gem dollar, and purple, gold-tan, and steel-blue toning concentrates at the margins. The design elements are well struck, except for weakness in the centers. A few minute marks are within the parameters of the Gem designation.(#7186)

1353 1889 MS65 PCGS. VAM-19a, Bar Wing. A Top 100 Variety. A flashy Gem, brilliant except for lovely golden rim toning on both sides. Well struck and nicely preserved, save for a couple of minor scrape marks on the upper reverse, above the eagle's head. (#7188)

1354 1889-CC VF20 PCGS. Reddish-orange overtones grace otherwise steel-gray surfaces. A pleasing midrange example of this Carson City key, minimally marked save for a wispy abrasion to the left of the portrait.(#7190)

1355 1889-CC—Polished, Artificially Frosted—ANACS. XF40 Details. A buffed example with bright, chrome-like fields and cloudy, stone-gray devices. This coin has been worked over, but the 1889-CC is the key date of a Carson City collection of Morgan dollars.(#7190)

1356 1889-CC XF40 ANACS. The cream-gray surfaces exhibit slight golden-red and tan accents near the edges. Moderately worn with faint hairlines in the fields. An appealing XF example of this low-mintage key date in the Morgan dollar series.(#7190)

Attractive XF45 1889-CC Dollar

1357 1889-CC XF45 PCGS. Light silver-gray surfaces display subtle golden undertones and occasional wisps of bluish-purple. Traces of luster reside in the recessed areas, and the design features exhibit relatively strong detail, even after discounting high-point wear. While a few minute marks are visible, this is quite a clean specimen for having seen some circulation. It will fit nicely in a high grade collection.(#7190)

Illuminating 1889-CC Dollar, XF45

1358 **1889-CC XF45 PCGS.** Bright luster illuminates the stars, legends, hair, plumage, and wreath of this key date Carson City Morgan. Well defined and essentially untoned. Unabraded aside from a few faded marks on the field near the profile. A collectable example of this desirable issue. Encapsulated in a green label holder. (#7190)

Desirable Choice XF 1889-CC Dollar

1359 **1889-CC XF45 PCGS.** An appealing Choice XF example of this elusive issue, well struck with pleasing color. Attractive lemongrass and tan shadings drape otherwise silver-gray surfaces. An undeniably desirable Carson City survivor that would fit well with an otherwise AU or better Morgan dollar date set.(#7190)

Exuberant Choice XF 1889-CC Dollar

1360 **1889-CC XF45 PCGS.** The exuberant silver-gold surfaces display much remaining luster, along with considerable eye appeal. This obverse is from the die most commonly seen for the issue, diagnosed by a tiny die line that crosses from the left of the large maple leaf to the wheat stalk nearby. A tiny peripheral die crack is noted on the reverse, through a star and ONE DOLL. The few abrasions seen are consistent with the Choice XF grade level.(#7190)

1361 **1889-CC—Polished—NCS. AU Details.** Well struck for the issue with little actual wear. A misguided past polishing has left each light steel-gray side with an unnatural gleam.(#7190)

Radiant AU50 1889-CC Dollar

1362 **1889-CC AU50 PCGS. CAC.** Only light field chatter attests to this coin's relatively short duration in the channels of commerce, as most of the luster is still radiant underneath, and in the protected areas around the rim and central devices. The grayish-white surfaces still retain broad appeal, and this piece would fit nicely into a BU or high-grade circulated set. From the most commonly seen obverse die used for this key date, with a tiny die line left of the maple leaf.(#7190)

Appealing AU53 1889-CC Dollar

1363 **1889-CC AU53 PCGS.** The 1889-CC, despite having a larger mintage than the last Carson City Morgan dollar issue (struck back in 1885), was not preserved in government vaults like the 1885-CC, and significantly worn pieces are the rule. This minimally toned, scarcely worn AU53 coin remains strongly lustrous with soft silver-gray surfaces.
From The Mario Eller Collection, Part Four.(#7190)

1364 **1889-O MS64 PCGS.** Strongly struck and minimally toned with booming luster. Though a few wispy marks preclude Gem status, this remains a highly desirable Choice coin.(#7192)

1365 **1889-O MS64 PCGS.** Strongly lustrous with hints of orange toning at the centers. Aside from a degree of the usual softness at the high points, this near-Gem is well struck.(#7192)

1366 **1889-S MS65 PCGS.** Impressively lustrous with essentially untoned centers. The margins show scattered reddish-orange elements. PCGS has graded 61 finer pieces (2/09).(#7194)

1367 **1889-S MS65 NGC.** Strong, flashy luster with little patina save for hints of canary-yellow close to the rims. A well-defined Gem that has few superiors; NGC has graded just 25 numerically finer examples (2/09).(#7194)

1368 **1889-S MS65 PCGS.** A strongly lustrous Gem example of this lower-mintage S-mint issue, well struck with surfaces that shine beneath layers of blue, champagne, and plum patina. Carefully preserved with excellent visual appeal.(#7194)

Gorgeous Prooflike Gem 1889-S Dollar

1369 **1889-S MS65 Prooflike PCGS.** This S-mint issue only infrequently comes with strongly Prooflike surfaces, but this Gem delivers, with unquestioned reflectivity and minimal patina combining for great eye appeal. A few tiny flaws on the reverse contribute to the grade. Population: 5 in 65 Prooflike, 2 finer (2/09).(#7195)

1370 **1889-S MS63 Deep Mirror Prooflike ANACS.** Champagne peripheral accents grace both sides of this otherwise untoned example. Scattered abrasions account for the Select designation. This S-mint issue is anything but common with a Deep Mirror Prooflike finish.(#97195)

1371 **1890 MS65 PCGS.** Well struck with vibrant luster beneath rich patina. The obverse has a melange of green-gold, sky-blue, sage, and silver-gray toning, while the reverse has similar colors in a ring around a minimally toned center.(#7196)

1372 **1890 MS65 PCGS.** Solidly struck and shining with occasional glimpses of sky-blue patina against silver-white surfaces. Incredible eye appeal. PCGS has graded only one coin finer of this strike- and luster-challenged issue (2/09).(#7196)

1373 **1890 MS65 PCGS.** Deep blue and violet peripheral shadings cede to reddish-orange at the centers. The obverse is brighter in both color and luster, while the reverse offers its own subtle eye appeal. (#7196)

1374 **1890-CC Tail Bar MS62 PCGS.** Ex: Carson City Collection. VAM-4. A Top 100 Variety. A lustrous, crisply struck, and virtually brilliant example of this popular and easily recognized Carson City variety. Wispy grazes on the cheek deny a higher grade, but the reverse is generally well preserved.(#87198)

1890-CC Morgan Dollar, MS63
Popular Tail Bar VAM-4

1375 **1890-CC Tail Bar MS63 PCGS.** VAM-4. A Top 100 Variety. The heavy die scratch below the arrow feathers provides the name of this popular variety. This blindingly brilliant example exhibits tremendous mint frost over both sides. Sharply struck and nicely preserved, with minor scuff marks that seem appropriate for the Select Uncirculated grade level.(#87198)

1376 **1890-CC MS63 PCGS.** Sharply struck and minimally toned overall, though a dusting of violet appears at the reverse margins. A few small scuffs and abrasions on the portrait account for the grade. (#7198)

1377 **1890-CC MS64 PCGS.** Softly struck in the centers but well-defined elsewhere. Luminous silver-gray toning covers parts of the fields, while the rims show glints of gold.(#7198)

1378 **1890-CC MS64 PCGS.** Well-defined with a hint of frostiness at the high points. A strongly lustrous and essentially untoned near-Gem from this later Carson City dollar issue.(#7198)

1379 **1890-CC MS64 PCGS.** Warm gold-orange and pink patina graces most of the obverse and the reverse periphery. A well struck and strongly lustrous Choice example of this later Carson City Morgan dollar issue.(#7198)

1380 **1890-CC MS64 NGC.** VAM-3, with prominent recutting on the 90 in the date. This lustrous near-Gem has only light peripheral gold toning on the obverse, but the reverse is luxuriously patinated in ocean-blue, cherry-red, and honey-gold. A few light marks limit the grade.(#7198)

Radiant 1890-CC Morgan Dollar, MS65

1381 **1890-CC MS65 NGC.** Purple, golden-tan, and cobalt-blue toning concentrates at the margins of this radiantly lustrous Carson City Gem. Well struck throughout, including good detail in the hair over Liberty's ear and on the eagle's breast feathers. Some minor marks in the left obverse filed likely prevent an even higher grade. Census: 75 in 65, 3 finer (2/09).(#7198)

Brilliant 1890-CC Dollar, MS65

1382 **1890-CC MS65 PCGS.** This brilliant Gem 1890-CC Morgan silver dollar is entirely untoned, save for tiny dark specks on the reverse. The strike is excellent with strong central and peripheral details on both sides, including virtually full hair detail over the ear. PCGS has graded a mere nine finer examples (2/09).(#7198)

Eye-Appealing Gem 1890-CC Dollar

1383 **1890-CC MS65 PCGS.** This better date Carson City Gem has vibrant luster and only an occasional wisp of golden toning. The strike is bold, and the eye appeal is undeniable. Encapsulated in an old green label holder. PCGS has certified only nine pieces in higher grades (2/09).(#7198)

1384 **1890-CC MS63 Deep Mirror Prooflike PCGS.** Outstanding contrast between the fathomless silver-white mirrors and the thickly frosted devices. Though a handful of scattered abrasions preclude a finer designation, this Select coin remains appealing. (#97199)

1385 **1890-O MS65 PCGS.** Light golden overtones with powerful, swirling luster. This smooth Gem is well-defined with enchanting eye appeal. PCGS has graded 19 finer pieces (1/09).(#7200)

1386 **1890-O MS65 PCGS.** Shining centers are virtually brilliant, while the margins show crescents of gold and orange. Outstanding eye appeal for this O-mint issue, a rarity any finer.(#7200)

1387 **1890-O MS65 PCGS.** VAM-10. A Hot 50 Variety. The "Comet" variety, so named for the interesting die gouges to the right of the date. An appealing Gem, minimally toned save for a dot of reddish-brown below the M of UNUM on the obverse.(#7200)

1388 **1890-O MS65 PCGS.** Aside from the usual striking softness in the centers, this Gem is commendable in every respect. Luminous silver-white surfaces show faint peach accents that stand out in the pillowy luster. PCGS has graded 19 finer examples (2/09). (#7200)

Original, Richly Toned MS66 1890-S Dollar

1389 **1890-S MS66 NGC.** The obverse and reverse surfaces of this amazing Premium Gem have intense mint frost under medium-density toning. The obverse is mostly gold and ivory with splashes of peripheral russet and steel. The reverse is heavily mottled with gold, russet, lilac, sky-blue, sea-green, light yellow, and orange toning. Census: 45 in 66, 1 finer (1/09).(#7202)

1390 **1891-CC MS64 PCGS.** Solidly struck with powerful, swirling luster. Each side is white in appearance, either silver-white on the untoned surfaces or milky cloud-white in the patinated areas. (#7206)

1391 **1891-CC MS64 PCGS.** Brightly lustrous with a solid strike for this later Carson City Morgan dollar issue. Nearly untoned save for a dot of charcoal-gray in the left obverse field.(#7206)

1392 **1891-CC MS64 PCGS.** The design elements are crisply rendered, and the mildly frosted devices create light contrast with the watery fields. A mere handful of minor marks are noted on each side of this appealing near-Gem.(#7206)

1393 **1891-CC MS64 PCGS.** Well struck with tremendous mint frost that radiates from essentially untoned silver-gray surfaces. A handful of small marks on each side prevent a higher grade. (#7206)

1394 **1891-CC MS64 PCGS.** Splashes of burnt-orange, electric-blue, and lavender reside on the lustrous surfaces of this near-Gem. Generally well struck, save for some central area softness. Light marks and grazes preclude Gem classification.(#7206)

Sharp MS65 1891-CC Dollar

1395 **1891-CC MS65 PCGS.** Pretty glimpses of sunset-orange and grayish-silver accent the surfaces on this Gem example. The strike is pleasingly bold throughout, and the eye appeal is its equal. A small straight-line area of dark-gray toning is noted on Liberty's lower neck, but it is undistracting. PCGS has certified 34 coins finer (2/09).(#7206)

Appealing Gem 1891-O Dollar

1396 **1891-O MS65 NGC.** With above-average striking definition in the centers and strong, inviting luster beneath rich patina, this Gem offers incredible eye appeal. Subtle, luminous bands of green-gold, peach-rose, and ocean-blue blend into one another on each side. NGC has graded just two numerically finer examples (1/09). (#7208)

Frosty 1891-O Dollar, MS65

1397 **1891-O MS65 PCGS.** This frosty silver-white Gem shows some tiny dotlike marks in the obverse field, some of which appear to be planchet flaws and others appearing to be minor contact evidence. Liberty's cheek is free of major contact, and the strike is typical. PCGS has never certified a finer example (2/09).(#7208)

1398 **1891-S MS65 PCGS.** Well-defined and brightly lustrous with considerable silver-frost on the high points. A minimally toned example of this popular issue, one that is elusive any finer. (#7210)

Exceptional 1891-S Dollar, MS66

1399 **1891-S MS66 PCGS.** The toning is unusual but delightful, featuring irregular mottled patches of amber, heather, and grayish ice-blue on the obverse. The reverse displays more traditional silver centers with champagne-pink hues that are deepest at the upper rim. A well struck and thoroughly appealing Premium Gem for the toning enthusiasts. Population: 49 in 66, 7 finer (1/09). *From The Jack Lee Estate, Inventory.*(#7210)

1400 **1891-S MS65 Prooflike PCGS.** A delightful prooflike Gem with bold design details and excellent cameo contrast between the fields and devices. This fully brilliant example approaches the finest prooflike grade that PCGS has ever assigned. Population: 20 in 65, 1 finer (2/09).(#7211)

1401 **1891-S MS65 Prooflike NGC.** A razor-sharp Gem that combines moderate mirrors with strong cartwheels. Light silver-blue overtones in the fields with splashes of milky patina. Census: 16 in 65 Prooflike, 0 finer (1/09).(#7211)

1402 **1892-CC—Artificial Toning—ICG. MS60 Details.** Sharply struck with a vibrantly lustrous obverse that shows only hints of patina at the margins. On the reverse, a mix of green-gold, blue, and violet color (including an X shape) seems to float over the surfaces.(#7214)

1403 **1892-CC MS61 PCGS.** Attentively struck with minimal patina. The portrait shows more luster grazes than actual marks, though a handful of abrasions on each side suffice to determine the grade. (#7214)

1404 **1892-CC MS63 PCGS.** Intense mint frost radiates from brilliant, icy-white surfaces—a typical appearance for an Uncirculated Morgan dollar from the Carson City Mint. Sharply struck and typically abraded on the obverse, for the grade. The reverse is nearly blemish-free, and would separately score at least one point higher.(#7214)

1405 **1892-CC MS63 PCGS.** Largely untoned with powerful, swirling luster. This coin is well struck for the issue, though it shows slight striking softness at the highest design elements.(#7214)

1406 **1892-CC MS63 PCGS.** Frosty silver-white with typical light abrasions on the obverse and a much cleaner reverse. A popular collecting grade that keeps this piece at an affordable price level. (#7214)

1407 **1892-CC MS63 PCGS.** Rich red and orange peripheral toning appears on each side, though the patina on the obverse is more limited in scope. Well-defined with impressive luster and few overt abrasions.(#7214)

1408 **1892-CC MS63 PCGS.** Richly toned with subtle, pleasing luster beneath. Faint abrasions are also hidden beneath the deep slate-gray, rouge, and gold patina.(#7214)

1409 **1892-CC MS63 PCGS. CAC.** Well-defined with bright and shining luster. Though the silver-white surfaces show scattered abrasions, the eye appeal holds up. A pleasing later Carson City dollar.(#7214)

1410 **1892-CC MS63 PCGS.** Occasional hints of milky toning scarcely dim the luster of this noteworthy Select example. Well struck with only a handful of wispy abrasions that account for the grade. (#7214)

Flashy Near-Gem 1892-CC Dollar

1411 **1892-CC MS64 PCGS.** This is a flashy, brilliant piece with intense mint frost over both sides. Well struck with crisp definition in the centers and equally sharp peripheral details. The 1892 Carson City issue was not prominently represented in the great GSA sales of the 1960s and 1970s, and near-Gem survivors such as this one are not easily available.(#7214)

Pleasing MS64 1892-CC Dollar

1412 **1892-CC MS64 PCGS. CAC.** Excellent striking definition with whispers of frostiness across the highest design elements, particularly on the reverse. Flashy fields are minimally toned with powerful cartwheels. This penultimate Carson City Morgan dollar issue was not well-represented among GSA pieces compared to many earlier dates.(#7214)

Choice Mint State 1892-CC Morgan Dollar

1413 **1892-CC MS64 PCGS. CAC.** Slight striking softness at the central obverse, though the reverse is well-defined there. Shining luster with minimal patina and only a few stray marks. The 1892-CC is much scarcer than its immediate predecessor, the 1891-CC. In turn, the 1893-CC is more elusive than the 1892-CC. (#7214)

Near-Gem 1892-CC Silver Dollar

1414 1892-CC MS64 PCGS. Well-defined on the reverse with fresh, vibrant luster. Minimally marked for the grade with strong eye appeal, a great example of this penultimate Carson City Morgan dollar issue. Although San Francisco is also associated with the Old West, Carson City coins remain more popular.(#7214)

Crisp 1892-CC Dollar, MS64

1415 1892-CC MS64 PCGS. Partially prooflike fields establish modest contrast with the motifs, especially on the reverse. A well executed strike leaves strong definition on the design elements, including the hair above Liberty's ear, and whispers of barely discernible light tan-beige color occur on the central devices. Minute obverse marks keep from a higher grade.(#7214)

Well-Defined MS64 1892-CC Dollar

1416 1892-CC MS64 PCGS. A well-defined and strongly lustrous near-Gem, minimally toned save for glimpses of silver-gray patina over parts of the obverse fields. This penultimate Carson City Morgan dollar issue was little-represented in the GSA sales, and even lower-grade pieces—much less Choice Mint State examples such as this—are prized.(#7214)

Elusive 1892-CC Dollar, MS64 Prooflike

1417 1892-CC MS64 Prooflike PCGS. Thick mint frost covers the devices, and the fields display tremendous depths of watery reflectivity. Fully struck and nicely preserved, with scattered small abrasions that are magnified by the glassy fields. A scarce issue in fully Prooflike condition, especially at higher grade levels like this. Population: 71 in 64 Prooflike, 10 finer (2/09).(#7215)

Brilliant 1892-CC Morgan, MS64 Deep Mirror Prooflike

1418 1892-CC MS64 Deep Mirror Prooflike NGC. Higher grade Deep Mirror Prooflike dollars rank among the most attractive of all non-proof issues. This example, for instance, has fully brilliant silver surfaces with deeply mirrored fields and satiny devices that combine to create a lovely cameo appearance. Census: 17 in 64 Deep Mirror Prooflike, 1 finer (2/09).(#97215)

1419 1892-S AU50 ICG. Gold-gray patina overall with elements of sage scattered at the margins. Light wear is concentrated largely at the high points, leaving the lightly abraded fields luminous. (#7218)

1420 1892-S AU53 PCGS. Considerable remaining luster despite the light wear across the high points. This minimally toned piece has wispy abrasions that account for the grade.(#7218)

1421 1892-S AU53 NGC. Light golden overtones visit still-lustrous surfaces. Modestly worn at the high points with faint, scattered abrasions that contribute to the grade.(#7218)

1422 1893 MS63 PCGS. Excellent striking definition with smooth silver-white luster. This Select coin shows just a handful of wispy abrasions that account for the grade. A great example of this lower-mintage issue.(#7220)

1423 1893 MS63 PCGS. A faintly toned low mintage Morgan dollar with nicely struck devices and minimally abraded fields. Minor facial marks are all that prevent a finer grade.
From The Mario Eller Collection, Part Four.(#7220)

1424 1893 MS64 PCGS. Well-defined with impressive luster and colorful, eye-catching patina. The obverse offers a dramatic combination of green-gold, sage, blue, and violet shadings, while the reverse exhibits more subtle orange and violet peripheral toning that fades into silver-gray close to the center. The reverse of this low mintage dollar is nearly immaculate, although the right obverse field has an inconspicuous abrasion.(#7220)

1425 1893 MS64 PCGS. Essentially untoned with flashy cartwheel luster in the fields. A few small luster grazes and contact marks are apparent on each side, preventing a higher grade. A low mintage issue that is popular with date collectors, in lieu of a much more expensive '93-S, '93-O, or '93-CC.(#7220)

1426 **1893 MS64 PCGS.** This low-mintage Morgan dollar provides vivacious luster and a bold strike. The centers have a hint of golden toning. Well-preserved save for minor grazes on the left obverse. Housed in a green label holder.(#7220)

1427 **1893 MS64 PCGS.** Crisply detailed with strong, shining luster. Only occasional glimpses of cloud-white patina visit each side. Grand eye appeal for this lower-mintage issue.(#7220)

Pleasing Gem 1893 Dollar

1428 **1893 MS65 PCGS.** The 1893 leads off the low-mintage Philadelphia issues in a three-year "desert" that contains some of the greatest rarities of the series. This shining, minimally toned Gem is pleasingly detailed with only a few faint marks present on each side. PCGS has certified three finer pieces (2/09).(#7220)

1429 **1893-CC—Improperly Cleaned—NCS. Unc Details.** A well struck example of this final-year issue, minimally toned with subdued luster from a past cleaning. Still, with no trace of wear, this remains a highly collectible piece.(#7222)

Coveted 1893-CC Dollar, MS61

1430 **1893-CC MS61 NGC.** The attributes of this Uncirculated specimen include intense mint frost and sharply struck devices. Untoned with a slight distinction noted between mildly frosted devices and watery, semireflective fields. This was the final year of coinage at the Carson City Mint, and a low mintage of 677,000 pieces has helped ensure the key date status of the issue. (#7222)

Well Struck 1893-CC Dollar, MS62

1431 **1893-CC MS62 PCGS.** The bright surfaces of this Carson City representative display just a wisp or two of barely discernible tan-gray color. The design elements are better struck than usually seen, including the centers, areas that are typically weak. Several marks are scattered over each side.(#7222)

Lustrous MS62 1893-CC Dollar

1432 **1893-CC MS62 PCGS.** Each side is immensely lustrous with hints of central golden-tan toning framed by essentially brilliant fields. While the obverse shows numerous wispy abrasions, the only prominent marks on the reverse are clash marks in the right field. Overall, an interesting example of this final CC-mint Morgan dollar issue.(#7222)

Appealing 1893-CC Morgan Dollar, MS62

1433 **1893-CC MS62 PCGS.** Both sides offer flashy luster, though the mirrors as a whole are insufficiently strong for a Prooflike designation. Lightly abraded overall with strong central detail. Considerable frostiness highlights the eagle's feathers. A highly desirable example of this final-year Carson City Morgan dollar issue.(#7222)

Flashy 1893-CC Dollar, MS62

1434 **1893-CC MS62 PCGS.** A glittering, flashy Mint State example from the final year of Morgan dollar production at the Carson City Mint. The obverse is brilliant, while the reverse shows a small amount of golden toning near the lower periphery. Numerous small marks on Liberty's face, the left obverse field, and the reverse fields limit the grade.
From The Mario Eller Collection, Part Four.(#7222)

Impressive 1893-CC Dollar, MS64

1435 1893-CC MS64 PCGS. The intensely brilliant surfaces of this conditionally scarce example are snow-white, with slight reflectivity and splendid cartwheel luster observed in the fields. A handful of minor abrasions are seen on both sides, and a possible counting mark is noted across Liberty's jaw. As with many Carson City Morgan dollars, the design elements are rendered with impressive sharpness of detail, especially over the centers. According to Bowers (1993), this is the third-rarest issue in Mint State of the Carson City series, behind the 1889-CC and the 1879-CC; and also a collectors' favorite as the final CC-mint dollar. PCGS has only certified nine finer examples (2/09).(#7222)

1436 1893-O AU55 PCGS. Lightly abraded overall with modest wear across the well struck high points. This luminous piece is largely pale silver-gray with only occasional glimpses of peripheral gold. (#7224)

1437 1893-O AU58 NGC. Modestly worn on the well struck high points. This strongly lustrous example has vibrant eye appeal for this New Orleans issue of just 300,000 pieces.(#7224)

1438 1893-O MS60 NGC. This low mintage O-mint dollar has full luster and light peripheral apricot patina. Nicely struck, and without obtrusive abrasions.
Ex: Long Beach Signature (Heritage, 2/2001), lot 6374.
From The Mario Eller Collection, Part Four.(#7224)

Lightly Toned 1893-O Dollar, MS63

1439 1893-O MS63 NGC. Light sky-blue, lavender, and gold patina occupies the obverse of this Select O-mint dollar, while the reverse is color-free. The reverse fields are partially prooflike, establishing modest variance with the devices. Typically struck, in that the centers are somewhat weak. Scattered marks define the grade. (#7224)

Elusive Near-Gem 1893-O Dollar

1440 1893-O MS64 PCGS. The 1893-O is the lowest-mintage New Orleans Morgan dollar (300,000 pieces). This issue is scarce in circulated grades and in the lower levels of Mint State. It becomes rare in the better Uncirculated grades.

David Bowers, in his *Silver Dollars & Trade Dollars of the United States*, writes that: "A few bags of 1893-O dollars were paid out at face value from the Cash Room at the Treasury Building from about 1948 to 1955. I have no record of bags of 1893-O being included in the 1962-1964 Treasury releases."

Soft violet-gray and sky-blue patination is joined by orange-gold on the reverse. The design elements are typically struck, revealing softness in the central areas. A few minuscule marks on the lustrous surfaces preclude Gem classification. Population: 91 in 64, 7 finer (2/09).(#7224)

1441 1893-S—Damaged, Bent—ICG. Good 4 Details. Varying levels of gray-gold and orange patina drape each side. This significantly worn example shows several rim cuts at the upper obverse, though the coin's bend is difficult to see in the holder.(#7226)

Interesting 1893-S Dollar, Good 6

1442 1893-S Good 6 ICG. This heavily circulated example has primarily slate-gray surfaces with dusky blue undercurrents. An exception is the eagle's breast, which shows lighter silver-gray color, possibly owing to pocket-piece rub or something similar. A few rim bumps are noted on each side, but there are no singularly mentionable abrasions.(#7226)

1443 1893-S—Improperly Cleaned—NCS. VG Details. The surfaces are chalky-white from cleaning, and peppered with numerous small to medium-sized abrasions on each side. All the major design elements are still fully outlined, though, and the rims are complete. (#7226)

Popular Key-Date 1893-S Morgan, VG10

1444 1893-S VG10 PCGS. Although well circulated, this example has the tiny die dot within the foot of the R in LIBERTY, diagnostic for this rare issue. The diagnostic die line inside the top of the upright of the T in LIBERTY is also present. A slate-gray piece with no relevant marks. Encapsulated in an old green label holder. (#7226)

Pleasing 1893-S VF25 Dollar

1445 1893-S VF25 PCGS. The key date 1893-S is desirable in all levels of preservation. The semibright surfaces of this pleasing VF25 example display hints of luster in the protected areas, along with occasional traces of grayish-tan color. The design elements retain sharp detail, and both sides are minimally marked.(#7226)

Silvery 1893-S Dollar, XF40

1446 1893-S XF40 PCGS. The silver surfaces of this key date Morgan display traces of luster in the protected areas and are visited by whispers of light gray. Relatively strong detail remains on the design features, except for the hair over Liberty's ear and the eagle's breast feathers. This remarkably clean coin will be an excellent addition to a high grade Morgan dollar collection.(#7226)

Sharp 1893-S Morgan, XF40

1447 1893-S XF40 PCGS. CAC. The 1893-S is the unquestioned key to the Morgan dollar series. The business strike mintage of 100,000 pieces (or possibly less, if current estimates prevail) is the lowest of any known issue struck for circulation. This piece is well struck and retains a great deal of detail for the grade. The surfaces have toned to a light brown-gray, with faint rose accents. The only noteworthy mark is a shallow abrasion just above Liberty's head.(#7226)

Reflective 1893-S Dollar, XF45

1448 1893-S XF45 NGC. Much reflectivity radiates from the surfaces of this pleasing silver-white Choice XF key date, and the eye appeal is every bit as generous. The reverse even shows some faint contrast remaining between the fields and devices, and interestingly, the reverse die is rotated about 10 degrees clockwise with respect to the obverse. Relatively unabraded, a good choice for those who prefer their Morgans with little color.(#7226)

Marvelous AU 1893-S Dollar

1449 **1893-S AU50 NGC.** Just the merest touch of a golden tinge appears at the extreme rims on each side; elsewhere, the surfaces are grayish-white with pinkish accents, and deeply reflective. This coin presents absolutely marvelous eye appeal for the assigned grade, a function equally of the relatively light circulation wear, good remaining luster, and minor abrasions consistent with a short stay in circulation. The reverse die is rotated about 10 degrees clockwise with respect to the obverse, a second example from the same consignor. An interesting example, and a wonderful addition to a high-grade set.(#7226)

Popular Key-Date 1893-S Dollar, AU53

1450 **1893-S AU53 PCGS.** Lincoln cent collectors have their 1909-S VDB anchor coin, Mercury dime enthusiasts revel at the mere mention of a 1916-D ten cent piece, and Morgan dollar specialists covet the 1893-S issue. Demand for these special date/mintmark combinations is incessant as they are pursued not only by collectors of the series, but also by investors, general hobbyists, hoarders, and even non-collectors who remember learning of a certain key-date coin many years ago and now have the money to purchase an example.

The current offering is in the grade range most heavily sought by the majority of those seeking an 1893-S dollar; the cost of lesser examples provides an incentive to wait for a finer piece, yet the price tag for high grade specimens increases dramatically and quickly reaches the six-figure mark. This picture-perfect AU53 piece displays ample luster and is free of distractions requiring mention here.(#7226)

1451 **1894 Fine 15 PCGS.** A desirable issue in an infrequently offered grade. This minimally marked example has deep violet-gray color with contrasting gold-gray at the worn zones.(#7228)

1452 **1894 XF45 PCGS.** Lightly worn across the high points with small, scattered abrasions on each side. Pale silver-gray surfaces exhibit undercurrents of blue.(#7228)

1453 **1894 AU53 NGC.** A stone-gray example of this widely pursued low mintage issue. Luster beckons from the borders and devices, and the only relevant marks are relegated to the reverse field near the arrowheads.(#7228)

1454 **1894 AU53 NGC.** Rich silver-blue color overall with glimpses of green-gold at the margins. A lightly worn but strongly appealing representative of this popular lower-mintage Philadelphia issue. (#7228)

1455 **1894 AU58 PCGS.** Well-defined for the issue with strong luster beneath subdued patina. Subtle pink, violet, mauve, and gray-gold tints visit each side.(#7228)

Pleasing MS62 1894 Morgan

1456 1894 MS62 PCGS. Faint tan toning visits this lustrous and low mintage Philadelphia dollar. A minor graze on the cheek, but the fields are smooth, as is the remainder of the portrait. MS62 is perhaps the ideal grade to acquire the 1894, since prices climb rapidly in Select and finer.(#7228)

1457 1894-O MS61 PCGS. Aside from typical striking softness at the high points and a handful of scrapes, this is a pleasing survivor of the issue. Strongly lustrous surfaces are silver-gray save for elements of reddish-orange and violet near the rims.(#7230)

1458 1894-O MS62 PCGS. The obverse shows occasional golden-tan overtones, while the reverse is bright and essentially unpatinated. Excellent appearance for the grade with only a few wispy abrasions precluding Select status.(#7230)

1459 1894-O MS62 PCGS. The pale orange and violet patina that graces the obverse margins appears as deeper color over much of the reverse. Well struck with above-average, pleasing luster, though scattered abrasions affect Liberty's cheek and nose.(#7230)

Lustrous 1894-O Dollar, MS63

1460 1894-O MS63 PCGS. Lustrous surfaces display occasional hints of light gold at the margins. 1894-O specimens are nearly always poorly struck (David Bowers, 2006). The current example exhibits somewhat better definition; for example, the hair above Liberty's ear shows partial detail. A few scattered marks serve to limit the grade.(#7230)

Desirable MS63 1894-O Dollar

1461 1894-O MS63 PCGS. Aside from a touch of the usual striking softness at the high points, this is a well-defined Select example of an elusive O-mint Morgan dollar issue. Brightly lustrous silver-white surfaces show a handful of rim abrasions and several wispy marks on the portrait that contribute to the grade.(#7230)

Attractive 1894-O Dollar, MS64

1462 1894-O MS64 PCGS. For the 1894-O dollar, near-Gem is the highest grade most collectors will ever come across; PCGS has certified only eight pieces finer, and NGC has seen just five better (2/09). Light gold patina concentrates at the margins of this MS64 coin, joined by wisps of electric-blue and lavender at the reverse periphery. Well struck, save for the typical weakness in the centers. Light grazes account for the grade.(#7230)

Satisfying 1894-O Morgan Dollar, MS64

1463 1894-O MS64 PCGS. The 1894-O is a major condition rarity, and even at the modest MS64 grade level PCGS has only certified eight finer examples. The opportunity to acquire a Gem or finer piece is so rare that nearly every collector will be pleased with a Choice example. Carefully selecting a nice quality example for the grade is extremely important. A coin such as the present piece should satisfy nearly any connoisseur.(#7230)

1464 1894-S MS63 PCGS. This Select scarcer date dollar has booming luster and a hint of golden toning. The strike is above-average, and the reverse field has few marks.
From The Mario Eller Collection, Part Four.(#7232)

1465 1894-S MS64 PCGS. An amazing example of the scarce 1894-S at a highly collectible grade level. This piece has all the eye appeal of a brilliant Gem but a few tiny abrasions prevent such a grade. Both sides are fully lustrous with frosty surfaces and no evidence of toning.(#7232)

1466 1894-S MS64 PCGS. Well-defined with strong, swirling luster. Great eye appeal for the grade with little patina save for dots of tan in the fields.(#7232)

Original 1894-S Gem Dollar

1467 1894-S MS65 PCGS. CAC. A fully original Gem with intermingled ivory, russet, violet, and blue toning over frosty mint luster. Both sides are well struck and minimally abraded. Light roller marks are visible on the cheek. PCGS has certified only 11 finer examples of the 1894-S dollar (02/09).(#7232)

1468 **1895-O AU50 ICG.** Ample luster clings to the legends and devices of this key date New Orleans silver dollar. A faintly toned representative with unblemished fields and a few unimportant facial marks.(#7236)

1469 **1895-O AU55 NGC.** This partly lustrous and untoned rare date dollar has attractive surfaces and only a hint of wear on the high points. A worthy example of this challenging New Orleans issue. (#7236)

Deeply Toned 1895-O Dollar, AU58

1470 **1895-O AU58 PCGS.** A vibrant example with rich champagne and gold toning, surrounding by deeper lilac and russet color at the peripheries. The underlying surfaces are frosty with nearly full luster that is only broken on the highest design points. The luster breaks are the only reason that this example should sell for less than five figures.(#7236)

Delightful 1895-O Morgan Dollar, AU58

1471 **1895-O AU58 PCGS.** For the grade, this is an exceptional 1895-O dollar with fully reflective fields and satiny devices. Hints of champagne toning are evident on both sides of this virtual Mint State coin. Only the barest trace of high point friction keeps this from the full Mint State category.(#7236)

Brilliant Near-Mint 1895-O Dollar

1472 **1895-O AU58 PCGS. CAC.** Only a slight trace of highpoint wear on the obverse separates this lovely near-Mint coin from others that are full Mint State. It has brilliant silver surfaces with frosty luster and only a slight number of tiny surface marks, certainly less than usual. Highly desirable and destined for an excellent Morgan dollar collection.(#7236)

1473 **1895-S XF45 NGC.** VAM-4. A Top 100 Variety. The interesting "S Over Horizontal S" variety, although any 1895-S is desirable since the issue is very scarce. This is an untoned and slightly subdued example with moderate wear at the centers but noticeable luster within the wings.(#7238)

1474 **1895-S AU53 NGC.** A lightly worn example with rose-gray and gold toning on the obverse, and variegated steel-green, gold, and olive-gray coloration on the reverse. There are no severe marks on either side. A lightly circulated example of this key date Morgan dollar issue.(#7238)

1475 **1895-S AU53 PCGS.** Light wear is noted largely at the high points, leaving subtle luster in the pale silver-gray fields. Light, scattered abrasions and a few reed marks appear on each side. (#7238)

Elusive 1895-S Morgan Dollar, MS64

1476 **1895-S MS64 PCGS.** Untoned with shimmering luster and a light coating of cloudiness in the fields. The design features are boldly rendered, save for minor softness on the hair detail just above Liberty's ear. Shallow marks on Liberty's neck and jaw, and near her mouth, prevent an even finer grade.(#7238)

1895-S Dollar, MS61 Prooflike

1477 **1895-S MS61 Prooflike PCGS.** The 1895-S is an issue that is elusive in Mint State, especially the higher grades, and one that is also seldom seen with the Prooflike designation. Bowers notes that "the contrast is not strong" on Prooflike coins. This piece has the usual bagmarks expected in the fields and on the device high points for the MS61 level, yet the contrast is perhaps better than expected while still falling short of a Deep Mirror Prooflike label. The silver-white surfaces show just a light tinge of lilac on each side. Population: 9 in 61 Prooflike, 53 finer (2/09).(#7239)

Rare Prooflike Gem 1895-S Dollar

1478 **1895-S MS65 Prooflike NGC.** VAM-4. A Top 100 Variety. The "S Over Horizontal S" VAM, among the more interesting blundered mintmarks in the Morgan dollar series. Of course, any 1895-S is desirable, since only 400,000 pieces were struck and most went directly into Western circulation. Prooflikes are very scarce in all grades, and decidedly rare with Gem preservation. Light roller marks (as made) are seen in the central portions of both obverse and reverse, but these are not immediately apparent to the unaided eye. The fields are bright and well mirrored and each side is mostly brilliant with just the faintest trace of golden color around the margins. Census: 7 in 65 Prooflike, 0 finer (2/09).
Ex: Long Beach Signature (Heritage, 2/2005), lot 10481. (#7239)

Desirable MS67 1896 Dollar

1479 **1896 MS67 NGC.** Despite a mintage of nearly 10 million pieces for the issue, neither NGC nor PCGS has graded an example numerically finer than this Superb Gem (1/09). Brightly lustrous surfaces are minimally toned, save for a dot of deep reddish-tan above the S in PLURIBUS on the obverse. Well-defined and carefully preserved.(#7240)

Alluring MS67 1896 Dollar

1480 **1896 MS67 NGC.** This lustrous, frosty stone-white Superb Gem offers an excellent strike and equal surface quality. Though this issue of nearly 10 million pieces is readily available in most Mint State grades, MS67 pieces are scarce. None finer appear in the combined certified population data (2/09).(#7240)

1481 **1896 MS65 Deep Mirror Prooflike ANACS.** Intensely reflective with strong contrast between the frost of the devices and the gleaming fields. Light silver-gray patina overall with crescents of deeper peach and blue at the upper obverse and lower reverse. (#97241)

1482 **1896-O MS61 PCGS.** Slightly above-average detail with the subtle luster common to this O-mint issue. Few overt abrasions, though numerous wispy marks contribute to the grade. Pale silver-gray centers give way to reddish-orange at the margins. (#7242)

1483 **1896-O MS62 NGC.** This example presents lustrous surfaces with creamy color and relatively minor marks for the assigned grade level. A pleasing Uncirculated example of this scarce issue from the New Orleans Mint.(#7242)

1484 **1896-O MS62 PCGS.** Central weakness on both sides seems to prevent a higher numerical grade to this lustrous dollar. The obverse has light silver-gray surfaces while the reverse has splashes of vivid lemon-yellow toning.(#7242)

1485 **1896-S MS62 NGC.** Light tan toning visits the central obverse of this lustrous and moderately abraded silver dollar. The mintage of the 1896-S and 1897-S are similar, yet the 1897-S is common, while the 1896-S is very scarce in all grades.
From The Mario Eller Collection, Part Four.(#7244)

Challenging MS63 1896-S Dollar

1486 **1896-S MS63 PCGS.** A challenging issue. This example has exceptional luster and a good strike. A dash of toning on the branch denies full brilliance. The reverse is well preserved, and only a few marks on the face prevent a higher third-party assessment. The similar-mintage 1897-S is common in Mint State, unlike the 1896-S, one of the many anomalies of conditional survival within the Morgan dollar series.(#7244)

Lustrous 1896-S Select Dollar

1487 1896-S MS63 PCGS. The silvery surfaces of this Select S-mint Morgan are generally well defined, except for weakness in the centers. Excellent luster is apparent on both sides, though the obverse reveals scattered contacts and grazes that limit the grade. Light roller marks are visible in the central areas.(#7244)

Enticing 1896-S Morgan Dollar, MS64

1488 1896-S MS64 PCGS. A satiny and fully lustrous example with impressive gold and iridescent toning splashed on both sides, this near-Gem has excellent surfaces and only a few minuscule grade-limiting marks. The 1896-S Morgan dollar is a condition rarity with few finer examples certified. PCGS has only graded 54 better pieces in nearly 25 years of coin certification.(#7244)

1489 1897-O MS61 PCGS. A popular New Orleans issue that poses a challenge in Mint State. This unworn example, though moderately abraded, is pleasing with strong luster and only a few overt marks on the central devices.(#7248)

1490 1897-O MS61 PCGS. A satiny Mint State piece with full luster beneath peripheral gold and iridescent toning. The 1897-O dollar is a condition rarity, plentiful enough in circulated grades but elusive in all Mint State grades.(#7248)

1491 1897-O MS62 PCGS. Light peach patina visits the rims, while the centers are generally pale silver-gray. Moderate scattered abrasions on each side contribute to the grade.(#7248)

1492 1897-O MS62 PCGS. Delicate canary-yellow tints hover at the margins of this appealing MS62 example. Strongly detailed for the issue with a relatively clean reverse.(#7248)

1493 1897-O MS62 NGC. A lustrous and nearly untoned representative of this conditionally scarce New Orleans issue. Moderately abraded, and the centers show typical incompleteness.
Ex: FUN Signature (Heritage, 1/2001), lot 7585, which realized $1,610.
From The Mario Eller Collection, Part Four.(#7248)

1494 1897-O MS62 PCGS. Luminous with a slightly dusky appearance owing to pale silver-gray patina that has settled over each side. Curiously few marks for the grade assigned.(#7248)

Lovely 1897-O Morgan, MS63

1495 1897-O MS63 PCGS. Natural light gold and iridescent toning highlights the frosty luster of this Select Mint State piece. Both sides have excellent design definition, stronger than normally seen on the '97-O dollar. PCGS has only certified 48 finer examples of this rarity.(#7248)

Sharply Struck 1897-O Dollar
MS61 Deep Mirror Prooflike

1496 1897-O MS61 Deep Mirror Prooflike NGC. NGC and PCGS do not see many 1897-O Deep Mirror Prooflike coins. In fact, the two services have graded just 23 specimens with this particular finish, mostly in the MS60 to MS62 grade levels. The current MS61 coin displays excellent field-motif contrast, and is sharply struck, including the central areas, which are usually weak on this date. Untoned surfaces possess several light marks and grazes, accounting for the grade.(#97249)

1497 1898-O MS67 PCGS. Well-defined overall and amply lustrous. This carefully preserved Superb Gem has dappled peach and blue patina over much of the obverse, while the reverse shows similar colors only at the periphery. Tied for finest certified by PCGS (2/09).(#7254)

1498 1898-S MS65 PCGS. A solidly struck and essentially untoned Gem. The lustrous surfaces have only small marks that do not interfere with this piece's eye appeal. Housed in a prior-generation holder.(#7256)

1499 1898-S MS65 PCGS. Frosty surfaces show pale golden-tan patina over a portion of the obverse and reverse, intermingled with lighter silver luster. While the 1898-S dollar is a rather plentiful, higher mintage issue, Gem or finer examples are elusive. In fact, PCGS has only certified 62 finer examples (2/09).(#7256)

1500 1898-S MS65 PCGS. Delicate gold-orange and coral-pink peripheral shadings yield to pale silver-white at the lustrous centers. An impressive Gem, well struck overall and highly appealing. (#7256)

Splendid 1899-O Morgan, MS67

1501 **1899-O MS67 PCGS.** A brilliant Superb Gem with impressive luster and exquisite surfaces. The centers are slightly soft in strike, while the often-weak bow of the wreath has excellent detail. By no means a rare issue, it would take an exhaustive search to find one any finer. Population: 85 in 67, 1 finer (2/09).(#7260)

1502 **1899-S MS65 NGC.** A boldly defined Gem with brilliant and frosty silver surfaces and excellent eye appeal created by the bright silver surfaces. Difficult to locate any finer.(#7262)

1503 **1899-S MS65 PCGS.** This solidly struck Gem is untoned and has an amazingly clean reverse. The obverse displays a few small nicks, but none of them are substantial enough to call the MS65 grade designation into question. An attractive, conditionally scarce coin. (#7262)

1504 **1899-S MS65 PCGS.** A lovely, brilliant Gem with great luster and impressive striking definition. A trace amount of milkiness and just a few tiny marks are seen on each side.(#7262)

1505 **1899-S MS64 Prooflike PCGS.** Each side is significantly reflective, though also with cartwheels in the luster. A lightly marked piece that offers great eye appeal overall.(#7263)

Exceptional 1900 Dollar, MS67

1506 **1900 MS67 NGC.** The 1900 Morgan is readily available through MS65, and can even be located in Premium Gem without too much trouble. Specimens in the lofty grade of MS67 are scarce, however. A sharp strike leaves above-average definition on the design features, including the centers, areas that are often weak. Bright, untoned surfaces reveal impeccable preservation. Census: 31 in 67, 0 finer (1/09).(#7264)

1507 **1900-O/CC MS65 PCGS.** VAM-11. A Top 100 Variety. One of the less prominent overmintmarks for the year, but a pleasing and crisply struck example nonetheless. The vibrant silver-white surfaces show only occasional splashes of cloud-white patina. (#7268)

1508 **1900-O/CC MS65 NGC.** VAM-11. A Top 100 Variety. A lustrous Gem that appears brilliant at first glance, although a wisp of peach-gold is present here and there. Crisply struck with smooth fields and only minor contact on the face and neck.(#7268)

1509 **1900-S MS65 PCGS.** Both sides show gold-orange and reddish-tan peripheral toning, though the patina on the reverse hews more closely to the rims. Immensely lustrous and attractive. (#7270)

1510 **1900-S MS65 PCGS.** A lovely Gem with brilliant silver centers surrounded by reddish-brown and steel-blue toning at the obverse periphery. The reverse has just a trace of reddish-brown at the lower border. Lustrous surfaces exhibit generally well struck devices, and are minimally marked.(#7270)

1511 **1900-S MS65 PCGS.** A bold Gem with frosty silver surfaces and exceptional brilliance, accompanied by faint splashes of champagne toning. PCGS has only certified 92 finer examples of this date (2/09).(#7270)

Lustrous, Attractively Toned MS63 1901 Dollar

1512 **1901 MS63 PCGS.** Despite a mintage of nearly 7 million pieces, the 1901 Morgan dollar is difficult to locate in Mint State, especially the in better grades of Uncirculated. Paul Green, in a January 9, 2007 *Numismatic News* article titled "1901 Morgan Value Contrary to Mintage," attempts to explain this discrepancy by asserting that: "The 1901 was destroyed in large numbers in the Pittman Act melting. There is never certainty when it comes to that subject, but the 1901 had to have been melted and in large numbers."

Soft multicolored patination covers the lustrous surfaces of this Select specimen, and a strong strike brings out better-than-usual definition on the design elements. A few minute marks limit the grade to MS63.(#7272)

1513 **1901 Doubled Die Reverse AU53 NGC.** VAM-3. A Top 100 Variety. The most coveted doubled die variety of the Morgan dollar series. The tailfeathers exhibit a wide spread, as do the arrows, the branch, and the eagle's beak. This example has light golden-brown toning and a few minor marks on the portrait. Census: 9 in 53, 20 finer (2/09).(#7302)

1514 **1901-O MS65 NGC.** VAM-1A, R.5. A small die gouge (as made) is seen within the ear, but this VAM is best known for its double set of clashmarks that sometimes (although not in the present case) clearly show n and t clashes near the portrait. Lustrous and crisply struck with only a wisp of golden toning.(#7274)

Splendid Gem 1901-S Silver Dollar

1515 1901-S MS65 PCGS. A splendid Gem example of this conditionally scarce issue from the San Francisco Mint. Strong satiny luster and variegated, obviously original toning enhance the overall visual appeal of this impressive piece. Wispy horizontal roller marks are noted across the center of the obverse, but post-striking blemishes are minimal on both sides.(#7276)

Elusive 1901-S Morgan Dollar
MS63 Deep Mirror Prooflike

1516 1901-S MS63 Deep Mirror Prooflike PCGS. Ex: Naples II Collection. The 1901-S is a much better date in any event, but Deep Mirror Prooflike examples are extremely rare. The present lot would at first glance nearly pass for a true proof. It is virtually untoned and has a good strike. Minor facial marks correspond to the grade. Population: 2 in 63 Deep Mirror Prooflike, 2 finer (2/09).(#97277)

1517 1902 MS66 NGC. Well-defined for the issue with only a trace of weakness at the high points. Brightly lustrous and minimally toned with smooth surfaces.(#7278)

1518 1902-O MS64 NGC. VAM-25, R.5. A Hit List 40 Variety. An early die state without the die crack along the base of the date. This VAM is popular for the double berry on the eagle's branch. Thoroughly lustrous and close to brilliant.(#7280)

1519 1902-O MS64 NGC. VAM-25, R.5. A Hit List 40 Variety. A "Two Olive Reverse" VAM that also has minute die doubling near Liberty's ear. No die crack is present on the date. Lustrous and delicately toned with a good strike and well preserved fields. (#7280)

1520 1902-O MS65 NGC. VAM-25, R.5. A Hit List 40 Variety. Vamworld.com lists the condition census solely as ANACS MS64, PCGS MS63. This is the late die state with cracks along the base of the date. Liberty's eyelid is die doubled, and a double berry is present on the olive branch. Lustrous and only faintly faintly toned with minor central softness and small marks near the eagle's head. (#7280)

1521 1902-S MS64 PCGS. Peach-orange and denim-blue outer bands give way to silver centers. An appealing near-Gem that shows a strong strike and just a handful of tiny abrasions.(#7282)

1522 1902-S MS64 PCGS. Rose and orange shadings dominate the obverse fields, but this near-Gem is essentially untoned elsewhere. Sharply struck with vibrant luster beneath the patina. (#7282)

1523 1902-S MS64 PCGS. Glimpses of golden toning appear at the margins, while the centers remain immensely lustrous silver-white. Well-defined and minimally marked for the grade.(#7282)

1524 1903-O MS64 Deep Mirror Prooflike PCGS. Extraordinary mirrors for an issue that rarely comes with reflective surfaces. This minimally toned near-Gem also offers excellent detail. Population: 31 in 64 Deep Mirror Prooflike, 14 finer (2/09). *From The Burning Tree Collection.*(#97287)

1525 1903-S AU50 ANACS. Lightly worn but largely on the high points, leaving the fields luminous. Blue-green and golden-tan shadings accent the pale silver-gray surfaces.(#7288)

1526 1903-S AU55 NGC. A somewhat muted example with dove-gray color and light circulation wear on the high points of the design. Slight glints of remaining luster cling to the devices. A scarce issue that becomes a semikey date in Mint State.(#7288)

Desirable MS64 1903-S Dollar

1527 1903-S MS64 NGC. The elegant gold-orange and peach shadings that drape each side are more prominent on the obverse. A sharply struck and immensely lustrous near-Gem from this elusive 20th century Morgan dollar issue, minimally marked for the grade. NGC has graded just 46 numerically superior pieces (1/09). (#7288)

Well Struck 1904 Gem Dollar

1528 1904 MS65 PCGS. CAC. Lustrous surfaces are essentially untoned, and exhibit well struck design elements, including most of the detail in the hair over Liberty's ear. A few minuscule grade-consistent marks do not disturb. After the 1904 Philadelphia, New Orleans, and San Francisco issues, no more Morgan dollars were struck until 1921. PCGS has certified just 14 finer examples (02/09).(#7290)

Brilliant Gem 1904 Morgan Dollar

1529 1904 MS65 PCGS. An extremely important date that is rarely seen in Gem quality, and almost never in the finer grades. PCGS has only certified 14 finer pieces (2/09). This Gem has brilliant and highly lustrous silver surfaces with a trace of faint gold toning on the obverse.(#7290)

1530 **1904-S XF45 PCGS.** Light wear crosses each side, though the gold-kissed fields remain highly lustrous. A great example of what would prove to be the last S-mint silver dollar until 1921. (#7294)

Appealing MS63 1904-S Dollar

1531 **1904-S MS63 PCGS.** Glimpses of champagne-pink and olive-gold grace both sides of this lovely coin, with good luster and eye appeal. The 1904-S is well known as a late-series semikey to aficionados, and this piece is extremely attractive for the assigned grade. That grade is determined by a few abrasions well-hidden under the light patina, and by a single dark spot on the lower neck, but they nonetheless fail to perturb.(#7294)

Shining MS64 1904-S Dollar

1532 **1904-S MS64 PCGS. CAC.** Brightly lustrous with only scattered hints of cloud-white patina. The strike is solid overall, with only trifling softness affecting the high points on the obverse. After this issue of just over 2.3 million pieces, San Francisco (and the other mints) would strike no more silver dollars until 1921.(#7294)

1533 **1921-S MS65 PCGS.** Well struck for the issue with just a hint of golden peripheral toning. This smoothly lustrous Gem is minimally patinated elsewhere. PCGS has graded 24 finer pieces (1/09). (#7300)

1534 **1921-S MS65 PCGS.** Strongly struck for the issue with bright luster and interesting eye appeal. With just 24 finer examples graded by PCGS (1/09), a high-end piece that remains in range for many collectors.(#7300)

Satiny MS66 1921-S Morgan

1535 **1921-S MS66 NGC.** The 1921-S is an issue that was formerly little distinguished, if at all, from its P- and D-mint counterparts. In the last couple of decades, however, it has come to the fore as a condition rarity in the higher Mint State grades. This satiny piece has splendid surfaces with plum and gold accents near the rims. A sharp and pleasing Premium Gem.(#7300)

Outstanding MS66 1921-S Morgan Dollar

1536 **1921-S MS66 NGC.** Mint State examples of this mass-produced final-year S-mint are most often poorly struck, with drab luster and numerous surface marks. This exquisitely preserved example defies all those trends, untoned and shining on the obverse with a more satiny appearance on the reverse. NGC has graded only one numerically superior example (1/09).(#7300)

PROOF MORGAN DOLLARS

Impeccable 1878 8 Tailfeathers Dollar, PR66 Cameo

1537 **1878 8TF PR66 Cameo NGC.** VAM-14.8. Blunt upper beak. The key diagnostic here is the doubled spike in front of Liberty's eye and the string of small die chips below it. David Bowers writes in his *Silver Dollars and Trade Dollars of the United States:* "Probably 300 to 500 1878 8 TF Proof dollars were minted. The number is not known, and estimates have ranged from about 250 upwards. Today, Proofs are rare."

NGC and PCGS have certified a couple of hundred or so 1878 8 Tailfeather proof dollars, only about 35 of which are designated Cameos. This Premium Gem Cameo displays whispers of barely discernible gold color at the margins. The design elements are well brought up, including the hair over Liberty's ear and the eagle's breast feathers. Impeccably preserved surfaces reveal just a few minor ticks on the cheek. Light roller marks are visible on the chin. Census: 9 in 66 Cameo, 5 finer (2/09).(#87311)

Colorful PR64 1879 Morgan Dollar

1538 **1879 PR64 PCGS.** An outstanding survivor that surely ranks among the most colorful specimens known for the issue. Peripheral blue-green patina fades through a ring of reddish-orange before fading into a champagne center. The reverse offers highly suggestive contrast. PCGS has certified 34 numerically finer pieces (2/09). (#7314)

Gorgeous 1880 Morgan Dollar, PR64 Cameo

1539 **1880 PR64 Cameo PCGS.** This is a simply gorgeous coin, and a great example of how attractive original toning can be on a Morgan dollar. The central devices are heavily frosted, and just a modicum of gold-orange patina is seen on Liberty's portrait, mainly on some of the hair strands. Meanwhile, wondrously deep electric-blue, purple-rose, and golden-brown toning resides near the periphery on each side. Two or three faint slide marks on Liberty's cheek seemingly preclude a full Gem assessment. Population: 25 in 64 Cameo, 33 finer (2/09).
From The Burning Tree Collection.(#87315)

1540 **1881 PR62 PCGS.** Razor-sharp striking crispness confirms the proof status of this specimen. Murky forest-green, russet-brown, and electric-blue coloration covers both sides. Faint hairlines reduce the grade.(#7316)

Attractive Near-Gem Proof 1881 Morgan Dollar

1541 **1881 PR64 NGC.** Fully struck with lovely, smoky purple-violet toning on both sides and a mild degree of cameo contrast on the obverse, where Liberty's portrait is lightly frosted. One of only 975 pieces struck in the proof format this year. The 1881 Morgan dollar proofs are known to be well produced and attractive, and this near-Gem is no exception.(#7316)

Sharp 1881 Morgan Dollar, PR64

1542 **1881 PR64 PCGS.** Bluish-purple, lavender, and golden-brown patina displays slightly deeper hues on the reverse of this near-Gem proof Morgan. Sharp definition characterizes the design elements, and both sides are nicely preserved. Thin vertical toning streaks are visible on the reverse. Population: 70 in 64, 34 finer (2/09). (#7316)

Brilliant 1881 Morgan Dollar, PR64

1543 **1881 PR64 PCGS. CAC.** Both sides of this near-Gem proof are entirely brilliant with white-silver surfaces. The fields are deeply mirrored around lustrous devices that present pleasing cameo contrast, despite the lack of such a designation on the holder. A large number of proof dollars were struck in 1881, including 975 Morgans and 960 Trade dollars. At least half of those coins still survive today.(#7316)

Exceptional PR66 1881 Morgan Dollar

1544 **1881 PR66 NGC.** The 1881 is easily one of the best-produced proofs in the Morgan series. Survivors seem to be of consistently high quality, and contrasted examples are not uncommon. This piece has remarkably deep mirrors and slight mint frost is seen over the devices, giving the coin a moderate cameo contrast. The coin is mostly brilliant, but there is just a hint of pale golden toning around the margins on each side. Census: 25 in 66, 18 finer (2/09). (#7316)

Golden-Toned 1882 Morgan, PR63

1545 **1882 PR63 PCGS.** An affordable example of this early proof Morgan issue, from a mintage of 1,100 pieces. The surfaces are appealingly golden-toned, and considerable if uncredited contrast appears between the fields and devices. Some minor contact marks and light hairlines in the fields determine the grade, but much appeal is present.(#7317)

Impressive PR65 1884 Morgan Dollar

1546 **1884 PR65 NGC.** Although NGC did not designate this piece Cameo, the lightly frosted devices create moderate contrast against the watery, deeply mirrored fields, especially on the reverse. This boldly struck specimen has only a couple of light hairlines in the fields but is otherwise flawless. Only 875 proofs were struck. Census: 29 in 65, 21 finer (2/09).(#7319)

Moderately Contrasted 1885 Dollar, PR65

1547 **1885 PR65 NGC.** The mintage of the 1885 dollar was 930 pieces. Most were well-produced and strong strikes are the rule, not the exception. This is a mostly brilliant example that has notably deep mirrors in the fields. The devices are moderately frosted and give the coin a near-cameo appearance, a feature that is certainly desirable on a type coin and available here at no premium. (#7320)

Exceptional PR66 Cameo 1885 Dollar

1548 **1885 PR66 Cameo NGC.** While not a rare proof Morgan by any means, the 1885 was a well-produced issue, one that for collectors has the appeal of a type coin from the 1880s. The strike has pinpoint detailing on each side. The mirrors are deeply reflective, and the devices show noticeable frost on the devices that provides the cameo effect. The piece is mostly brilliant on each side, with a slight accent of light golden-brown patina at the peripheries. Near-perfect preservation. Census: 14 in 66 Cameo, 9 finer (1/09). *From The Jack Lee Estate Collection.*(#87320)

Brilliant 1886 Morgan, PR63 Cameo

1549 **1886 PR63 Cameo PCGS. CAC.** Deeply mirrored fields surround the lustrous and frosty silver devices. This delightful proof is mostly brilliant with wisps of champagne toning on each side that does little to mask the splendid cameo contrast. Population: 6 in 63 Cameo, 19 finer (2/09). *From The Burning Tree Collection.*(#87321)

Exquisite 1886 Morgan Dollar, PR67 Cameo

1550 **1886 PR67 Cameo NGC.** Q. David Bowers notes rather tersely about the proofs of 1886 in his *Guide Book of Morgan Silver Dollars*: "Strike is usually decent. Contrast medium to low. Nice 1886 Proof dollars exist, but they are harder to find than certain other dates mentioned up to this point in time." The present piece, both beautifully mirrored in the fields and sharply struck on the richly frosted devices, is a validation of the best in the issue. Exquisitely preserved with faint glimmers of reddish-gold patina visiting parts of the obverse. Census: 6 in 67 Cameo, 1 finer (2/09). (#87321)

1551 **1887 PR64 NGC.** Well struck with an attractive melange of green-gold and violet-blue over each side. The strike is pleasing for the issue, and few disturbances are noted.(#7322)

Impressive PR65 Cameo 1887 Morgan Dollar

1552 **1887 PR65 Cameo NGC.** Only 710 proofs were struck in 1887, and this is one of the finer ones we have seen recently. In addition to razor-sharp definition in the centers, this piece is notably frosted on all the devices on each side, thus the Cameo designation by NGC. Brilliant throughout and deeply reflective in the fields. Census: 9 in 65 Cameo, 16 finer (2/09).(#87322)

Elegant PR65 1888 Morgan Dollar

1553 **1888 PR65 NGC.** Though 1888 proof Morgan dollars can be located without too much trouble through the near-Gem level of preservation, Gem and finer coins are much more elusive. The current PR65 specimen displays some cameolike effects, especially on the reverse. Cobalt-blue, purple, and yellow-gold patina bathes both sides. A handful of unobtrusive obverse slide marks may well preclude an even finer grade. Census: 20 in 65, 18 finer (2/09). (#7323)

Snow-White PR64 Cameo 1888 Silver Dollar

1554 **1888 PR64 Cameo PCGS.** The quicksilver surfaces are snow-white and blindingly mirrored, with good contrast and much appeal. A few slide marks appear on Liberty's cheek, however, and a tiny fleck of dark toning appears near the E in the Latin motto. Other contact is minimal, and the strike is expectedly pleasing. Population: 16 in 64 Cameo, 7 finer (2/09).(#87323)

Scarce PR66 Cameo 1888 Dollar

1555 **1888 PR66 Cameo NGC.** This date is known to specialists as a challenging one because of the lack of high point definition and general absence of cameo contrast. This is generally considered the first year that quality control slipped in the Mint. This is an unusually nice example, however, that shows full definition in the centers and stark cameo contrast between the heavily frosted devices and the deeply mirrored fields. An impressive proof Morgan and a coin the specialist will appreciate. Census: 11 in 66 Cameo, 4 finer (2/09). (#87323)

Appealing 1890 Morgan, PR64

1556 **1890 PR64 PCGS.** Beautifully detailed with prominent mirrors. Only a few faint hairlines are visible beneath the rich gold-orange and blue-green peripheral patina that surrounds the narrow light silver-gray centers. Overall, a remarkably appealing Choice proof. Population: 46 in 64, 39 finer (2/09).(#7325)

Beautiful, Elusive 1890 Morgan Dollar, PR67 Cameo

1557 **1890 PR67 Cameo NGC.** This is a truly beautiful representative of the proof Morgan dollar type. Both sides display profound cameo contrast between showy, frosted devices and dark, deeply reflective fields. There is a slight degree of haze on the reverse, where faint creamy coral accents are noted. The obverse, however, is essentially untoned and nearly free of any cloudiness in the fields, except for a trace amount just behind Liberty's head. This issue had a scant mintage of 590 pieces, one of the lowest in the series. Survivors are especially scarce with the Cameo designation at both services. Census: 12 in 67 Cameo, 5 finer (2/09).(#87325)

Iridescent 1892 Morgan, PR64

1558 **1892 PR64 NGC.** Examination of this near-Gem proof reveals a veritable kaleidoscope of toning, ranging from deep blue to green, gold, gold, rose, and lemon, all intermingled on each side. Among proof Morgans, the 1892 had a high mintage of 1,245 coins, second highest of the entire series and exceeded only by the 1,355 coin mintage of 1880.(#7327)

Starkly Contrasted 1892 Dollar, PR65 Cameo

1559 **1892 PR65 Cameo NGC.** The best explanation for the large mintage (1,245 pieces) of proofs for this year is the introduction of the Barber dime, quarter, and half, and the demand for silver proof sets for this year. Not all are of high quality, as is this piece. The fields are deeply mirrored and establish a "black" background for the chalky-white devices. Just a bit of striking softness is noted over the ear of Liberty. An outstanding high grade type coin. (#87327)

Delightful 1892 Dollar, PR66 Cameo

1560 **1892 PR66 Cameo NGC.** An impressive white-on-black cameo that has a significant amount of mint frost on the devices. The fields, by way of contrast, have deeply reflective mirrors. Thus, the profound (nearly Ultra Cameo) contrast. There are no observable contact marks on either side of this exceptional proof dollar, which is brilliant throughout. The obverse shows some strike softness over the ear, but the reverse is fully defined on the eagle's breast. Census: 28 in 66 Cameo, 19 finer (2/09).(#87327)

Marvelous PR66 Cameo 1893 Dollar

1561 1893 PR66 Cameo NGC. Elegantly frosted central devices are sharply struck. The centers are virtually untoned, while crescents of ultramarine, violet, and champagne are noted at the margins. Notably well-preserved with fantastic eye appeal, among the most desirable specimens imaginable for the issue.(#87328)

Deeply Patinated 1894 Morgan, PR63

1562 1894 PR63 PCGS. Overall detail is pleasing on this lightly hairlined, moderately reflective example, particularly on the reverse. The main attraction for this coin is its patina, universally deep with hushed cerulean and dusky amethyst shadings dominant. A few glimpses of lighter gold-gray appear in the spaces around the eagle.(#7329)

Wonderfully Toned 1894 Morgan Dollar, PR67

1563 1894 PR67 NGC. As with most of the proof mintage from 1894, this piece is fully struck in the centers. The mintage was 972 pieces, and the general quality of proofs is much higher than seen in previous years. This coin appears flawless. Even a loupe reveals no contact marks on either side. Each side is well matched, with rose-gray centers that brighten to pale blue and yellow at the margins. An outstanding proof Morgan.(#7329)

Desirable PR64 Cameo 1894 Dollar

1564 1894 PR64 Cameo NGC. Pleasingly detailed with significant frostiness across the central devices. Though a thin veil of cloud-white patina drapes the fields, the mirrors shine through. Only a handful of faint hairlines on each side preclude an even finer designation. Census: 8 in 64 Cameo, 57 finer (2/09). (#87329)

Exceptional 1895 Dollar, PR68 Cameo

1565 **1895 PR68 Cameo NGC.** The 1895 Morgan dollar has been an object of great desire for many decades, and the mysterious alleged production of 12,000 business strikes, with none ever verified by numismatic experts, has only compounded that desire. The year 1895 has a special cachet all its own. Just as the 1879-CC, 1889-CC, and 1893-CC dollars constitute the "great triumvirate" of key-date CC-mint dollars, so the year 1895 boasts three issues, each incredibly difficult in its own right: the 1895 proof-only dollars; the 1895-O, which is one of the most intriguing and elusive Morgans in Gem condition; and the 1895-S which, while also a condition rarity, is the most available of the three.

Although earlier there was doubt concerning the possible existence of business strike 1895 dollars, Q. David Bowers' most recent utterances on Morgan dollars have shown capitulation on the issue. In the 2006 *Buyer's Guide to Silver Dollars & Trade Dollars of the United States*, third edition, Bowers writes:

> "Called 'the King of Morgan Dollars,' the 1895 is known to me only in Proof or impaired Proof form. I have never seen a business strike. It is believed that the 12,000 reported business strikes of the date represent an accounting entry error, and were never struck, or as mentioned earlier, probably were dated 1894. Recent research indicates the latter scenario is true."

Bowers continues his commentary on the 1895 proof dollars by saying that typical "nice" grades are PR63 through PR65. If that is so, the present PR68 Cameo piece must be put in the category of "marvelous." The silver-white, radiantly mirrored fields and thickly frosted devices verge on an Ultra Cameo designation and, as expected for the Superb Gem level, there is absolutely no visible distraction of even the most minute sort.

While several hundred 1895 proof Morgan dollars still exist today, precious few approach the quality of the present specimen. In PR68 Cameo this piece is one of seven so certified at NGC, and there are four PR68 Ultra Cameos at that service. All of these pieces are tied for numerically finest, with the sole exception of a PR69 Ultra Cameo NGC example (2/09). PCGS has certified a single Deep Cameo in PR68.

See: Video Lot Description(#87330)

Impressive PR66 Cameo 1896 Dollar

1566 **1896 PR66 Cameo NGC.** The 1896 is one of the best-produced dates among later date Morgans. Examples can be located with cameo contrast and strong eye appeal, such as this piece. The fields show illimitable depth of reflectivity and set up a strong contrast against the thickly frosted devices. Light, even golden toning is seen over both obverse and reverse of this exceptional type coin. (#87331)

1567 **1896 PR68 Ultra Cameo NGC.** An exquisite Superb Gem with ice-white motifs and darkly mirrored fields. The contrast easily merits an Ultra Cameo designation. Although a powerful loupe locates a few hair-thin striations, relics of the die preparation, no abrasions are observed. The present piece can be identified by a trio of pinpoint flecks between the AR in DOLLAR.

Only 762 proofs were struck, a reduction of 118 pieces from that of the prior year's proof issue, the famous 1895 silver dollar. According to Q. David Bowers in his monumental *Silver Dollars & Trade Dollars of the United States,* two obverse dies were used to coin proof 1896 dollars, "both with date further left than usual, one with two small die file marks below ear, the other with heavy die polish in [the] ear and curls." On the present piece, both the ear and the recesses of Liberty's hair exhibit a mirrored surface. Therefore, this is the second obverse die referred to in the Bowers reference.

Mintages of Morgan silver dollars declined after 1891 and bottomed out in 1895. 1895 was the only year without Philadelphia business strike production, and also was the only year that the combined mintages at all mints were less than 1 million dollars. It is surprising, then, that business strike emissions soared in 1896. The three mints struck close to 20 million pieces, with nearly 10 million coined at Philadelphia.

It is true that the economy had improved in 1896. But since Treasury vaults contained more than 100 million silver dollars by 1896, none needed to be struck for circulation. One possibility for the heavy coinage of silver dollars was that they were needed to back the issue of 1896 silver certificates (Friedberg-224). 1896 was also an election year, and agitation by the Free Silver movement may have compelled increased government silver purchases. Census: 17 in 68 Ultra Cameo, 3 finer (2/09).(#97331)

Bright, Lightly Toned PR64 1897 Dollar

1568   **1897 PR64 NGC.** The 1897 is sandwiched between the two best-produced dates in the Morgan series, the 1896 and 1898. The 1897 is another well-produced date, but it is not as well represented at the high end. This piece is more akin to a post-1900 proof, with little field-device contrast present. The surfaces are bright and make this a flashy coin. The only defects are a few light hairlines discernible with a magnifier. Just a trace of golden toning is seen over each side.(#7332)

1569   **1898 PR64 NGC.** Deep slate-blue, violet, and sea-green shadings appear when this apparently deep gray specimen is tilted under a light. Only a few faint hairlines appear beneath the toning. (#7333)

Sharp 1900 Morgan Dollar, PR64 Cameo

1570   **1900 PR64 Cameo PCGS.** A watery, nicely contrasted specimen with a touch of haziness overall in addition to olive-gold peripheral accents. Sharply struck throughout, with no contact marks and minimal hairlines. Popular turn-of-the-century issue, scarce with Cameo contrast. Population: 11 in 64 Cameo, 10 finer (1/09). (#87335)

1571   **1902 PR61 NGC.** Orange-gold toning clings to the borders of this lightly hairlined representative. A good strike with only minor merging of detail on the hair above the ear. A scant 777 proofs were struck.(#7337)

Deeply Reflective PR65 1902 Morgan Dollar

1572   **1902 PR65 NGC.** A highly pleasing Gem proof that displays somewhat more field-motif contrast than ordinarily seen on this issue, which usually has a partially polished portrait, rather than cameolike or frosty. Sharply struck on the design features, and devoid of toning and mentionable marks.(#7337)

Pleasing 1903 Morgan Dollar, PR64

1573   **1903 PR64 PCGS.** Only 755 proof Morgan dollars were struck in 1903. The present coin is notable for its sharp strike, which is unusual with this issue. The fields are deeply mirrored, but there is little contrast with the devices. Apparently, the dies were polished in the device areas, as well as the fields. A few handling marks are consistent with the grade.(#7338)

PEACE DOLLARS

1574   **1921 MS65 PCGS.** Rich gold and orange overtones with powerful luster. This Gem shows typical central striking softness, though the peripheral details are pleasingly well-defined.(#7356)

1575   **1921 MS65 PCGS. CAC.** The surfaces of this softly struck first-year Peace dollar are luminous beneath ample silver-gray patina that shows occasional gold and blue elements. Well-preserved on the central devices.(#7356)

1576   **1921 MS65 NGC.** Whispers of olive-tan make occasional visits to the lustrous surfaces of this Gem. Weakly struck in the centers, which is par for the course for this date. Light contact marks and grazes are visible on both sides.(#7356)

1577   **1921 MS65 NGC.** Softly struck as usual in the centers, though the peripheral definition is solid. Subtle blue-green and gold-gray shadings drape the pleasingly lustrous surfaces.(#7356)

1578   **1921 MS65 NGC.** This deeply toned Gem has frosty underlying surfaces with excellent design definition, save for the centers that are always weak on this issue. The surfaces are virtually pristine. (#7356)

1579   **1921 MS65 PCGS.** Slightly weak at the centers as always, but even the central reverse has stronger feather detail than normal for this issue. Both sides are fully brilliant and highly lustrous with exceptional mint frost.(#7356)

1580   **1921 MS65 PCGS.** A highly lustrous Gem with fully brilliant and frosty silver surfaces that are virtually free of distracting marks. Considerable weakness is noted at the centers as usual for this high relief issue.(#7356)

1581   **1921 MS65 PCGS.** An attractive first-year Peace dollar with soft luster and occasional hints of gold-gray peripheral toning. Slight striking softness at the centers is typical for this design. (#7356)

1582   **1921 MS65 PCGS.** Lustrous surfaces display golden-gray patina in the central areas and magenta and steel-blue at the borders. The usual weakness is seen in the centers. A few grade-consistent marks do not disturb.(#7356)

1583   **1921 MS65 NGC. VAM-1G.** Struck from the obverse die used to coin matte proofs. Research by Dr. David Close identified this VAM variety. A lustrous and suitably struck Gem with a lightly toned obverse and medium golden-brown patina on the reverse. Marks are limited to Liberty's neck and the field near the M in UNUM.(#7356)

1584   **1921 MS65 NGC.** Variegated light brown and violet toning rests on the lustrous surfaces of this lovely Gem. Lightly struck on the hair strands around the ear, which is typical for the issue. A handful of minute reverse marks may preclude an even higher grade.(#7356)

1585 **1921 MS65 PCGS.** A bright Gem from the first year of issue, essentially brilliant with above-average detail on the portrait. Only a few small marks on the eagle preclude an even finer designation. (#7356)

1586 **1921 MS65 PCGS.** Boldly struck with icy, grayish-silver surfaces that glow with pleasing satin luster. A paper-thin mark bisects the eagle's back; otherwise, both sides are well preserved. Housed in an early PCGS holder with a pale green label.(#7356)

Exceptional 1921 Peace Dollar, MS66

1587 **1921 MS66 PCGS. CAC.** An exceptional 1921 Peace dollar. The mint luster is bright and thick over each side and there are no mentionable abrasions. Sharply struck overall with uncommonly strong definition in the centers, the surfaces are mostly brilliant with just the slightest hint of light silver-gray color present. (#7356)

Bold Premium Gem 1921 Peace Dollar

1588 **1921 MS66 NGC.** Shades of ocher, olive, and charcoal tinge the otherwise powder-gray surfaces. A couple of minor marks through the center obverse are in keeping with the Premium Gem level, but the bold strike is likely the final determinant, more better-impressed than usual on Liberty's hair and the high points of the eagle's feathers. Interesting and widely spread strike doubling is noted throughout the obverse, most prominently on Liberty's profile. NGC has graded only a half-dozen coins finer (2/09). (#7356)

Frosty 1921 Peace Dollar, MS66

1589 **1921 MS66 NGC.** The collector who desires a fully struck 1921 Peace dollar will necessarily need to locate one of the few proof examples that exist. For everyone else, the present Premium Gem is virtually "all there." It is a frosty example with faint champagne toning and deeper golden peripheries. Census: 101 in 66, 6 finer (2/09).(#7356)

Amazing MS66 1921 Peace Dollar

1590 **1921 MS66 PCGS.** One of the keys to the Peace dollar set in most grades, along with the 1928 and 1934-S. The High Relief 1921 (discounting the ultrarare 1922 High Relief) is actually a one-year subtype, here represented by a dazzling example. The piece is satiny silver-gray with a touch of gold, accented on the obverse rim by sunset-orange. Pay attention to this lot, as most 1921 Peace dollars are not nearly so attractive. PCGS has certified only six coins finer (2/09).(#7356)

1591 **1922-D MS66 NGC.** Brightly lustrous and minimally toned with a hint of frostiness on the central devices. Well-defined for the issue and attractive. NGC has graded just 14 finer pieces (2/09). (#7358)

Exceptional 1922-D Dollar, MS67

Splendid Superb Gem 1922-D Peace Dollar

1592   **1922-D MS67 NGC.** This issue is readily available through the MS65 level, while Premium Gems can be acquired with patience and searching. Coins such as the present example in the lofty grade of MS67, however, are elusive, and anything finer is virtually unobtainable. Slivers of electric-blue, purple, and gold-brown patina cling to the lower obverse and upper reverse rims, and lustrous surfaces are well preserved. The design elements are better struck than ordinarily seen. Among the finest examples of this introductory Denver Mint issue. Census: 14 in 67, 0 finer (2/09). (#7358)

1593   **1922-D MS67 NGC.** Awesome luster beams from this splendid Superb Gem D-mint Peace dollar. Many 1922-D Peace dollars display die breaks, and the current offering is no exception. A circular break extends from the base of Liberty's neck, across the top of the 1 in the date, up through the N of the motto, and finally terminates at the bases of LI in LIBERTY. A smaller die break joins a minuscule rim cud at 8 o'clock on the obverse to the aforementioned break, and the bases of R and Y in LIBERTY are joined by a diagonal crack. An impressive and interesting 1922-D that is also fully struck. Census: 14 in 67, 0 finer (2/09). (#7358)

1594   **1922-S MS65 PCGS.** Soft orange-gold and violet patina is slightly deeper in hue on the obverse of this lovely Gem. Lustrous surfaces exhibit well struck devices, and are minimally marked (2/09). (#7359)

1595   **1922-S MS65 PCGS.** Speckles of sky-blue, purple, golden-orange, and russet pepper highly lustrous surfaces. A well directed strike leaves strong definition on the design elements, and a few scattered light marks are within the confines of the designated grade. PCGS has certified only six coins higher (2/09).(#7359)

1596   **1923 Tail on O MS61 PCGS.** VAM-1C. A Top 50 Variety. The late die state of this well known VAM, similar to photo #2 in the Top 50 reference, where the variety receives a five-star desirability rating. A lustrous example with dusky gold toning, a good strike, and a few moderate marks on the reverse.(#7360)

1597   **1923 MS65 PCGS.** VAM-1O. A Top 50 Variety. The "Bar Wing," which shows a spike-like projection from the top of the eagle's wing, just below the beak. Largely untoned with impressive frostiness to the luster.(#7360)

1598 **1923 MS65 PCGS.** VAM-1A. A Top 50 Variety. The "Whisker Jaw," though the die break at Liberty's jawline looks more like a remora than a whisker. A lustrous Gem with hints of peach peripheral toning. Essentially unpatinated otherwise. (#7360)

Splendid 1923 Peace Dollar, MS67

1599 **1923 MS67 NGC.** Peace dollars of any stripe are elusive at the MS67 level. Although the U.S. Mint at Philadelphia managed to churn out more than 30 million examples of the 1923 Peace, only a scant 100 or so specimens have ever achieved the Superb Gem level at NGC and PCGS combined. This silver-white example offers cartwheel luster more characteristic of a Morgan dollar, with creamy smooth surfaces and essentially no distractions other than a couple of stray abrasions away from the focal areas. Census: 53 in 67, 0 finer (2/09).(#7360)

Radiant 1923 Peace Dollar, MS67

1600 **1923 MS67 NGC.** This radiant Superb Gem has frosty silver luster and exceptional design details, with a hint of the faintest imaginable champagne toning on each side. It is tied for the finest that NGC or PCGS has ever certified, an excellent candidate for the specialist or type collector. Census: 53 in 67, 0 finer (2/09). (#7360)

1601 **1923-D MS65 NGC.** Occasional whispers of light gold attach themselves to the lustrous surfaces of this D-mint Gem. A well struck piece, revealing just a few inconsequential marks. (#7361)

1602 **1923-D MS65 PCGS.** Ex: Larry Shapiro Collection. Whispers of tan-gold make a somewhat greater presence on the obverse of this Gem Peace dollar, where they are joined by a couple of splashes of bluish-violet. An impressive strike sharpens the design features. None of the few minute marks are worthy of individual mention. (#7361)

Fantastic Gem 1923-S Dollar

1603 **1923-S MS65 PCGS.** A fantastically lustrous Gem with a smooth obverse, silver-white with a hint of lemon-gold. Central striking softness has minimal effect on the eye appeal, though two horizontal abrasions on the reverse influence the technical grade. PCGS has certified only three finer pieces (2/09).(#7362)

1604 **1924-S MS64 PCGS.** Well-defined with soft silver-gray patina over lustrous surfaces. The obverse shows a handful of scattered marks, while the reverse displays a small scrape on the eagle's tail. (#7364)

1605 **1924-S MS64 PCGS.** Radiant and essentially untoned with just a touch of satin to the luster. The strike is pleasing, and only a few stray marks are present on the portrait.(#7364)

1606 **1924-S MS64 PCGS.** Light golden overtones cross the horizontal centers of this near-Gem. Vibrantly lustrous with pleasing detail and grand eye appeal. PCGS has graded 74 finer pieces (1/09). (#7364)

1607 **1924-S MS64 PCGS.** A swath of light golden-tan toning traverses the centers of both sides, and lustrous surfaces project well defined design features. Minute contact marks deny Gem status. (#7364)

1608 **1924-S MS64 PCGS.** Bright luster exudes from both sides of this near-Gem, and a better-than-average strike imparts strong delineation to the devices. Freckles of light tan on the reverse are only visible under magnification. A few light grazes barely preclude Gem status.(#7364)

Astounding 1924-S Peace Dollar, MS65

1609 **1924-S MS65 NGC.** The 1924-S is one of several Peace dollar issues that becomes notably elusive at the Gem level, and the captivatingly toned example offered here is the real McCoy. Well-defined central devices and softly lustrous surfaces shine beneath general champagne toning with streaks of deeper golden-green. Census: 64 in 65, 1 finer (2/09).(#7364)

Scarce Gem 1924-S Peace Dollar

1610 1924-S MS65 NGC. This is a better date in the Peace dollar series, one that is quite scarce at the Gem level of preservation. This satiny example displays relatively bold striking definition for the date, with some wispy die striations in the fields and few marks on either side. The pearl-gray coloration is imbued with appealing undertones of rose. Census: 64 in 65, 1 finer (2/09).(#7364)

Lustrous 1925 Dollar, MS67

1611 1925 MS67 NGC. Dapples of olive-green and reddish-gold make occasional visits to this highly lustrous Superb Gem, mostly at the margins of both sides. Well struck, as are most examples of this issue. Nicely preserved surfaces reveal just a few minor obverse grazes, and minute contact marks on the lower left reverse. Census: 48 in 67, 1 finer (2/09).(#7365)

Satiny 1925 Peace Dollar, MS67

1612 1925 MS67 NGC. An impeccable Superb Gem with fully brilliant, untoned silver surfaces and satiny luster. Seldom do any Peace dollars appear so fine, regardless of the rarity (or non-rarity) of the individual issue. The 1925 is one of the common issues but seldom seen in Superb Gem quality. Census: 48 in 67, 1 finer (2/09).(#7365)

1613 1925 Missing Ray MS65 PCGS. VAM-5. A Top 50 Variety. Similar to the more famous 1937-D Three-Legged Buffalo nickel, the dies were lapped to remove clash marks, and the ray above the leg feathers was removed. A lustrous, crisply struck, and attractive Gem with light golden-brown toning. Specialists should note that the page for this variety within the Top 50 book has an inverted photograph (#4). VAM-5 Population: 7 in 65, none finer (1/09).

1614 1925-S MS64 PCGS. Well struck with a degree of radiance to the silver-white fields. Minimally marked for the grade with considerable eye appeal. PCGS has graded just 36 finer pieces (1/09).(#7366)

1615 1925-S MS64 PCGS. Well struck along the borders although slightly weak at the centers, as usual for this lower mintage issue. Light caramel-gold toning visits shimmering surfaces. A faint graze on the cheekbone prevents a higher grade.(#7366)

1616 1926 MS66 NGC. A strongly lustrous and attractively toned Premium Gem. The centers are subtly gold-gray, while champagne-orange and rose colors dominate the margins. Magenta and violet-blue visit the reverse rims.(#7367)

1617 1926 MS66 PCGS. CAC. Silver-white surfaces show little trace of color, but the generous luster is overwhelming in its intensity. A single nick on Liberty's nostril is perhaps all that separates this lovely coin from an even finer grade. Only a single example at NGC has achieved that level (2/09).(#7367)

1618 1926 MS66 PCGS. Delicate green-gold and blue-green patina graces the obverse periphery of this attractive Peace dollar. The luster is vibrant, and the strike is considerably above-average. Only a handful of faint marks appear on the surfaces. Tied for the finest example graded by PCGS (2/09).(#7367)

1619 1926-D MS65 PCGS. CAC. Brightly lustrous silver-white surfaces show no singularly mentionable marks. A well struck example of this popular Denver issue.(#7368)

1620 1926-D MS66 PCGS. The strike is razor-sharp, and the honey-gold and cream-gray obverse toning is attractive. The reverse displays only faint peripheral almond-gold patina. A well preserved and desirable Premium Gem. PCGS has certified a mere eight pieces finer (2/09).(#7368)

1621 1926-S MS65 PCGS. Softly lustrous and well-defined with considerable frostiness to the devices. Surfaces are subtly silver-gray with glimpses of gold and tan in the fields.(#7369)

1622 1926-S MS65 PCGS. The lustrous surfaces of this S-mint representative display occasional whispers of olive-green, somewhat more extensive and deeper on the reverse. Potent luster invigorates both sides, complementing well struck devices. Light surface and rim marks likely preclude an even higher grade.(#7369)

1623 1926-S MS65 PCGS. Delicate golden overtones enliven this slightly satiny Gem. Well-defined with excellent eye appeal. PCGS has graded just 67 finer examples (2/09).(#7369)

Vibrant Gem 1927 Dollar

1624 1927 MS65 PCGS. Beautifully detailed and carefully preserved with gorgeous luster. Silver-gray centers yield to cream-gold at the margins. The obverse is remarkably clean for the grade, and only a small abrasion on the reverse precludes an even finer designation. PCGS has graded five finer examples (2/09).(#7370)

Striking MS65 1927 Dollar

1625 **1927 MS65 PCGS.** Gorgeous swirls of lemon-gold, ice-blue, and rose-red invigorate this lustrous and impeccably preserved Gem. Booming luster further confirms the exemplary quality. A popular low mintage date, housed in a first generation holder. Only five pieces have been graded finer by PCGS (2/09).(#7370)

1626 **1927-D MS64 PCGS.** Satiny luster adorns both sides of this near-Gem, each of which is visited by wisps of olive-green. This sharply struck piece reveals no marks worthy of individual mention. (#7371)

1627 **1927-D MS64 PCGS.** Bright silver-white surfaces are strongly lustrous with few flaws for the grade. A well struck near-Gem that offers considerable eye appeal.(#7371)

Sumptuous 1927-D Peace Dollar, MS65

1628 **1927-D MS65 PCGS. CAC.** The 1927-D is one of the show-stopper pieces in the Peace dollar series in Gem condition or finer, and many collectors accordingly opt out for a nice near-Gem. This MS65 example brooks no compromise, however, with distraction-free silver-white satiny surfaces that have a small complement of plum toning. Abundant brilliant luster radiates from each side. A stunning Gem example.(#7371)

Conditionally Rare 1927-D Peace Dollar, MS65

1629 **1927-D MS65 NGC.** A remarkable Gem with subtle champagne toning over satiny luster on the obverse, and brighter silver luster on the reverse. The '27-D is one of the important condition rarities in the series. This one has a bold strike with excellent obverse and reverse definition. NGC has only certified three finer examples of this issue.(#7371)

1630 **1927-S MS64 NGC.** Freckles of golden-tan, sky-blue, and purple toning gravitate to the margins of this near-Gem Peace dollar. Typically struck, with weak central areas. A scattering of minute marks precludes Gem status.(#7372)

1631 **1927-S MS64 PCGS. CAC.** Whispers of light gold-tan color are slightly more extensive and deeper on the reverse of this S-mint near-Gem. This is a well struck piece, with just a few minuscule surface and rim marks.(#7372)

1632 **1927-S MS64 PCGS.** Over-the-top eye appeal for this semikey issue is a function of the glassy surfaces that are more prooflike than usually seen, with silvery centers accented at the borders by cinnamon and steel-blue tinges. Surface marks are minimal, and they pale in comparison with the overall quality. PCGS has certified only 60 coins finer (2/09).(#7372)

1633 **1927-S MS64 PCGS.** Solidly struck and shining with occasional splashes of green-gold peripheral toning. Silver-white elsewhere with few marks. PCGS has graded 60 finer pieces (2/09). (#7372)

1634 **1927-S MS64 PCGS.** Dazzling luster endows this impressively struck near-Gem S-mint specimen. Minimally marked surfaces display hints of soft champagne color. These attributes add up to provide pleasing eye appeal.(#7372)

Satiny 1927-S Peace Dollar, MS65

1635 **1927-S MS65 NGC. CAC.** Few high grade 1927-S dollars were set aside and this issue is very elusive today in Gem condition. Bright and satiny, the surfaces have a hard, metallic sheen and are virtually unblemished. Some mottled golden-brown color gravitates toward the borders. Census: 69 in 65, 1 finer (2/09). (#7372)

1636 **1928 MS63 PCGS.** Dappled golden-tan patina is joined by splashes of violet on the reverse, and pleasing lustrous surfaces exhibit sharply struck design elements. The presence of some inoffensive grazes precludes a higher grade, nevertheless, this is a highly attractive coin for the grade. Housed in a green label holder. (#7373)

1637 **1928 MS64 PCGS.** An attractive Choice example of this lowest-mintage Peace dollar. Each side is richly toned with colors ranging from tan to wheat-gold and vivid orange, not to mention splashes of green and russet.(#7373)

1638 **1928 MS64 PCGS.** Bright and minimally toned save for hints of silver-gray at the left obverse. A well-defined example of this key issue with only a few luster scrapes on each side.(#7373)

1639 **1928 MS64 PCGS.** The obverse is subtly gold-gray on this lustrous Choice key. The reverse has the color showing more overtly, as well as streaks of ruby and charcoal up and down in the center. (#7373)

1640 **1928 MS64 NGC.** A strong Choice example of this famous low-mintage issue. Delicate gold and pink patina visits otherwise silver-gray surfaces. A handful of reed marks in the fields account for the grade.(#7373)

1641 **1928 MS64 NGC.** Blushes of pastel sun-gold toning adorn this thoroughly lustrous and sharply impressed near-Gem. The 1928 has less than half the mintage of any other Peace dollar issue. *From The Mario Eller Collection, Part Four.*(#7373)

1642 **1928 MS64 PCGS.** Soft champagne and violet coloration graces the lustrous surfaces of this low mintage near-Gem representative, and a decisive strike leaves strong impressions on the design elements. A few minuscule marks prevents a higher grade. (#7373)

Lovely 1928 Peace Dollar, MS65

1643 **1928 MS65 PCGS. CAC.** Faint gray patina covers the lustrous surfaces of this attractive Gem, and a well executed strike leaves strong definition on the design features. A few grade-consistent marks, more so on the obverse, do not detract. PCGS has graded only 11 coins finer, and NGC only two higher (1/09). Housed in a green-label holder.(#7373)

1644 **1928-S MS64 NGC.** A strongly lustrous example with contrasting sides. The obverse shows orange on the portrait with dappled blue and green over the fields, while the reverse is nearly brilliant. (#7374)

1645 **1928-S MS64 PCGS.** Swirling luster with underlying frostiness. This gold-kissed silver-gray example is softly struck but with a bright and pleasing appearance.(#7374)

1646 **1928-S MS64 PCGS.** Bright luster exudes from both sides, each of which displays speckles of light gold-tan color, which is a tad deeper in hue on the obverse. Typical softness in the centers, especially on the reverse. Minuscule marks define the grade.(#7374)

1647 **1928-S MS64 PCGS.** Soft silver-gray luster overall with splashes of green-brown and silver-blue on each side. Well struck for the issue with just a few too many marks for a Gem designation. (#7374)

1648 **1928-S MS64 PCGS.** Minimally toned save for streaks of golden-tan and reddish-orange that run from top to bottom on each side. Brightly lustrous and well struck with just a few small marks on the portrait.(#7374)

1649 **1928-S MS64 PCGS.** Crisply struck and satiny with blushes of medium tan-gold toning. Marks are inconsequential for the grade. TRVST exhibits minor die doubling, as do most 1928-S dollars. (#7374)

1650 **1934-D Doubled Die Obverse Small D AU58 PCGS.** VAM-4, Top 50 Variety. FS-004. Strong doubling is evident on GOD WE, the two right rays, and Liberty's profile. The D mintmark is small. The fourth edition *Cherrypickers' Guide* says: "This VAM is quite rare and in very high demand by specialists." A crescent of smoky golden-tan patina resides on the left third of the obverse, and along the left reverse margin. Nicely defined with considerable luster, and minimal circulation marks.
From The Ed Lepordo Collection, Part Two.(#7376)

1651 **1934-D MS65 NGC. CAC.** Crisply detailed with fresh, vibrant silver-white luster. Hints of frostiness appear on the portrait, which shows a handful of minuscule luster grazes.(#7376)

1652 **1934-D MS65 PCGS.** Frosty with silver-gray toning over much of each side and crescents of gold and reddish-orange near the rims. A minimally marked and enticing Gem.(#7376)

1653 **1934-D MS65 NGC.** Strongly lustrous beneath subtle, pleasing patina. The obverse exhibits delicate gold-gray shadings, while the reverse shows hints of pink and blue with a touch of orange near the rims.(#7376)

1654 **1934-D MS65 PCGS.** Shining and minimally toned, a pleasing Gem example of this Depression-era Peace dollar issue. Solidly detailed central devices show whispers of frost.(#7376)

1655 **1934-D MS65 PCGS.** The obverse has light silver-gray color overall, while the reverse shows dots of deeper brown toning. Frosty and delightful, an intriguing Gem.(#7376)

1656 **1934-D MS65 PCGS.** A solid Gem example of this scarce, late-date Peace dollar. This is an attractive and original coin that displays varying amounts of golden-russet toning over each side with underlying mint luster abundantly evident. Well struck. (#7376)

Lustrous 1934-S Dollar, MS63

1657 **1934-S MS63 PCGS.** The lustrous surfaces of this Select Peace dollar display freckles of gray-tan patina at the margins, which transitions into golden-gray in the central areas, more evident on the reverse. The design elements are well impressed, save for minor softness in the obverse center. Some minute marks define the grade.(#7377)

Delightful MS64 1934-S Dollar

1658 **1934-S MS64 PCGS. CAC.** Enchantingly toned with layers of silver-blue and gold-green mingling on each side, the latter color more present near the rims and outlining the devices. Well struck with soft, pleasing luster beneath the toning. Marvelous visual appeal for a "mere" near-Gem example of this Depression-era issue. (#7377)

Captivating MS64 1934-S Dollar

1659 **1934-S MS64 PCGS.** Impressively lustrous, well-defined for the issue, and strikingly toned. The obverse patina is relatively tame, with gold-orange and powder-blue shadings mostly at the margins, but the reverse has bolder color that introduces violet and cerulean to the mix. One of just over a million pieces minted.(#7377)

Well Struck 1934-S Dollar, MS64

1660 **1934-S MS64 PCGS.** Dappled golden-brown, bluish-gray, and light purple toning races over the lustrous surfaces of this near-Gem, and a well executed strike imparts relatively strong definition to the design features. A few minute marks on each side preclude Gem classification.(#7377)

Lustrous 1934-S Dollar, MS64

1661 **1934-S MS64 PCGS.** Both sides of this near-Gem Peace dollar are awash in potent luster and essentially untoned, save for wisps of nearly imperceptible light tan on the lower obverse. The design features are generally well impressed. A few minute grazes preclude Gem classification.(#7377)

Appealing 1934-S Peace Dollar, MS64

1662 **1934-S MS64 PCGS.** A brilliant and highly lustrous near-Gem. While the strike is a trifle soft on Liberty's hair, as usually seen, the remaining details are boldly impressed. The fields appear remarkably clean for the grade and a careful inspection reveals only minor marks on the devices. An appealing example of this late Peace dollar issue.(#7377)

Exceptional 1934-S Dollar, MS64

1663 **1934-S MS64 PCGS.** Light apple-green patina adorns the lustrous surfaces of this near-Gem Peace dollar, accented with freckles of golden-brown on the obverse. A sharp strike leaves better design detail than ordinarily seen, and both sides are nicely preserved for the designated grade. The 1934-S is the rarest issue in Uncirculated condition (Roger Burdette, 2008).(#7377)

Desirable 1934-S Dollar, MS64

1664 **1934-S MS64 PCGS.** The 1934-S is considered a key-date in the series despite a substantial population. The mintage barely broke the million coin barrier at San Francisco throughout the year. A lustrous example with subtle grayish-lilac toning on both sides and excellent design definition.(#7377)

1665 **1935-S MS65 PCGS.** Three rays below ONE. Only a hint of golden toning visits this lustrous final-year Gem. The portrait is well preserved, while the eagle's wing displays wispy marks, and the left obverse field has a few superficial blemishes.(#7379)

Pleasing 1935-S Dollar, MS66

1666 **1935-S MS66 NGC.** Splashes of medium intensity apple-green, gold, and purple toning visit the upper right obverse border of this Premium Gem, and an exacting strike manifests itself in good detail on the design elements. Pleasing satiny luster adorns both sides, each of which is free of significant marks. Census: 53 in 66, 3 finer (2/09).(#7379)

SACAGAWEA DOLLARS

1667 **2000-P Sacagawea "Wounded Eagle" MS66 PCGS.** FS-901. Two prominent die gouges pass through the eagle's body. A strongly lustrous Premium Gem example of this increasingly popular issue; well defined with untoned surfaces.

'Cheerios' 2000-P Sacagawea Dollar MS66

1668 **2000-P Cheerios MS66 PCGS.** FS-401. The rare and much publicized "Cheerios" variety, which shows greater feather definition on the eagle's tail feathers. Found only on 2000-P Sacagawea dollars included in selected boxes of Cheerios cereal as a Mint promotion. The reverse hub was modified prior to circulation strikes. Well struck and satiny with undisturbed yellow-gold surfaces. Also included is a 2000 Lincoln cent MS65 Red PCGS and the laminated card from the Cheerios box, which once contained both coins.

Also part of the lot is a framed cover page of the January 31, 2000 issue of *Coin World*. Among the four stories is headlined **Jubilant collector finds dollar in Cheerios box.** That collector is the consignor, who undoubtedly became even more jubilant several years later when a rare hub variety was discovered on the Cheerios dollars. The Cheerios box itself is not included.

Listed in the *Cherrypickers' Guide* as FS-C1-2000P-901, but since renumbered by Fivaz-Stanton to avoid confusion with the "Wounded Eagle" FS-S1-2000P-901.(Total: 2 items) (#147231)

PROOF SACAGAWEA DOLLARS

1669 **2000-S Sacagawea PR70 Deep Cameo PCGS.** Gold-on-black surfaces jump out at the observer at certain angles. Pristine surfaces exhibit exquisitely struck devices.(#99598)

1670 **2000-S Sacagawea PR70 Deep Cameo PCGS.** A technically perfect example of this initial proof Sacagawea dollar. Flawless surfaces with absolute contrast and exquisite light golden color. (#99598)

COMMEMORATIVE SILVER

1671 **1893 Isabella Quarter MS64 PCGS.** A Choice Mint State survivor, well struck for the issue with enchanting patina. Zones of blue-green, cerulean, violet, rose-orange, and gold drape each side. (#9220)

1672 **1893 Isabella Quarter MS64 PCGS.** Hints of light tan-gold patina clinging to the reverse margin are the only signs of color on this lustrous commemorative quarter. Both sides are lightly frosted, and exhibit sharply struck design elements. A few trivial marks precludes Gem status.(#9220)

1673 **1893 Isabella Quarter MS65 PCGS.** Each side offers rich watermelon and sapphire peripheral toning. The obverse shows similar, lighter colors at the center, while the reverse is silver-gray in that zone with deeper shadings at the margins compared to the other side.(#9220)

Great Superb Gem 1893 Isabella Quarter

1674 **1893 Isabella Quarter MS67 NGC.** Fully struck and nearly pristine, this is a great Superb Gem example of the Isabella quarter, one of the first commemorative coins ever produced at the Philadelphia Mint. Variegated iridescent toning appears on each side, in shades ranging from orange-gold, rose, and sea-green to purple and electric-blue. Census: 42 in 67, 9 finer (2/09). (#9220)

1675 **1900 Lafayette Dollar MS63 PCGS.** DuVall 3-D. An elusive variety marked by repunching at the AT of STATES on the obverse. Softly lustrous and well struck for the issue with tan-gray toning draping much of the obverse.(#9222)

1676 **1900 Lafayette Dollar MS63 PCGS.** DuVall 1-B. This Select piece shows few overt abrasions, though a number of wispy marks are hidden beneath gold-orange and cloud-white patina. Softly lustrous with dots of deeper crimson near the portrait of Washington.(#9222)

Lovely Choice Mint State 1900 Lafayette Dollar

1677 **1900 Lafayette Dollar MS64 NGC. CAC.** DuVall 1-B. Soft, pleasing luster shines through a mixture of gold and gray on each side, with hints of claret also noted at the rims. The reverse is softly struck as always, though the obverse portraits show considerable hair detail. Minimally marked overall, though the few abrasions present combine to preclude Gem status.(#9222)

Popular 1900 Lafayette Dollar, MS64

1678 **1900 Lafayette Dollar MS64 PCGS.** DuVall 2-C. Our nation's first commemorative silver dollar was a tribute to General Lafayette, a historic figure in this country as well as France. This brilliant near-Gem has frosty luster with a few faint peripheral iridescent splashes. The Choice Mint State grade provides an excellent opportunity to acquire an attractive yet affordable example of this desirable issue. (#9222)

Attractive 1900 Lafayette Dollar, MS64

1679 **1900 Lafayette Dollar MS64 PCGS.** DuVall 1-B. A relatively plentiful Lafayette dollar variety. This example shows mottled golden toning over lustrous silver surfaces. The lightly marked surfaces are typical of most examples at this Choice Mint State grade level. It is an excellent candidate for the value-conscious collector.(#9222)

Pleasing 1900 Lafayette Dollar, MS64

1680 **1900 Lafayette Dollar MS64 PCGS.** DuVall 1-B. The A in DOLLAR leans sharply to the left, diagnostic of the obverse die. This natural and satiny near-Gem has light silver-gray surfaces that are intertwined with ivory toning, the whole accented through wisps of gold and darker patina.(#9222)

Lustrous Gem 1900 Lafayette Dollar

1681 **1900 Lafayette Dollar MS65 PCGS.** Ex: Richard Jewell. DuVall 2-C. There are numerous abrasions on the high points, but in keeping with the Gem rating they are fewer both in number and severity than usually seen. Generous luster proceeds from both sides, with attractive silver-gold coloration and excellent eye appeal throughout. All Lafayette dollars were actually struck from hand-engraved dies on December 14, 1899, the 100th anniversary of the death of George Washington.(#9222)

1682 **1921 Alabama MS65 PCGS.** Light golden-tan and silver-gray shadings mingle on each side of this Alabama Gem. Well struck for the issue with considerable eye appeal. PCGS has graded 69 finer examples (1/09).(#9224)

1683 **1921 Alabama MS66 NGC.** A minimally toned Premium Gem that is well struck save for slight softness on the devices. Pleasingly preserved surfaces are softly lustrous. With just six numerically finer examples known to NGC (1/09), this ranks among the best-preserved examples of this Laura Gardin Fraser issue.(#9224)

1684 **1921 Alabama MS66 NGC.** Russet, cobalt-blue, and purple toning hugs the margins of this lustrous, well preserved commemorative. Nicely struck, except for the usual weakness in the reverse center. Census: 78 in 66, 6 finer (2/09).(#9224)

1685 **1921 Alabama 2x2 MS65 NGC.** Delicate golden overtones visit parts of the obverse, while the reverse has a measure of peripheral tan. A well struck Gem with attractive luster.(#9225)

1686 **1921 Alabama 2x2 MS65 NGC.** Subtle gold and blue shadings drape both sides of this Gem, from the more elusive 2x2 variant of the Alabama design. Well struck for the issue with pleasing luster. (#9225)

1687 **1937 Antietam MS66 PCGS.** Delicate sun-gold toning ensures the originality of this coruscating and evenly impressed Premium Gem. Only trivial surface imperfections are present.(#9229)

1688 **1937 Antietam MS67 PCGS.** Impressive peach, lime-green, and ice-blue shades invigorate this satiny and undisturbed Superb Gem. A handsome example of this popular and low mintage Civil War type.(#9229)

1689 **1937 Arkansas PDS Set MS66 NGC.** A similarly toned and graded set of the popular Arkansas commemorative type. The set includes: **1937,** with much sharper-than-usual striking details, particularly on the obverse, and speckled russet-gold patina over steel-blue surfaces; **1937-D,** crisply detailed and unmarked with a toning scheme similar to its Philadelphia Mint counterpart; and a **1937-S,** well preserved and satiny with somewhat thicker mottled patina than the first two pieces.(Total: 3 coins)

1690 **1939 Arkansas PDS Set MS65 PCGS.** Each example minimally toned with soft, pleasing luster. This low-mintage PDS set hails from the last year of the Arkansas design.(Total: 3 coins)

1691 **1934 Boone MS67 NGC.** Bright luster invigorates the yellow-gold surfaces dappled with freckles of golden-brown, and a well directed strike leaves strong definition on the design elements. A few trivial marks do not disturb. Census: 19 in 67, 1 finer (2/09). (#9257)

1692 **1934 Boone MS67 PCGS.** Deep reddish-gold and apple-green toning gravitates to the right and lower obverse margins, ceding to pale violet and mint-green over the remaining surfaces. A sharp strike, pleasing luster, and impeccable preservation complement the attractive patination. Population: 27 in 67, 1 finer (2/09). (#9257)

1693 **1935/34-S Boone MS66 PCGS.** This low-mintage (2,004 pieces) issue has the addition of the commemorative date 1934 above the words PIONEER YEAR. Splashes of light orange-gold are visible over the lustrous surfaces of this Premium Gem. A sharply struck piece with great eye appeal.(#9264)

1694 **1936 Boone PDS Set MS65 NGC.** Each example has minimally toned centers with varying degrees of peripheral toning. The **1936** shows dots of crimson and forest-green at the lower reverse, the **1936-D** shows more even golden-tan peripheral color, and the **1936-S** shows a combination of the two.(Total: 3 coins)

1695 **1937-S Boone MS67 NGC.** Satiny and well struck with attractive olive-gray and gold toning across both sides. Essentially pristine, except for a single tiny nick in the upper reverse field. (#9272)

1696 **1937 Boone PDS Set MS65 NGC.** The three lustrous Gems in this lot range from near-brilliance to rich golden-tan color. In order from least to most patina, they are the **1937-S,** the **1937,** and the **1937-D.**(Total: 3 coins)

1697 **1938-S Boone MS67 PCGS.** Pastels of multicolored toning are a tad deeper in hue on the reverse of this Superb Gem. Radiantly lustrous surfaces are impeccably preserved, and exhibit sharply struck design features. Population: 30 in 67, 1 finer (2/09). (#9276)

Elusive Superb Gem 1936 Bridgeport Half

1698 **1936 Bridgeport MS67 NGC.** Highly lustrous, with ice-blue color in the fields and light, speckled russet patina on P.T. Barnum's portrait and near the peripheries. This Superb Gem example is fully struck on both sides, an unusual occurrence with this early silver commemorative type. Census: 18 in 67, 1 finer (1/09). (#9279)

1699 **1925-S California MS66 NGC. CAC.** Light silver-blue and lavender-tan shadings embrace each side of this gleaming Premium Gem. A powerfully appealing coin with delightful luster. (#9281)

1700 **1936-D Cincinnati MS66 NGC.** Emerald-green, ruby-red, and autumn-gold dominate the obverse, but reverse toning is limited to light peripheral apricot. Lustrous and well preserved. (#9284)

1701 **1936 Cincinnati PDS Set MS64 NGC.** Each piece has silver-gray centers with varying levels of peripheral toning. Includes the **1936 MS64,** subtly gold-tinged near the rims; the **1936-D MS65,** peach-orange at the periphery with a crescent of blue at the lower right reverse; and **1936-S MS64,** crescents of green-gold at the margins with a dot of deep reddish-orange at the LL in DOLLAR on the obverse.(Total: 3 coins)

1702 **1892 Columbian MS66 NGC. CAC.** Strongly lustrous with a hint of frostiness. Blue and gold-orange peripheral toning gives way to silver-gray over the centers. A graze is noted on the cheekbone. NGC has certified 38 numerically finer pieces (2/09).(#9296)

1703 **1892 Columbian MS66 PCGS.** Remarkably rich ruby-red, aquamarine, and orange-gold envelop this satiny Superb Gem. Splendidly smooth aside from a faint graze on the field near the chin. PCGS has certified just nine pieces finer (1/09).(#9296)

1704 **1936 Delaware MS67 NGC.** Silver-gray centers yield to violet and rust patina at the margins of varying thickness and extension from the rim. Soft, pleasing luster and pleasingly preserved surfaces. NGC has graded just three numerically finer pieces (2/09). (#9301)

1705 **1936 Elgin MS67 PCGS.** Both sides of this exquisite Superb Gem display marvelous luster, with purple and russet toning gravitating to the borders. A sharply struck coin with just a few minuscule contact marks.(#9303)

1706 **1922 Grant no Star MS66 PCGS.** Whispers of champagne-gold patina find their way to the margins of this highly lustrous commemorative half. Both sides are sharply struck and well cared for.(#9306)

1707 **1922 Grant with Star MS63 PCGS.** Luminous and dusky with golden-tan and violet patina over much of each side. This faintly abraded Select example is pleasing for the grade.(#9307)

1708 **1922 Grant with Star MS64 PCGS.** Blushes of rose, tan-orange, and wheat visit each side of this With Star Grant half. Softly lustrous beneath the patina with typical but few marks. (#9307)

1709 **1922 Grant with Star MS64 NGC.** Aside from the usual "bald spot" on Grant's head, this is a well struck near-Gem, minimally toned with subtle luster. A solid example of its popular subtype. (#9307)

Vibrant Gem 1922 Grant With Star Half

1710 **1922 Grant with Star MS65 NGC.** The Grant Memorial commemorative With Star is one of the most elusive issues in the classic series, with a net distribution of just 4,256 pieces. That figure is many multiples lower than the 67,405 No Star examples issued. This vibrantly toned Gem has an arc of amber-gold and ice-blue around the perimeter, with charming accents of saffron and jade on the reverse. Pleasing mint frost covers both sides. There are no mentionable marks, and the strike is razor-sharp.(#9307)

Satiny 1922 Grant With Star Half Dollar, MS65

1711 **1922 Grant with Star MS65 NGC. CAC.** An important rarity created by the mere addition of a star in the coinage die. This piece has the usual satin luster and heavy die polish that is characteristic of genuine pieces. Both sides are mostly brilliant with only a hint of champagne toning and peripheral iridescence. NGC has only certified 48 finer submissions (2/09).(#9307)

1712 **1928 Hawaiian—Improperly Cleaned—NCS. AU Details.** With many Hawaiian halves distributed to non-numismatists, it is unsurprising that a number of them, including the present coin, are now impaired. This oddly bright example has minimal patina with light rub across the highest design elements. Still, an interesting and affordable coin.(#9309)

1713 **1928 Hawaiian—Improperly Cleaned—NCS. AU Details.** Lightly rubbed with minimal patina, the latter resulting from a past cleaning that has left parts of the surfaces hairlined. Still, a readily collectible example of this challenging classic silver commemorative. *From The Pasadena Collection, Part Two.*(#9309)

1714 **1928 Hawaiian—Whizzed—ICG. MS60 Details.** No trace of wear affects the surfaces of this Hawaiian half. The silver-gray luster is unnatural and muted with the porosity common to whizzed examples.(#9309)

Well Defined 1928 Hawaiian Half Dollar, MS64

1715 **1928 Hawaiian MS64 PCGS.** A medley of orange-gold, lavender, violet, and steel-blue bathes the lustrous surfaces of this near-Gem commemorative, and a well executed strike translates into strong definition on the design features, including the tropical beach landscape on the reverse. An occasional inoffensive mark denies Gem status.(#9309)

Extraordinary 1928 Hawaii Half, MS65

1716 **1928 Hawaiian MS65 PCGS. CAC.** An important commemorative issue, the Hawaiian Sesquicentennial half dollar was coined in 1928 to commemorate the 150th anniversary of the discovery of those islands. Captain James Cook is depicted on the obverse and he is credited with discovery of the islands in 1778. This lovely Gem has subtle pink, blue-green, and gold toning over ivory surfaces with full satiny luster. PCGS has only certified 65 finer examples (2/09).(#9309)

1717 **1935 Hudson MS64 NGC.** Occasional hints of gold and pink enliven this otherwise silver-gray near-Gem. Minor abrasions on the whale and ship contribute to the grade.(#9312)

1718 **1935 Hudson MS64 PCGS.** Light silver-gray overall with soft luster and glimpses of gold. Softly struck, as are many examples of this issue, with a few too many marks to qualify as a Gem; still, an appealing survivor.(#9312)

1719 **1935 Hudson MS65 PCGS. CAC.** Green-gold accents appear at the rims, while the rest of the coin is pale silver-blue. An attractive Gem that is housed in a first-generation holder.(#9312)

1720 **1935 Hudson MS65 NGC. CAC.** Gray and tan toning caresses the surfaces of this Gem Hudson half. Slight striking weakness in the centers has minimal effect on the strong eye appeal. (#9312)

1721 **1935 Hudson MS66 PCGS. CAC.** A couple of shades of golden-gray and tan patination dominate both sides of this Premium Gem commemorative, accented with whispers of soft violet and reddish-gold. Sharply struck, with impeccably preserved, highly lustrous surfaces that are devoid of mentionable marks.(#9312)

1722 **1935 Hudson MS66 NGC.** The Hudson commemorative half dollar ranks among the scarce commemorative types, with a mintage of just 10,000 coins, along with eight additional pieces that were reserved for the next annual assay meeting. This gorgeous representative is frosty and immensely lustrous with glimpses of orange-gold peripheral toning. NGC has graded 26 finer pieces (2/09).(#9312)

1723 **1935 Hudson MS66 PCGS. CAC.** Golden-orange and olive-green patina, imbued with wisps of violet, cover the highly lustrous surfaces of this magnificent Premium Gem. Sharply struck, and devoid of mentionable marks.(#9312)

1724 **1924 Huguenot MS66 PCGS.** Satiny with gold-orange peripheral shadings surrounding pale silver-gray centers. A lovely Premium Gem that is carefully preserved. PCGS has graded 38 finer pieces (1/09).(#9314)

1725 **1925 Lexington MS66 PCGS. CAC.** Finely speckled, multicolored toning is seen over each side of this splendid, upper-end coin. The surfaces are also highly lustrous and show no obvious abrasions. (#9318)

1726 **1934 Maryland MS67 NGC.** Impressively lustrous and delicately toned silver-blue with whispers of gold and violet. Fabulous preservation and eye appeal. NGC has graded just three numerically finer examples (1/09).(#9328)

Gorgeous 1921 Missouri Half, MS65

1727 **1921 Missouri MS65 NGC.** A moderately toned Gem with original gold and iridescent patina on both sides. A few abrasions are hidden in the devices and under the toning. Typical flatness on Boone's cheekbone is apparent but all other devices are boldly defined. NGC has only certified 29 finer pieces (2/09). (#9330)

1728 **1921 Missouri 2x4 MS64 PCGS. CAC.** A dusky near-Gem with deep reddish-gold and peach patina over each side. Well struck for the issue, though typical softness is noted at the high points. (#9331)

Deeply Toned Gem 1921 Missouri 2x4

1729 **1921 Missouri 2x4 MS65 PCGS.** Deep shades of cinnamon and russet ring the obverse, while the reverse margin shows glints of amber. The high points of each side are largely free of the distracting contact evidence seen on so many examples, accounting for the Gem grade. PCGS has graded only 23 finer pieces (2/09). (#9331)

Attractive Gem 1921 Missouri 2x4

1730 **1921 Missouri 2x4 MS65 PCGS. CAC.** The silver-gray surfaces are ringed with attractive peripheral accents of amber, russet, and slate-blue on the obverse. The reverse is painted from a more-consistent cinnamon palette. Only light abrasions are noted on the high points. PCGS has certified only 23 pieces in a finer grade (2/09). (#9331)

Lovely Gem 1921 Missouri 2x4

1731 **1921 Missouri 2x4 MS65 NGC.** Shades of mauve and plum grace both sides of this lovely Gem coin, one of the popular keys to the commemorative silver series. The few relevant marks seen are mostly in out-of-the-way locations, and the generous strike and appealing luster more than compensate. NGC has certified only 16 pieces finer (2/09).(#9331)

Elusive 1921 Missouri 2x4 Half, MS65

1732 **1921 Missouri 2x4 MS65 NGC.** This example of the more elusive Missouri half dollar variety shows above-average detail on the portrait's coonskin cap, though the usual weakness obscures the strap across the shoulder of the frontiersman on the reverse. Strongly lustrous surfaces are well-preserved beneath light silver-blue, green-gold, and russet patina. NGC has graded 16 numerically finer coins (2/09).(#9331)

Highly Lustrous MS66 1921 Missouri 2x4 Half

1733 **1921 Missouri 2x4 MS66 PCGS.** The simple Robert Aitken design for the Missouri Centennial commemorative is suggestive of the earliest commemoratives struck by the United States, the Columbia half and Isabella quarter. Other than UNITED STATES OF AMERICA, the dual dates, and the denomination, no other federal statutory inscriptions appear on either side. A small subset of pieces, however, display an extraneous design element: the eponymous 2x4 in the left obverse field.

This subtly shimmering 2x4 Missouri half offers delicate sky-blue patina over much of each side, while partial rings of reddish-tan form a halo around the portrait and similar toning appears over parts of the stars on the reverse. Though the standing frontiersman shows the typical softness at the strap on his back, the devices are pleasingly defined otherwise, and the overall eye appeal is excellent. Neither NGC nor PCGS has graded a finer representative (2/09). (#9331)

1734 **1923-S Monroe MS65 NGC.** Softly lustrous with a slightly above-average strike for this popular issue. Occasional hints of peripheral tan enliven the obverse. NGC has graded 54 finer pieces (1/09). (#9333)

1735 **1923-S Monroe MS65 PCGS. CAC.** This Gem Monroe commemorative offers mottled orange-gold, russet, and blue-green toning across satiny, highly lustrous surfaces. Well struck and free of mentionable surface distractions, as expected for the grade. (#9333)

1736 **1938 New Rochelle MS67 PCGS.** Blushes of sea-green, powder-blue, lavender, beige, and orange patina adorn each side, with the obverse particularly colorful. Highly lustrous and exquisitely struck. The fields display only minimal grazes.
Ex: Palm Beach Signature (Heritage, 11/2004), lot 7825. (#9335)

1737 **1938 New Rochelle MS67 PCGS.** Dusky lemon-gold color visits both sides of this lustrous and sharply struck Superb Gem. What few grazes that show up under magnification are not distracting. (#9335)

1738 **1936 Norfolk MS68 PCGS.** Deep silver-gray toning dominates the centers, while the margins show more lively gold and ruby hues. Well-defined with seemingly impeccable surfaces.(#9337)

Bold 1936-S Oregon Commemorative Half, MS68

1739 **1936-S Oregon MS68 NGC.** Forest-green, crimson, and golden-orange concentrate at the margins of this marvelous commemorative half, leaving the silver-gray centers splashed with golden-orange. Sharply struck devices complement impeccably preserved, lustrous surfaces. Census: 13 in 68, 0 finer (2/09).(#9346)

1740 **1937-D Oregon MS68 NGC.** Well-defined with softly lustrous, nearly pristine surfaces beneath heavy, dappled patina. Blue-green, crimson, tan, and silver-gray are the main colors. NGC has graded only one numerically finer example (1/09).(#9347)

1741 **1938 Oregon PDS Set MS66 to MS67 PCGS. CAC.** All three holders display the CAC seal and have consecutive serial numbers. The set includes: **1938 MS67,** light golden-brown and lime toning; **1938-D MS67,** delicate chestnut and stone-gray patina; and a **1938-S MS66,** dappled sun-gold shadings.(Total: 3 coins) (#9351)

1742 **1939-S Oregon MS67 NGC.** Well-defined with silver-gray centers. The obverse has prominent sage, green, and tan peripheral shadings, while the reverse is little-toned. Census: 81 in 67, 7 finer (1/09).(#9354)

1743 **1915-S Panama-Pacific MS65 PCGS. CAC.** Fully original and highly lustrous with deep lilac-gray and lighter ivory toning on both sides. The strike is bold save for slight shoulder weakness on the obverse and head weakness on the reverse.(#9357)

Sharp 1915-S Panama-Pacific Half Dollar, MS66

1744 **1915-S Panama-Pacific MS66 PCGS. CAC.** Electric-blue, golden-orange, lavender, and silver-gray patina adorns the lustrous, nicely preserved surfaces of this Premium Gem commemorative. The design features exhibit a uniformly sharp strike, enhancing the coin's eye appeal, which is appropriately confirmed by the CAC green label.(#9357)

1745 **1936-D Rhode Island MS67 ★ NGC.** A distinctive and eye-appealing Superb Gem, silver-gray over much of each side with delightful tan-orange and rouge patina at the margins. Smooth and delightful. NGC has graded just three numerically finer pieces (1/09).(#9364)

1746 **1937 Roanoke MS67 ★ NGC. CAC.** An original, wonderfully preserved example of this popular commemorative half. The piece was obviously housed for many years in an original holder of issue, as seen by the distinctive toning configuration on each side. Glowing mint luster underlies the varying intensities of color. (#9367)

1747 **1936 Robinson MS67 NGC.** Exquisitely preserved, particularly on the broad expanses of the portrait. Subtly lustrous surfaces shine through silver-gray patina that cedes to deep indigo and pale gold close to the rims. Census: 26 in 67, 0 finer (1/09).(#9369)

1748 **1935-S San Diego MS67 PCGS.** Low intensity multicolored toning, being somewhat deeper on the reverse, concentrates at the margins of this radiantly lustrous commemorative. Well preserved surfaces exhibit sharply struck design elements.(#9371)

Popular Gem 1926 Sesquicentennial Half

1749 **1926 Sesquicentennial MS65 NGC.** Coruscating luster and splashes of light golden-brown toning ensure the eye appeal of this carefully preserved Gem. The strike is good for the type, although Washington's cheek retains faint planchet chatter. The Sesquicentennial is elusive at the MS65 level and a rarity any finer, with just 16 such pieces known to NGC (1/09).(#9374)

Extraordinary 1926 Sesquicentennial Half, MS66

1750 **1926 Sesquicentennial MS66 NGC.** The 1926 Sesquicentennial half dollar issue (as well as quarter eagle) was struck in a low relief design that was generally poorly received. Examples in Gem or finer grades are elusive, particularly with original color and good eye appeal. This is one such piece, displaying original pastel toning in shades of lilac and lavender on both sides. The eye appeal is over the top, and only under a loupe do a few stray marks appear, as usually seen, on the high points of the portrait. Generous luster proceeds from both sides. Between NGC and PCGS combined, an even two dozen examples of the issue (less duplicates) have been certified at the Premium Gem level, and there are none finer (2/09). An extraordinary coin, surely among the finest aesthetically as well as numerically.(#9374)

1751 **1935 Spanish Trail MS65 PCGS. CAC.** One does not locate many examples of this commemorative issue that display smoothness in the broad, exposed fields. This lustrous, well struck Gem comes about as close as can be expected. Only a few trivial ticks are concealed in the upper obverse. The only other mark is also unobtrusive, occurring in the southeastern corner of Alabama. Hints of light gold color are visible at the margins.(#9376)

1752 **1935 Spanish Trail MS66 PCGS.** Light orange and golden-brown color visits each side of this softly lustrous Premium Gem. Strong eye appeal for this challenging commemorative issue.(#9376)

1753 **1935 Spanish Trail MS66 PCGS.** Luminous silver-gray at the base with occasional hints of blue, pink, and violet intermixed. A well struck Premium Gem that shows no singularly mentionable flaws.(#9376)

1754 **1925 Stone Mountain MS67 PCGS.** An impressive example of this ever popular commemorative issue. The surfaces are essentially brilliant with a narrow crescent of deep golden-green and purple coloration on the lower left obverse margin. Soft violet and yellow-green fill out the remaining areas. Nicely struck, and free of significant marks.(#9378)

1755 **1934 Texas MS67 PCGS.** Silver-gray surfaces yield pleasing luster, and are well preserved. The design elements are well impressed. Population: 37 in 67, 1 finer (2/09).(#9381)

1756 **1936-D Texas MS67 PCGS.** A bold strike brings out the sculptural qualities of this design. Bright and frosty luster with occasional glimpses of sky-blue patina.(#9387)

1757 **1936-S Texas MS67 PCGS.** Both sides are fully lustrous beneath a light dusting of yellow-green toning that assumes deeper hues on the reverse. There are no significant imperfections on the well struck surfaces. Population: 57 in 67, 1 finer (2/09).(#9388)

1758 **1927 Vermont MS66 PCGS.** Golden-brown and navy-blue enrich the borders of this satiny and sharply struck Premium Gem. The fields appear immaculate, and Ira Allen has only minor contact. *Ex: Pleasant Valley Collection (Heritage, 5/2004), lot 11181, which realized $1,868.75.*(#9401)

1759 **1927 Vermont MS66 PCGS.** A highly lustrous example of this often-elusive and popular commemorative half. The gold, olive, and violet toning that covers the obverse appears in concentric rings on the reverse. Well struck and nicely preserved.(#9401)

1760 **1946-S Booker T. Washington MS67 PCGS.** Remarkable sea-green, rose-red, and golden-brown toning adorns this lustrous and exceptionally preserved Superb Gem. Better struck than is customary for the type, with only a hint of planchet striations above the jaw. A lovely piece from the initial year of the six-year Booker T. Washington program. Population: 47 in 67, 0 finer (2/09).(#9406)

Elusive 1947-S Booker T. Washington MS67

1761 **1947-S Booker T. Washington MS67 NGC.** This silver commemorative issue is available through the Gem level of preservation, and can even be located in Premium Gem with some searching. Superb Gems such as the present example are elusive, however, and represent the finest-certified examples. Soft golden-silver patina covers highly lustrous surfaces. Sharply struck and nicely preserved. Census: 15 in 67, 0 finer (2/09).(#9410)

1762 **1949-S Booker T. Washington MS67 PCGS.** Brightly lustrous with minimal patina. Though slight planchet roughness remains on Washington's jaw, the coin is well-defined for the issue. Population: 14 in 67, 0 finer (2/09).(#9418)

1763 **1950 Booker T. Washington MS67 NGC.** Green-gold overall with hints of blue and orange. This outstanding Superb Gem is tied for numerically finest known to NGC or PCGS (1/09). (#9420)

1764 **1952 Washington-Carver MS66 PCGS.** A beautiful array of light colors invigorates the highly lustrous surfaces of this Premium Gem. Minimally marked surfaces have been sharply impressed. (#9434)

COMMEMORATIVE GOLD

1765 1903 Louisiana Purchase/Jefferson MS64 PCGS. Impressively lustrous with considerable flash and a touch of satin. Strongly detailed in the centers and minimally marked for the grade. (#7443)

1766 1903 Louisiana Purchase/Jefferson MS65 NGC. Each side offers shining luster with a distinctly orange-gold cast. A well struck Gem that is carefully preserved with delightful visual appeal. (#7443)

Desirable Premium Gem
Jefferson Louisiana Purchase Gold Dollar

1767 1903 Louisiana Purchase/Jefferson MS66 NGC. CAC. A gorgeous example of this introductory commemorative gold dollar. Lime-green, orange, and yellow-gold luster bathes virtually pristine surfaces. Precisely struck, eye-catching, and a good value relative to the next higher grade. (#7443)

1903 Louisiana Purchase Gold Dollar
Jefferson Portrait, MS66

1768 1903 Louisiana Purchase/Jefferson MS66 PCGS. President Jefferson's cheek is remarkably free of the tiny abrasions that normally plague this issue, and the few stray ticks that are noted are mostly in out-of-the-way places. Some strike softness is noted at the A of PURCHASE—was the die filling in? An appealing example of this popular commemorative issue. (#7443)

Original 1903 Jefferson Gold Dollar, MS66

1769 1903 Louisiana Purchase/Jefferson MS66 NGC. A remarkable Premium Gem with deep orange-gold surfaces and frosty mint luster. This piece has delightful orange toning over part of the reverse, attesting to its originality. Boldly struck from a late state of both dies with peripheral die scaling. (#7443)

1903 Louisiana/Jefferson Dollar, MS66

1770 1903 Louisiana Purchase/Jefferson MS66 PCGS. The first of the commemorative gold dollars, issued for the centennial Louisiana Purchase Exposition in 1903. The present Premium Gem offers bold orange-gold coloration on both sides, with a couple of accents of deeper reddish-brown, although they appear more like natural attractive patina than copper alloy spots. Attractive in any event, and with minimal contact. (#7443)

1771 1903 Louisiana Purchase/McKinley MS63 NGC. A satiny sun-gold representative that has glimpses of peach toning within the crevices of the reverse design. McKinley's cheekbone and jaw are slightly subdued, but the fields are unabraded. (#7444)

1772 1903 Louisiana Purchase/McKinley MS64 NGC. The fields on each side of this yellow-gold piece are flashy with mild reflectivity. Both sides have well-defined central devices. An interesting near-Gem. (#7444)

1773 1903 Louisiana Purchase/McKinley MS66 PCGS. CAC. This lustrous piece has wonderful golden-orange color with tinges of hazel. Tiny die cracks from the rim to peripheral letters are noted on each side. Certified in a green-label holder. (#7444)

1774 1904 Lewis and Clark MS61 NGC. Flashy with generally yellow-gold surfaces. Impressively struck with few marks on the portraits, though wispy abrasions affect the fields. (#7447)

Excellent 1904 Lewis and Clark Dollar, MS64

1775 1904 Lewis and Clark MS64 PCGS. Both sides of this first-year Lewis and Clark dollar show a degree of reflectivity in the honey-tinged lemon-gold fields, though neither obverse nor reverse proves particularly prooflike. Excellent definition with few marks for the grade assigned and noteworthy visual appeal. (#7447)

Appealing Near-Gem 1904 Lewis and Clark Dollar

1776 **1904 Lewis and Clark MS64 PCGS.** A couple of tiny contact marks are noted on the cheeks of both Lewis and Clark, but otherwise this piece is close to a finer grade, with radiant luster and deep, mellow orange-gold coloration. The third gold dollar commemorative, but the first associated with the actual expedition. (#7447)

Vibrant 1904 Lewis and Clark Gold Dollar, MS64

1777 **1904 Lewis and Clark MS64 NGC. CAC.** The luster of this Lewis and Clark gold dollar is surprisingly vibrant, particularly in the lemon-gold obverse fields. The strike is crisp on both portraits, and aside from a handful of tiny marks on the obverse, the surfaces are beautifully preserved. A solid representative of this noted issue. (#7447)

Pleasing 1904 Lewis and Clark Dollar, MS64

1778 **1904 Lewis and Clark MS64 PCGS.** Bright lemon-yellow color with echoes of green-gold in the lustrous fields. The strongly struck central devices show only a handful of wispy marks that contribute to the grade. Despite a cool initial reception, the Lewis and Clark gold dollars are among the most desirable American commemoratives.(#7447)

Captivating MS64 1904 Lewis and Clark Gold Dollar

1779 **1904 Lewis and Clark MS64 PCGS.** Rich yellow-gold color with a substantially above-average strike for the issue. Only a handful of tiny marks on each side preclude a finer designation. Though the historical interest of this design is obvious, sales of this gold dollar were far more modest than its promoter's lofty ambitions. (#7447)

Lovely MS64 1904 Lewis and Clark Dollar

1780 **1904 Lewis and Clark MS64 PCGS.** A shimmering canary-gold Choice gold dollar that displays hints of olive-green near the rims. The strike is sharp, and the few delicate marks fail to distract. The only true double-headed U.S. coin. Although neither Lewis nor Clark are identified, Clark is the man with shoulder-length hair. (#7447)

Choice 1904 Lewis and Clark Gold Dollar

1781 **1904 Lewis and Clark MS64 PCGS.** This flashy Lewis and Clark gold dollar is thoroughly lustrous and features rich pumpkin-gold toning. The fields, especially on the obverse, are mildly prooflike. The strike is bold and only a faint mark near Clark's chin precludes a finer grade. This issue was distributed by Farran Zerbe at the 1905 Lewis and Clark Exposition in Portland, Oregon.(#7447)

Doubled Reverse 1904 Lewis and Clark Dollar, MS65

1782 **1904 Lewis and Clark MS65 PCGS.** The reverse of this example, like the reverse of about half of the examples observed, has distinct doubling at the bottoms of ONE DOLLAR and the tops of most letters in AMERICA. At least two examples in the present auction show identical doubling, proving that it is not a chatter or strike doubled piece, but actually doubling that was in the coinage die. We are unaware of any previous description of such a variety.

These attractive gold dollar coins were struck to commemorate the centennial of Lewis and Clark's famous expedition to map and explore the Northwest. This Gem is highly lustrous and boldly struck, if not quite full on some of the central details. An attractive, carefully preserved example, free of surface distractions. (#7447)

Desirable MS66 1904 Lewis and Clark Dollar

1783 **1904 Lewis and Clark MS66 NGC. CAC.** Generally deep yellow-gold but with strong orange overtones to the fields. The strike is solid, and the surfaces are smooth with powerful luster. This first Lewis and Clark gold dollar issue is rarely encountered any finer; NGC has graded just 24 pieces that qualified as Superb Gems (1/09). (#7447)

Appealing MS66 1904 Lewis and Clark Dollar

1784 **1904 Lewis and Clark MS66 PCGS.** A small affair by the standards of the World's Columbian Exposition and the Louisiana Purchase Exposition, the Lewis and Clark Centennial Exposition, which was held in Portland, Oregon, would be little-remembered today if not for the two commemorative issues struck to celebrate it. The first is represented here by a shining yellow-gold Premium Gem, crisply struck and carefully preserved. PCGS has graded a mere 15 finer examples (2/09). (#7447)

Blazing 1904 Lewis and Clark Gold Dollar, MS66

1785 **1904 Lewis and Clark MS66 NGC.** A blazingly lustrous and scintillating peach-gold representative of this popular issue. As of (2/09), NGC has certified a scant 24 pieces at a higher numerical grade. These Charles Barber-designed commemoratives are the only two-headed coins officially struck by a U.S. mint. Money generated from the sale of 1904 and 1905 Lewis and Clark gold dollars—together with donations for national women's organizations—financed the creation of a large bronze statue of Sacagawea for the Lewis and Clark Centennial Exposition in 1905. The statue proudly stands today in Portland, Oregon's Washington Park. (#7447)

Flashy MS64 Prooflike 1904 Lewis and Clark Gold Dollar

1786 **1904 Lewis and Clark MS64 Prooflike NGC.** Crisp and seemingly flawless definition is observed on the design elements. A small die lump is noted on the reverse field, just below the tip of Clark's nose. The fields display tremendous prooflikeness and just a few wispy, grade-limiting hairlines. Census: 4 in 64 Prooflike, 1 finer (2/09). (#77447)

1787 **1905 Lewis and Clark MS62 NGC.** This Uncirculated example displays lovely olive-green and red-gold coloration. The design elements are sharply struck, and there are only a few stray lines in the fields that limit the grade. The 1905 Lewis and Clark dollar is the most difficult of the small gold commemoratives. (#7448)

1788 **1905 Lewis and Clark MS63 PCGS.** Light yellow-gold surfaces are softly lustrous, and the devices have slightly above-average detail. Minimally marked save for a handful of wispy flaws. (#7448)

1789 **1905 Lewis and Clark MS63 NGC.** This second Lewis and Clark gold dollar issue was a poor seller like the first, and with an estimated net mintage of just 10,000 survivors, it is as popular today is it was not at the time of release. This yellow-gold piece is well struck with pleasing luster and small, wispy abrasions in the fields. (#7448)

Bold 1905 Lewis and Clark Gold Dollar, MS64

1790 **1905 Lewis and Clark MS64 PCGS.** An incredible near-Gem, this orange-gold example of the famous 1905 Lewis and Clark gold dollar has bold design definition, along with hints of pale lilac toning. These pieces were distributed at the Lewis and Clark Exposition, held in Portland, Oregon.(#7448)

Glowing 1905 Lewis and Clark Gold Dollar, MS64

1791 **1905 Lewis and Clark MS64 NGC.** Both sides of this near-Gem commemorative are wrapped in glowing luster, and each possesses sharply struck design features. Yellow-gold surfaces exhibit hints of light tan, and yield a mild "orange-peel" effect at the borders. A few stray, minuscule marks deny Gem classification.(#7448)

Pleasing Gem 1905 Lewis and Clark Dollar

1792 **1905 Lewis and Clark MS65 PCGS.** The fourth commemorative gold dollar issue, the 1905 Lewis and Clark gold dollar was unsuccessful, even by the low standards set by the first three. As a consequence, high-end survivors are elusive today. This pale green-gold example offers a solid strike and pleasing luster. PCGS has graded 71 finer pieces (2/09).(#7448)

Sharp 1905 Lewis and Clark Gold Dollar, MS65

1793 **1905 Lewis and Clark MS65 NGC.** Pale yellow-gold surfaces are flashy, as is often the case for this low-mintage issue. Crisply detailed portraits are carefully preserved. A great Gem example of this ill-fated commemorative issue, which sold even more poorly than its 1904 counterpart. NGC has graded 49 numerically finer examples (2/09).(#7448)

Important 1905 Lewis and Clark Dollar, MS65

1794 **1905 Lewis and Clark MS65 NGC.** The Lewis and Clark gold dollars were not swift sellers, and the tiny fraction of the original mintage actually distributed would disappoint all but the most die-hard optimist. In his *Commemorative Coins of the United States*, Q. David Bowers recounts that contemporary numismatists treated the coins as "anathema," especially after the secondary market prices for the Louisiana Purchase gold dollars fell below the original purchase price. A few high-end examples have survived, however, and this satiny butter-yellow Gem is among them. Well-defined and carefully preserved, it offers outstanding eye appeal. NGC has graded 49 numerically finer examples (2/09).(#7448)

Exceptional 1915-S Panama-Pacific Gold Dollar, MS66

1795 **1915-S Panama-Pacific Gold Dollar MS66 NGC.** The highly lustrous gold surfaces have a wonderful display of yellow and orange color on both sides. The pristine surfaces are exceptional, with few marks to distract the viewer. Although relatively plentiful in Premium Gem quality, few finer examples of this piece have been certified, including just 50 at NGC (2/09).(#7449)

Pristine 1915-S Panama-Pacific Dollar, MS66

1796 **1915-S Panama-Pacific Gold Dollar MS66 NGC. CAC.** Issued in connection with the Panama-Pacific Exposition in San Francisco, this nearly pristine Premium Gem exhibits wonderful lemon-yellow luster with attractive splashes of orange patina. An excellent value within the gold commemorative series. Housed in a former generation holder. NGC has only certified 50 finer piece (12/08). (#7449)

Splendid MS66 1915-S Pan-Pac Gold Dollar

1797 **1915-S Panama-Pacific Gold Dollar MS66 PCGS. CAC.** This is a simply splendid Premium Gem example of one of the most popular and attractive of all the classic U.S. gold commemorative dollar designs. The surfaces have mellowed to deep orange-gold, with tinges of hazel in a couple of the protected areas. Perusal with a loupe reveals only a single small dotlike tick on the worker's cheek. PCGS has certified 47 pieces in finer grades, from the original net distribution of 15,000 coins (2/09).(#7449)

1798 **1915-S Panama-Pacific Quarter Eagle AU58 NGC.** A softly lustrous yellow-gold piece with a touch of rub across the highest design elements. The surfaces are minimally marked with just a few subtle flaws in the reverse fields.(#7450)

Gem 1915-S Panama-Pacific Two and a Half

1799 **1915-S Panama-Pacific Quarter Eagle MS65 PCGS.** This sharply struck and coruscating Gem has apricot-gold toning and only a few inconsequential field grazes. The curious creature on the obverse is a hippocampus, a mythological beast that combines the foreparts of a horse with the body of a sea monster.(#7450)

Flashy 1915-S Pan-Pac Quarter Eagle, MS66

1800 **1915-S Panama-Pacific Quarter Eagle MS66 PCGS.** Among the most popular of the classic gold commemoratives, the 1915-S Panama-Pacific is seldom seen in grades finer than the present Premium Gem. This example offers flashy orange-gold coloration with few abrasions other than a single contact mark on the knee of Liberty. PCGS has graded 19 pieces finer (2/09).(#7450)

Attractive 1915-S Panama-Pacific Quarter Eagle, MS67

1801 **1915-S Panama-Pacific Quarter Eagle MS67 NGC.** A sumptuous Superb Gem that is in a tie for numerically finest certified by NGC or PCGS (2/09). Deep butter-yellow surfaces offer gorgeous, satiny luster, and the strike is substantially above-average. Even close scrutiny fails to turn up any but the most trivial of faults. This commemorative issue, sold on its own for $4 or as part of a variety of sets, did not meet sales expectations and the net mintage amounts to only 6,749 pieces, though later generations of collectors have warmed to the issue and examples in all grades command considerable sums.(#7450)

1802 **Original Holder for Octagonal 1915-S Panama-Pacific 50 Dollar Piece.** No coins are included in this lot. The black box of issue for an Octagonal 1915-S fifty dollar slug. The box is inlaid with purple felt, which bears a six-line legend in gold letters and has an opening for a fifty dollar piece. The cardboard card for the box is also included, and is visible from the octagonal opening of the felt inlay.

Popular 1916 McKinley Dollar, MS67

1803 **1916 McKinley MS67 NGC.** The 1916 McKinley Birthplace gold dollar was the second of what are currently three issues depicting the assassinated leader, with the fourth, his Presidential dollar, slated for release in 2013. This satiny Superb Gem is well-defined with deep peach, orange, and butter-yellow surfaces that are exquisitely preserved. Tied for numerically finest certified by NGC or PCGS (2/09).(#7454)

1804 **1917 McKinley MS61 Prooflike NGC.** Ex: Las Vegas Collection. Well struck and gleaming with only wispy abrasions on the pale lemon-gold surfaces. This is one of just seven Prooflike examples graded by NGC (1/09).(#7455)

1805 **1917 McKinley MS64 PCGS.** Deep orange-gold color prevails on each side, with hints of peach on the obverse and rose on the reverse. A luminous near-Gem that shows few marks overall. (#7455)

1806 **1917 McKinley MS65 PCGS.** Butter-yellow overall with occasional hints of peach. This smooth Gem is well struck overall with excellent visual appeal. An interesting coin.(#7455)

Appealing 1922 Grant No Star Gold Dollar, MS64

1807 **1922 Grant no Star MS64 PCGS. CAC.** Both sides display an intermingling of yellow-gold, mint-green, and peach coloration residing on highly lustrous surfaces. A well executed strike complements these attributes, as do well preserved faces that reveal just a few unobtrusive marks. The CAC label attests to the nice eye appeal.(#7458)

Gem 1922 Grant No Star Dollar

1808 **1922 Grant no Star MS65 NGC.** Seeming deserving a finer grade, this piece shows precious few marks on General Grant's cheek, and the lustrous orange-gold surfaces display to good effect. In the final essence, only the most minuscule field dotlike marks, and one on Grant's forehead, appear to make the difference. A nice coin for the grade.(#7458)

Gorgeous 1922 Grant No Star Dollar, MS66

1809 **1922 Grant no Star MS66 NGC.** A bold and satiny Premium Gem, this Grant gold dollar is extremely well detailed with frosty yellow surfaces. It has remarkable eye appeal and approaches the finest that has ever been certified. NGC has only certified 74 finer submissions of this popular commemorative issue.(#7458)

Sensational 1922 Grant No Star Dollar, MS66

1810 **1922 Grant no Star MS66 PCGS.** A sensational example of the Grant commemorative gold dollar with frosty and highly lustrous yellow-gold surfaces and bold design elements. A few tiny surface marks are evident on each side, strictly consistent with the grade. Highly desirable and attractive.(#7458)

Pristine 1922 Grant No Star Dollar, MS67

1811 **1922 Grant no Star MS67 NGC.** General Grant's cheek is the exposed high point of this tiny gold dollar, and here it is remarkably free of abrasions, the singularly most important criterion for membership in this exclusive Superb Gem grade. The orange-gold coloration and excellent luster are pluses.(#7458)

Flashy MS67 1922 Grant No Star Dollar

1812 **1922 Grant no Star MS67 NGC.** This is a flashy canary-yellow Superb Gem that shows essentially no distracting contact, unlike most examples of this popular issue. This is the finest quality practicably obtainable, as NGC has certified only two coins at the MS68 level and they are likely in quite strong hands. Only one time before, three years ago, have we offered an MS68.(#7458)

Superb Gem 1922 Grant No Star Dollar

1813 **1922 Grant no Star MS67 PCGS. CAC.** The grade, the highest practicably obtainable for the issue, is here determined by the lack of mentionable contact on General Grant's cheek. Pretty orange-gold surfaces also display wonderful luster and eye appeal. The net distribution of the Grant No Star was only 5,000 coins. (#7458)

1814 **1922 Grant with Star MS64 NGC.** Rich butter-yellow color with occasional elements of lighter gold. Well-defined for the issue, even at the often-weak hair at the back of the portrait.(#7459)

Beautiful 1922 Grant With Star Gold Dollar MS67 ★
One of the Finest-Graded Examples

1815 **1922 Grant with Star MS67 ★ NGC. CAC.** The Grant with Star dollar is a well known key issue among earlier commemorative gold issues, partly because of its low mintage of only 5,016 pieces. The obverse star was a deliberate device intended to create a separate variety for collectors. This is the finest example that we have ever seen, with impeccable design definition, immaculate surface preservation, and beautifully variegated toning on both sides. Census: 3 in 67 ★, 1 finer with the ★ (2/09).(#7459)

1816 **1926 Sesquicentennial MS64 PCGS.** Well struck with intense mint luster and beautiful yellow-gold color, this is a fine near-Gem representative of the popular Sesquicentennial quarter eagle. A few tiny nicks are located on each side, but the viewer will need a magnifier in order to see them.(#7466)

1817 **1926 Sesquicentennial MS64 PCGS.** Sharply struck and shining, an attractive near-Gem. Surfaces range from bright sun-yellow near the rims to pale wheat-gold at the centers.(#7466)

1818 **1926 Sesquicentennial MS64 PCGS.** Glowing luster exudes from peach-gold surfaces tinted with hints of light tan. A few minute marks on this well struck piece preclude Gem status.(#7466)

1819 **1926 Sesquicentennial MS64 PCGS.** A vibrant near-Gem with bright lemon-gold luster and a solid strike. Despite a handful of small abrasions, this Sesquicentennial quarter eagle offers amazing eye appeal.(#7466)

1820 **1926 Sesquicentennial MS65 PCGS.** This type is frequently weak on some of the design elements, but this Gem example appears to be fully struck, and a scarce item as such. Intense mint luster gleams over each side, illuminating bright yellow-gold surfaces. Well preserved with minimal marks.(#7466)

1821 **1926 Sesquicentennial MS65 PCGS.** A shining Gem example of this popular and conditionally elusive issue. Bright yellow-gold surfaces exhibit orange undercurrents. Strong visual appeal. (#7466)

Pleasing Gem 1926 Sesquicentennial Quarter Eagle

1822 **1926 Sesquicentennial MS65 PCGS.** Varying stages of yellow-gold, from butter to wheat and sun, enliven each side of this well-defined Gem. The surfaces are virtually untouched save for a single small tick on the obverse scroll that does not jeopardize the grade. A great example of this final classic gold commemorative issue. (#7466)

1823 **1926 Sesquicentennial MS65 NGC.** In 1926, the Philadelphia Mint coined 46,019 Sesquicentennial quarter eagles , the odd pieces being reserved for assay. This frosty Gem has brilliant yellow-gold luster with exceptional surfaces and sharp design elements. (#7466)

1824 **1926 Sesquicentennial MS65 NGC.** This coin offers splendidly lustrous orange-gold surfaces that are remarkably mark-free. A great Gem example of a commemorative issue rarely found as such. (#7466)

1825 **1926 Sesquicentennial MS65 NGC.** Powerful, swirling luster invigorates each side, and a hint of frostiness visits the well-defined high points. A Gem example of this famous condition rarity is a virtual prerequisite for a high-end commemorative gold collection. NGC has certified just 91 numerically finer representatives (2/09). (#7466)

Attractive 1926 Sesquicentennial Quarter Eagle, MS66

1826 **1926 Sesquicentennial MS66 NGC.** Attractive luster envelopes both sides of this Premium Gem commemorative gold dollar, and a decisive strike imparts sharp definition to the design elements. Brass-gold surfaces are laced with hints of mint-green, and reveal just a few unobtrusive grade-consistent marks. Census: 87 in 66, 4 finer (2/09).(#7466)

MODERN ISSUE

1827 **1995-P Olympic/Gymnastics Silver Dollar PR70 Deep Cameo PCGS.** One of 12 perfect specimens for this issue graded by PCGS (2/09). The obverse has gleaming fields and frosted devices, while the reverse shows mirrors only on the clasped hands and the flame, a look that anticipates the reverse proof American Eagles of 2006. (#9717)

MODERN BULLION COINS

1828 **1993-W One-Ounce Gold Eagle PR70 Deep Cameo PCGS.** Technically flawless with absolute contrast between the inky mirrors and the amply frosted devices. One of just 23 pieces assigned the ultimate grade by PCGS (2/09).(#9875)

1829 **American Eagle 10th Anniversary Proof Set Including 1995-W Silver One-Ounce.** The four gold American Eagles in the set, the **one-ounce, half-ounce, quarter-ounce,** and **tenth-ounce** are all valuable in their own right, but the prime attraction is the **1995-W One-Ounce Silver,** low-mintage key to its series. All pieces uncertified in original case of issue but with standard apparent excellent and contrast.(Total: 5 coins)(#9887)

1995-W Silver Eagle, PR67 Deep Cameo

1830 **1995-W Silver Eagle PR67 Deep Cameo ICG.** Profound white-and-black contrast characterizes both sides of this Superb Gem proof. An exacting strike adds to the appeal, as do mark free surfaces. A few minuscule milky spots show up under magnification. The 1995-W, with a mintage of 30,125 pieces, is the key to the silver American Eagle series.(#9887)

Gleaming PR69 Deep Cameo 1995-W One-Ounce Silver American Eagle

1831 **1995-W Silver Eagle PR69 Deep Cameo PCGS.** Astounding black-and-white contrast dominates the eye appeal of this virtually flawless specimen. Even under magnification, this coin's few trivial faults are difficult to spot, particularly within the rich silver-white frost of the central devices. One of just 30,125 proofs struck for the issue.(#9887)

1832 **1999-W Half-Ounce Gold Eagle PR70 Deep Cameo PCGS.** Fabulous black-and-gold contrast between the impeccably mirrored fields and the strongly frosted devices. At an angle, the surfaces take on a butter-yellow cast. Population: 59 in 70 Deep Cameo (1/09).(#9944)

1833 **2006-W 20th Anniversary One-Ounce Gold Reverse Proof PR70 NGC.** A technically flawless example of this distinctive one-off variant with highly polished devices and frosted fields. Artistic and desirable.(#89995)

COINS OF HAWAII

1834 **1847 Hawaii Cent MS62 Brown PCGS.** Medcalf 2CC-2. The most readily available variant of the 1847 cent, offered here in Mint State. Despite the "Brown" designation, the generally mahogany surfaces show significant unturned copper-orange, particularly at the upper left reverse.(#10965)

Attractive 1883 Hawaiian Dime, MS66
The Famous Umi Keneta

1835 **1883 Hawaii Ten Cents MS66 PCGS.** The 1883 one-year type Umi Keneta, or Hawaii one dime, had a reported mintage of 250,000 pieces, but a large number were likely melted when Hawaii became a Territory of the United States. Walter Breen writes in his *Complete Encyclopedia* that the U.S. Treasury at that time decided that the Islands should use American coins. As a result, orders went out to banks and commercial establishments in the Islands ordering withdrawal of all 1883 Hawaiian coins from circulation.

Soft luster resides on both sides of this Premium Gem example, each of which displays a delicate mix of gray, sky-blue, lavender, and yellow-gold patina. A well executed strike leaves virtually complete definition on the design elements. Nicely preserved throughout. Population: 10 in 66, 0 finer (2/09).(#10979)

Sharply Struck 1883 Hawaii Half Dollar, MS63

1836 **1883 Hawaii Half Dollar MS63 PCGS.** Whispers of golden-tan patina visit the obverse of this Select half dollar, joined by blushes of sky-blue, lavender, and olive-gray on the reverse. Lustrous and sharply struck with clean surfaces aside from a small curved granular streak near OF. Encapsulated in a first generation holder. (#10991)

Important 1883 Hawaiian Half Dollar, MS64

1837 **1883 Hawaii Half Dollar MS64 PCGS.** A deeply toned hapalua with bold design elements and excellent luster, all combining to create incredible aesthetic appeal. This desirable piece, like all 1883 Hawaiian silver coins, was struck at the San Francisco Mint, using planchets of U.S. coinage standards. Population: 52 in 64, 10 finer (2/09).(#10991)

1838 **1871 Hawaii Wailuku Plantation One Real Token VF25 NGC.** Medcalf 2TE-2A. The Narrow Starfish variety of this copper one real token. This example has a large reverse die break along the right border, unlike the 2009 *Guide Book* plate coin shown on page 391. The chocolate-brown surfaces are mildly granular, and a loupe reveals a few faint marks from circulation. Struck from rotated dies. (#600503)

WORLD

1839 **(1947) Saudi Arabia One Pound AU58 NGC.** KM-35. Struck in Philadelphia to facilitate oil transactions. Warm yellow-gold surfaces show only the slightest hint of rub and few marks.

ERRORS

Prooflike Lincoln Cent MS63
75% Off Center on a Silver Dime Planchet

1840 **Undated Lincoln Memorial Cent—Struck 75% Off Center on a 90% Silver Type One Dime Planchet—MS63 Prooflike NGC.** 2.5 gm. Struck far off center toward 1:30. Lincoln's nose and forehead is present, as is the lower right corner of his memorial. The unstruck area has a couple of small rim nicks. The fields of the struck portion are highly prooflike, although this piece has been designated as a business strike by NGC.

1984 Cent Struck on a 1984-P Dime MS66

1841 **1984 Lincoln Cent—Double Denomination, Struck on a Roosevelt Dime—MS66 PCGS.** The first three digits of the cent date are clear, as are the first three digits of the dime date, seen on the N in ONE on the reverse. The P mintmark of the dime is also evident. Roosevelt's head is horizontal relative to the Lincoln Memorial. A dramatic and always popular error.
Ex: June Long Beach (Heritage, 6/2005), lot 7315, which realized $1,150.
From The Ed Lepordo Collection, Part Two.

1997 Cent Struck on a 1997-P Dime
A Popular '11-Cent' Error, MS66

1842 **1997 Lincoln Cent—Struck on a 1997-P Dime—MS66 NGC.** The dual-denomination error category has enjoyed a surge in popularity in the past decade. This example, which features an impression from 1997-dated cent dies after beginning as a 1997-P dime, shows light pink and peach patina over carefully preserved surfaces. The obverse shows the dime reverse undertype and vice versa.

1843 **1864 Large Motto Two Cent Piece—Reverse Die Clash With Indian Cent Obverse—MS64 Brown PCGS.** FS-901, previously FS-001.8. A scarce variety, with the reverse die clashed from an Indian cent obverse die. A sharply struck coin, with dappled tobacco-brown, red-gold, and purple toning. Lustrous and nearly blemish-free.

Dramatic 1865 Three Cent Nickel Error, MS61
Flip-Over Double Strike in Collar

1844 **1865 Three Cent Nickel—Flip-Over Double Strike in Collar—MS61 NGC.** At first glance, this faintly gold-toned three cent nickel appears to have been struck from heavily clashed dies. Closer inspection, however, reveals the truth: This coin was struck once and then flipped over within the dies, only to receive a second impression. This appears most clearly at the lower obverse, which shows a second set of dentils and a fragment of the reverse undertype.

Appealing Choice AU 1898 Nickel
Struck on a Foreign Planchet

1845 **1898 Liberty Nickel—Struck on a Foreign Planchet—AU55 NGC.** Foreign planchet not specified, but almost assuredly the Nicaragua five centavos. This example circulated briefly before it was saved. Luminous and softly struck, as expected for the different planchet, with sage and nickel-gold patina across much of each side. Interesting eye appeal.

Rotated in Collar, Double Struck
Buffalo Nickel VG8

1846 **Undated Type Two Buffalo Nickel—Double Struck, Rotated in Collar—VG8 NGC.** This Buffalo nickel rotated approximately 90 degrees counterclockwise between its two strikes within the collar. The top of the Indian's head from the first strike overlaps LIBERTY, and the bison's lower flank from the first blow is seen within the bison's back. Toned pearl-gray with an unblemished appearance.

1943-P Nickel Struck on a
Steel Cent Planchet AU50

1847   **1943-P Jefferson Nickel—Struck on a Cent Planchet—AU50
NGC.** 2.7 gm. Struck on the zinc-plated steel planchets used to
coin cents (and conserve copper) in 1943. The bottom half of
all four date digits are present, and the mintmark is (as expected)
located over Monticello. The planchet appears to be Type Two
with raised rims. A lightly circulated deep silver-gray piece with
minor contact on the portrait and a hint of granularity.

MS63 Red 1980-P Nickel
Struck 20% Off Center on a Cent Flan

1848   **1980-P Jefferson Nickel—Struck 20% Off Center on a Cent
Planchet—MS63 Red PCGS.** Struck off center toward 10 o'clock
with a full date and mintmark. A lustrous orange-gold piece that
shows the expected softness on Monticello, since the flan was
undersized relative to the dies. The cent planchet appears to be
Type One, without a raised rim.

1961 Proof Jefferson Nickel
Struck 30% Off-Center, PR66

1849   **1961 Jefferson Nickel Proof—Struck 30% Off Center—PR66
NGC.** One wonders how this incredible proof coin could have
escaped whatever quality control measures were in place—or
not—at the Mint in 1961. Not only is it a 1961-dated Jefferson
nickel struck 30% off center, but the resulting coin is so large it
is encapsulated in a quarter-sized NGC holder. A coin that poses
more questions than it provides answers; we posit that this may
have actually been a broadstruck coin, struck completely outside of
the collar and therefore larger and thinner than normal. The left
side of the obverse, and correspondingly on the reverse, are off the
flan. Pretty shades of ice-blue and gold appear on both sides of this
no-questions proof.

Roosevelt Dime Struck Off Center
on a Type One Nickel Planchet, MS63

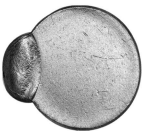

1850   **Undated Roosevelt Dime—Struck Off Center on a Five Cent
Planchet—MS63 ANACS.** The Type One planchet was intended
for Jefferson nickel dies, but ended up instead between dime dies. It
was struck approximately 80% off center toward 7:30, with only a
portion of the back of Roosevelt's head visible. The strike is uniface
obverse.

1851   **Undated Silver Roosevelt Dime—Obverse Obscured, Finned
Rim—PR64 PCGS.** An interesting error that shows only the ghost
of Roosevelt's portrait on the obverse but a characteristically sharp
reverse that does not show a mintmark; hence, the assumption of
a 1950-1964 Philadelphia origin and silver content. The lower
obverse and corresponding upper reverse rim shows a jagged rim
instead of the traditional squared edge.

1954 Franklin Half Struck on
Silver Quarter Planchet, MS63

1852   **1954 Franklin Half Dollar—Struck on Silver Quarter Planchet—
MS63 PCGS.** Well-centered overall with a full date and nearly all
of Franklin's profile and the Liberty Bell visible. Wrong planchet
errors are always popular, and this is an opportunity to acquire an
obsolete silver type. Light golden toning is seen over each side,
with good underlying mint luster.

80% Off Center Kennedy Half, MS63
Struck on a Type One Quarter Planchet

1853   **Undated Kennedy Half—Struck 80% Off Center on a Type One
Quarter Planchet—MS63 PCGS.** Struck widely off-center toward
6 o'clock. The BE in LIBERTY and HALF DO are present, as are
portions of Kennedy's hair and the eagle's tail. Struck on a quarter
planchet that missed the upsetting process to create the rim.
Ex: Central States Signature (Heritage, 4/2006), lot 5370.

1854 **1979-P Anthony Dollar—Struck on Quarter Planchet—MS63 NGC.** 5.7 gm. A lustrous first-year Anthony dollar with light peripheral golden toning and a single moderate mark on the neck of the suffragette. Despite the undersized wrong planchet, the strike is sharp except for the rims, which also vary widely in width.

1855 **1979-D Anthony Dollar—Struck on a Quarter Planchet—MS61 PCGS.** Struck slightly off-center, shifted toward 12 o'clock relative to the obverse, leaving a thin unstruck area at the bottom; a planchet split shows at 8 o'clock on the same side. Light golden toning overall. This faintly abraded piece may have gone undetected for some time, owing to the slight difference in size between quarter and Susan B. Anthony dollar planchets.

Double Struck 1999-P Anthony Dollar
Second Strike 40% Off Center, MS64

1856 **1999-P Anthony Dollar—Double Struck, 2nd Strike 40% Off Center—MS64 PCGS.** Both dates are evident on this fascinating and visually stunning error. The second impression is widely off center toward 10 o'clock. A planchet (not included) was fed between this piece and the reverse die for the second strike. Highly lustrous with light tan-gold toning.
Ex: New York Signature (Heritage, 7/2002), lot 7398; Central States Signature (Heritage, 4/2006), lot 5385.

Rare 2000-P '$1.25 Piece' MS65
Sacagawea Dollar Struck on a Maryland Quarter

1857 **2000-P Sacagawea Dollar—Struck on a Maryland Quarter—MS65 NGC.** The pearl-gray and pale gold color of this Sacagawea dollar provides the first clue it is struck on a wrong planchet. IN GOD WE TRUST and the P mintmark from the undertype are visible on Sacagawea's shoulder. On the reverse, STATE (from THE OLD LINE STATE) is faintly evident above PLURIBUS. A lustrous Gem that lacks the planchet chatter typically seen.

U.S. PRESIDENTS & STATESMEN

1858 **(1856) James Buchanan Political Medal MS63 NGC.** DeWitt-JB-1856-9. A brass campaign medal for the only bachelor president. Lustrous and untoned with a clashed lower reverse and a few delicate marks on the right obverse field.

U.S. MINT MEDALS

1876 Four-Piece Centennial
Set With Original Box

1859 **Four-Piece Centennial Medal Set With Original Box.** Four-piece set, includes: **large 1876 Centennial medal, Julian-CM-11,** gilt copper, 57 mm, lightly hairlined and one noticeable contact mark in the left reverse field; **large 1876 Centennial medal, Julian-CM-11,** copper, 57 mm, glossy reddish-brown surfaces; **small 1876 Centennial medal, Julian-CM-10,** silver, 38 mm, hairlined with gray-blue toning; and a **small 1876 Centennial medal, Julian-CM-10,** gilt copper, 38 mm, hairlined with bright color throughout. The box is showing signs of age with chipping on the top and weakness on the hinge, but the clasp still works. (Total: 4 medals)

Rare 1809 Madison Indian Peace Dollar, MS64

1860 **1809 James Madison Indian Peace Medal MS64 NGC.** Julian IP-5. Bronzed copper, 76 mm, 262.9 gm (4,057 gn), rim 7.1 mm. Reverse of 1809. A large-sized and thick example of this early Indian Peace medal portraying President James Madison. Signed "R" on obverse rim below bust. One this heavy was absent from the Ford sale (Stack's, Part XVIII, 5/2007), which had a Choice AU bronzed copper First Size, First Reverse with rim 5.4 mm-6.0 mm and weighing 3,215.3 gn. The present example shows still-lustrous medium-brown and red-brown semiprooflike fields with some light obverse spotting and a couple of small lacquered areas on the reverse. An NGC photo certificate is included.

1861 "1825" Bronze J.Q. Adams Indian Peace Medal MS64 NGC. Julian IP-11. Bronzed copper, 75.7 mm, 204.7 gm. Reverse of 1846. Obverse: Bust right, JOHN Q. ADAMS PRESIDENT OF THE UNITED STATES, 1825 below. Obverse signed F. **Die crack, rim to C in QUINCY into left field.** A second tiny crack joins the dot ornament left of the date with the nearby arrow. Reverse: PEACE AND FRIENDSHIP, pipe and tomahawk, right-hand index finger points to R in FRIENDSHIP. The surfaces show faded cherry and purple hues along with a couple of scattered verdigris spots, but much appeal is present. An NGC photo certificate accompanies the lot. The Ford example (Stack's, Sale XVIII, 5/2007, lot 82) brought $1,150.

HARD TIMES TOKENS

1862 1837 New York Feuchtwanger's Composition Three Cent Token VG8 NGC. HT-262. A well-worn but smooth example with silvery surfaces. Distinctive and affordable, likely a pocket-piece curiosity for a number of years.

Rare 1837 Feuchtwanger Three Cent Coat of Arms Obverse, HT-262, AU53

1863 1837 Feuchtwanger Three Cent, Coat of Arms AU53 PCGS. CAC. Low-117, HT-262, R.3. Much scarcer than the Feuchtwanger cent pieces. The obverse features the New York Coat of Arms. A typically struck and smooth example with moderate wear on the obverse and mottled olive patina on both sides. Listed on page 385 of the 2009 *Guide Book*. Population: 10 in 53, 14 finer (2/09).

Choice Mint State 1837 Feuchtwanger Three Cent New York Coat of Arms, Low-117, HT-262

1864 1837 Feuchtwanger Three Cent, Coat of Arms MS64 NGC. Low-117, HT-262. Choice Mint State examples of this scarce and popular token issue are rare, especially in comparison with the Feuchtwanger cents. Dr. Feuchtwanger struck two major three cent varieties in his German-silver alloy, an eagle obverse and the present design, which emulates the State of New York Coat of Arms. This piece has subdued gray luster with faintly mottled olive toning. The design elements are sharply defined on both sides. Surface marks are virtually nonexistent. As of (1/09), NGC has certified three pieces as MS64 with none finer, while PCGS has encapsulated none above MS63. Listed on page 385 of the 2009 *Guide Book*.

Near-Gem 1837 Feuchtwanger Three Cent Token Rare JMP Counterstamp, Eagle Obverse, HT-263

1865 1837 Feuchtwanger Three Cent, Eagle MS64 NGC. Ex: John J. Ford, Jr. Collection. Low-118A, HT-263, R.5. Cataloged in its Stack's Ford auction appearance as "the finest of the three known Low 118's with the JMP counterstamp (not JMB as reported by Miller). Counterstamp applied at the top of the reverse below [the] W in FEUCHTWANGER. The touchmark appears to be that of a silversmith but it has not been traced."

This is an exemplary piece with moderately prooflike fields and original pearl-gray toning. Void of marks aside from the small counterstamp, which is carefully applied and affects only the 3 in the date, opposite the counterstamp. A beautiful representative of this very scarce Feuchtwanger type. Listed on page 385 of the 2009 *Guide Book*.
Ex: Dupont Collection; Tilden Collection; Donald Miller; Ken Rendell FPL (9/1958); John J. Ford, Jr. Collection, Part IV (Stack's, 6/2004), lot 214; Stone 1837 Collection (Heritage, 1/2007), lot 8034.

Outstanding Superb Gem 1837 Feuchtwanger Cent, Breen 6-I

1866 1837 Feuchtwanger Cent MS67 NGC. Low-120, HT-268, Breen 6-I, R.1. Lovely powder-blue, peach, and yellow-gold hues endow this lustrous and magnificently preserved Superb Gem. The surfaces show none of the planchet streaks or laminations that often plague this popular issue. A bit soft on the EN in CENT, as always for the type, due to metal flow to the high relief eagle's body on the opposite side. Listed on page 385 of the 2009 *Guide Book*.

Exceptional Waterloo Medal Galvanic Molds

1867 **Pair of Waterloo Medal Negative Image Galvanic Molds by Pistrucci.** Copper. Undoubtedly the Waterloo medal is one of the most widely known and desired medals from the 19th century. Master engraver Benedetto Pistrucci took 33 years to complete the work on this medal. Its dimensions are mammoth: 140.8 mm in diameter. These galvanic molds are larger still, with an outer rim encircling each side. The background for the creation and execution of the medal was treated at length in our Tokens and Medals catalog from September 2008, lot 28829, when we offered (and sold) a copper medal.

The size of these medals precluded traditional striking on a press. All Waterloo medals were produced as electrotypes from an electroform such as this one. An in-depth discussion of this process is in a recent issue of the *E-Sylum* by Dick Johnson, volume 11, number 36, article #17. The exact source of these particular molds is not known as the consignor purchased them from an estate sale. The most desirable provenance would be the original Pinches mold from 1849. However, this is unprovable as far as we know, and several other molds have been produced over the years. An interesting passage in Johnson's article tells of the accuracy of this form of reproduction:

> "The most important thing you should remember about electroforming—it replicates minute detail. In comparison with other methods of making numismatic items, foundry casting reproduces detail down to 1/100 of an inch, die striking reproduces detail down to 1/1000th of an inch, but electroforming reproduces detail down to to the width of an atom!

> "Medalmakers have a saying about this: 'If it is in the model, it is in the medal.'"

These two molds have a thick layer of wax on the back of each and on the flange outside the design area. The wax is clear, milky-white, and red in various areas. The purpose of the wax, as again explained by Dick Johnson, is to provide resistant material where no metal is wanted to be deposited in the plating process. According to Johnson, "If this were not done the metal would deposit on both sides, all around and entomb the desired electroform." It was the consignor's belief that the different colors of wax most likely represent periodic touching up, thus indicating production over a long time period. Johnson agreed, and added "Electrotypers generally only keep one kind of wax on hand."

These two molds are magnificent. They appear almost perfectly preserved. The copper shows only the slightest oil-slick iridescence. Each mold has a loop at the top, enabling each to be hung on a wall for display. A wonderful and historic pair of medallic mementoes.(Total: 2 items)

MISCELLANEOUS MEDALS

1868 **1927 Charles Lindbergh Banquet Medal.** Bronze, 82mm. 220.4 gm. Plain edge. Dies by Kileny. Obverse: Woman stands on seashore raising symbols of France and the U.S. The Statue of Liberty at left, the Eiffel Tower right, Lindbergh flyer above. Reverse: globe with flight path depicted with dots, Lindbergh flyer above. The highpoints have a whisper of friction, and a thin mark is noted at 1 o'clock on the reverse, but this unabraded medal is otherwise as issued.

PROOF SETS

1869 **Lot of 15 Uncertified Proof Sets 1950-1964.** All 15 five-coin sets are out of their original packaging and housed in two screw-secured plastic holders. Cents vary from Red to Red and Brown, nickels have light to moderate patina, and the silver coins are generally minimally toned. Light hairlines are the norm but are rarely distracting. The 1960 set has a single Large Date cent.(Total: 15 sets)

1870 **Seven 1950s Five-Piece Proof Sets.** Seven five-coin proof sets of the 1950s, removed from original packaging and housed in screw-together plastic cases. Coins show light to moderate patina with Red to Red and Brown cents. Mild or null contrast is the rule. Sets are the **1950, 1951, 1952, 1953, 1954, 1955,** and **1957.**(Total: 35 coins)

MINT SETS

1871 **Uncertified 1947 Mint Set.** The coins individually grade between MS62 and MS65. Most of the silver coins display light to moderate original toning, and the cents are Red and Brown. No 1947-S Walking Liberty halves were struck. Housed in a vintage envelope.

1872 **Lot of 16 Early Mint Sets and a 1959 Proof Set.** Pieces housed in their original holders and envelopes with moderate to heavy patina. Includes a **1948,** a **1951,** a **1952,** a **1953,** a **1954,** a **1955,** a **1959,** and a **1960,** as well as two each of the **1949, 1956, 1957,** and **1958** sets. The lone proof set is a **1959.**(Total: 17 sets)

SETS AND PARTIAL SETS

1873 **Complete 1883-1912 Set of Proof Liberty Nickels PR65 to PR66 NGC.** Most examples show varying degrees of peach-gold and nickel-gray patina, each varying in intensity. The set includes: **1883 No Cents PR65 Cameo, 1883 With Cents PR65, 1884 PR65, 1885 PR65, 1886 PR65, 1887 PR66, 1888 PR65, 1889 PR65, 1890 PR65, 1891 PR65, 1892 PR65, 1893 PR65, 1894 PR66, 1895 PR66, 1896 PR65, 1897 PR66, 1898 PR65, 1899 PR65, 1900 PR65, 1901 PR65, 1902 PR66, 1903 PR65, 1904 PR65, 1905 PR65, 1906 PR65, 1907 PR66, 1908 PR65, 1909 PR65, 1910 PR65, 1911 PR65,** and the **1912 PR65.**(Total: 31 coins)

GSA DOLLARS

Prooflike GSA 1879-CC Dollar MS61

1874 **1879-CC MS61 Prooflike NGC.** This Clear CC representative appears at first glance to be fully brilliant, but has a faint hint of straw-gold toning. Sharply struck with flashy fields and the expected number of tiny facial marks. Scarce in a GSA holder as many were broken out for certification during the 1990s. Accompanied by a GSA box but no certificate.(#7087)

1875 **1880-CC Reverse of 1878 MS62 NGC.** Despite a number of abrasions on the portrait, this minimally toned and frosty piece remains fundamentally appealing. Band-certified in the holder of issue with box and certificate.(#7100)

1876 **1880-CC MS65 NGC. GSA Hoard.** A frosty and essentially untoned Gem example of this popular GSA issue. Band-certified in the government holder with accompanying box, certificate, and literature.(#7100)

1877 **1890-CC MS62 NGC.** Lustrous and lightly toned with clean fields, minor marks on the face, and a hint of striking softness at the centers. The 1890-CC is scarce within a GSA holder. The mint-issued black and silver box is included.(#7198)

1878 **1891-CC MS62 NGC.** VAM-3. A Top 100 Variety. The so-called "Spitting Eagle" VAM with a die lump (as made) beneath the eagle's beak. Lustrous and faintly toned with scattered lesser obverse marks. Accompanied by the box of issue.(#7206)

1879 **1891-CC MS63 NGC.** Band-certified in the holder of issue. This later-date Select piece is minimally toned and well-defined with only light, scattered abrasions.(#7206)

1880 **1885-CC MS66 NGC.** This Premium Gem is band-certified in the black holder of issue. Crisply detailed with vibrant luster and twinkling frost across the high points. Save for a hint of rose on the cheek, a minimally toned example.(#407160)

EARLY PROOF SETS

1881 **Partial 1879 Proof Set.** Five minor and silver proof coins, certified by PCGS. Includes a **cent PR63 Red and Brown, dime PR62, quarter PR62, half PR63,** and a **Morgan dollar PR62.**(Total: 5 coins)

1882 **Seven-Piece 1880 Proof Set.** All seven circulating denominations for the year are represented in this PCGS-graded set, including: **cent PR64 Brown, three cent nickel PR64 Cameo, five cent PR64, dime PR62, quarter PR62, half PR61,** and the **Morgan dollar PR61.**(Total: 7 coins)

1881 Five-Piece Silver Proof Set
Certified by PCGS

1883 **1881 Silver Five-Piece Proof Set PR62-PR63 PCGS.** Includes the Seated dime, quarter, and half dollar, and the Morgan and Trade dollars: **dime PR63,** silver-white and with light hairlines under a loupe, good cameo contrast on the reverse; **quarter PR63,** ice-white and sharply struck, with some minor obverse contact; **half dollar PR62,** snow-white with good contrast and some field contact, all of the proof dimes, quarters, and halves of the year had a mintage of only 975 pieces, with low emissions of their business strike counterparts; **Morgan dollar PR62,** silver-white and attractive with good contrast, a long, curving lintmark is noted through the last 1 in the date, sharply struck and pleasing; and **Trade dollar PR62,** also snow-white with good field-device contrast and minor contact.(Total: 5 coins)

1884 **Partial 1882 Proof Set.** Four pieces from an 1882 proof set, each certified by PCGS. Includes: **cent PR63 Brown, dime PR63, quarter PR63,** and a **half PR63.**(Total: 4 coins)

Pleasing 1894 Six-Piece Proof Set, PR63 to PR64

1885 **1894 Six-Piece Proof Set PR63-PR64 PCGS.** Includes: **cent PR64 Red and Brown,** attractively blended light to deep orange on each side; **nickel PR64 Cameo,** a hint of champagne toning over contrasting light gray surfaces; **dime PR64** and undesignated, although considerable contrast accompanies the brilliant silver surfaces with delicate golden peripheries; **quarter PR63 Cameo,** sharp details, brilliant surfaces, and excellent contrast; **half dollar PR64 Cameo,** gorgeous surfaces that are entirely untoned and nicely contrasted; and **dollar PR64 Cameo,** exceptional cameo contrast on both sides, approaching the Deep Cameo designation. (Total: 6 coins)

CERTIFIED MODERN PROOF SETS

1936 Five-Piece Proof Set, PR64 to PR66

1886 **1936 Five-Piece Proof Set PR64-PR66 PCGS.** The set includes: **cent PR64 Red and Brown,** medium orange-gold with a small patch of darker brown in the left obverse field, a few tiny flecks; **Satin Finish nickel PR66,** stunning bluish-gray with a couple of glints of gold, sharply struck and with lots of eye appeal; **dime PR65,** silver-white with only minuscule contact in the fields, pleasing and well struck; **quarter PR65,** silver-white and lustrous with a few gray flecks in the obverse fields; **half dollar PR65,** silver-white and sharply struck, with a few gray flecks but much eye appeal.(Total: 5 coins)

1887 **1939 Proof Set NGC Certified.** Encapsulated in a large NGC holder, each coin is individually graded. The **cent** is **PR64 Red and Brown**; the **nickel** is a **Reverse of '38** and grades **PR64**, deep golden and lilac toning; the **dime** is **PR65**, a real sparkler with completely brilliant surfaces and deeply mirrored fields; the **quarter** is **PR64**, mostly brilliant with just a few flecks of color on the obverse; and the **half** grades **PR65**, like the quarter, mostly brilliant with a couple of streaks of golden on the obverse.(Total: 5 coins)

1888 No lot.

End of Session Two

SESSION THREE

Floor, Telephone, Heritage Live!™, Internet, Fax, and Mail Signature® Auction #1126
Sunday, March 29, 2009, 1:30 PM ET, Lots 1889-2462
Baltimore, Maryland

A 15% Buyer's Premium ($9 minimum) Will Be Added To All Lots

Visit HA.com to view full-color images and bid.

EARLY HALF DOLLARS

Rare 1794 Half Dollar, VG10, O-101

1889 **1794 VG10 PCGS.** O-101, High R.3. The first-year 1794 Flowing Hair half is many times more elusive than its 1795 successor. The O-101 is the most available 1794 die marriage, yet it is only slightly less rare than the 1794 dollar, which invariably brings spectacular prices at auction. Toned dark brown with lighter dove-gray on the devices and lettering. Unabraded and mildly granular with a few faint adjustment marks (as made) concealed within the hair. (#6051)

1890 **1795 Y Over Star, Two Leaves VG8 PCGS.** O-121a, R.5. A heavy vertical die crack from the rim between 95 to the base of the bust affirms this later die state. Overton's third edition indicates that: "Some specimens also show a fine crack below 1 and the first star." This particular example exhibits no evidence of such a crack.

Battleship-gray patina imbued with tinges of light blue covers both sides, with hints of gold undertones showing through, particularly on the reverse. All of the design features are present, though the outer parts of the stars in the lower right obverse quadrant are worn smooth. The Liberty and eagle motifs display a modicum of internal detail, and about one-half of the dentils are visible on each side. None of the minute marks scattered about are worthy of individual mention.(#6052)

Collectible VG10 1795 Half Dollar O-115, Two Leaves Reverse

1891 **1795 2 Leaves VG10 PCGS.** O-115, R.5. The die crack near star 1 is nascent, although in the O-116 die pairing this crack extends to wander across the lower left obverse margin. This steel-gray Flowing Hair half is smooth save for a solitary small mark behind the upper point of Liberty's trailing curls. The right reverse border displays faint adjustment marks, as coined.(#6052)

1892 **1795 2 Leaves—Improperly Cleaned—NCS. Fine Details.** O-105, R.4. Reddish-gray toning drapes granular, lightly hairlined surfaces. Though this significantly worn piece shows a degree of impairment, it remains a readily collectible example of a very scarce die pair.(#6052)

Fine 1795 Two Leaves Half, O-125

1893 **1795 2 Leaves Fine 12 PCGS.** O-125, High R.4. Light tan-brown and silver-gray visit the obverse, while the slightly darker reverse provides russet, chestnut, and stone-gray toning. An unblemished representative with ample remaining definition within Liberty's hair. Most 1795 half dollar varieties are collectible if costly, but the R.8 O-132 precludes completion.(#6052)

Pleasing 1795 O-113a Half Dollar, Fine 15

1894 **1795 2 Leaves Fine 15 NGC.** O-113a, R.4. The A/E reverse. The obverse has a faint crack through the tops of LIBERTY and small die defect lumps among the stars at the lower right. Clashed near the chin and above the bust truncation. Light gray and chestnut surfaces show minor abrasions and handling marks that are consistent with the grade.
Ex: Les Bortner (5/1988); Bayside New York Collection (Heritage, 7/2008), lot 379.(#6052)

Very Fine 1795 Half, O-129
Curious STATES/D Error

1895 **1795 2 Leaves VF20 PCGS.** O-129, R.5. In 1795, two denominations, the half dollar and the five dollar, both show an overpunching of STATES over STATED. There is also a light crack from the border over A to the left side of M. This lovely collector coin has light silver surfaces with wispy gold color and deeper iridescent toning along the borders. Minor adjustment marks can be seen at the left side of the obverse.
Ex: Harry Laibstain, 6/1999; Westmoreland County Collection of Early Bust Halves, Part Two (Heritage, 4/2008), lot 955.(#6052)

Smooth VF 1795 Half, O-105

1896 **1795 2 Leaves VF20 PCGS. CAC.** O-105, R.4. Two points of star 1 are attached solidly to the lowest curl, and the point of star 2 lies entirely across the end of the second curl from the bottom. On the reverse the berries are arranged 10 and seven. Natural olive-gray patina resides on the remarkably clean surfaces of this well defined Flowing Hair half. A couple of light adjustment marks are noted in the lower right obverse quadrant.(#6052)

Attractive 1795 Half, O-131, VF25

1897 **1795 2 Leaves VF25 PCGS.** O-131, High R.4. The final A in AMERICA is recut on this penultimate Overton variety. Lavender and jade-green emerge when this nicely defined example is confronted with light. Completely problem-free except for a subtle rim ding on the reverse at 8 o'clock.(#6052)

Desirable O-125 1795 Two Leaves Half, Choice VF

1898 **1795 2 Leaves VF35 PCGS. CAC.** O-125, R.4. Original medium gray surfaces serve as a backdrop for intermingled gold and iridescent toning on both sides. This piece is slightly finer than the Overton plate coin, and it probably ranks among the top dozen known for the variety. An unusual and desirable opportunity for the Bust half enthusiast.(#6052)

Worthy XF 1795 Flowing Hair Half
O-122, Two Leaves Reverse

1899 **1795 2 Leaves XF40 NGC.** O-122, R.5. The obverse has light clash marks below the chin and hidden within the upper hair strands, extending into the field behind the top of Liberty's head. The reverse has a heavy die crack at the lower right, crossing the right ribbon end to the final A, the lower portion of the wreath, back to the border through the right wing tip, the left base of E, and the right top of M.

Pleasing pewter surfaces overall with darker gray color close to the borders. Both sides have light circulation marks that are expected for this grade. Moderate to heavy adjustment marks are present over portions of the reverse, especially at the lower left.
Ex: Sheridan Downey (8/1999); Westmoreland County Collection of Early Bust Halves (Heritage, 1/2008), lot 1338.(#6052)

Charming 1795 2 Leaves Half, O-105, XF40

1900 **1795 2 Leaves XF40 PCGS.** O-105, R.4. Star 1 connects by two points to the lowest hair curl, and star 2 lies across the next curl upward. The base of 1 is higher than 795. Although this piece is not yet in the O-105a die state, a tiny die crack does appear from the rim through the lowest point of star 15 and to the bust. Most of the other cracks that would characterize the later die state are as yet unformed. On the reverse the leaf point is between RI but closer to I, and M is recut at the left serif. This piece has considerable attractions that include moderate luster remaining, pretty silver-gold and grayish coloration, and little mentionable contact. Some old die clashing visible on the obverse only add to its charm.
From The Burning Tree Collection.(#6052)

Iridescent XF45 1795 Half Dollar
O-108a, Two Leaves

1901 **1795 2 Leaves XF45 NGC.** O-108a, R.4. Delicate die cracks are present from the bust tip and across the tops of AME. This splendid Choice XF coin takes a two-tiered approach to toning. The obverse offers iridescent gold, heather, and lilac in concentric rings, while the reverse is a more-subdued silver-gray with hints of iridescent sage and ice-blue. An attractively toned Flowing Half dollar that would highlight an early silver type set.(#6052)

Choice XF 1795 Flowing Hair Half, O-105

1902 **1795 2 Leaves XF45 NGC.** O-105, R.4. The lowest hair curl presses against two points of star 1. A radial die crack reaches the B in LIBERTY but fails to continue to Liberty's head. A lavender-gray and golden-brown representative with deeper toning in design recesses. Encased in a former generation holder.(#6052)

Splendid Choice AU 1795 Half
Popular STATES/D Variety, O-129

1903 **1795 Two Leaves AU55 NGC.** O-129, R.5. The popular Overton variety with an S punched over a D in STATES. The absent-minded engraver apparently thought he was entering UNITED. The darkly toned surfaces display golden-brown and ocean-blue when turned beneath a light. The obverse has moderate adjustment marks of mint origin, but the post-strike abrasions are inconsequential. Housed in a former generation holder.(#6052)

Dramatic 1795/1795 Three Leaves
Half Dollar, O-111, VG10

1904 **1795/1795 Three Leaves VG10 PCGS.** O-111, High R.4. The only Three Leaves Flowing Hair half variety, and also important for its dramatic repunched date (also seen on O-112). The coiner apparently cared little that the reverse die had a sizeable die break on its upper right quadrant, since all known O-111 examples show this break. Deeply toned silver-blue, aquamarine, stone-gray, and caramel-gold. The slightly glossy surfaces display occasional thin marks.(#6053)

1905 **1795/1795 VG8 PCGS.** O-112, R.4. Even in its worn state, this Flowing Hair half shows the doubled digits (or "Recut Date" in *Guide Book* parlance) boldly. The gold-gray obverse shows a number of cuts, but the slate-blue reverse is pleasingly preserved for the grade. Population: 2 in 8, 13 finer (1/09).(#6055)

Choice Fine 1795/1795 Half Dollar, O-112

1906 **1795/1795 Fine 15 PCGS.** O-112, R.4. A highly popular variety because of its widely repunched date. This slightly glossy Flowing Hair half displays lilac devices, powder-blue fields, and honey-gold margins. The right obverse has a couple of moderately granular areas. Population: 4 in 15, 5 finer (2/09).(#6055)

VF 1795/1795 Half Dollar
Two Leaves, O-112

1907 **1795/1795 VF20 PCGS.** O-112, R.4. The most distinctive of the 32 known 1795 half dollar marriages, since only O-112 has a widely and boldly repunched date. All four digits were initially punched too low, then entered a second time with normal position. This lightly abraded and nicely detailed example has attractive peach-gold, powder-blue, and sea-green toning.(#6055)

Dramatic 1795/1795 Two Leaves Half
O-112a, VF25

1908 **1795/1795 VF25 ICG.** O-112a, R.4. The date is double-punched, with the first entry very low, and corrected such that the second placement leaves the final date position much higher. The lower halves of the numerals from the first date position show clearly beneath, touching the border. A pleasing, natural appearance is presented on each side, with toning variations that range from pearl-gray and sky-blue to aqua-blue and golden-brown near the borders.(#6055)

1795 Small Head Half, O-126a, Fine 12

1909 **1795 Small Head Fine 12 PCGS.** O-126a, R.4. One of the three Small Head die marriages, the O-126 is the most "common" of the three while still very scarce. Star 1 is far below the lowest curl, and star 15 is 1 mm away from the bust tip. On the reverse the berries are arranged nine and eight (left-right), with two berries under each wing and only the upper right one having a stem. The die crack that characterizes O-126a is bold from the rim through E, along the stem and to the lowest left ribbon, although a bit of imagination is required to follow it thence to the rim. The olive-gray surfaces are mostly evenly worn, with a single light, straight scrape noted on each side. Still nice and collectible for the grade. (#6054)

Fine O-128a Small Head 1795 Half
Plate Coin in Second Edition of Overton

1910 **1795 Small Head Fine 12 PCGS.** O-128a, High R.5. **The plate coin in the second edition of Overton.** The reverse has a faint microcrack through the tops of CA into the field below the right ribbon. This is a single-use obverse and reverse die pairing. With no obvious die cracks on either side, it makes one wonder why the die pairing was retired. It may well be that this was the final die variety of the year.

Richly toned blue-gray surfaces with rose highlights on the devices. Short but prominent adjustment marks are noticed at the left obverse border to the stars, and the opposing point of the reverse is weak with the tops of ED nearly absent.
Ex: Michael Summers, 8/2006; Westmoreland County Collection of Early Bust Halves (Heritage, 4/2008), lot 954, which realized $4,887.50.(#6054)

Choice Fine 1795 Small Head Half, O-126a

1911 **1795 Small Head Fine 15 PCGS.** O-126a, R.4. The die crack through the E in UNITED is faint but apparent under magnification. From the scarce Small Head subtype, this Flowing Hair half is blanketed with deep cream-gray and chestnut toning. A pass beneath a loupe locates fewer than the customary number of small marks.(#6054)

Appealingly Fine 15 1795 Half
Scarce O-127 Small Head

1912 **1795 Small Head Fine 15 PCGS.** O-127, R.5. Faint traces of a crack can be seen extending in from the lower point of star 10. On the reverse is a faint crack between the left ribbon and stem, the start of a crack that continues through the left branch to the E of UNITED.

Subdued medium gray surfaces, with lighter tan color on the devices and deeper gray near the borders. Most of the known examples of O-127 are lower grade pieces with the exception of a single AU55. The second finest coin listed on Stephen Herrman's auction listing is a VF20, which should place this Fine 15 piece well within the Condition Census.
Ex: Michael Summers, 5/2005; Westmoreland County Collection of Early Bust Halves (Heritage, 1/2008), lot 1343, which realized $12,650.(#6054)

Collectible 1796 16 Stars Half, O-102
VG10 Details, Ely Specimen (1884)

1913 **1796 16 Stars—Plugged—ANACS. VG10 Details.** O-102, High R.5. Draped Bust Small Eagle half dollars, dated 1796 or 1797, have elicited serious collector interest since American numismatic auctions became widespread in the 1860s and 1870s. Even those coins revealing noticeable impairments, such as heavy scratches, holes, plugs, counterstamps, graffiti, re-engraved design elements, corrosion, gouges/punch marks, etc. found their way into 19th century collections, often after having realized relatively high prices.

The same situation exists in the present day. Early half dollar date/variety and type collectors, cognizant of the rarity of the series, place considerable demand pressure even on impaired specimens. Ongoing research by this cataloger indicates that at least 20 percent of surviving 1796-1797 halves exhibit one or more of the above-mentioned problems.

The 1796 16 stars offering in this lot is one of these coins. It has been crudely plugged in the field under Liberty's left (facing) bust. The plug's outline actually shows better on the reverse between the last S of STATES and O of OF. Both areas were then tooled, the obverse more so. A small dent is also visible in the drapery beneath this bust.

Aside from these impairments, this is a rather nice early half. Both sides display light bluish-purple and gray patina. The design elements show a good amount of definition, including Liberty's ear and lower hair curls, and some of the eagle's wing plumage. The date is strong, as is the 1/2 fraction. All in all, this piece probably falls more into the Fine Details grade range. No adjustment marks are visible. This coin will fit comfortably in a low to mid-grade collection.
Ex: Honorable Herman Ely Collection (W.E. Woodward, 1/1884), lot 157, where it realized $25 (a high price for that era); Western Reserve Historical Society Collection et al. (Stack's, 9/2002), lot 604. (#6058)

1914 **1797 VF25 PCGS. CAC.** O-101a, High R.4. The 1796-1797 Draped Bust half dollar with Small Eagle reverse was produced using three obverse and two reverse dies. The 1797 Overton-101 variety employed the third and final obverse paired with the same reverse die that was used for both 1796 issues (O-101, 15 stars, and O-102, 16 stars). 1797 O-101 eventually develops a crack from the rim through star 2 to Liberty's curl, as well as myriad reverse cracks (O-101a).

The present VF25 1797 O-101a example represents a later state of the reverse die. This is evident from a heavy crack that extends from the rim between D of UNITED and S of STATES, through the four laurel leaves and upper part of the wing to the lower neck. Another crack branches from this one to connect the lower parts of ST in STATES, where it joins a heavy crack running from the rim through the first T and the wreath to the eagle's upper neck. A light crack is also visible between the left (facing) leg and wing.

Bluish-gray toning on the obverse margin cedes to light silver-gray centers, while the former color dominates the reverse fields which then highlight the lighter gray design elements. The devices exhibit nice detail, including separation in much of Liberty's hair and about half of the eagle's wing plumage. The few small contacts scattered about are of little consequence, and adjustment marks are absent. A couple of minute marks on the forehead above Liberty's eye are mentioned for pedigree purposes. This pleasing, original coin is well deserving of the CAC green label.
(#6060)

Highly Attractive 1797 Fifty Cent, VF30
Intermediate Stage of O-101a

1915 **1797 VF30 NGC.** O-101a, High R.4. This 1797 O-101a specimen displays a faint crack from the rim through star 2 to Liberty's curl, and the reverse exhibits some of the incipient cracks that eventually led to the shattering of the reverse die. A light crack extends from the edge through the O in OF to the leaf point below F, and a thin crack travels from the rim at about 10 o'clock to the top of the leaf that is positioned to the lower right of the D in UNITED. Another light crack runs from the edge through the first T in STATES to the stem of the left, topmost berry, and yet another travels from the rim to the upper right serif of the U in UNITED. The relative lightness of these cracks, and the lack of any others, points to this particular coin being an intermediate stage of O-101a.

Light to medium gray patination dominates both sides, each of which exhibits subtle golden undertones and hints of luster in some of the protected areas. Liberty's hair is nicely delineated, as is a good portion of the drapery. The reverse design elements are also quite sharp, save for the typical softness on the eagle's breast, neck, and legs. Relatively strong dentilation is apparent on both sides, and no adjustment marks are evident on either. The reverse is remarkably clean, while the obverse reveals a few light marks, including a shallow hairline scratch across the neckline that does not detract from the overall appearance.

This is an attractive coin that will fit comfortably in a high quality type or date/variety collection.(#6060)

1916 **1801—Scratched—ICG. AU58 Details.** O-102, High R.4. Luminous violet and rose-orange overall with strong detail. Aside from an unfortunate scratch over the portrait, a well-preserved coin.(#6064)

Appealing Choice VF O-101 1802 Half Dollar

1917 **1802 VF35 PCGS. CAC.** O-101, R.3. The 1801 and 1802 half dollars, the first two years of the Heraldic Eagle reverse design, are both low mintage issues that are elusive in high grades. Mint records indicate a production of only 30,289 of the former and 29,890 of the latter. This wonderful piece has pale blue, heather, and gold toning with exceptional surfaces.(#6065)

1918 **1803 Small 3 XF40 ANACS.** O-104, R.3. The forest-green surfaces have lighter mint-green color on the high points of the design. Typically struck with generally flat stars, but Liberty's hair tresses and the eagle's wing feathers are nicely detailed. The obverse has many individually insignificant contact marks, while the reverse is smoother.(#6067)

Exquisite Choice XF O-104 1806/5 Half

1919 **1806/5 XF45 NGC.** Ex: Brown. O-104, R.4. The scarcest of the four die marriages that comprise the 1806/5 variety. The present Choice XF example has a pleasing amount of remaining luster, and the dappled tan-gold and silver-gray toning is clearly original. The strike is crisp save for softness near cloud 7. Encased in a prior generation holder.(#6077)

Scarce O-106 1806 Half Dollar, AU50

1920 **1806 Knobbed 6, Small Stars AU50 NGC.** O-106, R.4. Six berries on the olive branch instead of the usual five, and the 8 in the date is recut. An elusive die marriage: Stephen Herrman's list of Condition Census coins stops at the AU58 level, placing this piece just outside the top five known. Bright apricot-tinged luster fills the borders and the recessed areas of the devices. The major devices are crisply struck, although the sixth cloud is incompletely brought up. This dove-gray example has no distracting abrasions. NGC O-106 Census: 2 in 50, 3 finer (1/09).(#6075)

1921 **1806 Pointed 6, No Stem VF35 PCGS. CAC.** O-109, R.1. A relatively available variety that nonetheless enjoys considerable popularity thanks to its appearance in the *Guide Book*. Rich slate-blue toning overall with gray-gold at the margins and the worn zones on the high points.(#6073)

1922 **1806 Pointed 6, No Stem XF40 PCGS.** O-109, R.1. The familiar blundered die that lacks a branch stem, which makes it appear as if the branch is growing out of the claw. Powder-blue, golden-brown, steel-gray, and yellow-gold embrace this well defined Draped Bust half.(#6073)

1923 **1806 Pointed 6, Stem VF35 NGC. CAC.** O-116, R.3. Similar to O-114, with sharp recutting on TY in LIBERTY, but the recutting is less evident on Y for this variety. A broad die crack extends from the tip of Liberty's bust across the bottom of the date and through the first six obverse stars. This is an attractive Choice VF example with deep layers of original toning and normal wear for the grade. (#6071)

Charming Choice XF 1806 Bust Half O-116, Pointed 6, Stem

1924 **1806 Pointed 6, Stem XF45 PCGS.** O-116, R.3. Bold die cracks along the date and left-side stars make attribution easy. Glimmers of bright luster emerge from design crevices of this attractive Choice XF Draped Bust half. The golden-gray surfaces are smooth aside from a pair of faded thin marks near the forehead.(#6071)

1925 **1807 Draped Bust XF45 PCGS.** O-103, R.3. Dies strongly clashed but without the reverse cracks distinguishing O-103a. An olive-accented silver-blue and gold-gray piece that shows lighter areas at the rubbed high points.(#6079)

Lovely AU53 1807 Draped Bust Half, O-110a

1926 **1807 Draped Bust AU53 PCGS. CAC.** O-110a, R.3. Attractively toned powder-blue, sun-gold, and rose-red. Impressively void of abrasions, and the strike shows only moderate incompleteness limited to the stars near the beak and opposite on the curls above the shoulder. A partly lustrous representative of the final Draped Bust issue.(#6079)

Lustrous Near-Mint O-108
Draped Bust Half

1927 **1807 Draped Bust AU58 PCGS.** O-108, R.3. An untoned Borderline Uncirculated example from the final year of the type. Uncommonly free from marks except for wispy lines above the olive branch. Evenly struck, and the cartwheel luster is vivacious and virtually complete. Slight wear on the forehead curls precludes a Mint State assessment.(#6079)

Pleasing AU58 1807 Draped Bust Half, O-102

1928 **1807 Draped Bust AU58 NGC.** O-102, R.1. This is a lovely near-Mint representative of the final-year 1807 Draped Bust half dollar. The lightly toned surfaces reveal ivory-gray toning in the centers and pale golden color near the peripheries. High-point wear is evident on Liberty's hair detail above the forehead and on the eagle's head, but abrasions are nearly nonexistent.(#6079)

Desirable Near-Mint 1807 Draped Bust Half, O-102

1929 **1807 Draped Bust AU58 PCGS.** O-102, R.2. Though this variety's usual striking softness affects the centers, only a trace of friction is visible across the high points. Each side remains immensely lustrous with glimpses of gold and brown peripheral toning around centers in pale shades of silver-gray. Powerful eye appeal.
From The Mario Eller Collection, Part Four.(#6079)

BUST HALF DOLLARS

1930 **1807 Capped Bust 'Bearded Goddess' VF30 NGC.** Large Stars, 50 Over 20. O-111b, R.5. One of the few die crack varieties listed in the *Guide Book*, and a die pairing long coveted by Capped Bust specialists. This representative possesses deep tan-brown toning and is smooth aside from a couple of subdued thin marks on Liberty's neck.
Ex: Jules Reiver Collection (Heritage, 1/2006), lot 22595. (#6086)

1931 **1807 Large Stars, 50 Over 20 VF35 PCGS.** O-112, R.1. The more available of the two die pairs for this *Guide Book* variety, offered here in Choice VF condition with luminous silver-gray, violet-slate, and peach-gold patina.(#6086)

Luminous AU 1807 Half Dollar, Ex: Meyer
Large Stars, 50 Over 20, O-112

1932 **1807 Large Stars, 50 Over 20 AU50 PCGS. CAC.** Ex: Charlton Meyer Collection. O-112, R.1. The blundered denomination occurred when the engraver mistakenly grabbed the punch for a 2 instead of a 5. Either he thought he was working on a quarter die, or he simply grabbed the wrong punch due to a similarity in appearance. This lilac and medium gray piece has considerable lighter silver luster. Traces of an unknown black substance adhere to the reverse, but could probably be removed with little effort. Charlton Meyer is the only individual to ever own a complete die variety collection of Capped Bust halves.(#6086)

AU53 1807 Capped Bust Half
50 Over 20, Large Stars, O-112

1933 **1807 Large Stars, 50 Over 20 AU53 NGC.** O-112, R.1. Medium aquamarine and chestnut toning drapes this partially lustrous and lightly abraded type coin. The popular 0-112 variety with a partial blundered denomination. The reverse die would later be used to help coin the famous "Bearded Goddess" variety, O-111b. (#6086)

Choice AU 1807 Capped Bust Half
50 Over 20, Large Stars, O-112

1934 **1807 Large Stars, 50 Over 20 AU55 PCGS. CAC.** O-112, R.1. Golden-brown and ocean-blue adorn the reverse margin, while the obverse is comprehensively toned in gunmetal-blue and cream-gray. A slender strike-through (as made) reaches the S in PLURIBUS, but actual marks are minor and hard to locate. Population: 26 in 55, 41 finer (2/09).(#6086)

1807 Large Stars Half
O-114, AU50

1935 **1807 Capped Bust, Large Stars AU50 NGC.** O-114, R.3. The attribution is easy, aided by the die defect lumps visible beneath the 7 on the obverse and the two lowest arrowheads joined on the reverse. Substantial pewter-gray color on the obverse is accented by deeper peripheral gold with similar color across most of the reverse. Some luster remains visible, but it is subdued by the toning. This is a popular and important *Guide Book* variety, and the 1807-1808 First Style Capped Bust half dollars are an important two-year subtype, as the portrait and eagle were remodeled with the 1809 coinage.(#6088)

Boldly Struck 1809 Normal Edge
Gem Fifty Cent, O-106

1936 **1809 Normal Edge MS65 NGC.** O-106, R.3. Normal Edge. The N in UNITED is recut and a long, heavy engraver's scratch extends diagonally from the right corner of the shield into the eagle's right (facing) wing. A heavy die break connects all stars on the left side of the obverse.

Soft golden and ice-blue hues evenly blanket both sides of this lustrous Gem, and deeper electric-blue, purple, and golden-brown gravitate to the margins. An exacting strike leaves bold definition on the design features, and the eye appeal is memorable. Minor marks on Liberty's cheek likely preclude an even higher grade. Census for the date: 8 in 65, 2 finer (2/09).(#6092)

1937 **1810 AU58 NGC.** O-110, R.2. Most of this momentarily circulated half dollar is untoned, although the lower right obverse is charcoal-gray and there are peripheral glimmers of sun-gold. Minimally abraded and attractive.(#6095)

1938 **1810 AU58 NGC.** O-102, R.1. Deep lavender and jade-green envelop this satiny representative. The strike is good overall, although soft to the left of the shield. Smooth aside from concealed marks beneath the left (facing) wing.
Ex: Diamond Collection, Part One (Heritage, 1/2006), lot 2642. (#6095)

1810 Gem Half Dollar, O-109

1939 **1810 MS65 NGC.** O-109, R.3. In practice, 1810 half dollars are attributed by reverse characteristics. Ten die varieties are known from nine obverse dies and 10 reverse dies. Only the obverse of O-102 and O-103 is shared. The reverse of O-109 has several horizontal crossbars extending right of the shield, and two lines of vertical stripe 6 extending beyond the lower shield border.

The reverse is rotated about 45 degrees clockwise. Both sides have frosty luster beneath a thick coat of champagne, ivory, gold, and iridescent toning. Although not a full strike, the design definition is sharper than usual. While a few grade-limiting blemishes occur on each side, the surfaces are exceptional for the grade. Census: 6 in 65, 2 finer (10/08).(#6095)

1940 **1811 Small 8 AU58 NGC.** O-105a, R.2. Tiny die breaks within the horizontal shield stripes confirm the Overton variety. Luster dominates the borders and devices of this momentarily circulated half dollar. Free from eventful marks, and moderately toned in orange-gold and stone-gray.(#6097)

Brilliant Late-State 1812 Half, O-108a

1941 **1812 MS63 PCGS.** O-108a, R.2. The first 1 in the date is high, and all the digits lean to the left. On the reverse there is a center dot between crossbars 4 and 5, and AM and CA appear nearly to touch. There are numerous die cracks, some quite heavy, through UNITED, STATES, 50C, and there are multiple die clashes visible on both sides. This reverse die was clearly close to shattering, and the obverse die is also in a late state. This piece is nonetheless brilliant silver-white, and well-produced and well-preserved, considering the state of the dies present at its creation. One could almost believe that the coin is undergraded for the late die state rather than the actual condition.(#6100)

Outstanding 1812 MS66 Half Dollar, O-105

1942 **1812 MS66 NGC.** O-105, R.1. The obverse can be identified by several die cracks, while the reverse has a large, crude center dot on crossbar 5. The crack along the left border connects the first six stars.

Magnificent luster radiates from both sides of this Premium Gem, and pleasing violet and electric-blue patina encircles the medium gray toning that covers the centers. The strike is razor-sharp, including virtual fullness on the star centers, Liberty's hair, and the eagle's plumage. The eye appeal is outstanding, and a couple of light grazes do nothing to distract. Census for the issue: 22 in 66, 0 finer (2/09).(#6100)

Interesting 1813 Half Dollar, O-110, MS63

1943 **1813 MS63 NGC.** O-110, R.1. A fascinating piece that shows dramatic die clashing just above the date from PLURIBUS UNUM. This feature parallels the clashing seen on the so-called 50C/UNI variety (O-101). Well struck and highly lustrous, with dappled champagne patina on both sides. An attractive and numismatically interesting coin.(#6103)

1944 1814 AU58 NGC. O-102, R.2. A lightly toned type coin with bright luster throughout the devices and borders. Sharply struck and without notable abrasions. The reverse has RT in LIBERTY separately die clashed within the shield and to the right of the shield. *Ex: FUN Signature (Heritage, 1/2007), lot 4361, which realized $1,380.*(#6105)

Luminous Select O-103 1814 Half

1945 1814 MS63 NGC. O-103, R.1. The prominent reverse die break is diagnostic. This Select example comes from a near-terminal die state with stars drawn to the rims and prominent clash marks on each side. Softly lustrous with fiery gold-orange centers and cooler blue and green shadings present at the rims. For all varieties, Census: 27 in 63, 49 finer (1/09).(#6105)

1946 1815/2 AG3 PCGS. O-101, High R.2. The only known die variety. A delightful coin for the grade with attractive light to medium gray surfaces. While both sides have a quota of tiny handling marks, only a single fresh mark by the date is of any significance. Otherwise, this piece presents excellent eye appeal for such a low grade.(#6108)

1947 1818 MS62 NGC. O-114, R.3. A scarce variety distinguished by a recut star 1 on the obverse and an E in STATES that is higher than the letters on either side. This unworn, well struck representative has soft, swirling luster beneath rich stone-gray and almond-gold patina.(#6113)

1948 1818/7 Small 8 AU58 NGC. O-102, R.2. Moderately toned silver-gray and chestnut-gold with an occasional glimpse of charcoal along the obverse border. Considerable luster shimmers across the unblemished surfaces.(#6114)

1949 1819/8 Large 9 AU55 PCGS. O-103a, R.4. Incorrectly labeled as a Small 9 by PCGS. The network of slender reverse die cracks confirms the late die state. Dusky dove-gray and caramel-gold shadings embrace this satiny and lightly abraded example. (#6119)

1950 1819/8 Large 9 AU58 PCGS. O-104, R.1. Easily identified by the multiple recuttings on star 2. Gold-orange, olive, and silver-blue toning drapes lustrous surfaces that show just a trace of wear. (#6119)

1951 1819/8 Large 9 AU58 NGC. O-105, R.2. Colorfully patinated with jade-green, golden-tan, and cherry-red margins that frame the golden-gray fields and devices. No marks are obvious, and ample luster illuminates the surfaces.(#6119)

1952 1819/8 Large 9 AU58 NGC. O-102, R.2. Splashes of powder-blue and straw-gold enrich this shimmering and evenly struck half dollar. No marks are of any consequence, and wear is limited to highpoints such as the eagle's head above the eye.(#6119)

1953 1821 MS62 PCGS. O-107, R.3. A scarce variety distinguished by star 7 on the obverse pointing to Liberty's cap rather than her headband. The lustrous obverse has light gold-gray toning overall, while the reverse shows several streaks of sage. *From The Burning Tree Collection.*(#6128)

1954 1822 AU58 PCGS. O-110, R.2. The obverse is predominantly silver-gray, while the reverse is bathed in deep peach-gold. A thin mark is noted above the cleavage. The reverse appears fully lustrous, and obverse luster is only diminished on the cheek and open field.(#6129)

1955 1822 MS61 NGC. O-106, R.3. Exceptionally lustrous, this Bust Half dollar displays attractive antique-gold patina that partially surrounds the gray centers. A thin mark is concealed near the drapery clasp. *Ex: Frank O. Fredericks Collection, Part Five (Heritage, 8/2004), lot 6195.*(#6129)

1956 1823 MS61 NGC. O-112, R.1. This sharply struck and satiny Capped Bust half exhibits rich autumn-gold, emerald-green, and lilac toning. Abrasions are hard to locate, and the eye appeal is attractive.(#6131)

1957 1823 MS62 PCGS. O-103, R.2. A well struck example with full satiny luster and a rich blanket of dove-gray and tobacco-brown patina. A shallow, curved pinscratch below the eagle's beak, which is all that precludes a decidedly higher grade. *From The Burning Tree Collection.*(#6131)

Attractive Near-Gem 1823 Bust Half, O-106

1958 1823 MS64 PCGS. O-106, R.3. The date shows a large, well formed 3 that is taller than 182. On the reverse, RI in AMERICA nearly touch. A boldly struck piece with lovely, rich rainbow toning near the obverse and reverse borders. Lustrous and nicely preserved, with a few minor field marks that keep it from a Gem holder.(#6131)

Appealing O-110 1823 Half Dollar MS64

1959 1823 MS64 PCGS. O-110, R.2. Incorrectly designated by PCGS as the Broken 3 variety, which would be O-101. The 3 on the present piece is awkward, however, and eventually was worked over by a mint worker to create the Ugly 3 variety, O-110a. Lustrous and unblemished with moderate golden-brown and sea-green toning. Liberty's profile is strike doubled.(#6131)

Lustrous and Originally Toned 1823 Half, MS65 O-106a

1960 **1823 MS65 NGC.** O-106a, R.2. Cobalt-blue and purple toning gravitate to the obverse margins of this Gem, leaving the center light silver-gray. Uniform grayish-orange covers the reverse. A well executed strike brings out sharp definition on the design elements. Devoid of significant marks.(#6131)

1961 **1824/4 AU55 NGC.** O-109, R.2. A lovely deep dove-gray Choice AU half with substantial luster and impeccably smooth surfaces. Light friction on the cheek and bust tip corresponds to the grade. *Ex: Long Beach Online Session (Heritage, 9/2005), lot 8578.* (#6140)

1962 **1824 MS61 NGC.** O-113, R.1. Light to medium pearl-gray and golden-brown with deeper swaths of jade-green across the margins. The strike is bold except for the upper two left side stars. Housed in a former generation holder.(#6137)

1963 **1824 MS63 PCGS.** O-105, R.2. A die lump on the edge of the chin below the lower lip identifies the variety. Lustrous surfaces display whispers of cobalt-blue, lavender, and brown toning at the margins. Well struck on the design elements. A few minute marks define the grade.(#6137)

1964 **1824 MS63 PCGS.** O-115, R.2. Both sides have splendid mint frost beneath variegated ivory and gold toning. Though a wispy abrasion on the portrait precludes a finer designation, this lovely piece is sure to delight its next owner. For all varieties, Population: 35 in 63, 59 finer (2/09).(#6137)

1965 **1824 MS63 PCGS.** O-116, R.3. Light olive and sage toning overall. This well-defined piece is identified by variety through the joined E and D in UNITED on the reverse. Liberty's profile shows interesting strike doubling.(#6137)

1966 **1825 AU58 NGC.** O-114, R.1. This coruscating Bust half features deep golden-brown toning with glimpses of olive and stone-gray. A thin mark beneath the beak, but smooth overall. The strike is crisp except for the RIB in PLURIBUS.(#6142)

Sharp 1825 Half Dollar, O-111, MS62

1967 **1825 MS62 NGC.** O-111, R.3. Star 13 touches a rear curl, and the heavy recutting on the reverse in 50 confirms the attribution. Nicely struck with pleasing luster overall, though the light golden patina that covers the silver obverse gives way to an arc of darker reverse toning that encompasses most of the denomination and the arrowheads.(#6142)

1968 **1826 AU58 PCGS.** O-112, R.2. Impressively lustrous with only a touch of friction on the high points of the well-defined devices. Deep gunmetal-blue and lighter gold-orange shadings embrace each side.(#6143)

1969 **1826 MS62 NGC.** O-112, R.2. Blended golden-brown and gunmetal-gray with slightly deeper shades along the borders. A satiny representative with smooth surfaces and a good strike. (#6143)

Handsome MS63 1826 Bust Half, O-118a

1970 **1826 MS63 PCGS.** O-118a, R.1. Die cracks atop UNITED STATES OF AMERICA confirm the late die state. Lightly toned and highly lustrous with few marks and exemplary eye appeal. Although it is a higher graded example is obtainable, even the advanced collector should consider the quality of the present piece. (#6143)

1971 **1826 MS63 PCGS.** O-117a, R.2. A moderately to deeply toned example with varying shades of reddish-brown and gray noted over each side. Lustrous, unmarked, and sharply brought up save for the left-side stars.(#6143)

1972 **1826 MS63 PCGS.** O-101a, R.2. The lower reverse die crack is present, albeit faint. Deep peach-gold and gunmetal-gray envelop this crisply struck and mildly prooflike representative. Liberty's profile is strike doubled.(#6143)

Impressive Near-Gem 1826 Half Dollar, O-108

1973 **1826 MS64 PCGS.** O-108, R.1. A beautifully toned example of this relatively common die marriage. Although the variety is readily available, this particular piece does not show the die crack that joins obverse stars 2 through 7, continuing to the upper rim, that is "nearly always visible" on this obverse, according to Overton. Well struck, lustrous, and free of any distracting marks. (#6143)

Gorgeous 1826 O-101a Half Dollar, MS66

1974 1826 MS66 PCGS. O-101a, R.1. This late die state example has an obverse die crack through the base of the date, and reverse cracks through the denomination and through the tops of ICA to the border adjacent to the arrows. An impressive Premium Gem, both sides are bold and fully detailed with every design element exactly as the engraver intended. The surfaces are smooth and highly lustrous with soft ivory color and splendid gold, rose, and blue toning, deeper near the borders. A gorgeous example for the Set Registry specialist or advanced type collector. Population: 3 in 66, 2 finer (2/09).(#6143)

1975 1827 Square Base 2 MS60 NGC. O-104, R.1. Dusky dove-gray toning embraces this satiny and well defined silver type coin. Impressively devoid from obtrusive marks, and a worthy representative of this available die marriage.(#6144)

1976 1827 Square Base 2 MS61 NGC. O-115, R.2. A lustrous and unblemished half dollar with lightly toned centers and rich russet-brown patina near the rims. One can form a sizable collection simply from the varieties and major die states of 1827 half dollars. (#6144)

1977 1827 Square Base 2 MS61 NGC. O-114, R.3. The reverse is essentially brilliant, although the obverse has a wisp of chestnut toning. Surprisingly free from marks aside from a tick on the jaw. A few stars lack full centril detail, but the major devices are well brought up.
From The Mario Eller Collection, Part Four.(#6144)

1978 1827 Square Base 2 MS62 NGC. O-131, R.2. This satiny representative is blanketed in blended slate, cobalt-blue, and tan patina. The fields are remarkably smooth, although the cheek has an inconspicuous mark.(#6144)

1979 1827 Square Base 2 MS62 NGC. O-125, R.3. Lavender-gray and tan-gold toning blankets this gently shimmering representative. Neither side has any remotely relevant marks, and only the left-side stars display inexactness of strike.(#6144)

1980 1827 Square Base 2 MS62 NGC. O-106, R.2. Attractively lustrous centers show only minimal patina. Reddish-orange peripheral shadings add rich color to the piece. Interesting eye appeal.(#6144)

Select 1827 Bust Half
Square Base 2, O-126

1981 1827 Square Base 2 MS63 PCGS. O-126, R.2. A die break within the lowest hair curl identifies the variety, per Glenn Peterson's useful attribution reference. Both sides display satiny luster beneath light gold and iridescent toning, somewhat deeper on the obverse. The stars are typically flat in the centers, but all other design elements are bold.(#6144)

Gem 1827 Square Base 2 Bust Half, O-120a

1982 1827 Square Base 2 MS65 NGC. O-120a, R.3. The obverse is recognized by heavy, wavy die lines left of the date below the bust. The reverse shows AT in STATES clearly separated, and a wispy die crack above UNITED STATES. This is a gorgeous Gem example, and probably one of the finest survivors of this scarce variety. Rich purple, rose, and cobalt-green toning adorns the peripheries. The surfaces are remarkably clean and free of even the smallest abrasion.(#6144)

Beautiful 1827 O-107 Half, MS65

1983 1827 Square Base 2 MS65 NGC. O-107, R.3. This die marriage is only moderately scarce, with a few Gem examples known, including the present lovely piece. Both sides are highly lustrous with satiny silver surfaces beneath original golden-brown and iridescent toning. The design elements are bold and the surfaces are virtually mark free.(#6144)

1984	**1828 Curl Base 2, No Knob MS61 ANACS.** O-101, R.1. A small tine protrudes from the left side of Liberty's drapery, and on the reverse, the upper region of the F in OF is filled. This well struck and luminous piece has bands of golden-brown, orange, violet, and teal patina at the margins and silver-gray color at the centers.(#6148)

Pleasing Near-Mint O-121 1828 Half Dollar

1985	**1828 Square Base 2, Small 8, Large Letters AU58 NGC.** O-121, R.4. An intermediate state that shows the faint beginnings of the die crack that defines the O-121a. Rich rose, gold, and violet shadings drape lustrous surfaces. Minimally marked with only a trace of friction on the high points separating this piece from a Mint State designation.(#6151)

1986	**1828 Square Base 2, Small 8, Large Letters AU58 NGC.** O-113, R.3. This crisply struck and satiny piece is bathed in deep lilac and autumn-gold patina. The reverse is splendidly smooth, and the obverse has only a few abrasions on the cheek and left field. (#6151)

Outstanding 1828 Half Dollar, O-114, MS65
Square Base 2, Small 8, Large Letters

1987	**1828 Square Base 2, Small 8, Large Letters MS65 NGC.** O-114, R.3. Attributable by star 13, which is lightly joined to a curl, and peripheral die cracks on the reverse. Even though a fairly common variety, this piece must surely be one of the finest known at the MS65 level. This is a sharply defined example that has bright mint luster with an overlay of golden-rose toning that deepens and includes royal blue around scattered parts of the peripheries. An outstanding high-grade Bust half.(#6151)

1988	**1829 Small Letters MS61 NGC.** O-117, R.2. Deep peach-red patina embraces this unabraded and coruscating Capped Bust half. The strike is above average. Encapsulated in a prior generation holder.(#6154)

1989	**1829 Small Letters MS62 NGC.** O-103, R.1. A triangular die defect left of the date, and an irregular shape to the top of 5 in the denomination, help to validate the attribution of this Overton variety. This Uncirculated example displays shimmering luster across untoned, pearl-gray surfaces. Boldly struck and free of abrasions.(#6154)

1990	**1829 Small Letters MS62 ICG.** O-105a, R.1. A later die state of the O-105 variety. On the reverse, according to Overton: "Same as D except for arrow shafts which are lapped away at claws in this late die state." A well struck and nicely preserved example, with light taupe coloration.(#6154)

Lovely Near-Gem 1829 Bust Half, O-105a

1991	**1829 Small Letters MS64 PCGS. CAC.** O-105a, R.1. Small date with a curved die crack from star 10 to the lower hair curls. On the reverse, the late die state is indicated by missing arrow shafts, from die lapping. A well struck representative with intense mint luster and rich, original toning. There are two or three small spots on the reverse, but no distracting marks on either side.(#6154)

Scarce Near-Gem 1829 Half Dollar
Small Letters, O-112a

1992	**1829 Small Letters MS64 PCGS.** O-112a, R.2. The Overton subvariety with the die lines east of the date no longer present. Blended golden-brown and apple-green embraces this satiny and well struck near-Gem. The highpoints display hints of deep dove-gray. Population: 42 in 64, 15 finer (2/09).(#6154)

Satiny Choice 1829 Bust Half
Small Letters, O-105

1993	**1829 Small Letters MS64 NGC.** O-105, R.1. Recutting on the upper arrow shaft is diagnostic. This precisely struck Choice Bust half is toned in cream-gray, russet, and forest-green shades. The satin luster is especially vivacious throughout the borders. Smooth save for a few faint marks clustered near star 5.(#6154)

Near-Gem 1830 Bust Half Dollar
Medium 0, O-119

1994 **1830 Medium 0 MS64 PCGS.** O-119, R.1. Overton calls this the "Medium 0" variety, but PCGS only acknowledges the Small 0 and Large 0 varieties, and designates this piece on the holder as a Small 0. Diagnostic recutting is observed on 0 in the date, and the horizontal shield lines are mostly flat. Well struck with luscious original toning and minimal surface distractions.(#6156)

Shimmering Choice 1830 Half
Small 0, O-106

1995 **1830 Small 0 MS64 PCGS.** O-106, R.2. Sharply struck and lustrous with medium olive-green and walnut-brown patina. The reverse is well preserved, as is the obverse field, and the cheek has only faint contact. Glenn Peterson's "Recut tail of C" variety, with a split end on the tail of the C in the denomination.(#6156)

1830 Small 0 Half, O-103, MS64

1996 **1830 Small 0 MS64 PCGS.** O-103, R.1. The obverse stars have round, blunt points, and the 3 in the date is somewhat lower than the remaining digits. On the reverse the bottom horizontal shield stripe extends to the right past the shield border. The flag of 5 and bottom of A2 are recut. The first S in STATES is high and distant from TATES. Line 1 of stripe 2 extends to the second crossbar. This coin has much luster remaining beneath a thin veneer of powder-gray and gold patina. Close perusal with a loupe reveals only the most minor contact, and it is perhaps only the slightly subdued luster that prevents an even finer grade. Nonetheless a nice and extremely appealing coin.(#6156)

Appealing MS64 1830 Half
Large 0, O-123

1997 **1830 Large 0 MS64 NGC.** O-123, R.1. A Large 0 obverse paired with a reverse that shows the vertical stripes on the reverse extending below the boundary of the shield. This near-Gem is strongly lustrous and well-defined. Generally silver-white surfaces show occasional glimpses of champagne over the minimally marked fields.(#6157)

1998 **1831 MS61 ANACS.** O-106, R.3. Dappled golden-brown toning enriches the centers, and the margins display glimpses of lime-green. Lustrous, unblemished, and housed in an ANA cache holder. (#6159)

1999 **1831 MS61 PCGS.** O-104, R.1. An early die state that retains the parallel die lines beneath the bust truncation. A lustrous and pleasing example with medium chestnut-gold toning. The middle letters in PLURIBUS are softly defined.(#6159)

Pleasing MS63 1831 Half, O-119

2000 **1831 MS63 PCGS.** O-119, R.3. A later state with the obverse die lines missing. Well-defined and attractively lustrous with rich patina, a delightful Select representative. The obverse shows predominantly blue, violet, and rose shadings, while the reverse exhibits lighter gold and peach overtones. Striking eye appeal. (#6159)

Lustrous 1831 Half Dollar, O-102, MS63

2001 **1831 MS63 PCGS.** O-102, R.1. Although this obverse is shared between O-101 and O-102, the reverse is confirmed by the second line in stripe 1, which is heavy and bent, and the top of the 5, which is short and V-shaped. This piece displays lustrous pinkish-gold centers, with the rims a deeper sky-blue. Die erosion draws the stars toward the rim, but there is little mentionable contact. Typically struck, with some softness visible around the shield border and in URI.(#6159)

Desirable Near-Gem 1831 Bust Half, O-103

2002 **1831 MS64 PCGS.** O-103, R.1. A slight die crack extends along the bottom of the date, and the stand of 5 in the denomination is recut. Highly lustrous with lovely gold-tan and purple-rose toning over the obverse. The reverse is untoned. This near-Gem is well struck and shows a mere handful of scattered, tiny marks that keep it from grading even higher.(#6159)

Late-State 1831 Half, O-119, MS64

2003 **1831 MS64 NGC.** O-119, R.3. A later die state without obverse die lines at 7:30. This lustrous near-Gem has light tan toning and is precisely struck near the centers. A few peripheral elements lack a full impression. Careful inspection fails to locate any remotely mentionable marks.(#6159)

Shining 1831 Gem Half Dollar, O-110

2004 **1831 MS65 NGC.** O-110, R.2. There is a small tine of metal above the R in LIBERTY. On the reverse, the A in STATES is flat, thickened, and rotated, with its right (facing) base beneath the left base of the second T. Violet and sky-blue patina covers lustrous surfaces, and the design elements are generally well struck. Nicely preserved throughout. Census for the date: 57 in 65, 16 finer (2/09).(#6159)

2005 **1832 Small Letters MS61 NGC.** O-113a, R.3. The scarce late die state with dramatic flow lines in the fields near the borders. This satiny dove-gray Bust half is remarkably smooth for the grade. The stars and much of PLURIBUS is incompletely brought up. Liberty's nose and chin are doubled.(#6160)

2006 **1832 Small Letters MS62 PCGS.** O-103, R.1. A relatively available issue distinguished by recutting on the 5 in the denomination. Luminous rose and silver-blue shadings drape each side.(#6160)

2007 **1832 Small Letters MS62 ICG.** O-110, R.1. The so-called "Spiked Cap" variety, which features a small spur (as made) from the top of the cap. A smooth and satiny representative with medium golden-brown and dove-gray patina.(#6160)

Originally Toned Near-Gem 1832 Half Small Letters, O-121

2008 **1832 Small Letters MS64 PCGS.** O-121, R.3. A distinctive Overton marriage due to recutting on the flag of the 1 in the date, a mint-made die gouge within the right-side vertical shield stripes, and die crumbling on the scroll between PLURIBUS and UNUM. This satiny half dollar is mostly lightly toned but has rich arcs of forest-green, rose-red, and mauve along the right borders. (#6160)

Lovely Gem 1832 Small Letters Half, O-103

2009 **1832 Small Letters MS65 NGC.** O-103, R.1. A die lump is noticeable on Liberty's drapery fold, between 18 and the clasp. Recutting on the upright of the 5 in the denomination is also diagnostic for this variety. A lovely Gem example with olive, cobalt-blue and reddish-gold toning. Well preserved and free of any significant surface blemishes.(#6160)

2010 **1833 MS63 PCGS.** O-110, R.1. A diagonal die line through the C in 50 C is diagnostic. This minimally abraded Select Bust half is blanketed in rich dove-gray toning. A satiny and clearly original offering.(#6163)

Pleasing Near-Gem 1833 Half, O-109

2011 **1833 MS64 PCGS.** O-109, R.3. An Overton marriage noted for a die line extending from the right foot of the I in AMERICA. A sharply struck and unmarked Choice Bust half graced with dusky original chestnut-tan and sea-green toning. For all die varieties combined, the PCGS population is 70 in 64, 18 finer (2/09). *From The Burning Tree Collection.*(#6163)

Graceful Near-Gem 1833 Half, O-102

2012 **1833 MS64 PCGS.** O-102, R.1. Star 1 is widely recut near its northeast point, diagnostic for O-102. Dynamic luster sweeps the light golden-gray fields and devices. Nicely struck and devoid of any consequential marks. Very scarce in such exemplary quality. Population: 70 in 64, 18 finer (2/09).(#6163)

Elusive Gem 1833 Bust Half, O-102

2013 **1833 MS65 NGC.** O-102, R.1. Star 1 is recut at multiple points, and a broad stubby top is seen on the 5 in 50 C. A die line (as made) extends from the olive branch stem to the C in the denomination. This Gem example is highly lustrous and displays attractive, obviously original toning across both sides.(#6163)

Dazzling MS66 1833 Half Dollar, O-108

2014 **1833 MS66 NGC.** O-108, R.1. A remarkable Capped Bust half that boasts ebullient luster and unabraded surfaces. Lightly toned on the fields and devices, while the margins offer medium fire-red and chestnut-brown patina. Condition Census quality. Census: 5 in 66, 4 finer (2/09).(#6163)

2015 **1834 Large Date, Large Letters MS63 PCGS.** O-101, R.1. A lovely Select example of this readily collectible variant. Each side is impressively lustrous beneath toning that ranges from thin gold-gray at the centers to deep rose, violet, and blue at the margins. (#6164)

2016 **1834 Large Date, Small Letters MS62 PCGS.** O-105, R.1. The 4 in the date is recut. Naturally toned with turquoise-green peripheral accents, and creamy-gray color in the centers. Generally well impressed, despite weakness on the first five obverse stars and the eagle's left (facing) wing feathers.(#6165)

1834 Small Date, Small Letters Half Dollar, O-113, MS64

2017 **1834 Small Date, Small Letters MS64 NGC.** O-113, R.1. Star 13 is 1 mm away from the lowest hair curl and recut at each point. The 3 in the date is small and nearly closed. On the reverse the arrowheads are narrow, sharp, and widely separated. The E in the scroll has been eradicated and recut further left. This piece offers stunning light original toning with iridescent ice-blue near the rim and cinnamon centers. Despite the moderate coloration, most of the original luster still manages to shine forth.(#6166)

1834 Small Date, Small Letters Bust Half, O-116, MS64

2018 **1834 Small Date, Small Letters MS64 PCGS. CAC.** O-116, R.1. A wavy outline is seen in the field to the left of Liberty's bust, and there is diagnostic flatness on the right stars and on A in STATES and URI of PLURIBUS on the scroll. Aquamarine peripheral toning is seen on both sides, along with coral-gold patina that extends into the fields and centers. Well struck and nicely preserved; a high grade example of this otherwise common die variety.(#6166)

2019 **1835 MS61 NGC.** O-108, R.3. Medium lavender-gray, blue-green, and straw-gold toning adorns this nicely struck Capped Bust half. A hair-thin mark on the cheek, but otherwise impressively unabraded.(#6168)

Lustrous 1835 Half, O-106, MS63

2020 **1835 MS63 PCGS.** O-106, R.1. The 1 in the date tilts to the right, and minor recutting shows on the stand of the 5. On the reverse each of four stripes have one line extending to the second crossbar. Rich powder-blue and sea-green peripheral patina frames golden-brown and lilac-gray centers. Luster sweeps the lightly abraded fields and devices. The 1835 is a "sleeper" date, a bit scarcer than other Lettered Edge dates from the final decade of the series.(#6168)

2021 **1836 Lettered Edge AU50 NGC.** O-105, Low R.4. A scarce die marriage identified by a space in the obverse dentils near 12 o'clock and faint vertical die lines to the left of the denomination. A lilac-gray piece whose strong peripheral luster threatens to penetrate the open fields.(#6169)

2022 **1836 Lettered Edge MS61 NGC.** O-119, R.3. This final year Lettered Edge half has extensive luster, and the strike is sharp aside from minor flatness on the eyebrow. The lilac-gray toning is consistent throughout. An interesting lintmark (as made) curls across the upper reverse.(#6169)

2023 **1836 Lettered Edge MS62 PCGS.** O-122, R.2. A small dot is to the right of the 6, opposite center of the loop, and a small tine extends to the left of the upper serif of the E in STATES. The depth of the golden-gray toning somewhat subdues the luster. Relatively well struck, except for softness in the curls near Liberty's ear. A few minute marks are visible on each side.(#6169)

Pleasing 1836 Lettered Edge Half Dollar, O-113, MS64

2024 **1836 Lettered Edge MS64 PCGS. CAC.** O-113, R.2. The inner points of the first four stars are recut, the drapery clasp has a double outline, and a center dot is located between crossbars 4 and 5. Intermediate between O-113 and O-113a, as a crack extends from the rim near star 13 through star 12, past star 11, then curves to the tip of the upper ribbon, but proceeds no further. Lustrous surfaces display whispers of blue, gray, and orange patina. This well struck piece reveals just a couple of trivial marks that deny Gem status. Pleasing overall, as indicated by the CAC label. For the issue, Population: 55 in 64, 14 finer (2/09).(#6169)

Scarce Choice 1836 Half Dollar Lettered Edge, O-113

2025 **1836 Lettered Edge MS64 PCGS.** O-113, R.2. Along with O-108, O-113 exhibits an unusual double outline to Liberty's drapery clasp. Dappled autumn-gold and olive-gray dominates this gently shimmering and well impressed near-Gem. Clearly original and only lightly abraded. Population: 55 in 64, 14 finer (2/09).(#6169)

Gem O-101a 1836 Bust Half

2026 **1836 Lettered Edge MS65 PCGS.** O-101a, R.1. Several stars are lightly recut, most noticeably on star 6. Rich golden-brown and green-gray shadings endow this coruscating and unmarked Gem. The borders are well struck, while the centers show minor inexactness. Population: 10 in 65, 4 finer (2/09).(#6169)

Uncommonly Nice 1836 O-112 Half, MS65

2027 **1836 Lettered Edge MS65 NGC.** O-112, R.1. A relatively common variety in an uncommon grade, the die pair distinguished by the die line connecting the lower two arrowheads on the reverse. Strongly lustrous and well-defined with splashes of blue, violet, and peach peripheral toning around light silver-gray centers. For unattributed Lettered Edge pieces, Census: 21 in 65, 6 finer (2/09).(#6169)

1836 Lettered Edge Half, O-117, MS65

2028 **1836 Lettered Edge MS65 NGC.** O-117, R.3. Star 8 is recut on this die marriage, and the date is quite low. The first line of stripe 2 is solid to the second crossbar. This deeply and originally toned Gem offers iridescent green, blue, and gold patina over each side. The toning gives the underlying lustrous surfaces a completely original appearance. A solid MS65 that displays a reasonably good strike, save for the motto on the reverse. For the variety, Census: 1 in 65, 0 finer; the next closest grades MS62 (2/09).(#6169)

REEDED EDGE HALF DOLLARS

Interesting AU Details 1836 Reeded Edge Half

2029 **1836 Reeded Edge—Improperly Cleaned—NCS. AU Details.**
The small Reeded Edge half dollar issue of 1836 ushered in a
new age of U.S. mintage techniques, and survivors are prized
whatever their state. Though the present piece shows dimmed
luster and hairlines from a past cleaning, the surfaces have retoned
tan and orange at the margins.
From The Pasadena Collection, Part Two.(#6175)

2030 **1837 MS60 ANACS.** Well-defined with no trace of wear, though
the devices show a number of wispy abrasions. Gold-orange and
tan peripheral shadings surround untoned centers.(#6176)

2031 **1837 MS63 NGC.** Originally toned in shades of jade-green, coral-
red, and grayish-brown. Boldly struck with appealing, satiny luster.
Small marks limit the grade.(#6176)

Lustrous MS64 1837 Reeded Edge Half

2032 **1837 MS64 NGC.** Dappled golden-brown and russet toning
enriches this brightly lustrous and surprisingly well struck silver
type coin. The fields are remarkably smooth, and only moderate
contact near the chin prevents an even higher grade. Second and
final year of the 50 CENTS reverse.(#6176)

Wonderful MS64 1837 Half Dollar

2033 **1837 MS64 NGC.** Beautifully detailed with electrifying eye
appeal. On the obverse, pale silver-green outer toning fades
into ocean-blue and rose, with similar colors on the reverse in
patches. Gorgeous luster shines through the rich patina. An
outstanding example of this popular Reeded Edge half dollar issue.
(#6176)

2034 **1838 AU58 NGC.** A radiant, satiny sheen encompasses the light
silver-gray surfaces of this attractive near-Mint example. Boldly
struck with mere traces of highpoint wear on each side, and a
handful of minor abrasions on Liberty's neck.(#6177)

Bold 1838 Half Dollar, MS63

2035 **1838 MS63 PCGS.** Pleasing drab-olive coloration gives way at
the peripheries to charcoal-gray, with copper and golden hints in
the fields. This piece has a wonderfully bold strike, and it is perhaps
only a couple of stray, undistracting scrapes near the rim that
preclude an even finer grade. Population: 58 in 63, 48 finer (2/09).
(#6177)

Desirable MS63 1838 Half Dollar

2036 **1838 MS63 PCGS.** Dappled gold, violet, and russet peripheral
shadings surround silver-gray centers. A luminous Select piece,
minimally marked and appealing for the grade but with a handful
of wispy abrasions in the fields surrounding the portrait. PCGS has
certified 48 finer examples (2/09).(#6177)

2037 **1839-O AU55 ICG.** Subtly lustrous with silver-gray centers. Each
side of this modestly worn piece shows reddish-orange, green-gold,
and blue peripheral toning.
From The Pasadena Collection, Part Two.(#6181)

Appealing 1839-O Half Dollar, MS64

2038 **1839-O MS64 NGC.** The mintmark is boldly doubled below, as usually (or always) seen. Both dies are noticeably cracked, also as often seen. This incredible near-Gem has ivory luster beneath intense gold, violet, and sky-blue toning on both sides, the deeper shades closer to the border. The surfaces are smooth and frosty, with few surface marks on either side. The 1839-O is the first collectible New Orleans half dollar, and the only collectible example of the Capped Bust design from that mint. The earlier 1838-O half dollar is a major rarity, with less than 20 pieces known. Census: 14 in 64, 9 finer (1/09).(#6181)

SEATED HALF DOLLARS

2039 **1842-O Small Date, Small Letters VF20 PCGS.** WB-101, "Reverse of 1839" as described by PCGS. Softly struck as always with moderate wear over each side. Deep reddish-tan toning dominates the fields. Minimally marked save for a few abrasions on the figure of Liberty. For the Small Date, Small Letters variety, Population: 5 in 20, 37 finer (2/09).(#6238)

2040 **1842 Medium Date, Large Letters MS62 NGC.** WB-105. FS-301. The "Tripled Date" variety with recutting beneath the 842. Golden-brown with peripheral ocean-blue. Well struck and lightly abraded with moderately diminished luster across the open fields.(#6239)

2041 **1843 MS62 PCGS.** Both sides are subtly lustrous beneath dusky patina. Lilac-gray centers cede to deeper violet and green-gold close to the rims. Population: 10 in 62, 25 finer (2/09).(#6243)

Late-State 1844 Half Dollar, MS63

2042 **1844 MS63 PCGS.** WB-101, Normal Date. This piece offers considerably more eye appeal than might be expected for the Select Mint State grade assigned. The lustrous surfaces show a bold strike, quite close to full, with reflective fields and silvery centers that cede to shades of amber and cinnamon at the margins. A few faint hairlines and minor evidence of contact apparently constitute the grade. There is little field-device contrast noted, however: The dies had clearly been in use for a long time, as despite the bold strike numerous peripheral die cracks are seen on both sides, sometimes intersecting one another and indicating a reverse die, in particular, close to shattering. An attractive and interesting example of this issue. Population: 25 in 63, 14 finer (2/09).(#6245)

Charming Select 1844 Half Dollar

2043 **1844 MS63 PCGS. CAC.** While the 1844 half dollar has a healthy mintage of over 1.7 million pieces, few Mint State examples have survived to the present day. This Select coin is a delightful exception, its emerald-accented silver-white surfaces bright and appealing. Scattered abrasions in the fields account for the grade. Population: 25 in 63, 14 finer (2/09).(#6245)

2044 **1844-O MS62 PCGS.** Strongly lustrous with minimal patina save for dots of reddish-tan near the rims. Struck from a heavily polished obverse die with a thin ring of die cracks through the stars. Population: 6 in 62, 13 finer (2/09).(#6246)

2045 **1844-O Doubled Date Fine 12 PCGS.** WB-103. FS-301, formerly FS-001. A dramatic repunched date, with the errant digits slanting into the base of the seated Liberty, pictured and listed in the *Guide Book*. Despite significant wear, this gold-tinged silver-gray piece shows the repunching clearly.(#6247)

2046 **1844-O Doubled Date Fine 15 PCGS.** WB-103. Described in Wiley-Bugert as a "Dramatically Doubled Date," and even on this significantly worn piece, the four underdigits are bold. Each side shows a combination of silver-gray and slate toning. For the variety, Population: 3 in 15, 30 finer (2/09).(#6247)

2047 **1844-O Doubled Date XF40 PCGS. CAC.** WB-103. FS-301, formerly FS-001. One of the most striking repunched dates in American coinage, represented here by an appealing XF coin. Deep slate-gray surfaces show glimpses of rose and gold close to the centers. For the variety, Population: 7 in 40, 18 finer (2/09). (#6247)

2048 **1845-O AU55 ANACS.** WB-106, FS-302, formerly FS-002. A prominent triple-punched date that shows underdigits to the south. Strongly lustrous with reddish-orange and blue peripheral toning around nearly brilliant centers. Wear is minimal.(#6249)

2049 **1850-O MS63 PCGS.** Lustrous surfaces display pastel ice-blue, beige, and faint lilac patina. The design elements are well executed, though the last two stars along the lower right (facing) border are a trifle soft. A few grade-limiting marks are noted on Liberty's portrait and in the left (facing) obverse field.(#6265)

Condition Rarity 1850-O Half Dollar, MS64

2050 **1850-O MS64 PCGS.** The 1850-O is a difficult acquisition in Mint State, where Randy Wiley and Bill Bugert (1993) assign the date a low R.5. Soft bluish-gray and champagne-gold patina adorn the lustrous surfaces of this near-Gem, and a decisive strike leaves strong definition on the design elements. Minute contact marks preclude Gem classification. Population: 17 in 64, 11 finer (2/09). (#6265)

2051 **1852 XF45 ANACS.** WB-101. Each side shows deep violet-gray and slate-blue color. Light wear crosses the design on each side, and the obverse fields show a handful of small digs.(#6268)

Lustrous 1853 Arrows and Rays Half Dollar, MS64

2052 **1853 Arrows and Rays MS64 PCGS.** Lustrous silver-gray surfaces display whispers of orange-gold, especially around the borders. The design elements are sharply struck, including separation of liberty's foot and sandal. Scattered light marks keep from Gem status. PCGS has seen only 20 coins finer (2/09).(#6275)

Shining 1853 Arrows and Rays Half, MS64

2053 **1853 Arrows and Rays MS64 PCGS. CAC.** The surfaces are pearl-gray, with considerable original luster readily apparent under a light, which also reveals shades of sunset-gold and ice-blue. The strike is neither soft nor bold but reveals the apparent celerity with which these pieces were struck. Despite the considerable mintage of more than 3.5 million pieces this type issue is seldom found at the Gem level or finer, where PCGS has certified only 20 pieces (2/09).(#6275)

2054 **1853-O Arrows and Rays AU55 NGC.** A popular one-year type with arrows beside the date and rays around the eagle, created after a slight weight change was instituted for the type. Boldly struck and untoned, with minor hairlines on each side. A thick die crack extends through HALF DOL., and a grease stain (as made) resides below the eagle's left (facing) wing. Census: 26 in 55, 43 finer (2/09).(#6276)

Desirable 1854-O Arrows Half, MS64

2055 **1854-O Arrows MS64 NGC.** Fresh luster with only glimpses of gold visiting the otherwise silver-white surfaces. A trifle softly struck at the margins, but the centers are well-defined. A pleasing near-Gem representative of this popular O-mint Arrows half, one of several popular type issues for the design variety. Census: 69 in 64, 21 finer (2/09).(#6280)

Notable 1855 Arrows Half Dollar, MS64

2056 **1855 Arrows MS64 PCGS. CAC.** A favorable strike leaves strong design detail on this near-Gem half, with the exception of softness on the last three stars and the eagle's left (facing) leg and claw. Lustrous surfaces are nearly untoned, save for hints of light gold-tan that show up under magnification on the obverse. A few minute handling marks preclude Gem classification. Population: 13 in 64, 6 finer (2/09).(#6281)

2057 **1856-O MS63 PCGS.** WB-102. A repunched date variety with the underlying date at an angle, such that the 1 has the underdigit to the south and the 56 with their underdigits to the north. Delicate golden tints enliven the obverse, while the shining reverse remains pale silver-gray.(#6288)

Condition Scarcity 1857 Gem Half Dollar

2058 **1857 MS65 NGC.** The 1857 is a common coin in circulated grades, but scarce in Mint State. This Gem displays pleasing satiny luster on silver-gray surfaces that are imbued with hints of light tan on the reverse. The design elements are well struck, save for softness in Liberty's hair and the star centers along the right border. A nicely preserved coin. Census: 12 in 65, 3 finer (2/09). (#6290)

2059 **1858 MS64 PCGS.** A lovely satin representative with hints of lilac and champagne toning on both sides. A nicely detailed piece, denied Gem status by a few minute marks. Population: 58 in 64, 15 finer (2/09).(#6293)

2060 **1859 MS64 NGC.** Both sides of this near-Gem are awash with potent luster, and each displays light to medium orange-gold patina, accented with an occasional splash of sky-blue. Excellent delineation shows on the design features, save for minor softness on the eagle's left (facing) leg and claw. Strong eye appeal. Census: 19 in 64, 10 finer (2/09).(#6296)

Attractive MS64 1860 Half Dollar

2061 **1860 MS64 PCGS.** Soft, swirling luster percolates beneath rich green-gold, amber, and sage patina. Solidly struck and minimally marked save for an abrasion in the upper right obverse field. A relatively available issue in circulated grades, the 1860 half dollar becomes conditionally rare at the near-Gem level. Population: 13 in 64, 9 finer (2/09).(#6299)

Bright, Lustrous MS64 1861-O Half

2062 **1861-O MS64 PCGS.** W-4, struck while the New Orleans Mint was under the authority of the State of Louisiana. This particular piece is highly lustrous and mostly brilliant, with a few abrasions scattered over each side that limit the upside potential of the grade. The striking details are strong in all areas except for the uppermost stars on the obverse and the top of Liberty's head, a common trait on Seated halves. Population: 22 in 64, 12 finer (2/09).(#6303)

Appealing MS64 1863 Half Dollar

2063 **1863 MS64 PCGS. CAC.** This Civil War-era half is well-defined with strong luster beneath rich patina. Green-gold and lavender-gray shadings are predominant, though a few dots of deeper toning appear at the liberty cap and on and to the left of the shield. Carefully preserved for the grade. Population: 19 in 64, 12 finer (2/09).(#6309)

2064 **1864 MS63 PCGS.** Softly lustrous and attractive. The glimpses of violet toning that frame a silver-white center on the obverse are out in full force on the reverse. Population: 14 in 63, 23 finer (2/09).(#6311)

Conditionally Elusive 1867 Half Dollar, MS64

2065 **1867 MS64 PCGS.** WB-101. Normal Date. Gorgeous, deep multicolored toning adorns each side of this visually alluring near-Gem. The design elements are sharply struck, and even the hair detail on the top of Liberty's head is crisply rendered. An abrasion on Liberty's upper chest and a few faint hairlines in the right obverse field limit the grade. Wiley and Bugert (1993) assigned this variety a Low R.6 rarity ranking in Mint State in their *Complete Guide to Liberty Seated Half Dollars*. Population: 9 in 64, 7 finer (2/09).(#6321)

Challenging 1870-CC Half, VF20 Details

2066 **1870-CC—Scratched—ICG. VF20 Details.** WB-101. The noted scratches appear to be of older vintage in the right field, and they are now worn over and undistracting. A small apparent planchet recession from star 1 into the rim nearby is filled with some old black buildup, and there is another small planchet depression near star 13. These minor planchet flaws actually add to the piquancy of the coin, attesting to the difficulty that the fledgling Carson City Mint had with striking the first of the denomination. The reverse displays only the expected grade-consistent wear.(#6328)

Noteworthy 1870-CC Half Dollar AU53

2067 **1870-CC AU53 PCGS.** While a surprising number of 1870-CC silver dollars were apparently set aside as souvenirs, the entire inaugural half dollar issue from Carson City went into circulation and stayed there. Only two pieces have been certified as Mint State, one each as MS62 by NGC and PCGS, which may represent the same ex: Reed Hawn, James Bennett Pryor example. By comparison, the 1870-CC dollar, which has about one-fifth the mintage of its half dollar counterpart, has a combined NGC and PCGS Mint State population of 34 pieces.

At the AU53 level, the present piece probably fits within the Condition Census for the issue. It is an untoned and impressively detailed example with unblemished surfaces. Luster is evident within the drapery, eagle, shields, and legends. Population: 2 in 53, 2 finer (2/09).
From The Belle Collection of Carson City Coinage.(#6328)

Desirable XF40 1871-CC Fifty Cent

2068 **1871-CC XF40 PCGS.** Whispers of subtle luster remain in the fields of this silver-gray example, struck in the second year of coinage for the Carson City Mint. Several wispy abrasions run vertically in the right obverse field, but these flaws have little impact on the overall visual appeal. Population: 12 in 40, 33 finer (2/09).(#6331)

Scarce 1871-CC Half Dollar, AU50

2069 **1871-CC AU50 PCGS.** This issue is very scarce overall, and extremely rare in Mint State, of which a mere five specimens have been certified by PCGS and NGC. This pleasing AU example displays traces of luster in the protected areas of the light orange-gold and violet surfaces. Both sides are sharply struck and reveal just a few minute circulation marks.
From The Belle Collection of Carson City Coinage.(#6331)

Impressive Near-Gem 1872 Seated Half

2070 **1872 MS64 NGC.** Perhaps the most remarkable aspect of this appealing near-Gem is the great sharpness and precision of striking definition on all design elements. Essentially untoned and free of distractions, although a hair-thin pinscratch extends from the upper obverse rim near 11 o'clock across Liberty's head and flag to end at star 11. Few examples of this issue survive in high grades, despite a plentiful mintage of 880,600 pieces. Census: 6 in 64, 5 finer (2/09).(#6333)

Challenging 1872-CC Seated Half, AU Details

2071 **1872-CC—Improperly Cleaned—NCS. AU Details.** WB-101. The 1872-CC Seated half dollar issue had a mintage of 257,000 pieces, not a small number for the type from the Carson City Mint. Survivors are few, however, and the 1872-CC remains a scarce issue at all grade levels. This improperly cleaned example displays somewhat streaky brownish-gray coloration across each side. This well defined, minimally worn piece shows a few noticeable abrasions on the obverse, the most prominent one extending beneath stars 5 through 7.(#6334)

Rare Choice AU 1872-CC Half

2072 **1872-CC AU55 PCGS.** Despite a reasonable production of 257,000 pieces, the 1872-CC is surprisingly rare in Choice AU or finer. Most survivors have greater wear from circulation, and many pieces are cleaned or damaged. But the present coin has nearly full detail, and marks are limited to unimportant contact on the obverse field. The rich sea-green and tan-brown toning only adds to the eye appeal. Population: 9 in 55, 7 finer (2/09).
From The Belle Collection of Carson City Coinage.(#6334)

1873 Open 3, No Arrows Half, Good 6
A Major Seated Half Dollar Rarity

2073 **1873 Open 3, No Arrows Good 6 PCGS.** WB-101. While the mintage of 214,200 pieces is unimpressive, the survivorship of the Open 3, No Arrows halves is exceptionally low. To understand why, think of this date as being struck in three different periods. First, the Closed 3 coins were produced. Second, the Open 3 halves were struck after it was discovered that the 3 in the date more closely resembled an 8 than a 3. It was during this period that this coin was minted. Third, the weight was slightly altered and arrows placed on each side of the date to signify the change. An unknown but apparently large percentage of the mintage was melted in order to produce the With Arrows coins, thus creating a No Arrows rarity. This is a pleasing piece for the grade with heavy, even wear over the devices. The centers are pinkish-gray with deeper gray peripheries. The only detracting marks are a couple of parallel scratches in the right obverse field to the right of Liberty's knee. (#6337)

Notable 1873-CC No Arrows Half, XF40

2074 **1873-CC No Arrows XF40 PCGS.** An appreciably worn but highly appealing representative of this old-tenor issue, modestly marked in the fields but with few flaws on the devices. The obverse has rose-gray patina with only subtle variations, though the reverse shows areas of teak-brown and charcoal near the eagle's talons and the denomination. Population: 12 in 40, 30 finer (2/09). (#6338)

Elusive Mint State 1873-CC No Arrows Half

2075 **1873-CC No Arrows MS61 NGC.** WB-101, Small Mintmark. Two obverse dies are known for this rare subtype, both, of course, lacking the arrows at the date and showing the Close 3 date style. Coins of this issue, due to extensive melting, are extremely rare in Mint State, given an R.7 rarity rating by Wiley-Bugert. In MS61 this piece is one of two so graded (or one twice) at NGC, with a mere four coins finer (2/09). This is an exceedingly nice piece for the grade, with plenty of luster emanating throughout the golden-tinged fields. The strike is bold, although numerous wispy die cracks appear on both sides.
From The Belle Collection of Carson City Coinage. (#6338)

2076 **1873 Arrows MS62 NGC.** Gold, orange, and pink peripheral shadings frame pale silver-gray centers. A satiny example that is minimally abraded for the grade. Census: 24 in 62, 56 finer (1/09). (#6343)

Extremely Scarce 1873-CC Arrows Fifty Cent, AU58

2077 **1873-CC Arrows AU58 PCGS.** The 1873-CC Arrows half is extremely scarce in the AU58 level of preservation and quite rare in Mint State. This sharply struck near-Mint State example retains considerable luster on the light golden-gray surfaces that are devoid of significant marks. Population: 9 in 58, 15 finer (2/09).
From The Belle Collection of Carson City Coinage. (#6344)

Seldom Encountered 1873-CC Half Dollar With Arrows, MS64

Choice AU 1874-CC Arrows Half

2080 **1874-CC Arrows AU55 PCGS. CAC.** WB-101. A small tine extends from atop the eagle's head, and there is a noticeable die line through ES in STATES. The Randy Wiley-Bill Bugert Seated half reference (1993) calls this issue, with a mintage of 59,000 pieces, "rare in XF and above." This lovely Choice AU example displays golden-gray and apple-green patina. Well struck, save for minor softness in some of the star centers and on portions of the reverse motto. Both sides show only meager marks despite a brief stint in circulation. Population: 7 in 55, 17 finer (2/09).
Ex: Dallas Signature (Heritage, 11/2007), lot 784, which realized $9,200.
From The Belle Collection of Carson City Coinage.(#6347)

2081 **1875 MS64 PCGS.** Rich golden-brown and apple-green integrate throughout this satiny and solidly struck Choice half. The reverse is remarkably smooth, and the obverse field has only faint grazes. Population: 34 in 64, 18 finer (2/09).(#6349)

Originally Toned MS65 1875 Half Dollar

2082 **1875 MS65 PCGS. CAC.** More than 6 million half dollars were struck in 1875. Yet the issue is hardly common in Uncirculated condition, and full Gems are rare. The present highly lustrous example has pleasing lime-green and copper-gold toning, and the strike is unimprovably sharp. Abrasions are virtually absent, and the eye appeal is exceptional. An excellent candidate for an enviable type set. Population: 13 in 65, 5 finer (2/09).(#6349)

2083 **1876 MS64 PCGS.** A remarkably well struck and blemish-free example of this low-mintage Seated half dollar issue. Deep, variegated patina across both sides is a testament to the originality of this visually alluring specimen. Population: 50 in 64, 17 finer (1/09).(#6352)

2078 **1873-CC Arrows MS64 PCGS. CAC.** Arrowheads were placed beside the date on all half dollars minted after April 1873 to indicate a small weight change in the planchet. The new coins contained slightly more silver than their earlier counterparts, and were designed to have an exact metric weight of 12.5 grams. At the Carson City Mint, 214,560 half dollars were struck using the new standard in 1873. The issue is scarce in all grades today, and Mint State examples are rare. NGC has graded four coins at the MS64 level, with two finer; while PCGS has certified eight examples in MS64, with two finer (2/09).

The coin offered here is sharply struck throughout, with attractive steel-gray toning, accented by horizontal streaks of russet and lilac. The surfaces show a minimum number of handling marks for the grade. Since this issue is virtually unobtainable at the Gem level, the present specimen represents an important opportunity for advanced type collectors and half dollar specialists.(#6344)

2079 **1874-CC Arrows VG10 ICG.** WB-101. A cream-gray and ice-blue example of this challenging early Carson City half. Considerably scarcer than the other Arrows issue, the 1873-CC. Most of the L and Y in LIBERTY are clear. No marks are evident. (#6347)

Satiny Gem 1876-CC Half Dollar

2084 **1876-CC MS65 PCGS.** Ex: Battle Born Collection. WB-102, Medium CC. Caramel-gold and dove-gray embrace this satiny and remarkably unabraded Gem. An intricate strike, fully brought up save for trivial incompleteness on the eagle's left (facing) ankle. An outstanding Carson City type coin. Population: 8 in 65, 4 finer (2/09).
Ex: FUN Signature (Heritage, 1/2009), lot 2880, which realized $6,900.
From The Belle Collection of Carson City Coinage. (#6353)

Impressive 1876-S Half Dollar, MS65

2085 **1876-S MS65 PCGS. CAC.** This piece is similar to WB-102 with a small mintmark, although the mintmark on this piece leans sharply to the left. A wonderful Gem with smooth surfaces and satin luster beneath splendid iridescent toning. The strike is essentially full with sharp definition on Liberty's head, bold feather details, and sharp claws. Population: 9 in 65, 3 finer (2/09). (#6354)

2086 **1877 MS64 PCGS.** Crisply detailed with great eye appeal for this popular type issue. Strongly reflective at the green-gold and blue margins with the gold-gray centers more satiny in appearance. Population: 50 in 64, 30 finer (1/09).(#6355)

2087 **1877 MS64 PCGS.** Sharply struck with considerable reflectivity to the cloud-white fields. Minimally marked overall, though a degree of field chatter is noted near Liberty's right (facing) foot. Population: 50 in 64, 30 finer (2/09).(#6355)

Popular Near-Gem 1877-CC Half

2088 **1877-CC MS64 PCGS.** Type Two Reverse. A richly patinated obverse is the most memorable feature of this near-Gem CC-mint half dollar. Russet coloration dominates the fields, with steel-blue toning at the peripheries and central device. The reverse is rich steel-gray aside from russet-gold near the rims. Precisely struck and well preserved with noticeable luster and good eye appeal. Population: 39 in 64, 19 finer (2/09).
Ex: Dallas Signature (Heritage, 10/2008), lot 917, which realized $2,760.
From The Belle Collection of Carson City Coinage. (#6356)

2089 **1877-S MS64 PCGS.** Type Two Reverse with a closed bud above the H in HALF. Lovely golden-brown toning fills the margins of this satiny and impressively unabraded Choice half dollar. The strike is irreproachably sharp.(#6357)

2090 **1877-S MS64 PCGS. CAC.** Ex: Gil Clark. A beautifully toned piece exhibiting various shades of cherry-red, antique-gold, and blue-green over the obverse and reverse. Well struck, a couple of minor contact marks on the obverse limit the grade. An excellent candidate for a type collection. PCGS has certified 36 finer pieces (2/09).
From The Burning Tree Collection.(#6357)

2091 **1878-CC VF25 PCGS.** WB-101. This is a low mintage issue of just 62,000 pieces; also the final year of half dollar production at the Carson City Mint. This example features moderate wear and variegated rose-gray and charcoal toning. A single noteworthy abrasion is located on the right obverse field, below and to the left of star 11. Population: 2 in 25, 35 finer (2/09).(#6359)

Low Mintage 1879 Half Dollar, MS67 ★
One of Two Certified With Star

2092 **1879 MS67 ★ NGC.** Only 4,800 circulation strike half dollars were produced in 1879. Randy Wiley and Bill Bugert (1993) attribute this low mintage to the implementation of the Bland-Allison Act of 1878. This MS67 with Star example displays partially prooflike fields that nicely offset the motifs. A medley of light cobalt-blue, yellow-gold, lavender, and orange patina enriches impeccably preserved surfaces, and a decisive strike lends sharp definition to the design elements. Census: 2 in 67 ★, 0 finer (2/09). (#6361)

2093 **1885 MS63 PCGS.** A pleasing Select example that shows ample luster beneath rich patina. Green-gold, blue, and violet shadings cover modestly abraded surfaces. Population: 19 in 63, 29 finer (1/09).(#6367)

2094 **1886 MS63 NGC.** Frosty across the central devices with a sharp strike and flashy luster. Peripheral blue and gold accents yield to untoned centers. Census: 15 in 63, 42 finer (1/09).(#6368)

Elusive 1888 Seated Half, MS66

2095 **1888 MS66 PCGS. CAC.** Well struck, save for typical slight weakness on the top of Liberty's head and on star 8 nearby. Satiny, coruscating luster shimmers over each side. The rose-gray central toning yields to mottled sea-green, russet, and olive-drab patina in the fields and near the borders. Population: 18 in 66, 4 finer (2/09). (#6370)

Marvelous MS66 1888 Half Dollar

2096 **1888 MS66 NGC.** With just 12,000 pieces struck, this Philadelphia issue's token mintage has low availability from the start, and it is a condition rarity at the Premium Gem level. This MS66 coin is immensely lustrous with russet and violet peripheral toning giving way to pale silver-gray centers. Census: 20 in 66, 9 finer (2/09). (#6370)

2097 **1890 MS61 NGC.** Strongly reflective and well-defined for a business strike, though slight cartwheels in the fields confirm this coin's Mint State status. Blue, violet, and gold-orange peripheral shadings yield to silver-white elsewhere. Census: 3 in 61, 55 finer (2/09).(#6372)

PROOF SEATED HALF DOLLARS

Scarce 1856 Proof Half Dollar

2098 **1856—Altered Surface—NCS. Proof.** The surfaces show the details grade of a PR60 coin, but this is not designated on the insert. Significant because of the scarcity of pre-1858 proofs, only 25 pieces are estimated to have been struck of this date. The surfaces are brilliant throughout, and each side is heavily hairlined. Nevertheless, slight field-device contrast can still be seen on each side.(#6410)

Impressive 1856 Half Dollar, PR65

2099 **1856 PR65 NGC.** Mintage figures for this rare proof half dollar issue are unknown. Randy Wiley and Bill Bugert (1993) say less than 25 specimens are known, approximately the same estimate given by Walter Breen in his 1988 *Encyclopedia*. Breen lists 11 examples in his 1989 *Proof Encyclopedia*, and the possibility of three more. NGC and PCGS have certified 29 examples, some of which may be resubmissions.

The obverse has short diagonal lines from and in the border below and left of the 1, and a tiny diamond die chip inside star 13. The reverse has unfinished areas between the leaves and arrowheads, and imperfect lines in the first vertical shield stripe. The same lines extend upward through several horizontal shield lines. Lavender and golden-tan toning concentrates at the margins of this Gem, leaving the centers light champagne color. An exacting strike completes the design features. A few minute contact marks and some faint field hairlines do not detract in the least from the coin's overall appeal. Census: 3 in 65, 2 finer (2/09). (#6410)

Lovely 1864 Seated Half Dollar, PR64 Cameo

2100 **1864 PR64 Cameo PCGS.** A relatively large number of the 470-piece half dollar proof mintage for 1864 has survived, if the population data are any indication. PCGS and NGC have seen a total of about 300 examples (including resubmissions). Only 38 Cameo coins have been certified, however. The near-Gem offered here displays stunning field-motif contrast. Moreover, the frosted design features are exquisitely struck throughout, adding to the coin's outstanding eye appeal. Hints of light tan color gravitate to the margins. A few minute obverse marks preclude an even higher grade. Population: 14 in 64 Cameo, 1 finer (1/09).(#86418)

Gorgeous 1866 Motto Half, PR66

2101 **1866 Motto PR66 NGC.** Vivid iridescent hues of gunmetal-blue, purple, and sunset-gold gravitate to the margins on each side of this first-year With Motto issue, leaving the centers a soft champagne-gold. Sharply struck and nicely preserved. Certainly one of the finest survivors from a mintage of 725 proofs. Census: 7 in 66, 1 finer (2/09).(#6424)

Patinated Gem Proof 1867 Half

2102 **1867 PR65 NGC.** Jade-green and peach-gold envelop this penetratingly struck and unblemished Gem. The flashy fields and iridescent patina combine to provide dramatic eye appeal. Perusal beneath a loupe fails to find any noticeable hairlines. A meager 625 proofs were struck. Census: 26 in 65, 6 finer (2/09).(#6425)

Splendid 1867 Half Dollar, PR65 Cameo

2103 **1867 PR65 Cameo NGC.** The relatively low business strike mintage was less than a half-million coins, but this proof would see collector pressure in any case, just due to its superior aesthetics. The silver-white surfaces are almost devoid of distraction, save for a faint patch of hairlines in the right obverse field, where a single dot of dark color also rests. There is splendid field-device contrast, and the strike is razor-sharp. A minor contact mark above the F in HALF also fails to detract. Census: 10 in 65 Cameo, 7 finer (2/09). (#86425)

2104 **1869 PR64 PCGS.** Diverse sea-green, plum-red, and caramel-gold patina emerges when this unabraded near-Gem is rotated beneath a light. The strike is crisp save for slight incompleteness on the eagle's left (facing) ankle. A mere 600 proofs were coined. Population: 46 in 64, 16 finer (2/09).
From The Burning Tree Collection.(#6427)

2105 **1870 PR64 Cameo NGC.** In spite of a considerable proof mintage for the series, of 1,000 pieces, Cameo proof 1870s are exceedingly difficult to locate. In fact, this is the only Cameo proof of this issue at NGC, while PCGS has certified five Cameo proofs in all grades (2/09). This lovely specimen has untoned, brilliant ice-white surfaces that contrast well against the mildly frosted devices. Slight striking weakness on the central reverse and a few stray hairlines in the right obverse field seemingly preclude a Gem grade. (#86428)

Razor-Sharp 1872 Half Dollar, PR65

2106 **1872 PR65 NGC.** Gunmetal-blue, purple, and gold-beige patina is slightly deeper in hue on the obverse of this Gem proof. Razor-sharp delineation endows the design features, including complete separation of Liberty's foot from the sandal and straps. No mentionable marks are apparent on either side. Census: 12 in 65, 11 finer (2/09).(#6430)

Sharply Struck 1872 Gem Proof Half Dollar

2107　**1872 PR65 PCGS.** Deep electric-blue, lavender, sky-blue, and beige-gold toning covers both sides of this Gem proof, and a well executed strike sharps the design elements. Some inoffensive, grade-consistent handling marks are concealed in the toning. Population: 11 in 65, 3 finer (2/09).(#6430)

Beautiful PR66 1872 Half Dollar

2108　**1872 PR66 NGC.** This needle-sharp Premium Gem is principally silver-gray, but the borders display bands of cherry-red, honey-gold, and lime-green. Among the nicest survivors from the low proof mintage of 950 pieces. Certified in a former generation holder. Census: 8 in 66, 3 finer (2/09).(#6430)

Colorful 1874 Arrows Half, PR65

2109　**1874 Arrows PR65 PCGS.** The toning enthusiast will find plenty to love about this crisp Gem proof. Blue-green and sapphire peripheral bands yield to violet before fading into the central color, a pale orange on the obverse and dusky rose on the reverse. An utterly enchanting specimen. Population: 14 in 65, 5 finer (2/09). (#6435)

Pleasing 1874 Arrows Half, PR63 Cameo

2110　**1874 Arrows PR63 Cameo PCGS.** A thin ring of reddish-russet patina circles both sides of this otherwise silver-gray specimen. Nearly every design element is fully defined, and there is little evidence of mishandling on either side. A problem-free Select proof specimen with pleasing eye appeal. Perfect for high grade proof type purposes. Population: 4 in 63 Cameo, 15 finer (1/09). (#86435)

2111　**1875 PR64 Cameo PCGS.** The strike has left this piece with mostly brilliant, white, mirrored surfaces and wonderful frost on the devices. Milky patina gives way to champagne color on the reverse. Population: 4 in 64 Cameo, 2 finer (2/09).(#86436)

Flashy Cameo Gem Proof 1876 Half

2112　**1876 PR65 Cameo NGC.** One of the interesting aspects of 1876 proof halves is that most show evidence of a dropped C letter punch on Liberty's neck. This C is similar in size to the punch used to form Carson City mintmarks. The fields are deeply reflective, and there is noticeable frost on the devices to confirm the cameo effect. The centers of each side are brilliant and encircled by wide bands of golden-brown, cherry-red, and navy-blue at the margins. Census: 8 in 65 Cameo, 6 finer (2/09).(#86437)

2113　**1878 PR64 PCGS.** A sumptuous Choice proof that combines a crisp strike with notable army-green and gunmetal-blue color. A few hairlines are hidden beneath the toning. Population: 48 in 64, 18 finer (1/09).(#6439)

2114　**1880 PR64 Cameo NGC.** Crisply detailed with ample frost on the devices and minimally toned, pleasingly mirrored fields. A few small patches of hairlines to either side of Liberty account for the grade. Census: 23 in 64 Cameo, 28 finer (1/09).(#86441)

2115　**1881 PR64 NGC. CAC.** Strong field-motif variance characterizes this near-Gem proof. Champagne-gold surfaces are accented with purple at the margins, and exhibit well struck design features. Light handling marks deny Gem classification. A strikethrough is visible on Liberty's pole hand. Census: 78 in 64, 66 finer (2/09). (#6442)

2116　**1881 PR64 PCGS. CAC.** Richly toned and gorgeous. Each side shows a touch of contrast, the lightly toned and frosted central devices standing out against the more dusky ocean-blue, orange, and gold fields. A few faint hairlines account for the grade but do not compromise the eye appeal.
From The Burning Tree Collection.(#6442)

Imposing Gem Proof 1882 Half

2117 1882 PR65 NGC. Exquisitely detailed and carefully preserved for this issue of 1,100 proofs. The fields and devices are richly toned, with gunmetal, ocean-blue, and orange-gold shadings prevailing across each side. Worthy of a quality matched Gem set of proofs. Census: 36 in 65, 23 finer (2/09).(#6443)

2118 1882 PR64 Cameo PCGS. A bright and essentially untoned survivor with strong field-to-device contrast. Modest hairlines in the fields account for the grade. Population: 15 in 64 Cameo, 13 finer (1/09).(#86443)

2119 1883 PR64 PCGS. Remarkably crisp and clear definition is seen on every element of this classic design. The devices are lightly frosted and the fields are mildly reflective. A couple of tiny contact marks are noted on the reverse.(#6444)

2120 1885 PR63 PCGS. Exquisitely detailed with prominent mirrors beneath subtle peach patina. A handful of wispy hairlines in the fields preclude a finer designation. Strong eye appeal nonetheless. (#6446)

Gorgeous PR65 ★ Cameo 1886 Half Dollar

2121 1886 PR65 ★ Cameo NGC. A strongly contrasted later proof Seated half of astonishing beauty. The silver-black fields are profoundly reflective, and the icy white frost of the devices is rich and bold. Careful preservation adds to the already-considerable eye appeal. NGC has graded just eight numerically finer Cameo specimens (2/09).(#86447)

2122 1887 PR63 PCGS. CAC. Strongly mirrored with minimal patina. This crisply detailed Select proof is well-preserved save for a few scattered hairlines in the fields. Housed in a green label holder. (#6448)

Cameo Gem Proof 1888 Half

2123 1888 PR65 Cameo PCGS. This delightful Gem has good cameo contrast between the luminous devices and the mirrored fields. The strike is intricate, and the eye appeal is obvious. A meager 832 proofs were produced, in addition to just 12,001 business strikes. Population: 11 in 65 Cameo, 2 finer (2/09).(#86449)

Boldly Struck 1889 Gem Proof Fifty Cent

2124 1889 PR65 NGC. Electric-blue, lavender, and yellow-gold patina endows the luminous surfaces of this Gem proof, and a powerful strike lends bold delineation to the design elements. Close examination reveals no marks worthy of individual mention. Census: 27 in 65, 24 finer (2/09).(#6450)

BARBER HALF DOLLARS

2125 1892 MS64 PCGS. This first-year entry is a solid near-Gem example that leans toward the higher end of that grade designation. Lustrous and essentially untoned, with pearl-gray coloration that merges with mild rose undertones in the obverse fields. Nicely preserved and free of major distractions.(#6461)

2126 1893-O MS64 PCGS. One of several elusive O-mint Barber halves, this earlier issue is scarce at the near-Gem level and a rarity any finer. The lustrous surfaces offer original shades of golden-orange and purple, with flashes of turquoise at the margins. Minute abrasions on Liberty's cheek are all that limit the grade. Population: 41 in 64, 7 finer (2/09).(#6466)

2127 1893-O MS64 PCGS. Well struck and satiny, with smoky rose-gray toning on the obverse and lighter steel-blue and peripheral gold patina on the reverse. Clash marks are noticeable just to right of Liberty's face on the obverse, and in the upper reverse field (clash marks are unusual on Barber halves). An attractive near-Gem example of this New Orleans issue. Population: 41 in 64, 7 finer (2/09).(#6466)

2128 1894 MS64 NGC. Satiny with strong detail and eye appeal. Rose-accented silver-gray surfaces exhibit considerable deepening at the margins and orange elements on the reverse. Census: 36 in 64, 21 finer (1/09).(#6468)

2129 1894 MS64 PCGS. Softly lustrous beneath gold-gray and rose patina with deeper outlines at the devices. Minimally marked and appealing. Population: 28 in 64, 24 finer (2/09).(#6468)

Scarce 1894-S Barber Half, MS64

2130 **1894-S MS64 NGC.** Reflective fields are accented by medium gray toning around the periphery. This piece is fully struck, and dazzling luster radiates from the fields. Numerous die polish lines (as made) are visible on the obverse, and only a few minor marks are noted on each side. Faint die cracks encircle the reverse lettering, and there is a small die crack on the truncation of the bust. A conditionally scarce example. Census: 28 in 64, 4 finer (1/09).(#6470)

Desirable Gem 1895 Half

2131 **1895 MS65 PCGS. CAC.** Powerful, satiny luster shines through the silver-blue, green-gold, and violet-magenta shadings that drape most of each side. Sharply struck devices are impressively preserved. This little-saved Philadelphia issue is a condition rarity at the Gem level. Population: 17 in 65, 6 finer (1/09).(#6471)

2132 **1899 MS64 PCGS.** Strong, swirling luster with hints of silver-gray patina on each side. Strongly appealing for a "merely" Choice example of this Barber half. Population: 46 in 64, 23 finer (2/09). (#6483)

2133 **1901 MS64 PCGS.** A fabulous near-Gem example of this turn-of-the-century issue, strongly lustrous beneath dusky honey, sage, and pomegranate patina. Moving eye appeal. Population: 43 in 64, 12 finer (1/09).(#6489)

2134 **1901-S AU53 PCGS.** The San Francisco Mint only produced 847,044 Barber quarters in 1901, and survivors are even scarcer than such a low original mintage would suggest. This example is boldly struck on the obverse, with a bit of softness observed on some parts of the reverse eagle, including the right (facing) talons and the tail feathers. Slightly worn with a few marks and minor hairlines on each side.(#6491)

Appealing Choice AU 1901-S Half

2135 **1901-S AU55 ANACS.** The obverse shows primarily gold-gray patina, while the reverse has dusky silver-blue toning over the fields. A few small marks on and around the well struck portrait have scant effect on the eye appeal. A briefly circulated example of this popular turn-of-the-century S-mint half, one with a mintage in the high six figures.(#6491)

2136 **1902 MS64 PCGS.** A lovely, bright satiny sheen encompasses each side of this untoned near-Gem example. Only the faintest of marks appear on the high points of the obverse design. Population: 47 in 64, 18 finer (1/09).(#6492)

2137 **1902 MS64 NGC.** Light golden tints visit generally silver-gray surfaces with swirling luster. An appealing example from this higher-mintage 20th century Barber half issue. Census: 39 in 64, 15 finer (1/09).(#6492)

Splendid Gem 1902-O Half

2138 **1902-O MS65 PCGS.** Sharply defined on the obverse, the reverse shows just a bit of softness in the usual areas. The right obverse field has noticeable die polishing marks, which give the coin additional brightness through the golden toning seen on each side. A magnificently preserved Gem. Population: 3 in 65, 3 finer (2/09).(#6493)

Impressive 1903-O Half Dollar MS64

2139 **1903-O MS64 PCGS.** Russet-red borders gradually cede to cream-gray centers. A satiny near-Gem with splendidly unabraded fields and devices. Only moderate incompleteness on strike on the eagle's neck and right shield corner denies a higher grade. Population: 44 in 64, 11 finer (2/09).(#6496)

Lovely 1904 Fifty Cent, MS65

2140 1904 MS65 PCGS. A predominance of cobalt-blue and reddish-gold greets the viewer of this lovely Gem. Some deep crimson is seen at the center of the reverse. Sharply struck and fully lustrous. There are a couple of minor abrasions on Liberty's cheek, the only signs of contact readily apparent with a loupe. Despite the large mintage (nearly 3 million business strikes), few were preserved in grades that even approach the present specimen. Population: 7 in 65, 5 finer (2/09).(#6498)

2141 1904-S VF30 PCGS. An appealing piece, pale silver-gray with light, scattered abrasions on each side. This midrange representative offers strong value for its lower-mintage issue. Population: 7 in 30, 71 finer (1/09).(#6500)

2142 1906 MS64 PCGS. Minimally toned save for a subtle streak of gray at the central reverse. Well-defined overall with just a handful of stray marks. Population: 71 in 64, 26 finer (1/09).(#6504)

2143 1906-D MS64 PCGS. Untoned surfaces exhibit well struck devices, save for weakness in the upper right corner of the shield and the adjacent feathers. Handling marks on the cheek and neck limit the grade. Population: 54 in 64, 23 finer (2/09).(#6505)

Pleasing 1906-O Half, MS64

2144 1906-O MS64 PCGS. Beautiful pink-gold obverse coloration predominates, with a sliver of ice-blue at the extreme rim. The reverse adds a counterpoint of olive-gold to the main theme. The strike is pleasingly well detailed for an O-mint production, and despite the moderate color both sides show a considerable amount of attractive luster radiating from beneath. A nice coin for the grade. Population: 25 in 64, 12 finer (2/09).
From The Burning Tree Collection.(#6506)

Lustrous 1906-S Fifty Cent, MS64

2145 1906-S MS64 PCGS. Whispers of olive-green, purple, gold, and ice-blue patina cover both sides of this near-Gem, each of which is awash with potent luster. A well executed strike imparts strong delineation to the design features, save for minor softness on the arrow feathers and adjacent claw, and in the upper right shield corner. Precluded from Gem status by a few minute marks. Population: 31 in 64, 17 finer (2/09).(#6507)

2146 1908-O MS64 PCGS. Both sides of this O-mint half are well-preserved and satiny. The obverse shows subtle rose and orange tints, while the reverse is essentially silver-white.(#6514)

2147 1909 MS64 PCGS. Glimpses of pink and orange emerge from the mostly silver-gray patina that drapes each side. Smoothly lustrous with a hint of satin to the fields.(#6516)

Desirable MS64 1909-O Half, Ex: Pittman

2148 1909-O MS64 NGC. Ex: Pittman. Strongly lustrous for this issue from the final year of strikings at the New Orleans Mint. Overall detail is pleasing, even on the often-weak claws. Several shallow depressions are noted on the portrait. Minimally toned at the centers with dots of blue and gold toning near the margins. Census: 15 in 64, 21 finer (1/09).(#6517)

Condition Rarity 1911 Half Dollar, MS66

2149 1911 MS66 PCGS. Variegated golden-russet coloration is moderate on the obverse and light on the reverse, but both sides demonstrate undiminished cartwheel iridescence. This well-preserved Premium Gem displays above average definition for the type, though a hint of softness is visible at the upper right shield corner. Rare in this grade. Population: 9 in 66, 0 finer (2/09). (#6521)

2150 1912 MS64 PCGS. Well struck for the issue with lustrous silver-gray centers. The margins show elements of gold and orange with a dot of deeper toning at the R in TRUST. Population: 77 in 64, 16 finer (1/09).(#6524)

Gem 1912 Barber Half

2151 **1912 MS65 PCGS.** Blazing luster emanates from both sides of this Gem Barber half, and each possesses a delicate blend of golden-brown and stone-gray patina. The design elements are sharply impressed, except for weakness in the upper right shield corner and adjacent feathers. The reverse appears immaculate, and the obverse is equally smooth save for a few faint ticks on the face. Population: 14 in 65, 2 finer (2/09).(#6524)

2152 **1913-D MS63 NGC.** Impressive, swirling luster is the hallmark of this D-mint Barber half. Light rose and silver-gray shadings overall with a soft strike and few abrasions. Census: 34 in 63, 50 finer (1/09).(#6528)

Sharp 1913-S Half Dollar, MS64

2153 **1913-S MS64 PCGS. CAC.** Splendid luster radiates from the silver-gold and olive-tinged surfaces of this low-mintage late-series S-mint issue. The dearth of dies in faraway (from Philadelphia) San Francisco is evinced by a couple of wispy die cracks seen around the obverse periphery, but the strike is admirable, both for the issue and the design. The tiny marks that show on Liberty's cheek likely determine the grade but are nonetheless undistracting. A prime candidate for a nice date or type set. *From The Burning Tree Collection.*(#6529)

2154 **1914 MS62 NGC.** This low mintage half dollar has good luster and light powder-blue and almond-gold toning. Crisply struck, and marks are minimal. In a prior generation holder. Census: 15 in 62, 64 finer (1/09). *From The Mario Eller Collection, Part Four.*(#6530)

Low Mintage 1915 Half Dollar, MS64

2155 **1915 MS64 PCGS.** This low mintage date (138,000 pieces) is one of the more difficult Barber halves to obtain in the better grades of Mint State. Soft violet, champagne-gold, and lavender patina endows the lustrous surfaces of this near-Gem, and a decisive strike imparts strong definition to the design elements. A few unobtrusive handling marks keeps from full Gem. Population: 23 in 64, 18 finer (2/09).(#6532)

2156 **1915-D MS64 PCGS.** This Barber type coin has only a glimpses of sun-gold toning, and the lustrous fields appear unabraded. The devices are well struck and exhibit only infrequent minor marks. (#6533)

2157 **1915-D MS64 PCGS.** Untoned save for a hint of gold at the peripheral reverse. Slight striking softness at the eagle's claws is of little concern. PCGS has graded 57 finer pieces (1/09). (#6533)

Splendid 1915-D Half Dollar, MS65

2158 **1915-D MS65 NGC. CAC.** Well struck overall with only trifling softness where the eagle's wings meet the shield. The strongly lustrous surfaces show whispers of gold against otherwise pale silver-gray fields. An excellent representative of this final Barber half issue struck at Denver. Census: 49 in 65, 8 finer (1/09).(#6533)

Impressive MS65 1915-D Half

2159 **1915-D MS65 NGC.** A relatively low-mintage striking (under 1.2 million pieces) from the waning years of the design, this Denver issue was little-saved and is a rarity any finer than this minimally toned Gem. Attractive luster and an above-average strike greatly enhance the visual appeal. NGC has graded just eight numerically superior pieces (1/09).(#6533)

Delightful Gem 1915-D Half

2160 **1915-D MS65 PCGS. CAC.** This shimmering and virtually unabraded Gem has blended medium autumn-gold and cream-gray toning. The strike is precise save for slight blending on the right shield corner. A solitary tiny aqua fleck is noted beneath the 5 in the date. Population: 45 in 65, 13 finer (2/09).(#6533)

2161 **1915-S MS64 NGC.** An arc of deep violet toning covers the left side of the obverse, while a touch of rose accents the remaining silver-gray surfaces. Pleasing satiny luster shimmers on both sides, and the surfaces show only a handful of faint grazes.(#6534)

Lustrous 1915-S Half Dollar, MS66

2162 **1915-S MS66 PCGS. CAC.** PCGS/NGC data show the 1915-S half to be available through the near-Gem grade level. Gems are scarce, and higher grade coins are rare (at least in the certified population). The silvery surfaces of this Premium Gem are awash in coruscating luster and display occasional freckles of light olive-green color. A well struck piece that is nicely preserved. Population: 6 in 66, 2 finer (2/09).(#6534)

PROOF BARBER HALF DOLLARS

2163 **1892 PR65 PCGS. CAC.** An interesting Gem proof with unusual toning patterns. The obverse is bright silver at the left, with gold, rose, and iridescent toning over most of Liberty and the right field. A curved untoned line is evident on the cheek and neck. The reverse has much deeper lilac and steel coloration.(#6539)

Great 1893 Barber Half, PR65 Cameo

2164 **1893 PR65 Cameo NGC.** A great proof specimen, with watery reflectivity in the fields and softly frosted devices. Essentially untoned, with slight haze over each side. The design elements are fully struck, and even the eagle's right (facing) talons show crisp definition. A conditionally scarce Gem with the Cameo designation. Census: 12 in 65 Cameo, 30 finer (2/09).(#86540)

2165 **1894 PR64 PCGS.** Sharply struck and free of contact marks, the surfaces overall display a richness of color and originality that is virtually impossible to duplicate. The obverse is blanketed in deep purple-rose and electric-blue coloration. The reverse shows the same electric-blue and purple-rose patina, intermixed with golden-orange.(#6541)

2166 **1894 PR64 NGC.** A bright, untoned proof. The eagle's right (facing) wing lacks definition at its juncture with the shield. A couple of small contact marks are seen on Liberty's cheek. (#6541)

Nicely Toned PR66 1895 Half Dollar

2167 **1895 PR66 PCGS.** The mintage for proof halves from 1895 is the same as that for the famous dollars; that is, 880 pieces. However, the difference is 1.8 million pieces were struck for circulation, thus relieving the date pressure for the halves that is seen for the dollars. This piece has lovely toning on each side, a bit deeper on the obverse than the reverse. The fields are brightly mirrored on each side, and there are no mentionable contact marks.(#6542)

Sharp 1895 Half Dollar, PR66 Cameo

2168 **1895 PR66 Cameo NGC.** By 1895 whatever languid enthusiasm might have existed for the Barber designs had evaporated, and from the first-year total of more than 1,200 proof half dollars, by this fourth year of production the net coinage had slumped to 880 pieces. This coin is among the finer survivors, with good field-device contrast and untoned, silver-white surfaces that betray the slightest blush of champagne tint on the reverse. Census: 19 in 66 Cameo, 19 finer (2/09).(#86542)

2169 **1898 PR64 PCGS.** Surprisingly, this piece did not receive a Cameo designation. While the green-gold toning over the obverse fields disguises the effect on that side somewhat, the reverse shows full-on contrast that borders on Deep Cameo territory. (#6545)

Gorgeous 1898 Barber Half, PR65 Cameo

2170 **1898 PR65 Cameo PCGS.** Gorgeous iridescent hues of steel-blue hug the rims, with rose-pink, gold, and silver working inward toward the centers of each side. The silver centers and deep field-device contrast justly merit the Cameo designation, although it is unusual for PCGS to award it to a coin with so much peripheral color. Well struck throughout. From a proof mintage of 735 coins. Population: 10 in 65 Cameo, 10 finer (2/09).(#86545)

2171 **1899 PR64 PCGS.** The obverse has faint gold-gray overtones, while the reverse shows similar color only at the rims. Well-defined and strongly mirrored with only a few wispy hairlines on each side. Population: 56 in 64, 28 finer (2/09).
From The Burning Tree Collection.(#6546)

2172 **1899 PR64 Cameo NGC.** Soft uniform beige patina covers both sides of this Barber half, and an exacting strike leaves crisp definition on the frosted design elements that are highlighted by reflective fields. Incused lines traverse Liberty's cheek. There is disagreement in the cataloging department as to whether these are roller marks or post-strike. In any event, we recommend that prospective bidders personally inspect this coin.(#86546)

Charming PR67 Cameo 1899 Half Dollar

2173 **1899 PR67 Cameo PCGS. CAC.** Though deep blue and green patina consumes much of each side, this coin's essential cameo contrast shines through, both at the minimally toned and thoroughly frosted centers and at the edges of the devices where the toning spreads up from the fields. Carefully preserved and gorgeous. Population: 4 in 67 Cameo, 0 finer (2/09).(#86546)

Sharply Struck 1900 Gem Proof Fifty Cent

2174 **1900 PR65 PCGS.** The 1900 proof half dollar comes from a relatively high mintage of 912 pieces, of which a few hundred have been certified by PCGS and NGC, primarily through PR64. Medium intensity gray, apple-green, and orange patina adorns both sides of this Gem, each of which exhibits exquisitely struck design features and is nicely preserved. Housed in a green label holder. Population: 39 in 65, 19 finer (2/09).(#6547)

Splendid 1900 Barber Half, PR66 Cameo

2175 **1900 PR66 Cameo PCGS.** This midseries proof production saw a slight bump from the previous year's total, probably due to the nominal turn of the century. The snow-white surfaces display splendid field-device contrast and an impressive strike, with limited softness in the right shield corner, as usually seen. Population: 8 in 66 Cameo, 3 finer (2/09).(#86547)

Vibrant PR67 1901 Half

2176 **1901 PR67 NGC.** A dynamic Superb Gem specimen from this turn-of-the-century issue, carefully preserved with interesting patina. The obverse has largely light gold-gray toning with a dramatic streak of blue-violet close to the upper rim, while the reverse has deep blue-green and green-gold patina, the former color at the center and the latter at the margins. Census: 16 in 67, 7 finer (2/09).(#6548)

Enchanting PR66 1902 Half

2177 **1902 PR66 NGC.** Light golden-tan patina dominates both sides of this Premium Gem proof, with cobalt-blue and lavender accents at the borders. An attentive strike imparts strong definition to the design elements, with the sole exception being minor softness on the upper right corner of the shield. A few wispy flaws are noted on the cheek. Census: 28 in 66, 16 finer (2/09).(#6549)

Flashy PR66 1902 Barber Half

2178 **1902 PR66 PCGS.** Each side is beautifully toned with light golden-brown and sky-blue oval areas bounded by deeper cobalt-blue and jade-green, the latter is more prominent on the reverse. A pristine example of this elusive date, from the first issue in the brilliant-proof era for Barber halves. Population: 23 in 66, 5 finer (2/09). *From The Burning Tree Collection.*(#6549)

Beautiful PR65 Cameo 1903 Half Dollar

2179 **1903 PR65 Cameo NGC.** Though it lacks the thick frost found on the devices of pre-1902 Cameo coins, this Gem shows distinct contrast nonetheless. Mauve and russet peripheral toning gives way to gleaming silver-gray at the central obverse with champagne in the middle on the reverse. Census: 1 in 65 Cameo, 4 finer (2/09). (#86550)

2180 **1904 PR64 PCGS. CAC.** Ex: Benson. Beautiful golden-brown dominates both sides, although glimpses of blue and green illuminate the peripheries. Sharply struck and undeniably attractive.
Ex: Benson Collection, Part II (Ira & Larry Goldberg, 2/2002), lot 1081, which realized $1,782.
From The Burning Tree Collection.(#6551)

2181 **1905 PR64 PCGS. CAC.** Densely toned across both sides in shades of dark-orange and turquoise. The design elements are crisply struck, and neither side reveals any noteworthy flaws. An attractive near-Gem proof for the connoisseur of original patina.
From The Burning Tree Collection.(#6552)

Exquisitely Struck 1905 Gem Proof Fifty Cent

2182 **1905 PR65 NGC.** Richly toned in electric-blue, magenta, and beige-gold, all of which predominate around the borders, leaving the centers nearly color free. An exquisite strike emboldens the design elements, which show some contrast with the reflective fields. A hair-thin mark is visible on Liberty's lower right cheek. (#6552)

Impressive 1905 Barber Half, PR66

2183 **1905 PR66 NGC.** Luminous surfaces are covered in a medley of olive-green, sky-blue, violet, purple, and golden-tan patina, somewhat more extensively on the obverse. A solid strike leaves strong detail on the motifs, save for the slightest bit of softness on the upper right corner of the shield. Some nearly imperceptible slide marks on the cheek are only visible under high magnification. Census: 25 in 66, 16 finer (2/09).(#6552)

2184 **1906 PR64 NGC.** Whispers of low intensity multicolored toning grace the luminous surfaces of this near-Gem proof, and a sharp strike brings out strong definition on the design elements. A few trivial marks prevent Gem status.(#6553)

Colorful PR66 1906 Half Dollar

2185 **1906 PR66 PCGS. CAC.** Iridescent steel-blue and mint at the rims melds into pinkish-gold and silver at the centers of each side of this late-series example, from a proof production of only 675 coins. A prize for the color aficionados, and with the expected sharp strike, save on the usually soft right shield corner. Population: 17 in 66, 10 finer (2/09).
From The Burning Tree Collection.(#6553)

Fantastic PR67 1906 Half Dollar

2186 **1906 PR67 NGC.** A Superb Gem that is marvelously well-preserved, though this coin also draws attention for its magnificent patina. Generally gold-orange centers give way to blue-green hues at the margins, a light aqua shade on the obverse with deeper cerulean on the reverse. Census: 19 in 67, 5 finer (2/09). (#6553)

2187 **1907 PR64 PCGS.** Instantly appealing and lustrous, boasting generous dollops of fuchsia, jade-green, and copper-gold on the obverse, while the reverse sports similar colors with more green. Boldly struck, save for the usual right-side reverse weakness. Largely abrasion-free, and choice for the grade. Population: 48 in 64, 40 finer (2/09).
From The Burning Tree Collection.(#6554)

Patinated Gem Proof 1908 Half

2188 **1908 PR65 PCGS.** This well struck Gem is delightfully toned in magenta, peach, and powder-blue. The reverse appears immaculate, and the obverse has only a couple of faint hairlines. A treat for the enthusiast of attractively patinated silver type. A mere 545 proofs were issued. Population: 23 in 65, 18 finer (2/09).
From The Burning Tree Collection.(#6555)

PR66 1908 Barber Half With Dappled Toning

2189 **1908 PR66 NGC.** With only 545 pieces minted and few of those surpassing the Gem level, the 1908 proof half dollar is a borderline condition rarity in the state offered here. This piece is elegantly detailed with beautifully preserved, luminous surfaces beneath rich, dappled blue-green, rose, and silver-gray patina. Census: 31 in 66, 15 finer (2/09).(#6555)

Gem Cameo Proof 1908 Half

2190 **1908 PR65 Cameo PCGS.** Essentially brilliant with bright, watery mirrors and noteworthy contrast for this generally monochromatic proof issue. The strike is exceptionally sharp on the fletchings, and even on the right shield corner. Population: 3 in 65 Cameo, 6 finer (2/09).
Ex: Long Beach Signature (Heritage, 1/2004), lot 5992, which realized $4,370.(#86555)

Magnificent 1908 Half Dollar, PR66 Cameo
From the Eliasberg Collection

2191 **1908 PR66 Cameo PCGS. CAC.** Ex: SDC-Eliasberg Collections. The 1908 has one of the lowest proof mintages in the Barber half dollar series (545 pieces). Magnificent field-motif contrast shows on both sides of this Premium Gem. Exquisitely struck, save for the usual minor softness on the upper right shield corner. Whispers of cobalt-blue and gold-orange make occasional visits to this impeccably preserved specimen. Population: 5 in 66 Cameo, 1 finer (2/09).(#86555)

Enchanting PR67 1910 Barber Half

2192 **1910 PR67 NGC.** A sharply impressed specimen with exquisite gold, blue, and iridescent toning on both sides. The devices have slight evidence of frosty luster, and they are framed by reflective fields. Not quite enough contrast exists for a Cameo designation. Few finer examples of this date have been certified. This issue is also elusive in business strike format, furthering demand for proofs. Census: 19 in 67, 7 finer (2/09).(#6557)

Notable Superb Gem Proof 1910 Half

2193 **1910 PR67 NGC.** The 1910 proof half dollar saw a mintage of 551 pieces and is relatively available today through the near-Gem level of preservation. Superb Gems, such as the present piece, are quite scarce. Whispers of pastel olive-green and golden-brown visit impeccably preserved surfaces that exhibit crisply struck design elements. Modestly contrasted and delightful. Census: 19 in 67, 7 finer (2/09).(#6557)

Elegant PR65 1913 Half Dollar

2194 **1913 PR65 NGC.** An appealing Gem with impressively reflective surfaces, though each side shows only a hint of contrast between the sharply struck devices and the faintly gray-toned fields. Pleasingly preserved for the grade and for the issue of just 627 proofs. Census: 26 in 65, 37 finer (2/09).
From The Mario Eller Collection, Part Four.(#6560)

WALKING LIBERTY HALF DOLLARS

Blazing 1917 Walking Liberty Half, MS67 Among the Finest Certified

2195 1917 MS67 NGC. In the context of early date Walking Liberty half dollars, the 1917 is a common issue. The original mintage of 12.3 million pieces is the highest total for any date in the series before 1936, and its availability in Mint State makes the coin a favorite candidate for a type collection. Surprisingly, the issue's availability drops off sharply above the Gem level. Examples at the MS66 level are scarce, and only six coins have been certified in the Superb Gem grade by NGC and PCGS combined, with none finer (2/09).

The present coin is a spectacular specimen, with nearly perfect matte-like surfaces and thick, frosty mint luster. The pale brilliant and lilac centers are highlighted by a streak of golden-rose color along the right obverse. Overall eye appeal is awesome. Census: 4 in 67, 0 finer (2/09).(#6569)

Desirable Gem 1917-D Half Dollar With Obverse Mintmark

2196 1917-D Obverse MS65 PCGS. Silver-gray and gold-gray shadings mingle in the centers, while the margins show dots of deep crimson. Highly appealing for this low-mintage Obverse Mintmark variety of the 1917-D half, strongly lustrous and minimally marked. PCGS has certified just four finer pieces (1/09).(#6570)

Gorgeous Gem 1917-S Obverse Walking Liberty Half

2197 1917-S Obverse MS65 NGC. This is a truly lovely example of the 1917-S Obverse Walking Liberty half dollar, an issue that is important because of its comparatively low mintage, its conditional scarcity, and its status as a brief two-year subtype in a series that was produced from 1916 to 1947. Apparently, according to numismatic researcher and author Roger Burdette, the branch mintmark was moved from obverse to reverse in 1917, because the obverse mintmark had been misconstrued by some as a prominent die defect.

This frosty, snow-white, unmarked Gem will serve as a welcome addition to someone's high grade collection of Walking Liberty half dollars. Census: 22 in 65, 2 finer (2/09).(#6572)

2198 1917-S Reverse MS63 PCGS. Splashes of olive-green and violet-gray visit the lustrous surfaces of this Select S-mint representative. Well struck, except for Liberty's head. Minor marks define the grade.(#6573)

Choice 1917-S Reverse Mintmark Half

2199 1917-S Reverse MS64 PCGS. CAC. Despite a seemingly plentiful mintage of 5.554 million pieces, the 1917-S Reverse S is scarce in Mint State, particularly when compared with the much promoted 1938-D. 1917-S halves were set aside during the 1930s, when albums became readily available, but most survivors were well worn by then. This is a lustrous and brilliant Gem with minimal marks and a suitable strike.(#6573)

2200 1918 MS64 PCGS. Dabs of gold and violet patina appear largely at the margins. A strongly lustrous near-Gem, well-defined for the issue and pleasing. PCGS has graded 94 finer pieces (1/09). (#6574)

Highly Lustrous 1918-D Half Dollar, MS64

2201 1918-D MS64 PCGS. 1918 was a new hub year and the first year of the series that has all mint marks on the reverse. This '18-D displays potent luster emanating from silvery surfaces that show just a hint of faint gold color on the lower reverse margin. Well struck, and revealing a couple of minor marks precluding Gem status. This is a difficult issue to obtain any finer.(#6575)

2202 1918-S MS63 PCGS. Satiny and typically struck, with an even layer of blue-gray toning over each side, confirming the originality of the piece. Specks of russet and olive patina are likewise noted on both obverse and reverse. Free of distracting marks.(#6576)

2203 1918-S MS63 PCGS. Typically struck and lightly toned, with mostly silver-gray surfaces that reveal satin luster and very decent preservation. Light luster grazes in the right obverse field limit the grade.(#6576)

Pleasingly Toned 1919 Half, MS64

2204 1919 MS64 PCGS. CAC. The 1919-P Walking Liberty half, with a mintage of only 962,000 pieces, has the lowest mintage of the three issues for the year, but the 1919-D and 1919-S are less often seen in Mint State despite their higher mintages. (One wonders if there were more collectors in the vicinity of the longstanding Philadelphia Mint at the time, a not unreasonable assumption.) As the Gem level is approached, however, all three issues become scarce. This near-Gem has much luster radiating from liberally toned surfaces that feature shades of russet, charcoal, and silver-gold. Only minor contact marks on the eagle's lower right (facing) leg appear to limit the grade. The strike is bold and pleasing. (#6577)

2205 1919-S AU53 ICG. Typically softly struck on the high points, with minor wear and a few small marks from circulation. Each side displays a deep coating of variegated purple, tan, and gray coloration. An important semikey date in the Walking Liberty half dollar series.(#6579)

2206 1920 MS64 PCGS. Choice with pleasing luster and soft blue and cloud-gray patina overall. The devices are well struck, with a modicum of definition on the branch hand. A small scrape in the right obverse field accounts for the grade.(#6580)

Well Struck 1920-D Walker, MS65

2207 1920-D MS65 PCGS. Numismatic writers present different opinions regarding strike on the 1920-D half dollar. Bruce Fox (1993), for example, writes that: "... low striking pressure and/or inadequate die spacing produced weaker than average strikes." Jeff Ambio, on the other hand, contends that the typical example is quite bold.

The strike is very well executed on the current Gem offering, including nearly complete definition on the branch hand. Soft frosted luster rolls gently beneath mostly light coppery-gold toning imbued with splashes of powder-blue, deepening slightly along the lower portion of the reverse. A few grade-consistent obverse marks do not significantly distract. Population: 42 in 65, 6 finer (2/09). (#6581)

Beautiful Choice 1920-S Walker

2208 **1920-S MS64 NGC. CAC.** This coruscating near-Gem has a good strike and a refreshingly unabraded appearance. Lightly dappled straw-gold toning confirms the originality. Interesting for its heavily striated right obverse field, the result of aggressive die polishing at the Mint. A bold clashmark is nonetheless present beneath the base of the flag.(#6582)

Impressive Near-Gem 1921 Half

2209 **1921 MS64 PCGS. CAC.** A coin with both above-average detail for the issue, particularly on Liberty's head and hands, and gorgeous, satiny luster. Subtle golden accents are present mostly at the margins, and only a few stray marks appear in the fields. Just 52 finer examples are known to PCGS (2/09).(#6583)

Borderline Uncirculated 1921-D Walker

2210 **1921-D AU58 PCGS.** The lowest mintage issue in the series, and usually encountered well worn instead of nearly fully lustrous. A hint of friction on the eagle's breast is all that denies an Uncirculated assessment. The essentially untoned fields and devices display no remotely relevant marks, and the eye appeal is superior to many that have been certified as Mint State.(#6584)

Dazzling 1921-D Walking Liberty MS62

2211 **1921-D MS62 NGC.** The 1921-D is the lowest mintage date in the business strike Walking Liberty half dollar series (208,000 pieces). As usually seen with this date, the skirt lines and the eagle's right (facing) leg show blending of detail. The incomplete strike is the limiting factor in the grade, since all other aspects of this coin are exemplary. The surfaces display coruscating mint luster and lack consequential marks. The obverse is particularly unabraded.(#6584)

2212 **1921-S VF25 PCGS.** An appealing midrange example of this popular low-mintage San Francisco issue. Silver-gray fields yield to gold-orange at the margins and deeper slate patina close to the devices.(#6585)

Key 1921-S Half Dollar, XF40

2213 **1921-S XF40 NGC.** An elusive issue seldom seen in the middle circulated grades, but one in demand at all levels. In this XF grade, the present coin shows flatness on the head, thumb, and breast, and the eagle's breast and leg on the reverse. Some of the luster is still present, however, and a great deal of pleasing deep detail remains. A nice example of this key coin for a circulated set.(#6585)

Uncirculated Details 1921-S Half

2214 **1921-S—Cleaned, Retoned—ANACS. MS60 Details.** An unworn example of this famously low-mintage post-World War I issue. Overall detail is strong, and abrasions are few. Close examination reveals a number of hairlines visible on the luminous surfaces, hidden beneath dusky crimson and gold toning that seems to float over each side.(#6585)

Better Defined 1927-S Half Dollar, MS64

2215 **1927-S MS64 PCGS.** This near-Gem displays a better-than-average strike. Many survivors from this issue are terribly struck, especially in the central areas, where Liberty's branch hand is often completely gone on Mint State coins. While the division between the index finger and thumb is not visible on this coin, the latter is partially separated from the branch. The gown lines are sharply incised, and most of Liberty's head detail shows. Lustrous surfaces exhibit occasional speckles of gold color and are minimally abraded.(#6587)

Colorful MS64 1928-S Half

2216 **1928-S MS64 NGC.** This lustrous near-Gem's most promising attribute is its patina, swirling peach-gold and blue-green with glints of original silver. The striking softness seen at the centers is typical, though the reverse shows a better impression than the norm. NGC has graded just 42 numerically finer pieces (2/09). (#6588)

2217 **1929-D MS65 PCGS.** Radiant luster emanates from the silver surfaces accented with pinkish-gold. The strike is bold throughout, with a split thumb, articulation on LIberty's face, and both legs of the eagle. A nice satiny Gem for a fine collection.(#6589)

2218 **1929-S MS64 PCGS. CAC.** This is an attractive near-Gem example with intense mint luster and bright silver-white surfaces. Liberty's head and branch hand exhibit typical minor weakness, while the eagle's right (facing) leg feathers are also quite soft. A handful of small abrasions are noted in the right obverse field and on Liberty's trailing leg.(#6590)

2219 **1933-S MS63 PCGS.** Soft green-gold and silver-blue shadings embrace each side of this Depression-era Select survivor. Well struck for the issue with strong eye appeal despite wispy abrasions. (#6591)

2220 **1934-S MS64 PCGS.** Minimally toned with strong and desirable luster. This modestly marked piece has pleasing definition on Liberty's often-weak branch hand.(#6594)

2221 **1934-S MS64 PCGS.** A shining near-Gem, minimally toned save for a golden aura over the right obverse field. Strongly struck with few marks of any significance.(#6594)

Vibrant 1934-S Walking Liberty MS65

2222 **1934-S MS65 PCGS.** A needle-sharp strike, booming luster, and a pristine reverse attest to the quality of this handsome Gem. A few inconspicuous obverse ticks are mostly concealed within the flag. This Great Depression half dollar appears brilliant at first glance, although the borders display hints of apricot-gold.(#6594)

2223 **1935-D MS65 PCGS.** Delicate tan toning visits this lustrous Great Depression Gem. A small mark on the head, but otherwise smooth. The branch hand displays customary incompleteness of strike. *From The Mario Eller Collection, Part Four.*(#6596)

Exceptional 1935-D Half Dollar, MS66

2224 **1935-D MS66 PCGS.** This issue is nearly impossible to find fully struck. While we do not contend that this Premium Gem offering displays full delineation, it does show bold detail on the gown lines, and partial definition on the thumb and adjacent branches. Bluish-purple surfaces are accented in champagne-gold and exhibit pleasing luster. A few minute grade-consistent marks do not detract. Population: 88 in 66, 0 finer (2/09).(#6596)

Sharp Gem 1935-S Walking Liberty Half

2225 **1935-S MS65 PCGS.** Delicate golden patina visits the silver-white surfaces of this well struck and attractive S-mint Gem Walker. A few faint marks are present in the reverse fields, but they are consistent with the grade. Generous luster is abundant throughout. This Depression-era issue is available in Mint State, but Gems remain elusive.(#6597)

Striking MS66 1935-S Half

2226 **1935-S MS66 PCGS.** Slightly above-average design definition with satiny luster. The centers are silver-gray, while crescents of gold-orange and tan toning are visible near the rims. With just two finer examples known to PCGS (1/09), this must be considered among the finest survivors available.(#6597)

2227 **1936-D MS66 PCGS.** A creamy-white Premium Gem with impeccable fields and just a trace of striking deficiency in the centers. Only rarely is this 1930s Denver issue found finer. (#6599)

2228 **1936-S MS66 NGC.** Subtle hints of gold visit the margins of this softly lustrous Premium Gem. Solidly struck for the issue and delightfully well-preserved. NGC has graded 12 numerically finer pieces (2/09).(#6600)

2229 **1936-S MS66 PCGS.** A crisply struck example with subtle lilac accents over highly lustrous fields. Excellent eye appeal, even by Premium Gem standards. Housed in a first-generation holder. PCGS has graded six finer pieces (2/09).(#6600)

2230 **1937 MS67 PCGS.** Well struck and lustrous with medium olive-green and straw-gold patina. The reverse appears pristine, and the obverse is nearly as undisturbed. PCGS and NGC have each certified just two pieces finer (1/09).
From The Mario Eller Collection, Part Four.(#6601)

2231 **1937-D MS66 PCGS.** Pastel blue and canary-gold patina with a touch of tan graces the shining surfaces of this enticing Premium Gem. Solidly struck for this Denver issue with carefully preserved central devices. PCGS has graded 36 finer pieces (2/09). (#6602)

Fabulous MS67 1937-D Half

2232 **1937-D MS67 NGC.** With its powerful and frosty luster, this Superb Gem is an absolute delight. The strike is substantially above-average, and whispers of silver-pink and amethyst toning grace each side. An additional zone of golden-brown is noted at the upper right obverse. NGC has graded just one numerically finer example (2/09).(#6602)

2233 **1937-S MS66 PCGS. CAC.** Well-defined with smooth luster and stirring eye appeal. This is a wonderful Premium Gem, minimally toned and attractive. PCGS has graded 17 finer pieces (1/09). (#6603)

2234 **1937-S MS66 NGC.** A beautiful, entirely untoned example with scintillating luster over the bright silver-white surfaces. Generally well struck, with just the slightest weakness on Liberty's head and branch hand. Surface marks are nearly nonexistent. NGC has graded a mere 10 pieces finer (2/09).(#6603)

2235 **1937-S MS66 PCGS.** Glowing mint luster illuminates lovely pale yellow-gold and streaky purple toning. Well struck and impeccably preserved; an alluring and conditionally scarce Premium Gem. (#6603)

2236 **1937-S MS66 NGC.** Both the surfaces and coloration are immediately suggestive of an even finer grade, with considerable prooflikeness appearing in the fields and stray glints of gold and mint-green flashing under a light. Some tiny luster grazes in the fields perhaps are the ultimate decider, but the eye appeal is over the top.(#6603)

2237 **1937-S MS66 PCGS.** Traces of gold and red patina appear over the fields on each side. The fields have pleasing luster, and the strike is above average. An appealing piece. PCGS has graded 17 finer examples (2/09).(#6603)

2238 **1937-S MS66 PCGS.** This is an elegant Premium Gem example, with soft glowing luster and light bluish-silver toning that yields to antique-gold patina near the peripheries, and on the eagle's lower wing feathers. Fully struck and exquisitely preserved. (#6603)

2239 **1938-D MS65 PCGS.** A lovely Gem with watery obverse fields that exhibit faint die striations. The untoned, silver-gray surfaces are free of distracting blemishes on both sides.(#6605)

2240 **1938-D MS65 PCGS.** Well struck, except for Liberty's branch hand, with shimmering mint frost and smooth, virtually unmarked surfaces. The obverse is untoned, while the reverse shows an even layer of vibrant champagne-gold color.(#6605)

2241 **1938-D MS65 PCGS.** Well struck and highly lustrous, with surfaces that show a faint golden cast, and a few tiny bits of speckled russet patina on the obverse. Carefully preserved with a small number of superficial marks that prohibit an even finer grade. A popular issue with the lowest mintage of any Walking Liberty business strike from 1923 through 1947.(#6605)

2242 **1938-D MS66 PCGS.** A light coating of creamy, ivory-gray toning covers each side. Well struck with a couple of insignificant milling marks on the reverse, but no severe blemishes on either side. A slight degree of russet-red, green, and gold patina decorates the peripheries.(#6605)

2243 **1938-D MS66 PCGS. CAC.** An intensely lustrous beauty, this important half dollar has ivory surfaces with lovely peripheral gold toning. The brilliant surfaces are highly lustrous, and the design elements are boldly defined. PCGS has only certified 23 finer examples (2/09).(#6605)

2244 **1939-S MS67 PCGS.** An enchanting Superb Gem, brightly lustrous with hints of burgundy peripheral toning around bright silver-white centers. Tied for numerically finest known to NGC or PCGS (2/09).(#6608)

2245 **1939-S MS67 NGC.** A beautiful sheen of satin luster encompasses both sides of this fully untoned silver-white piece. Boldly struck overall, if typically soft on Liberty's branch hand, with nearly pristine surfaces. A diagonal die crack bisects the eagle on the reverse, from the top of the left (facing) wing through the right (facing) talons. Census: 86 in 67, 0 finer (2/09).(#6608)

2246 **1941 MS67 NGC.** Dappled blue and golden-tan peripheral bands yield to pale silver-gray in the centers. A well-defined Superb Gem with stirring visual appeal.(#6611)

2247 **1941-S MS66 PCGS. CAC.** A dazzling, brilliant, intensely lustrous Premium Gem that has tremendous visual allure. Boldly struck with the usual highpoint weakness. A tiny alloy spot resides on the eagle's upper right (facing) wing. Otherwise, the surfaces are virtually immaculate. PCGS has only graded six pieces finer (2/09). (#6613)

2248 **1941-S MS66 PCGS.** This brilliant short set key has potent luster and exceptional preservation. The skirt lines are close to complete, although the cheek and branch hand lack complete detail. PCGS has graded only six pieces finer (1/09).(#6613)

2249 **1942 Doubled Die Reverse MS65 PCGS.** FS-801, formerly FS-009. HALF DOLLAR and the lower right feathers are nicely die doubled. Lustrous, well preserved, and impeccably struck with delicate gold and lime toning.(#6614)

2250 **1942-S MS66 PCGS.** A shining Premium Gem, minimally toned save for a zone of champagne at the central obverse. Typical striking softness at Liberty's branch hand but well-defined elsewhere. PCGS has graded only one finer example (2/09).(#6617)

Frosty 1943 Half, MS68

2251 **1943 MS68 NGC.** This frosty silver-white coin undoubtedly appears much as it must have when it first popped out of an original roll. Fortunately it must have been recognized as extraordinary early on, as its subsequent preservation is equally impressive. The exacting strike is complemented by a noteworthy lack of abrasions, even when the coin is examined under a loupe. Among the finest few certified at either service.(#6618)

2252 **1944 MS67 PCGS.** This issue is plentiful at most grade levels, up to and including MS66. Superb Gems are scarce, however, and none have been rated any higher than MS67 at either service as of (1/09). This is a beautiful, brilliant coin, with a great satiny sheen over both sides. Well struck and virtually pristine.(#6621)

2253 **1944-S MS66 PCGS.** Strong and frosty luster lends this essentially silver-white Premium Gem immense eye appeal. Softly struck at the centers but well-defined elsewhere. PCGS has graded just five finer pieces (2/09).(#6623)

2254 **1945 MS67 NGC.** Brilliant and flashy, with heavy mint frost over both sides. Well struck and impressively preserved, with remarkably clean surfaces that are nearly pristine. A great Superb Gem Walker from the final year of the second World War. Census: 93 in 67, 0 finer (2/09).(#6624)

2255 **1945-S MS67 NGC.** Well struck for this often-weak issue with modest definition on the branch hand. Frosty and untoned in the centers with gold-orange and violet peripheral shadings. Census: 22 in 67, 0 finer (2/09).(#6626)

2256 **1946 MS67 NGC.** A splendid Superb Gem that gets high marks for technical merit as well as great visual appeal. Well struck, lustrous, and essentially pristine, with lovely sea-green, mauve, and yellow-gold toning intermingled across the untouched surfaces. Census: 31 in 67, 1 finer (2/09).(#6627)

2257 **1946-S MS67 NGC.** Ex: Nevada Silver Collection. Knob S. Lustrous and essentially unabraded with only a whisper of caramel-gold. Better struck than most San Francisco Walkers, since the head and skirt lines have impressive detail. Census: 50 in 67, 0 finer (2/09).(#6629)

2258 **1947 MS67 NGC.** Splashes of watermelon and orange peripheral toning offset the neutral silver-gray of the centers. Well-defined for this final-year issue.(#6630)

2259 **1947-D MS67 NGC.** Well-defined for this final-year issue with strong luster and minimal patina. This interesting Superb Gem is tied for numerically finest known to NGC or PCGS (1/09). (#6631)

2260 **1947-D MS67 NGC. CAC.** A striking Superb Gem example of this final-year issue, pleasingly lustrous with blue, green-gold, and claret peripheral toning framing silver-gray centers. Census: 39 in 67, 0 finer (2/09).(#6631)

PROOF WALKING LIBERTY HALF DOLLARS

Splendid 1936 Walker, PR66

2261 **1936 PR66 NGC.** The surfaces are simply splendid silver-white, with neither a trace of cameo effect, as usual for the issue, nor any singularly mentionable distractions. A nice type coin, and one much less often seen at the next grade level. NGC has certified 74 coins of the issue, less duplicates, at the Superb Gem rank (2/09). (#6636)

Impressive Premium Gem Proof 1936 Walker

2262 **1936 PR66 PCGS.** Fully struck and impeccably preserved, with distraction-free surfaces. On the obverse there is light haze in the fields, along with trace amounts of speckled orange patina near the edges and on the upper field areas. The reverse shows a complete layer of pastel terra cotta-orange toning, with numerous russet specks. The first proof issue in the series, and the rarest. (#6636)

2263 **1938 PR66 PCGS. CAC.** Gleaming mirrors are essentially untoned save for occasional hints of cloud-white. This crisply detailed Premium Gem offers gorgeous eye appeal.(#6638)

2264 **1938 PR67 NGC.** The blindingly mirrored silver-white surfaces show no mentionable distraction on either side, save for the near-total lack of contrast that is the norm for pieces of the era. NGC has certified 50 finer (2/09).(#6638)

Luminous 1938 PR68 Half Dollar

2265 **1938 PR68 NGC.** Luminous surfaces exhibit yellow-gold patina imbued with whispers of violet, golden-tan, and mint-green. The design elements are crisply defined, befitting a proof strike, and each side is impeccably preserved. The motifs display a slight amount of contrast with the fields. Census: 49 in 68, 0 finer (1/09). (#6638)

Reflective 1938 Walker, PR68

2266 **1938 PR68 NGC.** Hazy patina covers most of the surfaces, but translucent amber-orange and pale gold toning appears at the periphery, where this coin's deep reflectivity shines through. A remarkable specimen that lacks any mentionable distractions and is tied for the finest certified by either NGC or PCGS (2/09). (#6638)

Wonderful 1938 Half Dollar, PR68

2267 **1938 PR68 NGC.** A wonderful Superb Gem from early in the proof Walking Liberty series, this coin offers light gold toning around the reverse rim, while the obverse has just the barest suggestion of similar color. Under a loupe some microscopic grayish flecks can be discerned that cumulatively add to the color, but mentionable contact is nonexistent. Census: 50 in 68, 0 finer (2/09). (#6638)

2268 **1939 PR67 NGC.** A dazzlingly brilliant Superb Gem example of this Walking Liberty proof issue, with a low original mintage of 8,808 pieces. Crisply struck and virtually pristine on both sides. (#6639)

2269 **1939 PR67 PCGS.** Strongly struck overall with excellent reflectivity and eye appeal. Subtle green-gold tints visit the margins. Highly appealing and housed in a green label holder. PCGS has graded 24 finer pieces (2/09). (#6639)

Sharp 1939 Half Dollar, PR68

2270 **1939 PR68 NGC.** Yellow-gold patination is slightly more extensive and deeper on the reverse, and both sides are accented with freckles of light brown and sky-blue. An exacting strike fully delineates the design features, and both faces are immaculately preserved. Census: 85 in 68, 1 finer (2/09). (#6639)

Outstanding 1939 Walking Liberty Half, PR68

2271 **1939 PR68 NGC.** Walking Liberty half dollars were only struck as proofs for seven years, 1936 through 1942, and were never produced in large quantities. Really high grade specimens such as this one are relatively rare, compared to the high demand from collectors. This piece is fully struck and seemingly pristine, in the absence of any contact marks or hairlines. Creamy tan, sea-green, and mauve toning occurs on each side, becoming heaviest near the borders. Census: 85 in 68, 1 finer (2/09). (#6639)

2272 **1941 No AW PR67 NGC.** The variant without designer's initials, offered here as a Superb Gem proof. Light golden overtones enhance the eye appeal of this sharply struck specimen. (#6641)

2273 **1941 No AW PR67 NGC.** This essentially brilliant Superb Gem proof type coin has a precise strike and a pristine appearance. The reverse die was lapped, removing the designer's monogram and the tail of the R in PLURIBUS.
From The Mario Eller Collection, Part Four. (#6641)

Exceptional 1941 PR68 Walker
No Designer's Initials

2274 **1941 No AW PR68 NGC.** Breen believed the proofs lacking the designer's initials were more common than those that show the AW on the reverse. We have not found that to be the case, though. Such pieces do, however, provide the collector with a variant in the otherwise limited 1936-1942 proof series. This is a beautifully preserved coin that is lightly toned over most of each side with a dab of golden color at the margins. (#6641)

2275 **1942 PR67 NGC. CAC.** Strongly struck with subtle golden overtones to the fields. A carefully preserved Superb Gem that offers impressive visual appeal for the final proof Walking Liberty half dollar issue. (#6642)

FRANKLIN HALF DOLLARS

2276 1948-D MS66 Full Bell Lines PCGS. Unusually well-defined for the issue with fresh luster and strong eye appeal. Unlike many examples, this is a minimally toned piece with just a hint of peripheral gold.(#86652)

2277 1951-D MS66 Full Bell Lines PCGS. CAC. A lovely dusting of lilac toning covers the centers, while a ring of gold surrounds the perimeter. Vivid satiny luster gives this razor-sharp Premium Gem outstanding eye appeal. Neither NGC nor PCGS has certified any examples finer (2/09).(#86659)

PROOF FRANKLIN HALF DOLLARS

White PR67 Cameo 1950 Half

2278 1950 PR67 Cameo NGC. A brilliant and undisturbed Superb Gem that exhibits especially noticeable cameo contrast on the reverse. First-year proof Franklin halves have the lowest mintage of the series, and are highly elusive in cameo format. Population: 11 in 67 Cameo, 1 finer (4/05).
Ex: Elite Cameo #1 NGC Registry Set for 1950 Proofs (Heritage, 5/2005), lot 7907, which realized $8,625.(#86691)

Impressive 1951 Franklin Half, PR67 Cameo

2279 1951 PR67 Cameo NGC. Fully struck with mildly frosted devices and deeply reflective, inky-black fields. The surfaces are impressively preserved and free of even the smallest mark or hairline. A conditionally scarce representative of this early proof Franklin issue. Census: 14 in 67 Cameo, 0 finer (2/09). (#86692)

2280 1952 PR67 Cameo NGC. Strongly contrasted with subtle golden overtones across the centers. The frost on the portrait is thick and creamy. NGC has graded just one finer Cameo coin (2/09). (#86693)

2281 1956 Type Two PR69 Ultra Cameo NGC. The Type Two reverse (so indicated on the insert), identified by its high relief eagle with three feathers left of the perch. This near perfect specimen has nearly unimprovable deep cameo contrast on both sides. Census: 39 in 69 Ultra Cameo, 0 finer (2/09).(#96697)

1963 Franklin Half, PR69 Ultra Cameo

2282 1963 PR69 Ultra Cameo NGC. While the 1963 Franklin half in PR69 Ultra Cameo is not as difficult to find as other dates in the series, savvy collectors are increasingly putting away the finest pieces for the long term. This piece, as expected for the grade, reveals essentially nothing other than perfection on both silver-white sides. Census: 6 in 69 Ultra Cameo, 0 finer (2/09). (#96704)

KENNEDY HALF DOLLAR

2283 1964 MS67 NGC. Well struck and appealing, a solid Superb Gem example of this beloved first-year issue. Dappled amber-olive and silver-gray shadings dominate the obverse, while the reverse is minimally toned.(#6706)

Unpublished 1794 Silver Dollar, Fine 12

No. 60

J. C. MORGENTHAU & CO., Inc.

1 WEST 47th STREET

NEW YORK, June 9 193 7

Sold to *W. G. Sunderland*
Sunderland Farms Exeter R.I.

FOR LOTS PURCHASED AT *378* AUCTION SALE
ACCORDING TO YOUR BIDS.

Lot No.		Price	Lot No.		Price
212		111 –	*1794 Silver dollars.*		
606		8 –	*4 Gold dollars.*		
	fwd'g	119 –			
		119 24			

J. C. MORGENTHAU & CO., Inc.
1 WEST 47TH STREET
NEW YORK, N. Y.

W62729
REGISTER.

Mr. W. G. Sunderland
Sunderland Farms
Exeter
R.I.

2284 **1794 Fine 12 PCGS.** B-1, BB-1, R.4. The late Jack Collins spent considerable time and effort studying the 1794 silver dollars, and his manuscript was nearly completed at the time of his death. The Collins manuscript included individual provenances and illustrations of approximately 125 different specimens, and formed the basis for the published study of Martin Logies. Both works relied heavily on past auction appearances, especially those that included plates of the coins being offered. However, there were many auction appearances over the last 150 years that had no plates, and those coins are nearly impossible to track today. It is assumed that most of those earlier appearances have reappeared in recent times, and are now included in the roster.

Every now and then, a previously unpublished 1794 silver dollar makes an appearance, but such occurrences are rare. This example last appeared in the 378th sale held under the auspices of J.C. Morgenthau and Company in April 1937. This coin was not plated in the Morgenthau catalog, and carried a brief description:

212 1794 Good, really very good for this date, although the usual weakness on left side of coin. Very rare.

Morgenthau's 378th sale included large cents from the Gillette Collection, and other properties but the earlier provenance of this 1794 dollar remains unknown. The coin realized $111 in that 1937 sale. The original invoice and mailing envelope from June 1937 accompany the coin. The same invoice also included lot 606 from that sale, a group of four gold dollars that realized eight dollars. The purchaser was Mr. W.G. Sunderland of Sunderland Farms in Exeter, Rhode Island. Exeter, Rhode Island, is located in the east central portion of the state, just a few miles from Narragansett Bay. We have been unable to learn anything else about Mr. Sunderland.

J.C. Morgenthau and Company was primarily a rare stamp company. Morgenthau (1858-1929) was Julius Caesar Morgenthau of New York City. His career as a stamp dealer began in Chicago in 1893, and he established the J.C. Morgenthau and Company firm in 1905. At the time of his death, he had built the term into the premier philatelic auction house in the U.S., holding the most important sales of the time. The numismatic branch was operated by James Macallister and Wayte Raymond who conducted more than 50 coin auctions under the Morgenthau banner. Perhaps the most famous of those were the two sales that offered the Howard Newcomb Collection in 1945.

The present example, housed in a green label PCGS holder, is an attractive pewter-gray specimen with traces of gold and iridescent toning on both sides. The left obverse and reverse are typically weak. A single diagonal scratch from the hair to the neck passes below the ear and follows the jaw line. This pedigree marker will serve to identify the coin in the future. A tiny rim bruise below the 4 and final star are evident, as are a few other insignificant abrasions. Fine peripheral adjustment marks can be seen at the top of the obverse and a few faint hairlines are evident across portions of the reverse design elements. Overall this is a remarkable middle grade circulated piece that will garner considerable interest at the auction.(#6851)

2285 **1795 Flowing Hair, Three Leaves VG8 PCGS.** B-6, BB-25, R.3. The lowest curl dips between two arms of star 1 on the obverse. A well-circulated yet pleasing example with green-gold shadings mixed in with the sage patina on each side.(#6852)

2286 **1795 Flowing Hair, Three Leaves VG10 NGC.** B-7, BB-18, R.3. A scarce variety, offered here as a significantly circulated yet pleasing Very Good example. Silver-gray surfaces show extensive golden-tan overtones with few digs or overt marks. *From The Pasadena Collection, Part Two.*(#6852)

1795 Flowing Hair Dollar, Fine 15
Three Leaves, B-5, BB-27

2287 **1795 Flowing Hair, Three Leaves Fine 15 NGC.** B-5, BB-27, R.1. A familiar Flowing Hair die marriage identified by the die line or "bar" behind Liberty's uppermost hair curl. Toned dove-gray with deeper shadings near the rims. A few inconsequential adjustment marks are encountered near 4:30 on the obverse.(#6852)

Pleasing 1795 B-5, BB-27 Dollar, VF25

2288 **1795 Flowing Hair, Three Leaves VF25 PCGS. CAC.** B-5, BB-27, R.1. An attractive example of this plentiful die variety with modest amounts of wear on the high points. Both sides have light silver-gray surfaces with traces of gold toning. Housed in a first generation holder. It would not surprise us if this piece were eventually certified at a higher grade. Traces of luster seem to remain in a few protected areas close to the devices.(#6852)

Attractive 1795 Three Leaves
Silver Dollar, B-5, BB-27, VF30

2289 **1795 Flowing Hair, Three Leaves VF30 PCGS.** B-5, BB-27, R.1. Deeply toned over both sides, with unusually strong definition on most of the design elements. A number of moderate adjustment marks are evident along the lower obverse border, between 5 o'clock and 8 o'clock, and a few thinner adjustment marks are located over Liberty's ear and lower hair detail. Several moderate abrasions are noted on the reverse, below the eagle's left (facing) wing. A single moderate mark on the obverse resides near the tip of the bust. Evenly worn and quite attractive for the grade.(#6852)

Choice XF 1795 Flowing Hair Dollar
Three Leaves, B-5, BB-27

2290 **1795 Flowing Hair, Three Leaves XF45 NGC.** B-5, BB-27, R.1. Bowers-Borckardt Die State III. Early dollar veterans of the bourse floor know to look for the die line behind Liberty's upper hair curl to identify this familiar variety. But this is a much nicer example than usually encountered. Golden-brown luster glimmers from the wreath, wings, curls, and borders. Powder-blue enriches the devices and open fields. Evenly struck save for the upper reverse dentils, and impressively unabraded save for minor marks near the A in STATES.(#6852)

Appealing AU50 1795 Dollar, B-5, BB-27

Splendid 1795 B-5, BB-27 Dollar, AU53
Flowing Hair, Three Leaves

2291 1795 Flowing Hair, Three Leaves AU50 NGC. B-5, BB-27, R.1. Die State II or III. A splendid example in a rather early die state. Bowers notes that about one in 20 examples of the variety exist without the reverse die crack, but our experience suggests that nearly every known specimen has a crack at that location. Sometimes, however, it is very light and nearly invisible after a slight amount of wear.

This splendid early dollar has lustrous ivory surfaces with splashes of steel-blue and iridescent toning, especially on the devices. A few faint lines and tiny abrasions are evident with careful examination, but they are of little significance.(#6852)

2292 1795 Flowing Hair, Three Leaves AU53 PCGS. B-5, BB-27, R.1. Bowers-Borckardt Die State III. Blue-green and russet shades overlie the slate-gray obverse. The reverse has rich mottled cobalt-blue and stone-gray patina. Mint-caused adjustment marks cross the central obverse and make a peripheral appearance near the date and the L in LIBERTY. However, both sides are nearly unabraded save for a faded mark beneath star 8 and an inconspicuous pinscratch aligned with the contour of Liberty's neck. Luster shimmers from the hair, stars, wreath, and legends. The familiar Bolender-5 variety is readily identified by a diagonal die line behind Liberty's highest hair curl.(#6852)

Delightful 1795 B-5, BB-27 Dollar, AU58

2293 1795 Flowing Hair, Three Leaves AU58 NGC. B-5, BB-27, R.1. Bowers-Borckardt Die State III. A crack joins the left stem end and the border according to the BB reference, and that feature is clearly visible on this piece. It is possible that the "crack" is actually a die scratch, as it seems to be constant on most observed specimens. The reverse has numerous raised die pits over much of its surface.

Somewhat lightly struck at the centers, as nearly always for this variety. Wispy abrasions are consistent with the grade. This lovely example has pleasing light silver-gray at the centers, framed by peripheral iridescence. Faint champagne toning highlights the central design elements.(#6852)

Fine 1795 Flowing Hair Dollar
B-1, BB-21, Two Leaves Reverse

2294 1795 Flowing Hair, Two Leaves Fine 12 PCGS. B-1, BB-21, R.2. Deep aquamarine, lilac, and apricot hues envelop this scarce Flowing Hair dollar. Faint thin abrasions are noted above the date, behind the eye, and near star 7. The reverse has a pair of inconsequential rim nicks at 12 o'clock and 3:30, and the central obverse displays minor mint-made adjustment marks.(#6853)

Pursued 1795 Flowing Hair Dollar Fine 15
Two Leaves Reverse, B-1, BB-21

2295 1795 Flowing Hair, Two Leaves Fine 15 PCGS. B-1, BB-21, R.2. Forest-green and tan-brown enrich this collectible Flowing Hair dollar. Liberty's eye is sharp, and all legends and stars are bold. Some feather and hair detail remains. Prolonged examination with a glass locates only thin marks near the profile and adjacent to the peak of the left (facing) wing.(#6853)

Rare B-3, B-11 Two Leaves
VF 1795 Flowing Hair Dollar

2296 1795 Flowing Hair, Two Leaves VF20 PCGS. B-3, BB-11, R.5. The stone-gray devices contrast with charcoal-tinged fields. Lightly abraded aside from a few trivial rim nicks. There appears to be a die break on the denticles near the C in AMERICA, although no such break is discussed in either the Bowers and Rulau references. Housed in an old green label holder.(#6853)

Desired VF 1795 Flowing Hair Dollar
Two Leaves, B-4, BB-14

2297 1795 Flowing Hair, Two Leaves VF20 PCGS. B-4, BB-14, R.3. This cream-gray Flowing Hair dollar also displays traces of chestnut-gold. Uncommonly smooth for the grade despite a few hairlines on the portrait and a minor mark near star 11. Among the most desirable silver types. Certified in an old green label holder. (#6853)

Desirable 1795 Flowing Hair Dollar VF25
Two Leaves, B-4, BB-14

2298 **1795 Flowing Hair, Two Leaves VF25 PCGS.** B-4, BB-14, R.3. Attractively toned orange-gold and lime-green. The surfaces are pleasing to the unaided eye, although a loupe reveals faint hairlines, and a few thin marks are noted near the BER in LIBERTY. B-4 is seen much less often than the usual Two Leaves variety, B-1. Housed in a green label holder.(#6853)

Appealing XF45 1795 Flowing Hair Dollar
Two Leaves, B-2, BB-20

2299 **1795 Flowing Hair, Two Leaves XF45 NGC.** B-2, BB-20, R.3. A bold die line near star 4 provides ready attribution. Luster brightens the stars, wreath, and legends of this briefly issued and important early large silver type coin. Predominantly medium tan-gold, although the borders display aqua-green. Slightly glossy and devoid of reportable marks.(#6853)

Choice XF B-2, BB-20 Two Leaves
1795 Flowing Hair Dollar

2300 **1795 Flowing Hair, Two Leaves XF45 NGC.** B-2, BB-20, R.3. Straw-gold and gunmetal-gray blend throughout this charming better grade Flowing Hair dollar. Glints of luster emerge when the piece is rotated beneath a light. A few faded adjustment marks (as made) cross the central reverse.(#6853)

Popular Blundered Date 1795 B-1, BB-21
Flowing Hair Dollar, AU55

2301 **1795 Flowing Hair, Two Leaves AU55 NGC.** B-1, BB-21, R.2. Die State I. The popular blundered date variety is always from perfect dies. The obverse die made its first appearance on the B-1 die combination, and continued with two other reverse dies for the B-10 and B-16 rarities. The reverse die was first used for B-2, followed by its appearance here in the B-1 marriage, and finally for B-13. The bright silver surfaces display hints of steel and gold toning on each side. The fields are reflective with considerable original luster, and the reverse is fully mirrored. Impressive and desirable.(#6853)

Unique Silver Plug B-5, BB-27
1795 Flowing Hair Dollar VF25

2302 **1795 Flowing Hair, Silver Plug VF25 PCGS.** B-5, BB-27, R.1. Not to be confused with an out-of-the-mint repair, a silver plug was added to the center of the planchet in the mint before striking. Such plugs are a relatively recent discovery, and it is believed they were the opposite of adjustment marks, i.e., metal was added to the planchet to bring an underweight planchet up to proper weight. The plug is somewhat difficult to distinguish on this pleasing medium-gray example, but its oval-shaped outline is faintly apparent on the central obverse. Two small depressions on and near the bow of the wreath could also be of mint origin. This coin was the subject of a cover story for the May 20, 2002 issue of *Coin World*. It is the discovery piece, and only known example, of a silver plug on a 1795 Bolender-5 dollar.
Ex: Long Beach Signature (Heritage, 2/2003), lot 7935; New York Signature (Heritage, 7/2004), lot 6850, which realized $12,075. (#6854)

Rare XF Silver Plug B-3, B-11
1795 Flowing Hair Dollar

2303 **1795 Flowing Hair, Silver Plug XF40 PCGS.** B-3, B-11, R.5. A much better die marriage, and made even more desirable by its obvious mint-made silver plug, visible from both sides. The Mint, ever conscious of economy, added a silver plug to the center of underweight silver dollar planchets, rather than melt them down and try again. This procedure was abandoned later in 1795, probably because the plug remained visible on struck examples.

This is a well-defined Flowing Hair dollar with rich walnut-brown, cream-gray, and aqua-blue toning. Marks are surprisingly sparse, and the somewhat cloudy surfaces have good eye appeal. (#6854)

Sharp VF 1795 Draped Bust Dollar
Centered Bust, B-15, BB-52

2304 **1795 Draped Bust, Centered VF20 ANACS.** B-15, BB-52, R.2. Bowers-Borckardt Die State IV. Aquamarine and peach embrace this attractively detailed and lightly abraded representative. Trivial adjustment marks (as issued) are noted near 5 o'clock on the reverse. The Draped Bust punch was well centered when the obverse die was made, distinguishing B-15 from its somewhat more available B-14 counterpart.(#6858)

1795 Draped Bust Dollar, VF Details
Centered, B-15, BB-52

2305 **1795 Draped Bust, Centered—Improperly Cleaned—NCS. VF Details.** B-15, BB-52, R.2. The highest wave of Liberty's hair is directly below the E in LIBERTY. Numerous wispy hairlines on each side identify this as an improperly cleaned example, but the piece is not without attributes. The medium-gray surfaces are smooth, and free of any severe marks, although a pair of shallow scratches are evident on the reverse. The design elements retain a considerable amount of detail for the grade. (#6858)

Centered Draped Bust 1795 Dollar
Choice VF, B-15, BB-52

2306 **1795 Draped Bust, Centered VF35 PCGS.** B-15, BB-52, R.2. Bowers-Borckardt Die State V. Stone-gray overall with a blush of steel-blue on the ground beneath the eagle and a small faded spot on the right obverse field. Luster shimmers within the lower hair curls and on the centers of the wings. The reverse has a couple of unimportant rim nicks, and a few adjustment marks of mint origin pass through the hair and the rim near the bust tip.(#6858)

VF 1795 Draped Bust Dollar
Uncentered Bust, B-14, BB-51

2307 **1795 Draped Bust, Off Center VF20 PCGS.** B-14, BB-51, R.2. Dove-gray fields and devices contrast slightly with the deeper stone-gray fields. Ample wing and hair detail remains. The right reverse border has a few unimportant adjustment marks, as made. This quality collector coin is certified in a green label holder. (#96858)

Pursued VF 1795 Silver Dollar
Off Center Draped Bust, B-14, BB-51

2308 **1795 Draped Bust, Off Center VF20 PCGS.** B-14, BB-51, R.2. A nicely detailed piece with iridescent powder-blue, stone-gray, and olive patina. There are no mentionable abrasions, and the faintly hairlined fields lack evidence of adjustment marks. The Draped Bust design is said to be based on a drawing by noted American portrait artist Gilbert Stuart.(#96858)

Bold 1795 Silver Dollar VF30
B-14, BB-51, Uncentered Draped Bust

2309 **1795 Draped Bust, Off Center VF30 NGC.** B-14, BB-51, R.2. A deep stone-gray midgrade Draped Bust dollar. Gunmetal and almond-gold tints emerge here and there. The fields have a few unimportant ticks, and the reverse rim has minute nicks at 7:30 and 11:30, but the eye appeal is undeniably attractive.(#96858)

Choice VF 1795 Draped Bust Dollar
Uncentered Bust, B-14, BB-51

2310 **1795 Draped Bust, Off Center VF35 NGC.** B-14, BB-51, R.2. Chestnut toning is consistent throughout apart from glimpses of steel-gray on the devices. Both sides are surprisingly unabraded aside from a minor obverse rim ding at 3 o'clock. Close inspection of the reverse reveals faint adjustment marks, as produced. (#96858)

Notable AU 1795 Draped Bust Dollar
Off Center Bust, B-14, BB-51

2311 **1795 Draped Bust, Off Center AU50 PCGS.** B-14, BB-51, R.2. A pleasing stone-gray example that has faint vertical obverse streaks of charcoal-gray toning. Luster beckons from the hair, wings, wreath, clouds, stars, and legends. Examination beneath a glass fails to locate any distracting marks. Bolender-14 is believed to be the first Draped Bust die marriage, since the bust punch was entered off center, an engraving blunder not made on the subsequent B-15. Partly lustrous examples of this first year large silver type are coveted by early American numismatists. Population: 5 in 50, 32 finer (2/09).(#96858)

Challenging Very Fine 1796 Dollar
Small Date, Large Letters, B-4, BB-61

2312 **1796 Small Date, Large Letters VF20 PCGS.** B-4, BB-61, R.3. Bowers-Borckardt Die State I. Almond-gold and gunmetal-gray envelop this collectible better date early dollar. Refreshingly bereft of adjustment marks or noticeable abrasions, and the devices display partial detail within the wings and hair. Housed in a green label holder.(#6860)

Elusive Choice VF 1796 Dollar
Small Date, Large Letters, B-4, BB-61

2313 **1796 Small Date, Large Letters VF35 ICG.** B-4, BB-61, R.3. Bowers-Borckardt Die State I. Medium sea-green and cobalt-blue envelop this midgrade representative. The curls and wings exhibit much fine detail. Attractive despite a couple of ticks beneath the neck and a faint thin mark beneath the right (facing) wing. (#6860)

Collectible VG 1796 Dollar
Large Date, Small Letters, B-5, BB-65

2314 **1796 Large Date, Small Letters VG8 PCGS.** B-5, BB-65, R.2. Bowers-Borckardt Die State IV. Some wing and hair details are present on this olive-gray and gunmetal-blue example. Softly brought up on star 3 and the first letters in STATES, customary for the die state, which features a large die break between the IC in AMERICA. Housed in a green label holder.(#6861)

1796 Large Date, Small Letters Dollar
B-5, BB-65, VF20

2315 **1796 Large Date, Small Letters VF20 PCGS.** B-5, BB-65, R.2. Die State II, with a large die lump above I in AMERICA, but not touching C or the rim above. The 6 in the date is doubled. As noted in Bowers-Borckardt: "... this is visible at the underside of the top of 6 and the upper inside of the bottom loop." This is a pleasingly original VF example with natural rose-gray toning over both sides. Obverse stars 2 and 3 are weak, as are STA of STATES on the upper reverse. Evenly worn with few marks on either side. (#6861)

1796 Large Date, Small Letters
Dollar, B-5, BB-65, VF35

2316 **1796 Large Date, Small Letters VF35 PCGS.** B-5, BB-65, R.2. Die State III. The slightly larger numerals are in the style of the 1797 dollars, although it is not immediately obvious. The most prominent diagnostic for the obverse is the bold repunching visible on the 6 of the date. Another quick pickup is the broken lower right tip of the R in LIBERTY. On the reverse the letters are small, of course, and a leaf tip ends under the A in STATES. The die lump at I in AMERICA has begun its travel toward the adjacent C, although here it is still a broad die line rather than a solid lump touching the C. The surfaces still offer some muted luster over attractive silver-gray surfaces. ST are somewhat weakly struck, as often seen on this die marriage.(#6861)

2317 **1797 10x6 Stars, Large Letters—Repaired—NCS. VF Details.** B-3, BB-71, R.2. Moderately worn with slate-gray and gold shadings in the fields and lighter elements at the high points. On the central reverse are a number of scratches, as well as evidence of attempts to repair them.(#6865)

Scarce 1797 Dollar VF25
10x6 Stars, Large Letters, B-3, BB-71

2318 **1797 10x6 Stars, Large Letters VF25 PCGS.** B-3, BB-71, R.2. Bowers-Borckardt Die State III. A lilac-gray example with slightly deeper toning throughout the fields. Generally pleasing despite a minute aqua spot on the cleavage and faint marks on the reverse border near 2:30. There are only three 1797-dated die varieties, compared to the 33 marriages dated 1798. In a green label holder. (#6865)

Impeccable 1797 10x6 Stars Dollar VF35
Large Letters, B-3, BB-71

2319 **1797 10x6 Stars, Large Letters VF35 NGC.** B-3, BB-71, R.2. Bowers-Borckardt Die State III. The sole variety with a 10x6 star alignment. Deeply patinated in olive, steel-gray, and golden-brown. The reverse is unmarked, as is the obverse field, while the center of the portrait has a few faded reed marks. Encapsulated in a prior generation holder.(#6865)

Desirable 1797 10x6 Stars Dollar
B-3, BB-71, XF40

2320 **1797 10x6 Stars, Large Letters XF40 ICG.** B-3, BB-71, R.2. The lone 10x6 Stars variety for the year, represented here by a luminous gold-gray survivor. Light wear is concentrated largely on the high points. The central devices are minimally marked, though a few small digs are noted between the D of UNITED and the first S of STATES on the reverse.(#6865)

XF45 Details 1797 10x6 Stars Dollar
B-3, BB-71, Large Letters

2321 **1797 10x6 Stars, Large Letters—Cleaned—ICG. XF45 Details.** B-3, BB-71, R.2. Bowers-Borckardt Die State III. This well defined Small Eagle dollar is blanketed in consistent deep brown toning. The surfaces are minutely granular. The only mark of any consequence is a slender pinscratch near the eagle's neck. (#6865)

Appealing VF30 1797 Dollar
9x7 Stars, Large Letters, B-1, BB-73

2322 **1797 9x7 Stars, Large Letters VF30 PCGS.** B-1, BB-73, R.3. Bowers-Borckardt Die State IV. A charming lavender-gray collector coin without the rim nicks and noticeable abrasions often encountered on this large silver type. 1796 and 1797 are the two scarcest collectible dates in the early dollar series. In a green label holder.(#6863)

Scarce XF 1797 9x7 Stars Dollar
Large Letters, B-1, BB-73

2323 **1797 9x7 Stars, Large Letters XF40 NGC.** B-1, BB-73, R.3. Bowers-Borckardt Die State V with several advanced peripheral die cracks. A charming dove-gray Small Eagle Bust dollar. A number of breast feathers are visible, and the wings and tail have exemplary detail. Evaluation beneath a loupe locates only inconsequential contact.(#6863)

Elusive VF Small Letters 1797 Dollar
9x7 Stars, B-2, BB-74

2324 **1797 9x7 Stars, Small Letters VF20 PCGS.** B-2, BB-74, R.4. A deep dove-gray silver dollar that displays rich green-gray hues when rotated beneath a light. The only abrasion of any significance is a thin mark through the eagle's head. The scarcest of the three Bolender varieties of the date, each of which receive separate *Guide Book* listings. Housed in a green label holder.(#6866)

Challenging VF 1798 Small Eagle Dollar
13 Stars, B-1, BB-82

2325 **1798 Small Eagle, 13 Stars VF20 PCGS.** B-1, BB-82, R.3. Bowers-Borckardt Die State III. The tan-gold toning is moderately deeper on the obverse. A problem-free example of this popular Bolender variety, which receives its own Guide Book listing since the other Small Eagle marriage (B-2) has 15 stars. In a green label holder.(#6867)

2326 **1798 Large Eagle, Pointed 9 VF20 PCGS.** B-14, BB-122, R.3. A midrange piece characterized by rich violet-gray patina over the fields and lighter silver color at the worn zones on the central devices. A few small, scattered ticks are to be expected for the grade. Housed in a green label holder.(#6873)

2327 **1798 Large Eagle, Pointed 9 VF30 PCGS.** B-24, BB-124, R.2. Moderately worn with a mix of deep ocean-blue and lighter gold-gray shadings. Well struck save for noticeable softness at the cloud below and to the left of OF on the reverse.(#6873)

Noble VF30 Heraldic Eagle 1798 Dollar
Pointed 9, B-15, BB-112

2328 **1798 Large Eagle, Pointed 9 VF30 PCGS.** B-15, BB-112, R.3. Designated as a Wide Date variety by PCGS, but we believe only B-16, B-19, B-20, B-22, and B-23 merit that notation. Dusky golden-brown alternates with deep forest-green. A few of the right-side reverse stars are softly brought up, but wing detail is substantial, and the only mark of any import is seen near the 8 in the date.(#6873)

1798 Four Berries Dollar, B-8, BB-125, XF40

2329 **1798 Large Eagle, Pointed 9 XF40 PCGS.** B-8, BB-125, R.2. This die marriage is instantly recognized as the only 1798 silver dollar variety that only has four berries in the olive branch. Both sides are pleasing pewter-gray with a single tiny obverse rim bump at 9 o'clock. Die failure causes stars 5 and 7 on the obverse to be indistinct, although all other stars are bold. This late state has numerous die cracks, clash marks, lumps, and other die defects on both sides.(#6873)

Rare B-4, BB-92 1798 Dollar
Five Stripes, Knob 9, XF45 Details

2330 **1798 5 Stripes, Knob 9—Cleaned—ANACS. XF45 Details.** B-4, BB-92, R.5. A very scarce Bolender variety noted for its wide date and ten bold arrows. There are three additional faint arrow shafts, one of which has a weak arrowhead. This cream-gray and chestnut example is a bit subdued from cleaning, although the reverse has substantial luster. The right obverse has a few faint marks.(#6874)

2331 **1798 Large Eagle, 10 Arrows VF20 PCGS.** B-13, BB-108, R.3. Die State II with the die flaw noted at the L of LIBERTY. Medium-gray with blue accents overall. Prominent adjustment marks are noted at the center obverse.(#6876)

1798 Heraldic Eagle Dollar VF25
10 Arrows, B-13, BB-108

2332 **1798 Large Eagle, 10 Arrows VF25 PCGS.** B-13, BB-108, R.3. Bowers-Borckardt Die State IV. A deep cream-gray early dollar with golden-brown and russet toning near the rims. The wings have pleasing definition, and both sides are free from remotely mentionable marks. Housed in a green label holder.(#6876)

XF 1798 10 Arrows Dollar
Heraldic Eagle, B-13, BB-108

2333 **1798 Large Eagle, 10 Arrows XF40 PCGS.** B-13, BB-108, R.3. Bowers-Borckardt Die State IV with a delicate die crack through the initial obverse stars. Predominantly golden-brown and steel-gray with peripheral mauve and cobalt-blue. The central reverse displays adjustment marks of mint origin, but the surfaces lack post-strike contact save for an obverse rim nick at 10 o'clock. Population: 18 in 40, 24 finer (2/09).(#6876)

2334 **1798 Large Eagle, Pointed 9, Wide Date—Improperly Cleaned—NCS. VF Details.** B-23, BB-105, R.3. On the obverse, 8 in the date firmly touches the bust, and star 7 points directly at the lower left serif end of L in LIBERTY. On the reverse, there are five small berries on the branch, the two above being closest together; a leaf point is under the left foot of I in AMERICA. The pearl-gray surfaces of this improperly cleaned example display relatively good detail. Some hair-thin marks are noted across Liberty's portrait, and several dark spots appear along the upper obverse border. (#6877)

Popular XF 1798 Large Eagle Dollar
Wide Date, Pointed 9, B-23, BB-105

2335 **1798 Large Eagle, Wide Date, Pointed 9 XF40 ANACS.** B-23, BB-105, R.3. Dusky sun-gold, lilac, and blue-green embrace this well detailed dollar. The wings display ample luster, and all letters in E PLURIBUS UNUM are clear. Smooth except for a couple of tiny rim dings on the upper reverse and a few moderate marks on the right obverse field.(#6877)

AU Large Eagle 1798 Dollar
Better Variety B-16, BB-110, Wide Date

2336 **1798 Large Eagle, Wide Date, Pointed 9 AU50 PCGS. CAC.**
B-16, BB-110, R.5. Bowers-Borckardt Die State II. Predominantly
silver-gray with peripheral glimpses of fire-red and apple-green.
An interesting slender strike-through beneath the E in STATES,
but actual abrasions are minimal. Luster brightens design recesses.
Early dollars with CAC seals are difficult to find.(#6877)

Scarce 1798 Large Eagle, Wide Date Dollar
B-23, BB-105, AU53

2337 **1798 Large Eagle, Wide Date, Pointed 9 AU53 NGC.** B-23,
BB-105, R.3. Chestnut-tan toning fills the borders and encroaches
upon the centers. Luster illuminates the devices and margins.
Minimally abraded, although a roundish mark right of the M
in UNUM is mentioned as an identifier. Very scarce relative to
demand at the AU53 level.(#6877)

Desirable 1798 Large Eagle, Wide Date Bust Dollar
B-20, BB-102, AU55

2338 **1798 Large Eagle, Wide Date, Pointed 9 AU55 ICG.** B-20,
BB-102, R.5. Die State IV with lump above the date. A rare variant
that is increasingly popular, represented here by a barely-circulated
piece. Warm gold-gray color drapes each side, and occasional dots
of deeper slate toning are present near the well struck central
devices.(#6877)

2339 **1799 7x6 Stars Fine 12 ICG.** B-14, BB-167, R.3. A stone-gray
early dollar with lilac undertones along the reverse periphery. A
curved mark is noted near the second 9 in the date, and the devices
exhibit a few wispy hairlines.(#6878)

2340 **1799 7x6 Stars Fine 12 PCGS.** B-11, BB-161, R.3. Though
significantly worn, this piece retains strong outlines on the
devices. Deep blue patina shows occasional lighter gold accents.
(#6878)

2341 **1799 7x6 Stars Fine 15 ANACS.** B-8, BB-165, R.3. This
Choice Fine example has a nice, original appearance and plenty
of remaining design detail. The surfaces display a combination of
tan-gray and blue-green toning that is quite attractive. There are
no severe marks on either side.(#6878)

2342 **1799 7x6 Stars VF20 PCGS.** B-12, BB-160, R.3. Die State III,
with cracks to both the left and the right of the 1 in the date. A
luminous midrange piece with largely medium-gray toning that
shows elements of orange at the fringe. Well struck and appealing.
(#6878)

Dusky 1799 Dollar VF30
7x6 Stars, B-5, BB-157

2343 **1799 7x6 Stars VF30 PCGS.** B-5, BB-157, R.2. Bowers-Borckardt
Die State IV with many reverse peripheral die cracks. Charcoal-
gray with glimpses of lighter slate-gray toning. A minutely granular
representative that lacks consequential marks and has traces of
remaining luster in design crevices. Encased in a green label holder.
(#6878)

Choice XF 1799 7x6 Stars Dollar
B-10, BB-163

2344 **1799 7x6 Stars XF45 PCGS.** B-10, BB-163, R.2. Bowers-
Borckardt Die State III. Deep cobalt-green patina covers the
obverse, yielding to lighter shades of ochre on the high points. The
reverse shows aqua and gold peripheral toning, with brownish-rose
color over the fields and centers. An attractive specimen with
moderate wear and few abrasions. A shallow scratch is noted on
the lower reverse, from the rim to the top right edge of the eagle's
tailfeathers.(#6878)

Impressive Choice XF 1799 Dollar
7x6 Stars, B-17, BB-164

2345 **1799 7x6 Stars XF45 PCGS.** B-17, BB-164, R.2. Bowers-Borckardt Die State V. Medium caramel-gold toning enriches this handsome Choice XF Draped Bust dollar. The cheek, shoulder, and drapery show light wear, but luster glimmers from design recesses, and relevant marks are fortuitously absent. Certified in a green label holder.(#6878)

Exquisite AU 1799 Dollar
B-14, BB-167

2346 **1799 7x6 Stars AU50 NGC.** B-14, BB-167, R.3. Die State II. Small die chips to the right of Liberty's eye, along with a small crack beneath the AM in AMERICA identify this variety. Deep olive and golden-brown toning envelops both sides, which shimmers with luster beneath the patina. The reverse is particularly clean, and the obverse field shows only a couple of areas of minor granularity, found beneath the hair ribbon and above the cleavage. An outstanding, better grade example.(#6878)

Exceptional 1799 7x6 Stars Dollar
B-14, BB-167, Choice AU

2347 **1799 7x6 Stars AU55 NGC.** B-14, BB-167, R.3. Bowers-Borckardt Die State IV. This is the latest die state recorded in the Bowers-Borckardt reference, with a die crack connecting the tops of AME. That crack extends left nearly to the wing, and appears to emerge from the right top of the E. The surfaces are excellent, with nearly full luster beneath medium rose-gray toning and hints of steel-green on the reverse. An exceptional example of a plentiful variety that is normally found in lower grades.(#6878)

Mint State 1799 Draped Bust Dollar
7x6 Stars, B-10, BB-163

2348 **1799 7x6 Stars MS61 ICG.** B-10, BB-163, R.2. Bowers-Borckardt Die State I-II. It ranks among the most plentiful die varieties of the year, yet Mint State examples are seldom encountered. Both sides of this piece are exquisitely detailed, with only a hint of bluntness on Liberty's shoulder and on her hair near the forehead. Underneath the deep forest-green and walnut-brown toning rests substantial satin luster. A thin mark near the bust tip, but generally free from detracting marks. Apparently an early die state with a faint crack through the final three stars on the obverse, but there is no evidence of any reverse die cracks.(#6878)

Early Die State 1799 B-8, BB-165 Dollar, MS62

2349 **1799 7x6 Stars MS62 PCGS. CAC.** B-8, BB-165, R.3. This example is a die state that is intermediate between Die States I and II as described in the Bowers-Borckardt reference. The obverse has a bold die crack through the upper two points of star 7 to LIB as described for Die State II. However, the reverse has no cracks or flaws other than the constant die flaw through the top of the final S in STATES, a diagnostic feature of the B-8 die marriage. The reverse matches the description of BB Die State I.

An outstanding Mint State piece, this example shows some weakness at the centers that is typical of the variety. The peripheral details including the border are nicely defined, although the strike is imperfectly centered. Both sides have original gray-gold surfaces with pale blue toning in the fields. It is fully lustrous with excellent mint frost. Population: 25 in 62, 24 finer (2/09).(#6878)

Important 1799/8 15 Stars Reverse Silver Dollar, B-3, BB-141, MS63

2350 **1799/8 15 Stars Reverse MS63 NGC.** B-3, BB-141, R.3. Toned in dark golden-gray hues over the entire surface, with darker flecks on the reverse. The mint luster is present but generally overwhelmed by the toning. Close examination of the obverse shows crisscrossing adjustment marks on Liberty's face, neck, and hair, some of which extend into the surrounding fields. There is also an excellent pedigree marker in the form of a shallow nick that extends horizontally behind Liberty's eye into the nearby curl. The strike is fairly sharp for this variety. Clean surfaces as expected for the grade, with no noteworthy bumps or nicks.

This variety is always a favorite to examine. The overdate feature is bold, as no effort was made to hide the underdigit 8 beneath the second 9 of the date. For the mint engraver, a less than perfect day unfolded. Without thinking, he placed 15 stars over the eagle's head and then noticed the mistake. Rather than discard the die or simply strike coins with it, he decided to "hide" two of the stars. Dies are difficult to erase errors from (thankfully for die variety collectors today), so the engraver decided to cover two of the stars by extending the clouds down over them, figuring no one would notice. Perhaps no one noticed until decades later, since coinage continued using this pair of dies until they failed in the normal course of events. However, *two little star points peek out from the enlarged cloud on the left, and one and a fraction star points extend from the enlarged cloud on the right.* The engraver's bad day, and his attempt to obscure, are recalled by collectors today. Certainly one of the finer examples known of this important and popular overdate. Census: 6 in 63, 7 finer (2/09).(#6883)

2351 **1799 Irregular Date, 13 Stars Reverse Fine 15 NGC.** Ex: Jules Reiver Collection. B-15, BB-152, R.3. Bowers-Borckardt Die State IV. Irregular date, first 9 high, leans left; Line star pattern. Reiver die state b. Bowers-Borckardt die state IV. Bright silver with a hint of incipient gold toning. A very late die state of this popular variety, the obverse has well developed die cracks through the stars, and the reverse die shows weakness in the strike over the eagle's head. Identifiable by a small toning spot between star 6 and the upper ribbon, and a minor rim tick above the first T of STATES. (#6880)

AU53 1799 Irregular Date Dollar
B-15, BB-152, 13 Stars Reverse

2352 **1799 Irregular Date, 13 Stars Reverse AU53 NGC.** B-15, BB-152, R.3. Bowers-Borckardt Die State IV. This is a surprisingly lustrous example for the grade, with a rich complement of champagne-gold toning across both sides. Olive-green specks are also prominent on the obverse and reverse fields. Well struck and nicely preserved, with few marks noted on either side. (#6880)

Difficult B-5, BB-189 VF35 1800 Dollar

2353 **1800 VF35 PCGS.** B-5, BB-189, R.5. Sea-green consumes the centers, while deep golden-brown frequents the margins. This Choice VF better variety early dollar has unblemished surfaces and pleasing detail. Evaluation beneath a loupe uncovers no mentionable marks. Encased in a green label holder.(#6887)

2354 **1800—Improperly Cleaned—NCS. XF Details.** B-12, BB-184, R.3. The smooth, dove-gray surfaces are satiny and free of distracting marks. The fine-grained field textures are indicative of improper cleaning. An attractive example nonetheless.(#6887)

Choice XF 1800 Dollar, B-16, BB-187

2355 **1800 XF45 PCGS.** B-16, BB-187, R.2. Bowers-Borckardt Die State III. The faint curved die crack near Liberty's chin is diagnostic for this interesting Bolender marriage. A nicely detailed early dollar with stone-gray centers and deeper gunmetal toning toward the rims. The surfaces are attractive despite a pair of faint marks near obverse star 9 and a hint of granularity on the upper reverse. (#6887)

XF Details 1800 Wide Date, Low 8 Dollar
B-10, BB-190

2356 **1800 Wide Date, Low 8—Altered Surfaces—ICG. XF40 Details.** B-10, BB-190, R.3. A lightly worn, minimally marked example with the reverse rotated slightly counterclockwise. Several flaws in the plastic holder visible at the lower obverse do not affect the piece. Each side shows thick mocha and violet patina that is at odds with the wear patterns on the coin.(#6888)

2357 **1801 Fine 15 PCGS.** B-4, BB-214, R.4. The first 1 in the date is nearly touching the curl. This example retains strong detail for the grade assigned. Medium-gray toning overall with splashes of violet at the lower obverse periphery.(#6893)

Very Fine 1801 Dollar, B-2, BB-212

2358 **1801 VF20 PCGS.** B-2, BB-212, R.3. Bowers-Borckardt Die State II with a double "collar" (from clash marks) beneath Liberty's neck. A sharply defined Heraldic Eagle dollar with nearly full wing feather detail. E PLURIBUS UNUM is bold, and the slightly bright stone-gray surfaces are devoid of obtrusive marks. Encased in a green label holder.(#6893)

Interesting 1801 Dollar, B-1, BB-211, XF Details

2359 **1801—Improperly Cleaned—NCS. XF Details.** B-1, BB-211, R.3. Die State III. The Wide Date obverse, with 180 more widely spaced than 01. On the reverse the leftmost arrowhead is under the U of UNITED. The charcoal-gray surfaces are fairly lackluster, the telltale of a past cleaning. Much pleasing detail remains, however, in keeping with the XF Details grade. The usual die crack appears to the left of the date, and the multiple interesting cracks on the reverse that show the slow but inexorable eventual breakup of that die.(#6893)

Choice XF 1801 Dollar, B-3, BB-213

2360 **1801 XF45 PCGS.** B-3, BB-213, R.3. Bowers-Borckardt Die State II. Luster emerges from protected areas of this chestnut-gray Large Eagle dollar. The surfaces are pleasing despite a pair of faint straight hair-thin marks on the right obverse field. An irregular planchet flaw beneath the 01 in the date is of mint origin. In a green label holder.(#6893)

Impressive 1801 B-3, BB-213 Dollar, MS62

2361 **1801 MS62 NGC.** B-3, BB-213, R.3. Die State III with minor rust marks and tiny die cracks on the obverse. Four 1801 dollar varieties are known, and each is scarce or rare in Mint State grades. The varieties designated BB-211 and BB-213 were each coined from a reverse die that saw no other service. The other two varieties were coined from reverse dies that were also used in 1802 and 1803, and in both instances the 1801 dollars were coined after those dated 1802. Since the obverse die of this BB-213 variety is found in a later state than for BB-212, it is also certain that this die combination was struck no earlier than 1802. The study of emission sequences, in an effort to establish the events that took place at the first Mint, parallels the work of a detective who seeks to solve a crime. There is little or no documentation, and the primary evidence appears only on actual surviving coins.

This nearly flawless Mint State example has full satin luster beneath delicate ivory, gold, and iridescent toning. The surfaces have a few wispy hairlines and minuscule marks, fewer than normally associated with the grade. Perhaps just a trace of cabinet friction limits the numerical assessment of this lovely piece.

In his *Silver Dollar Encyclopedia*, Dave Bowers records a single Mint State example from the Bareford Collection, followed by two AU58 coins, two AU55 pieces, and two AU50 examples. This example appears different from any of those that Bowers listed in his reference. Census: 4 in 62, 3 finer (2/09).(#6893)

Worthy VF30 1802/1 Silver Dollar
Narrow Date, B-4, BB-232

2362 **1802/1 Narrow Date VF30 PCGS.** B-4, BB-232, R.3. Bowers-Borckardt Die State II. The underdigit 1 is obvious. Caramel-gold, pearl-gray, and jade-green enrich this impressive midgrade Draped Bust dollar. Rotation reveals pockets of luster, although the cheek, shoulder, and hair display wear appropriate for the grade. In a green label holder.(#6898)

XF 1802 Heraldic Eagle Dollar
Narrow Date, B-6, BB-241

2363 **1802 Narrow Date XF40 NGC.** B-6, BB-241, R.1. Bowers-Borckardt Die State III. A stone-gray representative with rose-gray undertones. Glimpses of luster emerge from border elements, and the surfaces are attractive despite a couple of faint thin marks above the hair ribbon and arrows.(#6895)

Desirable XF45 1802 Dollar
Narrow Date, B-6, BB-241

2364 **1802 Narrow Date XF45 ICG.** B-6, BB-241, R.1. Bowers-Borckardt Die State III. A splendid Choice XF example with impressive detail and noticeable glimmering luster. No marks can be seen with the unaided eye, and a loupe locates only a thin line beneath the RT in LIBERTY. A desirable addition to an early silver type set.(#6895)

XF 1802 Wide Date Dollar
Important B-5, BB-242 Variety

2365 **1802 Wide Date XF40 ANACS.** B-5, BB-242, R.5. Bolender-2 is a very scarce die marriage, but it is also important as the only Wide Normal Date 1802 variety. Thus, it receives its own *Guide Book* listing, where it is priced above the other 1802 listings aside from the non-collectible novodel proof. Well detailed, particularly on the reverse, and deeply toned in stone-gray, sun-gold, and lavender shades.(#6896)

Elusive 1803 Small 3 Silver Dollar
VF25, B-4, BB-254

2366 **1803 Small 3 VF25 PCGS.** B-4, BB-254, High R.3. Dappled ocean-blue and pearl-gray endow the obverse, while golden-tan and aqua shades embrace the reverse. All letters within E PLURIBUS UNUM are readable, and most are sharp. A few faint thin obverse marks are of little account. Housed in an old green label holder. (#6900)

1803 Large 3 Bust Dollar, B-6, BB-255, VF25

2367 **1803 Large 3 VF25 PCGS.** B-6, BB-255, R.2. Bowers-Borckardt Die State II to III. Cobalt-blue and mauve fields with lighter stone-gray on the highpoints. Careful inspection beneath a lens fails to locate any noticeable abrasions. All letters in E PLURIBUS UNUM are discernible, and most are sharp. Certified in a green label holder.(#6901)

VF30 Large 3 1803 Dollar, B-6, BB-255

2368 **1803 Large 3 VF30 ICG.** B-6, BB-255, R.2. Bowers-Borckardt Die State II. Deep green-gray and lilac consume this refreshingly unabraded example. The cheek, forehead, and shoulder display wear, but traces of luster cling to the stars and letters. The Large 3 variety likely comprised the 1804 delivery of Bust dollars, long mistaken for an 1804-dated coinage.(#6901)

2369 **1803 Large 3—Scratched—ANACS. VF35 Details.** B-6, BB-255, R.2. The Large 3 variety is the ideal choice for a type collection, as it is more plentiful than all other 1803 varieties combined. This Large 3 dollar has pleasing light gray surfaces with a few minor reverse scratches between S and O.(#6901)

XF Large 3 1803 Dollar, B-6, BB-255

2370 **1803 Large 3 XF40 PCGS.** B-6, BB-255, R.2. Bowers-Borckardt Die State III. Incorrectly designated as a Small 3 variety by PCGS. Medium orange-gold and olive-gray toning drapes this attractively detailed representative, which retains glimpses of luster within the wings and other design recesses.(#6901)

Impressive AU Large 3 1803 Dollar, B-6, BB-255

2371 **1803 Large 3—Lamination Obverse at 8:00—AU50 PCGS.** B-6, BB-255, R.2. Bowers-Borckardt Die State III. Luster brightens the design of this lightly toned and partly lustrous tan-gray Draped Bust dollar. The lamination is charcoal-gray and affects the lower half of star 1. A few faint field marks are of little import. Choice AU early dollars are enthusiastically contested on the auction floor. Population: 10 in 50, 20 finer (12/08).(#6901)

GOBRECHT DOLLARS

Richly Toned 1836 Original Gobrecht Dollar Judd-60, Die Alignment I, Proof AU Details

2372 **1836 Name on Base, Judd-60 Original, Pollock-65, R.1—Environmental Damage—NCS. Proof AU Details.** Silver. Plain Edge. Die Alignment I (the center of Liberty's head is opposite the DO in DOLLAR). The die scratch plainly shows above the eagle's wing pointing toward the AT of STATES. This die scratch is seen only on so-called First Originals struck in late December 1836 and the Second Originals from March 1837. One of the most popular 19th century type coins, and a difficult type to locate in high grade as a good portion of the original mintage was released into circulation. This example is sharply struck in all areas. Each side is richly toned with pinkish-rose centers and much deeper blue-green color around the margins. Beneath the toning each side shows obvious signs of cleaning, and there are numerous small abrasions in the fields. However, at a distance the toning does an excellent job of camouflaging each of these surface imperfections. (#11225)

Deeply Mirrored 1836 Gobrecht Dollar, PR62 Judd-60, Die Alignment I

Toned Judd-60 1836 Gobrecht Dollar, PR63 Die Alignment I, So-Called 'Second Original'

2373 1836 Name on Base, Judd-60 Original, Pollock-65, R.1, PR62 PCGS. Silver. Plain Edge. Die Alignment I (the center of Liberty's head is opposite the DO in DOLLAR). First issue of 1836, struck prior to the die clashing that produced the diagonal line above the eagle's wing. Always a popular type coin because of the majestic design and limited availability of all three dates, Gobrecht dollars are one of the classic issues in United States numismatics. Gobrechts are also one of the few U.S. coins that were struck in proof format and released into general circulation. This piece is mostly brilliant on the obverse with very light toning on the reverse and the fields are deeply reflective. A few shallow scratches and contact marks in the right obverse field account the coin's grade.(#11225)

2374 1836 Name on Base, Judd-60 Original, Pollock-65, R.1, PR63 NGC. Silver. Plain Edge. Die Alignment I (the center of Liberty's head is opposite the DO in DOLLAR). Struck in either late 1836 or March 1837 from clashed dies, as evidenced by the diagonal line above the eagle's wing. This piece also shows the dentil chip above the second A in AMERICA, which first shows on the die state prior to the die clashing. The jury is still out on the exact striking sequence of the various Die Alignment I, II, and IV coins, but this is a fertile area of investigation for researchers.

The coin is fully struck in all areas, even the foot of Liberty is completely defined. The surfaces are toned in deep shades of gray-green and rose, and this toning helps conceal several field marks present on each side. A well-preserved example of this always-popular 19th century type coin.

From The Burning Tree Collection.(#11225)

SEATED DOLLARS

Important 1843 Seated Dollar, MS64

2375 **1843 MS64 NGC.** A relatively common coin in lower circulated grades but difficult to locate in the better grades of Mint State. In fact, the 1843 Seated dollar is highly elusive in any Uncirculated grade, and this Choice piece is tied for numerically finest in the combined certified population (1/09). This frosted, highly lustrous example has just a hint of natural patina circling the rims on each side. Well struck overall and largely mark-free.(#6929)

Choice AU 1845 Seated Dollar

2376 **1845 AU55 NGC.** Luster shimmers across the devices and borders of this low mintage No Motto silver dollar. The obverse is ocean-blue with glimpses of plum-red, while the reverse is lightly toned except for golden-brown and russet-red near the right border. Minor field marks pose no distraction.(#6931)

Desirable 1846-O Seated Liberty Dollar, MS63 Choice Condition Rarity

2377 **1846-O MS63 PCGS. CAC.** The 1846-O Seated Liberty dollar is the first silver dollar coined at any of the branch mints. A small mintage of 59,000 pieces was accomplished, and the coins circulated extensively in the Mississippi Valley. The issue is available in circulated grades today, but Mint State coins are rare. Q. David Bowers comments, "A top grade 1846-O is an object of desirability. In MS-63 or better grade it is a prime rarity."

The present coin has bright, semi-prooflike fields, as often seen on Seated dollars. The reflective surfaces are overlaid with attractive layers of original toning. Pale shades of lilac and rose predominate, with occasional highlights of deeper blue. All design elements are sharply defined, and the surfaces are free of obvious defects. Population: 8 in 63, 1 finer (2/09).(#6933)

2378 **1847 AU58 NGC. CAC.** This piece is close to Mint State, with almost all of its original luster present. There are smoky gray toning stripes on the obverse, along with accents of gold. A few light abrasions consistent with a short spate in circulation appear under a loupe, and the strike on Liberty's upper torso is somewhat soft. Nonetheless, an appealing coin with a choice reverse.(#6934)

2379 **1850—Improperly Cleaned—NCS. AU Details.** Lightly hairlined fields have retoned deep moss-green, sage, and slate-blue. A degree of wear is noted on the light gray high points, but the surfaces show no rub elsewhere.(#6937)

2380 **1856—Improperly Cleaned—NCS. AU Details.** Breen-5454. This appears to be one of the coins described by Walter Breen as being from an 1856/4 overdate variety, which is not universally accepted by numismatists. The current example presents a mottled appearance, with mostly deep green-gray coloration across each side. Somewhat bright from improper cleaning.(#6944)

2381 **1860-O AU58 PCGS.** Somewhat baggy, with semireflective fields and well struck devices. Essentially untoned except near the edges. A common date in the series; recommended for type purposes. (#6950)

Pleasing Select 1860-O Seated Dollar

2382 **1860-O MS63 PCGS.** Each side shows soft, pleasing luster beneath rich, dappled gold-orange and silver-gray patina. Delicate blue accents visit the margins. Slight striking softness at the margins, though the faintly abraded centers are well-defined. A great example of this antebellum issue. Population: 65 in 63, 25 finer (2/09).(#6950)

Scarce 1866 Dollar Motto, MS63

2383 **1866 Motto MS63 NGC.** The 1866 Motto, coming from a mintage of 48,900 circulation strikes, is scarce in all grades. A medley of medium intensity gold, gray, electric-blue, and magenta toning runs over both faces of this Select offering. Modest field-device variance is visible when the coin is tilted ever so slightly under a light source. Typically struck, with softness in some of the star centers and the hair atop Liberty's head. Census: 10 in 63, 21 finer (2/09).(#6959)

Appealing 1866 With Motto Dollar, MS64

2384 **1866 Motto MS64 PCGS. CAC.** This is the first year that the motto IN GOD WE TRUST appeared on the Seated Liberty dollar. Partially prooflike fields offset the devices, and a mix of orange-gold, violet, cobalt-blue, yellow-gold, and golden-brown visits both sides. Typically struck, in that Liberty's hair and the star centers are weak. The reverse is sharply impressed. All in all, a highly appealing coin. Population: 16 in 64, 8 finer (2/09). (#6959)

2385 **1870-CC Fine 12 NGC.** Deep heather and gold-gray patina embraces each side of this heavily circulated example. Despite the extensive wear, the present coin has strong outlines to the devices, though only the letters L and Y of LIBERTY are present at the shield. Dots of toning are present on the rims.(#6964)

2386 **1870-CC—Improperly Cleaned—NCS. XF Details.** This lightly worn silver dollar comes from the Carson City Mint's first year of strikings. Slate-blue, silver-gray, and steel shadings combine on each side, and moderate hairlines indicate a past cleaning. (#6964)

Attractive 1871 Silver Dollar MS62

2387 **1871 MS62 PCGS. CAC.** Blushes of autumn-gold iridescence drape this high mintage but conditionally rare representative. Luster is vibrant although slightly diminished across the open obverse field. The 1871 is plentiful in circulated grades by Seated dollar standards, but is certainly more difficult in Mint State than the 1859-O or 1860-O.
From The Burning Tree Collection.(#6966)

Elusive Near-Gem 1871 Seated Dollar

2388 **1871 MS64 NGC.** A frosty near-Gem example of an issue that is plentiful in lower Mint State grades, but conditionally rare in better grades. The present piece is one of those conditionally rare coins that specialists will find most desirable. Both sides have delicate champagne-gold toning over fully lustrous surfaces with excellent eye appeal. Although not full, the strike is bold. Census: 35 in 64, 6 finer (2/09).(#6966)

Rare 1871-CC Seated Dollar, VF Details

2389 **1871-CC—Improperly Cleaned—NCS. VF Details.** One of the rarest Seated dollars with only 1,376 pieces struck, and second-rarest of the four Carson City issues. This example has obviously been cleaned, but displays an ample measure of remaining design detail which is sufficient for the VF grade level. A few shallow marks and wispy hairlines appear on each side.(#6967)

Rarely Seen 1871-CC Dollar, XF45

2392 **1872-S XF45 PCGS.** Reddish-orange, violet, and denim-blue shadings dominate the fields, while the devices are generally silver-gray. Lightly worn but with considerable remaining luster. Population: 22 in 45, 49 finer (1/09).(#6970)

Silver-White 1873 Seated Dollar, MS64

2393 **1873 MS64 PCGS.** All Seated dollars of this year were struck from the Close 3 date style, while all Trade dollars use the Open 3 variant, a factoid apparently first brought to light by "Mr. 1873," Harry X Boosel. (The date is not "closed," hence the disfavor into which the former term has fallen.) The loops are large and closer together. This lustrous piece has silver-white surfaces with minimal visible contact for the grade. An attractive example for a type or date set. Population: 24 in 64, 14 finer (2/09).
From The Burning Tree Collection.(#6971)

Historic XF Details 1873-CC Seated Dollar

2390 **1871-CC XF45 NGC.** This is a problem-free example with no abrasions that are out of context with the XF45 level of preservation. A warm blanket of steel-gray patina blankets both sides, and the features are well defined with only slight wear evident over the high points. The 1871-CC boasts the lowest mintage (1,376 pieces) among CC-mint Seated dollars. Only 85-125 pieces are believed extant in all grades, and these coins are rarer than survivors from the 1870-CC and 1872-CC deliveries. NGC and PCGS have seen only five coins in Mint State, the finest two grade MS64. A significant silver dollar rarity from both absolute and condition standpoints.
From The Belle Collection of Carson City Coinage.(#6967)

2394 **1873-CC—Scratched—NCS. XF Details.** Last but arguably foremost among Carson City Seated dollars, the 1873-CC has been a collector favorite for decades. This lightly worn example has generally pale silver-gray surfaces with occasional reddish-brown accents. Though a number of fine scratches are present in the fields, this remains a readily collectible piece.(#6972)

1872-CC Seated Dollar, AU53

2391 **1872-CC AU53 NGC.** From an initial mintage of 3,150 pieces, although far fewer exist in the marketplace today. Most of the original luster is intact on this gold-tinged specimen, which shows the light wear and moderate contact marks expected of a short spate in circulation. The strike is somewhat soft on the upper obverse, leaving some peripheral stars and some of the details of Liberty's face less than full. Census: 6 in 53, 26 finer (2/09).
From The Belle Collection of Carson City Coinage.(#6969)

Outstanding 1857 Seated Dollar, PR64

Elusive 1857 Seated Dollar, PR65

2395 1857 PR64 PCGS. CAC. Breen-5455. Most of the business strike 1857 Seated dollars were used for the export trade, and few ever saw domestic circulation. Circulated 1857 dollars are almost equally as rare as their Mint State counterparts. The proof Seated dollars saw an emission of a few dozen pieces at most, and today there are fewer than two dozen pieces graded PR64, with nine coins finer at both services combined (2/09). This piece has the beardlike protrusion below Liberty's chin seen on some proof specimens as described in Bowers-Borckardt, with the left side of the 1 in the date slightly to the right of a denticle edge. Both sides show considerable reflectivity and moderate field-device contrast, with light gold patina predominating against areas of smoke-gray and a patch of teal on the obverse. An attractive, problem-free, and rare specimen. Population: 10 in 64, 1 finer (12/08).(#7000)

2396 1857 PR65 NGC. Although proof mintages prior to 1858 are lost to today's collectors, Bowers (*Silver Dollars and Trade Dollars of the United States*, 1993) estimates an original mintage of 50-100 pieces for the proof 1857 Seated dollar and claims the issue is "more available than the 1855, but scarcer than the 1856." He also warns that many prooflike 1857 business strikes masquerade as proofs. This example shows faint evidence of the diagnostic "beard" below Liberty's chin, ensuring the NGC attribution. This is a conditionally rare member of a very scarce issue; the NGC *Census Report* reveals four examples in PR65, with just four finer (2/09). Neither side reveals any conspicuous handling marks, and the finish shows faint cameo tendencies over the devices and legends. Pinpoint detail is seen on all design elements, and the surfaces offer gray-rose toning in the centers, with cobalt-blue at the margins.(#7000)

PR62 1859 Seated Dollar

2397 **1859 PR62 ICG.** Proofs of this issue are actually more available than are Mint State business strikes, which remain quite elusive. This proof example is nonetheless still conditionally scarce. The obverse is covered with a kaleidoscope of colors including green, purple, and charcoal, with the reverse slightly lighter ice-blue, green, and amber. A nick in the obverse field near star 1 requires singular mention.(#7002)

Sharp 1862 Seated Dollar, PR63

2399 **1862 PR63 NGC.** The obverse has generally gold-orange patina with blue-green shadings at the upper margin, while the reverse is mostly silver-gray with touches of color close to the rims. A well-defined Select proof from this Civil War-era issue, attractive despite minor hairlines and a few isolated points of contact in the fields.(#7005)

Enthralling 1860 Seated Dollar, PR65

2398 **1860 PR65 NGC.** Though this proof issue has a stated mintage of 1,330 pieces, that figure grossly overestimates the number of coins actually sold. As recounted by Q. David Bowers in his *Silver Dollars and Trade Dollars of the United States*, "Only 527 were eventually sold, and the rest were consigned to the melting pot." Among those specimens surviving today is this precious Gem, sharply struck, carefully preserved, and beautifully toned. Pale silver-gray centers yield to bands of rich blue-green, cerulean, amethyst, and reddish-orange. A powerfully appealing coin not to be missed. Census: 16 in 65, 9 finer (2/09).(#7003)

Fabulous Premium Gem Proof
1866 Motto Seated Dollar

2400 1866 Motto PR66 NGC. The upsurge of religious sentiment that occurred during the dreadful War Between the States saw the placement of the motto IN GOD WE TRUST on many U.S. coin designs. The first U.S. regular issue coin to bear the motto was the two cent piece that debuted in 1864, but by 1866 a panoply of issues bore those words, as the Mint rushed new dies into production. Several denominations for the year are known both with and without the motto.

 The 1866 Motto Seated dollar is elusive in high grades, with a recorded production of only 725 pieces. NGC has certified only four pieces in PR66 with two finer, and PCGS has graded two PR66 coins with none finer (2/09).

 Even if the surfaces of this piece were not as close to technical perfection as they are, the toning would bring a significant premium. The interior of each side is fiery red and surrounded by deep blue at the margins. The fields are brightly reflective and flash forcefully through the toning. This nice, high-grade example would fit perfectly in a first-year type set.(#7014)

2401 1868 PR58 PCGS. In addition to scattered hairlines and contact marks in the fields, this silver-gray specimen also shows rub on the high points. Still, this remains a readily collectible (and now comparatively affordable) representative of the proof Seated dollar type.(#7016)

2402 1868—Obverse Scratched—NCS. Proof. Minor evidence of rub affects the high points, and a shallow near-vertical scratch runs just above Liberty's outstretched foot. Moderate mirrors show a number of small, scattered hairlines.(#7016)

Impressive 1869 Seated Dollar, PR64

2403 1869 PR64 PCGS. An impressive near-Gem proof, this Seated dollar exhibits wonderful cobalt-blue, russet, and light gold toning with considerable underlying cameo contrast. The fields are exceptionally deep and crisply meet the devices. Both sides are well preserved with few imperfections, limited to a few grade-consistent hairlines that are only visible with a glass. A wonderful example for the specialist or the type collector. Population: 56 in 64, 25 finer (2/09).(#7017)

Choice Proof 1870 Seated Dollar

2404 1870 PR64 NGC. Although the reported proof mintage is 1,000 pieces, Duncan Lee states that "many were melted at year's end, making the 1870 scarcer than its mintage would indicate." This Choice proof has dusky caramel-gold toning and a needle-sharp strike. Census: 46 in 64, 32 finer (2/09).(#7018)

TRADE DOLLARS

Appealing 1873 Trade Dollar, MS63

2405 **1873 MS63 PCGS.** All Trade dollars of 1873 show the Open 3 date style, as here. The 1873 Trade dollar is quite scarce in all Mint State grade levels. The luster is slightly subdued on this silver-gold specimen, although the fields are only lightly scuffed and show minimal evidence of contact. There is faint field-device contrast present. Certified in a green-label holder. Population: 26 in 63, 38 finer (2/09).
From The Burning Tree Collection. (#7031)

Elusive 1873-CC Trade Dollar, MS62

2406 **1873-CC MS62 PCGS.** A slight trace of repunching is evident above the 7. Just 124,500 Trade dollars were minted in Carson City in 1873, following an extremely limited production of 1873-CC Seated dollars. The currently offered example is brilliant with white-silver surfaces and satin luster. Each side has a hint of champagne toning. Population: 16 in 62, 15 finer (2/09).
From The Burning Tree Collection. (#7032)

Rarely Seen 1873-CC Trade Dollar, MS64 One of the Finest Known

2407 **1873-CC MS64 NGC.** The Trade dollar, substantially heavier than its predecessor the Seated dollar, was the eventual destination of much of the silver mined from Nevada and California in the early to mid-1870s. In particular, the Comstock Lode's silver mines saw much of their output go to the various Mints to be made into Trade dollars, though the majority of Nevada silver actually crossed the border into California to be minted at San Francisco, rather than be struck in-state at Carson City.

The Carson City Trade dollars are particularly elusive due to a lack of savings, with the first and last issues, the 1873-CC and the heavily melted 1878-CC, the most challenging of all. To quote from the Q. David Bowers reference *Silver Dollars & Trade Dollars of the United States,* "So far as is known, not a single numismatist in 1873 was interested in collecting trade dollars by mintmark varieties. Nearly all coins were shipped to the Orient, although a few apparently saw domestic use. Many of the exported pieces saw heavy use and were chopmarked ..."

It is only through the purest happy accident that a handful of unworn examples have survived to the present day. This Choice coin is one of the best-preserved, crisply detailed and immensely lustrous beneath a melange of rich gold-orange, rose, claret, silver, and plum shadings. A handful of stray marks preclude Gem status, but the eye appeal remains impressive. Census: 5 in 64, 1 finer (2/09).
From The Belle Collection of Carson City Coinage. (#7032)

Scarce 1873-S Trade Dollar, MS63

2408 **1873-S MS63 PCGS. CAC.** Unquestionably original, the mostly lavender-gray surfaces reveal speckled russet shadings in the more protected areas around the devices. The toning adequately conceals the few wispy abrasions that are present, but it also mutes the luster ever so slightly. Still, this is an attractive representative of this underrated Trade dollar rarity. Population: 18 in 63, 29 finer (2/09).
From The Burning Tree Collection.(#7033)

Desirable 1873-S Trade Dollar, MS64

2409 **1873-S MS64 PCGS. CAC.** This exceptional quality 1873-S Trade dollar is housed in an older green-label holder. The surfaces have pale lilac and gold toning, with splashes of iridescence that is most notable on the obverse. High quality 1873-S Trade dollars are extremely difficult to locate. Population: 25 in 64, 4 finer (2/09).
From The Burning Tree Collection.(#7033)

Sharp 1874 Trade Dollar, MS64

2410 **1874 MS64 PCGS.** Smoke-gray at the centers cedes to brownish-gray at the rims on each side. Considerable luster and silver color remains in the fields, accentuating the gray and charcoal devices. This piece is sharply struck, and shows fewer signs of contact than might be expected at this grade level. Population: 24 in 64, 7 finer (2/09).
From The Burning Tree Collection.(#7034)

Attractive 1874-CC Trade Dollar, MS63

2411 **1874-CC MS63 PCGS.** The 1874-CC and 1875-CC Trade dollars are the two common dates from that Mint, each having a production in excess of 1 million coins. Behind those, the 1877-CC had the next highest mintage with 534,000 coins. It is the first two dates mentioned above that are candidates for a type collection. This pale lemon example has underlying satiny luster with pleasing surfaces for the grade. Population: 37 in 63, 20 finer (2/09).
From The Burning Tree Collection.(#7035)

2412 **1874-S MS62 PCGS.** Impressively lustrous with delightful patina. Blue, violet, and gold peripheral shadings yield to brighter silver-gray centers. Minimally marked for the grade.
From The Burning Tree Collection.(#7036)

Splendid Near-Gem 1874-S Trade Dollar

2413 **1874-S MS64 NGC.** Breen-5784, Medium S, as most of the issue. No period after FINE. This is a splendid near-Gem of this available date in delightful shades of pearl and ice-blue. The strike is fairly soft on the upper obverse and lower reverse especially, where parallel roller marks appear through the lower eagle, the mintmark, and DO(LLAR) below. For mintage exceeding 2.5 million pieces, this issue is seldom found finer: NGC has certified 20 in MS64 with two finer, while PCGS has certified 23, with one finer (2/09). (#7036)

Superlative 1874-S Trade Dollar, MS64

2414 **1874-S MS64 PCGS.** The 1874-S Trade dollar was the first of the common dates from the San Francisco Mint, with a mintage of 2.5 million coins. This issue, and the next four S-Mint Trade dollars through 1878, are the true common dates of the design. The strike is a little blunt at the top of the obverse, and both sides show typical abrasions. However, the excellent eye appeal trumps those few imperfections. Population: 23 in 64, 1 finer (2/09).
From The Burning Tree Collection.(#7036)

Elusive 1875 Trade Dollar, MS62

2415 **1875 MS62 NGC. CAC.** Type Two Reverse. An impressive Mint State piece, from a limited mintage of only 218,200 business strikes, the lowest mintage of any P-Mint Trade dollar, aside from the proof-only issues. Frosty luster is visible beneath pleasing gold toning with peripheral iridescence. Census: 13 in 62, 42 finer (2/09). *From The Burning Tree Collection.*(#7037)

Important 1875 Trade Dollar, MS63

2416 **1875 MS63 NGC.** Type Two Reverse. A brilliant silver representative of this scarce, low-mintage issue of uncommon quality. While the upper obverse and lower reverse details are weak, the overall appearance is exceptional. Brilliant silver surfaces are splashed with pale gold toning on each side. Census: 16 in 63, 26 finer (2/09).(#7037)

Scarce Near-Gem 1875 Trade Dollar

2417 **1875 MS64 PCGS.** Type Two Reverse. An attentively struck near-Gem example of this lower-mintage Philadelphia Trade dollar issue, softly lustrous beneath delicate rose-gray and sea-green shadings. A small depression on Liberty's extended forearm appears to be of Mint origin. Population: 18 in 64, 3 finer (2/09).(#7037)

2418 **1875-CC MS61 PCGS.** Type One Reverse. Hints of cloud-white and golden-brown peripheral toning enliven each side of this Carson City Trade dollar. Moderately abraded but well struck overall with only slight softness around the eagle's talons. (#7038)

Attractive 1875-CC Trade Dollar MS62

2419 **1875-CC MS62 PCGS.** Type One Reverse. This lightly toned Carson City representative features unbroken cartwheel luster and an above average strike. Only Liberty's hair lacks intricate detail. Faint field marks are present but none distract. A good value relative to higher grades.(#7038)

Lovely MS63 1875-CC Trade Dollar

2420 **1875-CC MS63 PCGS.** Type One Reverse. The berry is seen below the eagle's left (right facing) claw. The 1875-CC Trade dollar is readily available in the lower Mint State grades, is elusive in MS63, and very difficult to obtain in higher grades. Pale orange, sky-blue, and lavender toning overlays lustrous surfaces that exhibit well struck motifs. Small contact marks are seen on Liberty's cheek, neck, arms, and foot, and in the obverse fields. A few light nicks are also apparent on the reverse rim. Population: 45 in 63, 26 finer (2/09). *From The Burning Tree Collection.*(#7038)

Dazzling Choice 1875-CC Dollar

2421 **1875-CC MS64 PCGS.** Type One Reverse. Generally brilliant, although freckles of tan patina endow the reverse. This Choice Carson City Trade Dollar gains instant appeal with its bright cartwheel sheen and attentive strike. A few minor field marks discount the possibility of Gem status, but fail to diminish the coin's admirable appearance.
Ex: San Francisco ANA Signature (Heritage, 7/2005), lot 6674, which realized $8,050.
From The Belle Collection of Carson City Coinage.(#7038)

2422 **1875-S MS63 PCGS.** Type One Reverse. Large S. Vibrant luster and a wisp of golden toning ensure the originality of this attractive Trade dollar. Obscure marks beneath the right scroll end are all that limit the grade.(#7039)

2423 **1875-S MS63 PCGS.** Type One Reverse. Large S. Brightly lustrous with glimpses of peripheral golden toning against the shining silver-white found elsewhere. A minimally marked Select piece that offers great eye appeal. *From The Burning Tree Collection.*(#7039)

Desirable MS64 1875-S Trade Dollar

2424 **1875-S MS64 PCGS.** Type One Reverse. Large S. Strongly lustrous with hints of golden patina visiting the fields. Minimally marked with no trace of wear. Softly struck at the high points, with roller marks also noted at the eagle's softly struck right (facing) claw, adding interest to the piece. PCGS has graded 33 finer examples (2/09).(#7039)

2425 **1876 MS63 ANACS.** Type One Obverse, Type Two Reverse. Light golden-brown patina. A well struck piece with good luster and relatively unabraded surfaces. Although priced as a type coin, the 1876 is actually scarcer than several other issues, especially those from the San Francisco Mint.
Ex: Long Beach Signature (Heritage, 9/2002), lot 7248.
From The Burning Tree Collection.(#7041)

Smooth Choice 1876 Trade Dollar

2426 **1876 MS64 PCGS.** Type One Obverse and Reverse. This satiny near-Gem features lovely golden-brown, pearl-gray, and aqua patina. Only the eagle's right (facing) leg lacks an exacting strike. Refreshingly unabraded, a worthy representative of this relatively low mintage Centennial issue.
From The Burning Tree Collection.(#7041)

Coveted 1876 Trade Dollar, MS64
Transitional Hub Combination

2427 **1876 MS64 PCGS.** Type One Obverse, Type Two Reverse. This amazing 1876 Trade dollar represents the elusive transitional variety with an old hub obverse and a new hub reverse. Perhaps only about 10% of surviving 1876 Trade dollars represent the transitional die combination. This one is boldly detailed with satiny luster and fully brilliant silver surfaces. In our auctions dating back to 1993, we have only handled three finer examples of this hub combination.
From The Burning Tree Collection.(#7041)

2428 **1876-CC Doubled Die Reverse—Cleaned—ANACS. AU58 Details.** Type One Obverse and Reverse. FS-801, formerly FS-014. The doubling is most prominent on the olive branch, the eagle's claws, the right wing tip, the top arrowhead, and markedly on E PLURIBUS UNUM. Evidence of wear is scant, and only a few faint hairlines point to a past cleaning. Otherwise, a radiant near-Mint example of this desirable *Guide Book* variety.
From The Burning Tree Collection.(#7042)

Impressive MS62 1876-CC Trade Dollar

2429 **1876-CC MS62 PCGS.** Type One Obverse. Type Two Reverse. Tall CC. This coin was previously offered as lot 4112 in our April 2002 sale of the Morris Silverman Collection, where it was described as: "The Carson City Mint halted Trade Dollar production in April 1876 after only 509,000 coins were produced with that date. While not the rarest Trade Dollar in an absolute sense, the '76-CC is particularly elusive in Mint State. Interestingly, the 1876-CC is just as rare, if not *rarer*, than the key date 1878-CC in grades above the AU level. This fact is not, however, widely known, probably because the former issue is generally available in worn condition whereas the 1878-CC is elusive in all grades. The 1876-CC is also a difficult coin to locate with any degree of eye appeal, as most technically Uncirculated coins are plagued by poor luster and/or excessive bagmarks. Not so the present BU example. True, the surfaces display scattered, grade-defining abrasions that include a few reeding marks in the left obverse field, but the luster is pleasing and the eye appeal benefits greatly from a moderate overlay of champagne-apricot patina around the obverse border and throughout the reverse. The needle sharp strike is also noteworthy for the type, every feature displaying virtually full definition. Clearly, this is an impressive representative of this often overlooked CC-mint Trade Dollar. Most 1876-CC are of the Type I Obverse / Type II Reverse combination." To this description we add that the Tall CC variety of this issue is not at all common in Mint State, with most survivors displaying some degree of wear.
From The Burning Tree Collection.(#7042)

2430 **1876-S MS63 NGC.** Type One Obverse and Reverse. Large S. Orange-gold and olive-gray compete for territory across this satiny and crisply struck Centennial year Trade dollar. Both sides are generally free from the noticeable small marks usually associated with the MS63 level. An elusive type with rich original toning. (#7043)

Lustrous 1876-S Trade Dollar, MS64

2431 **1876-S MS64 NGC. CAC.** Breen-5802, Type One Obverse, Type Two Reverse, Minute S. The end of the scroll points left on the obverse, while on the reverse there is no berry under the eagle's claw. Lustrous surfaces exhibit light hazy toning. Well struck, save for the usual softness on the upper obverse and on the eagle's left (facing) leg and wing. A few light peripheral cracks are visible, but this is a nicely preserved coin.(#7043)

Near-Gem 1876-S Trade Dollar

2432 **1876-S MS64 PCGS.** Type One Obverse and Reverse. Large S. A lustrous Choice type coin with light golden-brown toning and an above average strike. Surprisingly mark-free aside from a minor reverse rim nick at 1 o'clock. Trade dollars are scarce in such pleasing quality. Population: 92 in 64, 5 finer (2/09). *From The Burning Tree Collection.*(#7043)

Lustrous 1876-S Trade Dollar, MS64

2433 **1876-S MS64 PCGS. CAC.** Type One Obverse and Reverse. Housed in a green label PCGS holder, this near-Gem has exceptional aesthetic desirability for the grade. Light champagne toning graces both sides of this lovely Trade dollar. Population: 92 in 64, 5 finer (2/09). *From The Burning Tree Collection.*(#7043)

Well Struck 1877 Trade Dollar, MS64

2434 **1877 MS64 PCGS.** Well known for soft definition on Liberty's head and stars 5-7, this piece has nearly complete definition on the head and is almost fully detailed on the upper stars as well. The surfaces are softly frosted and each side is covered with golden-rose toning with an accent of sea-green around the peripheries. *From The Burning Tree Collection.*(#7044)

Desirable 1877-CC Trade Dollar, MS63

2435 **1877-CC MS63 PCGS.** Despite having the third highest Carson City Trade dollar mintage, the 1877-CC is an elusive and desirable issue, especially in Mint State grades. This one has light gold toning and frosty silver luster with excellent eye appeal. Population: 27 in 63, 10 finer (2/09). *From The Burning Tree Collection.*(#7045)

Outstanding MS64 ★ 1877-CC Trade Dollar

2436 **1877-CC MS64 ★ NGC.** The logic behind producing just over half a million Trade dollars, a denomination originally intended for overseas consumption, at Carson City, a Mint located in a thoroughly landlocked state that borders no other nation, clearly had more to do with domestic boondoggle than any sort of mercantile practicality. Said boondoggle, however, led to the creation of this gorgeous near-Gem, arguably a worthy trade-off. The shining, moderately reflective obverse shows deep yellow-orange central toning with blue and aqua patina near the rims, while the reverse shows echoes of champagne and russet at the margins. NGC has graded just one numerically finer survivor (2/09).(#7045)

Fully Mirrored 1877-S Trade Dollar, MS64

2437 **1877-S MS64 PCGS. CAC.** Although PCGS seldom recognizes prooflike Mint State coins, the present piece has fully reflective or mirrored fields on both sides, with excellent design details. Satiny silver luster is visible on the devices. Business strike Trade dollars are seldom encountered with such characteristics.
From The Burning Tree Collection.(#7046)

Lovely 1877-S Trade Dollar, MS64

2438 **1877-S MS64 PCGS.** Dusky silver surfaces have accents of pale toning over the underlying Mint frost. The few scattered surface marks that are visible on each side are entirely consistent with the grade and of little concern. PCGS has only certified 32 finer pieces (2/09).
From The Burning Tree Collection.(#7046)

Pleasing Choice XF 1878-CC Trade Dollar

2439 **1878-CC XF45 NGC.** The official mintage for this final Carson City Trade dollar issue is 97,000 pieces, though as the *Guide Book*'s footnote for the issue indicates, "44,148 trade dollars were melted on July 18, 1878. Many of these may have been 1878-CC." Certainly, the issue is far more elusive than the stated mintage would suggest, even for lightly worn coins such as the present example. Deep violet-gold toning embraces each side, with lighter shadings where the high points are worn. Census: 10 in 45, 43 finer (2/09).(#7047)

Difficult 1878-CC Trade Dollar MS62

2440 **1878-CC MS62 ICG.** In terms of total number of coins known, the 1878-CC is the rarest Trade dollar. Federal records indicate that 97,000 pieces were produced. On July 19, 1878, however, the Carson City Mint melted 44,148 Trade dollars, many of which were probably dated 1878-CC.

An important Mint State representative, the present example is sure to elicit strong bids at auction. The cartwheel luster is dazzling, and although there is a hint of caramel-gold toning, the overall appearance is one of sparkling brilliance. Clean for the grade aside from a few scuffs on the right obverse field.
Ex: Morris Silverman Collection (Heritage, 4/2002), lot 4117, which realized $10,350.
From The Burning Tree Collection.(#7047)

Outstanding 1878-S Trade Dollar, MS64

2441 **1878-S MS64 PCGS. CAC.** A wonderful near-Gem, this 1878-S Trade dollar is boldly defined with full obverse and reverse details. The surfaces are highly lustrous, beneath light gold and iridescent toning. This is the final business strike Trade dollar, struck just before the beginning of huge Morgan dollar production. More than 4 million coins were minted but PCGS has only graded 37 of them any finer than this one (2/09).
From The Burning Tree Collection.(#7048)

PROOF TRADE DOLLARS

Glorious PR64 1873 Trade Dollar

2442 **1873 PR64 PCGS. CAC.** Under a light the surfaces reveal glorious deep orange-purple and forest-green tones on both sides, along with a bold strike and little mentionable contact. The proofs of this year all share a common obverse die with an unusual straight, deep die line extending from the cotton bale to the waves of the sea. More lines, shorter, appear just above Liberty's ankle, running in the same direction—apparently an earlier die state than normally seen. Population: 30 in 64, 6 finer (2/09). *From The Burning Tree Collection.* (#7053)

Gorgeous 1874 Trade Dollar, PR64

2443 **1874 PR64 PCGS. CAC.** This exceptional Choice proof Trade dollar has vibrant gold and iridescent toning over the fully mirrored obverse and reverse fields. Both sides show additional peripheral rainbow patina. Population: 42 in 64, 8 finer (2/09). *From The Burning Tree Collection.* (#7054)

Vividly Toned 1875 Trade Dollar, PR63

2444 **1875 PR63 PCGS.** Type One Reverse. The first of two transitional years in the Trade dollar series, 1875's are known from two different reverse hubs identified simply as Type One and Type Two. Business strikes and proofs alike were coined from both hub types. This Select example has vivid gold toning at the center of the obverse, framed by deep violet and blue. The reverse is almost entirely bluish-gold. Population: 62 in 63, 74 finer (2/09). *From The Burning Tree Collection.* (#7055)

Impressive 1875 Trade Dollar, PR64

2445 **1875 PR64 PCGS. CAC.** Type Two Reverse. This glorious near-Gem has medium gold at the centers with rich blue and lilac along the borders. While business strike 1875 Trade dollars are celebrated as key-date coins, proofs are no rarer than any other date in the series. Population: 60 in 64, 14 finer (2/09). *From The Burning Tree Collection.* (#7055)

Lovely Gem Proof 1876 Trade Dollar

2446 **1876 PR65 PCGS.** Type Two Obverse and Reverse. Splendidly patinated in rose-red, apple-green, navy-blue, orange, and lilac. The strike is good, although Liberty's hair and the eagle's right (facing) leg lack absolute detail. Study beneath a loupe is unable to locate any detractions. Population: 16 in 65, 3 finer (2/09). *From The Burning Tree Collection.* (#7056)

Spectacular 1876 Trade Dollar, PR66

2447 1876 PR66 NGC. CAC. Type Two Obverse and Reverse. The Act of July 22, 1876 demonetized the Trade dollar, revoking its legal tender status. The denomination nearly vanished from domestic circulation, and was used almost exclusively in the China trade after the Act took effect. Collectors continued to order proof sets every year, and 1,150 proof Trade dollars were included in the sets for 1876. Even as proofs, the coins were worth very little at the time. An example in the Stickney Collection (Henry Chapman, 6/1907), lot 901, realized only $1.20 thirty-one years later. Today these coins are prized by collectors, and Premium Gem examples are extremely rare. NGC has certified only eight specimens at the PR66 level, with one finer; while PCGS has graded three PR66 examples, with none finer (2/09).

The present coin features spectacular toning in concentric rings over the amazingly deep, watery fields. The obverse is nearly brilliant at the center, with widening bands of rose and blue color, growing deeper toward the rims. A couple of spots of planchet roughness are noted in the left obverse field, below the arm. The overall visual appeal is outstanding.(#7056)

Appealing 1878 Trade Dollar, PR64

2448 1878 PR64 PCGS. The first of the Philadelphia proof-only issues, although both Carson City and San Francisco would produce business strikes for the year. The P-mint emission was 900 coins, of which this survivor shows dusky pearl and orange surfaces with considerable luster under the light color. A few stray contact marks, mostly on the reverse, account for the grade, but the eye appeal is right. Population: 69 in 64, 17 finer (2/09).(#7058)

Choice Proof 1878 Trade Dollar

2449 1878 PR64 ANACS. The rich golden-brown fields and devices are bounded by ocean-blue, plum-red, and forest-green. An exactingly struck and attractive near-Gem. The scarcest of the collectible proof-only issues, since just 900 pieces were struck, less than half the number coined in 1880.
From The Burning Tree Collection.(#7058)

Gem Cameo Proof 1878 Trade Dollar

2450 1878 PR65 Cameo NGC. Light honey toning adorns this decisively struck Gem. Careful evaluation beneath a loupe locates only faint field hairlines. Both sides yield profound field-motif contrast. The 1878 was the first in a run of proof-only issues that extended through 1885. The mintage for the 1878 was only 900 pieces. Census: 22 in 65 Cameo, 6 finer (2/09).(#87058)

Choice Proof 1879 Trade Dollar

2451 1879 PR64 PCGS. This near-Gem displays deep gunmetal-gray, autumn-gold, and powder-blue patination. An attentive strike sharpens the design features, and the surfaces appear undisturbed beneath the blanket of toning. Although the general public despised Trade dollars by 1879, the proof-only Philadelphia dates of 1878 to 1883 were popular with advanced collectors.(#7059)

Impressive 1879 Trade Dollar, PR65 Cameo

2452 1879 PR65 Cameo NGC. Lavish reflectivity turns the fields into dark, watery pools. The central devices are richly frosted. All of the design elements are struck with razor-sharp precision, which gives this Gem proof a much finer overall appearance than the average business strike Trade dollar (from earlier years), even at the same grade level. The surfaces are impressively preserved on both sides. (#87059)

Proof-Only 1880 Trade Dollar, PR63

2453 1880 PR63 PCGS. CAC. A solid coin for the grade, with decent contrast between the mirror fields and frosted devices. A few of the lower obverse stars are weak, as always seen on the proofs from this date. The mintage came in at 1,987 pieces for the year, and this issue was only struck in proof for collectors. Certified in a green-label holder.(#7060)

Pleasing Choice Proof 1880 Trade Dollar

2454 1880 PR64 NGC. This highest-mintage proof-only Trade dollar issue is readily accessible in lesser states, but beginning with the Choice level, examples become elusive. This near-Gem specimen is well-defined in the centers with strongly reflective fields beneath rich blue-green, olive, and violet patina.(#7060)

Exquisite Near-Gem 1880 Trade Dollar

2455 1880 PR64 ANACS. This dramatically toned Choice Trade dollar has peripheral bands of emerald-blue, sun-gold, and champagne-rose. The centers are peach-gold. The strike is exemplary, as is the eye appeal. The 1880 is the most available of the proof-only dates that round out the series, but examples with remarkable patina are few and far between.
From The Burning Tree Collection.(#7060)

Luminous PR64 1880 Trade Dollar

2456 1880 PR64 NGC. A flashy and moderately toned near-Gem that appears golden-gray or yellow-gold depending upon its rotation relative to a light. The right-side stars are lightly impressed, but the remainder of the design is sharp. A popular proof-only date.
From The Burning Tree Collection.(#7060)

Lovely 1880 Trade Dollar, PR64 Cameo

2457 **1880 PR64 Cameo PCGS.** Fully struck, except for a couple of Liberty's toes, with imposing cameo contrast between fields and devices. Excellent preservation leaves no evidence of contact on either side. The second proof-only date at the end of the Trade dollar series, with a total mintage of 1,987 pieces. Population: 44 in 64 Cameo, 28 finer (2/09).(#87060)

Desirable 1881 Trade Dollar, PR64

2458 **1881 PR64 PCGS.** This year's proof-only issue of 960 pieces is less than half of the mintage for the previous year. The present near-Gem specimen offers excellent reflectivity beneath ample green-gold, sapphire, and sage patina. A handful of faint hairlines are also present beneath the toning.(#7061)

Deeply Toned PR64 1882 Trade Dollar

2459 **1882 PR64 PCGS. CAC.** The 1882 is a popular, proof-only issue with an impressively low mintage of only 1,097 pieces. This is a mildly cameoed example that has rich sea-green, Prussian-blue, and rose coloration on each side. The fields are exceptionally deep in their reflectivity with no obvious blemishes to the unaided eye. *From The Burning Tree Collection.*(#7062)

Brilliant PR64 Cameo 1882 Trade Dollar

2460 **1882 PR64 Cameo NGC.** All the post-1878 Trade dollars are popular because they are only available in proof format. Only 1,097 pieces were struck and most of the survivors are not as starkly cameoed as this coin. Both sides are brilliant and the fields are deeply reflective against the thickly frosted devices. An impressive example of this low-mintage date. Census: 35 in 64 Cameo, 48 finer (2/09).(#87062)

Charming PR63 1883 Trade Dollar

2461 **1883 PR63 PCGS. CAC.** The 1883 is the last of the readily collectible proof Trade dollar issues. Though this Select specimen shows a few minor hairlines and points of contact, the overall eye appeal is grand, boosted by strong gold-toned mirrors and appealing blue, violet, and peach peripheral shadings that appear intermittently. *From The Burning Tree Collection.*(#7063)

Gem Proof 1883 Trade Dollar

2462 **1883 PR65 NGC.** The last of the proof-only Trade dollar issues save for the fabulous clandestine 1884 and 1885 emissions. The 1883 coinage was reported at 979 pieces, with most survivors today averaging PR63 or thereabouts. Gem specimens such as this piece are occasionally found, but anything in higher grade must be considered elusive. The present piece has lovely deep steel-blue and coral obverse toning, with steel-blue and jade on the reverse. Census: 49 in 65, 38 finer (2/09).(#7063)

End of Session Three

SESSION FOUR

Floor, Telephone, Heritage Live!™, Internet, Fax, and Mail Signature® Auction #1126
Sunday, March 29, 2009, 5:00 PM ET, Lots 2463-3494
Baltimore, Maryland

A 15% Buyer's Premium ($9 minimum) Will Be Added To All Lots

Visit HA.com to view full-color images and bid.

PATTERNS

PR61 1850 Three Cent Silver Pattern
Judd-125 Original

2463 **1850 Three Cent Silver, Judd-125 Original, Pollock-147, R.4, PR61 NGC.** The design for this three cent silver is similar to the famous Judd-67 gold dollar pattern from 1836, but the date has been moved to the obverse below the cap, and the denomination within the palm frond is expressed with a large Roman numeral III. Struck in silver with a plain edge. This popular design was executed by Franklin Peale from designs by James Longacre. This silver-gold piece with tinges of ice-blue and lilac shows good luster and eye appeal, but is lightly hairlined.(#11536)

Transitional 1859 Indian Cent Pattern
Judd-228, Pollock-272, MS65

2464 **1859 Indian Cent, Judd-228, Pollock-272, R.1, MS65 PCGS.** This is a transitional pattern that combines the standard Indian Head cent obverse with the adopted reverse design of 1860-1909. Struck in copper-nickel with a plain edge. The surfaces are well preserved, with lovely gold-tan color. A few scattered flyspecks are noted, but there are no distracting marks on either side of this appealing Gem. Population: 60 in 65, 10 finer (1/09). (#11932)

Gem Brown 1863 One Cent Pattern, Judd-299

2465 **1863 One Cent, Judd-299, Pollock-359, R.3, PR65 Brown PCGS.** An experimental piece struck from the regular Indian cent dies but without the L on the ribbon. Struck in bronze with a plain edge, with the dies in medal alignment. The fields display shallow mirrors, and the surfaces show a deep overlay of red-brown and blue-green patina. Crisply struck and free of hairlines or contact marks. Population: 6 in 65 Brown, 6 finer (1/09).(#60454)

Desirable Judd-350 1863 Ten Dollar, PR65 Brown

2466 **1863 Ten Dollar, Judd-350, Pollock-422, Low R.6, PR65 Brown PCGS.** Similar to the then-contemporary Liberty eagle design, except that GOD OUR TRUST is placed on a scroll in the upper reverse field. Struck in copper with a reeded edge. A decisively detailed specimen with rich mocha-cinnamon hues. Carefully preserved with strong eye appeal. Housed in an earlier large-format holder. Population: 3 in 65 Brown, 2 finer (2/09). (#60512)

Judd-371 1864 Two Cent Piece, PR60 Details

2467 **1864 Two Cents, Judd-371, Pollock-440, Low R.6—Damaged—ANACS. PR60 Details.** From regular issue plain edge Large Motto dies, but struck in copper-nickel instead of bronze. A glossy specimen with sea-green and medium brown toning. The damage is difficult to locate, but appears to be subtle crimping on the obverse rim at 5 o'clock and opposite on the reverse at 1 o'clock. (#60541)

Elusive 1864 Ten Cent, Judd-381
R.7, PR65 Red and Brown

2468 **1864 Ten Cents, Judd-381, Pollock-449, R.7, PR65 Red and Brown PCGS.** Struck from regular issue 1864 Seated dime dies, but in copper with a reeded edge. A chestnut-brown specimen with olive and sea-green hues. This well struck and seemingly unabraded Gem is separated from an even higher grade by only a few tiny flyspecks. Population: 2 in 65 Red and Brown, 0 finer (1/09).(#70552)

Copper 1865 Liberty Quarter Eagle
Judd-439, PR64 Brown

2469 **1865 Quarter Eagle, Judd-439, Pollock-512, Low R.7, PR64 Brown PCGS.** A dies trial piece from regular Liberty quarter eagle dies, struck in copper with a reeded edge. A well struck near-Gem richly toned plum-red, sun-gold, and olive-green. Extended study beneath a loupe locates only a few minute obverse toning flecks. (#60624)

Scarce 1865 Five Dollar Pattern
Judd-446, High R.6, PR66 Brown

2470 **1865 Five Dollar, Judd-446, Pollock-518, High R.6, PR66 Brown NGC.** The obverse is of the regular die, while the reverse is similar to the regular issue of 1865 except for a scroll above the eagle reading IN GOD WE TRUST. This reverse was adopted for regular coinage in 1866. Struck in copper with a reeded edge. Deep rose-brown and cobalt-blue colors merge over both sides, with pristine surfaces. Census: 5 in 66 Brown, 0 finer (1/09). (#60633)

1866 Washington Copper Five Cent
Judd-462, PR64 Red and Brown

2471 **1866 Five Cents, Judd-462, Pollock-536, Low R.7, PR64 Red and Brown PCGS.** A five cent pattern featuring George Washington in profile, facing right, on the obverse. The date has minute digits. The reverse has the 5 of the denomination central on that side, surrounded by a laurel wreath. Struck in copper with a plain edge. Lovely orange-red dominates but cedes to rose-lilac on the central reverse. Well struck and mark-free with a solitary small spot on the reverse rim at 9 o'clock.(#70657)

Appealing 1866 Shield Five Cent
Judd-508, PR66 Brown

2472 **1866 Shield Five Cents, Judd-508, Pollock-592, High R.6, PR66 Brown NGC.** Struck from a regular obverse die of the 1866 Shield nickel, while the reverse suggests the No Rays design that was produced for circulation the following year. Struck in copper with a plain edge. Deep brown surfaces are only slightly luminous, but they are carefully preserved. Overall definition is strong.(#60704)

1866 Shield Nickel, Judd-510
R.8, PR64 Brown

2473 **1866 Shield Five Cents, Judd-510, Pollock-594, R.8, PR64 Brown PCGS.** 60.34 gn, too heavy to be a planchet for an Indian cent. From regular Shield nickel dies with a plain edge, but struck in an alloy of 99.3% copper and 0.7% aluminum, per the PCGS insert. Although designated as Brown, both sides display orange and rose-red when angled beneath a light. A sharply struck specimen and an extremely rare dies trial piece.(#60707)

1868 One Cent Pattern, Judd-605, R.5, PR62

2474 **1868 One Cent, Judd-605, Pollock-670, R.5, PR62 PCGS.** A diminutive pattern cent with an obverse similar to the adopted three cent nickel design, and a reverse with a large Roman numeral I in the center surrounded by a wreath. Struck in nickel with a plain edge. These are relatively common patterns that were issued in sets along with the three cent and five cent patterns of the same design. The 1 in the date is lightly repunched. A well struck dove-gray piece that is clean for the assigned grade.(#60817)

Choice Proof Judd-633 1868 Five Cent

2475 **1868 Five Cents, Judd-633, Pollock-705, R.4, PR64 NGC.** The obverse design is that of the three cent nickel, as adopted, but on a larger planchet, with minor design modifications appropriate to the larger diameter. The reverse features a Roman numeral V in the center, with a wreath encircling, scroll with IN GOD WE TRUST and Maltese cross above. Struck in nickel with a plain edge. This attractive piece displays faint chestnut toning and a few light-gray toning flecks.(#60851)

Elusive 1868 Half Dime, Judd-638
Low R.6, PR66 Cameo

2476 **1868 Half Dime, Judd-638, Pollock-710, Low R.6, PR66 Cameo NGC.** Regular die trials striking of the 1868 half dime, but struck in nickel alloy with a plain edge. A well struck and flashy Premium Gem that is completely untoned. Lovely cameo contrast is evident between the frosted devices and the deeply reflective fields. Exquisitely preserved and conditionally scarce. Census: 1 in 66 Cameo, 2 finer (1/09).(#60856)

1870 Quarter Dollar, Judd-887
High R.7, PR66

2477 **1870 Quarter Dollar, Judd-887, Pollock-986, High R.7, PR66 PCGS.** The obverse is designed by William Barber and features Liberty seated and facing left, surrounded by 13 stars. She supports a shield with her right hand and has an olive branch in her left hand. A Liberty pole arises behind the shield, and the date is in the exergue. The reverse is the regular issue With Motto Seated Liberty quarter design. Struck in aluminum with a plain edge. Sets of these patterns in various diameters, from the half dime through the silver dollar, were struck in 1870 with regular issue reverses. This is a crisply struck and attractive example. The reverse die is lightly rusted, and the upper right obverse has a lengthy, curled die scratch (as made) through two of the stars. PCGS has certified only three examples in all grades, one as PR65 and two as PR66 (1/09). (#61131)

Lovely PR65 1870 Standard Silver Quarter, Judd-888

2478 **1870 Standard Silver Quarter Dollar, Judd-888, Pollock-987, R.5, PR65 NGC. CAC.** A bust of Liberty faces right and wears a cap ornamented with three stars. The legend UNITED STATES OF AMERICA surrounds the figure, and a scroll with IN GOD WE TRUST is below. The reverse reads 25 CENTS 1870 in the center, and is surrounded by a wreath of cotton and corn. Struck in silver with a reeded edge. Sea-green, blue, and violet-rose patina graces each side of this charming Gem. Sharply struck with powerful mirrors beneath the toning. Census: 2 in 65, 6 finer (2/09).(#61132)

Interesting Judd-939 1870 Standard
Silver Half, PR62 Cameo

2479 **1870 Standard Silver Half Dollar, Judd-939, Pollock-1052, R.5, PR62 Cameo PCGS.** Obverse with a bust of Liberty facing right, wearing a cap ornamented with two stars. A ribbon across Liberty's shoulder has LIBERTY inscribed in incuse letters. Legend UNITED STATES OF AMERICA around the periphery, motto IN GOD WE TRUST on a scroll below. The reverse with denomination 50 CENTS and date 1870 within a wreath of corn and cotton, STANDARD above. Struck in silver with a reeded edge. A strongly mirrored and contrasted coin with hints of reddish-brown peripheral toning. Hairlines in the fields account for the grade. (#61185)

Beautifully Toned PR63 Judd-1015
1870 Indian Princess Silver Dollar

2480 **1870 Dollar, Judd-1015, Pollock-1149, Low R.7, PR63 NGC.** Ex: Share Collection. The Indian Princess obverse shows Liberty seated, with her left hand resting on a globe and right hand holding a Liberty pole with cap on top. There are two conjoined flags behind, one ornamented with 22 stars. The reverse is the regular-issue Seated dollar design. Struck in silver with a plain edge. Beautifully toned in golden-brown and pearl-gray. Boldly struck and visually impressive despite a few trivial field hairlines. Per USPatterns.com, the Share Collection of pattern Liberty Seated dollars was referred to as a "renowned Florida collection" within the Pollock reference.
Ex: Share Collection (American Numismatic Rarities, 9/2003), lot 68, which realized $8,050.(#61263)

1871 Copper Seated Quarter, Judd-1102
High R.7, PR65 Brown

2481 **1871 Quarter Dollar, Judd-1102, Pollock-1238, High R.7, PR65 Brown NGC.** The regular dies issue of 1871, but struck in copper with a reeded edge. Examples of other silver and gold denominations struck in copper are known for this year with similar rarity, which suggests that sets were purposely made. The brown surfaces show an occasional speckling of blue on each side, with the original mint red just below the brown patina. Sharply defined throughout, with moderate reflectivity in the fields. (#61361)

Judd-1293 1873 Trade Dollar, PR64

2482 **1873 Trade Dollar, Judd-1293, Pollock-1435, R.4, PR64 NGC.** The design is similar to the issued Trade dollar, but Liberty's left hand rests on a globe, her right hand holds a staff, and plow handles sprout from behind the globe. On the reverse, the banner bearing E PLURIBUS UNUM is clutched by the eagle in its beak, and the eagle clutches a Federal shield in place of the usual olive branch. Struck in silver with a reeded edge. This prominently mirrored near-Gem has beautiful ocean-blue, rose-red, and straw-gold obverse patina. The reverse has similar shades in addition to a deeper blush of mauve along the left border.(#61578)

Desirable 1876 Sailor Head Dollar in Copper
Judd-1463, PR64 Brown

2483 **1876 Sailor Head Dollar, Judd-1463, Pollock-1613, R.7, PR64 Brown NGC.** William Barber's Sailor Head motif is on the obverse, with her coronet inscribed LIBERTY. The periphery includes IN GOD WE TRUST, the date, and 13 stars. The reverse displays an open laurel wreath with ONE DOLLAR at the center, and UNITED STATES OF AMERICA and E PLURIBUS UNUM across the border. Struck in copper with a reeded edge. This Sailor Head dollar pattern issue, although similar to the Judd-1457 through Judd-1461 silver dollar pattern, has a slightly larger head and broader neck, with a jawline that is only faintly demarcated. The copper Judd-1463 is practically the only representative of the Sailor Head issue that most collectors can expect to acquire, as most of the remaining Centennial-year patterns of this design are essentially unobtainable. This piece offers deeply tinged orange-brown and bluish surfaces that lack overly distracting abrasions, although some minor contact is evident.(#61784)

1879 Goloid Metric Dollar, Judd-1626
Proof, AU Details

2484 **1879 Goloid Metric Dollar, Judd-1626, Pollock-1822, R.4— Heat Damage, Whizzed—NCS. Proof, AU Details.** William Barber's design for the Goloid Metric dollar. A capped head of Liberty appears on the obverse; the crowded reverse carries verbose statutory inscriptions and details relating to the coin's purported chemical composition. A circle of stars about the central inscriptions breaks the otherwise continuous wording. Struck in goloid, according to the NCS attribution, with a reeded edge, but USPatterns.com notes that "it is unknown if any of these have undergone metallurgical testing." The present piece shows grayish-white surfaces that are fairly lackluster, certainly showing the uniform microscopic evidence of whizzing. Nonetheless attractive, with some faint tinges of charcoal-gray on the reverse. (#62004)

Impressive 1882 Shield Five Cent
Judd-1693, Low R.7, PR64 Cameo

2485 **1882 Shield Five Cents, Judd-1693, Pollock-1895, Low R.7, PR64 Cameo PCGS.** The dies are similar to those used on the regular issue 1882 Shield nickel, but the base of the shield is designed differently, lacking the ornamental ball. Struck in nickel with a plain edge. This modified design was also struck in copper, aluminum, and white metal. Deeply mirrored, the devices are also nicely frosted and give a strong contrast against the reflective surfaces. Brilliant throughout. There is only a subtle difference between this pattern and a regular issue proof, and we would not be surprised if a few of these patterns still reside unrecognized in proof type sets that contain Shield nickels. Population: 4 in 64 Cameo, 1 finer (1/09).(#62098)

1896 One Cent, Judd-1769, PR63

2486 **1896 One Cent, Judd-1769, Pollock-1985, High R.6, PR63 PCGS.** The obverse displays a shield with 13 stripes, having the motto E PLURIBUS UNUM above and the date 1896 below. There are 13 stars at the border arranged seven left and six right, and the border is beaded. On the reverse, the denomination 1 CENT is centered within a curved olive sprig, with the legend UNITED STATES OF AMERICA surrounding both. The reverse also has a beaded border. Struck in one of four different compositions of aluminum, with a plain edge. At least a dozen examples are known in aluminum. Bright overall with significant portions of oxidation at 7 and 9 o'clock on the obverse rim. Population: 3 in 63, 2 finer (1/09).(#62223)

GOLD DOLLARS

2487 **1849 No L MS63 NGC.** Breen-6000. The initial Open Wreath variety, identified at a glance by the repunching on the lowest two stars. Well struck and lustrous with rich lemon patina and a few subtle marks above DOLLAR.(#7501)

2488 **1849 Open Wreath MS63 PCGS.** Breen-6001. Rich butter-yellow color that offers considerable lightness where the satiny luster is strongest. A minimally abraded and attractive Select piece. (#7502)

2489 **1849 Open Wreath MS64 PCGS.** Breen-6003, With L, Heavy Date. The first 1849 gold dollars had an Open Wreath Reverse, with a Small Head obverse and no designer's initial L (for James B. Longacre) on the bust truncation. At the end of the year, the final 1849 gold dollars had a Close Wreath Reverse, with designer's initial and a Large Head obverse. The Open Wreath varieties, With L, come in Small or Large Head and are transitional issues, with the Small Head the scarcer of the two subtypes. Both Open Wreath varieties, however, are scarcer than the Close Wreath type, only known with Large Head. This Large Head, Open Wreath example displays sharp design elements and frosty yellow-gold luster, accented by pale orange toning. A few tiny marks on the obverse prevented a Gem grade for this lovely example. Certified in a green-label holder.(#7502)

2490 **1849 Open Wreath MS64 NGC.** Breen-6004. Thin date numerals. Smooth yellow-gold surfaces show only occasional hints of satin. A pleasing Choice example of this first-year gold dollar issue with above-average preservation.(#7502)

2491 **1849 Open Wreath MS64 NGC.** Breen-6002. A "distant stars" die marriage that has a sharply repunched star near 5 o'clock. The obverse field is moderately prooflike, while the reverse provides cartwheel luster. Crisply struck save for a couple of star centers. Incorrectly designated as a No L variety by NGC.
From The Ed Lepordo Collection, Part Two.(#7502)

2492 **1849 Open Wreath MS64 PCGS.** Breen-6002. The star at 5 o'clock is widely repunched. Excellent strike and luster. A great sun-yellow example of this popular first-year gold dollar variant. PCGS has graded 63 finer representatives (2/09).(#7502)

Radiant 1849-D Gold Dollar, AU58

2493 **1849-D AU58 NGC.** Variety 1-A, with reverse mintmark strongly left. Midway through the short existence of the Dahlonega Mint, it added the gold dollar to its repertoire. The present example is minimally worn with only minor wear on the brightly lustrous yellow-gold surfaces. An interesting survivor.(#7507)

Bright 1849-D Gold Dollar, MS62

2494 **1849-D MS62 PCGS.** Variety 1-B, with the D mintmark centered, and a crack through its top. An unworn example of this initial Dahlonega gold dollar issue with bright lemon-gold surfaces that show unusual radiance. Though scattered, wispy marks appear on and around the portrait. Generally well struck throughout. Population: 24 in 62, 11 finer (2/09).(#7507)

Charming Near-Mint 1850-C Gold Dollar

2495   **1850-C AU58 PCGS.** Variety 1. Glowing luster dominates the smooth fields of this handsome Charlotte gold dollar. Abrasions are trivial aside from a concealed mark on the prominent 1. Wear is minimal, and the mintage of 6,966 pieces ensures the paucity of high grade survivors. Population: 8 in 58, 12 finer (2/09). (#7510)

Popular MS61 1850-C Gold Dollar

2496   **1850-C MS61 NGC.** Variety 1. An earlier Charlotte gold dollar issue that can pose a challenge to the Southern gold collector, though it does have limited availability even at the Mint State level. This example has radiant yellow-gold surfaces that show fewer abrasions than the grade might suggest. Census: 15 in 61, 6 finer (2/09).(#7510)

2497   **1850-D—Damaged—ANACS. XF40 Details.** Variety 2-C. The yellow-gold surfaces of this rare issue have traces of original luster and the usual softness of strike on the obverse. Several heavy abrasions on each side account for the "damaged" designation. (#7511)

2498   **1851-C AU50 PCGS.** Variety 1. Strong yellow-gold luster with glimpses of green-gold. A minimally marked piece despite light wear across the high points. Housed in a green label holder. (#7514)

2499   **1851-D—Scratched, Cleaned—ANACS. XF Details, Net VF30.** Variety 3-E. Deep orange-gold surfaces are oddly bright from a past cleaning. Modestly worn with few abrasions, though an unfortunate scratch appears in the left obverse field.(#7515)

2500   **1851-D AU50 PCGS.** Variety 3-E. Rich yellow-gold color with a splash of orange, well struck for the issue but with a degree of typical central softness. Housed in a first-generation holder. Population: 22 in 50, 67 finer (2/09).(#7515)

2501   **1851-D—Ex-Jewelry—ANACS. AU53 Details.** Variety 3-E. Solder remnants are noted on the wreath, and a determined attempt has been made to pinscratch away these former mounts. The obverse shows signs of cleaning but is otherwise unimpaired. (#7515)

2502   **1852 MS64 NGC.** Sharply struck with slight frostiness to the pale lemon-gold luster. Crisp eye appeal with only a few tiny marks on each side. An ideal type coin for the grade.(#7517)

2503   **1852-O MS61 NGC.** Light yellow-gold color overall with just a touch of duskiness near the rims. Softly struck on the high points with wispy abrasions that contribute to the grade.(#7520)

2504   **1852-O MS62 NGC.** Variety One. A radiant straw-gold example that has soft, pleasing luster. Well struck and appealing despite a handful of light marks. Census: 42 in 62, 32 finer (1/09). (#7520)

2505   **1853 MS64 PCGS.** An immensely lustrous yellow-gold representative of this popular type issue. Boldly impressed with a touch of satin present on each side.(#7521)

2506   **1853 MS64 PCGS.** Rich apricot-gold patination is imbued with traces of lavender and sky-blue on the reverse. Lustrous fields host sharply struck and pleasingly preserved devices.(#7521)

Stunning MS66 1853 Gold Dollar

2507   **1853 MS66 NGC.** Although due to the enormous pre-Civil War mintage exceeding 4 million pieces the 1853 is the commonest gold dollar, most certified examples are found in the higher AU or lower Mint State grades. At this Premium Gem level, examples are scarce. This stunning piece has remarkable even, consistent frosty surfaces throughout, with a bold strike and pretty khaki-gold coloration. A small planchet lamination appears below the upper knob of the 3 in the date. Census: 65 in 66, 11 finer (2/09). (#7521)

2508   **1853-C—Damaged—NCS. AU Details.** Variety 1, the only known die marriage. A heavy reverse scrape at 1 o'clock distorts the edge and obverse rim of this piece. Otherwise, it is a lustrous green-gold example with bold design details.(#7522)

Interesting AU53 1853-D Gold Dollar

2509   **1853-D AU53 NGC.** Variety 5-G, sole recorded variety for the year. This issue is most often found in XF to low AU grades, with Mint State examples proving elusive. This AU53 coin has rich yellow-gold color with substantial liquid luster remaining in the fields. Softly struck in the centers, as usual. The reverse is rotated approximately 90 degrees counterclockwise.(#7523)

Rare Mint State 1853-D Gold Dollar

2510 **1853-D MS60 PCGS.** Variety 5-G. The orange-gold surfaces are fully lustrous on both sides, but the fields show numerous light hairlines and tiny abrasions that account for the grade. There are no consequential marks, however, and no sign of high point rub. Some planchet roughness is as expected. A rare issue in Mint State. Population: 1 in 60, 10 finer (2/09).(#7523)

2511 **1853-O MS62 NGC.** Deep yellow-gold color with hints of orange. A well-defined and unworn representative of this popular O-mint gold dollar issue, immensely appealing.(#7524)

2512 **1853-O MS63 PCGS.** Lustrous yellow-gold surfaces are laced with mint-green, and exhibit sharply struck design features, except for softness in LLA of DOLLAR and the 3 in the date. Some minor die rust is noted on Liberty's portrait.(#7524)

2513 **1853-O MS63 NGC.** Shining yellow-gold surfaces are peculiarly radiant. Well-defined on the obverse but with significant weakness at the 1 in the denomination, as sometimes seen.(#7524)

Pretty 1854-S Gold Dollar, MS61

2514 **1854-S MS61 NGC.** A tiny gold treasure from the first-year coinage of the fabled San Francisco Mint, which finally opened its doors in 1854 to serve the growing local populace. Only 14,632 gold dollars were produced of this issue. The present piece offers pretty orange-gold coloration, with some moderate clashing noted on the reverse. A few stray abrasions account for the grade, but much appeal remains. Census: 24 in 61, 35 finer (2/09).(#7527)

Marvelous MS64 1854-S Gold Dollar

2515 **1854-S MS64 PCGS. CAC.** A blend of light lemon-yellow and sun-gold invigorates each side of this shining near-Gem, part of the first gold dollar issue struck at the San Francisco Mint and the only Type One variety of the same. Sharply struck central devices are largely untroubled. A noteworthy piece. Population: 7 in 64, 2 finer (2/09).(#7527)

2516 **1854 Type Two MS62 ICG.** Butter-yellow surfaces are smoothly lustrous, and the devices are well-defined for the issue. This Type Two dollar would make an excellent type piece.(#7531)

2517 **1855 AU58 PCGS.** A satiny, well struck example with only faint wear on the high points. Struck from lightly clashed dies. (#7532)

2518 **1855 AU58 PCGS.** Pale yellow-gold at the centers with deeper orange overtones at the margins. Just a touch of friction separates this immensely lustrous Type Two gold dollar from a Mint State designation.(#7532)

2519 **1855 MS61 NGC.** Satiny and boldly struck, with attractive green-gold color and few blemishes on either side. Die clash marks are noted near the reverse center.(#7532)

Vibrant MS64 1855 Gold Dollar

2520 **1855 MS64 NGC.** As found on many 1855 gold dollars, the present piece displays strike weakness in the central reverse design and bold clash marks. Redeeming qualities are the vibrant luster, well preserved surfaces, and attractive straw-gold coloration throughout. The 1854 and 1855 gold dollars are typically selected by those building type sets, since both dates were struck in relatively large quantities and are the most available of the six different Type Two issues. However, in near-Gem or better condition, neither date is common. NGC has graded 48 numerically finer pieces (2/09).(#7532)

Attractive 1855 Gold Dollar
Type Two, MS64

2521 **1855 MS64 PCGS.** Due to striking difficulties, the Type Two gold dollar was only produced for three years, 1854-1856. As a consequence of its short lifespan, the Type Two is the rarest gold dollar type by a wide margin. Thanks to its large initial mintage of 758,269 pieces, the 1855 gold dollar is the most available date of the type in ultra-high grades, and vies with the 1854 date for most obtainable in lower grades. These circumstances make the issue an extremely popular choice with type collectors.

The present coin displays remarkably clean surfaces, accented by light reddish tints of color. Q. David Bowers remarks that nearly all examples seen are weakly struck in some areas, and clash marks are common. We are pleased to note the obverse of this specimen is fully struck, and the characteristic softness is limited to the LL in DOLLAR and the 18 in the date on the reverse. Some light clashing is evident on both sides. Altogether, visual appeal is excellent.(#7532)

Spectacular 1855 Gold Dollar
Type Two MS66

2522 1855 MS66 NGC. The tiny gold dollar was quite popular with numismatists of the 19th century. While larger denomination gold coins were prohibitively expensive for the common man, collectors found the gold dollar attractive, available, and affordable. Apropos of the denomination, Augustus Heaton remarked, "It has attracted great attention from many collectors who have sought no other gold series." The coins' popularity even extended to foreign collectors, such as John G. Murdoch, a member of the Numismatic Society of London. In the catalog of the Murdoch Collection (Sotheby, Wilkinson & Hodge, 7/1903), there were no less than 143 examples of the U.S. gold dollar. Lot 800 was a typical listing, "**Dollars** of the larger size, With an Indian's head to left, dated 1854, 1855, 1857 (2), and 1862." Note that the Sotheby's cataloger was familiar enough with the series to distinguish between the smaller Type One gold dollars and the larger Type Two and Type Three coins. Apparently, he was not familiar with the more subtle design differences of the later two types.

The design of the gold dollar was changed in 1854 to make the coins easier to handle in everyday commerce, creating the Type Two style. The coins featured a high relief bust of an Indian princess on a larger diameter, thinner planchet. Unfortunately, the new design was impossible to strike satisfactorily, with universal weakness showing on the central reverse design. The design had to be modified after only three years, and was replaced by the lower relief Type Three in 1857. The short-lived Type Two is the least available gold dollar type, and examples are highly prized by type collectors.

A substantial mintage of 758,269 gold dollars was achieved by the Philadelphia Mint in 1855. Q. David Bowers believes this date is the most obtainable Type Two gold dollar in ultra-high grades, making it the logical choice for advanced type collectors. A PCGS graded MS67 example of this date sold for $86,250 in January 2005.

The present coin is a spectacular specimen, with terrific reddish tinted mint frost. The strike is better than average, but shows the characteristic softness on the central reverse. Some light clashing is evident, but there are no obvious marks or luster grazes. Only nine coins have been certified above the MS66 level by NGC and PCGS combined (2/09).(#7532)

Extraordinary 1855 Type Two Gold Dollar, MS66

2523 1855 MS66 PCGS. CAC. Intense luster joins forces with pristine surface quality on this straw-gold Premium Gem Type Two gold dollar. The unusually strong strike for the issue confirms the lofty grade assigned by PCGS and subsequently verified by CAC. A typical 1855 gold dollar will display weakness in the LL of DOLLAR and the 8 in the date. While those features are not bold on the current offering, they are more defined than one would expect for the date. Poorly placed design features on the obverse and reverse caused metal flow problems on the Type Two gold dollars, hence the inadequately defined areas described above. The characteristic die clash marks are observed on both sides and are mentioned here only for the sake of accuracy, as they do not detract from the overall eye appeal of this splendid coin.

Demand stemming from type collectors keeps the prices strong on all Small Head Indian Princess Type Two gold dollars, especially in the higher grades. And, while the 1855 Philadelphia issues are not difficult to find in general, the competition for superior examples is fierce. Those collectors seeking Gem or better specimens have fewer than 100 coins from which to select, regardless of the grading service. As of (1/09) PCGS has certified 13 pieces at the MS66 level, with only four coins finer, and no example has achieved a grade higher than MS67. The tally at NGC is similar. As a point of reference, the Smithsonian Institution coin is considered to grade no finer than MS63.(#7532)

Elusive 1855-D Gold Dollar, XF Sharpness

2524 **1855-D—Removed From Jewelry—NCS. XF Details.** Variety 7-J. The tip of the last 5 in the date points to the right side of the A in DOLLAR, and the topmost portion of the right bow points to the left side of the ball in 5. The 1855-D is among the rarest Dahlonega gold dollars, with the added appeal of its status as the only Dahlonega Type Two issue. This piece shows moderate wear in the centers of both sides (and the typical original strike weakness), but plenty of eye appeal remains on the orange-gold surfaces. The rim shows faint evidence of mounting, and a couple of small scrapes appear in the upper obverse field. A collectible and attractive example of this rare date, from a tiny mintage of 1,811 coins.(#7534)

2525 **1855-O XF40 NGC.** A popular type coin, the 1855-O is the only Type Two gold dollar struck at the New Orleans Mint. Charming olive-green patina overlies the fairly smooth surfaces. The centers are soft, as typically seen, but there is still plenty of detail throughout.(#7535)

Interesting AU55 1855-O Gold Dollar

2526 **1855-O AU55 NGC.** As the last O-mint gold dollar and the only issue for the denomination with the Type Two design, the 1855-O is highly prized by Southern gold enthusiasts, particularly this close to Mint State. Richly lustrous lemon-gold and butter-yellow surfaces show only trifling wear on the high points.(#7535)

Type Two 1855-O Gold Dollar AU58

2527 **1855-O AU58 NGC.** The 1855-O would have been a better issue in any event, because of a low production of 55,000 pieces. But the fact that it is the sole New Orleans issue of the Type Two design makes it even more desirable. Soft luster is present throughout the legends and coronet, and no marks are remotely worthy of discussion.(#7535)

Important 1855-O Gold Dollar, MS61

2528 **1855-O MS61 PCGS.** As the last New Orleans gold dollar issue and the only one of the Type Two design, this issue is highly prized by Southern gold enthusiasts. This orange-inflected sun-yellow example offers dramatic luster with glimpses of reflectivity in the flashy fields. The few wispy abrasions on each side do not fully account for the grade. In a green label holder. Population: 9 in 61, 23 finer (2/09).(#7535)

2529 **1856-S Type Two AU50 NGC.** FS-501. Double S. Distinct orange tints visit the obverse, while the reverse is lighter yellow-gold. A briefly circulated representative of the last Type Two gold dollar issue.(#7536)

1856-S/S Type Two Gold Dollar AU58

2530 **1856-S Type Two AU58 NGC.** FS-501. Double S. Sharply struck and nearly mark-free with clean, subdued yellow gold surfaces. Walter Breen claimed the discovery of the repunched mintmark 1856-S. The right border of the additional S is obvious, clumsily placed too far northeast and also tilted to the left. Both sides exhibit heavy clash marks, and the obverse has two bold die cracks. But the 1856-S is best known as the final Type Two issue, struck a year after the other mintmarked Type Two issues presumably due to the geographical distance between Philadelphia (where the dies were made) and San Francisco.(#7536)

Appealing Choice XF 1857-D Gold Dollar

2531 **1857-D XF45 NGC.** Variety 9-L. A pleasing Choice XF example of what Winter has labeled "the most underrated Dahlonega gold dollar," rich yellow-gold with glimpses of this issue's signature frosty luster in the fields. Light wear on the high points merges with a typically soft strike, but the eye appeal holds up well. (#7546)

2532 **1857-S AU55 PCGS. CAC.** The C in AMERICA is faint, but the remainder of this partially lustrous olive-gold example is evenly struck. A mere 10,000 pieces were struck.
Ex: Dallas Signature (Heritage, 4/2007), lot 1552.(#7547)

2533 **1858-D—Cleaned, Damaged, Ex-Jewelry—ANACS. XF45 Details.** Variety 10-M. Lightly worn at the high points with unnatural glossiness to the butter-yellow surfaces. Scarcely perceptible in the holder is rim damage, suggestive of the piece once being mounted in jewelry.(#7549)

High-Grade 1858-D Gold Dollar, AU58

2534 **1858-D AU58 NGC.** Variety 10-M. Only 3,477 pieces were struck of this rare Dahlonega Mint gold dollar. Although a Mint-made lint mark curls across the obverse at 9 o'clock, the surfaces are otherwise clean, and the remaining luster is noticeable. Both sides display original reddish-orange color. As with most examples, the 5 in the date and the R in AMERICA are softly struck, as are occasional portions of the devices. This issue is reasonably obtainable in AU and even occasionally in Uncirculated grades in spite of the low mintage.(#7549)

Exquisite 1858-D Gold Dollar MS62

2535 **1858-D MS62 NGC.** Variety 10-M. From a small mintage of 3,477 pieces, the 1858-D is surprisingly available in circulated grades. At the Mint State level, the situation is less clear. Q. David Bowers believes this issue is frequently overgraded, and notes population data seems deceptive on this issue. The typical coin shows a weak strike, due to improper placement of the dies. Clash marks and planchet irregularities are often seen as well. David Akers observed, "It is almost impossible to obtain an 1858-D in full Mint State (I have seen only two or three), VF and EF examples are reasonably obtainable."

The present coin is an attractive example of this uncommon date. The strike is typical of this issue, with softness on the central features of both obverse and reverse. The fields are brightly reflective, and handling marks are minimal. Overall eye appeal is excellent. Census: 15 in 62, 10 finer (2/09).(#7549)

2536 **1858-S AU50 NGC.** Luminous honey-gold surfaces show traces of orange. Lightly circulated but strongly detailed, a modestly marked coin for the grade. Census: 8 in 50, 67 finer (1/09).(#7550)

Appealing MS61 1859-D Gold Dollar

2537 **1859-D MS61 NGC.** Variety 11-N. Well struck for the issue, though a degree of the usual softness is noted at the hair over Liberty's eye and the date on the reverse. Wispy abrasions affect the fields, yet the overall eye appeal remains solid, with rich yellow-orange color dominating each side. Census: 10 in 61, 24 finer (2/09).(#7553)

2538 **1860 MS64 NGC.** Ex: Richmond Collection. An exceptionally attractive example of this pre-Civil War issue, with deep antique-gold surface coloration accented by shades of lilac and blue. The 1860 gold dollar issue is many times rarer than the 1861 or 1862 emissions. Census: 12 in 64, 10 finer (2/09).(#7555)

2539 **1860-D—Polished—ANACS. AU50 Details.** Variety 12-P. Only slight wear is noticed on the high points of the devices, but the design elements are weakly defined, a trait common to all 1860-D gold dollars. The surfaces are unusually bright from polishing, and a shallow scratch is noted in the reverse field to the right of the denomination.(#7556)

2540 **1861 MS64 PCGS.** Subtle, swirling luster invigorates each side of this golden-tan beauty. An interesting near-Gem with pleasing detail overall. PCGS has graded 40 finer examples (2/09). (#7558)

Flashy 1867 Gold Dollar, MS66

2541 **1867 MS66 PCGS.** Bright yellow-gold surfaces adorn this Premium Gem. The fields on both sides yield considerable "flash," thereby accentuating the frosty, sharply struck motifs. Impeccable preservation enhances the coin's eye appeal. Relatively heavy clash marks are visible, including a crisp impression of LIBERTY below the date. Housed in a green label holder. Population: 4 in 66, 1 finer (2/09).(#7566)

2542 **1868 MS64 PCGS.** With swirling, flashy luster and a sharp strike, this yellow-gold survivor offers impressive eye appeal. Notably well-preserved for a near-Gem. Population: 12 in 64, 17 finer (1/09).(#7567)

Beautiful 1869 Gold Dollar, MS66

2543 **1869 MS66 PCGS.** According to Garrett and Guth (2006): "The 1869 gold dollar is still a scarce coin that is not encountered very often at auction or on the bourse floor. Most of the known coins are well struck, and prooflike surfaces are the norm." The current offering is certainly well struck, and the fields exhibit tremendous, shimmering mint frost. Surface flaws are virtually absent, save for a small disturbance directly above R in DOLLAR. Housed in an earlier PCGS holder with a pale green label. Population: 2 in 66, 11 finer (2/09).(#7568)

Gleaming 1873 Closed 3 Select Gold Dollar

2544 **1873 Closed 3 MS63 PCGS.** With a commonly cited mintage of just 1,800 business strikes, this variety of the 1873 gold dollar is far more elusive than its Open 3 counterpart. This gleaming Select piece is generally yellow-gold with a patch of orange alloy between UNITED and STATES. Population: 10 in 63, 9 finer (2/09).(#7574)

Impressive 1874 Gold Dollar, MS66

2545 **1874 MS66 NGC. CAC.** This radiantly effulgent Premium Gem boasts superior eye appeal and impressive technical merit. Most of the design elements are crisply produced, except for brief lapses on N in UNITED and O in DOLLAR, possibly from minor die wear. Beautifully preserved, with exceptionally clean surfaces that help to explain the coin's lofty grade assessment by NGC. Census: 44 in 66, 50 finer (2/09).(#7575)

Wonderful 1874 Gold Dollar, MS67

2546 **1874 MS67 NGC.** This Superb Gem approaches the finest available quality for the otherwise common 1874 gold dollar. It has amazing bright yellow luster with fully frosted surfaces. Although LIBERTY is essentially invisible, all other design elements are bold. Census: 41 in 67, 9 finer (2/09).(#7575)

Superb Gem 1879 Gold Dollar

2547 **1879 MS67 NGC.** Well struck with orange-gold toning over both sides, some noticeable clash marks are on the reverse. A few wispy die striations show on each side of this attractive, essentially unmarked Superb Gem. Census: 18 in 67, 0 finer (2/09). *Ex: Palm Beach Signature (Heritage, 3/2005), lot 6830.*(#7580)

Splendid 1880 Gold Dollar, MS66 ★

2548 **1880 MS66 ★ NGC.** The combination of exceptional quality and a low mintage of only 1,600 coins means that few have survived. At the same time, the 1880 gold dollar failed to circulate at the time of issue, meaning that most survivors are in higher grade. Garrett and Guth report that 98% of the certified population are Mint State coins. However, Premium Gem quality pieces are difficult to locate, especially when those coins have excellent eye appeal. This piece exhibits reflective surfaces and bold devices with brilliant yellow-gold luster.(#7581)

Glorious MS67 ★ 1880 Gold Dollar

2549 **1880 MS67 ★ NGC.** Nearly a perfect coin, technically speaking, this Superb Gem is also a visual feast of the first order. Glorious mint frost highlights the clean, honey-gold surfaces that are virtually immaculate on both sides. The striking definition is clean and crisp on every design detail. Interestingly, there is a complete wire rim around the obverse and reverse peripheries. Census: nine in 67 ★, two finer with the ★ (1/09).(#7581)

2550 **1881 MS65 PCGS.** Flashy yellow-gold fields are typical for this popular 1880s gold dollar issue. The strike is crisp, and the eye appeal is great. A delightful Gem.(#7582)

2551 **1882 MS64 PCGS.** Brightly lustrous with generally wheat-gold surfaces that cede to bolder yellow near the rims. A well-defined near-Gem that is housed in a green label holder.(#7583)

Outstanding 1882 Gold Dollar, MS67 Prooflike

2552 **1882 MS67 Prooflike NGC.** A simply gorgeous and technically outstanding representative of this low mintage gold dollar issue, which Garrett and Guth refer to as a "hoard" date. The design elements are reproduced with razor-sharp precision down to the last denticle, although DO in DOLLAR and the lower loops of both 8s and 2 in the date are filled. A shimmering, frosty, near-flawless Superb Gem with noteworthy reflectivity in the fields, as attested by NGC's Prooflike designation. Census: 3 in 67 Prooflike, 0 finer (2/09).(#77583)

Impeccable 1883 Gold Dollar, MS67

2553 **1883 MS67 PCGS. CAC.** Housed in an older green-label holder, this Superb Gem possesses exceptional aesthetic appeal. The fields are fully and completely mirrored with lustrous and mildly frosty devices. Both sides have a few splashes of deeper orange toning that add to its overall look. PCGS has only certified eight finer examples.(#7584)

2554 **1884 MS64 Prooflike NGC. CAC.** A solid strike endows this brassy-gold specimen, and modest field-motif variance is evident over both sides. Faint handling marks visible under magnification preclude Gem status, nevertheless, a highly appealing coin. Census: 11 in 64 Prooflike, 7 finer (2/09).(#77585)

2555 **1886 MS66 PCGS.** Sharply struck and gleaming with pale yellow-gold color overall. A touch of deeper sun-yellow graces the center and its carefully preserved portrait. Population: 17 in 66, 3 finer (2/09).(#7587)

Splendid 1887 Gold Dollar, MS65 Deep Mirror Prooflike

2556 **1887 MS65 Deep Mirror Prooflike NGC.** The mintage was only 7,500 coins in one of the last years of the series, so it is expected that a percentage of those coins would be prooflike, as the first fresh strikes from the dies. The wonderful state of preservation of this coin is also likely due either to coin dealers of the era or collectors, aware that the series would likely soon end. This splendid Gem has lovely canary-yellow coloration, with considerable contrast and relatively unscathed surfaces. NGC has certified six Deep Prooflike examples of the issue in all grades, but this is the only MS65, with a single MS66 Deep Prooflike finer (2/09).(#7588)

Extraordinary 1888 Gold Dollar, MS66

2557 **1888 MS66 PCGS. CAC.** A remarkable orange-gold representative with faint traces of green and blue toning, this Premium Gem is boldly detailed and possesses intensely lustrous surfaces with a full quota of mint frost. PCGS has only certified 46 finer examples of the date (2/09).(#7589)

2558 **1889 MS66 NGC. CAC.** Yellow-gold surfaces overall with hints of orange and wheat. A well-defined Premium Gem with impressive, swirling luster and strong visual appeal.(#7590)

2559 **1889 MS66 NGC.** Bold design features and exquisite surfaces unite with satiny yellow-gold luster to create an exceptional visual presentation. Although the mintage was limited to 29,000 coins, the date is rather plentiful, making the 1889 an ideal choice for type collectors.(#7590)

Outstanding 1889 Gold Dollar, MS67

2560 **1889 MS67 NGC. CAC.** Both sides of this lovely Superb Gem possess frosty luster and a delicate blend of yellow-gold, mint-green, lilac, and apricot patina. An impressive strike imparts sharp delineation to the design elements, and immaculate preservation shows on the mark-free surfaces. All of these attributes contribute to the coin's outstanding eye appeal, as intimated by the CAC green label.(#7590)

Uncommon Superb Gem 1889 Gold Dollar

2561 **1889 MS67 NGC. CAC.** This was the final year of issue for the gold dollar denomination, and numerous examples were undoubtedly saved both as souvenirs by non-numismatists and by collectors/investors. As a result, many are available at all grade levels. This Superb Gem example, however, seems anything but common, and displays luxuriant mint frost over both sides. Pretty lime-green and peach toning is intermingled over the clean, nearly pristine surfaces.(#7590)

PROOF GOLD DOLLARS

Splendid PR65 Ultra Cameo 1860 Gold Dollar

2562 **1860 PR65 Ultra Cameo NGC.** Garrett and Guth estimate that perhaps only 15 to 20 examples survive today of this rare prewar issue. This piece appears simply splendid for the assigned grade, with high-contrast canary-yellow surfaces and lots of eye appeal. It takes a loupe to reveal the tiny abrasions—one on Liberty's cheek, a thin field scrape, some tiny lint marks on the reverse—that account for the overall grade. But this is one of those coins where one can also put down the high-powered loupe and simply bask in the sheer beauty. Census: 4 in 65 Ultra Cameo, 1 finer (2/09). (#97610)

Notable PR63 Cameo 1868 Gold Dollar

2563 **1868 PR63 Cameo NGC.** Exquisite contrast for a "mere" Cameo specimen, with razor-sharp central devices coated in mint frost and yellow-gold mirrors offering watery reflectivity. Only a few small hairlines and points of contact in the fields preclude a finer designation. Housed in a prior-generation holder. Census: 1 in 63 Cameo, 7 finer (2/09).(#87618)

1870 Gold Dollar, PR63, Ex: Pittman

2564 **1870 PR63 NGC. Ex: Pittman.** This attractive yellow-gold specimen has flashy mirrors and noticeable cameo contrast. The strike is precise, and the only relevant marks are limited to the border near the A in STATES. Rare, since only 35 proofs were struck. The NGC encapsulation bears the misspelling PTTMAN. Census: 2 in 63, 0 finer (4/08).
Ex: Will W. Neil Collection (B. Max Mehl, 6/1947), lot 2319, which realized $28.50; John Jay Pittman Collection, Part One (David Akers, 10/1997), lot 905, which realized $4,400.(#7620)

Appealing 1884 Gold Dollar
PR64 ★ Ultra Cameo

2565 **1884 PR64 ★ Ultra Cameo NGC.** Repunching shows on the 18 of the date, as usually seen. The splendid yellow-gold surfaces show only a few stray contact marks, none large, but collectively determining the grade. The appeal is high, however, with excellent contrast and eye appeal well deserving of the Star designation. From a proof mintage of slightly more than 1,000 pieces.(#97634)

Reflective 1886 Gold Dollar, PR66 Cameo

2566 **1886 PR66 Cameo NGC.** As one of the later proof gold dollar issues with a four-figure mintage, the 1886 makes an "excellent type coin," per Garrett and Guth. While Select and even Choice specimens trade hands with some regularity, the frequency of appearances for Premium Gems is substantially smaller. This strongly contrasted yellow-orange survivor offers powerful mirrors with a strong aura of originality. The surfaces are carefully preserved, and the portrait shows pleasing, if mild frost. A noteworthy candidate for the condition-conscious type collector. Census: 20 in 66 Cameo, 3 finer (2/09).(#87636)

Pleasing 1887 Gold Dollar, PR64 Deep Cameo

2567 **1887 PR64 Deep Cameo PCGS. CAC.** Outstanding contrast with bright lemon-gold surfaces that supply powerful mirrors in the fields and rich frost on the devices. Crisply detailed with only a few small disturbances on each side that account for the grade. One of just two Deep Cameo coins graded at this level by PCGS with only three finer (1/09).(#97637)

Rare 1796 With Stars Quarter Eagle, MS62
A Seldom-Seen and Overlooked Issue, BD-3

2568 **1796 Stars MS62 NGC.** Ex: Ed Price Collection. BD-3, R.5. The obverse die has sixteen stars arranged point to point. This unusual arrangement is similar to the orientation on 1794 silver dollars but on no other early U.S. coins. The serif of the 1 is very close to the hair curl, the bottom of the 7 almost touches the right side of a dentil, and the top of the 6 overlaps the drapery. In LIBERTY, IBE are more closely spaced than other letters, the L is slightly low, and the Y is high and leans right. Eight stars to the left and eight to the right. Stars 11, 12, 13, and 14 are more widely spaced than others. A long triangular dentil is positioned over the center of the T.

The reverse die shows several prominent die scratches that extend through the tops of TATE with one through the middle of that A. The legend is well-spaced with most letters distant from the border. The lower right curve of the D joins the fourth feather. AT are high, the final S touches a cloud, and the F touches a cloud. The final A is close to the claw and stem, touching neither. The branch has four berries and the top berry is merged with the upper edge of the leaf below R. The lowest of eight arrows is below the space between U and N, and the longest arrow is below the right foot of the left base of N. Sixteen stars appear to have been placed at random. A star at the right has two points merged with the top of the wing. A double dentil is found below the left side of the eagle's tail. A faint die crack connects all stars on the left with LIBE. Short cracks or die lines join stars 3, 5, and 7 to the border. The reverse has a short die crack from the right arm of the first T in STATES to the right base of that letter. Parallel lines through TATE are constant in all die states.

While the No Stars design of 1796 is the higher visibility coin with its one-year type design, the With Stars variant is actually considerably rarer. Less than half as many With Stars were struck as No Stars (432 vs. 963 pieces), and since the With Stars has the same design type as the successive years through 1807, it is an overlooked issue among early quarter eagles. The estimates of the number of survivors range from as few as 20 to 25 coins (Akers) to a high of 30 (Breen). Virtually all are in the VF-XF grade range. Most show central striking weakness, and adjustment marks are prevalent.

Today, most numismatists accept the January 14, 1797 delivery of 432 coins as the striking date for this variety. The current estimated surviving population of each of the first three quarter eagle varieties is almost exactly 10% of the first three deliveries. Either five or six examples of BD-1 are known, nearly 10% of the 66 coins delivered on September 21, 1796. Approximately 90 examples of BD-2 are known, almost exactly 10% of the 897 coins delivered on December 8, 1796. Finally, about 40 examples of this BD-3 die variety are known, about 10% of the 432 coins delivered on January 14, 1797.

This piece shows soft detailing in the center of each side and there are a few light adjustment marks located in the center of the reverse. Struck from a slightly rough planchet; there are tiny planchet flecks out of each side, and pronounced die file marks are seen above and through the tops of S(TATE)S. Rich reddish-orange patina covers each side of this attractive coin with bright, semi prooflike fields apparent (especially so on the reverse).

One of just half a dozen or so known Mint State specimens. This piece was plated in the 1982 Eliasberg catalog, the 1999 Bowers and Merena catalog, and our 2005 FUN catalog.

Ex:Spedding Sale (S.H. & H. Chapman, 12/1894); J.H. Clapp; Clapp Estate (1942); Louis E. Eliasberg, Sr. (Bowers and Ruddy, 10/1982), lot 80; Long Beach Connoisseur Collection; Bowers and Merena (8/1999), lot 337; Heritage (1/2005), lot 8761; Ed Price Collection (Heritage, 7-8/2008), lot 1452.(#7647)

R.6 1797 Quarter Eagle, BD-1, Fine Details

2569 1797 PCGS Genuine. BD-1, R.6. We grade this coin Fine Details, Cleaned. Only the single die variety for the year is known, from an original mintage that Bass-Dannreuther estimates as from 427 to 585 coins. The stars are arranged seven and six. As on all known examples, there is a massive die break extending from near the rim above the left top of Y in LIBERTY, down through the left side of star 8, downward through the right (facing) field before Liberty's face, to the left side of star 12, two points of star 13, and thence to the rim. One example, currently unique, listed in Bass-Dannreuther shows a retained cud in that area. While this piece of course does not show that feature, the die break is well advanced, to the point that the portions of the obverse on either side appear to verge on ceasing to be coplanar.

The reverse die, in a later state than here, was also used on the 1798/7 JR-1 dime, as documented in our recent sale of the Ed Price Collection. This piece shows all major types clearly, with orange-gold surfaces that, while still attractive, are overbright for the details grade. Darker brownish-black buildup is noted around the device edges. A rare and collectible example of this type, which Bass-Dannreuther estimate has 20 to 25 survivors in all grades. (#7648)

Elusive AU 14 Star Reverse
1804 Two and a Half, BD-2

2570 1804 14 Star Reverse AU50 PCGS. Breen-6119, BD-2, R.4. From the original mintage of 3,327 pieces, estimates of the number of extant pieces range from 50 to 60 (Akers, 1975) to Harry Bass's *Sylloge*, which places the number of survivors at 125. This is a popular variety for its obvious counting error: While for its first few years of existence the Mint added stars as new states were admitted to the Union, by the early 1800s it had standardized at the "Original 13." This coin's reverse shows a partial star punched into the leftmost cloud, perhaps providing the impetus for the 14 Stars error. This piece shows only light circulation wear, with considerable mint luster remaining, and lovely, distraction-free yellow-gold surfaces with copper-gold highpoints. Certified in a green label holder.(#7652)

1804 Quarter Eagle, 14 Star Reverse
BD-2, AU50 Details

2571 1804 14 Star Reverse—Damaged, Cleaned—ANACS. AU50 Details. Ex: ANS. Breen-6119, BD-2, R.4. The 14 reverse stars are arranged in two arcing rows of six, plus two single stars flanking the eagle. This is one of the quarter eagle issues whose reverse was also used to strike silver dimes, in this case the 1804 JR-2. The present piece shows rim damage above IBE, above star 6, and between stars 11 and 12 on the obverse. Some of the denticulation is faint, on the obverse from 7 to 10 o'clock, and around much of the reverse. The noted cleaning is not overly harsh, but has left a few scattered hairlines and a somewhat bright appearance. Minor adjustment marks are noted at ED on the reverse. Despite the minor problems, much appeal remains on this historic piece.
Ex: B. Peyton; American Numismatic Society; Stack's ANS (1/2007), lot 2010, which realized $10,350.(#7652)

Unworn 1826/6 Two and a Half, BD-1

2572 **1826/6—Cleaned—ICG. MS60 Details.** BD-1, R.5. As noted in Bass-Dannreuther, "Traditionally, this coin has been called an overdate and the mintage figure has been reported to be a *firm* [italics theirs] 760. Both of the assumptions are probably wrong, as the 6 of the date appears only to have been recut and some of the coins delivered in 1827 were probably dated 1826." That said, this date remains notably rare in all grades, much less with all original detail intact as this yellow-gold and orange-gold piece boasts. Only subdued luster from a past cleaning keeps this coin from a stratospheric price tag.(#7665)

CLASSIC QUARTER EAGLES

2573 **1834 Classic AU58 NGC.** Breen-6138, Small Head, R.1. Arguably the most available of the varieties for this year, represented here by a pale yellow-gold example. Only a trace of rub is visible on the devices.(#7692)

Attractive 1834 Classic Quarter Eagle, MS61

2574 **1834 Classic MS61 NGC.** Breen-6138, Small Head, R.1. The most plentiful of four known 1834 Classic Head quarter eagle varieties. This lustrous green-gold example has excellent surfaces for the grade, with only a few small abrasions on each side. The central obverse and reverse design details are remarkably well defined.(#7692)

Luminous 1834 Classic Two and a Half MS62

2575 **1834 Classic MS62 PCGS.** Breen-6138, Small Head, R.1. Honey-gold toning, a crisp strike, and luminous luster confirm the quality of this introductory year Classic quarter eagle. The sole remotely consequential mark is a hair-thin line above the eagle's head. A good selection for an advanced gold type set.(#7692)

Exceptional MS64 Prooflike 1834 Classic Head Quarter Eagle

2576 1834 MS64 Prooflike NGC. Large Head, Breen-6140, McCloskey-A, R.3. The Classic Head design made its debut in 1834, to mark a change in weight of the U.S. gold coinage. This change was necessary to halt the exportation and melting that plagued the old-tenor gold coinage. From a mintage of 112,234 pieces, the 1834 quarter eagle is one of the most available dates of the Classic Head design. The date is available in all grades, making it a favorite choice for type collectors, as well as gold specialists.

The present example is a beautiful specimen of this first-date-of-issue coin. The fields are deeply reflective, and the devices are strongly impressed. Handling marks are minimal for the grade. Overall eye appeal is outstanding. Census: 6 in 64 Prooflike, 2 finer (2/09).(#77692)

2577 1835 AU58 PCGS. McCloskey-1, R.2. The most available variety with wide AM in AMERICA on the reverse. Brightly lustrous yellow-gold surfaces show few marks. Softly struck on the central devices with modest friction. For all varieties, Population: 23 in 58, 43 finer (2/09).(#7693)

Dazzling MS61 1835 Quarter Eagle

2578 1835 MS61 NGC. McCloskey-1, R.2. The dentils and stars are needle-sharp, as are the eagle's neck and wings. The indifference of strike at the centers is unavoidable for the type. Luster dominates all but the open fields, which are prooflike, and the absence of remotely consequential abrasions ensures the eye appeal. (#7693)

2579 1836 Script 8 AU53 NGC. Head of 1835, Breen-6143, McCloskey-D, R.2. Rich yellow-gold color with flashy fields. From a later die state with prominent crack through star 6. A copper alloy streak is noted to the left of Liberty's nose.(#7694)

2580 1836 Script 8—Cleaned—ANACS. MS60 Details. Head of 1835, Breen-6143, McCloskey-D, R.2. This well struck Classic quarter eagle shows no trace of wear. Pale lemon-gold surfaces retain hints of reflectivity, though hairlines indicate a past cleaning. (#7694)

2581 1836 Block 8 AU55 PCGS. Head of 1837, Breen-6144, McCloskey-C, R.2. Luster illuminates the margins and devices of this canary-gold Choice AU type coin. Void of consequential marks, and scarce any finer.
From The Ed Lepordo Collection, Part Two.(#97694)

Lustrous 1836 Quarter Eagle, MS61

2582 1836 Block 8 MS61 NGC. Head of 1837, Breen-6144, McCloskey-C, R.2. The reverse has a single small berry in the branch, a common 1836 quarter eagle variety, although still rare in Mint State. This attractive green-gold example is fully lustrous. The design motifs are weak at the center, but otherwise nicely defined.(#97694)

2583 1837 AU50 NGC. McCloskey-B, R.2. Each vertical stripe of the shield has three distinct lines, and the lowest arrowhead touches the second A in AMERICA, identifying the variety. Splashes of apricot adhere to the yellow-gold surfaces of this quarter eagle. Well struck, save for softness in the stars along the left border. There are no more marks than what might be expected for a coin that has seen some circulation.(#7695)

Choice AU 1839-C Quarter Eagle

2584   **1839-C AU55 NGC.** Variety 3, R.4. The 1839-C is a scarce issue, and enjoys high demand from collectors of Southern gold. The present coin is a desirable example, with a bold strike and mint luster throughout the legends, curls, and plumage. Abrasions are moderate for the grade. Census: 37 in 55, 89 finer (2/09). (#7699)

2585   **1839-D Fine 15 PCGS.** Winter 1-A, McCloskey-A, R.3. A rich yellow-gold representative with even wear. Generally abraded aside from a faint V-shaped mark on Liberty's neck and a few faint slide marks on the left border of the eagle. The only Dahlonega issue of the type, and scarce due to a low reported mintage of 13,674 pieces. (#7700)

2586   **1839-O—Scratched—ANACS. AU53 Details.** High Date, Wide Fraction, Breen-6152, McCloskey-A, R.3. Softly struck, the surfaces are generally free from abrasions, and tiny portions of mint luster can still be seen near the devices. A shallow pinscratch vertically bisects the obverse, from approximately 3 o'clock to 9 o'clock. Always a popular issue as the only Classic quarter eagle from the New Orleans Mint, the '39-O is also popular because of the obverse mintmark, another distinctive one year feature. (#7701)

Well Struck 1839-O Quarter Eagle
Unc Details, McCloskey-A

2587   **1839-O—Improperly Cleaned—NCS. Unc Details.** High Date, Wide Fraction, Breen-6152, McCloskey-A, R.3. Peach-gold surfaces have a greenish cast, and have been muted by the cleaning. Fine hairlines are visible under magnification. The design elements are well brought up, and no significant contact marks are visible on either side.(#7701)

LIBERTY QUARTER EAGLES

Desirable Near-Mint 1840-C Quarter Eagle

2588   **1840-C AU58 NGC.** Variety 1, lone variety for the year. Bright yellow-gold fields show considerable radiance despite slight friction on the high points and abrasions in the fields. Pale yellow-gold centers give way to richer orange elements close to the rims. A highly-graded example of this earlier issue. Census: 27 in 58, 13 finer (2/09).(#7718)

2589   **1841-C VF35 NGC.** Variety 1. A charming C-mint quarter eagle with smooth and original yellow-gold surfaces. Only 10,281 pieces were produced, and survivors are scarce at all grade levels. Struck from widely rotated dies.(#7721)

Luminous AU55 1841-C Quarter Eagle

2590   **1841-C AU55 NGC.** Variety 1, the only variety for the year. Though lightly worn, this modestly abraded yellow-gold piece offers considerable watery luster in the fields. The portrait shows slight striking softness, yet the eagle is well-defined for the issue. Census: 26 in 55, 33 finer (2/09).(#7721)

Exceptional 1841-C Quarter Eagle, AU58 ★
The Sole Example With a ★ Designation

2591 **1841-C AU58 ★ NGC.** Variety 1 (previously Variety 2-B), the only variety for the year. NGC has bestowed the coveted "Star" designation, denoting exceptional eye appeal, on this conditionally rare quarter eagle from the Charlotte Mint. It is the *only* 1841-C quarter eagle to have received the "Star," as of (2/09). Upon viewing the coin it is easy to understand why, although AU examples generally do not merit such consideration. Well struck except for a few of the obverse star centrils, with minimal high point wear and some wispy hairlines on each side that may have precluded a Mint State grade. Lime-green over the fields and centers, with vivid copper-orange coloration near the borders. A mere seven examples have been certified in Uncirculated condition by NGC and PCGS combined, but this number is virtually certain to include resubmissions. Doug Winter suggests a total of four or five Mint State survivors, in the latest edition of his book on Charlotte gold coinage.(#7721)

Pleasing VF30 1841-D Quarter Eagle

2592 **1841-D VF30 NGC.** Variety 2-C. An early Dahlonega Mint issue, with a scant mintage of 4,164 pieces and limited survival in this grade and higher, further enhancing its desirability. This example is characterized by uniform, even wear. A pleasing example of this vintage piece, given the grade.(#7722)

2593 **1842-O VF35 PCGS.** Light to moderate wear on the central devices blends with the issue's typical striking softness. A minimally abraded yellow-orange example that offers interesting eye appeal. Population: 14 in 35, 61 finer (2/09).(#7726)

2594 **1843 AU50 ICG.** Deep yellow-orange color with astounding reflectivity remaining in the fields. Excellent strike with only modest wear affecting the highest design elements.(#7727)

2595 **1843 AU53 ICG.** Rich lemon-gold color with scattered butter-yellow accents. Modestly abraded for the grade with only trivial wear across the high points.(#7727)

2596 **1843 AU58 NGC.** Lovely lime-green and peach-gold coloration adorns the satiny, slightly worn surfaces of this appealing near-Mint example. Boldly struck with just a few trivial marks observed on each side. Census: 57 in 58, 20 finer (2/09).(#7727)

2597 **1843-C Large Date, Plain 4 XF40 NGC.** Variety 1. The more available of the two date sizes, this 1843-C quarter eagle variety displays honey-gold surfaces with occasional glimmers of luster. Typically struck, in that the centers are weak. Minimally marked for a coin that saw some circulation.(#7728)

2598 **1843-C Large Date, Plain 4 XF40 PCGS.** Variety 1. Glimpses of orange-gold luster persist within protected areas of this attractively toned XF Charlotte quarter eagle. The fields are clean, and the moderate contact on the chin and cheekbone fails to distract.
From The Ed Lepordo Collection, Part Two.(#7728)

Popular AU 1843-C Quarter Eagle
Large Date, Plain 4

2599 **1843-C Large Date, Plain 4 AU50 NGC.** Variety 1, the only known Large Date die marriage, as expected given the scant mintage of 23,076 pieces. This is unmarked and typically struck example with attractive dusky yellow gold surfaces. The borders display noticeable luster.(#7728)

2600 **1843-D Small D VF30 NGC.** Variety 4-D. An interesting midrange piece that has luminous orange-gold centers and deep violet-copper alloy at the margins. Minimally marked for the grade. (#7730)

Sharp 1843-D Small D Quarter Eagle
MS60, Ex: Ashland City

2601 **1843-D Small D MS60 PCGS.** Variety 4-F. Ex: Ashland City. The die crack that passes through the F in OF and into the field distinguishes this most common variety of the year. The 1843-D is the most frequently encountered D-mint quarter eagle, with 36,209 pieces produced, and Winter also calls it the "best struck of the early Dahlonega quarter eagles." Curiously, though, high grade pieces are very rare. Winter estimates that only 4-5 Uncirculated coins exist, although the combined Mint State PCGS and NGC population is 23 pieces, a figure that undoubtedly includes resubmissions. This crisply struck lemon-gold piece offers a bold strike, aside from slight softness on the vertical shield lines. Refreshingly devoid of obtrusive contact or planchet difficulties, with superior eye appeal as a result. This ex: Ashland City piece is listed in a tie for fifth place in the Condition Census Winter provides in his 2003 D-mint reference.(#7730)

High-End 1843-D Quarter Eagle
Small D, MS62

2602 **1843-D Small D MS62 PCGS.** Variety 4-D. The 1843-D quarter eagle is a "common" date in the context of Dahlonega gold coins, with a "large" original mintage of 36,209 pieces. Doug Winter estimates a surviving population of 250-300 examples in all grades. Most examples seen are in lower grades, and the issue is surprisingly scarce at the AU level. Mint State coins are rare, and only three coins have been certified in grades above MS62 by NGC and PCGS combined (2/09).

   The coin offered here is a particularly attractive specimen, with bright, semi-prooflike fields. The surfaces are bright yellow, with hints of red around the devices. The strike is sharp, except for slight softness on the eagle's leg. A few handling marks are consistent with the grade. Population: 5 in 62, 2 finer (2/09).(#7730)

Popular MS62 1843-O Quarter Eagle
Small Date, Crosslet 4

2603 **1843-O Small Date, Crosslet 4 MS62 PCGS.** Razor-sharp striking definition combines with immense luster for potent eye appeal. Each side has attractive yellow-gold coloration with few significant marks, though wispy abrasions are noted in the fields. The Small Date variant is highly elusive at this level. Population: 12 in 62, 12 finer (1/09).(#7731)

2604 **1844-C XF40 NGC.** Variety 6-E, the only known. The 1844-C is the worst-struck quarter eagle from the Charlotte Mint. In fact, Douglas Winter (1998) contends that "all are weakly struck." This brassy-gold piece unfortunately falls into this category. Liberty's forehead and temple curls and the eagle's plumage adjacent to the shield are especially weak. Minute circulation marks are slightly more apparent on the obverse.(#7735)

2605 **1844-D—Scratched—ANACS. VF30 Details.** Variety 5-I. The upper reverse has scrapes, and both sides have several wispy pinscratches. Yellow-gold surfaces are unusually bright for the amount of wear. Just 17,332 pieces fell from the dies. (#7736)

Attractive 1844-D Quarter Eagle, AU55

2606 **1844-D AU55 PCGS.** Variety 5-H. Feathers fill the upper part of the opening in the mintmark. Yellow-gold, orange, and mint-green colors compete for territory on this attractive Choice AU quarter eagle. Ample luster resides in the recessed areas. Peripheral elements are sharply struck, but the centers reveal the weakness seen on most examples. A small mark on the chin does not significantly detract.(#7736)

Sharp 1845-D Quarter Eagle, MS61

2607 **1845-D MS61 PCGS.** Variety 6-I. Very rare in high grades, with likely fewer than a dozen known in this MS61 level at both services combined. A scrape along Liberty's nose and cheek appears to be the primary grade determinant, although a small planchet indentation is noted near the rim at 3 o'clock on the obverse. Elsewhere, the coin just shows the light abrasions and minor hairlines that characterize most examples of the issue. Moderate die clashing appears on the reverse, along with some curious parallel die lines that pass from the last S in STATES under the eagle's wing to the rim. The strike is pleasing: Despite the minor softness on the curl over Liberty's ear, all of the reverse details and the remainder of the obverse is well brought up. The pretty orange-gold surfaces are faintly reflective. According to the Condition Census in Winter's 2003 edition, this piece would qualify for a fourth-place tie with an MS61 NGC piece. Population: 4 in 61, 3 finer (2/09). (#7738)

MS62 1846 Two and a Half

2608 **1846 MS62 PCGS. CAC.** The low mintage 1846 is very scarce in all grades, and is unknown above MS63. This is a moderately prooflike example, perhaps one of the first coins struck from this die pairing. The striking details are strongly brought up, and there is only faint chatter in the obverse fields to account for the grade. (#7740)

Condition Census 1846-D/D Quarter Eagle, AU58 Variety 7-K, Rare Early Die State

2609 **1846-D/D AU58 PCGS. CAC.** Variety 7-K. The rare early die state that shows remnants of an errant mintmark above the 1 in the fraction. Both sides exhibit overlapping sets of clash marks, as made. This well struck near-Mint Dahlonega five has an orange-red obverse. The reverse is mainly lime-gold. Smooth aside from a hair-thin mark beneath the hairbun. Population: 4 in 58, 1 finer (2/09).(#97742)

Elusive Near-Mint 1846-O Quarter Eagle

2610 **1846-O AU58 NGC. CAC.** This scarce date O-mint representative displays ample luster on the bright yellow-gold surfaces. The design elements are well struck, except for the usual weakness on the left (facing) leg. Refreshingly clean surfaces add to the coin's overall appeal. Census: 56 in 58, 23 finer (2/09). (#7743)

Attractive 1847-C Two and a Half, AU53

2611 **1847-C AU53 PCGS.** Variety 1. The most available C-mint quarter eagle, produced to the extent of 23,226 examples in antebellum Charlotte. This piece is slightly better than the average certified specimen, with a bold strike and attractive antique-gold and amber coloration. A small dotlike planchet indentation is noted above the eagle's head. Population: 20 in 53, 59 finer (2/09). (#7745)

Pleasing MS61 1848 Quarter Eagle

2612 **1848 MS61 NGC.** With a low mintage of 6,500 business strikes (less than five times the number of 1848 CAL. quarter eagles), the 1848 two and a half offers a worthy challenge for the collector who seeks an unworn example. This bright yellow-gold piece offers significant reflectivity and strong eye appeal despite moderate abrasions. Well-defined and desirable.(#7748)

Historic VF30 1848 CAL. Quarter Eagle

2613 1848 CAL. VF30 PCGS. While the traditional survey of U.S. commemoratives begins with the Columbian Expedition half dollars of 1892, when one thinks about commemorative coinage in a broader, more international sense, a different candidate emerges: the CAL. quarter eagles dated 1848, struck from California gold with ceremony. The present example likely served as a pocket-piece, judging from the brightness of the moderately worn surfaces and its scattered marks, including a faint pinscratch near the countermark. Color is generally yellow-gold save for elements of peach at star 10 on the obverse and in a crescent along the lower reverse. An attractive and comparatively affordable representative of this historic variety. Population: 1 in 30, 55 finer (2/09).(#7749)

Luminous AU55 1848-D Quarter Eagle

2614 1848-D AU55 NGC. Variety 10-M. Yellow-gold surfaces are startlingly radiant on this Choice AU coin. A well struck and minimally abraded example from a Dahlonega issue Winter has described as "much scarcer than believed, especially in high grades." Including the inevitable resubmissions, NGC has graded 72 finer examples (2/09).(#7751)

Appealing 1848-D Quarter Eagle, AU58

2615 1848-D AU58 PCGS. CAC. Variety 10-M, the more common of two known varieties for the date. This piece has lustrous and fully brilliant green-gold surfaces with exceptional eye appeal. A few tiny marks are evident on each side, and they are entirely trivial in nature. Population: 26 in 58, 18 finer (2/09). (For both varieties.) (#7751)

2616 1849 AU58 NGC. A scarce low mintage date, with just 23,294 pieces produced. Both sides exhibit faintly hairlined fields. The devices are quite well struck, particularly the on obverse, and a trace amount of wear further accounts for the grade.(#7752)

2617 1849-C—Improperly Cleaned—NCS. AU Details. Variety 1. Well-defined with only modest wear. The pale mustard-tan surfaces are mildly granular with peculiar luster, the result of a past cleaning. (#7753)

2618 1849-D—Ex-Jewelry, Damaged—ANACS. XF40 Details. Variety 11-M. High date with the 1 distant from the border. The obverse presents a relatively clean and well detailed appearance, along with pleasing honey-gold color. The reverse displays a heavy bluish-gray residue, some to the left side and a smaller amount near the right edge. Damage from jewelry usage and possible repair exists near the lower left reverse border.(#7754)

Attractive 1849-D Quarter Eagle, AU58

2619 1849-D AU58 NGC. Variety 11-M. High Date, with the 1 in the date nearly touching the bust, the more common of the two obverses for the year. Most of the luster still clings to this marvelous example of one of the rarest quarter eagle issues from the late 1840s. The surfaces are honey-gold, revealing under a loupe considerable eye appeal and mostly minor abrasions expected for the grade. A patch of tiny scrapes below STATES OF requires singular mention. A well struck and ultimately pleasing example. This piece would, according to the Condition Census in Winter's 2003 reference, be tied for fifth place with an apparently large number of AU58 pieces (likely including multiple resubmissions). Census: 50 in 58, 14 finer (2/09).(#7754)

Low Mintage 1850-C Quarter Eagle AU53

2620 **1850-C AU53 NGC.** Variety 1 with the mintmark over the 1 in the fraction. A richly detailed straw-gold Charlotte representative. Smooth aside from a faint mark between STATES and OF. At least four sets of closely spaced clashmarks are present in the fields. A meager 9,138 pieces were struck.(#7756)

2621 **1850-D XF45 PCGS.** Variety 13-M. Pale lemon-gold surfaces are radiant on this lightly marked Choice XF piece. Well struck for the issue with distinctive eye appeal. Population: 22 in 45, 68 finer (2/09).(#7757)

2622 **1850-O AU58 PCGS.** This honey-gold low mintage New Orleans quarter eagle has a suitable strike and lacks relevant marks. Luster beckons from raised areas. The flag of the 5 in the date is repunched. Housed in a green label holder. Population: 8 in 58, 17 finer (2/09). (#7758)

Brilliant 1851-C Quarter Eagle, AU58

2623 **1851-C AU58 NGC.** Variety 1, the only known die combination for the issue. The date is quite large for this small coin, and the first 1 is solidly joined to the bust, and very nearly touches the border. Somewhat matte-like surfaces exhibit bright green-gold coloration with brilliant luster. Only a few tiny imperfections are evident on each side. Census: 20 in 58, 16 finer (2/09).(#7760)

Lovely Gem 1852 Quarter Eagle

2624 **1852 MS65 PCGS. CAC.** Because of the plentiful mintage of 1.16 million pieces in antebellum Philadelphia, the 1852 quarter eagle is fairly available today, although Gems or finer become quite scarce. The strike is well executed throughout the obverse, but the eagle's claws are weak on the reverse. The preservation is quite lovely, however, with minimal abrasions noted and attractive amber-gold coloration throughout. This piece is one of only nine so certified at PCGS, with but two in higher grades (2/09).(#7763)

Attractive 1852-D Quarter Eagle, MS62

2625 **1852-D MS62 NGC. CAC.** Variety 15-M, the single variety identified for the year. This attractive survivor from an issue of just 4,078 pieces exhibits most of the noteworthy characteristics of the date; to wit, it has vibrant luster and bold central detail, with a degree of the usual softness noted at the dentils on each side. Unlike most of its peers, this straw-gold and lemon-gold piece shows few overt distractions, and the few wispy abrasions that preclude Select status are generally inoffensive. A top-notch piece that can stake a plausible claim to a place on the Condition Census. Census: 2 in 62, 3 finer (9/08).(#7765)

Challenging 1854-C Quarter Eagle, AU50

2626 **1854-C AU50 NGC.** Variety 15-I. The 1854-C always catches the attention of collectors with its mintage of only 7,295 pieces. It is ranked sixth out of the 20 C-mint quarter eagles in overall rarity and 12th in high grade. Out of the 105-145 pieces known in all grades, only 34-43 examples are believed known in AU grades. This piece shows a few light marks on each side, but none are individually distracting. The devices are softly struck on each side, as usually seen. Both obverse and reverse display a slight accent of reddish patina around the margins.(#7770)

2627 **1855-C—Improperly Cleaned—NCS. AU Details.** Variety 16-I. Only 3,677 pieces were struck and this is the rarest quarter eagle from the Charlotte Mint in terms of its overall rarity. This example has been improperly cleaned but presents a smooth, unmarked appearance, with substantial detail remaining on both sides. (#7775)

Desirable 1856-C Quarter Eagle, MS61

2628 **1856-C MS61 NGC.** Variety 1 and the only known die combination for the 1856-C quarter eagles. Although some mint-made surface roughness is characteristic of all known examples, few survivors have the intense luster and mostly sharp design elements that are seen on this piece. A few small planchet depressions are also mint-made, and again they are typical of surviving 1856-C quarter eagles. Census: 6 in 61, 3 finer (2/09).(#7778)

2629 **1856-S AU55 NGC.** Strongly struck with hints of the original mirrors in the fields. Tan shadings visit otherwise mustard-gold surfaces. Minimally marked for the grade with little actual wear. (#7781)

2630 **1856-S AU58 PCGS.** Lime and apricot shades enrich this unmarked and partially lustrous slider. A trace of friction on Liberty's eyebrow and the eagle's neck feathers confirms momentary non-numismatic handling. Population: 12 in 58, 19 finer (2/09). (#7781)

Elusive Near-Gem 1857 Quarter Eagle

2631 **1857 MS64 NGC.** Pleasing satin luster accompanies lovely lime-gold and peach toning. The carefully preserved surfaces are essentially distraction-free. A conditionally scarce example from this issue of 214,130 pieces which is considered common, but only in lower grades. Census: 13 in 64, 4 finer (2/09).(#7782)

2632 **1857-S AU55 NGC.** Pale yellow-gold surfaces remain immensely lustrous despite a degree of wear. Uncommonly sharp detail contributes to the notable eye appeal.(#7785)

Bold AU55 1858-C Two and a Half

2633 **1858-C AU55 PCGS.** Variety 1. A sharply defined and unmarked Choice AU Charlotte gold piece. Generally green-gold, with orange patina near the rims. As often seen for this very scarce issue, shallow strike-throughs are present beneath the beak and right (facing) wing. A mere 9,056 pieces were struck. Population: 25 in 55, 37 finer (2/09). *From The Burning Tree Collection.*(#7787)

Lovely Near-Mint 1858-C Quarter Eagle

2634 **1858-C AU58 NGC.** Variety 1, the only die pair for the year. Strongly struck for the issue with particularly pleasing detail on the fine strands of Liberty's hair. Wispy abrasions appear in yellow-gold fields with an uncharacteristic gleam. An interesting survivor with just a touch of friction on the high points. Census: 33 in 58, 40 finer (2/09).(#7787)

Reflective 1858-C Quarter Eagle, MS63

2635 1858-C MS63 NGC. Variety 1, the only known die pair. An extremely large mintmark for the denomination slightly displaces the 1 in the fraction. It is probably from a punch intended for half eagles. With a mintage of only 9,000 coins, it is hardly surprising that only one die pair was necessary. This piece has an excellent strike that only shows slight weakness on the eagle's left (facing) leg. The fields are reflective, and both sides exhibit brilliant yellow luster with few blemishes. NGC has certified two examples at this grade level, with none finer, while PCGS has certified three, also with none finer (1/09).(#7787)

2636 1859 Old Reverse, Type One AU58 NGC. Brightly lustrous with elegant lemon-gold color. A well-defined example that shows just a trace of friction across the high points and few marks. Census: 42 in 58, 34 finer (2/09).(#97788)

Scarce 1860 Old Reverse Quarter Eagle, AU55

2637 1860 Old Reverse, Type One AU55 PCGS. Relatively few of the 22,563 quarter eagles produced by the Philadelphia Mint in 1860 were struck from the old reverse hub type of pre-1859, which featured larger reverse letters and arrowheads than the new reverse design. The exact numbers are unknown, however; in fact, the Old Reverse (Type One) quarter eagle variant was not even discovered until the 1990s (per Garrett and Guth). This is a fresh-looking Choice AU representative with boldly defined motifs and a couple of minor pinscratches on the reverse. Only the faintest degree of highpoint wear seems evident on the eagle's head, neck feathers, and wing tips. Population: 3 in 55, 11 finer (1/09).(#97791)

2638 1860 New Reverse, Type Two MS61 NGC. Rich lime-gold and apricot toning adorns the lustrous surfaces of this conditionally scarce Uncirculated example. From a new reverse design with smaller letters and arrowheads. Census: 23 in 61, 13 finer (2/09). (#7791)

2639 1860-C—Improperly Cleaned—NCS. AU Details. Variety 1. Nicely detailed with a few shallow marks and wispy hairlines in the fields. A bit bright from improper cleaning. From the final year of Charlotte Mint production, and one of only 7,469 pieces struck. (#7792)

Vibrant AU 1860-C Two and a Half

2640 1860-C AU50 PCGS. Variety 1, as always. The final Charlotte quarter eagle issue has a mintage of only 7,469 pieces, and is rare in AU grades. This sun-gold representative displays some softness on the eagle's shield, but the strike is otherwise nice. The slightly bright fields display a few subtle marks. Population: 12 in 50, 27 finer (2/09). *From The Burning Tree Collection.*(#7792)

Elusive 1861 Old Reverse Quarter Eagle, MS63

2641 **1861 Old Reverse, Type One MS63 PCGS.** The large letters and arrowheads on the reverse confirm this important and elusive variety, one that Garrett and Guth describe as "... very rare in any grade and ... many times rarer than the 1861 New Reverse quarter eagle." Mint-green and apricot compete for territory on this lustrous Select specimen. Well struck and minimally abraded. Population: 5 in 63, 4 finer (1/09).(#97794)

2642 **1861 New Reverse, Type Two MS62 NGC.** The modified reverse with small letters and arrowheads. This unworn example has subtle, yet pleasing luster with deep butter-yellow surfaces that show peripheral orange accents.(#7794)

2643 **1861 New Reverse, Type Two MS63 PCGS.** This is a lustrous, sharply struck coin with lovely lime-gold coloration and minimal surface marks for the grade. The New Reverse (Type Two) design features smaller arrowheads that are well away from the R and C in AMERICA.(#7794)

2644 **1862 AU58 NGC.** Pale yellow-gold fields are profoundly reflective on this well-defined piece. Just a touch of rub affects the high points. NGC has certified only 50 Mint State examples (2/09). (#7796)

2645 **1866-S AU55 NGC.** The obverse has a jagged die crack from the border between stars 2 and 3 through the field to Liberty's chin. Considerable luster remains, with light yellow-gold around the devices, accompanied by considerable olive patina in the fields and on the devices. Census: 22 in 55, 26 finer (2/09).(#7804)

2646 **1866-S AU58 NGC.** An attractive near-Mint specimen that only has a trace amount of high point wear and some wispy field hairlines separating it from Mint State. Boldly struck with good color and plenty of luster.(#7804)

Scarce, Flashy 1867 Quarter Eagle, AU58

2647 **1867 AU58 NGC.** Bright and flashy, with considerable prooflikeness evident in the fields. Well struck with mere traces of high point wear on either side. One of just 3,250 pieces produced, and very scarce at all grade levels. Garrett and Guth indicate that this issue is underrated because it hails from the Philadelphia Mint, which is less popular with collectors than its Southern counterparts. Census: 7 in 58, 6 finer (2/09).(#7805)

2648 **1867-S AU50 NGC.** Softly struck as usual at the high points, though the light yellow-gold surfaces show little actual wear. Minor, scattered abrasions contribute to the grade. Census: 15 in 50, 68 finer (1/09).(#7806)

2649 **1869-S AU55 NGC.** A subtly lustrous, lightly worn lemon-gold example, softly defined with a pleasing appearance overall. While this issue's P-mint counterpart has a much lower mintage, attrition has made the 1869-S quarter eagle more valuable in higher grades. NGC has certified 66 finer pieces (1/09).(#7810)

Appealing 1869-S Quarter Eagle, MS61

2650 **1869-S MS61 NGC.** Many of the post-Civil War S-mint quarter eagles are rare and underrated, low-mintage productions. The 1869-S is no exception, with an emission of only 29,500 pieces. And apparently, those few pieces made were mostly absorbed instantly into commerce in the hard-metal-trusting West of the era: Most certified examples average only Choice XF or so. This piece is strictly Mint State, with good luster and a bold strike. A few grade-defining contact marks appear in the fields on both sides, but the orange-gold surfaces offer plenty of appeal. Census: 8 in 61, 4 finer (2/09).(#7810)

2651 **1870 AU58 NGC.** Bright yellow-gold luster with impressive reflectivity. This well-defined piece shows only a trace of friction across the high points, though scattered marks are also visible. NGC has graded just 14 Mint State examples of this low-mintage issue (2/09).(#7811)

2652 **1870-S AU55 NGC.** An attractive straw-gold representative with plenty of luster for the grade. The fields display wispy hairlines and small marks, and moderate wear exists on the design's high points. A conditionally scarce Choice AU example. Census: 15 in 55, 36 finer (2/09).(#7812)

2653 **1872-S AU55 NGC.** Strongly lustrous and highly appealing with pale straw-gold surfaces that show only trifling wear. Modestly marked and attractive for the grade. Census: 32 in 55, 59 finer (1/09).(#7816)

2654 **1873 Closed 3 MS64 PCGS.** An excellent survivor with the earlier Closed 3 logotype. Satiny luster graces generally khaki-gold surfaces that show occasional mustard and tan elements. Minimally flawed for the grade with solid overall eye appeal. A rarity in Gem; PCGS has graded just nine coins finer (1/09).(#7818)

2655 **1876 AU55 NGC.** The 1876 quarter eagle is a low mintage issue of 4,100 pieces that is very scarce at the AU grade level. This example is softly struck over the centers, with appealing olive-orange coloration. Minor marks and light wear define the grade. Census: 17 in 55, 49 finer (2/09).(#7824)

Attractive 1878 Quarter Eagle, MS65

2656 **1878 MS65 NGC.** Perusal of NGC/PCGS population figures reveals the 1878 quarter eagle to be relatively plentiful through the MS63 level of preservation. The certified population drops somewhat in MS64, and declines precipitously in higher grades. The present Gem exudes excellent luster, and its wheat-gold surfaces exhibit well defined motifs. A couple of ticks and tiny copper spots do not detract. Census: 25 in 65, 4 finer (2/09). (#7828)

Marvelous Gem 1878 Quarter Eagle

2657 **1878 MS65 NGC.** While the quarter eagle mintage in excess of a quarter-million pieces does not approach the prodigious Morgan dollar productions of the year, it is nonetheless substantial enough that marvelous survivors such as the present Gem are sometimes available. There is splendid prooflikeness visible on each side, with near-immaculate orange-gold surfaces and a bold strike. Census: 27 in 65, 4 finer (2/09).(#7828)

2658 **1879 MS63 NGC.** Pale yellow-gold surfaces offer gorgeous luster. This sharply struck example is minimally marked for the grade, though the fields show a few wispy abrasions.(#7830)

2659 **1880 MS60 NGC.** Well-defined with no trace of wear. Though numerous light to moderate abrasions affect each side, this remains a desirable example of its low-mintage issue. Census: 12 in 60, 47 finer (2/09).(#7832)

2660 **1880 MS62 NGC.** Each side of this crisply detailed quarter eagle offers its own form of eye appeal. The yellow-gold obverse offers significant reflectivity in the fields, while the orange-suffused reverse is more dusky and luminous. Either way, an attractive example of this low-mintage business strike issue. Census: 15 in 62, 13 finer (2/09).(#7832)

Charming MS64 1882 Quarter Eagle

2661 **1882 MS64 PCGS. CAC.** A delightful quarter eagle, strongly struck with watery luster in the fields. Deep butter-yellow shadings dominate, though glimpses of green-gold flank the portrait. Excellent eye appeal for this low-mintage issue of just 4,000 business strikes. Population: 19 in 64, 9 finer (2/09).(#7834)

Splendid Low-Mintage 1883 Quarter Eagle, AU58

2662 **1883 AU58 NGC.** Garrett and Guth rightly opine, "With so few made for the nation's commerce, one wonders why the coins were struck at all." Only 1,920 pieces were made. The fact is, however, that quarter eagles for much of the nation's coinage history were the red-headed stepchild, much more likely in any given year to be produced to a small degree—or not at all. This piece has the expected prooflikeness such a small emission nearly ensures, with only light field chatter and small abrasions appearing on the orange-gold surfaces under a loupe. Census: 21 in 58, 20 finer (2/09).(#7835)

2663 **1886 MS62 PCGS.** A mildly prooflike representative whose powerful strike and relatively clean fields ensure the eye appeal. A scant 4,000 pieces were struck. Population: 15 in 62, 17 finer (2/09). *From The Burning Tree Collection.*(#7838)

Elusive 1887 Quarter Eagle, MS64

2664 **1887 MS64 PCGS.** The 1887 quarter eagle, with a mintage of 6,160 coins, is scarce in all grades. This near-Gem displays strong luster emanating from yellow-gold surfaces laced with traces of light tan and peach. Well struck, save for minor weakness in some of the star centers. Light handling marks on both sides preclude Gem status. Population: 13 in 64, 0 finer (2/09).(#7839)

2665 **1889 MS63 PCGS.** Rich sun-gold and butter-yellow color dominates on this lustrous Select piece. Modestly abraded for the grade with stirring eye appeal. Population: 45 in 63, 52 finer (1/09). (#7841)

2666 **1891 Doubled Die Reverse AU55 ICG.** Breen-6310. This is Breen's Doubled Die Reverse, with AMERICA and the top two arrowheads boldly doubled. A briefly circulated example of this underrated variety, bright sun-gold on the obverse with orange overtones on the reverse.

2667 **1891 AU58 NGC.** Ex: Richmond Collection. Deep orange-gold surfaces with occasional rose accents. Lightly abraded, yet immensely lustrous and appealing for this lower-mintage issue. (#7843)

2668 **1892 AU53 PCGS.** A lightly circulated survivor of this lower-mintage issue, modestly marked with light wear on the well-defined devices. Deep gold-orange fields are flashy. Population: 10 in 53, 89 finer (1/09).(#7844)

2669 **1892 AU58 NGC.** Sharply struck and gleaming with pale lemon-gold and straw shadings. Just a touch of friction affects the high points, and marks are few.(#7844)

2670 **1893 MS63 PCGS.** Orange-gold with hints of sun-yellow and strawberry. Each side of this minimally abraded Select coin hosts well-defined devices and fields with effusive luster.(#7845)

Vibrant MS66 ★ 1897 Quarter Eagle

2671 **1897 MS66 ★ NGC.** In keeping with other quarter eagle issues of the late 19th century, this Philadelphia issue has a low business strike mintage of just under 30,000 pieces. This sharply struck survivor offers high-end eye appeal, with strong reflectivity and flash to the yellow-gold fields. The central devices exhibit razor-sharp striking definition. NGC has graded a mere 16 numerically finer pieces (2/09).(#7849)

2672 **1898 MS61 PCGS.** A well-defined example of this lower-mintage late 19th century quarter eagle issue. Yellow-gold fields are impressively lustrous, though each side shows its share of wispy abrasions.(#7850)

2673 **1900 MS66 NGC.** Peach-gold and mint-green patina is joined by lavender on the reverse, where the overall hues are somewhat deeper. Well struck lustrous surfaces are devoid of mentionable marks.(#7852)

2674 **1901 MS65 PCGS.** An exquisitely detailed Gem from the dawn of the 20th century, bright yellow-gold with swirling luster. Remarkable eye appeal for the issue.(#7853)

2675 **1903 MS62 ICG.** Solidly struck with attractive luster. The yellow-gold fields show a scattering of light abrasions, which have surprisingly little impact on the overall eye appeal.(#7855)

2676 **1903 MS65 NGC.** Shining yellow-gold with swirling luster in the carefully preserved fields. A well-defined and delightful Gem that would fit well in a 20th century gold type collection. (#7855)

2677 **1904 MS63 PCGS.** Excellent honey-gold and yellow-orange color with slight variations from obverse to reverse. Well struck for the issue with impressive eye appeal for the grade.(#7856)

2678 1904 MS65 NGC. Gleaming yellow-gold with sharp striking definition. This pale but pleasing Gem would make an excellent addition to a type collection.(#7856)

2679 1905 MS66 NGC. The 1905 is one of the more available dates in the Liberty Head quarter eagle series. Peach-gold color graces this Premium Gem, complemented by a well executed strike. Vibrant luster exudes from both sides, each of which is devoid of mentionable marks. This lovely example is an excellent choice for a high grade type set.(#7857)

2680 1905 MS66 NGC. Sharply struck with shining luster. Peach and orange hints grace mostly yellow-gold surfaces. A delightful Premium Gem with winning eye appeal.(#7857)

PROOF LIBERTY QUARTER EAGLES

Appealing 1898 Quarter Eagle, PR64 Ultra Cameo

2681 1898 PR64 Ultra Cameo NGC. The mintage of the issue is recorded as 165 pieces, of which Garrett and Guth estimate that perhaps 100 survive today. This piece displays optimal contrast over the honey-gold surfaces, but a loupe reveals light grade-defining contact marks, primarily on the obverse. Still quite appealing, and well suited for a gold type set. Census: 7 in 64 Ultra Cameo, 28 finer (2/09).(#97924)

Superlative 1899 Quarter Eagle PR65 Ultra Cameo

2682 1899 PR65 Ultra Cameo NGC. In the *Encyclopedia of U.S. Gold Coins 1795-1933*, Jeff Garrett and Ron Guth estimate perhaps 100 specimens of the 1899 proof quarter eagle are extant, from an original mintage of 150 pieces. Population data is suspect for this issue, due to rampant resubmissions.

The present coin is a delightful specimen, with thick mint luster on the devices and subtle hints of rose and lilac color on both surfaces. The contrast between the deeply reflective fields and the sharply delineated, frosty devices creates a dazzling cameo effect. NGC has awarded this piece the coveted Ultra Cameo designation. Census: 3 in 65 Ultra Cameo, 24 finer (2/09).(#97925)

2683 1899 PR67 Ultra Cameo NGC. The gold fields of Colorado and Alaska were at their peak of production in the 1890s. The fabulous gold fortunes taken from excavations in the Klondike in the last decade of the 19th century rivaled the output of the more famous 1849 California Gold Rush. In the same decade, the mineral wealth discovered in the Cripple Creek area gave impetus to the long-promised establishment of the Denver Mint.

Paradoxically, this vast influx of gold did not result in large mintages of quarter eagles. The quarter eagle denomination saw extremely limited circulation in the 1880s and 1890s. The public had come to accept paper money to a much greater degree than it had before the Civil War. The U.S. government issued millions of Gold Certificates and Coin Notes which had to be backed by gold reserves. Gold was also the preferred medium of exchange in foreign trade. For these purposes, double eagles were much more convenient than lower denomination gold coins. Thus, the great majority of gold bullion received at the Mint was dedicated to the production of double eagles. Eagles and half eagles sometimes had substantial mintages during this time frame, but production of quarter eagles was uniformly small. The business strike mintage of quarter eagles at the Philadelphia Mint in 1899 was only 27,200 pieces, augmented by a further 150 proof strikings.

Surprisingly, Walter Breen identified two obverse dies used in the production of this tiny proof mintage. The present coin is a representative of the B-2 variety, characterized by the location of the left base of the numeral 1 in the date over the center of a denticle. The population data for this issue has been badly distorted by resubmissions. More than 250 proof examples of this date have been certified by the two leading grading services, far more than the total number minted. Experts believe perhaps 100 examples of this issue are extant today. The 1899 quarter eagle in proof trades as a type coin, with some pressure from date collectors due to the small business strike mintage. In *Collecting & Investing Strategies for United States Gold Coins,* Jeff Ambio believes high-quality proof quarter eagles from the 1890s have strong potential for price appreciation under the right market conditions.

The present coin is one of the most beautiful examples of the Liberty Head quarter eagle surviving today. The exquisitely detailed, frosty devices contrast boldly with pristine, reflective fields to produce the gold-on-black Ultra Cameo effect. Eye appeal is equal to the high numeric grade. This offering is a rare opportunity for the discerning collector. Census: 12 in 67 Ultra Cameo, 7 finer (2/09).(#97925)

Important 1902 Quarter Eagle, PR65 ★
The Only Star Designation of the Date

2684 **1902 PR65 ★ NGC.** A glittering Gem proof, this example also carries the additional Star designation for excellent eye appeal, and it truly is a beautiful piece. The fields are completely and deeply mirrored, while the devices are satiny and mildly reflective with a hint of cameo contrast. Census: 9 in 65, 12 finer (2/09) but this single coin is the only proof 1902 quarter eagle that has received the Star designation.(#7928)

2685 **1903 PR50 PCGS.** Distinct rub on the high points of the obverse and in the lightly hairlined fields, though the yellow-gold mirrors are largely intact. An interesting and affordable example of this more available proof Liberty quarter eagle issue.(#7929)

2686 **1905 PR58 PCGS. CAC.** An exactingly struck specimen that possesses orange and lemon tinged luster near design elements. The devices show no evidence of friction, but the open fields are subdued from brief non-numismatic handling. Proof gold coins were often spent by heirs or cash-crunched owners, since in many cases such pieces commanded little premium over face until after the FDR gold recall. A stingy 144 proofs were struck.(#7931)

Glittering 1907 Quarter Eagle, PR67 Cameo

2687 **1907 PR67 Cameo NGC.** The last quarter eagle issue, this Superb Gem Cameo proof has glittering light yellow surfaces with deep mirrors around lustrous devices. The current certified population substantially exceeds the original mintage of 154 coins. NGC and PCGS have combined to grade 229 coins. Census: 17 in 67 Cameo, 8 finer (2/09).(#87933)

INDIAN QUARTER EAGLES

2688 **1908 MS64 PCGS.** Giving the immediate impression of a higher grade, this example displays the intense radiance and careful surface preservation more typical of Gems. Careful inspection with a loupe reveals a couple of faint pinscratches on the upper left obverse field, and a small mark on the Indian's cheekbone, which may have prevented a finer grade assessment.(#7939)

2689 **1908 MS64 NGC.** Rich yellow-gold color with slight satin on the surfaces. Minimally marked for the grade and well-defined with strong visual appeal.(#7939)

2690 **1908 MS64 NGC.** Strongly struck with striking yellow-gold color. This lustrous near-Gem is minimally marked for the grade with elegant eye appeal.(#7939)

Striking MS66 1908 Quarter Eagle

2691 **1908 MS66 ICG.** Warm yellow-gold luster shows glints of orange close to the margins. An enchanting and well-defined example that offers remarkably smooth surfaces and winning visual appeal. Coins of such quality are elusive for the design as a whole, not only for this desirable first-year issue.(#7939)

2692 **1909 MS63 PCGS.** High-end for the Select Uncirculated grade level, with soft golden-tan color and only the slightest evidence of contact on either side. The strike is also notable as all of the device detail is intricately displayed.(#7940)

2693 **1909 MS64 NGC.** Whispers of greenish-tan visit the lustrous peach-gold surfaces of this near-Gem, and an exacting strike leaves sharp definition on the design elements, including the bonnet feathers and the eagle's plumage. Faint pinscratches under the Indian's chin limit the grade. Nevertheless, this is still a nice type coin.(#7940)

2694 **1909 MS64 PCGS. CAC.** Strong yellow-gold color with hints of peripheral orange. A pleasingly lustrous near-Gem that offers slightly above-average definition for the issue.(#7940)

2695 **1909 MS64 PCGS.** A wonderful light-yellow example that resembles the Roman Finish proof gold pieces of the same date. The strike is bold with exceptional design details on both sides. High grade examples of this design are relatively scarce, as few collectors saved pieces at the time of issue.(#7940)

2696 **1909 MS64 PCGS.** Yellow-gold toning overall with hints of tan. This pleasingly lustrous near-Gem is well struck without any singularly mentionable marks.(#7940)

2697 **1909 MS64 PCGS.** Well struck with rich khaki-gold coloration and smooth, matte-like surfaces. Only a small graze near obverse stars 5 and 6 prevents an even finer grade designation. (#7940)

2698 **1909 MS64 PCGS.** Dusky butter-yellow and sun-gold hues dominate the eye appeal of this softly lustrous near-Gem. Well-defined in the centers with only slight peripheral weakness, which is noted on the lowest pendant in the necklace. Available across all circulated grades but a scarce issue any finer.(#7940)

Lovely 1910 Indian Quarter Eagle, MS64

2699 1910 MS64 NGC. Just missing Gem quality by virtue of a few nicks on the upper right reverse field, this piece is satiny and appealing, with a pleasing mattelike appearance. Lime-green and peach-gold colors merge across both sides. Only 492,000 quarter eagles were produced in 1910; examples at the MS64 level represent a small percentage of the survivors.(#7941)

Sharp 1910 Quarter Eagle, MS64

2700 1910 MS64 NGC. A delicate mix of peach-gold and mint-green patina covers the lustrous surfaces of this near-Gem. Sharp definition is visible on the design elements, including the eagle's shoulder feathers. A few light handling marks deny Gem classification. Nice overall eye appeal for the grade designation. (#7941)

Well Struck 1910 Quarter Eagle, MS64

2701 1910 MS64 PCGS. The brassy-gold surfaces of this near-Gem yield a faint greenish cast. A well executed strike leaves strong definition on the design features, including the bonnet feathers and the eagle's plumage. A few minor marks on the raised, exposed fields preclude Gem status.(#7941)

Crisply Struck 1910 Near-Gem Quarter Eagle

2702 1910 MS64 NGC. Orange-gold coloration adorns this near-Gem quarter eagle, and a superior strike leaves crisp detail over the design features. Each side possesses strong luster. Minute surface and rim marks preclude Gem classification. This is one of the more elusive dates for the Indian Head quarter eagle series in Gem grades (Jeff Garrett and Ron Guth, 2006).(#7941)

Elusive Gem 1910 Indian Quarter Eagle

2703 1910 MS65 PCGS. Satiny and boldly struck, with light orange-gold and steel-green toning, this is an alluring Gem example of the low mintage 1910 quarter eagle. Mattelike surface textures are noted on both sides, along with careful preservation and minimal marks. This issue is scarce at the Gem level of preservation, and rare any finer. Housed in a first-generation holder.(#7941)

2704 1911 MS64 NGC. A highly attractive example of this Philadelphia Mint issue, with excellent luster and pretty sunset-gold and steel-green toning. Minimally marked for the grade, and only on the reverse field.(#7942)

2705 1911 MS64 PCGS. CAC. Elegant lemon-gold surfaces are strongly lustrous with a hint of honey. Well-defined and marvelously appealing, a fantastic near-Gem. PCGS has graded 67 finer examples (2/09).(#7942)

2706 1911 MS64 NGC. Strong gold-orange luster with winning eye appeal. A well-defined example for this earlier Philadelphia issue that shows few marks.(#7942)

2707 1911 MS64 NGC. Well-defined with bright, almost brassy luster. The strike is particularly solid on the peripheral devices, compared to the norm. Modestly marked and pleasing.(#7942)

2708 1911 MS64 PCGS. Rich yellow and sun-gold color abounds on this shining near-Gem. Well struck overall with only a small graze below the T in LIBERTY precluding a finer designation. (#7942)

2709 1911-D—Mount Removed, Improperly Cleaned—NCS. AU Details. Formerly affixed to jewelry at 12 o'clock. The mount was removed and the area smoothed, which affects the ER in LIBERTY. The R has been re-engraved. An oval area opposite on the reverse at 6 o'clock has a scuffy surface. Glossy from cleaning. The mintmark is faint but unmistakable upon magnification. (#7943)

AU 1911-D Two and a Half

2710 1911-D AU50 PCGS. An attractively toned representative of this always popular series key. Rich orange patina predominates, which cedes to steel-gray on the highpoints and open fields. The mintmark is low relief but fully evident. Smooth overall with a few whispery hairlines on the upper reverse. Encapsulated in a green label holder.(#7943)

Key 1911-D Quarter Eagle, AU50

2711 1911-D AU50 PCGS. The light rub shows on the high points of the Indian's cheek, the eagle's beak and upper wing, but most of the original luster is still intact. The margins show pretty accents of lilac and mint-green, with the centers offering more traditional amber-gold patina. The mintmark is bold. Popular in all grades. This piece is certified in an old small-size PCGS holder.(#7943)

Choice AU 1911-D Two and a Half

2712 1911-D AU55 PCGS. This orange-gold key date quarter eagle has considerable luminous luster, and the mintmark is sharply defined. The strike is equally exemplary, and the fields are smooth save for inconsequential ticks near the motto and a solitary mark concealed within the headdress.
From The Ed Lepordo Collection, Part Two.(#7943)

Unworn 1911-D Quarter Eagle

2713 1911-D—Reverse Scratched—NCS. Unc Details. The lemon-gold surfaces of this series key show strong luster, and the detail on each side is laudable. Though the upper reverse shows an unfortunate staple scratch, the coin still displays beautifully and offers a comparatively affordable alternative to an MS61 or MS62 representative.(#7943)

Uncirculated 1911-D Two and a Half

2714 1911-D MS60 PCGS. Rich apricot-gold patination imbued with blushes of lilac and sky-blue adorns both sides of this '11-D key date. This is a well defined piece, including most of the feathers on the eagle's shoulder and a clear mint mark. Some light marks are visible in the raised fields. Housed in a green-label holder. (#7943)

Mint State Sharpness
1911-D Quarter Eagle

2715 1911-D—Ex-Jewelry—ICG. MS60 Details. This magnificently detailed but overly bright key date Indian quarter eagle has a bold mintmark and no obvious abrasions. The rims appear problem-free. Although wiped at one time with a jeweler's cloth, many collectors would nonetheless be proud to own it.(#7943)

Pleasing MS61 1911-D Quarter Eagle

2716 1911-D MS61 PCGS. An appealing Mint State representative of the most coveted Indian quarter eagle issue, one of just 55,680 pieces minted. The surfaces are lustrous yellow-gold with hints of deeper sun color close to the margins. Well-defined and minimally marked for the grade, with solid eye appeal.(#7943)

Famous 1911-D Quarter Eagle, MS63

2717 1911-D MS63 PCGS. Widely known as the key date Indian quarter eagle, the 1911-D had an original mintage of 55,680 coins, only about 20% of the next lowest mintage total. Because few examples were saved at the time of issue, most of those that survive today are in various circulated grades.

This splendid 1911-D quarter eagle has full yellow-gold luster with only a few minor abrasions, including a line of tiny marks on Liberty's cheek that prevent a higher grade. The strike is bold throughout, with one of the sharpest mintmarks we can remember handling.(#7943)

Key-Date 1911-D Quarter Eagle, MS64

2718 1911-D MS64 NGC. The 1911-D Indian Head quarter eagle boasts the lowest mintage of the series, with only 55,680 pieces coined. To quote David Akers, "This is by far the rarest and most valuable date of the Indian Head quarter eagle type." Many specimens are seen with a weak mintmark, but the D on the present coin is sharp. An exemplary strike imparts crisp definition to all design elements. The granular, matte-like surfaces are overlaid with rich, satiny mint luster, and are enhanced by light, even shades of red throughout. The only noticeable flaw is a small dark spot at the top of the eagle's legs.(#7943)

Appealing 1911-D Quarter Eagle, MS64

2719 **1911-D MS64 NGC.** The acknowledged key to the Indian Head quarter eagle series, the 1911-D is from a low mintage of only 55,680 pieces. This mintage is less than one-fourth the production figure of the next lowest issue, the 1914. Apparently, few examples were saved at the time of issue, and survivors are usually seen in lower Mint State grades. Specimens are often seen with a weak mintmark, but the D on this example is sharp. The strike is above average, with slight softness on the bottom feather in the headdress and the top of the eagle's wing. The surfaces display rich, satiny luster, overlaid by an even reddish patina. A few shallow handling marks are consistent with the grade.(#7943)

2720 **1912 MS63 PCGS.** Rich yellow-gold color with impressive luster. A highly desirable example for the Select designation, well struck and attractive.(#7944)

2721 **1912 MS63 NGC.** Boldly struck with intense apricot-gold coloration and shimmering mint luster. A couple of small marks are detected on the upper right reverse, including one just behind the eagle's head.(#7944)

2722 **1912 MS64 PCGS.** Lovely satiny luster with khaki-gold surfaces and excellent design definition. PCGS has only certified 59 finer examples of the date (2/09). A small dark toning spot is visible on the reverse.(#7944)

2723 **1913 MS64 NGC.** Rich yellow-gold color with glimpses of orange toning. A beautiful near-Gem, immensely lustrous with few distracting marks.(#7945)

2724 **1913 MS64 NGC.** Delightful yellow-gold patina graces this bright and lustrous representative. This sharply struck piece is remarkably clean for the grade, with only a couple of microscopic marks in the fields. A wonderful type coin. NGC has certified only 53 pieces finer (2/09).(#7945)

Gorgeous 1913 Indian Quarter Eagle, MS65

2725 **1913 MS65 PCGS.** This delightful Gem has amazing multi-hued toning over light yellow surfaces. Both sides are fully brilliant with frosty gold luster. Only a few tiny marks and abrasions are evident on each side, preventing a higher grade. Population: 86 in 65, 5 finer (2/09).(#7945)

2726 **1914 MS62 PCGS.** Warm sun-yellow luster invigorates each side. Though this well struck piece shows a scattering of the usual abrasions, the eye appeal remains high.(#7946)

Desirable MS64 1914 Quarter Eagle

2727 **1914 MS64 NGC.** Luminous peach-gold surfaces show occasional ruby accents. A well-defined and satiny near-Gem example of this lower-mintage Indian quarter eagle issue, not so elusive as the key 1911-D overall but of comparable condition rarity any finer than the MS64 designation. NGC has graded just 40 coins as Gem or better (1/09).(#7946)

Pleasing 1914-D Quarter Eagle, MS64

2728 **1914-D MS64 PCGS.** A gorgeous near-Gem, this quarter eagle has highly lustrous and frosty yellow-gold surfaces with delicate pink toning. A few marks on the cheek and other abrasions in the fields are all that keep it from the coveted MS65 grade level. PCGS has only certified 38 finer examples (1/09).(#7947)

Wonderful MS64 1914-D Quarter Eagle

2729 **1914-D MS64 NGC.** Bright yellow-gold with an almost brassy appearance on the reverse. This highly lustrous near-Gem, housed in a prior generation holder, offers excellent eye appeal with few marks. This D-mint issue is largely unavailable any finer, with just 30 numerically superior pieces known to NGC (1/09). (#7947)

Captivating MS64 1914-D Two and a Half

2730 **1914-D MS64 PCGS.** Light yellow-orange color prevails on each side, though hints of deeper sun-orange are noted near the rims. An appealing Choice coin, strongly lustrous with substantially above-average definition at the necklace. Just 38 Gem or better examples appear in the PCGS *Population Report*.(#7947)

Attractive 1914-D Quarter Eagle, MS64

2731 **1914-D MS64 PCGS.** A vibrantly lustrous example of this popular D-mint quarter eagle, shining yellow-orange with splashes of peach. Excellent definition, with the pendants and even Pratt's oft-obscured initials visible at the lower obverse. Carefully preserved and highly attractive. PCGS has graded 38 finer pieces (1/09). (#7947)

Near-Gem 1914-D Indian Quarter Eagle

2732 **1914-D MS64 NGC.** This is a boldly struck, satiny example with the faint outline of an extra inner rim on the obverse, and bolder inner rim on the reverse. The highly lustrous surfaces are more frosty than satiny, and the coloration is a pleasing shade of greenish honey-gold. This issue is relatively easy to obtain at the near-Gem level, but it becomes rare (and quite expensive) any finer. (#7947)

Elusive Near-Gem 1914-D Indian Quarter Eagle

2733 **1914-D MS64 NGC.** Bright and brilliant, with semiprooflike fields and boldly struck design elements. Several wispy die cracks are noted on the obverse. A luster graze on the Indian's cheekbone and jaw, and a few faint pinscratches in the reverse fields seem to limit the grade. The second-rarest Indian quarter eagle in Gem condition (behind the '11-D), according to Garrett and Guth. (#7947)

Boldly Defined 1914-D Quarter Eagle, MS64

2734 **1914-D MS64 PCGS.** The Denver Mint struck just three different quarter issues, including the 1911-D, 1914-D, and 1925-D. The first is the key issue of the series, and the last is a common date. In the middle falls the 1914-D from a mintage of 448,000 coins. The present is bold with rich yellow surfaces and a trace of orange patina. PCGS has only certified 38 finer pieces (2/09). (#7947)

2735 **1915 MS64 NGC.** Rich sun-gold color with glimpses of rose and wheat near the margins. This lustrous near-Gem is well struck with excellent overall eye appeal.(#7948)

2736 **1915 MS64 NGC.** An interesting Choice example from just before the design's decade-long hiatus, generally yellow-orange with an element of deeper pumpkin near the date. Strong visual appeal.(#7948)

Well Struck Gem 1915 Quarter Eagle

2737 **1915 MS65 PCGS.** The peach-gold surfaces of this Gem are joined by splashes of mint-green on the reverse, and yield pleasing luster. A well executed strike imparts sharp definition to the design features, including the eagle's shoulder, and both sides are nicely preserved. Encapsulated in a green label holder.(#7948)

Elusive Gem 1915 Two and a Half

2738 **1915 MS65 ICG.** Although workers at the Philadelphia Mint were presumably unaware of it at the time, the 1915 would be the final date from the mint until 1926. Gold coins no longer circulated, and export demand was removed by World War I. This is a handsome orange-red and apple-green example with unabraded fields and a meticulous strike.(#7948)

2739 **1925-D MS64 NGC.** Intense mint frost shimmers over both sides of this near-Gem, which grades more than two points higher than the typical survivor from this Denver Mint issue. Boldly struck and nicely preserved, with a few wispy nicks and pinscratches on each side.(#7949)

2740 **1925-D MS64 NGC.** Rich yellow-gold and wheat color with occasional orange accents. Satiny and pleasingly preserved for the design with a solid strike. Winning eye appeal.(#7949)

2741 **1925-D MS64 PCGS.** Warm sun-yellow surfaces show glimpses of wheat and orange. A well-defined and interesting Choice coin that shows few marks on either side.(#7949)

2742 **1925-D MS64 NGC.** Fresh yellow-gold luster with occasional hints of frostiness. A well struck Choice Mint State coin that offers excellent eye appeal for the grade.(#7949)

2743 **1925-D MS64 NGC.** The satiny surfaces are mattelike and clean, with crisply struck design elements and attractive honey-gold surfaces. The last branch mint quarter eagle of the series. (#7949)

2744 **1925-D MS64 NGC.** Sharply struck with an "extra", inner rim detected on each side. This is a highly frosty straw-gold near-Gem from the Denver Mint, with just a few trivial surface distractions. (#7949)

2745 **1925-D MS64 PCGS.** This near-Gem has clean, satiny surfaces that display light khaki-orange and rose toning. Surface marks are absolutely minimal for the grade.(#7949)

2746 **1925-D MS64 NGC.** Strongly lustrous with satiny wheat-gold surfaces. Occasional pink accents visit parts of the carefully preserved fields. Well-defined and interesting.(#7949)

Appealing Gem 1925-D Indian Quarter Eagle

2747 **1925-D MS65 NGC. CAC.** The lustrous surfaces are well preserved and clean on both sides. Faint parallel striations on the lower left obverse field are mint-made and undistracting. The subtly variegated toning includes elements of peach, mint-green, and rose. A well preserved and attractive Gem example of this final Denver Mint Indian quarter eagle issue.(#7949)

Elegant Gem 1925-D Quarter Eagle

2748 **1925-D MS65 NGC.** After a decade of idling, the quarter eagle denomination came back to life with this popular Denver issue. The present Gem is warmly lustrous with minimally marked yellow-gold surfaces. Only a tiny flaw in the right reverse field precludes a finer designation. NGC has certified 39 higher-graded examples (2/09). (#7949)

Captivating Gem 1925-D Quarter Eagle

2749 **1925-D MS65 NGC.** Peripheral peach toning encompasses the green-gold centers. The surfaces are pleasantly smooth, and the strike is precise save for the usual minor blending within the lower reaches of the headdress. A great example from this Denver-only year for quarter eagles, certified in a prior generation holder. (#7949)

2750 **1926 MS64 NGC.** Clearly nicer than the typical example, this near-Gem Indian quarter eagle displays shimmering mint frost and lovely honey-gold color. Not a rare coin at this grade level, but an appealing piece that would serve admirably for type purposes. (#7950)

2751 **1926 MS64 NGC.** Strong, frosty luster characterizes this near-Gem. On the obverse, the color is slightly dusky tan, while the reverse has paler yellow-gold.(#7950)

2752 **1926 MS64 NGC.** Rich orange-gold color with hints of dusky pink. Luminous surfaces show glimpses of twinkling luster at the margins. Appealing for this first 1920s Philadelphia quarter eagle issue.(#7950)

2753 **1926 MS64 PCGS.** Crisply detailed centers and uncommonly strong luster combine for powerful eye appeal. This elegant yellow-orange piece is beautifully preserved.(#7950)

Shimmering 1926 Gem Quarter Eagle

2754 **1926 MS65 PCGS.** Orange-gold and olive-green compete for territory across this shimmering, original Gem, and the design elements benefit from a sharp strike. Examination beneath a glass locates smooth surfaces, aside from a slender mark above the 19 in the date. Housed in a green label holder.(#7950)

Magnificent 1926 Quarter Eagle, MS65

2755 **1926 MS65 NGC. CAC.** While the 1926 is one of the most plentiful dates in the Indian Head quarter eagle series, it is improbable that many will achieve the technical quality and aesthetic appeal of the present Gem. Outstanding luster issues from well preserved surfaces meticulously blended in apricot-gold, mint-green, and lilac coloration. Exquisitely defined motifs top off the coin's magnificent eye appeal.(#7950)

2756 **1929 MS64 NGC.** Rich yellow-gold color with hints of frostiness in the fields. A marvelously appealing near-Gem example from this final Pratt quarter eagle issue.(#7953)

2757 **1929 MS64 NGC.** Subtly frosted with wheat-gold surfaces overall and hints of orange on the reverse. Strongly struck and attractive for this final quarter eagle issue.(#7953)

Appealing Gem Proof 1910 Quarter Eagle

Bold 1910 'Roman Finish' Quarter Eagle, PR66

2758 **1910 PR65 PCGS. CAC.** The second edition of David Akers' *Handbook of 20th Century United States Gold Coins 1907-1933* rather succinctly dismisses the anomalous recorded mintage of 682 proof coins as "simply too high in relation to the number of coins that have survived." The number is either a bookkeeping error, or a record mintage that was subsequently melted. In the latter scenario, the Mint, after producing the unpopular proofs in two different styles for 1908 and 1909, anticipated record sales for the 1910 that simply failed to materialize. Akers comments that the Mint probably released no more than 200 examples of the 1910 proof quarter eagle.

Nearly all of the 1910 proofs were produced with the so-called Roman or satin finish, a cross between a matte and mirrored texture. This is a remarkably attractive example, with scant evidence of contact save for a single, hair-thin scrape beneath the Indian's chin. The semireflective surfaces are consistently honey-gold, with broad and generous eye appeal. Population: 10 in 65, 6 finer (2/09). (#7959)

2759 **1910 PR66 NGC.** In the early part of the 20th century, there were essentially three different finishes used for proof coins. Initially the Liberty Head gold proofs had brilliant mirrored surfaces. They were followed by matte or "sandblast" finish coins that featured dull and non-reflective surfaces. The third finish is seen on this coin, featuring a satiny finish without a mirrored surface, but also lacking the normal mint frost seen on most circulation strike coins.

This boldly defined "Roman Finish" Premium Gem proof has exquisite bright yellow surfaces with nary a blemish on either side. Few 1910 proof quarter eagles have survived in such high grade, with just 13 pieces that NGC has certified at finer grade levels (1/09). The finish is satiny with a fine-grained surface that exhibits faint die polishing lines in the fields on each side.(#7959)

Elusive 1913 Quarter Eagle, PR63

2760 **1913 PR63 PCGS.** A rare issue in proof format, like all matte proof coinage, the 1913 matte proof shows a combined survivorship between NGC and PCGS of 91 coins, less duplicates. The 1913 issue was struck with a fine-grained, multifaceted surface like the 1912 pieces. This example shows deep color somewhere between olive-green and olive-brown. A glancing scrape from the rear headdress feathers to near star 8 likely explains the grade. Population: 3 in 63, 28 finer (2/09).(#7962)

Pristine Matte PR67 1913 Quarter Eagle

2761 **1913 PR67 NGC.** The official mintage for 1913 proof quarter eagles was 165 pieces, and the number of survivors today is estimated to be in the range of 60 to 75 coins. This is an outstanding matte proof specimen with fine-grained surfaces that are pristine, as far as we can determine. Even upon close inspection using a jeweler's loupe, we see no spots, contact marks, or hairlines whatsoever. The design elements are flawlessly reproduced throughout. Lovely khaki-green and reddish-peach colors are beautifully intermingled across both sides. Simply impeccable technical quality, and truly magical eye appeal. Census: 11 in 67, 3 finer (2/09).(#7962)

THREE DOLLAR GOLD PIECES

2762 **1854—Mount Removed—NCS. XF Details.** Mounts have been removed at 3 and 9 o'clock on the reverse, with the nearby rim repaired and the fields sunken and smoothed. The reverse also displays two lengthy straight pinscratches, presumably used to guide placement in jewelry.(#7969)

2763 **1854 AU55 PCGS.** This piece is well struck and still shows a great deal of luster. Rich lime-green and reddish patina are noted, along with faint highpoint wear on both sides. First year of issue and always a popular date with collectors.(#7969)

Smooth 1854 Three Dollar MS62

2764 **1854 MS62 PCGS.** This minimally abraded piece is deep yellow-gold aside from a wisp of steel-gray on the cheek. Luster traverses the designs, and the eye appeal is superior. The first-year 1854 issues also comprise a single-year type, since DOLLARS is larger on subsequent dates.(#7969)

Delightful 1854 Three, MS63

2765 **1854 MS63 PCGS.** A pleasing first-year three dollar gold coin, this Select Mint State piece has satiny yellow-gold luster, bold design features, and high-quality surfaces for the grade. Curious raised spines are visible between the LI and IB of LIBERTY. The reverse has light clash marks that are typical of these coins.(#7969)

Lustrous and Richly Patinated MS64 1854 Three Dollar

2766 **1854 MS64 NGC. CAC.** Always popular as the first year of the unusual three dollar type, it is a fortuitous coincidence that large numbers were set aside at the time of issue. This is an especially well-preserved example, as verified by the CAC sticker. The mint luster is especially thick on this piece and each side shows pronounced reddish color with subtle streaks of lilac on the reverse. The devices are sharply struck, and the only mark that keeps this piece from a Gem grade is a short mark just behind Liberty's nose.(#7969)

2767 **1854 MS66 NGC.** Compared to the straightforward treatment accorded the other gold denominations, the Garrett and Guth overview of the three dollar coin in their *Encyclopedia of U.S. Gold Coins* begins with a paragraph that borders on arch:

> "Introduced in 1854, the $3 gold coin's primary purpose was to facilitate the purchase of sheets of 100 postage stamps—in other words, it was the rich man's three-cent piece. Today, their 'numismatic purpose' often is to compete sets of gold type coins, particularly the 12-piece sets [that cover all basic designs and denominations]. Because they are one of the most valuable coins in the set, the $3 piece is usually the last one needed or added."

Later, Garrett and Guth quote Q. David Bowers, who suggests that while "It could have been that the owner of a $3 piece could have purchased a sheet of 100 three-cent stamps without requiring change, or could go to a bank and easily obtain 100 silver trimes," any such theory is "a stretch in reasoning."

Meanwhile, the logic for numismatists is clear: The coins exist, so they can be collected! A coin such as this Premium Gem is a notable prize, coming from the highest-mintage year of issue, which also happened to be its debut (a clear sign, echoed in the two cent piece and three cent nickel, that a denomination either rapidly became obsolete or was unnecessary in the first place). Smooth surfaces sport swirling yellow-orange luster, and the sharply struck devices are as carefully preserved as the fields. Each side borders on faultlessness to the unaided eye. Census: 6 in 66, 1 finer (2/09). (#7969)

2768 **1854-O Fine 15 PCGS.** The 1854-O is popular as the sole New Orleans issue of the denomination. Its mintage of 24,000 pieces is low, since the facility concentrated on Seated coinage that year. This green-gold and sun-yellow example exhibits wear appropriate to its grade, but is without any bothersome abrasions.(#7971)

Scarce XF 1854-O Three Dollar

2769 **1854-O XF40 PCGS.** The sole O-mint issue of this popular denomination, which makes an example necessary to complete a New Orleans type set. Customary for the '54-O, the present piece has a lapped wreath bow and a die crack to the rim from the right ribbon end. Well detailed, and luster glimmers within the coronet. The subdued and clean pale gold surfaces are bereft of mentionable abrasions.(#7971)

2770 **1855 XF45 ICG.** A satiny, faintly hairlined example with slightly muted luster. The khaki-gold surfaces show a few minor nicks and a pair of shallow planchet flaws located, respectively, near UN and T in UNITED.(#7972)

2771 **1855 AU58 NGC.** Yellow-gold surfaces exhibit a fair amount of contrast when the coin is tilted just slightly beneath a light source. Well defined, except for weakness on the ribbon bow. Light circulation marks are visible over each side.(#7972)

Historic 1855-S Three Dollar, XF40

2772 **1855-S XF40 NGC.** The first S-mint three dollar issue, the 1855-S was produced to the extent of only 6,600 coins. Examples are in demand in all grades, both for the desirability of the odd three dollar denomination in general and the historicity of early S-mint gold. Considerable luster remains for the grade on both sides, and the yellow-gold surfaces are relatively free of singular contact. The slanting 5s preferred by Mint Chief Engraver James B. Longacre, visible here, are to this cataloger a plus.(#7973)

Desirable Choice XF 1855-S Three

2773 **1855-S XF45 NGC.** The first three dollar gold issue produced at San Francisco, the 1855-S, amounted to just 6,600 pieces, a paltry figure but one that is in line with the modest mintages of later years. This example shows light but distinct wear on the high points, though marks are few on the butter-yellow surfaces. Strong eye appeal. Census: 42 in 45, 56 finer (1/09).(#7973)

Lightly Circulated 1855-S Three Dollar, AU50

2774 **1855-S AU50 PCGS.** The forehead and hair show slight wear, but noticeable luster glimmers from the tan-gold surfaces. A mere 6,600 pieces were struck for this difficult issue, the first of the three dollar gold denomination from the then-new San Francisco Mint. Population: 9 in 50, 18 finer (10/08).(#7973)

Rare AU 1855-S Three Dollar

2775 **1855-S AU50 ANACS.** Although its Philadelphia Mint counterpart is plentiful by the standards of the type, the 1855-S is very scarce regardless of grade. Just 6,600 pieces were coined, since the fledgling San Francisco Mint concentrated on double eagles, which were desperately needed for large Gold Rush financial transactions. This example has unblemished fields and only moderate highpoint wear.(#7973)

2776 **1856 AU58 NGC.** Rich butter-yellow color with soft, pleasing luster remaining in the fields. Well-defined devices show just a trace of rub on the high points.(#7974)

2777 **1856-S XF40 NGC.** Light wear is concentrated largely at the high points. The deep lemon-gold fields retain considerable luster, though they also show a number of marks.(#7975)

2778 **1856-S XF40 NGC.** Breen-6356. Small S mintmark. Glimpses of luster outline the devices and legends. Wear is generally restricted to Liberty's curls and brow on the obverse. San Francisco three dollar pieces are scarce. Just 34,500 pieces were struck.(#7975)

Elusive 1856-S Three Dollar Gold, AU58

2779 **1856-S AU58 NGC.** Medium S. Somewhat bright and lightly hairlined, with nearly complete design detail on both sides. A slight degree of wear is noted on Liberty's hair. This issue had a modest mintage of 34,500 pieces, and, while not rare, becomes scarce any finer than XF. The current example seems nicer than average for the grade.(#7975)

2780 **1857 AU53 NGC.** Well struck for this earlier three dollar issue with bright yellow-gold surfaces that are modestly worn and only lightly abraded. Faint clash marks are visible on the reverse. (#7976)

2781 **1857-S PCGS Genuine.** Our grading XF Details, Ex-Jewelry. The area to the left of the mintmark shows evidence of disturbed metal, such as might be seen where a mount was removed. Otherwise, a lightly worn example with wheat-gold fields and a handful of abrasions, including one that crosses the 7 in the date. (#7977)

2782 **1859—Cleaned—ANACS. AU55 Details.** Well struck with light wear across the high points. Modestly hairlined yellow-gold surfaces show remnants of original luster and traces of tan.(#7979)

2783 **1859 AU55 NGC.** A remarkably clean and attractive Choice AU example of this three dollar gold issue. The rich khaki-gold toning is imbued with strong elements of rose. Faint hairlines are noted in the fields.(#7979)

Desirable MS61 1859 Three Dollar Gold

2784 **1859 MS61 PCGS.** The production increase the three dollar gold denomination enjoyed from 1858 to 1859 was short-lived, and the next year, the downward spiral of mintages continued. This unworn piece from a small five-figure mintage has luminous yellow-gold surfaces that show elements of orange. Minimally marked and pleasing. Population: 13 in 61, 72 finer (1/09).(#7979)

Scarce Select 1860 Three Dollar

2785 **1860 MS63 PCGS.** This date is scarce in all grades and is extremely difficult to locate in Mint State. Like nearly all surviving Mint State examples of this issue, the surfaces have frosty and brilliant yellow-gold luster and the design elements are sharply detailed. In addition to 7,036 business strikes that were coined in January 1860, the Philadelphia Mint produced 119 proofs, which were made after the business strikes. Population: 11 in 63, 15 finer (2/09).(#7980)

2786 **1860-S VF35 PCGS.** The 7,000 business strikes of the 1860-S would prove to be the last regular-issue three dollar gold pieces struck at San Francisco. This Choice VF piece is luminous with hints of dusky tan mingling with the dominant yellow-gold of the surfaces.(#7981)

Low Mintage 1861 Three Dollar, Choice AU

2787 **1861 AU55 PCGS. CAC.** Although mintages rose for most gold denominations in 1861, the three dollar was an exception. Only 5,959 pieces were coined. The present example has original green-gold toning aside from protected areas that display peach luster. Slight highpoint friction confirms only a brief stint in commerce. (#7982)

Exceptional 1861 Three Dollar, AU55

2788 **1861 AU55 PCGS. CAC.** An incredible representative of the rare 1861 three dollar gold piece, this example is housed in a green label holder and retains exceptional aesthetic appeal. The mintage was a mere 5,959 coins at the start of the Civil War. The attractive lemon-yellow surfaces are satiny and lustrous, with only a few scattered and unimportant marks. Population: 29 in 55, 65 finer (2/09).(#7982)

Lovely 1861 Select Three Dollar

2789 1861 MS63 PCGS. This lovely piece, from a low mintage of only 5,959 coins, is an exceptional Select Mint State representative with satiny surfaces, bold design features, and delightful orange-gold luster. Distributed minute marks limit the grade. Population: 14 in 63, 14 finer (2/09).(#7982)

Attractive 1863 Three Dollar, AU53

2790 1863 AU53 NGC. This Civil War-era date has a mintage of only 5,000 pieces, but examples are obtainable up through AU55. This AU53 piece shows much luster still remaining. While there are light abrasions and wear as expected, there are no singular abrasions noted. The surfaces are honey-gold, with some pretty pinkish overtones around the devices. An attractive piece from the historic 1860s decade.(#7984)

Appealing 1864 Three Dollar, MS62

2791 1864 MS62 PCGS. Bowers estimates in his 2005 reference volume on the series that only 200 coins exist from the original mintage of 2,600 pieces, "of which nearly all show evidence of wear, sometimes extensive." The average grade of the certified survivors at NGC and PCGS—surely the top end of all known examples—is Choice AU or so. The present coin is expectedly prooflike, with minor field chatter appearing on the appealing yellow-gold surfaces. A couple of minor abrasions on Liberty's cheek help determine the grade. Population: 16 in 62, 14 finer (2/09).(#7985)

Desirable 1865 Three Dollar, AU53

2792 1865 AU53 PCGS. The coloration is unusual but quite appealing, with rose-pink shades around the protected device areas complementing mint-green overtones in the still-lustrous regions of the fields. This lower-mintage Civil War-era issue is well-defined, although light wear crosses the high points. Scattered wispy marks contribute to the grade. Population: 12 in 53, 31 finer (2/09).(#7986)

2793 1866 XF45 PCGS. A lightly worn but pleasing example of this lower-mintage issue, yellow-gold with hints of deeper sun color near the rims. Strong luster remains in the fields.(#7987)

Elusive Near-Mint 1866 Three Dollar

2794 1866 AU58 NGC. A crisply struck apricot-gold Borderline Uncirculated example. Tiny field marks are distributed, but none merit singular mention. A scant 4,000 pieces were struck, and unlike later dates, relatively few pieces were hoarded by Philadelphia-area dealers. Census: 35 in 58, 41 finer (2/09).(#7987)

Lustrous 1866 Three Dollar, MS61

2795 1866 MS61 NGC. This is a mighty attractive coin from the original mintage of only 4,000 coins. While a loupe reveals a couple of scrapes and ticks in the obverse fields, the excellent luster and pretty orange-gold coloration, with faint tinges of ice-blue, more than compensate. Census: 23 in 61, 16 finer (2/09). (#7987)

2796 1868 XF40 PCGS. Vibrant yellow-orange luster has persisted despite the wear on the high points. A well struck example that shows a few light abrasions on the cheek, hence the grade. (#7989)

Spectacular 1870 Three Dollar, MS64

2797 **1870 MS64 NGC.** For a number of years after the Civil War, gold and silver coins were rarely seen in commerce. Instead, they were hoarded by those people who could afford to do so. As a result, the Philadelphia Mint produced small amounts of coins at the time, seeing little reason to produce coinage that would also be hoarded. James Pollock addressed the situation in the 1870 Mint report: "...Emerging from a tremendous Civil War which shook every social interest to the very foundation, it is no wonder that our currency continues in an abnormal condition. Most of our people rarely get the sight of a gold or silver coin."

This amazing example is tied for the finest that NGC or PCGS has ever certified. It is fully lustrous and satiny with brilliant orange-gold surfaces and faint pink highlights. Few grade-limiting surface marks are evident on either side. Census: 3 in 64, 0 finer (2/09).(#7991)

Choice AU 1871 Three Dollar Gold

2798 **1871 AU55 NGC.** Light but distinct wear crosses the high points of this briefly circulated three dollar gold piece, which hails from an issue of just 1,300 business strikes. Generally bright yellow-gold surfaces show a slight duskiness when away from a light source. The fields show a few minor distractions, such as a line of shallow reed marks to the right of the portrait and a shallow pinscratch just above and to the right of the knot in the bow on the reverse. (#7993)

Seldom-Seen Choice AU 1872 Three Dollar Gold

2799 **1872 AU55 PCGS.** The 1872 is a much better date. A stingy 2,000 pieces were struck, and most of the couple hundred survivors are in XF or AU grades. The present coin has prooflike luster throughout the legends and about the devices. There are no mentionable marks, and any collector would be proud to show it.(#7994)

Prooflike 1872 Three Dollar, MS62

2800 **1872 MS62 PCGS.** An amazing example of a scarce date, seldom encountered finer. This 1872 three dollar piece has fully mirrored fields with deep orange-gold surfaces. The low business-strike mintage of 2,000 pieces is responsible for the considerable prooflikeness appearing throughout, with pretty yellow-orange color, a few stray, undistracting abrasions, and some light field chatter. The devices are highly lustrous and the overall appearance resembles that of a Cameo proof, although it is clearly a business strike. The reverse die is rotated perhaps 20 degrees counterclockwise from the obverse. Population: 16 in 62, 10 finer (2/09).(#7994)

2801 **1874 XF40 NGC.** An evenly worn example of this popular date. Original reddish-tinted surfaces show only a handful of shallow flaws on the obverse. An ideal circulated type coin.(#7998)

2802 **1874 XF45 NGC.** A lightly worn mustard-gold example of this popular type issue, minimally marked with above-average definition. Considerable eye appeal for the grade.(#7998)

2803 **1874 AU53 PCGS.** Strong yellow-gold color with a touch of pink-orange at the upper obverse. Light but distinct wear crosses the highest design elements.(#7998)

2804 **1874 AU58 NGC.** With flashy luster and just a trace of friction across the high points, this light yellow-gold example would be ideal for a near-Mint State type set. Minimally marked with great eye appeal.(#7998)

2805 **1874 AU58 NGC.** Bright yellow-gold patina enhances both sides of this resplendent specimen. Although the highpoints show light rub, bright mint luster dominates the remarkably clean surfaces. Well struck overall and a great type coin.(#7998)

2806 **1874 AU58 NGC.** A lustrous example that appears to be very close to Mint State. The rich green-gold and reddish coloration is this coin's best attribute. Wispy hairlines and a few shallow marks limit the grade.(#7998)

Undisturbed MS62 1874 Three Dollar

2807 **1874 MS62 PCGS.** A lovely representative whose sun-gold and lime surfaces display only a few minor marks. Boldly struck and pleasing for this often lackluster grade. The 1874 has a higher mintage than surrounding dates, perhaps because the Treasury anticipated Federal paper money would finally trade at par with gold, which would allow three dollar pieces to again circulate in commerce.(#7998)

Brilliant 1874 Three Dollar, MS63

2808 **1874 MS63 PCGS.** Although it is a common date, and many similar quality or higher grade examples survive, this piece has exceptional luster for the grade. Both sides are bright yellow with hints of pink toning. A few scattered and entirely trivial surface marks are expected at the Select Mint State grade level. (#7998)

Attractive MS64 1874 Three Dollar Gold

2809 **1874 MS64 PCGS.** With strong, swirling luster and an excellent strike on the fine details of Liberty's hair, this orange-kissed yellow-gold survivor offers amazing eye appeal. Only a few tiny marks in the fields preclude Gem status. This type issue is a rarity any finer; PCGS has certified just 12 higher-grade examples (2/09). (#7998)

Impressive 1874 Three Dollar, MS64

2810 **1874 MS64 PCGS.** An extraordinary three dollar gold piece, this 1874 is fully lustrous with hints of green and lovely orange toning over the brilliant yellow-gold surfaces. Both sides are impressively free of distracting marks, with only the tiny ticks that one expects on a near-Gem. PCGS has only certified 12 finer examples (2/09). (#7998)

Attractive 1877 Three Dollar, MS61

2811 1877 MS61 PCGS. The paltry production of business strikes in this year amounted to only 1,468 pieces for a denomination that had long since become a quaint anachronism. The surfaces are prooflike as expected, and although some abrasions, field chatter, and a mediocre planchet and strike account for the grade, without a loupe the piece appears rather undergraded and quite attractive. Bowers' 2005 reference on the denomination estimates that only seven to 11 Mint State coins exist. The piece is lustrous throughout, with highly contrasted orange-gold surfaces that show strike weakness at the bottom and sides of the wreath and on the headdress feathers. The population data are almost certainly inflated by resubmissions. Population: 5 in 61, 4 finer (2/09). (#7999)

2812 1878 AU53 PCGS. A reasonable amount of design detail remains evident for the grade. Both sides display lime and red-gold coloration. The fields show some wispy hairlines.(#8000)

2813 1878 AU58 NGC. Ex: Las Vegas Collection. This straw-gold piece is softly struck and faintly worn on the highpoints. There are wispy hairlines in the fields, but abrasions are minimal for a lightly circulated coin.(#8000)

2814 1878—Reverse Scratched—NCS. Unc Details. Both sides offer impressive luster and strong detail. While the wheat-gold obverse displays beautifully, the reverse shows a horizontal scratch to the left of the 3 in the denomination.(#8000)

2815 1878 PCGS Genuine. Our grade Uncirculated Details, Reverse Cleaned. Strongly struck with vibrant, swirling luster on the yellow-gold obverse. Though the reverse has been dulled by cleaning, the coin still displays attractively.(#8000)

Favored 1878 Three Dollar Gold, MS62

2816 1878 MS62 PCGS. A favored issue among type collectors, the 1878 three dollar gold issue had an original mintage of 82,304 pieces, which is high for the series. Only the 1854 had an even higher business strike production of 138,618 coins. This example is well struck and nicely preserved, with rich coloration and few marks on either side. It is housed in an early PCGS holder with a green label.(#8000)

Shimmering MS64 1878 Three Dollar

2817 1878 MS64 NGC. Rich, shimmering luster and deep orange-gold toning are hallmarks of this unusually attractive near-Gem. Even under close scrutiny with a loupe, the surfaces appear minimally disturbed. A well struck example of the second-largest issue in the three dollar gold series, an ideal choice for type collectors. (#8000)

Fantastic Near-Gem 1878 Three Dollar Gold

2818 1878 MS64 NGC. Paul M. Green, in an October 10, 2006 article for *Numismatic News*, suggests that the reason for the unusually high coinage of three dollar pieces in 1878 was "due to the government preparing for 1879, which under the terms of the Resumption Act, would see paper [money] and gold coins trading as equals again for the first time since 1861." Whatever the reason, the 1878 has long proved a boon for gold type collectors. This near-Gem is no exception, with slightly dusky yellow-gold surfaces that are nonetheless immensely lustrous.(#8000)

Charming MS64 1878 Three Dollar

2819 **1878 MS64 NGC.** Garrett and Guth note for this issue: "The 1878 issue usually features a rich, coruscating luster and good to great eye appeal." The present near-Gem follows type to the hilt, with swirling wheat-gold luster invigorating each side. Well struck and immensely appealing, a wonderful type coin.(#8000)

Popular 1878 Three Dollar Gold, MS64

2820 **1878 MS64 NGC.** Attractively toned in peach shades, which are slightly deeper in hue on the reverse. The coruscating surfaces are only minimally abraded. The ARS in DOLLARS and the upper right portion of the wreath exhibit minor die doubling, as often seen on this issue. The loops of the 8s in the date display subtle recutting.(#8000)

Near-Gem 1878 Three Dollar

2821 **1878 MS64 PCGS.** A lovely orange-gold near-Gem that boasts an exemplary strike and coruscating cartwheel luster. Only a few faint field grazes exclude an even finer third party assessment. The 1878 is a frequent choice for gold type set collectors, who soon realize the scarcity of the denomination.(#8000)

Worthy Choice 1878 Three Dollar

2822 **1878 MS64 PCGS.** Orange and rose-red enrich this lustrous and attractively toned near-Gem. Smooth aside from a delicate obverse luster graze past 6 o'clock. While the collector may locate only 1878 three dollar pieces in the marketplace, few will demonstrate the rich original patina of the present representative.(#8000)

Wonderful Gem 1878 Three Dollar Gold

2823 **1878 MS65 NGC.** A wonderful type coin, the 1878 three dollar gold is the obvious late-series choice for type collecting. While the 1854 and 1874 also have relatively large mintages for the series, the earlier coins are seldom found in the highest Mint State grades, the Gem level or finer. This piece displays delightful orange-gold coloration on both sides, with flowing luster over the smooth, creamy surfaces and essentially no contact beyond the most minor sort. NGC has certified a few dozen finer, but they are likely held in some strong hands in today's "interesting times." Expect fervent bidding on this coin.(#8000)

Exquisite Gem 1878 Three Dollar Gold

2824 **1878 MS65 NGC.** Between the fine detail on Liberty's hair, the textured, swirling luster of the pale lemon-gold fields, and the remarkably well-preserved nature of the surfaces, even the most discerning collector will find plenty to enjoy on this three dollar gold Gem. The 1878 three dollar issue is the last chronologically among the trio of popular type issues for the denomination (the others being the 1854 and 1874), with an unusually large mintage of over 82,000 pieces that was saved in quantity. Even so, anything finer than this coin is scarce, and type enthusiasts should take notice.(#8000)

Lovely MS64 1879 Three Dollar

2825 **1879 MS64 PCGS.** Light yellow-gold color overall with potent, swirling luster. The boldly impressed central devices are pleasingly preserved for the grade. After the last high-mintage issue of three dollar gold pieces the previous year, production for 1879 fell to a token 3,000 business strikes.(#8001)

Radiant 1880 Three Dollar, MS62

2826 **1880 MS62 PCGS.** The mintage for the 1880 three dollar issue was even more meager than the years surrounding it, a picayune 1,000 business strikes and 36 recorded proofs. The surfaces on this radiant yellow-gold example are expectedly prooflike, especially in protected areas around the lettering and central devices. Some light field chatter and minor abrasions account for the grade, but much eye appeal emanates from this delightful coin.(#8002)

Famous 1881 Three Dollar, AU58

2827 **1881 AU58 NGC.** With just 500 business strikes produced, the 1881 has the lowest mintage of any three dollar gold issue made for circulation. This impressively lustrous yellow-gold piece is well-defined and shows just a touch of rub across the high points. Census: 40 in 58, 32 finer (2/09).(#8003)

Low Mintage 1882 Three Dollar AU58

2828 **1882 AU58 PCGS. CAC.** An attractive slider with plentiful luster, a bold strike, and an unmarked appearance. The date for the 1882 was obviously entered using two logotype punches, an 188 and a 2. The 2 was initially entered much too high. That 2 was partially effaced from the die, then the 2 was entered again, this time slightly too low. This feature is plain on the entire business strike mintage of just 1,500 pieces. *From The Burning Tree Collection.*(#8004)

Extremely Rare 1883 Three, MS64 ★

2829 **1883 MS64 ★ NGC.** At first glance this important business strike actually looks like a proof due to its fully mirrored fields and satiny devices. The light yellow surfaces have hints of the watery or wavy surface that is typical of proof gold coins. The borders on both sides have pale lemon-yellow color.

The 1883 three dollar gold piece is extremely popular due to its low mintage of just 900 business strikes. Another 89 proofs were also coined. The current NGC Census Report shows that just two 1883 three dollar pieces have been certified in MS64 ★ , the only Star designated examples of the date (2/09).(#8005)

Lovely 1885 Three Dollar MS62

2830 **1885 MS62 PCGS.** Ex: South Texas Collection. A minuscule mintage of 801 pieces confirms the rarity of this much better three dollar date. This is a sharply struck example with clean surfaces, attractive peach toning, and moderate field reflectivity. Population: 19 in 62, 58 finer (2/09).(#8007)

Important 1885 Three Dollar Gold, MS64

2831 **1885 MS64 PCGS. CAC.** In 1885 the Philadelphia Mint coined a mere 801 circulation strikes and 109 proofs of the three dollar gold piece, perhaps prompting Thomas Elder to state that this date was the rarest of all later three dollar issues. By the 1880s, the denomination was essentially obsolete. It was originally issued to aid in the sale of postage stamps, as the postal rate in 1854 was three cents. That rate eventually dropped to two cents as costs declined, and the three dollar gold piece was no longer necessary.

This remarkable example is boldly detailed with bright orange-gold surfaces. The fields are fully mirrored as usual for the low mintage issue. Trivial surface marks prevent a higher grade but do little to distract the viewer. Population: 29 in 64, 16 finer (2/09). (#8007)

2832 **1886 XF45 NGC.** Lovely lilac patina graces the rims of this low-mintage survivor from late in the Indian Princess three dollar series, with orange-gold centers and good eye appeal. A few light marks are consistent with the Choice XF grade, but none is individually distracting. Just 1,000 business strikes were coined.(#8008)

Lovely Choice AU 1886 Three Dollar Gold

2833 **1886 AU55 PCGS.** A lovely Choice AU representative with essentially complete design detail remaining on both sides, along with mere traces of high point wear on the obverse. Minuscule hairlines are prominent in the obverse and reverse fields, preventing a higher grade assessment, but severe marks or abrasions are absent. (#8008)

Impressive Prooflike 1886 Three Dollar, MS62

2834 **1886 MS62 PCGS.** An impressive prooflike example of this important issue from a mintage of only 1,000 circulation strikes, with sharp design elements, mirrored fields, and wonderful orange-gold coloration. The surfaces are delightful, with few blemishes on either side. Although some dates are rarer, the low production total of this issue explains its limited availability. Population: 16 in 62, 11 finer (2/09).(#8008)

High-End 1888 Three Dollar, MS62

2835 **1888 MS62 PCGS.** Among the more common issues from the later series in high grade. The present example shows some doubling on UNITED, a diagnostic of the business strikes. This piece has spectacular deep orange-gold coloration with tinges of jade at the obverse borders. Although a few stray abrasions account for the grade, the eye appeal and overall aesthetic quality appear high-end for the assigned level.(#8010)

Low Mintage 1888 Three Dollar, MS65

2836 **1888 MS65 PCGS.** In the penultimate year for the denomination, only 5,000 business strike 1888 three dollar gold pieces were minted. Melting may have further limited the supply of these coins per a comment by S.H. Chapman, "Of the later years of the $3, large numbers were remelted at the Philadelphia Mint." In spite of these circumstances, the 1888 is an available issue today, in the context of the series. Business strikes of this date frequently show a mixture of cartwheel luster and semi-prooflike finish in the fields, and the present coin is a good example of this combination. The strike is remarkably sharp for this issue, with nearly complete definition on all design elements. The bright yellow-gold color is accented by a faint, reddish patina on both sides. Population: 83 in 65, 30 finer (2/09).(#8010)

Beautiful 1888 Three Dollar, MS65

2837 **1888 MS65 NGC. CAC.** From a small business strike mintage of just 5,000 pieces, the 1888 three dollar gold piece is surprisingly available today. Q. David Bowers estimates a surviving population of 550-750 examples in all grades, which correlates well with current population data. The high survival rate may be due to 19th century dealer J.W. Scott, who purchased a large group of coins from the Mint and distributed them to collectors in the normal course of business. Scott's hoard may have amounted to several hundred pieces, as he had them readily available for years after 1888.

The present coin is an attractive specimen, with a sharp, but not quite full strike. The devices are dripping with thick mint frost, and the play of colors on the surfaces is a visual treat. A lovely intermixture of rose and lilac shades on the obverse is matched by the even, reddish tones on the reverse. There are no observable handling marks to limit the grade. Census: 40 in 65, 22 finer (2/09).(#8010)

Elusive 1860 Three Dollar Gold, PR65

2838 **1860 PR65 NGC.** Ostensibly, 119 proof three dollar gold pieces were delivered by the coiner on April 5, 1860. However, the issue's appearances on the market are extremely infrequent. Numismatists believe most of those proofs went unsold and were melted at the Mint. Walter Breen speculated that many specimens were later spent or carried as pocket pieces until they became indistinguishable from business strikes. In *The United States $3 Gold Pieces 1854-1889*, Q. David Bowers reports, "Although Mint records state that 119 Proofs were struck, it is likely that no more than 20 were actually distributed. For decades the 1860 has been viewed as a first-class rarity among Proofs in the $3 series." Bowers goes on to estimate a surviving population of 10-12 examples.

Harry Bass noticed that proofs of this date were struck from the same dies as circulation strikes. The dies were simply repolished to produce a mirror finish. This process (called lapping) resulted in some loss of detail in certain areas. Longacre's initials, on the truncation of the neck, were nearly eradicated by the lapping, and the spacing of the obverse dentils was also disrupted.

The present coin is a small masterpiece of the coiner's art. Despite the aforementioned lapping, this coin features a sharp strike. Exquisite detail is present in the hair and feathers on the obverse, and in the wreath on the reverse. The fields are fully reflective, and complement the crisply delineated devices to produce fantastic eye appeal. This specimen is tied with two other pieces, one at PCGS and another at NGC, for the honor of finest certified. Census: 2 in 65, 0 finer (2/09).(#8023)

Rare 1882 Three Dollar, PR58

2839 **1882 PR58 PCGS.** A delightful, lightly circulated proof example, from a mintage of just 76 coins in 1882. Although a trace of rub is detected on the highpoints, and the fields exhibit myriad hairlines and abrasions, this specimen still retains excellent eye appeal. A desirable piece for the budget-minded collector of rarities. (#8046)

2840 **1887 PR66 Cameo NGC.** A review of empirical data sheds light on the habits and interests of late 19th century coin collectors. In 1887, two proof gold denominations were struck in comparable quantities. The quarter eagle proof mintage is recorded in Mint archives as 122 coins, against 160 three dollar pieces struck in the same year. Even the business strike figures for both issues are analogous, with approximately 6,000 coins produced for each denomination. Fast forward 121 years to the time of the current sale. A review of the combined NGC and PCGS population data reveals that 44 1887 proof quarter eagles have been certified in all grades, against a total of 183 three dollar gold pieces—more than the recorded mintage and surely the result of multiple resubmissions in pursuit of a higher designation. A study of auction appearances indicates a similar ratio.

How could the majority of the 1887 three dollar proof issue still exist to this day, while less than half of the proof quarter eagles of the same year survived the past century? The answer, in a word, is popularity. Proof three dollar gold pieces were desirable to collectors of the late 1800s just as they are to numismatists of our time. It is likely that other denominations struck in proof format, such as the quarter eagle referenced above, eventually found their way into circulation. At the turn of the century the collector value of a proof two and a half would have been close to the face value. Of course the same can be said of the three dollar, but the odd denomination and unfamiliar, quirky design provided an incentive to save such pieces, proof or otherwise.

Proof three dollar gold pieces are as popular today as ever. Even though the availability of 1887 proof threes is nearly four times as great as their quarter eagle counterparts, collector demand for the threes keeps the prices approximately twice as high. In reality, both issues are scarce—even rare—and cherished by aficionados of proof gold. The honey-gold specimen offered here is of memorable quality, displaying deep, dark fields that contrast elegantly with the cameo devices of both sides. And, as one would expect to find on a Premium Gem proof, the surfaces are well preserved and attractive. The orange peel effect observed on the obverse is common to the type and confirms its status as a genuine proof issue. Census: 21 in 66 Cameo, 11 finer, including those designated as Ultra Cameo (2/09).(#88051)

EARLY HALF EAGLES

Rare BD-9 1795 Small Eagle Five, AU Details

2841 **1795 Small Eagle—Mount Removed—NCS. AU Details.** Breen-6415, BD-9, High R.5. The many die varieties of 1795 half eagles provide a formidable challenge to the dedicated specialist. The 1795 Small Eagle has historic significance, since it represents the first gold issue from the U.S. Mint. This is a whizzed example with smoothed fields and softer definition on the devices, yet it suffices to provide a midrange example of this rare type.(#8066)

Desirable BD-4 1800 Five Dollar, AU Details

2842 **1800—Scratched—NCS. AU Details.** Breen-6439, BD-4, R.4. The distinctive reverse with repunched M in AMERICA, matched with the Blunt 1 obverse showing a flagless 1 in the date. Butter-yellow surfaces retain a surprising degree of radiance. Though several scratches on the portrait make the details grade necessary, this early half eagle will reward the collector who can look past its imperfections.(#8082)

Appealing 1800 Select Half Eagle, BD-5

2843 **1800 MS63 NGC.** Breen-6438, BD-5, High R.3. Attributed by the blunt 1 in the date, reverse star 13 touching the eagle's neck, both feet of last A in AMERICA touching the claw, and the last S of STATES over cloud space.

Yellow-gold and mint-green patina cover both sides of this Select example, and traces of luster reside in the recessed areas. Sharply defined design features are well centered on the planchet, and the dentilation is relatively strong. A few trivial marks keep from a higher grade, but do not detract from the overall appeal. Census for the issue: 25 in 63, 8 finer (2/09).(#8082)

Bright 1802 BD-7 Half Eagle, AU55

2844 **1802/1 AU55 NGC.** Breen-6440, BD-7, R.5. The 2 in the date touches the bust, the 1 is left of center in the two, and the reverse Ts are missing the right foot. The bright yellow-gold surfaces of this Choice AU example display whispers of apricot and pale green, along with relatively well defined design features. Each side reveals the expected number of marks seen on coins experiencing brief circulation.(#8083)

Luminous BD-1 1803/2 Half Eagle, XF40

2845 **1803/2 XF40 PCGS.** Breen-6441, BD-1, R.4. The obverse with missing right foot of the T in LIBERTY, the reverse with a weak arrowhead halfway below the N in UNITED. This lightly worn example offers a mixture of rich butter-yellow and "old-gold" colors. Modestly abraded overall, though a few small digs are noted at the margins. The line on the portrait is a possible adjustment mark. *From The Ed Lepordo Collection, Part Two.*(#8084)

Mint State Sharpness 1803/2 Half Eagle, BD-4

2846 **1803/2—Obverse Repaired, Improperly Cleaned—NCS. Unc Details.** Breen-6441, BD-4, R.4. BD State e/b. The only one of the four varieties for the year with a perfect T in LIBERTY. The reverse confirmation comes from star 12, whose two points respectively nearly touch the lower part of the beak and the ribbon below. The obverse field behind Liberty's head and below the stars has been repaired and shows a somewhat different texture than the remainder of that side. The surfaces are overbright from the noted cleaning. Nonetheless much pleasing detail is present, as expected for the Unc Details grade. A die crack extends through the lower date and thence through stars 1-6, while on the reverse a crack runs from the rim through the left (facing) wing, the shield, and E(RICA) back to the rim. There are no visible adjustment marks. (#8084)

Lustrous AU55 1804 Five Dollar, BD-1

2847 **1804 Small 8 AU55 PCGS.** Breen-6443, BD-1, High R.4. The 1 in the date has a blunt top, and the 8 is normal (formerly called the Small 8, but Bass and Dannreuther say it is the correct size). The 4 is small. There is a die crack from the rim through the 0, running upward into the portrait. On the reverse a straight graver's line appears, connecting the left (facing) shield point with the B in the motto, through star 12, and to the upper beak. TE are apart, with the right side of the upright of E above the break between two clouds.

A wonderful example with lustrous green-gold surfaces and light peripheral rose toning. The surfaces have a few typical abrasions, but overall this piece is fully consistent with the grade. (#8085)

Choice AU 1804 Overdate Five Dollar, BD-7

2848 **1804 Small 8 Over Large 8 AU55 NGC. CAC.** Breen-6442, BD-7, R.4. The date is dramatically repunched, most noticeably on the base of the 1 and the top of 8. This obverse die was paired with three different reverses; Miller-59 is promptly identified by the location of the upright of the E in STATES between two clouds. This impressive early half eagle is well struck and presents clear breast feathers. Light friction on the curls, cap, and drapery precludes a Mint State assessment, and only slight abrasions are present, which ensures the eye appeal. The upper left reverse border has a few faint adjustment marks, as made.(#8086)

Dramatic 1804 BD-7 Half Eagle, AU58
Small Date Over Large Date

2849 **1804 Small 8 Over Large 8 AU58 NGC.** Breen-6442, BD-7, R.4. This is one of the most dramatic and unusual repunched dates in all of American numismatics. Initially the date was placed in the die with punches that were probably intended for eagle dies, and the smaller half eagle digits were then punched on top of the 1 and 8, almost perfectly centered so that the 8 is completely outlined by the previous 8. Both sides have bright yellow surfaces with virtually complete luster, and only the usual quota of minor abrasions that are expected at this grade level.(#8086)

Near-Mint 1805 Half Eagle
Close Date, BD-2

2850 **1805 AU58 NGC.** Close Date, Breen-6445, BD-2, R.4. Bass-Dannreuther Obverse State g, Reverse State d. The BD-1 and BD-2 1805 half eagle varieties are the so-called Perfect 1, Close Date types, sharing a common obverse but with different reverses. This is the final, terminal die state of this variety, with numerous die cracks and clash marks noted on each side. This greenish-gold example is almost fully lustrous, with minimal highpoint wear and few marks on either side.(#8088)

Charming 1806 Round Top 6
Half Eagle, BD-6, AU55

2851 **1806 Round Top 6, 7x6 Stars AU55 NGC.** Breen-6448, BD-6, R.2. Also known in numismatic circles as the Round Top 6, 7x6 Stars, this "available" variety is much more often seen than the five Pointed 6, 8x5 Stars die marriages known. This piece has original orange-gold surfaces that have most of their original luster still intact, with much eye appeal present. While light high point wear and a few minor abrasions are as expected for the grade, there are no adjustment marks or singular contact in evidence on either side, save for a couple of faint scrapes on the cap. A charming Choice AU example suited for a nice type set.(#8089)

Popular 1806 Half Eagle, BD-6, MS62
Round Top 6, 7x6 Stars

2852 **1806 Round Top 6, 7x6 Stars MS62 NGC.** Breen-6448, BD-6, R.2. Six different die varieties are known for the 1806 half eagle, five varieties with a pointed 6 in the date, and the present BD-6 variety, with a round top, or knobbed 6. The Capped Head Right design was retired midway through 1807, but a substantial mintage of 64,093 pieces was accomplished in 1806. John Dannreuther believes 35,000 to 50,000 of these pieces were of the BD-6 variety, as it is the most available today. The surviving population is believed to total 600-900 examples in all grades. The issue's availability in Mint State makes it a logical choice for type collectors.

The present coin is an appealing example, with bright, semiprooflike fields and attractive yellow-gold color. The strike is uneven, as often seen, with the left obverse stars nearly complete, but the right stars weak. The reverse shows some softness on the shield and wings, and a few shallow adjustment marks over cloud 6 and at the right margin.(#8089)

Appealing 1806 Round Top 6
7x6 Stars Five, BD-6, MS62

2853 **1806 Round Top 6, 7x6 Stars MS62 NGC.** Breen-6448, BD-6,
R.2. Also known as Knobbed 6. BD Obverse/Reverse States d/e.
The reverse of this variety is shared with the R.7 BD-5, 1806
Pointed 6 variant. Bass and Dannreuther point out that the Pointed
6 *dies* were produced first, since the numeral and obverse letter
punches were created to replace the Knobbed 6 BD-6. But we can
also deduce that the BD-5 was *produced* first, as the BD-6 reverse
shows later die states than the common reverse of the BD-5.

Specifically here, after lapping the dies clashed again, showing
clash marks on the reverse in the region of stars 1, 7, 12, and the
eagle's beak nearby. More clashing appears above the arrowheads
in the field. An obverse rust lump shows on the upright of the R in
LIBERTY. A small die crack travels upward from the obverse rim
to the lowest hair curls, which are quite thin. Another crack runs
from the obverse rim to star 4. This piece offers pretty greenish-
gold color and generous, glowing luster, but the piece is struck
slightly off-center, missing the reverse denticulation above ED and
AM, respectively. There are no adjustment marks visible on either
side. An altogether interesting and desirable type coin, with much
eye appeal and historic value.(#8089)

Scarce 1807 Half Eagle, AU55
Small Reverse Stars, BD-1

2854 **1807 Bust Right AU55 NGC.** Small Date, Small Obverse Stars,
Small Reverse Stars, Breen-6449, BD-1, High R.4. Possibly from the
terminal die state of this reverse die, with a heavy rim cud above T in
UNITED. This Choice AU example is lightly worn across both sides,
with bold striking details and deep green-gold and red-orange toning.
A scarce die marriage which is seldom seen at any grade level.
(#8092)

AU Sharpness 1807 Bust Left Five, BD-8

2855 **1807 Bust Left—Damaged—NCS. AU Details.** Breen-6453,
BD-8, R.2. This first-year Capped Bust Left half eagle has original
olive-gold toning and impressive sharpness, but a mark on the
cap and a cluster of ticks on nearby stars have left a slight bend.
The reverse has minor rim nicks at 7 o'clock, 8:30, and 11:30.
(#8101)

Splendid MS61 1807 Bust Left Five, BD-8

2856 **1807 Bust Left MS61 NGC.** Breen-6453, BD-8, R.2. This new mid-1807 Capped Bust to Left design is the result of the Mint's hiring of John Reich in this year, a career that would last precisely 10 years. Reich's signature notched star, star 13, is seen on every issue of this design through 1817. On the BD-8, the lowest arrow fletchings are at the tip of the flag on the 5. This piece shows splendid antique-gold and greenish-gold surfaces with much luster evident. A faint scrape is noted at the rim near star 11, but abrasions are minor otherwise. Adjustment marks occur on the reverse, near the rim at AT in STATES and URI in the Latin motto below. (#8101)

Coveted 1807 Bust Left Five, BD-8, MS62

2857 **1807 Bust Left MS62 NGC.** Breen-6453, BD-8, R.2. A satiny and exactingly struck olive-gold representative. A loupe reveals a few wispy marks, but the surfaces are much nicer than it is often encountered for the grade. BD-8 is the most plentiful die pairing of the date, but as a gold type coin, it is extremely scarce. (#8101)

Impressive 1810 Capped Bust Left Five Small Date, Tall 5, BD-1, MS62

2858 **1810 Small Date, Tall 5 MS62 NGC. CAC.** Breen-6462, Miller 114, BD-1, High R.3. Four die varieties are known for the 1810 Capped Bust Left half eagle, of which BD-1 is the second most available. John Dannreuther estimates an original mintage of 20,000-30,000 pieces and a surviving population of 150-225 examples. Mint State specimens are scarce, but can be found with some patience.

The present coin is sharply struck, with full definition on all design elements except the lower hair curls. Thick mint luster and impressive reddish patina highlight the surfaces, and the superior visual appeal has resulted in the coveted CAC designation. Census: 19 in 62, 10 finer (2/09).(#8106)

Magnificent 1810 Capped Bust Left Five
Large Date, Large 5, BD-4, MS64

2859   1810 Large Date, Large 5 MS64 NGC. Breen-6459, BD-4, R.2. A large mintage of 100,287 half eagles was accomplished in 1810. The BD-4 variety, characterized by the large date and the squat, large 5 in the denomination, is the most available of the four die marriages of this popular issue. Its availability in Mint State makes this date the most popular choice with type collectors.

Historically, collectors have always prized the 1810 half eagle, as it is one of the few dates of the design type that has been readily available for study. Numismatists were making the distinction between Large Date and Small Date varieties at least as far back as 1890, when both types appeared in the Parmelee Collection (New York Coin & Stamp Company, 6/1890), lots 868 and 869. It is remarkable to find catalogers differentiating between die varieties at a time when most collectors did not even care about mintmarks.

While the Large Date, Large 5 may be the most commonly encountered type of this date, there is nothing common about it in MS64 condition. Demand will always outstrip supply for early gold type. This is a beautiful coin with thick mint luster that shows the attractive green-gold coloration usually seen on early U.S. gold. The striking details are sharp throughout and there are no singularly distracting blemishes on either side, just the usual accompaniment of small ticks and luster grazes. In the center of the reverse, there are a series of parallel roller marks, shallow lines impressed into the planchet as it was passed through large rollers that reduced the thickness of the planchet stock. Extraordinary eye appeal and great historic interest combine in this delightful offering. Census: 35 in 64, 7 finer (2/09).(#8108)

1811 Small 5 Half Eagle, BD-2, MS62

2860   1811 Small 5 MS62 NGC. Breen-6464, BD-2, R.3. Bass-Dannreuther Die State e/b with prominently clashed dies. This lemon-gold early half eagle has a lustrous reverse and full luster across the obverse periphery. Friction is minimal, and both sides are refreshingly devoid of singular abrasions. Only two die varieties are known for the 1811. The obverse die is the same, but the reverses are readily distinguished by the size of the 5. The Large 5 variety is believed moderately scarcer. Both marriages are much more elusive than the 1807 BD-8 or the 1810 Large Date, Large 5, BD-4. (#8109)

2861 **1811 Small 5 MS64 PCGS.** Breen-6464, BD-2, R.3. BD Die State e/b. Only one obverse die was used for this year, but it was paired alternately with Large 5 (the numeral in the denomination 5D) and Small 5 reverses. There was another reverse die used in 1810 that also has a Small 5, but the 1811 is a different reverse: On the 1810 Small 5 varieties (BD-2 and BD-3), the tip of the lowest arrow fletchings points to the tip of flag on the 5. On the 1811 Small 5, the feather tip is over the center of the flag.

Bass-Dannreuther note that while numismatists earlier considered the 1811 Large 5 with this obverse (BD-1) to be much scarcer, "auction data indicate this variety [BD-2] appears only 25 to 50 percent more often than the [BD-1]. Neither variety is scarce and both are available at all major coin shows and appear with frequency at auctions." The BD reference rates the BD-1 as High R.3 (175-250 known), and the BD-2 as R.3 (225-300 known).

Be that as it may, precious few of either variety are likely to approach the marvelous aesthetics of the present piece. The greenish-gold surfaces glow with generous, frosty luster, with some areas of prooflikeness seen close to the devices on each side. The few stray ticks are completely in line with the near-Gem level of preservation. The strike is uniformly bold and well-centered throughout, with no mentionable weakness in evidence. The reverse adds a dollop of cinnamon hues over the letters of AMERICA, and a faint apparent die grease stain in that same area fails to detract in any meaningful way.

The obverse show the faint "shield clash" below Liberty's ear, and the small die crack appears between stars 9 and 10. A tiny raised scribe line or straight die line in the reverse field, near the rim between (O)F and A(MERICA), appears unrecorded, and the "vertical lump on beak below nostril hole" is visible, as well.

With its wonderful combination of superior luster and eye appeal and its status as one of the more relatively "common" issues in this difficult U.S. series, this piece should be given serious consideration by the many potential bidders considering adding some high-grade early gold type to their numismatic holdings. Among the finest certified at PCGS. Population: 13 in 64, 0 finer (2/09).(#8109)

Splendid 1812 BD-1 Half Eagle, AU58

2862 **1812 AU58 NGC.** Wide 5D, Breen-6466, BD-1, R.3. A lovely 1812 half eagle with satiny luster and attractive medium yellow surfaces, faint traces of orange patina adding to its overall aesthetic appeal. Only a trace of high point wear prevents a Mint State grade assessment, and the surfaces have few imperfections to take away from its attractive appearance.(#8112)

2863 **1812 MS64 NGC.** Narrow 5D, Breen-6465, BD-2, High R.4. The two varieties of the 1812 half eagle both have the same obverse. The BD-1 has the reverse feather tip positioned over the right edge of the flag of the 5, and a widely spaced 5D, with the D wholly under the branch. BD-2, the Narrow 5D, has the D mostly under the feather. Perhaps an easier way to identify the two reverses is to inspect the I of PLURIBUS relative to STATES. BD-1 shows the I beneath the left serif of E, while the I is below the right serif of the second T on the BD-2 variety.

John Dannreuther and Harry Bass Jr., in their *Early U.S. Gold Coin Varieties* reference, estimate that 80 to 100 specimens of the scarcer BD-2 variety are known. The authors write that 300 to 450 of BD-1 are believed to exist. The 2009 *Guide Book* reports a mintage of 58,087 for the date.

MS64 is the highest grade that most collectors can expect to acquire of this date. NGC and PCGS have certified 14 Gems, a number of which are likely resubmissions. The finest graded 1812 half eagle is a PCGS MS66.

The lustrous brassy-gold surfaces of this near-Gem offering display hints of light tan, and give off a slight greenish cast. A well executed strike imparts strong definition to the design elements; the sole exception is minor softness on the upper right corner of the shield. While a few minor handling marks preclude Gem classification, they do not detract from the coin's overall appeal. Faint adjustment marks are visible at the obverse margins. Census: 36 in 64, 9 finer (2/09).(#8112)

Elusive 1814/3 Half Eagle, BD-1, AU58

2864 **1814/3 AU58 NGC. CAC.** Breen-6468, BD-1, High R.4. The 1814 overdate half eagle, the only variety of the year, is generally unrecognized as an important rarity in the series. It is much rarer than the 1813, but overshadowed by the 1815 half eagle. This near-Mint example has rich green-gold surfaces with excellent luster, and only a trace of high-point wear.(#8117)

2865 **1833 Large Date MS61 PCGS.** Breen-6498, BD-1, High R.5. The actual size of the digits in the Small Date and Large Date variants is just barely distinguishable, but the style of the number punches is distinctly different. The 3s on the Large Date have pronounced knobs and the 8 is more blocklike rather than the italic (or belted) style seen on the Small Date.

An article by Paul Gilkes in the June 26, 2000 issue of *Coin World* deals directly with the rarity of the 1829 half eagle, but the explanation applies just as effectively to the 1833:

"The main reason the 1829 Capped Head, Large Planchet half eagle is so difficult to obtain is that it and many of its predecessors fell victim to the great melts, a byproduct of the flood of Mexican and Peruvian silver. The influx of silver on the world market compared to gold supplies lowered the silver price, but appeared as an unstoppable increase in the value of gold reckoned in Mexican dollars. The result was widespread hoarding and melting of older gold coins when their bullion value exceeded their face value by enough to warrant a profit over the cost of melting. Tens of thousands of half eagles and other gold denominations of recent vintage were melted soon after their production and reclaimed ..."

As a result, few people in the 1820s and 1830s ever saw or handled a U.S. quarter eagle or half eagle. The few that did survive are often encountered in relatively high grades. For the 1833, the average grade is 57.6. This coin is noticeably finer at the MS61 level. It would, in fact, grade higher but there is a long, vertical abrasion on the shield on the reverse, and we are at a loss to explain its origin. A bit softly struck on the obverse stars and the left portion of the eagle's wing, the surfaces otherwise are bright and the fields semireflective. Even, light reddish-yellow color is seen over each side of this rarely seen Capped Head issue. Population: 3 in 61, 9 finer (2/09).(#8157)

CLASSIC HALF EAGLES

2866 **1834 Plain 4 AU50 PCGS.** Second Head, Breen-6502, McCloskey 2-A, R.2. Light wear merges with the striking softness on this piece's high points. Still, deep yellow-gold fields retain considerable luster. Wispy abrasions contribute to the grade. Housed in a green label holder.(#8171)

2867 **1834 Plain 4 AU50 PCGS.** First Head, Breen-6501, McCloskey 1-A, R.3. Originally toned orange-red where luster persists. The cheek and open fields are yellow-gold. Bereft of consequential marks, and certified in a green label holder.
From The Ed Leporco Collection, Part Two.(#8171)

2868 **1834 Plain 4 AU55 NGC.** Second Head, Breen-6502, McCloskey 2-A, R.2. A well struck, lightly worn mustard-gold example of this first-year Classic half eagle issue. A handful of small, scattered marks affect each side.(#8171)

2869 **1834 Plain 4 AU55 PCGS.** Second Head, Breen-6502, McCloskey 2-A, R.2. Surprisingly flashy with pale yellow-gold centers that cede to deeper color at the margins. Well struck with only light abrasions and modest wear.(#8171)

2870 **1834 Plain 4 AU55 NGC.** First Head, Breen-6501, McCloskey 3-A, R.3. A modestly worn example with considerable luster remaining in the wheat-gold fields. Just a touch of rub crosses the high points.(#8171)

2871 **1834 Plain 4 AU55 PCGS.** Second Head, Breen-6502, McCloskey 4-C, R.3. A nice Choice AU example with unabraded green-gold surfaces that display coppery-reddish alloy near the margins, on both sides. Noticeably worn over the obverse center. (#8171)

2872 **1834 Plain 4 AU58 NGC.** Second Head, Breen-6502, McCloskey 2-A, R.2. A good amount of luster remains on the peach-gold surfaces of this near-Mint State example. Well struck, except for softness in the hair at the temple and forehead and the eagle's left (facing) leg. A few minute circulation marks are of no consequence. (#8171)

2873 **1834 Plain 4 AU58 NGC.** First Head, Breen-6501, McCloskey 3-B, R.2. A nice, near-Mint example of this Classic Head half eagle. The centers are a bit weak, as usual, but the surfaces are decently preserved overall.(#8171)

Remarkable, Lustrous MS63 1834 Classic Five

2874 **1834 Plain 4 MS63 NGC.** McCloskey 2-A, R.2. This common variety has an obverse with the 4 tripled at the upper right side of the upright, although the repunching is difficult to see on this example. John McCloskey has identified nine differed die varieties of the 1834 Classic Head half eagles. Only three of the nine varieties are common, the normal choice for type collectors.

This lovely Mint State example has satiny medium yellow luster and exquisite surfaces for the grade. Most of the design details are bold, although the hair details over Liberty's ear are weaker than the remaining features.(#8171)

Scarce 1834 Crosslet 4 Half Eagle, AU53

2875 **1834 Crosslet 4 AU53 NGC.** Second Head, Crosslet 4, Breen-6503, McCloskey 5-D, R.4. The Crosslet 4 variety is the undisputed key to the Classic half eagle series, and is many times scarcer than its Plain 4 counterpart. This AU survivor is boldly struck, and only the left side obverse stars exhibit partial incompleteness. Still quite lustrous, with bright lime-gold toning and wispy field hairlines on each side.(#8172)

2876 **1835 AU55 NGC.** First Head, Breen-6504, McCloskey 1-C, R.5. A very scarce die marriage that shares a reverse die with the extremely rare M. 2-C proof. A richly detailed Choice AU example with apricot toning and no detrimental marks.(#8173)

Lustrous 1836 Second Head Five, MS62

2877 **1836 MS62 NGC.** Second Head, Large Date, Breen-6509, McCloskey 4-D, R.2. The large digit 1 in the date, much larger than the other digits, identifies the obverse, and on the reverse the TES is tight, with a wide OF, and the D in the denomination is almost entirely under the stem. This lustrous greenish-gold piece shows light field chatter under a loupe, but there are no singular abrasions, and good eye appeal is present.(#8174)

2878 **1837 XF45 NGC.** Large Date, Small 5, Breen-6511, McCloskey 1-A, R.4. One of three die marriages for this date and type, all of which are quite scarce. This is a pleasing XF example with light green and red-gold toning.(#8175)

2879 **1837 AU53 NGC.** Small Date, Breen-6513, McCloskey 3-C, R.4. A lightly worn, moderately abraded example with significant remaining luster in the wheat-gold fields. Interesting eye appeal. (#8175)

Exceptionally Well-Preserved
1837 Classic Five, MS64

2880 1837 MS64 PCGS. McCloskey 2-B. The 1837 half eagle is one of the important dates in the Classic Head series, much rarer than either the 1834 or 1836. The mintage of 207,121 coins does not suggest its true rarity. Jeff Garrett and Ron Guth discuss the 1837 half eagle in their *Encyclopedia of U.S. Gold Coins 1795 to 1933*: "Despite a seemingly high mintage, this is actually a semi-scarce date, with a raw rarity on par with that of the 1838-D. Examples up to About Uncirculated are relatively easy to find, but Mint State examples are decidedly rare. The number of Mint State examples is fairly well distributed from MS-60 to MS-64, but drops off dramatically in MS-65."

Three varieties of the 1837 half eagle are known, and they are distinguished by either a single curl hanging over the forehead, or a double curl in that location. The McCloskey 2-B is a Single Forehead Curl variety, and is clearly the most plentiful of the three known die pairs for the date. It may also be the only variety known in Mint State grades.

This gorgeous near-Gem is highly lustrous with brilliant, frosty yellow-gold surfaces and excellent design details. A few minuscule abrasions on each side are all that prevent a higher MS65 grade for this beautiful half eagle. PCGS has certified 42 submissions in all Mint State grades, but only three are finer than the present piece. Population: 8 in 64, 3 finer (2/09).(#8175)

2881 1838 AU55 NGC. Small Arrows, Large 5. Breen-6515. A scarce Classic Head half eagle and quite a find in Choice AU condition. This piece shows numerous small abrasions in the fields, but the design elements are quite well brought up on both sides. (#8176)

2882 1838—Cleaned—ANACS. MS60 Details. Small Arrows, Large 5, Breen-6515, McCloskey 2-B, R.2. Excellent definition throughout with no trace of wear. Lemon-gold surfaces are a trifle overbright from a past cleaning.(#8176)

2883 1838—Improperly Cleaned—NCS. Unc Details. Large Arrows, Small 5, Breen-6514, McCloskey 1-A, R.2. Strongly struck with no trace of rub or friction across the high points. Light yellow-gold surfaces show a degree of dulling from a past cleaning, as well as scattered hairlines in the fields.(#8176)

Elusive 1838 Small Arrows Half Eagle, MS61

2884 1838 MS61 NGC. Small Arrows, Large 5. Breen-6515. Brilliant and satiny luster graces the yellow-gold surfaces of this nicely detailed beauty. Aside from the typical grade-consistent abrasions and a small spot at star 9, the overall surfaces are exceptional. This seldom encountered date is usually only seen in circulated grades. Census: 33 in 61, 49 finer (1/09).(#8176)

1838-D Five Dollar, VF30
One-Year Type Coin

2885 1838-D VF30 NGC. McCloskey 1-A, R.3. The 1838-D is a popular coin because of its status as a one-year type within the Classic series. It is also generally not found in high grades, and when it is, such pieces are invariably pricey. This coin shows deep, even reddish patina over each side. The high-point definition is somewhat uneven, most likely because the hair curls were softly struck when the coin was new. This caused the coin to show less of the design in that area. Lightly abraded.(#8178)

LIBERTY HALF EAGLES

Smooth Choice AU 1839 Half Eagle

2886   1839 AU55 NGC. CAC. A charming first year Liberty half eagle with pleasing definition and ample luster, particularly on the reverse. Neither side has any remotely mentionable marks, which ensures the eye appeal. 1839-dated fives exhibit a sleepy-eyed portrait of Liberty that differs from subsequent issues. (#8191)

Near-Mint 1839-C Half Eagle

2887   1839-C AU58 NGC. Variety 1, the sole variety of the year, in an earlier die state with no rim cud below the date. This well struck near-Mint piece is surprisingly bright, and the faintly granular lemon-gold obverse surfaces exhibit few significant faults. The 1839 half eagle issue is one of just two struck at the Charlotte Mint to bear the C mintmark on the obverse, and the only issue of the Coronet or Liberty Head design to do so (the other, the 1838, has a Classic Head portrait); as such, it is immensely popular with both type and date collectors of Southern gold. Census: 8 in 58, 13 finer (2/09).(#8192)

2888   1839-D Fine 12 NGC. Variety 2-A. The obverse-mintmark Southern gold issues enjoy widespread popularity, and the 1839-D five is no exception. This significantly worn yet attractive yellow-orange example shows khaki and sage accents.(#8193)

Scarce 1840-C Five Dollar, AU53

2889   1840-C AU53 PCGS. Variety 1 (formerly Variety 2-B). The right edge of the C mintmark is over the left edge of the E in FIVE while its left edge is over the V. Very scarce early Charlotte five that is most often available in VF or low-end XF condition, with pieces grading as high as AU being quite rare. This example is softly struck in areas, but there is little actual wear present. Scattered abrasions that are typical for this issue are present on both sides. (#8196)

Lustrous 1840-C Half Eagle, AU55

2890   1840-C AU55 PCGS. Variety 2 with the point of the arrow feather over the inner curve of the mintmark. An exceptional example for the grade, this Choice AU piece has brilliant light yellow surfaces with few abrasions on either side. The lower obverse border has some stray marks extending up from the dentils, reminiscent of digits erroneously punched into the die. Population: 7 in 55, 4 finer (2/09).(#8196)

Borderline Uncirculated 1840-C Five

2891   1840-C AU58 NGC. CAC. Variety 2. This luminous near-mint example has an above average strike, and is smooth aside from a solitary pinscratch beneath the lowest arrow shaft. The Charlotte branch produced 18,992 examples of the issue, and most saw considerable circulation. The typical survivor grades just XF40, and few exist in Mint State grades. Census: 9 in 58, 5 finer (2/09). (#8196)

Pleasing 1840-D Tall D Half Eagle, AU50

2892 **1840-D Tall D AU50 NGC.** Variety 3-B. The Tall Mintmark variety fills about half of the space between the arrow feather and the VE in FIVE. There is a "prong-like" die defect extending from the denticles toward the thirteenth star. This pleasing green-gold example has attractive surfaces, although a minor obverse rim bruise is evident at 5 o'clock. Census: 10 in 50, 38 finer (2/09). (#8198)

2893 **1840-D Small D—Altered Surfaces—ANACS. AU55 Details.** Variety 4-C. A rare variant with a repunched date on the obverse and a die crack running through a small mintmark on the reverse. Luminous orange-gold overall with significant granularity, which ANACS has termed "altered surfaces" but the cataloger for the Harry W. Bass, Jr. Collection described as "seawater surfaces." *Ex: Lester Merkin (3/1969), lot 210; The Harry W. Bass, Jr. Collection, Part II (Bowers and Merena, 10/1999), lot 890.* (#8199)

2894 **1842-D Small Date—Cleaned—ANACS. VF20 Details.** Variety 8-E. This hairlined Southern gold piece has unnatural orange patina in areas where luster would reside if the grade were higher. The wings exhibit ample plumage detail.(#8210)

2895 **1842-D Small Date VF25 NGC.** Variety 8-E. Although this Dahlonega No Motto five served its duty in Georgian commerce, the wings retain most of their initial definition, and most star centrils are clear.(#8210)

2896 **1842-D Small Date VF30 PCGS.** Variety 8-E. A moderately worn example with light, scattered abrasions on the orange-gold surfaces. Interesting eye appeal with an aura of originality.(#8210)

Lustrous AU53 1842-D Small Date Five

2897 **1842-D Small Date AU53 NGC.** Variety 7-E. The left base of the 1 is over the left side of a denticle, and the left side of the D mintmark is over the left side of the V in FIVE. The latter part of 1842 saw simultaneous enlargements both of the date and the reverse lettering on half eagles struck in Philadelphia, Charlotte, and Dahlonega (but not New Orleans). Of the two D-mint coins, the Small Date, Small Letters (as Winter terms it) is much more available than the Large Date, Large Letters. This piece boasts still-lustrous pinkish-gold surfaces that offer good eye appeal, despite the moderate abrasions noted on both sides. Census: 8 in 53, 60 finer (2/09).(#8210)

2898 **1843 MS61 NGC.** An appealing yellow-gold example with soft, pleasing luster. Sharply struck, though a number of fine marks and a handful of digs are present on each side. Census: 28 in 61, 36 finer (1/09).(#8213)

2899 **1843-D Medium D XF45 NGC.** Variety 10-H. The usual mintmark size, although a seldom-seen Small D variety is known. This sharply defined straw-gold Dahlonega type coin lacks noticeable marks and has a mildly bright appearance. *From The Ed Lepordo Collection, Part Two.*(#8215)

Radiant 1843-D Medium D Five Dollar, AU55

2900 **1843-D Medium D AU55 NGC.** Variety 10-H. Strongly struck in the centers with considerable radiance to the yellow-gold surfaces. Despite a number of light to moderate abrasions on each side, this modestly worn example retains great eye appeal. An excellent representative of this popular earlier Dahlonega half eagle. Census: 33 in 55, 52 finer (2/09).(#8215)

Boldly Struck 1843-O Large Letters Half Eagle, MS61

2901 **1843-O Large Letters MS61 PCGS.** Early branch mint New Orleans half eagles are difficult to find in Mint State, since few gold coins were held as bank reserves until the late 1870s. This is a boldly struck example with butter-gold and straw-gold toning. Minute marks are scattered about both sides. Population: 2 in 61, 1 finer (2/09).(#8216)

2902 **1844-D—Damaged, Cleaned—ANACS. XF40 Details.** Variety 11-H. Khaki-gold surfaces with elements of mustard and orange show numerous hairlines from a past cleaning. Well struck and lightly worn. Two scratches are noted above the eagle's right (facing) wing.(#8221)

2903 **1844-O AU55 PCGS.** Almost uniformly yellow-orange save for a dot of purplish alloy near the U in UNITED on the reverse. Sharply struck and mildly abraded with a touch of rub on the high points. Population: 29 in 55, 54 finer (2/09).(#8222)

Appealing MS61 1844-O Half Eagle

2904 **1844-O MS61 PCGS.** Subtle, swirling yellow-gold luster dominates the eye appeal of this unworn O-mint example. Though the centers show slight striking softness and wispy abrasions populate the fields, this coin offers strong eye appeal that the grade alone might not suggest. Population: 10 in 61, 15 finer (2/09). (#8222)

Rare Select 1844-O Five Dollar
Ex: *S.S. New York*

2905 **1844-O MS63 NGC.** Ex: *S.S. New York.* A satiny straw-gold representative with only a few minor marks and just a hint of surface granularity. The centers show unimportant incompleteness of strike. NGC certified 19 examples of the 1844-O from the 1846 *S.S. New York* shipwreck, with three graded MS63 and only two pieces certified finer, both as MS64.(#8222)

Notable MS63 1844-O Five Dollar

2906 **1844-O MS63 NGC.** The 1844-O five offered here is well struck, with just the slightest weakness on the curls that is often seen with this issue. The surfaces have only minimal abrasions for the grade, none individually distracting. The frosty mint luster of the devices underscores the bright, orange-gold color of the fields. This coin combines excellent eye appeal, condition rarity, and the cachet of the old Southern mint. A great opportunity for the type collector and the specialist. Census: 10 in 63, 6 finer (2/09).(#8222)

2907 **1845-O AU53 NGC.** Light yellow-gold color overall with substantial radiance to the fields. Well-defined with only minor, scattered abrasions on each side. Census: 12 in 53, 57 finer (2/09). (#8225)

Attractive Choice AU 1845-O Half Eagle

2908 **1845-O AU55 NGC.** An issue that is common in lower grades but rare in Mint State. This piece has semireflective yellow-gold fields with good luster and eye appeal. An attractive Choice AU example of this antebellum half eagle from the historic New Orleans Mint. Census: 13 in 55, 44 finer (2/09).(#8225)

1846 Large Date Five Dollar MS61
From the *S.S. New York* Shipwreck

2909 **1846 Large Date MS61 NGC.** Ex: *S.S. New York.* According to an NGC press release, the *S.S. New York* "foundered during a hurricane on September 7, 1846. 17 of the 53 crew and passengers were lost, along with thirty to forty thousand dollars in gold, silver, and bank notes." Only three 1846 half eagles were recovered, including two Large Date examples in MS61. Sharply struck and only moderately abraded.(#8226)

Amazing 1846 Large Date Five, MS64
Tied for Finest at NGC

2910 1846 Large Date MS64 NGC. Half eagles of this issue are known with two distinctly different date sizes logically called Large Date and Small Date varieties. The Small Date variety is much rarer but both are rare in Choice Mint State grade. In fact NGC has certified just four examples of the Large Date in MS64 (2/09) with none finer. The same service has certified an MS63 Small Date, the single finest of that variety.

This incredible piece just misses the Gem category due to a few light abrasions on each side. However, it has the luster and eye appeal of a full Gem, with brilliant yellow surfaces, reflective fields, and bold design details. The reverse has a curved bisecting die crack from the border and upright of the D in the denomination, through the eagle just below the shield, to the border just left of the first S.(#8226)

2911 1846-D XF45 NGC. Variety 16-K. A well struck, lightly abraded piece that shows considerable radiance remaining in the pale yellow-gold fields. An interesting survivor from this higher-mintage Dahlonega half eagle issue.(#8228)

Choice XF 1846-D/D Half Eagle

2912 1846-D/D XF45 PCGS. Variety 15-J. The mintmark is punched twice, with wide separation between them. The first punch was much too high, well up into the branch and the lower part of the eagle, with the second punch in the normal mintmark position. Garrett and Guth, calling it the "High 2nd D/D" variety, say that the variety makes up in popularity what it lacks in rarity. This piece has some smoky gray-gold haze, along with the light abrasions and circulation wear expected for the Choice XF level. Population: 19 in 45, 52 finer (2/09).(#8229)

2913 1846-O XF45 PCGS. Softly struck at the margins as usual, but pleasingly detailed on the central devices despite light wear. Green-gold overall with a few areas of reddish alloy. Population: 14 in 45, 35 finer (1/09).(#8230)

Attractive 1847 Half Eagle, MS62

2914 1847 MS62 PCGS. CAC. Pleasingly lustrous, with mildly prooflike fields and lovely lime-gold toning. Boldly struck throughout; the 4 in the date is filled by a die chip and the 7 is recut. Nicely preserved with a few stray marks and wispy hairlines that restrict the grade. One of the most common No Motto half eagles, and recommended to type collectors. Population: 48 in 62, 27 finer (2/09).(#8231)

2915 1847-C—Improperly Cleaned—NCS. XF Details. Variety 1. A sharp Charlotte five that has been lightly cleaned with baking soda to bring out its remaining luster. Both sides are minimally abraded for the grade aside from an unimportant obverse rim ding at 4 o'clock.(#8233)

2916 1847-C—Scratched, Improperly Cleaned—NCS. XF Details. Variety 1. Several fine scratches are noted in the zones around the portrait, and each lemon-gold side has dulled and granular surfaces that show evidence of cleaning. Actual wear is minimal.
From The Pasadena Collection, Part Two.(#8233)

Worthy 1847-C Half Eagle AU53

2917 **1847-C AU53 NGC.** Variety 1. A Charlotte Mint representative whose subdued lime-green and apricot-gold surfaces lack consequential abrasions. Luminous luster is especially evident near the rims. An opportunity to acquire a better grade, problem-free example from this popular and challenging Southern facility. (#8233)

2918 **1848-D Good 4 NGC.** Probable variety 19-N, though no repunching is visible. An unusual opportunity for the Southern gold enthusiast, since examples only rarely receive this amount of wear without being cleaned, scratched, or otherwise impaired. Deep orange and purple shadings dominate each side. The single lowest-graded example of this issue certified by NGC (2/09). (#8238)

2919 **1848-D—Improperly Cleaned—NCS. AU Details.** Variety 18-M. Struck after the obverse dies sustained considerable clash marks. Yellow-gold surfaces are suspiciously bright, but the strike is crisp and wear is minimal. *From The Pasadena Collection, Part Two.*(#8238)

Popular 1849-C Half Eagle AU53

2920 **1849-C AU53 PCGS.** Variety 2 with the date more centered beneath the bust. Scarcer than its Variety 1 counterpart. A partly lustrous and bright Charlotte representative with light wear on the hair and plumage. There are no reportable abrasions. Population: 18 in 53, 38 finer (2/09).(#8241)

Choice AU 1850-C No Motto Five

2921 **1850-C AU55 NGC.** Variety 1 with a radial reverse die crack at 7 o'clock. Four die marriages are currently known, despite a mintage of only 63,591 pieces. A straw-gold Choice AU Charlotte five with clean surfaces and generous glints of green-gold luster, particularly on the reverse. Census: 27 in 55, 42 finer (2/09).(#8244)

2922 **1851-C XF40 NGC.** Variety 1. A scarce Charlotte half eagle, this piece is typical for the issue in both quality and appearance. There is some bluntness on the eagle's neck and right (facing) talons, along with numerous, but basically light abrasions over both sides. (#8247)

2923 **1851-C XF45 NGC.** Variety 1. Lightly worn with glimmers of warm luster enlivening the yellow-orange surfaces. The sole individually mentionable flaw is a vertical abrasion to the left of star 11 on the obverse.(#8247)

2924 **1851-C AU50 NGC.** Variety 1. The more common variant with mintmark close to the olive branch. A well struck example, lightly worn in the centers with radiant lemon-gold fields. Census: 14 in 50, 67 finer (2/09).(#8247)

Rare 1851-C Five Dollar, MS60

2925 **1851-C MS60 NGC.** Variety 1. Attributed by a small mint-made punch mark on Liberty's ear lobe, and a large, bold C mintmark centered over the upright of E in FIVE. This well defined piece has bright green-gold surfaces with clearly visible die polish on both sides, along with light handling marks. The 1851-C is a rare date in any Mint State grade, with only 16 such examples certified by NGC and PCGS combined, a number of which are likely resubmissions. Census: 3 in 60, 9 finer (2/09).(#8247)

2926 **1851-O XF40 NGC.** Considered very scarce in any grade, an XF 1851-O half eagle should be considered a prize. Although not quite full, the strike is certainly adequate for the date. Some luster is still seen under the devices, and there are numerous small abrasions in the fields.(#8249)

Overlooked 1851-O Five Dollar, AU55

2927 **1851-O AU55 NGC.** Like the quarter eagle of this date and mint, the 1851-O half eagle is a scarce and curiously overlooked issue. There are approximately 125-150 pieces known in all grades, most in the Very Fine to Extremely Fine grade range. In About Uncirculated, this is a rare coin with just 15 to 20 pieces known. Mint State 1851-O examples are very rare, as are all O-mint half eagles from the 1850s. The devices show some of the usually found weakness, especially in the central reverse, and the bright yellow-gold surfaces still retain significant amounts of luster in the fields. Numerous small, medium, and large abrasions are scattered over each side, and a shallow strike-through appears above the eagle on the reverse. Census: 15 in 55, 24 finer (1/09).(#8249)

2928 **1852-C VG8 PCGS.** Variety 1. A substantially worn yet highly pleasing example of this popular Charlotte half eagle issue. Light abrasions affect the lemon-gold fields, as expected for the grade, but these flaws do not seriously affect the eye appeal. At the lower reverse, there is slight merging between the lettering and the rim. (#8251)

Near-Mint 1852-C Five Dollar

2929 **1852-C AU58 NGC.** Variety 1. Bright luster glints from the borders and devices of this lovely near-Mint Charlotte No Motto five. The eagle's neck is softly brought up, which is par for the course on this issue, but the overall strike is good. Marks are minor for the AU58 level. Census: 41 in 58, 35 finer (2/09). (#8251)

Notable Mint State 1852-D Half Eagle

2930 **1852-D MS60 NGC.** Variety 27-U. Though any number of AU examples appear in the combined certified population, few Mint State examples of this higher-mintage issue are known. This example has gleaming yellow-gold surfaces with no trace of wear. Considerable peripheral weakness and the scattered abrasions that account for the grade have surprisingly little impact on the eye appeal. Census: 3 in 60, 17 finer (2/09).(#8252)

Attractive 1853-D Five Dollar, AU53

2931 **1853-D Large D AU53 NGC.** Variety 29-V. The 1853-D is always of interest to collectors, as it is the most frequently seen of all the Dahlonega fives. This is one of the better-struck examples, with the high-point softness generally limited to slight friction from brief handling in the channels of commerce. Medium reddish-gold color with no mentionable abrasions.(#8255)

Luminous AU55 1853-D Five Dollar

2932 **1853-D Large D AU55 NGC.** Variety 29-V. Strongly struck in the centers with only light wear across the highest design elements. This subtly lustrous butter-yellow piece shows only mild abrasions overall, though a shallow pinscratch is noted in the field to the right of Liberty's neck. In sum, an intriguing survivor. (#8255)

Remarkable MS62 1853-D Half Eagle

2933 **1853-D Large D MS62 PCGS. CAC.** Variety 29-V. This honey-gold representative has nearly full luster, and the strike is intricate save for the fletchings and a couple of star centers. Marks are minor for the grade, and the eye appeal is considerable. A wonderful addition to a high quality Dahlonega gold type set. Population: 8 in 62, 6 finer (2/09).(#8255)

2934 **1854 AU58 NGC.** Excellent strike with just a touch of rub on the high points. This minimally marked No Motto five has rich yellow-orange color and lovely luster. NGC has graded 61 finer pieces (1/09).(#8256)

Elusive 1854 Half Eagle, MS62

2935 **1854 MS62 NGC.** An elusive pre-Civil War issue, despite the generous mintage of more than 160,000 business strikes, the 1854 half eagle is seldom seen in grades above AU. Indeed, Garrett and Guth call the date "much rarer than most price references would indicate." This piece shows a bold strike and good luster over orange-gold surfaces. The eye appeal is considerable, despite the small scrapes in the left obverse field and one on Liberty's cheek. Census: 21 in 62, 19 finer (2/09).(#8256)

Frosty 1854 Five Dollar, MS63

2936 **1854 MS63 NGC.** A lovely piece with excellent orange-gold luster and frosty surfaces. A moderate antebellum mintage of 160,675 coins suggests an issue that should be available without difficulty, but high grade representatives are nearly impossible to find. Census: 12 in 63, 7 finer (2/09).(#8256)

1854 'Doubled Earlobe' Five Dollar, MS62 FS-101

2937 **1854 FS-101 MS62 PCGS. CAC.** FS-101, formerly FS-004.5. Liberty's earlobe is widely die doubled, reminiscent of the *Guide Book* doubled ear 1984 Lincoln cent. Of course, *any* No Motto half eagle is desirable at the MS62 level, since few examples of the denomination were set aside until the late 1870s. Nicely struck and lightly abraded with abundant peripheral luster. FS-101 Population: 3 in 62, none finer (2/09).(#145713)

2938 **1854-D Large D XF45 NGC.** Unlisted in Winter; reverse has a bold, large mintmark. Bright lemon-gold surfaces are minimally abraded, and only slight striking weakness affects the centers. Modest wear crosses the high points.(#8258)

Flashy 1854-D Medium D Five Dollar, AU58

2939 **1854-D Medium D AU58 NGC.** Variety 31-W. Definitely scarcer than its Large D counterpart, and also preferable to the Weak D variety. This orange-gold near-Mint example has an impressive amount of flashy luster, especially across the borders and within the devices. The strike is intricate for a Dahlonega product. (#88258)

2940 **1854-O AU50 NGC.** Deep gold-orange color with isolated areas of rose near the margins. A modestly abraded and pleasingly lustrous example of this antebellum five dollar issue.(#8259)

Difficult 1856-C Half Eagle AU58

2941 **1856-C AU58 NGC. CAC.** Variety 1 as always for this issue. The entire mintage of 28,457 coins were apparently produced from this single die pair. Examples are scarce in all grades, and near-Mint pieces are decidedly rare. This one has a sharp strike and ample glimmering luster. The straw-gold surfaces are smooth aside from a solitary mark on the shield. Census: 26 in 58, 14 finer (2/09). (#8267)

2942 **1856-D XF40 NGC.** Variety 33-BB. Light wear is concentrated at the high points, leaving the mustard-gold fields a measure of luster. Scattered abrasions overall, though the eye appeal is strong for the grade. Census: 6 in 40, 87 finer (1/09).(#8268)

Lustrous MS62 1857-C Half Eagle

Impressive MS63 1859-D Medium D Five

2943 **1857-C MS62 PCGS.** *Variety 1.* The 1857-C is one of the more frequently encountered Charlotte fives, but it is seldom located in Mint State. The numbers of Uncirculated coins certified by both of the major services are greatly inflated by resubmissions. Probably only 10-12 pieces actually exist in Mint State out of the 225-275 coins believed to exist in all grades today. This is an attractive, sharply struck example. It lacks the usually seen heavy abrasions, with just a few scattered field marks and ticks appearing on the devices, mainly with a loupe. The margins show a pronounced reddish patina on each side.(#8272)

2944 **1857-S AU55 NGC.** Traces of luster reside in the recessed areas of this Choice AU five dollar, and a well executed strike leaves sharp definition on the motifs. Peach-gold surfaces reveal distributed light marks.(#8275)

2945 **1858 AU55 NGC.** Decisively struck with just a trace of rub across the high points. Rich yellow-orange color with glimpses of dusky peach close to the rims. A small depression is noted at the upper shield on the reverse. Census: 17 in 55, 28 finer (2/09). (#8276)

2946 **1858-C XF40 NGC.** *Variety 2,* the more elusive variety. Satiny yellow-orange surfaces host devices that remain well-defined despite a degree of wear. Modestly abraded but pleasing.(#8277)

2947 **1859-D Medium D—Scratched, Cleaned—ANACS. AU50 Details.** *Variety 36-CC.* Each side shows light, scattered abrasions and modest wear. Yellow-gold fields show numerous hairlines as well as a scratch in the left obverse field.(#8282)

2948 **1859-D Medium D MS63 PCGS.** *Variety 36-CC.* Easily one of the finest survivors known for this elusive late-date Dahlonega half eagle issue, listed in Doug Winter's condition census for the issue and previously part of the Chestatee Collection offered by Heritage in August 1999, which consisted of duplicates (!) from the incomparable Duke's Creek Collection. The two small abrasions below the truncation of the bust are unmistakable pedigree markers.

Rich orange-tinged yellow-gold luster shows slight granularity but is fine and pleasing nonetheless. Slight striking softness as usual on the central devices, though each side shows few marks for the grade. A great opportunity for the dedicated Dahlonega gold lover.(#8282)

Almost Uncirculated 1860-D Five Dollar

2949 1860-D Medium D AU50 NGC. Variety 38-FF. While the mintage for the 1860-D is only 14,635 pieces, it is actually one of the more obtainable dates in the Dahlonega series of half eagles. This is an attractive, problem-free example that shows even reddish-gold color throughout. Well struck for the grade with only slight friction evident over the high points.(#8286)

2950 1861 MS61 NGC. Excellent strike and luster for this heavily produced issue, a popular type date for No Motto half eagle enthusiasts. Surfaces range from pale lemon-gold to strong sun-yellow.(#8288)

2951 1861 MS61 PCGS. Decisively detailed with light yellow-gold color overall. Though each side exhibits a number of tiny marks, the overall eye appeal holds fast.(#8288)

Desirable AU55 1861-C Half Eagle

2952 1861-C AU55 NGC. Variety 1. A pleasing example for this final Charlotte half eagle issue. Rich yellow-gold luster radiates from each side, and though a number of fine abrasions are apparent, neither the fields nor the devices show the "choppy" appearance noted by Winter. Modest wear crosses the high points. Census: 20 in 55, 30 finer (2/09).(#8289)

Impressive 1863-S Half Eagle, AU58

2953 1863-S AU58 NGC. Only one die variety is known, with a large S mintmark on the reverse that Walter Breen attributed as the "Reverse of 1856." A single known variety is unsurprising, given a mintage of only 17,000 coins. The obverse has some curious raised die lines behind LIBERTY, near the eye, on the neck, and on the bust, visible on several examples that we checked in our Permanent Auction Archives.

A wonderful example, this half eagle has highly lustrous yellow-gold surfaces with traces of pink, green, and blue patina. The surfaces are lightly abraded, consistent with the grade, and the strike is excellent. PCGS has certified one finer example of the date, and NGC has never graded a Mint State piece. Census: 22 in 58, 0 finer (1/09).(#8295)

Appealing Near-Mint 1864 Five Dollar

2954 1864 AU58 NGC. The central detail is excellent on this orange-inflected yellow-gold survivor. The luster is strong and virtually unaffected by wear, and only small, scattered marks dot each side. If not for a trace of friction on the high points, a strong claimant to Select status. Census: 9 in 58, 4 finer (1/09).(#8296)

2955　**1867-S XF40 PCGS.** A delightful honey-gold example of this scarce, low-mintage issue. The San Francisco Mint struck 29,000 pieces that entered circulation at the time of issue, leaving few higher grade pieces for collectors. Population: 6 in 40, 21 finer (1/09).(#8314)

2956　**1870 XF40 PCGS.** Light yellow-gold color overall with a surprising amount of luster remaining in the fields. Numerous small abrasions contribute to the grade. Overall, a desirable example of this lower-mintage issue. Population: 5 in 40, 25 finer (2/09). (#8319)

Elusive 1871 Half Eagle, AU55

2957　**1871 AU55 NGC.** The 1871 Liberty Head, With Motto half eagle has an extremely low mintage of 3,200 pieces. The date is rare in all grades today, with a total surviving population of about 100 examples. Small mintages were the pattern for this era, as gold was being hoarded and banks had not resumed specie payments. The coin offered here is a pleasing example of this rare date. The fields are bright and semi-prooflike, with just a few small abrasions on each side. The attractive yellow-gold centers yield to reddish margins, with traces of mint luster at the peripheries. Census: 10 in 55, 22 finer (2/09).(#8322)

Notable AU55 1871 Five Dollar

2958　**1871 AU55 NGC.** Subtly green-gold fields offer excellent reflectivity despite the modest wear across the high points of the well-defined devices. Scattered, wispy abrasions contribute to the grade, but overall, this is a pleasing example from a low-mintage issue of just 3,200 business strikes. Census: 10 in 55, 22 finer (2/09).(#8322)

Popular 1871-CC Five Dollar, AU50

2959　**1871-CC AU50 PCGS.** Despite the numerous duplications evident in the NGC and PCGS population data, only two or three dozen 1871-CC half eagles at most exist in AU or finer condition. Only four Mint State pieces make up the certified population.

　　The pleasing surfaces on this AU50 orange-gold coin are well struck, like most of the issue, and there is only moderate softness on the eagle's legs and the fletchings. The obverse strike is also bold, although an abrasion on Liberty's neck is noted. A collectible example of a rare and popular issue. Population: 5 in 50, 15 finer (2/09).(#8323)

Impressive Near-Mint 1871-CC Half Eagle

2960 **1871-CC AU58 NGC.** Lustrous surfaces are deep yellow-orange with a horizontal alloy streak on the eagle's right (facing) wing. Lightly marked overall with just a touch of friction on the high points precluding a Mint State designation. Rusty Goe, writing in 2003, noted in his book *The Mint on Carson Street* that "As the collector base for 'CC' gold coins increases, examples of this date will quickly disappear." Six years later, chances to acquire high-end Carson City coins such as this one are becoming increasingly rare. Census: 6 in 58, 2 finer (2/09).
From The Belle Collection of Carson City Coinage. (#8323)

Elusive 1872-CC Half Eagle, AU50
Unknown in Mint State

2961 **1872-CC AU50 NGC.** As of the current writing (2/09), neither NGC nor PCGS has ever certified an example of this issue in Mint State. There are currently five AU58s combined at both services, a figure that almost surely includes some duplication. Rusty Goe writes in *The Mint on Carson Street* that "survival estimates for the 1872-CC half eagles are lower than for any other date in the series, with less than 1/2 of 1% extant." The present AU50 example still retain about half of the original luster, with khaki-gold coloration deepening to antique-gold at the rims. The few marks and high-point wear are completely in line with the grade. A rare coin from this legendary era of U.S. numismatics.
From The Belle Collection of Carson City Coinage. (#8326)

Sharply Struck 1872-S Five Dollar, AU55

2962 **1872-S AU55 NGC.** Traces of luster adhere to the honey-gold and mint-green surfaces of this Choice AU S-mint representative. The design elements exhibit sharp definition, though the eagle's neck feathers are a touch soft. Minute marks are scattered about, more so on the obverse. (#8327)

2963 **1873 Closed 3 MS64 PCGS.** Rich peach-gold toning endows this lustrous and exceptionally preserved half eagle. A good strike with only minor blending of detail on the eagle's neck. Unlike many later issues in the series, the 1873 Closed 3 is very scarce in Mint State and is desirable as a near-Gem. Population: 4 in 64, 3 finer (2/09).(#8329)

Desirable AU55 1874 Five Dollar

2964 **1874 AU55 PCGS.** A number of tiny abrasions affect each side, and a dig is noted behind Liberty's hair bun. Still, this lightly worn coin retains considerable eye appeal, with the strongly reflective lemon-gold luster foremost. An interesting piece from one of the few half eagle issues to have a lower mintage than its three dollar counterpart. Population: 13 in 55, 5 finer (2/09).(#8333)

Intriguing 1874-CC Half Eagle, AU58

2965 **1874-CC AU58 NGC.** The mintage was somewhat more than 21,000 pieces, and although Goe calls it "easily the most accessible date from the first nine years of half eagle production at the Carson City Mint," he also estimates its survival rate at only 1%, or 210 pieces. This AU58 coin is clearly tied for the lower end of the Condition Census for the issue, as NGC and PCGS together have certified a maximum of three pieces finer (2/09).

This example displays a bold strike, with relatively mark-free surfaces for the grade and some moderate reflectivity noted in the fields. An intriguing and thoroughly attractive specimen. Census: 18 in 58, 1 finer (2/09).
From The Belle Collection of Carson City Coinage.(#8334)

Appealing Choice AU 1875-CC Half Eagle

2966 1875-CC AU55 NGC. The production total for half eagles in 1875, at 11,828 pieces, was barely half of the previous year's total, for two reasons: First, double eagle coinage took precedence. Second, and probably more influential, silver coinage was greatly increased at all mints in preparation for specie redemption that was slated to begin in January 1878. This Choice AU example offers radiant luster and considerable reflectivity remaining under a light overlay of field chatter. There are few individually relevant marks and, although the central strike is somewhat soft, much eye appeal remains throughout. Census: 10 in 55, 6 finer (2/09).
From The Belle Collection of Carson City Coinage.(#8337)

Very Rare MS62 1876 Half Eagle

2967 1876 MS62 NGC. A formidable rarity within the Liberty half eagle series. Only 45 proofs and 1,432 business strikes were coined. Since nobody collected contemporary gold coins in 1876 except in proof format, the commercial pieces went directly into circulation, and most were eventually melted. A handful of Mint State examples are known, including the present moderately prooflike representative. It is crisply struck and has a few inconsequential field marks.(#8339)

Low Mintage 1876-CC Half Eagle, XF45

2968 1876-CC XF45 PCGS. Winter 1-A. The top of Liberty's hair is not fully struck, although the eagle's wings have rich definition. The reddish-khaki surfaces retain glimpses of the original luster. A faint diagonal pinscratch in the left obverse field reaches the fourth star, and is mentioned primarily for pedigree purposes. Only 6,887 pieces were struck, which is the lowest mintage of any Carson City half eagle issue. Population: 13 in 45, 18 finer (2/09). (#8340)

Significant AU55 1877-CC Liberty Five

2969 1877-CC AU55 NGC. Another rare Carson City issue from the 1870s. A meager 8,680 pieces were struck, and all went into circulation since NGC has yet to certify any as Mint State. The present piece has light peach toning and a good strike. No marks merit comment. Census: 15 in 55, 6 finer (2/09).
From The Belle Collection of Carson City Coinage.(#8343)

2970 1878 MS63 PCGS. Strongly struck with a hint of frostiness to the fields. This elegant Select coin shows butter-yellow peripheral elements with softer straw-gold elsewhere.(#8345)

Rare 1878-CC Half Eagle, AU53

2971 **1878-CC AU53 PCGS. CAC.** Variety 1-A. The 1878-CC five dollar, from a mintage of only 9,054 pieces, is one of the rarest Carson City half eagles. Douglas Winter (2001) contends that an XF40 specimen is the best that collectors can expect to acquire. The certified population data more or less bear this out. PCGS and NGC have seen only about 25 pieces in the two XF grades, a number of which are likely resubmissions. Likewise, the two services have certified about 35 examples in the four AU grades, several of which are probably resubmitted coins. One Mint State specimen has been graded—an NGC MS63.

   This yellow-gold AU53 coin displays apricot and lavender accents, along with traces of luster in the protected areas. The design elements are well defined, save for some typically seen localized minor softness. Both sides are relatively unblemished, except for a faint hair-thin mark on the cheek.
From The Belle Collection of Carson City Coinage. (#8346)

Well Defined 1879-CC Half Eagle, AU50

2972 **1879-CC AU50 NGC.** Variety 2-A, identifiable by a die scratch through the bottom right serif of the E in LIBERTY. Traces of luster reside in the recessed areas of this yellow-gold specimen. Well defined, except for softness on the eagle's neck feathers. A few expected light marks are seen, but the surfaces do not have a "scruffy" appearance that most examples of this issue have.
From The Belle Collection of Carson City Coinage. (#8349)

Glowing MS61 1879-CC Half Eagle
Tied for Finest Certified

2973 **1879-CC MS61 NGC.** Rusty Goe names the 1879-CC the most accessible half eagle from the first decade of the denomination's production in Carson City. This piece is certainly among the finest known, as neither NGC nor PCGS has certified a single coin finer (2/09). Glowing luster proceeds from both sides, and the bold strike and relatively abrasion-free surfaces are a definite plus. The average certified survivor only grades VF35 or a bit better. Clearly at the top of the Condition Census for the issue. Census: 3 in 61, 0 finer (2/09).
From The Belle Collection of Carson City Coinage. (#8349)

2974 **1880 MS64 PCGS.** Exquisitely detailed with inviting, satiny luster. On the obverse, straw-gold shadings prevail, while the reverse offers richer butter-yellow coloration with a hint of orange. Population: 63 in 64, 10 finer (1/09).(#8351)

2975 **1880-CC XF45 NGC.** Well-defined for this middle-date issue with considerable luster remaining in the dusky yellow-gold fields. Minimally abraded devices contribute to the eye appeal. (#8352)

2976 **1880-CC AU50 PCGS.** Rich yellow-orange color with reddish alloy toward the margins. Amply lustrous despite light wear. Housed in a first-generation PCGS holder. Population: 30 in 50, 66 finer (2/09).(#8352)

2977 **1880-CC AU50 NGC.** Excellent detail despite the light wear that crosses each side. A lightly abraded yellow-gold piece that offers substantial remaining luster in the reflective fields.(#8352)

Attractive Mint State 1880-CC Half Eagle

2978 **1880-CC MS60 NGC.** The increased output of half eagles in Carson City during this year—52,027 coins as opposed to 17,281 for the previous year—was due to the Treasury's increased emphasis on lower-denomination coinage, although that emphasis came in Carson City at the expense of the double eagle. This piece is fully lustrous and sharply struck, with pretty honey-gold surfaces. There is a long scrape along Liberty's cheek, and a hair-thin mark in the obverse field between stars 11 and 12. Other contact is consistent with the grade, but the eye appeal is considerably nicer than might be inferred. Census: 2 in 60, 10 finer (2/09).
From The Belle Collection of Carson City Coinage.(#8352)

Splendid 1880-S Half Eagle, MS65

2979 **1880-S MS65 NGC.** The generous mintage exceeding 1.3 million pieces is responsible for the existence of splendid Gems such as the present piece. Orange-gold centers are bounded by antique-gold rims, with a glint of mauve through the date area. The strike is full throughout. Were it not for some small abrasions in the reverse fields, this wonderful piece might actually be a candidate for an even finer grade. As it is, this coin is one of 15 so certified at NGC, and there are none finer at either service (2/09).(#8353)

2980 **1881/0 MS60 NGC.** FS-005. Relatively unmarked for the MS60 grade, this crisply struck example has abundant, bright luster. Although the 1881 is quite common, the 1881/880 overdate is scarce in Mint State. Census: 6 in 60, 55 finer (1/09). (#8355)

2981 **1882 MS64 NGC.** Strongly struck with powerful luster. Pale wheat-gold surfaces overall, though with slight deepening at the margins. NGC has graded 30 finer pieces (2/09).(#8358)

1882-CC Half Eagle, AU58

2982 **1882-CC AU58 NGC.** The 1882-CC half eagle is an issue seldom seen in Mint State, although this AU58 specimen is quite close. It shows a few light scuffs and abrasions like many examples, but most of the original luster is still intact. The strike is fairly well executed, with localized softness on the eagle's claws. NGC has certified 33 pieces finer (2/09).(#8359)

Fabulous 1882-CC Five Dollar Gold, MS62

2983 **1882-CC MS62 NGC.** This mid-date Carson City issue has a markedly higher mintage than its neighbors, and as a result, it is more available in a variety of grades than any date that came before. At the MS62 level, however, the 1882-CC five is a rarity, with just six such pieces known to NGC and only one coin graded finer (2/09). This shining example is well-defined with rich butter-yellow color and undercurrents of orange. Scattered wispy marks define the grade, though the coin offers eye appeal more reminiscent of an MS63 or better representative.
From The Belle Collection of Carson City Coinage.(#8359)

Popular AU55 1883-CC Five Dollar

2984 **1883-CC AU55 NGC.** Following the boom year of 1882, production of half eagles at Carson City plunged to 12,958 pieces in 1883. This is an appealing survivor with light wear across the well-defined high points. Modestly abraded lemon-gold fields have essentially undimmed luster. Census: 24 in 55, 37 finer (2/09). *From The Belle Collection of Carson City Coinage.*(#8362)

Attractive 1884-CC Five Dollar, AU58

2985 **1884-CC AU58 PCGS.** The year 1884 would see the last half eagles minted at the Carson City Mint until the 1890 issue. Only 16,402 examples were produced in 1884. This piece displays deep, mellow orange-gold coloration on both sides, highly attractive. Only a touch of high-point rub on the boldly struck surfaces separates this piece from Mint State, and contact is minimal. Population: 13 in 58, 3 finer (2/09). *From The Belle Collection of Carson City Coinage.*(#8365)

Captivating 1885-S Half Eagle, MS66

2986 **1885-S MS66 NGC. CAC.** Although the 1885-S is one of the more common dates of the Liberty Head Reverse Motto five dollar series, it is rare in the higher-level Mint State grades. The impeccably preserved surfaces of this Premium Gem specimen display radiant luster and soft orange-gold patina imbued with whispers of mint-green and lilac. A well executed strike leaves sharp definition on the design elements, rounding out the captivating eye appeal. A milling mark beneath the eagle's beak may help identify the coin. Census: 15 in 66, 2 finer (2/09).(#8368)

Sharp Gem 1886 Half Eagle

2987 **1886 MS65 NGC.** The strike is nearly full, save for a whisper of softness on the high point hair and the lower eagle details. The surfaces are pretty ice-blue and orange-gold, with some faint prooflikeness peeking through on portions of each side. This piece is the only Gem certified of this issue at NGC, but there is one piece finer each at NGC and PCGS (2/09).(#8369)

2988 **1891-CC MS62 NGC.** Crisply detailed with immense luster gracing the orange-tinged yellow-gold surfaces. Minor abrasions overall with three reed marks in the right obverse field accounting for the grade.(#8378)

2989 **1891-CC MS62 NGC.** Deep orange-gold surfaces show occasional rose tints. A well-defined example of this popular Carson City gold type issue, modestly marked for the grade.(#8378)

Scarce Select Mint State 1892-CC Half Eagle

2990 **1892-CC MS63 NGC.** A gorgeous orange-gold example of this popular issue. With a mintage of 82,968 pieces, it would seem that examples should be available in all grades. In fact, PCGS has never certified an example above MS63, and NGC has only graded three finer. This specimen is boldly detailed and exhibits scattered surface marks that are consistent with the grade. Census: 6 in 63, 3 finer (2/09). *From The Belle Collection of Carson City Coinage.*(#8380)

2991 **1893 MS64 NGC.** Excellent detail with strong, satiny luster. The surfaces are generally yellow-orange with hints of rose and a degree of coppery alloy on the reverse.(#8383)

Elegant Gem 1893 Five Dollar

2992 **1893 MS65 NGC.** With a mintage of over 1.5 million pieces, it is unsurprising that a number of high-grade 1893 fives have survived to the present day, though Gems are conditionally scarce. This satiny orange-gold example exhibits crisp detail on the well-preserved portrait. NGC has graded just nine coins finer (2/09). (#8383)

2993 **1893-CC AU50 PCGS.** Warm sun-orange surfaces show slight evidence of alloy near the rims. A lightly worn, modestly abraded example with an overwhelming aura of originality.(#8384)

Bold 1893-CC Half Eagle, MS61

2994 **1893-CC MS61 NGC.** The final year of production from the fabled Carson City Mint, but this piece is certainly a worthy representative of that fabled facility and time. The 1893-CC half eagle is usually found no higher than AU55 or so. This MS61 piece displays a sharp strike throughout, if a bit short of full, and only scattered light abrasions, in keeping with the grade, possible prevent an even finer assessment. Liberty's cheek, in particular, is remarkably clean. A tiny scrape on the first C in the mintmark is noted under a loupe. *From The Belle Collection of Carson City Coinage.*(#8384)

Scarce Select Mint State 1893-CC Five

2995 **1893-CC MS63 PCGS.** The 1893-CC is one of the more commonly seen CC half eagles and it is also one of the more available Carson City fives in Mint State. It is still a very scarce coin in MS63 condition, however. This is a sharply defined example that displays radiant cartwheel luster and no abrasions that are readily apparent to the unaided eye. Population: 5 in 63, 4 finer (2/09). *From The Belle Collection of Carson City Coinage.*(#8384)

1897 Liberty Half Eagle MS65

2996 **1897 MS65 NGC.** This precisely struck Liberty half eagle has sweeping luster and no objectionable marks. Pale peach-gold on the fields and devices with a glimpse of sea-green throughout the peripheries. Difficult to secure any finer, since the typical example is scuffy from contact with peers. Census: 68 in 65, 8 finer (2/09). (#8394)

Wonderful 1897 Half Eagle, MS66

2997 **1897 MS66 NGC.** Despite a mintage of more than 800,000 pieces, the 1897 is difficult to acquire in the higher grades of Mint State. This delightful Premium Gem is tied for the finest certified, with NGC reporting just eight coins in MS66 and none finer. PCGS has certified none above MS65, at which level they have graded 15 examples (2/09). Pleasing apricot-gold and mint-green patina endows the surfaces, which exhibit only minuscule handling marks. Crisply defined motifs and eye-catching satiny luster enhance the wonderful eye appeal.(#8394)

2998 **1899 MS65 NGC.** Well-defined and strongly lustrous with a touch of satin to the peach-kissed fields. Strong eye appeal for the issue. NGC has graded 87 numerically finer pieces (2/09). (#8398)

Bold Gem 1899-S Half Eagle

2999 1899-S MS65 NGC. An issue that is much rarer in Gem condition than the original mintage exceeding 1.5 million pieces would indicate, the 1899-S must have seen many examples melted later. Less than two-dozen Gem or finer specimens are certified at both services combined. This piece is nearly fully struck, with bold frosty straw-gold coloration. The surfaces are also nearly pristine, with the sole exception of a series of scrapes on the lower bust truncation and in the right obverse field nearby. Census: 12 in 65, 4 finer (2/09).(#8399)

3000 1901/0-S MS64 PCGS. FS-301, formerly FS-006. The underdigit 0 shows most prominently to the right of the top of the second 1 in the date. Well-defined and strongly lustrous with a peach blush over the centers of otherwise yellow-gold surfaces. PCGS has graded just 14 finer examples for the variety (2/09) (#8403)

Shining MS66 1901-S Five Dollar

3001 1901-S MS66 PCGS. The 1901-S half eagle is a well-established choice for the 20th century type collector, readily available even at the Gem level. A Premium Gem, however, is another matter entirely. This sharply struck example is carefully preserved with rich yellow-orange luster. PCGS has graded only two finer pieces (1/09).(#8404)

Attractive 1901-S Five Dollar, MS66

3002 1901-S MS66 NGC. CAC. The 1901-S, from a mintage of 3.648 million pieces, is one of the most common dates of the series in most grades. Even MS65 examples can be obtained with patience, but the certified population then falls dramatically. This Premium Gem specimen possesses frosty luster residing on apricot-gold and mint-green surfaces that are nicely preserved. The design elements are well defined, save for weakness in some of the star centers. (#8404)

Notable MS66 1901-S Five Dollar

3003 1901-S MS66 NGC. Satiny and carefully preserved with strong visual appeal. Butter-yellow shadings are the norm, though distinct orange and tan accents visit the margins. The central devices offer marvelous detail. This issue is a rarity any finer, with just 13 such pieces graded by NGC (2/09).(#8404)

3004 1902-S MS64 NGC. A lovely near-Gem example with shimmering mint luster and light honey-gold toning. Exceptionally well struck in the centers and nicely preserved, with a modicum of wispy marks on each side.(#8406)

Lovely Gem 1904 Five Dollar

3005 1904 MS65 PCGS. Excellent design definition with satiny yellow-gold surfaces. Occasional glimpses of green-gold and lavender appear near the rims. A lower mintage issue, much scarcer than, for example, the 1901-S. Housed in an old green label holder. Population: 52 in 65, 17 finer (2/09).(#8409)

Radiant Near-Gem 1904-S Five Dollar

3006 1904-S MS64 NGC. Only 97,000 examples of this issue were coined—a precipitous drop from the totals of the previous few years—and Gem examples are expectedly elusive. This splendid near-Gem offers radiant luster over lovely orange-gold surfaces. The strike is quite close to full, as often seen on S-mint productions of the era. It is perhaps only a hair-thin mark on Liberty's cheek that prevents an even finer grade assessment, but the eye appeal is considerable. Census: 6 in 64, 3 finer (2/09).(#8410)

3007 1908 MS64 NGC. Glowing luster exudes from both sides of this near-Gem representative, and a well directed strike leaves strong definition on the design features. A few minor marks on the brass-gold surfaces limit the grade.(#8418)

Impressive MS66 1908 Liberty Five Dollar

3008 **1908 MS66 PCGS.** Each side of this final-year Liberty half eagle sports fresh, vibrant luster. Pale straw-gold centers and deeper sun-yellow margins are equally well-preserved, and the strike is crisp. An ideal Premium Gem for the discerning type or date collector. Population: 26 in 66, 7 finer (2/09).(#8418)

Singular MS66 1908 Liberty Head Five

3009 **1908 MS66 NGC. CAC.** The year 1908 saw the last production of the long-running Liberty Head type, and only in Philadelphia of the five dollar denomination. This original Premium Gem displays boldly struck orange-gold surfaces with greenish-gold coloration near the rims. The obverse is essentially pristine, and the reverse show only a single diagonal contact mark in the left field above the eagle's wing. The eye appeal is off the charts. Census: 50 in 66, 7 finer (2/09).(#8418)

Elusive 1908 Liberty Head Five, MS67

3010 **1908 MS67 NGC.** This visually impressive Superb Gem is conditionally scarce at the current grade level, as one of just 13 pieces so graded by NGC and PCGS combined. Scintillating mint frost abounds over the yellow-gold surfaces, which reveal mint-green peripheral accents. The design elements are crisply struck, including the eagle's shield and talons, and only a handful of the obverse stars are less than fully defined. This was the final year of the relatively long-lived Liberty half eagle series, and the first year of the new Indian Head design. In fact, the 1908 half eagle is the only so-dated coinage of the Liberty Head design. Census: 6 in 67, 1 finer (1/09).(#8418)

PROOF LIBERTY HALF EAGLE

Outstanding 1903 Half Eagle PR65 Cameo

3011 **1903 PR65 Cameo NGC. CAC.** Most gold proofs struck in 1902 and later are lacking in contrast, in accordance with the alteration of Mint procedures that led to the evolution of the brilliant finish (and later, the satin, matte, and Roman gold finishes as European influences waxed and waned). The present Gem, though it does not offer the thick frost that defined the devices on many earlier proofs, does display substantial contrast between the sharply struck portrait and the gleaming lemon-gold fields. Excellent preservation out of the 154 proofs struck. Census: 9 in 65 Cameo, 11 finer (2/09).(#88498)

INDIAN HALF EAGLES

3012 **1908 MS63 NGC.** Brightly lustrous with pale wheat-gold surfaces that take on a brassy cast. Though the well struck devices show scattered abrasions, the eye appeal remains strong.(#8510)

Pleasing MS64 1908 Five

3013 **1908 MS64 PCGS.** Deep yellow-orange color shows occasional butter and honey accents. This near-Gem is strongly struck in the centers with only trifling weakness at the margins. Though the 1908 five benefited from the usual first-year savings to a limited extent, the nature of the design means that few finer survivors exist today.(#8510)

1908 Indian Five Dollar, MS65

3014 **1908 MS65 PCGS. CAC.** As a first-year issue, the 1908 half eagle experienced a savings bonus to high-grade examples, though the number was not as high as it could have been, owing to the design's initial unpopularity. Select and even Choice examples are readily available for a price, though the 1908 half eagle becomes elusive at the Gem level and is a condition rarity any finer. This immensely lustrous orange-gold piece shows hints of salmon that add vibrancy to the minimally marked surfaces. The strike is bold in the centers, with only the slightest hint of softening visible at the margins. PCGS has graded 17 finer examples (2/09).(#8510)

Lustrous 1908 Indian Half Eagle, MS65

Appealing 1908 Indian Five, MS65

3015 1908 MS65 NGC. As the first year of issue, the 1908 Indian half eagles are required for date and mintmark collectors, and are in great demand from type collectors. The Indian Head design that appeared on quarter eagles and half eagles was the creation of Bela Lyon Pratt, a Boston sculptor who once studied under Augustus Saint-Gaudens. Pratt was acquainted with Dr. William Sturgis Bigelow, a close friend of President Theodore Roosevelt, and this was the connection that eventually resulted in the sunken design. Bigelow felt that the fields would protect the design from wearing away.

Wisps of orange and green accompany the brilliant and highly lustrous yellow surfaces that exhibit a full quota of original mint frost. All of the design definition on each side is bold and intricately defined. This remarkable Gem has pristine surfaces and excellent eye appeal. NGC has only certified 18 finer examples (2/09).(#8510)

3016 1908 MS65 NGC. Bela Lyon Pratt's Indian Head-Eagle design was unpopular with the public, who felt that the design would trap germs and promote unsanitary conditions, spreading disease. Breen noted in his *Complete Encyclopedia* that Philadelphia coin dealer Samuel Hudson Chapman was an outspoken critic of the design, alleging "that the designs were antinaturalistic, unhygienic, incapable of stacking, and too easily counterfeited."

Pristine and lustrous yellow-gold surfaces exhibit frosty mint luster with excellent aesthetic appeal. This boldly detailed Gem is a coin that will please the connoisseur, destined for a high-quality date or type collection. NGC has only certified 18 finer examples (2/09).(#8510)

Admirable 1908 Half Eagle, MS65

3017 1908 MS65 NGC. While the Indian Head design had its critics, it also had many admirers. In *Numismatic Art in America*, for example, Cornelius Vermeule writes: "The Native American is far from emaciated [as described by S.H. Chapman], and the coins show more imagination and daring of design than almost any other issue in American history. Pratt deserves to be admired for his medals and coins ..."

The soft, frosty yellow-gold surfaces of this brilliant and highly lustrous Gem retain subtle hints of pale green and rose toning on each side. Every individual detail side is remarkably well defined. NGC has only certified 18 finer pieces (2/09).(#8510)

Gorgeous 1908 Gem Indian Five

3018 1908 MS65 NGC. As a type, the Indian Head half eagle is the single most challenging gold issue of the 20th century to locate in Gem quality. NGC has certified more than 78,000 Indian half eagles in all grades, but only 572 coins have graded MS65 or finer, or 1 out of every 137 coins. As a point of comparison, one out of every 45 Indian quarter eagles are graded MS65 or finer, and the figures for Indian eagles and Saint-Gaudens double eagles are 1 out of 23 and 1 of 8, respectively.

This gorgeous Gem has exceptional mint frost with brilliant yellow luster and frosty gold surfaces. Both sides exhibit lovely green and rose highlights. All of the design details are extraordinarily well defined. NGC has only certified 18 finer coins (2/09).(#8510)

Pristine 1908 Indian Five, MS66

Pleasing Gem 1908-S Five Dollar

3019 1908 MS66 PCGS. CAC. Bela Lyon Pratt developed the unusual sunken Indian Head design for the quarter eagles and half eagles introduced in 1908. The design work is such that the highest point of the motifs is at the same level as the surrounding fields. At one time, Pratt had actually studied under the tutelage of Augustus Saint-Gaudens. Regarding his design, Jeff Garrett and Ron Guth observe: "Pratt's bold and dynamic incuse designs were sunk into the coin, as opposed to raised by the dies, a new concept for regular-issue coinage of the U.S. Mint." The word "incuse" is often associated with these coins, but technically it is incorrect. The actual design is raised, but then sunk below the surrounding surfaces.

Dr. William Bigelow was a friend of Pratt, and he was also a friend of President Theodore Roosevelt. It was through Bigelow's efforts that Pratt was selected to prepare the new Indian design for the quarter eagle and half eagle gold coins. Both denominations first appeared in 1908 and continued until 1929, with various intermissions during the time span. The design had its critics who came up with some imaginative reasons that it should not be produced. Among the most imaginative: The design would trap germs and disease-bearing dirt, proving unhealthy.

This amazing Premium Gem is boldly detailed and fully brilliant with impressive light yellow luster. The surfaces are essentially pristine without any visible blemishes on either side. Population: 16 in 66, 1 finer (1/09).(#8510)

3020 1908-S MS65 NGC. Between the limited mintage of 82,000 pieces and a lack of interest among West Coast collectors and hoarders, the 1908-S Indian half eagle was little-saved and the pool of available examples is small. Add in the poor Gem-level survival rate for the design as a whole, and it is little wonder that this popular S-mint issue is a borderline condition rarity in MS65. This shining sun-gold example offers warm luster and well-preserved surfaces. Only a handful of tiny grazes separate this appealing piece from an even finer designation. Census: 24 in 65, 21 finer (2/09). (#8512)

Fantastic Gem 1908-S Five Dollar

Desirable MS65 1909 Half Eagle

3021 1908-S MS65 PCGS. Of the three Mints that produced Indian half eagles in 1908, San Francisco had the lowest output, with five-figure production of just 82,000 pieces. It is one of just three Indian half eagle issues with fewer than 100,000 coins produced, yet unlike the 1909-O and 1911-D issues, the 1908-S is not a condition rarity through most Mint State grades, though at the Gem level, even this highly saved issue begins to run short on supply. This impressively lustrous survivor shows vibrant and well-preserved yellow-orange surfaces. Aside from a touch of weakness at the lowest pendant on the necklace, the strike is crisp, and the overall visual appeal is excellent. Population: 44 in 65, 21 finer (2/09).(#8512)

3022 1909 MS65 PCGS. Among the stated goals of the recessed-relief Indian quarter eagle and half eagle designs was to protect the central devices from wear for an extended period of time. While this goal was achieved to a degree, another problem cropped up: With the devices protected, the fields became the most exposed areas, leaving them vulnerable to unsightly abrasions, particularly on the larger half eagle.

As a result, Gems are scarce for virtually all issues in the series, and the 1909 is hardly an exception. This honey-gold example is in esteemed company, with vibrantly lustrous, largely untouched surfaces that show hints of rose and orange near the margins. Well struck and desirable. PCGS has graded just seven finer examples (2/09).(#8513)

3023 1909-D MS64 PCGS. CAC. Warm honey-gold surfaces show elements of orange on this piece, which would be ideal for a type collection. A minimally marked and immensely lustrous Choice example of this popular Indian five dollar issue, one that is surprisingly unavailable any finer; PCGS has certified just 93 such pieces (1/09).(#8514)

3024 1909-D MS64 NGC. Pleasing luster exudes from the honey-gold surfaces of this near-Gem five dollar. This is a sharply struck piece that reveals a few minor but grade-limiting marks. The 1909-D becomes quite challenging any finer.(#8514)

3025 1909-D MS64 PCGS. Light golden toning overall with glimpses of pink. An appealing near-Gem from the single highest-mintage Indian half eagle issue, an ideal type piece.(#8514)

3026 1909-D MS64 PCGS. Strongly lustrous with attractive wheat-gold surfaces. Well-defined and appealing with only a handful of small marks visible in the fields.(#8514)

3027 **1909-D MS64 PCGS.** Bright wheat-gold surfaces show occasional hints of sun-yellow. A well-defined piece that displays few abrasions, though a luster scrape is noted at the T of LIBERTY. This popular type issue is available at the MS64 level, but anything finer is scarce; PCGS has graded 93 such pieces (2/09). *From The Burning Tree Colletion.*(#8514)

In-Demand 1909-O Half Eagle, AU50

3028 **1909-O AU50 PCGS.** The 1909-O half eagle is an anachronistic issue, the last gold coin struck at the New Orleans Mint, the only 20th century O-mint half eagle (New Orleans struck eagles in 1901, 1903, 1904, and 1906) and the last half eagle struck in New Orleans since the 1894-O. It is also, of course, easily the series key, and in "feverish demand" according to Garrett and Guth. This piece has deep reddish-orange patina on both sides, with mild wear visible on the high points and tinges of ice-blue in the protected recesses. The mintmark is fairly bold, and double-punched as on most examples. Certified in a green-label holder.(#8515)

Low Mintage 1909-O Half Eagle, AU53

3029 **1909-O AU53 PCGS.** The 1909-O five dollar saw a mintage of 34,200 pieces. It is one of the most sought-after issues in the Indian Head half eagle series because of the low mintage and general scarcity in any Mint State grade.

The mintmark is very weak on this AU53 coin. The remaining design features are quite sharp, though the eagle's shoulder reveals minor softness. Yellow-gold surfaces display a fair amount of luster, and are lightly abraded.(#8515)

1909-O Five Dollar, AU55

3030 **1909-O AU55 NGC.** The 1909-O is one of the more sought-after issues in the Indian Head five dollar series because of the low mintage of 34,200 pieces. The yellow-gold surfaces of this Choice AU specimen are tinted with light tan, and retain a good amount of luster. Both sides are nicely defined and minimally marked. (#8515)

Important Near-Mint 1909-O Indian Five

3031 **1909-O AU58 NGC.** By the time of the "Renaissance of American Coinage," to borrow Roger Burdette's memorable phrase and book title, the New Orleans Mint was an increasingly antiquated operation, with its last coinage coming in 1909. New Orleans had struck its last eagles in 1906 and its last double eagles in 1879, meaning that no Saint-Gaudens design ever appeared with an "O" mintmark. Only through a tiny mintage of 34,200 Bela Lyon Pratt-designed five dollar pieces in 1909 did the Louisiana facility put its stamp on the Renaissance.

This near-Mint survivor hails from that coveted issue, today a prominent series key. Bright yellow-gold surfaces are amply lustrous, with few abrasions and only a trace of rub. An interesting and high-end survivor from this memorable issue.(#8515)

Key Date 1909-O Indian Half Eagle, AU58

3032 **1909-O AU58 NGC.** Variety One. The mintmark is weakly impressed and shows doubling on its left side. The satiny surfaces have considerable eye appeal, with even khaki-gold color and considerable remaining mint luster for the grade. A few small marks appear on each of the two sides, but none of them are overly distracting. This issue has the lowest mintage of any Indian half eagle and is scarce at all grade levels.(#8515)

Luminous MS61 1909-S Five Dollar

3033 **1909-S MS61 NGC.** Though it does not rank among the lowest-mintage Indian half eagle issues, the 1909-S five is nonetheless surprisingly elusive in all Mint State grades. This sun-gold piece, though significantly abraded, offers pleasing luster and detail. NGC has certified 70 finer examples (1/09).(#8516)

3034 **1911-D AU55 ICG.** This low mintage Choice AU example has slight wear on the cheekbone and headband, but luster emerges from the design. The right reverse field is moderately abraded. The Denver mintmark is faint but unmistakable.(#8521)

3035 1911-D AU55 NGC. Despite light wear that crosses the central devices, this yellow-orange piece retains substantial luster and shows few marks. A desirable example of this lower-mintage issue. (#8521)

3036 1911-S MS61 NGC. Rich gold-orange color and solid overall detail. Though each side shows a number of light to moderate abrasions, this unworn piece retains considerable eye appeal. (#8522)

Elusive MS64 1911-S Half Eagle

3037 1911-S MS64 PCGS. The 1911-S is an elusive issue as the Gem level is approached, despite its original mintage exceeding 1.4 million examples. Apparently there were few collectors of the pre-World War I period in San Francisco who desired (or could afford) to salt away five dollars for an unlimited time by putting back an example. The khaki-gold surfaces offer plenty of mint luster, and the only singularly mentionable abrasions are a small patch in the obverse field before the Indian, near the rim at 9 o'clock. In MS64 this piece is one of 19 so certified at PCGS, and there are eight finer at that service (2/09).(#8522)

Shimmering 1912 Five Dollar, MS64

3038 1912 MS64 NGC. Shimmering luster emanates from both sides of this near-Gem half eagle, and attractive yellow-gold coloration bathes each. An exacting strike manifests itself in strong delineation on the design features, enhancing the coin's eye appeal. A few minute marks in the raised exposed fields preclude Gem status. (#8523)

Appealing 1912 Near-Gem Five Dollar

3039 1912 MS64 PCGS. Bright luster endows both sides of this near-Gem half eagle, and a well executed strike leaves sharp delineation on the design elements, including the bonnet feathers and the eagle's plumage. A few trivial marks apparently deny Gem classification. Nice overall appeal.(#8523)

Desirable MS64 1912 Five Dollar

3040 **1912 MS64 PCGS.** Most striking about this near-Gem is its color and luster, shining orange-gold at the margins with a slight fading to sun-yellow closer to the centers. The well struck obverse displays beautifully, and though minor alloy and marks on the reverse preclude a finer designation, this remains a choice example. PCGS has graded 45 finer pieces (2/09).(#8523)

Lustrous 1913 Five Dollar, MS64

3041 **1913 MS64 NGC.** The lustrous surfaces of this near-Gem five dollar yield soft greenish-gold patina, and a well executed strike leaves sharp delineation on the design elements, except for minor weakness on the eagle's shoulder. Marks are visible on the Indian's cheek and the back of the eagle's neck.(#8525)

Lovely MS64 1913 Half Eagle

3042 **1913 MS64 NGC.** Rich orange-gold color with strong and pleasing luster. Though a handful of wispy surface marks affect each side, this near-Gem shows none of the overt abrasions that so often plague the wide-open fields on this design. As always for the series, an elusive issue any finer; NGC has graded just 42 such coins (1/09).(#8525)

Brilliant 1913 Half Eagle, MS64

3043 **1913 MS64 NGC.** Among all the Indian half eagles, the 1913 is one of the common dates, but it is rarely seen any finer than the present Choice Mint State piece. NGC has only certified 42 finer examples (2/09). This beauty has brilliant honey-gold luster with frosty surfaces. Close examination is necessary to see the few trivial marks on either side. Clearly at the top of the MS64 grade level. *From The Burning Tree Colletion.*(#8525)

Well Struck 1913-S Half Eagle, MS62

3044 **1913-S MS62 PCGS.** The luminous surfaces of this S-mint specimen display a delicate blend of brass-gold and mint-green color, accented with splashes of apricot, especially on the reverse. The mintmark is somewhat mushy, which is characteristic of this issue, but the overall strike is better than ordinarily seen. A few minute marks are visible, slightly more so on the reverse. (#8526)

Attractive 1914 Five Dollar, MS64

3045 **1914 MS64 NGC.** Variegated apricot, mint-green, lilac, and yellow-gold coloration enriches the lustrous surfaces of this near-Gem. The design elements are well brought up, including the Indian's hair and bonnet feathers; the eagle's shoulder feathers are a tad soft, though all show. Minuscule marks preclude Gem status. (#8527)

Bright 1914-D Select Half Eagle

3046 **1914-D MS63 PCGS.** Bright luster radiates from both sides of this Select half eagle. Yellow-gold surfaces are tinged with wisps of light tan, and exhibit crisply defined design features, including the Indian's hair and bonnet and the eagle's shoulder and mintmark. Small marks on the Indian's cheek and in the fields preclude a higher grade.(#8528)

Uncirculated 1914-S Five Dollar

3047 **1914-S MS61 NGC.** The 1914-S is scarce in mint condition, as are most S-mint five dollar issues. This is a satiny example with highly lustrous surfaces and exceptional eye appeal for the grade. Numerous light abrasions are scattered over each side. Traces of pale green add to the overall desirability of this piece.(#8529)

Sharply Defined 1915 Five Dollar, MS64

3048 **1915 MS64 NGC.** A mix of yellow-gold, mint-green, and apricot takes on slightly deeper hues on the reverse of this near-Gem, and a well executed strike delivers sharp definition to the design features, a characteristic of this issue. Minute handling marks, more so on the obverse, deny Gem status.(#8530)

Pleasing MS64 1915 Five Dollar

3049 **1915 MS64 NGC.** The 1915 is one of the more frequently encountered type coins in this short-lived series, and it is also one of the best produced which makes it excellent for type purposes. This is a particularly attractive piece that has smooth, lustrous surfaces that are free from the usually heavy abrasions normally seen on this type. The striking details are well defined, and both sides display light, even reddish patina.(#8530)

Well Struck 1916-S Five Dollar, MS62

3050 **1916-S MS62 PCGS.** Lustrous brassy-gold surfaces display occasional glimpses of rose and light green under magnification. The design features are well impressed, including the eagle's shoulder feathers, while the mintmark shows the usual mushiness. Small contact marks, especially on the exposed raised fields, limit the grade.(#8532)

Impressive PR67 1908 Five Dollar Indian

3051 **1908 PR67 NGC.** There were few proof gold collectors in 1908. Only 167 proof half eagles were struck, an increase from the 92 proofs produced the prior year. The 1908 quarter eagle had a comparable increase in proof mintage from its 1907 predecessor. The cause for the additional pieces struck was presumably the new designs by Bela Lyon Pratt. These replaced the long-lived Liberty types, which had been struck throughout the entire lifetime of most collectors of the era.

Some who ordered the new Indian half eagle proofs were surely surprised when they received and examined their specimens. Unlike prior designs, the devices were sunken into the field, with the high points at the same level as the field. These designs are often referred to as incuse, but this is a misnomer, since an incuse design would have opposite relief, with areas such as the cheekbone the lowest point of the design, instead of the highest. The proof finish of the Indian half eagle was also dramatically different than the Liberty type. Proof Liberty half eagles have mirrored fields and (at times) frosty devices, similar to the proof gold American Eagles in production today. The proof Indian and Saint-Gaudens types are matte proofs, with the same microgranular finish on both the fields and devices.

Proof Indian half eagles are easily distinguished from their business strike counterparts. The color is comparatively dark, since the fields lack reflectivity, and luster is diffused. Since the pieces were well made, the abrasions that plague bag-stored business strikes are absent on proofs. Finally, the proofs are fully struck, the extra detail most noticeable on the eagle's shoulder and the lower reaches of the headdress. The present piece shows all of these characteristics, and is essentially perfect, save for a tiny Mint-made planchet flaw located directly beneath, but relatively distant from, the U in TRUST. This minuscule flaw serves as an identifier for any auction appearances. Census: 11 in 67, 1 finer (2/09).(#8539)

3052 **1909 PR68 NGC.** Mint officials most likely anticipated strong collector demand for the new Indian half eagle when they delivered 167 proofs in 1908. Sales, however, were disappointing, a fact that one can easily see in the limited mintage of the 1909. This second-year issue was produced to the extent of just 78 coins, and the finish was markedly different from that employed for the 1908. The 1909, as well as the 1910, was struck with a Roman Gold finish, which is actually a hybrid between brilliant and satiny. Those issues are the only two in the proof Indian half eagle series to display that texture; survivors of both deliveries are equally rare, despite a considerably higher reported mintage for the 1910.

The inability of some to distinguish between business and specimen strikes of the two issues may mean that a not-insignificant number of the proofs were inadvertently lost to circulation. In the case of the 1909, we estimate just 30-40 survivors, examples of which have been graded from PR63 through PR68 at the two major grading services.

This piece is tied for the single finest proof 1909 five dollar at NGC and PCGS (2/09)—or that figure may represent one coin presented twice for grading and certification. It is easily one of the most appealing specimen strikings we have ever offered. The surfaces are pleasingly bright for the finish, with considerable satin texture evident. The strike is full in all areas, and outwardly distracting and/or grade-limiting blemishes are nonexistent. It is solely for pedigree concerns that we mention a tiny swirl of overlying color in the obverse field at the upper left corner of the first digit in the date. Medium intensity orange-gold shadings blanket both sides. Census: 2 in 68, 0 finer (2/09). (#8540)

Interesting VF Details 1795
13 Leaves Eagle, BD-2

3053　**1795 13 Leaves—Repaired, Improperly Cleaned—NCS. VF Details.** Breen-6830, Taraszka-2, BD-2, High R.4. The more elusive of the two 13 Leaves varieties for the year, a borderline rarity when all grades are combined. The 13 Leaves reverse is in common with the BD-1, believed to be the die pair for the first eagles struck, and the obverse is in common with the famous 9 Leaves variety, the BD-3. The present piece, though altogether too bright with a degree of porosity to the moderately worn butter-yellow surfaces, remains readily collectible. Smoothing and other repair is noted at the left and right reverse margins.(#8551)

Elusive 1795 BD-5 Eagle, AU Details

3054　**1795 13 Leaves—Improperly Cleaned—NCS. AU Details.** Breen-6830, Taraszka-5, BD-5, R.5. Five 1795 eagle varieties are known, four with 13 leaves on the reverse (BD-1, BD-2, BD-4, BD-5) and the one remaining variety (BD-3) with just nine leaves in the branch. John Dannreuther estimates a surviving population of only 35 to 45 examples of BD-5, the rarest of the four 13 leaves die marriages. Light yellow surfaces are a bit too bright, a result of cleaning. A few obverse and reverse marks are mostly concentrated along the right border on each side. The reverse has a heavy raised lump between OF and AMERICA that is a defect seen on all known examples BD-4 and BD-5, the two varieties sharing the same reverse die.(#8551)

3055 1795 13 Leaves MS63 PCGS. Breen-6830, Taraszka-1, BD-1, High R.3. The United States Mint produced gold coins for the first time in 1795, starting with half eagles, and beginning the ten dollar gold series in September. A modest mintage of 5,583 eagles dated 1795 was achieved during the fiscal year, with deliveries taking place from September 27, 1795 through March 30, 1796. Five different die marriages are known for the date, with BD-1 the most "common" variety. The BD-1 obverse die is characterized by the closely spaced date, with the 1 close to the curl, and the tip of the 5 overlapping the bust. Star 11 is extremely close to Y in LIBERTY, and there are two lumps visible in the field near Y. The reverse die has 13 leaves in the palm branch, one of which nearly touches U in UNITED.

In *Early U.S. Gold Coin Varieties*, John Dannreuther estimates a total surviving population of 225-325 examples of the BD-1 variety in all grades. The date may be available in the context of early U.S. gold coinage, but it is scarce in absolute terms. In Choice Uncirculated grades, it is quite rare. NGC has certified only 13 coins at the MS63 level, with eight finer; and PCGS has graded only 12 examples at the Choice level, with eight finer (2/09).

The present coin is a fantastic representative of this historic date. The strike is admirable for such an early issue. Some softness is noted on the central details, but the peripheries are sharp, with bold detail on the stars. The surfaces display thick mint frost, with some semiprooflike areas in the reverse field. The surfaces are amazingly clean, with just a few field marks and tiny planchet flaws visible through a glass. A truly extraordinary prize for the type collector or early gold aficionado.(#8551)

1799 Small Stars Ten Dollar, BD-8 PCGS Genuine

3056 1799 Small Stars Obverse PCGS Genuine. Irregular Date. Breen-6840, Taraszka-20, BD-8, R.5. This piece shows AU Details and it is Damaged and Cleaned. The 17 in the date are evenly spaced but tilted far right, the star point of star 12 touches the upper beak, and star 13 touches the scroll. The estimated mintage was 2500 to 3500 pieces, and of that number it is believed that 45 to 55 examples are known in all grades today. Slight traces of mint luster can still be seen around the devices. The surfaces are bright from cleaning and light hairlines are evident with a magnifier. The center of the reverse shows damage on the horizontal shield lines. Well struck. (#98562)

Extremely Rare 1799 BD-1 Eagle, AU Details
Unique Early Die State

3057 **1799 Small Stars Obverse—Improperly Cleaned—NCS. AU Details.** Breen-2182; Taraszka-13; BD-1, High R.7. The reverse die has a small die chip between the U and N of UNITED, and that reverse is common to four different varieties. The present specimen has star 9 joined to the Y and star 13 nearly touching the bust. This extremely rare variety was unknown in gold until an example appeared in a 1972 Lester Merkin sale. Prior to that time, the die combination was known in the form of a unique copper trial piece. The existence of the same die combination in both copper and gold is a strong indication that the copper example, known as Judd-26, is a true die trial rather than a later-date concoction.

Two distinct die states are known among survivors of the BD-1 die marriage. Early die state pieces have a short crack from the rim to star 8. Late die state pieces have a second crack from the rim to the L and across Liberty's cap.

John Dannreuther estimates that between five and seven examples of the BD-1 variety are known. Today we are aware of the following five pieces:

1. AU55. Late die state. Superior (10/2001), lot 2874. Unattributed in the Superior catalog.

2. AU, cleaned. Early die state and the only one currently known. Benson Collection (Goldberg Coins, 2/2003), lot 2083. **The present specimen.** This piece has pleasing light yellow color with a shimmering appearance that indicates it has been cleaned. A few scattered surface marks are consistent with the grade. However, it is still the second finest known example that we are aware of.

3. XF or finer. Late die state. Lester Merkin (2/1972), lot 433; Harry W. Bass, Jr. Illustrated in the Bass Sylloge and the Bass-Dannreuther reference. The Merkin description emphasized the importance of this piece: "Breen 1-A, with unpublished heavy breaks down through 8th star and L. Obv. a little short of EF, rev. EF plus. Rarity 8, the only one actually traced as the original Guttag-Newcomer coin has not been located. Rarity explained by the obverse breaks."

4. XF45. Late die state. 1994 ANA (Heritage, 8/1994), lot 5817. Illustrated in the Taraszka reference. Unattributed in our 1994 ANA catalog.

5. AU58, scratched and retooled. Late die state. Goldberg Coins (2/2006), lot 1232. Unattributed in the Goldberg catalog.(#98562)

1800 Ten Dollar, XF Details
A Single-Die Pairing Issue, BD-1

3058 **1800—Damaged—NCS. XF Details.** Breen-6842, Taraszka-23, BD-1, High R.3. Only one die pairing is known for this year and the reverse was a reuse of Reverse F from 1799. The damage refers to heavy scrapes above the date and above the end of the bust of Liberty. The bright yellow-gold surfaces have numerous small abrasions over each side. A bit softly defined in the centers. (#8563)

Desirable Mint State 1801 Eagle, BD-2

3059 **1801 MS60 PCGS.** Breen-6843, Taraszka-25, BD-2, R.2. Obverse: star 8 near cap, star 13 nearly touches bust. Reverse: eagle's upper beak nearly touches star point just below. Boldly struck and highly lustrous, with vibrant lime-gold toning and nicely preserved surfaces that only show scattered, minor blemishes and a small number of trivial hairlines. According to the Garrett-Guth reference: "The 1801 eagle has a high mintage and is noted for having the second-highest surviving population (after 1799), thus it is an excellent choice as one of the more affordable dates of the type."(#8564)

Bright 1801 Eagle, BD-2, MS61

3060 **1801 MS61 NGC.** Breen-6843, Taraszka-25, BD-2, R.2. There are two known die marriages for this date, and they share similar (but not identical) reverse dies. The obverse diagnostics are keys, however, according to the Bass-Dannreuther reference on *Early U.S. Gold Coin Varieties*. These include: Star 1 away from the lowest hair curl; Star 8 close to Liberty's cap (with two points toward the cap); Star 13 almost touches Liberty's bust.

This is a bright Mint State example with flashy yellow-gold surfaces that include semireflective fields and generally well struck devices; only the eagle's arrow fletchings and talons and some of the obverse stars show striking weakness. A number of superficial marks, mostly located in the fields, prevent an even finer grade. (#8564)

3061   **1801 MS62 NGC.** Breen-6843, Taraszka-25, BD-2, R.2. The attribution is a cinch, since there are only two obverses known for this year, and on the BD-2 star 1 is considerably farther from the lowest hair curl. Star 8 is close to the cap, and star 13 nearly touches the bust. The obverse stars are different, longer and spindlier than on the BD-1. The reverses are different, too: The BD-1 1801 has a different die held over from its use in 1799 (BD-10) and 1800 (a single-variety year, BD-1), which shows the eagle's beak touching a star point at two different places. On the BD-2 as here, the eagle's beak does not touch a star point, although it is quite close.

Bass-Dannreuther estimate the mintage of this available variety to be in the range of 30,000 to 40,000 pieces from the total recorded mintage of 44,000-plus coins for the year.

It is precisely the relatively generous production for the era and denomination that enables the existence of outstanding type coins such as the present specimen. To begin with, for such a large gold coin the surfaces, at least to the naked eye, are remarkably free of abrasions, large or small. Indeed, even a loupe reveals only the expected faint ticks and abrasions. Neither the tiny mark in the right obverse field before Liberty's nose nor a couple of scrapes on the cheek are worthy of more than passing mention. The adjustment marks noted in the central hair and lightly on the cheek are undistracting, and scarcely visible without magnification. Radiant luster proceeds forth from both sides of this bright greenish-gold coin, unimpeded by color or patina.

While this issue has seen a few dozen certified in this grade at NGC and about an equal number finer, there is no doubt that it will become a cornerstone of a fine numismatic collection. (#8564)

3062 **1803 Small Stars Reverse AU53 NGC.** Breen-6844, Taraszka-26, BD-1, High R.5. Official records indicate a mintage of 15,017 eagles for the year 1803. This mintage is shared between six different die marriages, all with the same obverse die. Anthony Taraszka and Harry Bass both concluded that the present variety was first in the die emission sequence because of the number of edge reeds. Eagles from 1799 through 1801 all have 131 edge reeds. There are no eagles dated 1802. The 1803 BD-1 eagle has 131 edge reeds, in keeping with the earlier years. All other 1803 eagle varieties and the eagles of 1804 have either 130 or 126 edge reeds, indicating a break in the production series after BD-1. The variety is very scarce today, with only 30-40 survivors extant.

The obverse die is perfect, with no clashing, lapping or cracks. The reverse can be distinguished by the small stars combined with the long arrows (one extending past N and another extending to the foot of I in UNITED). The reverse die must have failed quickly because the obverse was still perfect when paired with the BD-2 reverse.

The surfaces are even and bright with some luster remaining on both sides. Both sides have attractive, green-gold color and a moderate number of abrasions. A few adjustment marks can be seen on the reverse, primarily in the dentils.(#8565)

3063 1803 Small Stars Reverse MS63 NGC. Breen-6844, Taraszka-28, BD-3, R.4. The 1803 Capped Bust Right, Heraldic Eagle ten dollar gold piece boasts a small mintage of 15,017 pieces. Six different die varieties are known for this issue, with one obverse die used in all six marriages. The reverse die used for BD-3 is characterized by the position of the eagle's beak nearly touching the star below its point, and the right foot of E in STATES positioned over a cloud space. BD-3 is the most available variety of the date, but it is still scarce in absolute terms. In *Early U.S. Gold Coin Varieties*, John Dannreuther estimates 150-200 examples of this issue are still extant in all grades. Mint State 1803 eagles are rarities, even the "common" varieties. NGC has certified 17 examples of this issue at the MS63 level, with nine finer; while PCGS has graded nine Choice specimens, with only nine finer (2/09).

Die marriages were of little interest to collectors of the 19th century, and catalogers seldom differentiated between varieties in their lot descriptions. Numismatists became more conscious of these important differences in the early part of the 20th century, and auction catalogs began to describe the small stars reverse in basic detail. In the Stickney Collection (Henry Chapman, 6/1907), lot 623, an 1803 eagle is described thusly, "1803 R. Small stars. Extremely fine. Mint lustre. See plate." The coin sold for $25, a good price at the time.

The present coin is sharply struck, with complete detail on the feathers on the eagle's breast. The surfaces display bright, satiny luster, with attractive reddish patina on each side. A few light obverse abrasions can be detected with a loupe. Rarity, historic interest, and strong visual appeal combine to make this offering an important opportunity for the early gold specialist. (#8565)

LIBERTY EAGLES

1841-O Eagle, XF Details

3064 **1841-O PCGS Genuine.** Our assessment XF Details, Improperly Cleaned. A comparatively affordable example of this famous O-mint eagle rarity. Light wear is present largely at the high points of the design, though the orange-gold surfaces also show light hairlines and a number of scattered abrasions.(#8583)

Appealing AU55 1842 Large Date Eagle

3065 **1842 Large Date AU55 NGC.** Despite having a much larger estimated mintage than its Small Date counterpart, the 1842 Large Date ten is almost equally desirable today. This scarcely worn example shows a number of fine abrasions on each side, yet the yellow-orange obverse is virtually devoid of significant abrasions. Census: 5 in 55, 9 finer (2/09).(#8584)

Rare Mint State 1842 Large Date Ten

3066 **1842 Large Date MS60 PCGS.** The date is noticeably larger than on the Small Date, and the clear crosslet on the 4 cinches the deal. Garrett and Guth note that the Large Date, while more common overall, is equally as rare in Mint State as the Small Date. The PCGS population data provide confirmation. This piece is much more attractive than the MS60 grade suggests, with deep orange-gold coloration and considerable prooflikeness present under light haze in the fields. Numerous light abrasions pepper the surfaces, but a single scrape in the reverse field between STATES and OF, extending downward almost to the eagle's neck, is the determinant. A die break is noted from the eagle's left (facing) claw down to the E in TEN and to the rim. Population: 1 in 60, 4 finer (2/09). (#8584)

3067 **1842-O XF45 PCGS.** Despite this coin's wear on the high points, the orange-gold fields remain flashy. Only a few marks of note appear on each side. Housed in a green label holder. Population: 30 in 45, 35 finer (2/09).(#8587)

3068 **1843 AU53 NGC.** Subtly lustrous yellow-gold surfaces show tan and peach elements at the margins. Lightly abraded overall but with only modest wear on each side. Census: 14 in 53, 43 finer (2/09).(#8588)

Pretty Choice AU 1843-O Ten Dollar

3069 **1843-O AU55 NGC.** As with most antebellum O-mint eagles, the 1843-O is common in lower grades (through Choice XF, scarce in AU, and exceedingly rare in Mint State). The surfaces on this pretty orange-gold Choice AU piece are semireflective under a light layer of field chatter. There are few singular abrasions noted, however. The bold strike is a plus. Census: 57 in 55, 63 finer; the great majority of those are AU58 (2/09).(#8589)

3070 **1844 Fine 12 ICG.** A well-worn but readily collectible example of this low-mintage issue, modestly abraded for the amount of wear with mustard-accented khaki-gold surfaces. Interesting eye appeal. (#8590)

3071 **1844-O AU50 NGC.** Boldly struck for the issue, with uniform sharpness on the central and peripheral design elements. A slight degree of wear is noted on each side, and numerous small marks are observed in the fields.(#8591)

Uncirculated 1844-O No Motto Eagle

3072 **1844-O MS60 NGC. CAC.** The 1844-O eagle is one of the more available No Motto dates from the New Orleans Mint, but it is still a scarce coin in high grade. Recently, 32 examples of this date were recovered from the wreck of the S.S. *Republic*, but they were primarily in AU grades. Garrett and Guth report Mint State coins are exceedingly rare. The present coin features a better than average strike, with fine detail in the hair and feathers. Attractive yellow-gold color blends with honey toning on the surfaces. Scattered handling marks are consistent with the grade. Census: 5 in 60, 8 finer (2/09).(#8591)

Pleasing 1846/'5'-O Eagle, AU53

3073 **1846/5-O AU53 PCGS.** PCGS certifies this with quotation marks around the date, e.g. 1846/'5'-O, on the theory that many numismatists believe that the underlying "digit" is actually a die defect. Nonetheless, with its own *Guide Book* listing and much popularity, the variety is always in demand. This well-struck piece is semiprooflike under a light layer of field chatter, with rich honey-gold color and lots of eye appeal. Population: 3 in 53, 7 finer (2/09). (#8596)

Choice XF 1848-O No Motto Ten

3074 **1848-O XF45 PCGS.** A canary-gold example with attractive surfaces and a suitable strike. Only 35,850 ten dollar pieces were struck in New Orleans in 1848, and nice survivors are strongly contested by Southern gold specialists. A shield ring, better known on the 1851-O issue, is also present on the current coin, located (as usual) atop the second vertical shield stripe. Population: 26 in 45, 31 finer (2/09). *From The Burning Tree Colletion.*(#8600)

Low Mintage 1848-O Ten Dollar, AU50

3075 **1848-O AU50 NGC.** Most of the high-point softness on each side of this AU example can be attributed to poor striking definition rather than circulation wear. The light green-gold surfaces are somewhat muted, however, and show scattered marks that probably indicate at least a brief stay in the channels of commerce. A scarce, low mintage New Orleans Mint issue of only 35,850 pieces. Census: 19 in 50, 58 finer (2/09).(#8600)

Delightful 1848-O Eagle, AU50

3076 **1848-O AU50 PCGS.** A delightful survivor from a mintage of just 35,850 coins. Although PCGS has certified 24 submissions in the various AU grades, the typical certified 1848-O eagle averages only Choice XF or so. Orange-gold surfaces show numerous small abrasions and a somewhat soft strike on the lower reverse, but the only singular mark is a light scrape on Liberty's cheek. Population: 7 in 50, 23 finer (12/07).(#8600)

Interesting Breen-6888 1849 Eagle

3077 **1849 MS61 PCGS.** Breen-6888. Described by Breen as an 1849/1848 overdate and "very rare." Diagnostic is the die crack running through the 4 in the date. Warmly lustrous yellow-gold surfaces show few marks for the grade, and though the devices are softly struck with blending of detail at the high points, the eye appeal remains high.(#8601)

3078 **1849-O XF40 NGC.** Still-luminous yellow-gold surfaces show light, scattered abrasions. Well struck for this often-weak issue, though the stars are ill-defined. Zones of alloy appear at the reverse rims.(#8602)

Scarce 1849-O Ten Dollar, XF40

3079 **1849-O XF40 NGC.** The 1849-O ten dollar comes from a sparse mintage of 23,900 pieces. This Extremely Fine example displays honey-gold patina laced with tan. The design features are uniformly well defined, and the surfaces are cleaner than typically found on this heavily bagmarked issue, revealing just a few minor circulation marks. Census: 10 in 40, 63 finer (2/09).(#8602)

Desirable MS61 1851 Ten Dollar

3080 **1851 MS61 NGC.** As noted by Garrett and Guth, "The 1851 eagle might appear to be a common coin at first glance, but in reality it is much scarcer than the mintage indicates." Mint State examples such as the present coin are actually condition rarities. This piece offers warm yellow-gold luster and above-average detail. Scattered reed marks and wispy abrasions account for the grade. Census: 8 in 61, 8 finer (2/09).(#8606)

Lustrous Near-Mint 1851-O Eagle

3081 **1851-O AU58 PCGS.** Almost 100 examples of the 1851-O eagle were found on the submerged wreck of the *S.S. Republic*, which foundered in a hurricane off the Georgia coast in 1865, 100 miles southeast of Savannah. Examples are still today rare in Mint State; in AU58 this coin is one of 15 so certified at PCGS, with eight finer (2/09). This piece, while we do not know if it is one of the *S.S. Republic* survivors, offers bold appeal, with canary-yellow surfaces that retain nearly all of their original luster. The strike is bold.(#8607)

3082 **1853/2 AU50 PCGS.** FS-301, formerly FS-007. This is a bright example that retains nearly complete design detail, save for the slightest degree of wear on the center of the obverse, and on the eagle's wing tips. Numerous small contact marks limit the grade. A popular overdate variety, listed on page 256 of the 2009 *Guide Book*. Population: 11 in 50, 20 finer (2/09). (#8611)

3083 **1854-S AU55 NGC.** An untoned example with pockets of luster and relatively clean surfaces. From the first year of production at the fledgling San Francisco Mint, which struggled to provide gold coinage for local commerce. The facility concentrated on double eagle production after 1855.(#8615)

Unworn 1855 Ten Dollar Gold

3084 **1855 MS60 NGC.** Excellent striking definition in the centers with no trace of wear, though the peripheral elements show slight softness. Deep yellow-orange surfaces show myriad fine abrasions that account for the grade, yet the eye appeal remains much better than the MS60 designation might suggest. Overall, an interesting and desirable example of this challenging No Motto issue. Census: 13 in 60, 30 finer (2/09).(#8616)

3085 **1856-S AU53 NGC.** Light yellow-gold color with considerable bright luster. This well struck example shows a handful of scattered abrasions that contribute to the grade.(#8621)

3086 **1857 XF40 PCGS.** Despite the light wear across each side, considerable reflective yellow-gold luster remains. A trifle softly struck, as often seen. Population: 22 in 40, 60 finer (2/09). (#8622)

3087 **1858-O AU55 NGC.** A delightful green-gold example, this Choice AU piece has nearly full luster and presents excellent aesthetic appeal. Of the three eagle issues coined in 1858, the O-mint issue has the highest mintage and is clearly the most available, but it is hardly common. Just 20,000 were coined, and the average survivor only grades AU50 or so. Census: 43 in 55, 45 finer (1/09).(#8626)

3088 **1860 AU53 NGC.** A pleasing combination of lime-gold and reddish patina is seen over both sides of this rare survivor, from a low-mintage issue of just 15,105 pieces. This example shows a few marks and some faint hairlines, from brief circulation. Census: 18 in 53, 51 finer (1/09).(#8631)

3089 **1862-S Fine 12 PCGS.** Reasonably well detailed for the grade, with even wear and smooth fields. One of the more elusive S-mint dates of the No Motto type, and initially a low-mintage issue of only 12,500 pieces.(#8636)

Rare 1863-S Eagle, AU50

3090 **1863-S AU50 NGC.** Lightly circulated and showing traces of highpoint wear on both sides. Green-gold with bits of vibrant reddish luster apparent near the peripheral devices. A rare and highly respected date in the No Motto series of gold eagles, with a low mintage of just 10,000 pieces. Census: 7 in 50, 12 finer (1/09). (#8638)

Elusive Choice AU 1870-S Eagle

3091 **1870-S AU55 PCGS.** The 1870-S is very scarce in all grades, and is a great rarity in Choice AU quality. Just 8,000 pieces were struck, and unlike the three dollar gold pieces struck at Philadelphia that year, none were set aside by collectors. The present piece has uncommonly smooth fields, plentiful luster, and attractive peach and lime toning. The cheek has moderate parallel roller marks, there is a faint vertical line on the cheek, and a few wispy abrasions are noted near the eagle's head. Population: 3 in 55, 3 finer (2/09). (#8659)

Important AU53 1871 Eagle

3092 **1871 AU53 PCGS.** With just 1,790 business strikes produced, it stands to reason that the 1871 eagle is a rarity, particularly at the AU level. This yellow-gold example, though modestly worn, still retains much of its original reflective luster in the fields. The obverse shows several significant abrasions on either side of the portrait. Population: 4 in 53, 4 finer (2/09).(#8660)

3093 **1872-S XF45 NGC.** A modestly worn but pleasing S-mint ten, butterscotch-yellow with some deepening of color around the devices. Strong eye appeal for this low-mintage issue.(#8665)

Impressive Choice AU 1874-CC Ten

3094 **1874-CC AU55 NGC.** Peach-tinged luster is extensive, an unusual trait for a Carson City ten from the 1870s—a decade with many low mintage CC-mint issues. The present example also benefits from a crisp strike and a near-absence of detrimental marks. Only five 1874-CC eagles have been certified as Mint State, two of the most notable being an NGC MS65 formerly from the Warren Miller collection offered by Heritage in October 1995, and a PCGS MS63 once owned by Louis Eliasberg, Sr. and Harry W. Bass, Jr. While the present piece has witnessed brief circulation, its eye appeal is certain to please the advanced specialist. Census: 18 in 55, 3 finer (2/09). *From The Belle Collection of Carson City Coinage.*(#8670)

Scarce 1874-S Ten Dollar, XF45

3095 **1874-S XF45 PCGS. CAC.** Dusky orange-gold surfaces show light, even wear with glimmers of luster at the margins. Despite the time this piece spent in circulation, marks are few. Minor bits of verdigris are present near the first and last stars on the obverse. Overall, a solid Choice XF example of this lower-mintage San Francisco eagle issue, produced to the extent of only 10,000 pieces. Population: 19 in 45, 16 finer (2/09).(#8671)

Desirable XF Details 1875-CC Eagle

3096 **1875-CC—Improperly Cleaned—NCS. XF Details.** This low-mintage issue is hotly contested in virtually any state, and though the yellow-gold surfaces of this lightly worn example show evidence of a past cleaning, there should still be healthy bidding. Small, scattered abrasions dot the fields. Light wear is restricted to the portrait.(#8673)

High Grade 1875-CC Ten, AU53

3097 **1875-CC AU53 PCGS.** Like other Carson City eagles from the 1870s, the 1875-CC has a meager mintage of just 7,715 pieces. This figure is much lower than the 1875-CC double eagle production of 111,151 pieces. Undoubtedly, bankers and exporters preferred the largest gold denomination possible, since this made payments of large amounts more convenient.

The 1875-CC was rare to begin with, but there were no coin collectors in the Old West, and few could afford to set aside a coin that constituted at least a week's pay. It comes as little surprise that PCGS has certified only one example as Mint State, and also only one piece as AU58. Thus, AU53 and AU55 coins are the finest that can be practically obtained. The present peach-gold representative is uncommonly smooth, although a small mark above the jaw is mentioned as a pedigree indicator. The luster is especially ample on the reverse.

From The Belle Collection of Carson City Coinage.(#8673)

Rare Choice VF 1876-CC Ten

3098 **1876-CC VF35 PCGS.** Much better struck than the typical '76-CC, since the issue is usually mushy at the centers. The hair near the ear shows only minor bluntness. Any 1876-CC is desirable due to the Carson City mintmark and a meager mintage of 4,696 pieces. Orange and yellow-gold with moderate, even wear and no consequential marks. *From The Burning Tree Colletion.*(#8675)

3099 **1876-S VF25 PCGS.** A nice, original-looking piece with khaki-green and orange-gold toning, and plenty of remaining design definition for the grade. Only superficial marks and hairlines are noted on either side. A scarce and underrated With Motto issue, with a low mintage of 5,000 pieces.(#8676)

3100 **1878-S AU55 NGC.** Varying stages of yellow-gold with hints of brassiness in the still-lustrous fields. Though a handful of abrasions affect the well struck portrait and wispy marks are noted in the fields, this piece remains fundamentally pleasing. Census: 33 in 55, 30 finer (1/09).(#8682)

Choice XF 1879-CC Eagle

3101 **1879-CC XF45 PCGS.** The '79-CC Ten Dollar has an impressively low mintage of only 1,762 pieces, the lowest output of any gold coin ever produced at the Carson City Mint. Possibly the second rarest Carson City eagle, behind only the extremely rare 1870-CC. This luminous yellow-gold example has only a single relevant mark, a thin obverse line near 3 o'clock. Population: 3 in 45, 12 finer (8/05). *Ex: Long Beach Signature (Heritage, 9/2005), lot 4798. From The Belle Collection of Carson City Coinage.*(#8684)

Conditionally Scarce MS63 1880 Ten

3102 **1880 MS63 NGC.** The 1880 has a relatively high mintage, and is available in scuffy AU58 to MS62 grades. Nonetheless, the issue is very scarce at the MS63 level, and none have been certified above MS64. This Select example is crisply struck and provides unencumbered luster. Census: 28 in 63, 7 finer (2/09). (#8687)

3103 **1881-CC AU53 NGC.** Strong, satiny luster remains in the fields of this lightly circulated piece. Small, scattered abrasions have little impact on the eye appeal.(#8692)

3104 **1881-CC AU53 PCGS.** The fields exhibit pale steel-green color, while the high points and the peripheries display exuberant orange-gold luster. Tiny marks and faint hairlines limit the grade, along with a slight degree of wear on both sides. Population: 14 in 53, 79 finer (2/09).(#8692)

Near-Mint 1882-CC Ten Dollar

3105 **1882-CC AU58 NGC.** The Carson City Mint produced a mere 6,764 eagles in 1882, concentrating most of their coinage effort on half eagles and double eagles, in addition to the silver dollars that were coined and put into storage. As a result, the 1882-CC eagle is a rarity, especially in top grades. PCGS has never certified a finer example, and NGC has only graded three submissions in MS60 or better grades. Past commentaries have called the date "underrated" or a "sleeper." Today, attractive examples remain extremely difficult to locate. This one has vibrant peripheral luster with satiny light yellow surfaces and few abrasions of any kind, aside from a tiny patch of marks at the lower left obverse. Census: 35 in 58, 3 finer (2/09). *From The Belle Collection of Carson City Coinage.*(#8696)

Beautiful Mint State 1882-O Eagle

3106 **1882-O MS60 PCGS.** This piece is beautifully toned in shades of deep orange-red, with glints of hazel-gray near the rims and on the high points. Due to the mintage of only 10,820 pieces and the circulation of most of the issue, Mint State pieces are seldom encountered. Well struck, and certified in a green-label holder. Population: 3 in 60, 5 finer (2/09).(#8697)

Attractive AU53 1884-CC Ten Dollar

3107 **1884-CC AU53 NGC.** A lovely piece with considerable luster retained over medium yellow surfaces. The design definition is bold, and the overall appearance is exceptional for the grade. The 1884-CC eagle is a scarce issue from a mintage of just 9,925 coins, and examples are always in demand in most any grade. Census: 25 in 53, 80 finer (2/09).(#8704)

Elusive 1884-CC Ten Dollar, AU55

3108 **1884-CC AU55 PCGS.** This is a low-mintage Carson City eagle issue with a mintage of only 9,925 pieces and a condition rarity as well, seldom seen above the VF-XF level. This Choice AU example is an especially attractive coin that has virtually abrasion-free surfaces. The design details are well struck, and there is abundant mint luster that still surrounds the devices. Population: 15 in 55, 19 finer (2/09).(#8704)

Low-Mintage 1884-CC Ten Dollar, AU55

3109 **1884-CC AU55 NGC.** The arm's-length appearance of this piece suggests a Mint State specimen, with an abundance of shimmering mint luster and lovely, rich shades of apricot-gold and lime-green on each side. Closer inspection reveals a trace amount of highpoint wear and a few minute hairlines in the fields. An alluring Choice AU example of this low-mintage Carson City issue. Census: 29 in 55, 51 finer (1/09).(#8704)

Desirable Select 1885 Eagle

3110 **1885 MS63 NGC.** A desirable yellow-orange example that offers well-defined centers and strong luster. Though a number of small marks are present on each side, significant abrasions are few. Despite a mintage of just over a quarter of a million pieces, the 1885 eagle is a borderline condition rarity so fine. Census: 22 in 63, 11 finer (2/09). *From The Burning Tree Collection.*(#8706)

3111 **1888 MS62 PCGS.** Primarily yellow-orange with a streak of alloy between the E and D of UNITED on the reverse. Modestly abraded for the grade assigned, though the chin does show a significant mark. Population: 12 in 62, 6 finer (2/09).(#8712)

3112 **1891-CC MS60 NGC.** Crisply struck and immensely lustrous with no trace of wear. Numerous light to moderate abrasions pepper the obverse, and the upper obverse rim shows several alloy spots. (#8720)

3113 **1891-CC MS60 NGC.** Strongly struck with bright and intact luster. Yellow-gold surfaces show hints of orange and violet. Though each side is moderately abraded, the MS60 designation seems harsh. Housed in a prior-generation holder.(#8720)

3114 **1891-CC MS61 NGC.** Sharply struck with blindingly reflective surfaces that are pale lemon-gold. Though moderately abraded, an undeniably appealing Carson City eagle.(#8720)

3115 **1891-CC MS62 PCGS.** Variety 3-C. Some interesting die characteristics are found on this Carson City eagle, including obvious repunching on the mintmark. "This variety should sell for a premium," according to Doug Winter. Intense mint frost and well struck devices are also evident on each side. Scattered, tiny marks limit the grade.(#8720)

Condition Scarcity 1891-CC Ten Dollar, MS63

3116 **1891-CC MS63 NGC.** Comprehensive luster and an exacting strike confirm the quality of this original almond-gold example. Faint marks are present, but fewer than is typical of the Select grade and of the issue, which is usually heavily abraded. The 1891-CC ten dollar is readily available in the lower Uncirculated grades, but is scarce in MS63 and rare any finer. Census: 84 in 63, 9 finer (2/09).(#8720)

Rare Uncirculated 1892-CC Eagle

3117 **1892-CC MS61 NGC.** An impressive Mint State piece with good yellow-gold luster. The strike is bold with excellent central and peripheral details. The left obverse field has a few small marks. The 1892-CC has the second highest mintage (40,000) of any Liberty ten from the Carson City Mint, yet examples are difficult to obtain in Mint State. Census: 21 in 61, 10 finer (2/09). *From The Belle Collection of Carson City Coinage.*(#8722)

3118 **1892-S MS62 PCGS.** Warm yellow-orange luster with above-average detail. This satiny example shows light marks and several alloy streaks on Liberty's portrait.(#8724)

3119 **1892-S MS62 PCGS.** Rich yellow-gold color overall with occasional straw and orange elements. Though scattered wispy abrasions preclude Select status, this well-defined coin remains highly appealing. PCGS has certified 41 finer examples (2/09). (#8724)

Borderline Uncirculated 1893-CC Ten

3120 **1893-CC AU58 NGC.** The 1893-CC ten is generally not seen above the AU58 level and this grade represents excellent value for this final-year issue. A significant amount of mint luster remains on each side and the surfaces are sun-gold with sharply defined devices. Both sides are minimally abraded save for moderate marks on the upper left obverse field. Census: 38 in 58, 10 finer (2/09). *From The Belle Collection of Carson City Coinage.*(#8726)

3121 **1895 MS64 NGC.** The top of the 95 in the date is lightly repunched. Original orange-gold and olive-green toning endows this lustrous and sharply impressed representative. The portrait is well-preserved, and the fields show only a few light grazes. NGC has graded just four finer pieces (2/09).(#8732)

3122 **1895-O MS60 Prooflike NGC.** Probably because of their low mintages, prooflike New Orleans eagles are seldom encountered. The present typically abraded example is sharply struck and has flashy fields. Census: 1 in 60 Prooflike, 2 finer (1/09).(#78733)

Scarce 1896-S Ten, MS62

3123 **1896-S MS62 PCGS.** A scarce but not unobtainable S-mint issue in Uncirculated. However, it is almost never found finer than MS62. In fact, only two coins have been sold recently at public auction (both were MS63). One was sold in 2005, the other in 2007. This is an attractive coin that displays rich, frosted mint luster. Both sides have pronounced reddish patina with an accent of olive at the top of the reverse. Sharply defined.(#8736)

3124 **1897-S MS62 NGC.** Light yellow-gold at the centers with elements closer to sun and orange at the margins. Modestly abraded for the grade with strong detail. Census: 24 in 62, 6 finer (2/09). (#8739)

3125 **1899 MS64 NGC.** Sharply struck with satiny wheat-gold surfaces that show subtle rose inflections. An abrasion between stars 9 and 10 on the obverse seems to be the only obstacle to a Gem designation.(#8742)

3126 **1899 MS64 PCGS.** Boldly impressed with potent luster that offers both cartwheels and reflectivity. Peach-tinged tan-gold surfaces are immensely appealing. PCGS has graded 28 finer examples (2/09). (#8742)

Elegant Gem 1900 Eagle

3127 **1900 MS65 PCGS.** Rich and satiny luster enlivens gold-orange surfaces. The strike on the portrait is exquisite, particularly the fine strands of Liberty's hair. Though a few tiny marks appear in the fields, the central devices are clean, and the eye appeal is consistent with the Gem designation. Population: 11 in 65, 1 finer (2/09).(#8745)

Challenging 1900-S Select Ten Dollar

3128 **1900-S MS63 PCGS.** Partially prooflike fields highlight the motifs of this Select S-mint representative, especially on the reverse. The strike is sharp, leaving none of the design elements with even a hint of weakness. Light contacts and grazes account for the grade. Mint Sate pieces are difficult to locate. Population: 13 in 63, 3 finer (2/09).(#8746)

Splendid MS66 1901 Eagle

3129 **1901 MS66 NGC.** This piece is every bit as splendid as the grade implies, with rich and even antique-gold coloration over surfaces that are nearly abrasion-free. The cartwheel luster is equally appealing, and the strike is full. There is a tiny planchet lamination in the obverse field near star 5, and a tiny bit of dark toning appears near the last two digits of the date. The reverse shows a couple of field marks away from the focal points, but nothing that could conceivably dampen the enthusiasm of even the fussiest viewer. Census: 71 in 66, 7 finer (2/09).(#8747)

3130 **1901-S MS61 ICG.** Exquisitely detailed with warm honey-gold luster. Though each side shows a number of fine abrasions, this turn-of-the-century S-mint remains fundamentally appealing. (#8749)

3131 **1901-S MS64 NGC.** Strongly struck for this turn-of-the-century S-mint issue with impressive, satiny luster. Paler yellow-gold centers give way to deeper sun-gold shadings at the margins.(#8749)

Lustrous MS66 1901-S Ten

3132 **1901-S MS66 PCGS.** With a mintage of over 2.8 million pieces, the 1901-S is among the most heavily produced eagles of the 20th century, and the issue has strong availability even at the Gem level. Premium Gems are elusive, and anything finer is a rarity. This MS66 coin offers flashy cartwheel luster that invigorates beautifully preserved yellow-gold and honey-orange surfaces.(#8749)

Charming Premium Gem 1901-S Ten Dollar

3133 **1901-S MS66 NGC.** Both sides of this Premium Gem ten dollar are awash with pleasing satiny luster. The design features are well impressed, with only star 13 revealing a hint of softness. Peach-gold surfaces exhibit a few grade-consistent luster grazes, somewhat more so on the obverse. Splendid eye appeal.(#8749)

Wonderful MS66 1901-S Ten Dollar

3134 1901-S MS66 NGC. A top-flight survivor from this turn-of-the-century issue, crisply struck with impressive, satiny luster. Both sides show rich gold-orange color, with that of the reverse slightly deeper. Beautifully preserved with elegant eye appeal, a great choice for the type collector. NGC has graded 25 finer examples (2/09).(#8749)

3135 1902-S MS64 NGC. Greenish-gold patina imbued with whispers of apricot rests on highly lustrous surfaces. This well struck piece shows just a few minor marks that preclude Gem classification. (#8751)

Elusive 1903-O Ten Dollar, MS63

3136 1903-O MS63 PCGS. The design elements are crisply reproduced, and the surfaces display satiny, unbroken mint luster over golden-orange surfaces. A typical number of superficial blemishes are noted for the grade on each side, mostly in the fields. A conditionally scarce issue at the Select Uncirculated level. Population: 86 in 63, 12 finer (2/09).(#8753)

Scarce Premium Gem 1905 Liberty Eagle

3137 1905 MS66 NGC. Powerfully struck with attractive orange-gold coloration throughout. The intense luster of the current offering is suggestive of an even finer grade designation, but closer examination reveals a few abrasions in the field in front of and behind Liberty's lower neck. Although the 1905 eagle is considered "one of the more common 'tough' dates of the 20th century," according to the Garrett-Guth reference, the issue is undeniably challenging in grades higher than MS65. As of (2/09), NGC has certified a mere 13 examples at the MS66 level, with only seven finer pieces—all grading MS67.(#8757)

3138 1906-S MS62 PCGS. All of the design elements are crisply reproduced. Highly lustrous with pleasing orange-gold coloration and mild marks that seem fewer than expected for the grade. Population: 51 in 62, 29 finer (1/09).(#8762)

3139 1907 MS62 Prooflike NGC. Well struck with rich golden coloration and, most notably, mirrored fields of more than modest depth. Abrasions are far more numerous on the obverse. Only a few 1907 Liberty eagles have been awarded a Prooflike designation by NGC. Census: 4 in 62 Prooflike, 2 finer (1/09).(#8763)

PROOF LIBERTY EAGLE

Proof 1892 Ten Dollar

3140 1892 PCGS Genuine. We net grade the coin PR60 and note it is harshly cleaned. From the PCGS insert all we learn is PCGS Genuine. However, the number on the insert (8832) corresponds to a proof 1892. Additionally, we note that the date is low, as seen on proofs from this year. Also, the fields on each side show noticeable orange-peel texture, a trait common to proof gold struck in the latter half of the 19th century. The surfaces are uniformly bright from cleaning and have a slight reddish hue. *From The Burning Tree Colletion.*(#8832)

Famous 1907 Wire Rim Saint-Gaudens Eagle, MS64

3141 **1907 Wire Rim MS64 PCGS.** The making of the 500 Wire Rim or Wire Edge Saint-Gaudens eagles dated 1907 was something of a command performance, according to letters reprinted in Roger W. Burdette's *Renaissance of American Coinage*. In one such letter, dated August 22nd, President Theodore Roosevelt sent to Secretary of the Treasury George B. Cortelyou an implicit threat to the superintendent of the Philadelphia Mint, suggesting that he would find a replacement who would "be put in charge to make the [Saint-Gaudens eagles] forthwith."

Two days letter, spurred by a letter received from William D. Sohier, a self-described "old friend" of the President's, Roosevelt sent another, more terse message to Cortelyou, the first paragraph of which read: "Perhaps the mint people ought to see the enclosed letter. Let them tell me when the new eagles and double eagles will appear. I hope a fortnight." Within a week, samples from a batch of 500 pieces, in high relief but with Charles Barber's knife-rim added to protect the design, were made available to Roosevelt, and he expressed his approval, largely defusing the tension between the President and the Mint.

This near-Gem comes from that prized early batch of Wire Rim eagles, struck on a medal press with the rims prominent and periods separating the words on the reverse. Orange-accented yellow-gold surfaces have the warm and dramatic luster peculiar to this issue, which has attracted generations of collectors to this famous variety. Pleasingly preserved for the grade assigned and housed in a green label holder.(#8850)

3142 **1907 Wire Rim MS65 PCGS.** The Wire Rim Saint-Gaudens eagles were the first examples of the late sculptor's design struck in quantity, though they were not made available until the release of the No Periods variant to banks. Despite today's collector appreciation of the Wire Rim ten dollar piece's inherent beauty, even the limited mintage of 500 pieces did not achieve full distribution right away, being at the disposal of others, including Secretary of the Treasury George Cortelyou and President Theodore Roosevelt. Roger Burdette, in his *Renaissance of American Coinage*, notes that "[t]he 500 [Wire Rim] eagles were to satisfy any possible request from Roosevelt. These were an 'insurance policy' put in place by Cortelyou against additional presidential rage."

After Saint-Gaudens eagles and twenties were released to the public, the coins were no longer necessary for that role, but rather than being melted, they were turned over to the Treasury for sale to collectors, at first for face value. Burdette notes that after the first wave of interested numismatists had made their purchases, the coins were next offered "to members of Congress and other influential persons in private transactions. In 1912 the balance was transferred to the mint cabinet where they were sold to coin dealers" for $15 apiece.

This warm sun-yellow Gem offers gorgeous luster and marvelous eye appeal. Each side is minimally marked with suggestions of patina. A small alloy fleck below the I of UNITED on the reverse is mentioned solely for accuracy. In sum, a marvelous example of this coveted early Saint-Gaudens eagle.(#8850)

Brilliant 1907 No Periods Eagle, MS63

3143 **1907 No Periods MS63 ANACS.** This is a splendid example of what might well be called the "Saint-Gaudens eagle," in emulation of the double eagle series styled after the famous sculptor. The surfaces are brilliant yellow-gold that is set off nicely by the ANACS gold-label insert. A couple of minor contact marks well hidden in the Indian's headdress account for the grade, but the luster is gorgeous and the eye appeal is right.(#8852)

Lovely Select 1907 Indian Ten

3144 **1907 No Periods MS63 PCGS.** A beautiful gold type coin that boasts dazzling cartwheel sheen and unabraded fields. A small mint-made planchet flaw (as made) is concealed in the wing, as is a solitary minor horizontal mark. This green-gold beauty has all the eye appeal of the next higher grade.
From The Ed Lepordo Collection, Part Two.(#8852)

Vibrant Near-Gem 1907 No Periods Ten

3145 **1907 No Periods MS64 NGC.** The luster is fresh and vibrant, the strike substantially above-average on the reverse. Warm yellow-gold color dominates the eye appeal. Despite its status as a first-year issue, the 1907 Saint-Gaudens ten comes to market surprisingly seldom in near-Gem and better states.(#8852)

Charming 1907 No Periods Ten Dollar, MS66

3146 **1907 No Periods MS66 NGC.** The 1907 No Periods is one of the most common dates in the Indian Head ten dollar series. As NGC/PCGS population data indicate, it is readily available through the MS64 grade level. The Gem population noticeably declines, as does that of Premium Gems. Anything finer is extremely difficult to come by.

The brass-gold surfaces of this MS66 example have a satiny texture with pleasing luster. The hair curls over Liberty's brow are softly struck, which is usual for the issue. The remaining design features are well impressed. A few trivial surface grazes and rim marks are within the parameters of the grade designation. In sum, this charming specimen generates great eye appeal.(#8852)

Memorable 1907 No Periods Eagle, MS66

3147 **1907 No Periods MS66 NGC.** The first widespread circulation issue of the new Saint-Gaudens design, as modified (or tinkered with) by the obstructionist Charles Barber. We can thank Barber nonetheless that the mintage was achieved to the extent of nearly a quarter-million coins, leading to the existence of memorable Premium Gems such as the present piece. The margins are greenish-gold, tending to orange-gold on the high points of each side. Only the faintest luster grazes on Liberty's cheek perhaps limit an even finer grade.(#8852)

Exceptional Gem 1908 No Motto Eagle

Lustrous 1908-D Motto Eagle, MS63

3154 **1908-D Motto MS63 ICG.** Erroneously described as No Motto on the holder. The surfaces show good luster and color on both sides, with orange-gold high points and greenish-gold in the recesses near the margins. However, those surfaces are also somewhat scuffy, with numerous light abrasions that dot the coin, including most notably several on Liberty's cheek.(#8860)

Appealing MS64 1908-S Ten

3148 **1908 No Motto MS65 NGC. CAC.** Beautiful lime-green and pastel peach coloration is highlighted by effulgent luster over both sides of this exceptional Gem example, from the second year of the Indian Head eagle series. The No Motto type was produced first, and approximately 10 times as many examples of the 1908 With Motto variety were struck afterward. The With Motto variation continued to the end of the series, making the No Motto Indian eagle a brief and scarce design type. Boldly struck and carefully preserved. Only a handful of tiny marks are found on the smooth surfaces with the aid of a magnifier. Census: 25 in 65, 19 finer (2/09).(#8853)

3149 **1908 Motto MS61 NGC.** A rich satiny sheen emanates from the fine-grained surfaces of this lovely Mint State example. The relatively small number of noticeable surface marks makes this piece seem conservatively graded.(#8859)

3150 **1908 Motto MS61 NGC.** The national motto IN GOD WE TRUST was omitted in the first year of this new gold coinage series. In 1908, however, Congress acted to restore the motto despite Theodore Roosevelt's objections. This example is lustrous and appealing, despite a small mark on Liberty's cheek that restricts the grade.(#8859)

3151 **1908 Motto MS61 NGC.** A gorgeous representative of this second-year issue, with bright, satiny, mattelike surfaces. There are numerous tiny marks and nicks on each side, limiting the grade. (#8859)

3152 **1908 Motto MS62 NGC.** Bright and satiny, with rich apricot and rose color. The mattelike surfaces are lightly marked, as expected for the grade.(#8859)

3153 **1908 Motto MS63 NGC.** Frosty yellow-gold luster shows on both sides of this attractive ten dollar piece, as do sharply impressed design features. Minuscule surface and rim marks limit the grade. (#8859)

3155 **1908-S MS64 NGC.** All San Francisco Saint-Gaudens eagles are of the With Motto variety, and that Mint's introductory issue of 1908 amounted to under 60,000 pieces; the variety has become particularly desirable as a conditionally scarce issue at the near-Gem and better levels. This example combines an unusually crisp strike with distinctive, satiny luster that enlivens the orange-accented wheat-gold surfaces. A coin devoid of overt abrasions, with only a handful of wispy marks in the fields accounting for the Choice designation. Census: 24 in 64, 23 finer (2/09).(#8861)

3156 **1909 MS62 NGC.** In the third year of Saint-Gaudens' Indian Head ten dollar design, the mintage remained a relatively small 184,700 pieces. This example is boldly struck with rich satin luster and a handful of small marks on each side.(#8862)

3157 **1909-D MS61 NGC.** Light yellow-orange color with generally minor abrasions, though the reverse shows a few more significant marks above the eagle's wing. Slightly satiny luster enlivens each side.(#8863)

Exceptional 1909-D Select Ten Dollar

3158 **1909-D MS63 PCGS.** Select examples of this issue are scarce, and higher-grade coins are quite rare, especially in MS65 and better. Peach-gold surfaces imbued with tints of light green possess a frosty texture and emit soft luster. The strike is better than usually seen. A few minuscule marks account for the grade.(#8863)

3159 **1909-S MS60 NGC.** No trace of wear, though this lustrous yellow-orange piece shows numerous wispy abrasions and a handful of more significant marks. Deep alloy accents appear in the feathers of the headdress.(#8864)

Glowing 1909-S Ten Dollar, MS64

3160 **1909-S MS64 NGC.** The 1909-S ten dollar is more difficult to obtain in Mint State than its nearly 300,000-piece mintage might suggest. Glowing luster emanates from its peach-gold surfaces imbued with hints of apricot, mint-green, and light tan. This is a well struck piece that reveals just a few minor grade-defining marks. Census: 38 in 64, 13 finer (2/09).(#8864)

3161 **1910 MS64 NGC.** Excellent definition overall, though the hair above the ear shows slight softness. Strong yellow-gold luster with great eye appeal.(#8865)

Glorious Gem 1910 Eagle

3162 **1910 MS65 NGC.** Beautiful Gem examples of this late gold type are a glory to behold, and this piece is no exception. The frosty surfaces are evenly colored orange-gold, with splendid cartwheel luster and premium eye appeal. Only the most minor marks appear on each side, in keeping with the grade.(#8865)

Beautiful Gem 1910 Indian Ten

3163 **1910 MS65 PCGS.** The 1910 is an issue that appears frequently in MS62 but is rare as a Gem. This is due to a combination of soft gold alloy, indifferent bag shipment and storage, and a design that tends to collect scuffs on the cheek and open fields. But such a fate has eluded the present coin, which has gorgeous preservation, dazzling luster, and a precise strike. Population: 53 in 65, 22 finer (2/09).(#8865)

3164 **1910-D MS64 PCGS.** Strongly detailed on the hair over the ear, among other places, and pleasingly lustrous. This orange-tinted yellow-gold example offers grand eye appeal for the grade. PCGS has certified 91 finer examples (2/09).(#8866)

3165 **1910-D MS64 NGC.** Well-defined overall with only trivial striking softness noted at the hair over Liberty's ear. Pale yellow-gold color with a touch of frostiness at the high points.(#8866)

3166 **1910-D MS64 NGC.** Satiny yellow-gold overall with a touch of cloudiness at the upper reverse. Well-defined with strong visual appeal for the grade.(#8866)

High Grade 1910-D Ten Dollar, MS66

3167 **1910-D MS66 NGC. CAC.** Perusal of NGC/PCGS population data indicate that this date is readily available through MS64. The Gem population decreases significantly, and higher-grade coins are difficult to acquire. Moreover, Jeff Garrett and Ron Guth (2006) contend that: "Many show a form of die damage that weakens definition through the date, stars, and reverse peripheral lettering." The current Premium Gem deviates from this profile, in that its sharply struck devices reveal none of the aforementioned weaknesses. Moreover, the highly lustrous surfaces display a beautiful mix of peach-gold, yellow-green, apricot, and mint-green patina, and are nicely preserved.(#8866)

3168 **1911 MS63 NGC.** Strongly struck with particularly laudable detail on the portrait. Rich yellow-gold color with a single dig to the left of the headband accounting for the grade. Housed in a prior-generation holder.(#8868)

3169 **1911 MS64 PCGS.** A brightly lustrous Choice coin with strong detail on the strands over Liberty's ear. The light yellow-gold obverse yields to a slightly deeper sun-yellow shading on the reverse. Minimally flawed for the grade with impressive visual appeal for this issue, one that becomes elusive any finer.(#8868)

3170 **1911 MS64 NGC.** Strongly struck with powerful, swirling luster. Generally yellow-gold surfaces show a darker alloy streak that runs diagonally on Liberty's neck.(#8868)

3171 **1911 MS64 PCGS.** With slightly over half a million pieces struck, the 1911 is not an obvious candidate to be a condition rarity, yet it is elusive any finer than this, with just 83 such pieces graded by PCGS (2/09). This shining example is generally yellow-gold with a touch of pebbling to the fields. Wispy marks on the portrait account for the grade.(#8868)

Shining Gem 1911 Eagle

3172 **1911 MS65 NGC.** Excellent striking definition, particularly on the often-weak hair over Liberty's ear. Each side has bright wheat-gold luster with hints of deeper sun-yellow over parts of the reverse. Pleasingly preserved and devoid of overt abrasions, a coin with top-notch eye appeal. NGC has graded 58 numerically finer examples (1/09).(#8868)

Impressive MS65 1911 Ten Dollar

3173 **1911 MS65 PCGS.** A meticulously struck Gem that boasts blended olive-gold and caramel-gold toning. Coruscating luster reveals only trivial surface imperfections. Not strictly a type coin, since the 1911 is much scarcer than the 1926 or 1932 at the MS65 level. Population: 56 in 65, 27 finer (2/09).(#8868)

Outstanding Gem 1911 Ten Dollar Indian

3174 **1911 MS65 NGC.** Radiant luster and light honey-gold coloration are hallmarks of this outstanding Gem example. The coin's surfaces have a pleasing fine-grain texture in the fields, similar to that of the Roman Finish proofs from 1909 and 1910. Well struck throughout, and free of serious distractions; there are just a handful of trivial surface marks that might preclude an even finer grade assessment. (#8868)

Frosty 1911 Indian Ten, MS65

3175 **1911 MS65 NGC.** Faint traces of pink toning enhance the light yellow-gold luster of this frosty piece. A few tiny imperfections on each side are entirely undistracting. Although more common than similar quality Gem half eagles, top grade Indian eagles are elusive. NGC has only certified 58 finer 1911 eagles (2/09).(#8868)

Borderline Uncirculated 1911-D Ten

3176 **1911-D AU58 NGC.** An uncommonly low mintage of 30,100 pieces ensures the scarcity of this charming orange-gold near-Mint Indian ten. Both sides shimmer with unbroken cartwheel luster, and both sides are smooth save for moderate contact on the cheekbone. Much more affordable than an MS61 example, yet the eye appeal is similar.(#8869)

Amazing 1911-S Indian Head Eagle, MS66
Among the Finest Certified

3177 **1911-S MS66 PCGS.** The 1911-S Indian Head ten dollar gold piece was once considered one of the rarest dates of the series in Mint State. The date boasts a low mintage of just 51,000 pieces, and the great majority of the coins must have been released into circulation at the time of issue. Before the discovery of a hoard of 50 pieces in Europe in the 1970s, Mint State specimens of this date were virtually unheard-of. The date began appearing in auction catalogs in the 1940s, but even great collectors like F.C.C. Boyd and King Farouk were content with specimens that graded only VF during that era. Louis Eliasberg, the "King of Coins", settled for an XF40 example in his extraordinary collection.

The situation changed radically in 1979 when Marc Emory, acting for New England Rare Coin Galleries, brokered a deal for a group of Gem Uncirculated 1911-S eagles through his contacts in Spain. The story of this remarkable find was told for the first time in *The Coinage of Augustus Saint-Gaudens*. The hoard was originally the property of the American governor of the Philippines in 1911, who gave a group of 50 ten dollar gold coins from the San Francisco Mint to a Spanish citizen who was residing in the Philippines at the time. The coins were preserved by that gentleman, who later returned to Spain, and the hoard became part of his estate when he died. The coins were retained by his family for many years until his grandson decided to sell them through a prominent coin collector from Barcelona. Marc Emory met with the collector and finalized a deal through a Swiss bank for 30 of the coins. The remainder of the hoard eventually became available, and NERCA became the conduit for their entry into the U.S. coin market. Nearly all Gem level 1911-S eagles in collector's hands today are from this fantastic hoard.

The present coin is sharply struck, with exquisite detail evident on all design elements. The usual granular surfaces are overlaid with soft, satiny luster that creates compelling visual appeal. Only 11 coins have been certified at the MS66 level by NGC and PCGS combined, with none finer (2/09). (#8870)

3178 **1912 MS63 PCGS.** Well-defined for the issue with strong, slightly frosty luster. Though this Select coin shows a handful of wispy abrasions, the yellow-gold surfaces show few overt marks. (#8871)

3179 **1912-S MS61 NGC.** Pale straw-gold color with impressive luster. Lightly abraded overall with two significant digs in the left obverse field, but strong eye appeal otherwise.(#8872)

3180 **1913 MS63 PCGS.** Slightly granular surfaces sparkle with satiny luster. A few scattered marks are seen, but this example is nicely struck and quite attractive for the Select Mint State grade level. (#8873)

3181 **1913 MS63 NGC.** Pleasing luster emanates from the yellow-gold surfaces of this Select ten dollar, and a decisive strike imparts strong detail to the devices. Minute contact marks limit the grade. (#8873)

Near-Mint State 1913-S Eagle

3182 **1913-S AU58 PCGS.** The 300,000 eagles produced in San Francisco in 1912 largely satisfied the area's demand for the issue, and in 1913 that mint coined just 66,000 pieces of the ten dollar denomination. This luminous orange-gold piece is minimally marked, with only a trace of friction across the high points. (#8874)

Rare 1913-S Indian Ten, MS60

3183 **1913-S MS60 NGC.** The 1913-S Indian eagle is one of the rare, low-mintage issues, with an original production of just 66,000 coins. Once considered the rarest date in the series, it is only called a scarce date today. This one has frosty light yellow luster with minor grade-consistent abrasions.(#8874)

3184 **1914 MS63 NGC.** A honey-gold type coin that boasts sweeping luster and unblemished fields. The strike is bold, and the mintage is less than any other Philadelphia issue.
From The Mario Eller Collection, Part Four.(#8875)

3185 **1915 MS63 NGC.** Attractive honey-gold coloration endows this Select eagle, complemented by sharply struck design elements and potent luster. Light marks and scuffs preclude a higher grade. (#8878)

Choice 1915 Ten Dollar

3186 **1915 MS64 NGC.** A splendid near-Gem with exceptional yellow-gold luster and bold design details, even at the centers. A few scattered pepper spots are visible on the reverse of this piece. Although Philadelphia had struck eagles annually since 1838, 1915 was the final issue struck at the facility until 1926.(#8878)

Attractive MS64 1915 Ten Dollar

3187 **1915 MS64 PCGS.** Well-defined and strongly lustrous for this popular Saint-Gaudens eagle issue, which would prove to be the last ten dollar coin struck at the Philadelphia Mint for more than a decade. Rich yellow-gold color dominates, though a touch of reddish alloy appears on the feathers of the headdress. Slightly satiny and thoroughly appealing.(#8878)

Gorgeous 1915 Eagle, MS64

3188 **1915 MS64 NGC.** Greenish-gold color enriches both sides of this near-Gem. Like most examples of this issue, this piece has excellent luster on its frosty surfaces, and the design elements are sharply struck. Impeccable preservation adds to the gorgeous eye appeal. A minute mark on the eagle's neck and a few minuscule rim ticks are all that stand in the way of Gem classification.(#8878)

Elegant 1915 Gem Ten Dollar

3189 **1915 MS65 PCGS.** The 1915 is one of the more available Saint-Gaudens eagle issues in MS65, but it is still scarce at that level and a condition rarity any finer. Both sides of this elegant Gem offer powerful luster with hints of frost and satin that enliven the generally well preserved peach-gold surfaces. The strike is pleasing, particularly at the often-weak hair over Liberty's ear, and the eye appeal is impressive. An interesting candidate for the 20th century gold type collector seeking a slightly better date for this series. Population: 40 in 65, 7 finer (2/09).(#8878)

3190 **1915-S—Cleaned—ICG. AU58 Details.** A touch of wear crosses the high points, and the bright lemon-gold surfaces are glossy from cleaning. Still, a readily collectible example of this lower-mintage issue.(#8879)

Appealing MS62 1915-S Ten Dollar

3191 **1915-S MS62 PCGS.** The 1915-S is one of the key dates to the Indian Head ten dollar series. Not only is this a low-mintage date (59,000 pieces), but most ended up being melted during the 1930s (Jeff Garrett and Ron Guth, 2006). This MS62 survivor displays pretty apricot-gold and mint-green patina and soft luster. Additionally, a well executed strike manifests itself in sharp definition on the design features. A few minor obverse marks define the grade; nevertheless, this piece generates pleasing overall eye appeal.(#8879)

3192 **1926 MS64 NGC.** Vibrantly lustrous with rich yellow-orange color on each side. Strong definition adds to the marvelous eye appeal. A great type piece.(#8882)

Sharp MS65 1926 Ten

3193 **1926 MS65 NGC.** Sharply struck with vibrant, frosty luster. Substantially better-preserved than the norm for this popular type issue, though a few insignificant abrasions are still present on each side. Excellent overall visual appeal. Housed in a prior generation holder. NGC has certified a mere 48 finer representatives (2/09). (#8882)

Amazing 1926 Indian Ten, MS66

3194 **1926 MS66 NGC.** An extraordinary Indian eagle, tied for the finest 1926 certified. Despite a mintage of more than 1 million coins, few have survived in the highest grades. The date rarely circulated, so the typical survivor is in the MS60 to MS66 grade range with an average grade of about MS62. Census: 48 in 66, 0 finer (2/09).(#8882)

3195 **1930-S MS66 PCGS.** The 1930-S ten dollar gold piece boasts a small mintage of 96,000 pieces. The reason for producing coins of this denomination at all is a mystery to modern numismatists, as they were clearly not needed in the regional economy. No eagles had been produced at any of the mints since 1926, and no more coins of this denomination would ever be minted at San Francisco. All examples seen today are in Mint State grades, indicating that none of the mintage was released into circulation at the time of issue. The great majority of the coins were held in Treasury vaults until the Gold Recall of the mid-1930s, when they were melted and stored as bullion at Fort Knox. Experts estimate a surviving population of 125-140 examples of this date, all preserved by coin collectors who saved them at the time of issue. In *A Handbook of 20th Century Gold Coins 1907-1933,* David Akers rates the 1930-S as the fourth rarest coin in the 32-coin series in terms of absolute rarity.

Both Walter Breen and David Akers tell of a small hoard of 1930-S eagles, probably from a single roll, that was dispersed in the San Francisco area. Breen relates that one coin would be released every three years, to avoid flooding the market. This supply has presumably been exhausted, and no other hoards are known.

The coin offered here is an extraordinary specimen of this elusive date. The surfaces display amazing, bright mint luster, and all design elements are sharply defined. Wide swathes of pale lilac and rose accent the lovely yellow-gold color of the pristine surfaces. Overall visual appeal is compelling. Only six coins have been certified at the MS66 level by NGC and PCGS combined, with three finer (2/09).(#8883)

3196 1932 MS64 NGC. Well struck overall with the swirling luster that distinguishes this Depression-era issue. Slightly orange-gold surfaces take on a green-gold cast at certain angles. An attractive MS64 piece.(#8884)

3197 1932 MS64 NGC. Strongly struck with swirling luster that enlivens yellow-gold surfaces. An intriguing Choice coin that would make an excellent addition to a type set.(#8884)

3198 1932 MS64 NGC. A shining near-Gem example of this high-mintage late-date issue, strongly struck and highly appealing. Surfaces are generally yellow-orange with a hint of tan. (#8884)

3199 1932 MS64 NGC. In the penultimate year of the series, the Philadelphia Mint produced more than 4.4 million examples of the Indian Head gold eagle. Enough of those coins have survived to make this issue a common date in the series, and an ideal choice for type purposes. This near-Gem is well struck and highly lustrous, with lovely yellow-gold color and minimal surface marks, nearly all of which are located on the reverse.(#8884)

3200 1932 MS64 PCGS. Solidly struck and shining. The obverse has deep butter-yellow shadings, while the reverse shows similar color at the center and paler elements near the rims.(#8884)

Desirable MS65 1932 Eagle

3201 1932 MS65 NGC. An appealing Gem example of this popular type issue, the highest-mintage Saint-Gaudens eagle despite its production during the Great Depression. Strongly detailed central devices are pleasingly preserved with only a few light luster grazes on each side. Yellow-orange surfaces are highly lustrous. (#8884)

Popular 1932 Gem Eagle

3202 1932 MS65 NGC. The 1932 ten dollar, with its 4.463 million mintage, is a popular type coin. This MS65 is especially suitable for a high grade type collection. Its radiantly lustrous yellow-gold surfaces exhibit well struck design elements. A few light contact marks and dark toning spots are visible over each side. (#8884)

Superlative 1932 Indian Eagle, MS66

3203 1932 MS66 NGC. Along with the 1926, the 1932 ranks as one of the most popular type coins, not merely among Saint-Gaudens eagles, but for any U.S. gold series. Examples in grades through Choice are readily available and even Gems can be had for a price, but demand substantially exceeds supply for anything finer. This lovely Premium Gem offers sharp detail and bright straw-gold and butter-yellow surfaces. The obverse on its own might even approach Superb Gem status, though a mark at the N in IN on the reverse precludes a finer designation. Still, a coin that displays beautifully. NGC has graded just seven numerically finer examples (2/09).(#8884)

LIBERTY DOUBLE EAGLES

3204 1851-O—Graffiti—ANACS. AU50 Details. The left obverse field has illegible cursive scribble and a small dig between stars 3 and 4. New Orleans is the most elusive double eagle mintmark, and examples with plentiful glimpses of remaining luster are in demand from Southern gold type collectors.(#8905)

Bright 1851-O Twenty, AU55

3205 1851-O AU55 PCGS. Bright yellow-gold surfaces offer substantial reflectivity with green-gold accents. Though a number of light to moderate abrasions affect the fields, flaws are few on the modestly worn devices. Despite a substantial mintage, this issue becomes challenging in the higher circulated grades. Population: 28 in 55, 25 finer (1/09).(#8905)

1851-O Double Eagle, AU55 Details

3206 **1851-O—Cleaned—ICG. AU55 Details.** The design elements show impressive, uniformly crisp definition throughout. High point wear is slight and exists on the eagle's wing tips, as well as on Liberty's hair. There are a few noticeable abrasions on each side, including one that extends from Liberty's earlobe to the top of her throat. The coin has a somewhat bright appearance due to improper cleaning.(#8905)

3207 **1852 XF40 PCGS.** Subdued yellow surfaces are lightly abraded and the design elements are moderately worn on this early twenty. Traces of residue adheres to the reverse.(#8906)

3208 **1852 AU53 NGC.** Pale yellow-gold overall with modest wear across the highest design elements. Scattered abrasions contribute to the grade, though the overall eye appeal remains strong. (#8906)

3209 **1852 AU53 NGC.** Strongly lustrous despite the light wear that crosses the high points. Yellow-gold fields are modestly abraded. Housed in a prior-generation holder.(#8906)

3210 **1852 AU55 NGC. CAC.** Pale straw-gold at the central obverse with slightly deeper yellow-gold shadings present elsewhere. Light, scattered abrasions cross each side, and the high points show mild wear.(#8906)

Scarce 1852-O Twenty, AU Details

3211 **1852-O—Obverse Damage—NCS. AU Details.** The scarcity of the New Orleans mintmark on double eagles has led to strong type demand for those few O-mint issues that appear with some regularity at auction. This is a green-gold example with glimpses of glowing luster in protected areas. The "damage" appears overstated and consists of a few moderate bagmarks on the portrait and above the hairbun.(#8907)

3212 **1853 XF45 ICG.** Light but distinct wear crosses the yellow-orange high points. Though several abrasions are present on the obverse, the reverse is comparatively clean.(#8908)

3213 **1853 AU50 NGC.** Actual wear is minor on this yellow-orange example, and the strike is pleasing. Several significant abrasions on the obverse account for the grade.(#8908)

3214 **1853 AU58 NGC.** Shining yellow-gold with bold detail. An interesting and desirable near-Mint survivor that shows only a few small, scattered marks. NGC has graded 44 Mint State coins (2/09).(#8908)

Seldom-Seen 1853/2 Double Eagle, AU58 Details

3215 **1853/2—Cleaned—ICG. AU58 Details.** FS-301. What appears to be the downstroke of a 2 is within the lower loop of the 3 in the date. The variety is further confirmed by a die lump beneath the tail of the R in LIBERTY. The peach-gold surfaces of this near-Mint State specimen retain a good amount of luster despite the light cleaning. Nicely defined, and revealing just a few small circulation marks. Very rare in Mint State.(#8909)

3216 **1854-S XF40 NGC.** A moderately abraded, lightly worn example from the San Francisco Mint's first year of operation as such. Generally yellow-gold surfaces show an element of alloy at the rim just above star 6.(#8913)

3217 **1855-S XF45 NGC.** Lightly worn on the high points but surprisingly well-preserved otherwise on the portrait. Numerous scattered abrasions are present in the fields. Overall, a pleasing Choice XF coin from the second year of the San Francisco Mint. (#8916)

Choice AU 1856 Double Eagle

3218 **1856 AU55 PCGS.** The fields of this Choice AU twenty dollar yield partially prooflike characteristics, leading to modest contrast with the motifs when the coin is tilted slightly under a light. Yellow-gold surfaces retain luster in the recessed areas, and reveal just a few minor circulation marks.(#8917)

3219 **1856-S AU53 NGC.** Numerous minor abrasions are noted on both sides of this pale greenish-gold example. A few small splashes of coppery-orange toning are evident on the reverse.(#8919)

Meritorious Choice AU 1856-S Twenty

3220 1856-S AU55 PCGS. This Choice AU twenty possesses considerable luster, and it exhibits sharply struck design elements. The lemon-gold surfaces are pleasing for a large gold coin that briefly entered circulation. Possibly from the *S.S. Central America* shipwreck, although undesignated as such.
Ex: Dallas Signature (Heritage, 11/2007), lot 2251, which realized $2,530.(#8919)

3221 1857 AU53 NGC. Light yellow-gold overall with glimpses of peripheral tan and orange. Wispy abrasions and a few more significant marks are present, but the eye appeal is high for the grade.(#8920)

3222 1857-S AU50 ICG. An appealing AU example with lovely rose-gold toning, light highpoint wear, and numerous wispy hairlines and contact marks on each side.(#8922)

3223 1857-S AU55 NGC. A lightly circulated example with flashy, almost prooflike fields that show scattered abrasions. Pale yellow-gold color is the norm, though a few spots of copper alloy appear around the date.(#8922)

Lustrous Select *S.S. Central America* 1857-S Twenty, Spiked Shield

3224 1857-S MS63 PCGS. Ex: *S.S. Central America*. SSCA 0128, Variety 20A, the "Spiked Shield." The surfaces of this shining example offer pleasing luster. The straw-gold fields show a ring of orange at the outer margins and thin strands of similar color near the centers. Minimally abraded overall, though a scrape runs from the E on Liberty's coronet through the hair and to star 9. Housed in a gold label holder. Comes with box and faux-book case. (#8922)

Vibrant 1857-S Twenty Dollar, MS63 From the *S.S. Central America*

3225 1857-S MS63 NGC. Ex: *S.S. Central America*. Vibrant luster radiates from the yellow-gold surfaces of this Select S-mint twenty dollar, and the design elements are impressively delineated. A scattering of marks over each side, including some noticeable ones on the cheek, limit the grade(#8922)

Popular 1857-S 'Bold S' Double Eagle, MS64

3226 1857-S MS64 PCGS. Bold S. Variety 20B. Vibrant luster exudes from both sides of this near-Gem, each of which displays yellow-gold coloration imbued with occasional splashes of apricot. The design elements are well delineated throughout. A few light surface and rim marks deny Gem classification, and a lamination is visible in the area of UN of UNITED. The "Bold S" mintmark is specified on the holder.(#8922)

Charming MS65 1857-S Double Eagle Spiked Shield, Ex: *S.S. Central America*

3227 1857-S MS65 PCGS. Ex: *S.S. Central America*. Spiked Shield. Variety 20A. SSCA 0364. A shining Gem with the signature "look" of the pieces recovered from the wreck of the *S.S. Central America*: pale yellow-gold interiors with a deepening to orange at the rims, a sharp strike, and powerful luster. Rewarding eye appeal with only a handful of luster grazes. Certified in a gold label holder. Comes with box and related ephemera.(#8922)

Gleaming MS66 1857-S Double Eagle
Ex: S.S. *Central America*

3228 1857-S MS66 PCGS. Ex: *S.S. Central America.* SSCA 4938. When the *S.S. Central America* gold recovery brought to light scores of freshly lustrous, never-worn 1857-S double eagles, conventional notions of the issue's rarity were turned on their head. Far from being an elusive early S-mint, it had become one of the top candidates for collectors seeking a No Motto Liberty double eagle for a high-end type set; though its role had changed, its importance had not.

The centers of this shining example are bright straw-gold, while elements of deeper sun-yellow grace the margins. Crisply struck and carefully preserved, as expected for the grade. Immensely appealing. Comes with certificate of authenticity, stand, faux-book case, and outer box.(#8922)

3229 1858 AU55 PCGS. Rich lemon-gold peripheral color yields to paler yellow-gold at the centers. Lightly abraded overall, yet pleasing with considerable remaining luster. Population: 19 in 55, 38 finer (1/09).(#8923)

3230 1858-S AU53 NGC. Well detailed with a slight degree of original luster evident near some of the devices. An appealing straw-gold representative of this scarce San Francisco Mint issue, which is usually seen in VF to XF grade levels.(#8925)

Pleasing AU55 1858-S Twenty

3231 1858-S AU55 NGC. A scarcely worn double eagle from the San Francisco Mint's early days, lightly abraded overall with only a touch of wear across the highest design elements. This still-lustrous yellow-gold piece boasts a strong strike, and despite its flaws, it retains considerable eye appeal.(#8925)

3232 **1859-O AU58 PCGS.** Every New Orleans double eagle coined after 1853 is an important rarity. While the 1854-O and 1856-O issues are recognized as premier U.S. coin rarities, other dates like this 1859-O (9,100-piece mintage) are less well-known. Doug Winter (2002) calls this issue the fourth rarest New Orleans twenty, following the 1855-O that ranks third. He writes:

"The 1859-O double eagle is a very scarce issue in all grades. It is most often seen in Very Fine to Extremely Fine grades and it is rare in About Uncirculated. Most pieces in this grade range are no better than AU53, and the 1859-O becomes very rare in properly graded AU55."

PCGS and NGC combined have certified about 110 1859-O double eagles. The two services rate a mere three coins as Mint State.

This near-Mint State example exhibits a better strike than ordinarily seen. Specifically, all obverse stars are bold, and most of Liberty's hair is strong. The wing tips and tail feathers reveal some of the usual softness, but the remaining reverse motif details are sharp. The surfaces display exceptional, nearly complete medium yellow luster and hints of reflectivity near the devices. A few minute contact marks are scattered about, but these are fewer and of less severity than ordinarily seen. This is significant, because Winter writes: "Almost every known 1859-O double eagle shows deep abrasions on the surfaces."

Considering the above-average strike and lightly marked surfaces, this is a truly exceptional offering that will draw serious attention from New Orleans Mint collectors and those of high quality, rare gold coinage. Population: 4 in 58, 1 finer (2/09).(#8927)

3233 **1859-S VF35 NGC.** Ex: *S.S. Republic.* Lemon-gold surfaces show splashes of orange. Surprisingly radiant for a Choice VF example, a well struck coin with considerable eye appeal. Comes with presentation box, DVD, and literature.(#8928)

3234 **1859-S AU50 NGC.** Luminous yellow-gold color with mustard overtones to the still-lustrous fields. Traces of alloy are noted at the softly struck stars. Lightly abraded and modestly worn. (#8928)

Choice AU 1859-S Double Eagle

3235 **1859-S AU55 NGC.** The remaining level of design detail is nearly complete, with really light friction on Liberty's hair. Even olive-green toning is quite attractive, and the fields are largely undisturbed by any evidence of contact, except on the lower right reverse. A nice grade for this San Francisco Mint issue, typically seen at lower levels of preservation.(#8928)

3236 **1860 AU55 PCGS.** A brightly lustrous and well-defined piece, pale lemon-gold with glimpses of green-gold in the fields. The modest wear present on each side has little effect on the eye appeal. *From The Ed Lepordo Collection, Part Two.*(#8929)

Scarce 1860-S Double Eagle, AU55

3237 **1860-S AU55 NGC.** Nicely detailed with slight, even highpoint wear and appealing green-gold toning. The faint hairlines and minor marks noted are typical for the grade. As one of the rarest double eagles from the San Francisco Mint, the 1860-S is difficult to locate in high grades. At the Choice AU level, however, this piece remains relatively affordable.(#8931)

3238 **1861 AU55 NGC.** Dusky butter-yellow surfaces retain ample luster in the protected areas. Scattered abrasions and light wear across the high points account for the grade.(#8932)

3239 **1861 AU58 NGC.** A softly lustrous yellow-gold piece, well struck with modest rub on the high points. Pleasing for the grade with few marks of any significance.(#8932)

Appealing Near-Mint 1861 Double Eagle

3240 **1861 AU58 NGC.** Boldly struck and still fully lustrous, with a bright satiny sheen across both sides. This is an appealing near-Mint example of the date and denomination. The Civil War was just about to begin and coin mintages would quickly diminish as a consequence, but the 1861 issue enjoyed a substantial production of almost 3 million coins. A great choice to represent the Type One double eagle.(#8932)

3241 **1861 AU58 NGC.** Shining with pleasing overall detail. The surfaces show light, wispy abrasions and two dots of deeper alloy on the rim to the right of the date.(#8932)

Desirable 1861 Twenty, MS61

3242 **1861 MS61 PCGS.** Warm yellow-gold color overall with hints of orange. Strongly lustrous and attractive despite a number of light abrasions. Though this Civil War-era double eagle issue has a mintage approaching 3 million pieces, most survivors are circulated, and Mint State pieces are elusive. *From The Burning Tree Collection.*(#8932)

Low Mintage AU55 1862 Double Eagle

3243 **1862 AU55 NGC.** Although the Philadelphia Mint coined more than 1.3 million gold dollars in 1862, the facility's production of double eagles was parsimonious. Just 92,133 twenties were struck, and since few were held as bank reserves, Uncirculated pieces are out of reach for most collectors. This Choice AU representative provides a viable alternative, and has ample luster in addition to a few abrasions on the right reverse field.(#8937)

3244 **1863-S—Cleaned—ICG. XF45 Details.** The yellow-orange surfaces show unnatural luminosity from a past cleaning. Well struck and appealing despite its flaws, which include scattered abrasions on the portrait.(#8940)

3245 **1863-S AU50 NGC.** Generally wheat-gold with elements of sun-yellow and orange on the reverse. Light wear overall with a number of tiny abrasions, but strong eye appeal nonetheless.(#8940)

3246 **1863-S AU55 NGC.** The butter-yellow obverse shows a number of light abrasions, but the reverse is minimally marked. Modest wear crosses the high points of the well struck devices.(#8940)

3247 **1863-S AU55 NGC.** Dusky yellow-gold overall with orange overtones. Several abrasions are present on and near Liberty's cheek, but the reverse offers solid eye appeal.(#8940)

Lustrous 1863-S Double Eagle, AU58

3248 **1863-S AU58 NGC.** The surfaces are lightly hairlined and exhibit noticeable highpoint wear, particularly on the obverse, but the luster is intense and nearly full over both sides. A few minor coin-to-coin marks are evident in the fields. Once a conditionally rare S-mint twenty, almost always seen in VF to XF grades; around 300 pieces were recovered from the S.S. *Republic* and S.S. *Brother Jonathan* shipwrecks, however, including many in AU condition. (#8940)

Important MS62 1864-S Twenty
Ex: S.S. *Republic*

3249 **1864-S MS62 NGC.** Ex: *S.S. Republic.* While 1865-S double eagles made up the bulk of the treasure recovered from the S.S. *Republic*, a scattering of older issues was included as well, such as the 1864-S twenty, as represented here. Pale yellow-gold centers are strongly lustrous with slight deepening of the color close to the rims. Softly struck with wispy abrasions that preclude Select status, yet the eye appeal remains high. Census: 11 in 62, 5 finer (2/09). (#8942)

Elusive 1865 Double Eagle, AU58

3250 **1865 AU58 NGC.** The 1865 (351,200 pieces struck) is a somewhat overlooked scarcity, particularly in grades at or near the Mint State level, even after the recovery of several hundred examples from the shipwreck of the S.S. *Republic*. Minimally worn with plenty of bold striking definition still in evidence, this yellow-gold example also possesses much of the original mint luster. The scattered abrasions from a short stint in circulation include no marks worthy of individual mention.(#8943)

Attractive Near-Mint 1865-S Double Eagle
Ex: S.S. *Brother Jonathan*

3251 **1865-S AU58 PCGS.** *Brother Jonathan 965.* An attractive example with almost all of the original mint luster still surviving. Back in 1982, when David Akers wrote his book on double eagles, the great majority of 1865-S survivors then known were in the VF to EF grade range, but the discovery of lustrous AU and Uncirculated pieces from the S.S. *Brother Jonathan* and S.S. *Republic* shipwrecks has served to greatly increase the number of high-grade survivors. *Ex: S.S. Brother Jonathan Treasure Coins (Bowers and Merena, 5/1999), lot 821.*(#8944)

Interesting MS62 1865-S Double Eagle
From the S.S. *Brother Jonathan*

3252 **1865-S MS62 PCGS.** *Brother Jonathan 830.* Most of the coins recovered in the early 1990s from the Brother Jonathan shipwreck in the 1990s were 1865-S double eagles, understandably, as the ship foundered after crashing into a rock off the California coast on July 30 of that year. The orange-gold surfaces of the present example show scant evidence of more than a century-long submersion in the waters of the Pacific Ocean, save for some slight haze and localized microporosity. Still-lustrous surfaces display orange-gold patina predominating, with deeper areas of smoky-gold. The reverse die is in a late stage, with many interesting cracks around the reverse periphery. In a special S.S. *Brother Jonathan* PCGS encapsulation. *Ex: S.S. Brother Jonathan Treasure Coins (Bowers and Merena, 5/1999), lot 716.*(#8944)

Affordable Fine 1866-S No Motto Twenty

3253 **1866-S No Motto Fine 12 NGC.** A more affordable example of this final No Motto double eagle issue than most, owing to the significant wear that crosses the devices. The yellow-orange fields remain surprisingly lustrous, however, and though light, scattered marks are present on each side, more-significant abrasions are few. (#8945)

XF45 Details 1866-S No Motto Twenty

3254 **1866-S No Motto—Cleaned—ANACS. XF45 Details.** Most S-mint Liberty double eagles are plentiful in circulated grades, since the denomination was the mainstay of the hard asset West Coast economy. The two exceptions are the 1861-S Paquet Reverse and the 1866-S No Motto, both of which have low mintages. Although subdued by a mild cleaning, this is a richly detailed pale gold example without any individually relevant abrasions. (#8945)

AU55 Details 1866-S No Motto Twenty

3255 **1866-S No Motto—Polished—ICG. AU55 Details.** A minimally worn example of this final No Motto double eagle issue, well struck with light, scattered abrasions. Yellow-gold surfaces show stark brightness from polishing, but this merely provides the budget-conscious collector with an opportunity to acquire a better-detailed representative.

3256 **1866 AU50 NGC.** Khaki-gold toning yields to vibrant orange luster remnants near the devices. Well struck and moderately worn, with a few noticeable abrasions on each side.(#8949)

3257 **1866 AU53 NGC.** Despite light wear, the fields remain immensely lustrous. A pleasing example of this initial Motto double eagle issue, minimally abraded for the grade.(#8949)

1866-S Motto Double Eagle AU53

3258 **1866-S Motto AU53 PCGS.** Struck too late to participate in the *Brother Jonathan* hoard, the Motto 1866-S becomes scarce in AU, although XF pieces are generally available. The present coin has plentiful luster on the reverse, and obverse luster brightens design recesses. Small marks are scattered, as expected for a lightly circulated large denomination gold coin.(#8950)

Desirable 1867 Double Eagle, MS61

3259 **1867 MS61 NGC.** The 1867 is a hoard date that was brought back to this country primarily in the 1960s. Most examples grade no finer than the present piece, whose surfaces have unusually pronounced mint luster for the grade and strong strike details throughout. A number of small abrasions and luster grazes account for the grade.(#8951)

3260 **1867-S XF45 NGC.** Strong yellow-gold luster for the amount of wear present. Light abrasions overall, but nothing that jeopardizes the grade. Interesting eye appeal.(#8952)

3261 **1867-S AU50 PCGS.** Honey-gold surfaces display traces of luster in the protected areas, and are generally well struck, except for portions of Liberty's hair. Both sides reveal several marks, including some rim nicks.(#8952)

3262 **1867-S AU50 NGC.** Impressively lustrous with light wear and abrasions. Pale yellow-gold surfaces show traces of wheat. Overall, a solid example of this Type Two issue.(#8952)

3263 **1867-S AU53 NGC.** Small spots of rub on the high points show as sage-colored alloy, contrasting with the honey-gold color present elsewhere. Modestly abraded for the grade.(#8952)

Exemplary MS62 1868 Double Eagle

Desirable MS63 1869 Double Eagle

3264 **1868 MS62 PCGS.** Any Type Two double eagles is desirable in Mint State, but the 1868 is the rarest Philadelphia issue of the type in such condition. As of (2/09), PCGS has certified only seven examples of the 1868 in Uncirculated grades, two each in MS60 through MS62 plus one finer as MS63. The present lot is therefore a rare and fleeting opportunity to acquire an 1868 with unbroken luster and only lightly abraded surfaces. This canary-gold piece has a good strike and pleasing eye appeal. It is among the finest survivors from a low mintage of 98,575 pieces.(#8953)

3265 **1868-S AU50 NGC.** An attractive yellow-gold Type Two double eagle that has only a single remotely reportable mark, beneath the eagle's right (facing) wing. The 1868-S is very rare in Mint State, and most collectors settle for a nice AU.(#8954)

Lustrous Near-Mint 1868-S Double Eagle

3266 **1868-S AU58 NGC.** This San Francisco Mint issue has a surprisingly high number of survivors at the AU58 grade level, but Mint State examples are genuinely scarce, and considerably more expensive. This specimen is well struck and quite flashy, with intense mint luster that seems nearly full. Highpoint wear is minimal, but both sides present a rather scuffy, moderately abraded appearance.(#8954)

3267 **1869 MS63 PCGS.** The 1869 was struck later than any of the famous shipwreck hoards, such as the S.S. Republic, the S.S. Central America, and the S.S. Brother Jonathan. 1869 was also prior to the wholesale export of gold coins to Europe, where they were retained by banks as bullion reserves. Thus, the 1869, along with other early Type Two dates, is confoundedly difficult to locate in quality Mint State. But here is a pleasing apricot-gold example that boasts full luster and lacks the unfortunate abrasions that tend to plague lower graded Uncirculated twenties. A strong bid will be needed to secure this prize. Population: 3 in 63, 2 finer (2/09). (#8955)

3268 **1869-S AU53 NGC.** A trifle softly struck, as often seen for this issue, with worn high points and lustrous yellow-gold fields. Wispy abrasions overall with more significant marks found in a line below star 6 on the obverse.(#8956)

3269 **1869-S AU55 NGC.** Appealing yellow-gold color with wheat overtones. This pleasingly lustrous Choice AU coin shows light, scattered abrasions that contribute to the grade.(#8956)

3270 **1870-CC XF45 NGC.** The 1870-CC double eagle combines many of the characteristics that collectors find most desirable in U.S. coinage. It combines the desired and legendary CC mintmark with the largest classic coinage denomination ever issued for circulation, and adds the historic first year of production for the historic Carson City Mint. In 1870 the double eagle denomination had been in existence only 20 years, owing its origin to the Fields of Gold found in nearby California. In that year the Carson City Mint was opened to produce local coinage from the precious gold and silver gleaned from the Comstock Lode discovered in 1859, obviating an overland or rail trip to transport metal to California for coinage.

According to *The Mint on Carson Street* author Rusty Goe, Abraham Curry, founder of the town of Carson City and superintendent of the eponymous mint, was especially proud of the large, heavy twenty dollar gold pieces flowing from the facility. The recorded mintage of double eagles from the first year was 3,789 pieces, although only a few dozen are known today.

By whatever route, most of them circulated heavily. The average certified survivor "only" grades about VF35 or a bit better—but into that must be factored the fact that not a single true Mint State example is known. (Although Goe quotes Q. David Bowers as once reporting that he had handled a Mint State coin at one time, it is unknown today. Goe comments: "If this piece were ever to hit the market, the sky would be the limit as far as price was concerned.") So, for every AU50 coin known, another only grades VF20. When Goe published his reference in 2003, the highest-graded pieces were a handful of coins in AU—two at NGC, four at PCGS. Since then NGC has certified two pieces in AU53 and one coin in AU55. The highest-graded example at PCGS is a single AU53. Pieces in XF condition, much less Choice XF, the condition of the present piece, are still considered high-end, and possibly within the Condition Census, as some of the above citations are almost certainly reappearances of the same coin.

The present Choice XF example shows the heavy abrasions on both sides that are typical of, literally, every known example. These soft and heavy coins circulated in the rough-and-tumble West until the survivors were plucked from the channels of commerce, and that has taken its toll. However, this piece offers the twin blessings of good original color and considerable luster remaining for the XF45 grade, qualities that most survivors lack. The surfaces are mellow orange-gold, with considerable reflectivity and even some faint prooflikeness remaining in some of the protected areas. The strike is somewhat soft around portions of the peripheries, although most of the stars display some detail to the centrils. The TAT in STATES is noticeably weak. Goe aptly paraphrases the nonetheless obvious appeal of this coin when he states, "More often than not all of these deficiencies are excused due to the date and mintmark combination, by 'CC' gold specialists who are able to pay the hefty price tag to own an 1870-CC double eagle, as there is no equal as far as they are concerned." Census: 7 in 45, 5 finer (2/09). *From The Belle Collection of Carson City Coinage.*(#8958)

See: **Video Lot Description**

3271 **1870-S AU53 NGC.** Potent yellow-gold color with glimpses of reflectivity in the luster. A lightly worn yet highly appealing piece that shows miscellaneous marks in the fields.(#8959)

3272 **1870-S AU55 NGC.** Considerable luster for the grade, though modest wear is apparent at the softly struck high points. Small, scattered abrasions have little effect on the eye appeal. (#8959)

3273 **1870-S AU55 NGC.** Both sides of this lustrous yellow-gold double eagle are lightly abraded, consistent with the grade. Typical examples of this date are found in lower circulated grades. This attractive example will be a nice addition to a top circulated collection of Liberty twenties.(#8959)

Choice VF 1871-CC Double Eagle

3274 **1871-CC VF35 PCGS.** Although more collectible than its famously rare 1870-CC predecessor, the 1871-CC is also a very difficult issue. Most of the mintage of 17,387 pieces circulated for years in the Old West, where no consideration was given to any *numismatic* value. PCGS has certified none above AU55. The present Choice VF example still has suggestions of luster along the borders, and the apricot-gold fields and devices lack individually noticeable marks. An opportunity to acquire this rare Carson City date in an economic yet attractive condition.(#8961)

Roswell K. Colcord, Carson City Mint Superintendent

Desirable 1871-CC Double Eagle, AU53
Second-Rarest CC-Mint Twenty

3275 **1871-CC AU53 NGC.** Well worn and heavily bagmarked is the usual state of most survivors of the 1871-CC double eagle issue. After opening in 1870, the Carson City Mint saw an increase of more than 800% in the gold deposits in the following year. However, that surge in deposits did not translate into a huge increase in double eagle coinage. This was due partly because the mint could equally supply assayed gold bars as well as coinage, and many miners preferred that medium to coins.

Nonetheless, the 1871-CC double eagle was produced to the extent of 14,687 coins. (Rusty Goe's *The Mint on Carson Street* notes, "Some references list the mintage for 1871-CC double eagles as 17,387, although official U.S. mint records have reported it as 14,687 since 1887.") While that was an improvement of nearly 290% over the previous year, it apparently failed to make a dent in the region's needs. Most were swallowed in the maws of commerce, and today the average certified survivor, estimated to be only a couple of hundred coins, only grades XF40 to XF45. This estimate gibes with the total NGC/PCGS certified population data, which show 276 submission events.

This splendid AU53 example is head and shoulders above the norm for the issue, with much original luster remaining on both sides and splendid deep, mellow orange-gold coloration. The strike is delightfully bold overall, with all stars showing their centrils and only minor softness on the high points of Liberty's hair. A few moderate abrasions that dot the surfaces are in keeping with the issue and grade, although they are neither numerous nor bothersome.

The 1871-CC double eagle is, by a wide margin, the second-rarest double eagle issue from the Carson City Mint. One fundamental distinction that numismatists would do well to keep in mind is that between *conditional rarity* and *fundamental rarity*. While there are many coins that are conditionally elusive in high grades (many of them awfully nice to look at), coins such as the present piece, which are rare in all grades and have been so nearly since their creation, are among the most desired issues in all of U.S. numismatics. And with good reason.
From The Belle Collection of Carson City Coinage. (#8961)

3276 **1871-S AU55 NGC.** Flashy on each side with above-average detail and wispy abrasions. The obverse is pale wheat-gold, while the reverse is slightly more dusky.(#8962)

Popular Near-Mint 1872-CC Twenty

3277 **1872-CC AU58 PCGS.** The 1872-CC double eagle is a low-mintage issue of 26,900 pieces. Most of the coins seen at auction are in Very Fine to Extremely Fine condition. About Uncirculated pieces are scarce, and Mint State examples are rare. The brass-gold surfaces of this AU58 example exhibit considerable luster and nicely defined motifs. Distributed light marks are slightly more prevalent on the obverse, but these are fewer and of less severity than typically seen on most surviving examples. Population: 29 in 58, 2 finer (2/09). *From The Belle Collection of Carson City Coinage.*(#8964)

3278 **1873 Closed 3 XF45 PCGS.** Well struck with light wear across the yellow-gold surfaces. Modestly abraded on the portrait with a horizontal pinscratch in the right obverse field.(#8966)

3279 **1873 Open 3 MS61 NGC.** This is a lovely Type Two example with gorgeous gold and khaki color and shimmering luster. A handful of minor marks are noted on each side, but these seem minimal for the grade. An extremely popular issue for type collectors. (#8967)

3280 **1873 Open 3 MS61 NGC.** Well struck for the issue with bright luster and pale yellow-gold surfaces. Though the obverse shows a number of abrasions, the reverse is comparatively clean. (#8967)

Bold AU53 1873-CC Double Eagle

3281 **1873-CC AU53 PCGS.** Its mintage of 22,410 pieces suggests that the 1873-CC is very scarce, and a quick glance at the PCGS Population Report provides confirmation. The grading service has certified just seven coins as Mint State, which indicates that nearly all collectors must settle for an AU example. The present sun-gold piece has a few marks on the cheek but is otherwise only moderately bagmarked.(#8968)

Desirable 1873-S Open 3 Twenty, MS61

3282 **1873-S Open 3 MS61 NGC.** Erroneously described as a Closed 3 on the holder; the two logotypes are close in appearance on the large twenty dollar pieces. Bright yellow-gold surfaces show few overt abrasions and are host to well struck devices. Extremely rare any finer, with just six such coins in the combined certified population (1/09).(#8979)

1874-CC Double Eagle, AU53

3283 **1874-CC AU53 NGC.** Luster resides in the protected areas of this Carson City representative, and the design features show relatively strong definition, except for weakness in portions of Liberty's hair. Minute distributed marks occur on each side, and a light grease streak is visible in the upper left reverse.(#8971)

3284 **1875-CC AU55 PCGS.** Rich yellow-gold luster with a hint of frostiness on the softly struck devices. Lightly abraded overall but with only trifling wear across the high points.
From The Belle Collection of Carson City Coinage.(#8974)

3285 **1876 MS60 NGC.** Light Motto subtype. A lustrous peach-gold double eagle from the final date of the Type Two design. Scattered abrasions are present, as befits the grade.(#8976)

3286 **1876 MS61 NGC.** Intense, flashy mint luster and alluring rose and peach-gold toning are highlights of this Mint State double eagle from the Philadelphia Mint. A number of small marks limit the grade, but the majority of them are superficial.(#8976)

Appealing MS62 1876 Twenty Dollar

3287 **1876 MS62 PCGS.** Heavy Motto. The last of the Type Two Philadelphia double eagles, offered here as an elegant MS62 coin with rich butter-yellow luster. Sharply struck design definition with considerable frostiness on the minimally marked obverse portrait. Scattered abrasions in the fields account for the grade. (#8976)

3288 **1876-CC XF45 NGC.** Reddish-gold patina visits both sides of this Choice XF double eagle, each of which is relatively well defined. Semibright surfaces reveal minute distributed marks. (#8977)

3289 **1876-CC AU50 PCGS.** Faint traces of frosty luster remain in the protected areas on this pleasing Carson City double eagle. Both sides have splashes of pinkish toning with hints of field reflectivity. (#8977)

Lovely 1876-CC Twenty, AU53

3290 **1876-CC AU53 NGC.** This attractive double eagle combines the CC mintmark with the Centennial-year date. Its allure is increased by considerable prooflikeness visible on both sides under the light field chatter. The orange-gold surfaces are well struck and display minimal heavy abrasions.(#8977)

Attractive 1876-CC Double Eagle, AU55

3291 **1876-CC AU55 PCGS.** An attractive Choice AU representative with a great deal of luster for the grade and luscious, deep apricot-gold coloration. Wispy hairlines are evident on each side, along with a few scattered abrasions. Final year of the Type Two design and a popular Carson City type coin.(#8977)

Near-Mint 1876-CC Twenty Dollar

3292 **1876-CC AU58 PCGS.** The final Type Two Carson City date, struck during our nation's Centennial. Cartwheel luster consumes the reverse of this nicely struck double eagle. The obverse luster is close to complete, and although small marks are distributed, none merit singular description. Popular for its comparatively low mintage and its Nevada origin.(#8977)

3293 **1876-CC—Cleaned—ANACS. AU58 Details.** This issue is always popular as a Type Two Carson City product, ensuring its steady demand among collectors. This is a bright, improperly cleaned example with numerous wispy marks and hairlines on each side.(#8977)

Notable AU55 Prooflike 1876-CC Twenty

3294 **1876-CC AU55 Prooflike NGC.** This popular Type Two Carson City double eagle issue is available through all circulated grades and into lower Mint State, but Prooflike representatives are another matter. This yellow-orange example is modestly worn with a handful of marks and slight cloudiness to the obverse fields, but the mirrors shine in full force on the reverse. Census: 1 in 55 Prooflike, 4 finer (2/09).(#78977)

3295 **1876-S MS61 PCGS.** The obverse is moderately abraded as expected for the grade. The reverse has fewer and lighter abrasions that are reminiscent of pieces graded a point or two higher. This attractive piece has brilliant yellow luster.(#8978)

1877 Double Eagle, MS62

3296 **1877 MS62 PCGS.** Yellow-orange surfaces display a nearly unbroken luster flow, even though both sides have their share of light to moderate distributed contact marks. The portrait and eagle are crisply detailed. Elusive any finer, with just 14 such pieces known to PCGS (2/09).(#8982)

3297 **1877-CC XF45 NGC.** First year of the modified Type Three design, the 1877-CC is one of the more available Carson City twenties of this type, primarily because of a small hoard that entered the market in the mid-1990s. This piece has even reddish patina over each side, and there is just the faintest trace of mirroring still visible in the fields. Even, light wear over the high points with no obvious abrasions on either side.(#8983)

3298 **1877-CC XF45 NGC.** Light yellow-gold color with glimpses of flashiness at the margins. A faintly abraded, modestly worn example of the first Type Three Carson City double eagle issue. (#8983)

3299 **1878 MS61 NGC.** Peach-gold surfaces exhibit sharply struck design features, and retain a considerable amount of luster, the most potent of which occurs in the recessed areas. Distributed small marks are visible over each side.(#8985)

Popular 1878-CC Double Eagle, XF45

3300 **1878-CC XF45 PCGS.** Splashes of pale bluish patina are evident over the light yellow-gold surfaces of this Choice XF double eagle, especially the obverse, and traces of luster can still be seen hugging the design motifs. The design elements are well defined. The Carson City Mint double eagles are one of the most popular collecting categories among all gold coins.(#8986)

Difficult AU 1878-CC Twenty Dollar

3301 **1878-CC AU50 NGC.** Luminous luster brightens the borders of this lightly circulated CC-mint double eagle. Carson City concentrated on Morgan dollar production in 1878, to the neglect of gold denominations. A scant 13,180 twenties were struck, most of which circulated since NGC has certified only five coins as Mint State, none above MS61.(#8986)

3302 **1879-CC XF40 PCGS.** The 1879-CC double eagle has one of the lower mintage figures for coins produced at the Carson City Mint (10,708 pieces). Yellow-gold color covers this specimen, which shows traces of luster in the recessed areas. This is a well detailed coin that has distributed minuscule marks consistent with light circulation.(#8989)

Challenging 1879-CC Twenty AU55

3303 **1879-CC AU55 NGC.** The Carson City Mint struck more than 100,000 double eagles each year between 1874 and 1876. By 1878, gold deposits had presumably dwindled, since only 13,180 pieces were struck. 1879 had an even smaller twenty dollar production, just 10,708 pieces, and only a handful are known in Mint State. Most survivors are XF to AU. The present sun-gold example is surprisingly bereft of abrasions, although a slight obverse rim bump is noted at 5 o'clock. Liberty's chin has only a whisper of wear, and luster dominates most of the reverse.(#8989)

Deeply Reflective 1880 Twenty, AU58 Prooflike

3304 **1880 AU58 Prooflike NGC.** The 1880 has an impressively low mintage of only 51,400 pieces. Over the past 15 years or so a number of coins have been repatriated from European sources. Nevertheless, it is still a scarce date. Apparently only one pair of dies was used for the entire run of strikes for circulation, which would indicate this coin must have been one of the first struck before the mirror-like finish diminished with successive strikings. The fields are brightly prooflike on each side. Additionally, the strike is strong throughout. A number of small to medium-sized abrasions are scattered over each side, as one would expect. Census: 1 in 58 Prooflike, 0 finer (2/09).(#78992)

3305 **1882 AU58 ICG.** The 1882 is the rarest Type Three double eagle in business strike form (571 circulation strikes). Michael Fuljenz and Douglas Winter write in their *Type Three Double Eagles, 1877-1907* reference that:

> "... it must be ranked among the rarest 19th century American gold coins in any series. The few remaining examples generally grade Extremely Fine-45 to About Uncirculated-50. Any 1882 Double Eagle which grades About Uncirculated-55 is extremely rare and only two pieces are believed to exist in Mint State."

PCGS and NGC have actually certified four Mint State 1882 double eagles, the highest grading MS62. Indeed, the two services have graded a total of 26 pieces in all levels of preservation.

The present ICG-certified AU58 coin displays prooflike fields, which is typical for the issue. These establish notable contrast with the motifs, especially when the coin is rotated under a light source. A penetrating strike delivers crisp definition to the design elements, including the reverse shield and eagle, areas that are sometimes soft. A few minor marks are visible over each side, but these are totally within the context of a large gold coin that has seen brief circulation.

Interestingly, Fuljenz and Winter say that: "The great rarity of this date makes its eye appeal relatively unimportant. When examining a coin which is as rare as the 1882 Double Eagle, the collector cannot be overly concerned with eye appeal." The fact that this particular specimen projects outstanding eye appeal thus makes it all the more special for the connoisseur of rare gold coins.(#8996)

Delightful 1883-S Double Eagle, MS63

3306 **1883-S MS63 PCGS. CAC.** Intense luster radiates from both sides of this Select S-mint coin. Orange-gold surfaces imbued with hints of light green and yellow-gold exhibit sharply struck design elements. Scattered light marks limit the grade, but this is nevertheless a highly attractive piece. Housed in a green label holder.(#9000)

3307 **1884-CC AU50 NGC.** Dusky yellow-gold surfaces show ample strawberry overtones and alloy streaks on and around the upper portrait. Lightly circulated with the usual scattering of marks. (#9001)

3308 **1884-CC AU53 PCGS.** Warm yellow-gold luster overall with hints of paler straw. Design definition is excellent with only modest wear and marks. A fundamentally pleasing example. *From The Belle Collection of Carson City Coinage.*(#9001)

3309 **1884-CC AU55 PCGS.** Substantial luster brightens the design elements of this nicely struck and briefly circulated Carson City double eagle. Marks are unexpectedly few. A quality (and hefty) gold type coin from the legendary Old West facility.(#9001)

Attractive 1884-CC Double Eagle, AU58

3310 **1884-CC AU58 PCGS.** Bright and flashy, with a great deal of remaining mint luster. The yellow-gold color is even and attractive across each side. In the absence of any noticeable highpoint wear, this example seems close to Mint State. Potentially an excellent choice for type purposes.(#9001)

3311 **1884-S MS62 NGC.** Sharply struck with strong, satiny luster and rich yellow-orange color. A modestly abraded coin for a piece that did not gain the Select designation.(#9002)

Beautiful Select 1884-S Twenty

3312 **1884-S MS63 PCGS. CAC.** Strongly lustrous and generally yellow-gold, though a touch of alloy is visible at the luster scrapes on the highest design elements. The strike is bold, and the overall eye appeal is grand. Despite a healthy mintage, this issue is elusive any finer, with just 18 such pieces graded by PCGS (1/09). (#9002)

3313 **1884-S MS61 Prooflike NGC.** Prooflike 1884-S double eagles are few and far between. Indeed, NGC has graded a mere nine pieces, none above the MS62 level. The moderately reflective fields of this MS61 example set off the design elements, all of which are sharply impressed. Distributed scuffs limit the numerical grade. Census: 5 in 61, 2 finer (2/09).(#79002)

Exceptional 1885-CC Double Eagle, VF35

3314 **1885-CC VF35 PCGS.** The low mintage 1885-CC double eagle (9,450 coins) is, according to Douglas Winter (2001): "... the rarest Carson City double eagle from this decade, both in terms of overall and high grade rarity." This Choice VF example retains a good amount of luster in the recessed areas and displays relatively strong design detail. Moreover, its yellow-gold surfaces are not excessively bagmarked, unlike most surviving examples.(#9004)

Lustrous 1887-S Twenty Dollar Gold, MS62

3315 **1887-S MS62 PCGS.** An intensely lustrous example that appears to be conservatively graded. Rich apricot-gold toning is imbued with subtle greenish accents over each side. The design elements are sharply struck, although the mintmark has a somewhat irregular shape and may be repunched.(#9007)

3316 **1888 MS62 PCGS.** Lime and peach coloration are intermingled across the satiny surfaces of this Uncirculated example. Quite attractive for the grade, despite several facial marks. A scarce issue in Mint State, and rare any finer than MS62.(#9008)

3317 **1888-S MS62 PCGS.** Strong yellow-gold color overall with glimpses of wheat and peach. A number of fine abrasions and a more significant one on the cheek contribute to the grade. (#9009)

Brilliant 1889-CC Twenty, AU58

3318 **1889-CC AU58 PCGS.** The Carson City Mint went on hiatus from mid-1885 through 1888, producing no coinage. The outputs of both silver dollars and double eagles when the facility reopened in 1889 were modest for their respective series, 30,945 coins in the case of double eagles. Examples are nonetheless available in all grades up to MS64—did denizens of Nevada realize the Mint might close soon? This piece offers strong eye appeal over brilliant orange-gold surfaces that show just the barest trace of high-point rub. Moderate abrasions are consistent with the grade.(#9011)

3319 **1889-S MS62 PCGS.** Rich yellow-orange color with a degree of reflectivity to the fields. Well-defined with only scattered modest abrasions precluding Select status.(#9012)

3320 **1890-CC—Reverse Scratched, Improperly Cleaned—NCS. AU Details.** Peach-gold surfaces reveal fine hairlines under high magnification, along with a good amount of luster in the recessed areas. A short field scratch is visible to the upper right of the eagle. All of the design elements benefited from a sharp strike. (#9014)

3321 **1890-CC AU50 PCGS.** Well-defined with rich sun-yellow color and traces of crimson at the margins. Light, scattered abrasions and modest wear contribute to the grade.(#9014)

Exceptional 1891-CC Twenty Dollar, XF45

3322 **1891-CC XF45 PCGS.** The 5,000-piece mintage for the 1891-CC double eagle is among the lowest for any Carson City issue. This yellow-orange Choice XF piece has the expected number of surface and rim marks for the grade, but they are much less severe than ordinarily seen, for as Douglas Winter (2001) opines: "... this is one of the most heavily abraded of all Carson City gold coins ... and any piece with only moderately abraded surfaces is in great demand." The design elements are well defined, except for the usual strike weakness on the lower obverse stars.(#9017)

Important Select 1892-CC Double Eagle

3323 **1892-CC MS63 NGC.** An attractive and unusually desirable Select representative of this penultimate Carson City double eagle issue, sharply struck on the portrait with considerable reflectivity in the fields. Yellow-orange hues are dominant, though glimpses of copper-red alloy are noted at the rims and as small dots in the fields. Each side shows only a handful of wispy abrasions, though these taken together define the grade. One of 10 pieces, five graded by NGC and five graded by PCGS, tied for finest certified in the combined condition census (2/09).
From The Belle Collection of Carson City Coinage.(#9020)

Bright AU55 1893-CC Twenty

3324 1893-CC AU55 PCGS. The last double eagle issue from the fabled Carson City Mint, the 1893-CC saw a modest emission of only a bit more than 18,000 coins. Examples are available up to MS63, however, probably because more of the issue were saved. This piece shows somewhat prooflike orange-gold surfaces that show light abrasions on both sides. For the grade, however, the luster is quite splendid, retaining essentially all of its original brilliance and beauty.(#9023)

Uncirculated 1893-CC Double Eagle

3325 1893-CC MS61 PCGS. An orange-gold Carson City twenty from the final year of coinage at the legendary Western facility. Lustrous and crisply struck with original orange-red and olive toning. The reverse is splendidly smooth, while the obverse has only faint scattered luster grazes.(#9023)

Scarce 1893-CC Twenty Dollar, MS62

3326 1893-CC MS62 NGC. Ex: Richmond Collection. The 1893-CC is most frequently seen in the About Uncirculated to MS60 grade range. It becomes scarce in MS62, and is rare in MS63 and finer. Both sides are somewhat frosty in finish, and display peach-gold color laced with mint-green. Distributed marks are light, and of less severity than typically seen. The design elements are well impressed throughout.(#9023)

Marvelous MS63 1893-CC Twenty

3327 1893-CC MS63 NGC. The Carson City double eagle series ends on a mixed note with the 1893 issue. While the mintage of 18,402 pieces is down compared to the year before, survival rates are up, and though MS63 examples of the issue are conditionally rare, they are more available than for any other Carson City double eagle date, with 37 instances in the combined certified population (2/09). This lovely MS63 coin has shining lemon-gold surfaces with hints of straw. Excellent detail on Liberty's hair with only a handful of wispy abrasions affecting each side.
From The Belle Collection of Carson City Coinage.(#9023)

3328 1895 MS64 PCGS. CAC. A pleasingly detailed example with wheat-gold outer zones that yield to a slightly paler center. Modestly marked for the grade with delightful eye appeal and slightly satiny luster. PCGS has graded just two finer pieces (1/09).(#9027)

Near-Gem 1896 Twenty Dollar
Ex: Eagle Collection

3329 **1896 MS64 PCGS.** Ex: Eagle Collection. Breen-7322, "very rare." All four date digits are repunched north. The 1896 is currently a much scarcer date than the 1895 or 1897. It is most often seen in MS60-63 grades. Properly graded MS64s, like the piece in the Eagle Collection, are scarce and Gems are very rare. Sharply defined, the surfaces are satiny and show subtle rose and orange-gold coloration. The only noticeable mark is a small rim nick near star 3 on the obverse.
Ex: Eagle Collection (Heritage, 1/2002), lot 4121; Long Beach Signature (Heritage, 6/2002), lot 6992.(#9029)

3330 **1896-S MS63 PCGS. CAC.** Deep yellow-orange color with potent, swirling luster. This S-mint issue is available at the Select level but becomes elusive any finer.(#9030)

3331 **1898 MS62 NGC.** Crisp striking definition with only small, wispy abrasions on the generally yellow-orange surfaces. On the reverse, an abrasion at 6 o'clock on the rim contributes to the grade.(#9033)

3332 **1899 MS61 Prooflike NGC.** Profoundly mirrored surfaces are deep yellow-gold with an undercurrent of orange. Moderately abraded, yet appealing. Census: 3 in 61 Prooflike, 5 finer (1/09). (#79035)

3333 **1899-S MS62 Prooflike NGC.** Razor-sharp striking definition and bright, brassy mirrors enliven this modestly abraded example. Interesting eye appeal despite the scattered flaws. Census: 9 in 62 Prooflike, 10 finer (1/09).(#79036)

3334 **1900 MS64 NGC.** Attractive champagne-gold and steel-green patina adorns the satiny, shimmering surfaces of this near-Gem double eagle. Well struck with a few minor marks and pinscratches that limit the grade.(#9037)

3335 **1900-S MS63 PCGS.** Dusky yellow-gold at the margins with lightening toward the centers. A modestly abraded Select coin that shows slight hints of patina over the fields.(#9038)

Blazing 1901 Gem Double Eagle

3336 **1901 MS65 PCGS.** This Gem is awash with blazing luster radiating from orange-gold surfaces imbued with traces of light green. A well executed strike imparts virtually complete definition to the design elements, and the handful of small marks is consistent with the designated grade. A couple of minute copper spots are visible on the lower obverse. PCGS has seen a mere three coins with a higher grade, and NGC has graded none finer (2/09).(#9039)

Sharp 1902-S Twenty, MS63

3337 **1902-S MS63 PCGS.** Large numbers of 1902-S double eagles were sent to Europe or South America for international trade, and many examples have returned to the States in recent years. Select coins are obtainable with patience and searching, but higher grade pieces are elusive. This sharply defined MS63 example displays lustrous yellow-gold surfaces imbued with traces of light green, grayish-blue, and lilac. Scattered light marks define the grade.(#9042)

Charming MS65 1903 Twenty

3338 **1903 MS65 NGC.** Crisply detailed and shining with pale yellow-gold surfaces. Excellent eye appeal and preservation with only two small reed marks noted on Liberty's neck. An attractive Gem from a lower-mintage issue that is conditionally rare any finer; NGC has graded just eight such pieces (2/09).(#9043)

3339 **1904 MS64 PCGS.** Intense mint luster radiates across each side of this lovely gold-orange near-Gem. Two or three small marks are noted on each side, limiting the grade. Housed in a first-generation PCGS holder.(#9045)

3340 **1904 MS64 PCGS.** Shining yellow-gold color with orange overtones in the fields. Powerful eye appeal and careful preservation for the MS64 designation. A treat of a type coin.(#9045)

Upper-End MS65 1904 Double Eagle

3341 **1904 MS65 NGC. CAC.** The prevalence of this date in Uncirculated grades cannot diminish the exceptional eye appeal of this coin. The surfaces are uncommonly smooth with lovely, satin-like mint luster. The striking definition is strong in all areas, and both obverse and reverse display light reddish coloration. (#9045)

Reflective MS65 1904 Twenty

3342 **1904 MS65 PCGS.** An excellent specimen for a type collection, this piece has sharp design features, save for a few flat stars on the obverse, and weakness at the base of DOLLARS on the reverse. Both sides exhibit wonderful orange-gold luster. The surfaces are reflective, and on the border of fully prooflike.(#9045)

Shining Gem 1904 Double Eagle

3343 **1904 MS65 NGC.** Rich yellow-orange color overall with impressive luster. This Gem is well-defined and pleasingly preserved. As one of the highest-mintage double eagles across the history of the denomination, the 1904 twenty is an obvious choice for the type collector, and this example's eye appeal is particularly rewarding.(#9045)

Vibrant Gem 1904 Twenty Dollar

3344 **1904 MS65 NGC.** An exquisite Gem that offers virtually flawless eye appeal. The deep yellow-gold surfaces are smooth with a silky mint sheen that rolls around the coin. An excellent piece, untouched by significant marks or unsightly abrasions, that would make an excellent addition to a similarly graded type set. (#9045)

Popular Gem 1904 Twenty

3345 **1904 MS65 PCGS. CAC.** The design elements are fully struck, as often seen on this well produced issue. The intensely lustrous surfaces only display a few small, unimportant marks. Demand for Liberty double eagles has soared in recent years, after slumbering for most of the 1990s. A perfect choice for a Gem type set. (#9045)

Splendid Gem 1904-S Twenty

3346 **1904-S MS65 PCGS.** Among the most plentiful double eagle issues save for it Philadelphia city cousin, the 1904-S has a population that nonetheless narrows considerably at the Gem level, before becoming all but unobtainable at the next grade level higher. The splendid cartwheel luster and near-total absence of distracting abrasions complement the bold strike and lovely orange-gold surfaces, tinged with mint-green. PCGS has certified two examples finer (2/09).(#9046)

3347 **1905 MS61 NGC.** Crisply detailed with warm yellow-gold luster. Though each side shows a number of significant abrasions, the coin's eye appeal holds together.(#9047)

Attractive 1906-S Double Eagle, MS64

3348 **1906-S MS64 PCGS.** A common issue in the lower Mint State grades due to the large production in excess of 2 million coins, the 1906-S becomes quite elusive in Choice or Gem condition. This piece offers splendid orange-gold and greenish-gold coloration, with relatively few marks and bold eye appeal, as expected at the near-Gem level. Certified in a green-label holder. PCGS has certified three coins finer (2/09).(#9051)

Stunning 1907-D Twenty, MS65

3349 **1907-D MS65 NGC. CAC.** Intense, shining luster lends this final-year D-mint Liberty double eagle stunning eye appeal. The strike is sharp, and the fields are pleasingly preserved. The obverse shows relatively even sun-gold shadings, while the reverse shows similar peripheral color with pale yellow-gold at the center.(#9053)

Extremely Rare 1897 Proof Twenty
PR64 ★ Cameo

3350 **1897 PR64 ★ Cameo NGC.** From a tiny proof mintage of only 86 pieces, the 1897 proof double eagle is one of the rarest issues from the turn-of-the-century era. Hard times in the financial sector, that began with the Panic of 1893, were still hanging on and probably limited the number of proof sets ordered by collectors. In the *Encyclopedia of U.S. Gold Coins 1795-1933*, Jeff Garrett and Ron Guth had this to say about the 1897 proof double eagle:

> "Although the mintage of the 1897 issue is fewer than for the 1896 double eagle in Proof, the date is considerably rarer. There are just 20-25 coins known in all grades. The population numbers are higher, but these do not take into account resubmissions. There are also several mishandled examples represented on the population reports. After 1897, Proof double eagles become much more available. The 1897 issue is underrated."

A search of auction records reveals only two prior appearances of 1897 proof Cameo double eagles at Heritage since 1990. NGC has graded only six 1897 double eagles in the PR64 Cameo category, and three finer; while PCGS has certified four example at this level, with one finer (2/09). Of course, these figures may include resubmissions.

The present coin is a visual treat, with bright yellow-gold surfaces and thick mint frost on the devices. The fields display the distinctive "orange peel" quality that is characteristic of proofs of the late 19th century. Only a few light field marks keep this specimen out of the Gem category. Overall eye appeal is outstanding on this rare numismatic treasure.(#89113)

Charming 1907 Liberty Head Twenty
PR63 Cameo

3351   **1907 PR63 Cameo NGC.** A small proof mintage of 78 Liberty Head double eagles was accomplished in 1907, the smallest proof mintage of the 20th century. Anticipation of the new Saint-Gaudens design, which began production in November, probably limited the mintage of the older design proof sets. The survival rate is high, with perhaps 40-50 examples still extant. An early auction appearance of a 1907 proof set was in the James Ten Eyck Collection (B. Max Mehl, 5/1922), lot 347. Mehl noted, "1907 Old type. $20., $10., $5., $2.50. Perfect brilliant proofs. Rare. The $20. in brilliant proof is far more rare than the rare variety St. Gaudens type."

The present coin is a splendid specimen of this historic issue. Attractive yellow-gold surfaces are enhanced by reflective fields and a sharp strike. In the *Encyclopedia of U.S. Gold Coins 1795-1933*, Jeff Garrett and Ron Guth note most examples of this date lack Cameo devices, but NGC has awarded this piece the coveted Cameo designation. A few small handling marks limit the grade. Census: 4 in 63 Cameo, 28 finer (2/09).(#89123)

HIGH RELIEF DOUBLE EAGLES

Low-Grade 1907 High Relief Twenty, Fine Details

3352   **1907 High Relief, Wire Rim—Ex-Jewelry, Cleaned—ANACS. Fine Details, Net VG8.** Apparently a pocket piece at one time, Liberty's body and the top of the eagle's front wing are well worn, but the medallic nature of the high relief design is still readily apparent. The surfaces are noticeably bright from cleaning. An affordable example of this ever-popular issue.(#9135)

Attractive Uncirculated Details
MCMVII High Relief, Wire Rim

3353   **1907 High Relief, Wire Rim—Altered Surface—NCS. Unc. Details.** Despite its NCS designation, even the experienced collector will have difficulty detecting the impairment on the present High Relief twenty. Friction is virtually absent, and the softly lustrous surfaces appear unperturbed. Well struck save for the usual incompleteness on the base of the rays above the sun. (#9135)

Desirable MCMVII High Relief Twenty Wire Rim, MS64

3354 1907 High Relief, Wire Rim MS64 PCGS. A first-year-of-issue coin, a one-year type, and arguably the most beautiful coin ever minted for circulation, the Saint-Gaudens 1907 High Relief double eagle is on every collector's list of dream coins. From a tiny mintage of 12,367 pieces, the High Relief is surprisingly available today. Collectors prized this issue from the first day of release, and a large number of specimens were saved in Mint State for future generations to enjoy. Intense competition is always the rule when a High Relief is offered, and we expect no less when this attractive example comes up for bidding.

The present coin is fully struck, with rich, satiny mint luster. The attractive reddish patina often seen on High Reliefs is especially pronounced on this example, particularly around the devices. One obverse mark above the date, near the rim, limits the grade.(#9135)

Near-Gem Wire Rim High Relief MCMVII Double Eagle

3355 1907 High Relief, Wire Rim MS64 PCGS. The population of 1907 High Relief twenties drops precipitously beyond the MS64 level. Collectors can expect a full Gem piece to cost nearly double that of an MS64 example. For this reason, near-Gems—such as the current offering—elicit much attention when appearing at auction. Dave Bowers, in his *Guide Book of Double Eagle Gold Coins* (2004), offers the following advice to those pursuing a 1907 High Relief double eagle: "Select an example with care, checking the high parts of the relief for rubbing or marks, particularly at Miss Liberty's bosom and, most obviously, on her knee." For the current offering we note only one mark worthy of mention; a small abrasion on Liberty's right (facing) shin. Otherwise, the high points are pleasantly well preserved and the luster is rich. The immediate eye appeal of this Wire Rim twenty is comparable to that of a finer piece. Housed in a green label holder.(#9135)

Desirable AU55 1907 High Relief, Flat Rim Twenty

3356   1907 High Relief, Flat Rim AU55 PCGS. Light but distinct rub is noted on Liberty's knee and upper gown. Despite the minor wear, the well-protected fields remain impressively lustrous with pale yellow-gold radiance. Neither side shows conclusive evidence of a wire rim. A more affordable example of this legendary American coin-turned-art.(#9136)

Near-Mint MCMVII High Relief Twenty

3357   1907 High Relief, Flat Rim AU58 PCGS. A satiny green-gold representative of this world-famous, low mintage, and much-hoarded issue. Only a hint of wear is seen on Liberty's knee and chest, and on the crest of the front wing. The reverse appears void of marks, and the obverse has merely a pair of minor field ticks. The key to a 20th century gold type collection.
From The Ed Lepordo Collection, Part Two.(#9136)

Unworn 1907 High Relief, Flat Rim Twenty

3358   1907 High Relief, Flat Rim—Reverse Rim Damage—NCS. Unc Details. Several shallow scrapes and nicks are present at the lower and left reverse rims on this High Relief Saint-Gaudens double eagle. Neither side shows any trace of wear, however, and the yellow-gold luster is intact. The minimally marked obverse, in particular, displays beautifully.(#9136)

Near-Gem Flat Rim High Relief MCMVII Saint-Gaudens Twenty

3359 **1907 High Relief, Flat Rim MS64 PCGS.** No American gold type is as internationally celebrated as the High Relief. Only the iron will of President Theodore Roosevelt could have been behind such an impractical issue. But before any bankers could complain that the coins would not stack, speculators removed most of the mintage of 12,367 pieces from commerce. However, most are not as nice as the present near-Gem, which has comprehensive satin luster and an unabraded appearance. The strike is impeccable, and the eye appeal is magnificent. A highlight of nearly any gold type collection.(#9136)

Elusive Flat Rim High Relief Double Eagle, MS64

3360 **1907 High Relief, Flat Rim MS64 PCGS. CAC.** This is a gorgeous example of the famous High Relief Saint-Gaudens double eagle type, from the Flat Rim variety that is significantly scarcer than its Wire Rim counterpart. The lime-gold surfaces shimmer with a lovely, even satiny sheen. As always, the central design elements are fully struck, while the peripheral details are somewhat weak, including the eagle's tailfeathers. This inherent striking weakness on some parts of the design was the ultimate downfall of the High Relief type, and a lower relief version was soon introduced to permanently replace it. Showing only a ghostly luster graze, in the upper left obverse field, and a handful of tiny nicks between both sides, this piece seems high-end for the grade, and close to Gem quality.(#9136)

Delightful 1907 Double Eagle
High Relief, Flat Rim MS65

3361 1907 High Relief, Flat Rim MS65 PCGS. From an original mintage of 12,367 pieces, the famous MCMVII High Relief Saint-Gaudens double eagles are known in both Wire Rim and Flat Rim varieties. Q. David Bowers believes the two varieties resulted from differences in milling and planchet diameter, and do not really constitute different die varieties. Whatever their origin, the dramatic physical differences were noted by numismatists at the time of issue, and the two types have historically been listed separately. It is believed that approximately one-third of the original mintage was of the Flat Rim variety, but the Wire Rims have a higher survival rate. In the *Encyclopedia of U.S. Gold Coins 1795-1933*, Jeff Garrett and Ron Guth estimate the Flat Rim double eagles are nearly five times as scarce as the Wire Rim variety today.

In the sale of the Keel, Griswold, and Johnson Collections (Henry Chapman, 2/1908), both varieties of the High Relief twenty were offered, illustrating how soon the difference was recognized. Lot 619 of the sale reads in part, "1907 1st issue, with the high or 'Wire Edge.' Uncirculated. Mint lustre. In great demand, selling now at $35 to $45." Lot 620 reads, "1907 $20 second issue, the same as last with the edge smooth made by using a flattening collar. Uncirculated. Mint lustre. In great demand, selling now at $35 to $40." Notice Chapman believed a different collar was used to efface the wire rim feature. It is also interesting to observe that the Wire Rim variety was selling for a slightly higher price than the Flat Rim in 1908.

The present coin is a magnificent specimen, fully struck, with bright, satiny luster. The surfaces are a pleasing yellow, with an even layer of reddish patina on each side. The surfaces are essentially pristine. Population: 92 in 65, 45 finer (2/09). (#9136)

PR64 MCMVII High Relief Twenty

3362 1907 High Relief PR64 NGC. Dr. Robert Loewinger researched proof High Relief double eagles for his treatise *Proof Gold Coinage of the United States*. According to Walter Breen, those pieces have the following characteristics:

a) Inner borders sharp on both sides.
b) Relief details fully brought up.
c) All berries rounded.
d) All Capitol pillars countable.
e) All tail feathers with clear ends.
f) Edge letters are bolder than on normal strikings in the same collar, with horizontal striations between them.
g) Only a minor trace of knife-rim.

Dr. Loewinger also lists the criteria used by NGC to distinguish proofs from business strikes:

1) Extreme sharpness in all details, both at the centers and toward the peripheries.
2) The complete absence of die erosion or distortion.
3) Numerous, raised die-polishing lines on both sides. These appear in a random, swirling pattern. While also evident on currency strikes, these are particularly bold on proofs.
4) Uniformly satiny surfaces, without any of the radial flowlines that produce conventional Mint luster.
5) A build-up of metal just inside both borders, though especially evident on the reverse. This appears as a slightly raised ridge forming a concentric circle with the coin's border. It probably resulted from the extreme compression to which the proofs were subjected by additional strikes.

The present piece meets the above requirements for a proof. The strike is full throughout, and the rich, satin luster is dissimilar to that seen on the typical High Relief twenty. There are no grade-limiting marks, which suggests that this coin was given special handling by the Treasury. Butter-gold toning cedes to hints of aqua near Liberty's torch.

The new NGC holder allows a better view of the edge and rim than on prior-generation encapsulations. This near-Gem proof has a slight wire rim on the obverse between 6 and 1 o'clock. The wire rim on the reverse is also slight and partial, present between 3 and 10 o'clock.

Die polish lines are prominent inside the rim and throughout the fields. They likely faded on later strikes, which suggests that the proofs were struck prior to "normal" High Relief production. Clearly, this is a special High Relief twenty, and it will hold the place of honor within the finest 20th century proof type set.(#9132)

3363 1907 High Relief PR65 NGC. Interesting numismatic events slated for 2009 are destined to tie some "modern" coinages—a damning phrase that some collectors automatically dismiss out of hand—with "classic" coinages of the past, those seemingly admired by all and collected by most, save for some contrarian sorts. One is the smallest denomination, and one is the former largest denomination. At the bottom end we see the U.S. Mint, with admirable symmetry, gearing up to release four different reverses for the Lincoln cent, emblematic of different periods in the life of "Honest Abe." Each reverse, if plans hold true, will be combined with an obverse that reflects the original relief and design of the 1909-dated Victor D. Brenner cents. Will the 2009 Lincolns be the last of the lot? Lower copper prices and a recession in the BRIC countries (Brazil, Russia, India, and China) may give the coins a reprieve—but only time will tell.

At the other end of the denominational spectrum, the Ultra High Relief pure gold, 1 troy oz. double eagle dated MMIX (2009), slated for issue in January 2009, will almost certainly spur increased collector interest in the original Ultra High Reliefs of 1907. Produced to the extent of only 20 or so proof coins, the 1907 Ultra High Reliefs (dated MCMVII) are today off-limits to all but the most well-heeled of collectors. As a result, we predict a flock of collector gold bugs will turn to the available High Relief, Roman Numeral coins.

As of this writing NGC only, not PCGS, recognizes the validity of the proof High Reliefs. The former service has certified 238 proofs in all grades, including six Flat Rim coins, 121 Wire Rim coins, and 111 others unspecified as to rim (but undoubtedly mostly of the Wire Rim kind). The present coin, a pleasing Gem proof, will return aesthetic rewards immediately when viewed by its new owner, and is almost certainly destined to provide increasing rewards in the future. The surfaces are bright yellow-gold with the usual, equally bright satiny mint luster. The swirling die polishing marks seen on all High Reliefs are abundantly evident on this piece. A couple of minor contact marks keep this piece from an even higher numeric designation. For collectors who plan to acquire one or more of the new MMIX Ultra High Relief coins, this specimen would make a splendid accompaniment. Census for Wire Rim coins: Census: 17 in 65, 24 finer (2/09).(#9132)

SAINT-GAUDENS DOUBLE EAGLES

3364 **1907 Arabic Numerals MS63 PCGS.** Satiny with deep yellow-orange luster. A modestly abraded Select piece that offers slightly above-average detail for this first low-relief Saint-Gaudens double eagle issue.(#9141)

Lustrous 1907 Arabic Numerals Twenty, MS65

3365 **1907 Arabic Numerals MS65 PCGS.** Occasional splashes of greenish-gray and lilac visit the lustrous, orange-gold surfaces of this Gem double eagle, and an exacting strike leaves strong definition on the design elements, including the panes of the Capitol building and the fingers on Liberty's branch hand. A scattering of light, grade-consistent marks does not detract. Housed in a green label holder.(#9141)

Impressive Premium Gem 1908 No Motto Saint-Gaudens Double Eagle

3366 **1908 No Motto MS66 PCGS. CAC.** Ex: Wells Fargo Nevada Gold. One of the most popular issues in the series for type purposes, the 1908 No Motto was produced to the extent of 4.27 million pieces, and Mint State survivors are plentiful even at the Premium Gem level of preservation. This example is well struck, highly lustrous, and impressively preserved, with just a single shallow abrasion, located directly beneath RT on the upper obverse, to prevent an even loftier grade assessment.(#9142)

Worthy MS66 1908 No Motto Twenty From the Famed Wells Fargo Hoard

3367 **1908 No Motto MS66 PCGS.** Ex: Wells Fargo Nevada Gold. Lovely honey-gold and pastel orange patina decorates the well preserved, lustrous surfaces of this Premium Gem, from the famous Wells Fargo hoard. Just one or two minor marks are noted on each side, preventing an even loftier grade assessment. Housed in a green label PCGS holder.(#9142)

3368 **1908-D No Motto MS64 PCGS.** Lustrous with pretty orange-gold coloration, a bold strike and only a few stray abrasions noted in the fields on each side. A popular coin to represent the No Motto issue. (#9143)

Sumptuous 1908 Motto Twenty, MS64

3369 **1908 Motto MS64 PCGS. CAC.** Compared to the millions of No Motto examples struck in this year, the total of Motto 1908 twenties is a paltry sum, scarcely over 150,000 pieces. This near-Gem survivor is satiny with deep sun-gold surfaces that show traces of orange. Well-defined and minimally marked for the grade. (#9147)

Amazing 1908 Motto Twenty, MS65

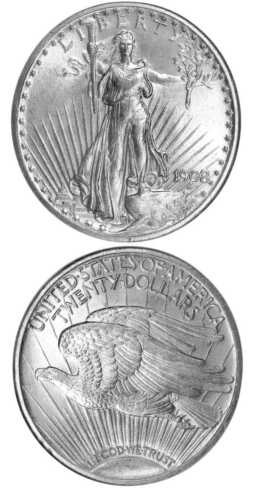

3370 1908 Motto MS65 NGC. During President Theodore Roosevelt's coinage redesign program, the motto IN GOD WE TRUST was omitted on the first coins issued in 1907 and 1908, and was restored to the reverse in 1908. The 1908 Motto double eagle is quite rare in Gem or higher grades, with only 54 examples certified MS65 or better by NGC and PCGS combined. An amazing Gem with highly lustrous and brilliant yellow-gold surfaces. It is sharply defined with virtually full design articulation on both sides. The surfaces have a few scattered ticks but are essentially pristine. Census: 16 in 65, 11 finer (1/09).(#9147)

3371 1908-D Motto MS64 PCGS. Dusky yellow-gold in the fields with slight lightening toward the centers. If not for a small horizontal mark on Liberty's upper gown, a candidate for Gem status. (#9148)

Lustrous Choice AU 1908-S Twenty

3372 1908-S AU55 PCGS. The small mintage of 22,000 coins is iconic in the Saint-Gaudens series, and most certified survivors are about AU55, the grade of the present piece. Faint rub is visible on the high points of Liberty's breast and exposed thigh and knee, and light abrasions are in keeping with a short spate in circulation. Most of the original cartwheel luster remains, over pretty orange-gold surfaces. Certified in a green-label holder.(#9149)

3373 **1908-S MS65 PCGS.** In 1908, all three active mints—Philadelphia, Denver, and San Francisco—struck Saint-Gaudens double eagles. Philadelphia produced over 4.2 million examples of the No Motto variety and an additional 150,000-plus With Motto pieces. Denver's production was more subdued, yet it managed to produce over 1 million double eagles that year, with a roughly two-for-one ratio between No Motto and With Motto representatives.

San Francisco's output, however, bordered on the nominal; in a striking contrast to that mint's multimillion-coin production of both the Liberty Head pieces of 1907 and the Saint-Gaudens twenties of 1909, it issued a mere 22,000 examples of the 1908, all With Motto coins. As one might surmise, acquiring a survivor is challenging. Q. David Bowers writes in his *Guide Book of Double Eagle Gold Coins*, "Today, examples are elusive in all grades, but thanks to importations of the current generation, such coins in MS-62 and MS-64 are much more available than they were prior to the 1980s."

Gems such as the present piece, however, have always been condition rarities. This coin offers marvelous eye appeal from a variety of sources, including immensely lustrous yellow-gold surfaces; bold detail, both on the central devices and the peripheral elements; and a delightful absence of significant distractions. Slight traces of alloy at the reverse rim add character to the coin. Population: 14 in 65, 14 finer (1/09). (#9149)

3374 1908-S MS65 PCGS. CAC. Ex: Brahin. With regard to third party certification, most coins are either accurately graded or conservatively graded; the latter observation applies to the current offering. Sumptuous, satiny luster gracefully swirls atop both sides of this well struck Gem. The apricot-gold coloration is even throughout, save for a small area of light copper toning at the 3 o'clock obverse rim.

At 22,000 pieces, the 1908-S double eagle has the lowest recorded mintage of all Arabic Numeral issues from 1907 through 1933. However, the 1908-S twenties are not the rarest in the series, since several 1920s and 1930s issues were subsequently melted in mass quantities. Nonetheless, the paltry mintage of 1908-S coins, combined with the fact that most of the coins struck entered circulation, make this issue legitimately rare in Gem or better condition. As of (2/09), PCGS has certified 14 examples at the MS65 level with only 14 finer.

Several theories have been put forth to explain why the San Francisco Mint managed to strike over 4 million Liberty double eagles from 1906 to 1907, yet struggled to produce just 22,000 1908-dated coins with the new Saint-Gaudens design. Some suggest that the Great Earthquake and Fire of 1906 was the cause, while others feel that the large production of double eagles in the previous two years created an excessively large supply, so the demand for new 1908 twenties was low. Another explanation is that the San Francisco Mint was awaiting new With Motto dies, resulting in a late production start.

Roger Burdette's *Renaissance of American Coinage, 1905-1908* sheds light on what could be the true reason for the small mintage of 1908-S double eagles. In his 2006 reference on the subject, Burdette explains the complications experienced by the Philadelphia Mint with regard to the new lettered edge mechanism: "It was not until September 1907 that the new mechanism was completely successful on the $10 gold coins, and it was December before the double eagle version was operating reliably at Philadelphia. Denver and San Francisco mints had additional problems with the mechanism and it was August 1908 before the San Francisco Mint could strike the new coins without damaging the presses." While four months left plenty of time to strike more than 22,000 coins, it may have been that mint officials decided to wait until January 1909 to ramp up production of the new double eagle design. In the end, all theories likely share a role in the low mintage of 1908-S twenties.(#9149)

3375 **1909 MS62 PCGS.** Excellent luster over lightly scuffed fields and pretty orange-gold coloration. A nice alternative for a With Motto type coin, about equally as rare as the overdate also known for this year.(#9150)

Scarce Choice 1909 Double Eagle

3376 **1909 MS64 PCGS.** This lustrous peach-gold near-Gem has a minor graze on the waist but the surfaces are otherwise unusually unabraded. The non-overdate variety is even scarcer than suggested by its mintage of 161,282 pieces, since about half of all survivors are the separately collected 1909/8 overdate. Only 26 examples have been certified finer by PCGS (2/09).(#9150)

3377 **1909/8 MS61 NGC.** This popular and bold overdate, the only such variety for the design, remains a collector favorite decades after its discovery. This satiny sun-yellow piece is well-defined with wispy abrasions in the fields.
From The Ed Lepordo Collection, Part Two.(#9151)

Popular 1909/8 Double Eagle, MS62

3378 **1909/8 MS62 PCGS.** The famous 1909/8 double eagle is about equal in rarity to the Normal Date twenty of the same year. This example has pleasing and satiny deep yellow surfaces with faint obverse reflectivity and reverse frostiness. A few scattered surface marks on each side prevent a higher and much more important grade. The present MS62 example should provide an excellent value.(#9151)

Desirable 1909/8 Double Eagle, MS62

3379 **1909/8 MS62 NGC.** Soft luster exudes from the yellow-gold surfaces of this popular overdate representative. The design elements are generally well impressed, including strong detail in Liberty's facial features and on the fingers of the branch hand. Minute surface and rim marks limit the grade.(#9151)

Lustrous 1909/8 Double Eagle, MS63

3380 **1909/8 MS63 PCGS.** The mintage of this issue is about equally split between the nonoverdate and overdate varieties. Every example of this overdate that we have seen has a distinctive and singular reverse, identified by a small diagonal die line inside the O of OF, running from northwest to southeast in the lower third of the letter. The present example shows moderate abrasions over lustrous orange-gold surfaces, with a bold strike and lots of eye appeal.(#9151)

Pleasing 1909/8 Select Twenty Dollar

3381 **1909/8 MS63 PCGS.** FS-301. A pleasing Select representative of this popular overdate, the only such error known for the Saint-Gaudens double eagle series. Peach-gold patina adorns lustrous, lightly marked surfaces, and a well directed strike imparts nice definition to the design features. Encapsulated in a green label holder.(#9151)

Elusive 1909/8 Twenty, MS64

3382 **1909/8 MS64 PCGS. CAC.** This piece has the arm's-length eye appeal of a Gem, with intense, shimmering mint frost and gorgeously deep apricot-gold and lime coloration across each side. Well preserved with a mere handful of wispy nicks in the obverse fields that seemingly preclude an even finer grade assessment. The design elements are boldly reproduced overall, even if Liberty's torch hand is somewhat weak.

This issue is the only overdate variety in the Saint-Gaudens double eagle series, and receives a considerable degree of attention from numismatists as a result. It is also something of a conundrum, as ongoing population estimates seem to indicate that the overdated coins comprise around half of the total mintage of 161,282 coins. How Mint officials were able to miss such an obvious "defect," on up to half of the twenty dollar pieces produced in 1909, is indeed a mystery.(#9151)

3383 **1909-S MS64 PCGS.** Luminous yellow-gold surfaces overall with hints of wheat. A well struck example that offers considerable eye appeal for the grade assigned.(#9153)

3384 **1909-S MS64 PCGS.** Both sides have satiny luster, while the reverse also possesses considerable vibrancy. Yellow-orange on each side with a dot of alloy at the lower left reverse margin. (#9153)

3385 **1910 MS64 PCGS.** Subtly lustrous surfaces are pale yellow-orange with glimpses of green-gold. A smooth and well struck near-Gem that offers excellent eye appeal.(#9154)

3386 **1910 MS64 PCGS.** Shining straw-gold surfaces are minimally marked for the grade. A gleaming and intriguing near-Gem that offers slightly above-average design definition.(#9154)

Radiant MS65 1910 Double Eagle

3387 **1910 MS65 PCGS.** Brightly lustrous with pale straw-gold fields that offer considerable radiance. Pleasingly detailed overall with subtle hints of orange-peel texture above Liberty's arm. This Philadelphia issue has a mintage of under half a million pieces; it is scarce in Gem and a rarity any finer.(#9154)

3388 **1910-S MS64 PCGS.** Light yellow-gold color overall with impressive luster. A desirable near-Gem that could serve as a slightly better date in a type collection.(#9156)

3389 **1911-D/D MS64 PCGS.** Repunched Mintmark, FS-501. A strongly lustrous yellow-gold example of this popular repunched mintmark variety. Well struck with light abrasions on the central devices.(#9158)

3390 **1911-D/D MS65 PCGS. CAC.** RPM FS-501. Pale straw-gold surfaces are brightly lustrous. This Gem is crisply struck with slight orange-peel texture near the rims.(#9158)

Unusual 1911-D/D Twenty, MS66

3391 **1911-D/D MS66 PCGS.** FS-501. The boldly doubled mintmark is clearly evident on this piece, although examples of the variety are frequently seen. Varieties such as repunched mintmarks, overdates, and doubled dies are seldom seen on any gold coins, due to the care that was taken in their production. This boldly defined piece has frosty yellow-gold luster with considerable rose toning. Population: 6 in 66, 0 finer (2/09).(#9158)

Desirable MS66 1911-D/D Twenty

3392 **1911-D/D MS66 NGC.** FS-501. A broadly repunched mintmark variety that enjoys considerable popularity, though it has not yet received its own entry in the *Guide Book*. This Premium Gem survivor is attentively struck with warm luster enhancing the sungold and pastel-yellow surfaces. Grand eye appeal.(#9158)

Marvelous MS65 1911-S Double Eagle

3393 **1911-S MS65 PCGS.** Rich yellow-orange color and impressive luster are the most striking attributes of this crisply detailed Gem. Impressively preserved surfaces show only a handful of trivial faults. With only 22 finer examples known to PCGS (2/09), this S-mint issue is a condition rarity any better.(#9159)

Enticing 1912 Saint-Gaudens Twenty, MS65

3394 **1912 MS65 PCGS.** Double eagles were not struck at any of the branch mints in 1912, leaving the Philadelphia mintage of 149,824 pieces as the total supply for the year. Two stars were added to the obverse, commemorating the entrance of Arizona and New Mexico to the Union. The addition of these stars technically created a new design type, but few collectors recognize this issue as the start of a separate type. The date is available in grades up to MS64, but it becomes rare at the Gem level. Only eight coins have been certified in grades above MS65 by NGC and PCGS combined (2/09).

The present coin is a desirable specimen, with soft, frosted mint luster and sharp definition on all design elements. The only mentionable mark is a tiny, diagonal tick in the left obverse field, just below the leftmost wave of hair. Population: 27 in 65, 5 finer (2/09).(#9160)

Lovely MS64 1913 Twenty

3395 **1913 MS64 PCGS.** A well-defined piece with rich color, generally wheat and yellow-orange but with a small dot of alloy near Liberty's torch hand. Softly lustrous with few marks. The low-mintage 1913 twenty is a condition rarity any finer, with only eight Gem or better coins graded by PCGS (1/09).(#9161)

3396 1913 MS65 PCGS. The 1913 Saint-Gaudens double eagle boasts a low mintage of just 168,780 pieces. In the context of early date Saint-Gaudens twenties, the issue is a scarce coin in all grades and is prohibitively rare above the Gem level. To quote David Akers in his 1998 sale of the Thaine B. Price Collection, "As a date, the 1913 is much more rare than the 1912; in fact, it is the rarest of the With Motto Philadelphia Mint issues from 1908-1915, especially in Choice Uncirculated or better condition." As of this writing, NGC has certified 17 examples in MS65, with one finer at MS66, while PCGS has graded only nine coins at the Gem level, with none finer (2/09).

Faced with the difficulty of obtaining a Gem level example of this date, some advanced collectors have endeavored to obtain a proof specimen instead. Louis Eliasberg and John Jay Pittman opted for this course. This option is not for the faint-of-heart, as only an estimated 30-40 proof examples are believed to be extant. All things considered, the odds of obtaining a matte-proof example of this date seem at least as good as the chances of acquiring a Gem level business strike. The importance of the present offering becomes clear when these facts are considered.

The present coin is an exciting example of this important issue. The coin is well struck, an area that is often a problem with this date. The surfaces are suffused with light, even reddish patina, enhancing the considerable visual appeal of the original gold color. The soft, frosted mint luster is typical of this issue. There are no individually distracting handling marks. (#9161)

3397 **1913-D MS64 PCGS.** Warm yellow-gold color overall with glimpses of wheat. An attractive near-Gem that offers strong luster and definition for the issue.(#9162)

3398 **1913-D MS64 PCGS.** Striking yellow-gold color with slight variations. The impressively lustrous fields are minimally marked for the grade, though a thin abrasion is noted to the left of Liberty's branch arm.(#9162)

3399 **1913-D MS64 PCGS.** Pale yellow-gold at the centers with deeper butter and sun elements near the rims. Well-defined and delightfully lustrous, an intriguing near-Gem.(#9162)

3400 **1913-D MS64 PCGS.** Light yellow-gold in the centers with deeper shadings near the rims. This is a well struck near-Gem, minimally marked with solid eye appeal.(#9162)

3401 **1913-S MS61 PCGS.** Lustrous and suitably struck with light apricot toning and fewer small abrasions than is usual for the grade. The 1913-S has long been a collector favorite due to its low mintage of 34,000 pieces. Encased in a green label holder. (#9163)

Desirable Near-Gem 1913-S Double Eagle

3402 **1913-S MS64 PCGS. CAC.** Satiny yellow-orange surfaces have unassuming, yet powerful luster that contributes greatly to this coin's eye appeal. Both sides are well-defined, and if not for a few light horizontal marks on Liberty, this piece could make a claim to Gem status. PCGS has graded 21 finer examples (1/09). (#9163)

Appealing MS64 1913-S Twenty

3403 **1913-S MS64 PCGS.** Warm, satiny orange-gold luster is foremost on this solidly struck and intriguing near-Gem. A few glimpses of copper alloy are noted at Liberty's head. Only a few wispy marks preclude a finer designation, and they have only minimal impact on the eye appeal. PCGS has graded 21 Gem or better coins (2/09). (#9163)

Low Mintage 1913-S Twenty Dollar, MS64

3404 **1913-S MS64 PCGS.** This low mintage issue (34,000 pieces) was, according to Jeff Garrett and Ron Guth (2006) subject to poor quality control, as many coins reveal copper spots from improperly mixed alloys. The lustrous peach-gold surfaces of this near-Gem example are devoid of this affliction. Moreover, the design elements exhibit above-average definition, except for incompleteness on the Capitol dome. A few minute marks define the grade. Housed in a green label holder.(#9163)

Choice 1913-S Saint-Gaudens Twenty

3405 **1913-S MS64 PCGS.** Despite its minuscule original mintage of 34,000 pieces, this issue's early date and sizable percentage of exported coins makes it only moderately difficult to acquire through MS64. The devices of this highly lustrous yellow-gold example have excellent detail, and the piece is kept from a Gem grade by only a few small abrasions on the surfaces. Higher-grade examples are decidedly rare; PCGS reports only 21 pieces finer (3/09). *Ex: Dallas Signature (Heritage, 10/2006), lot 3559, which realized $5,750.*(#9163)

Charming MS64 1914 Double Eagle

3406 **1914 MS64 PCGS.** This Philadelphia issue has gained a degree of notoriety for its five-figure mintage, though its high production standards should be winning more praise. This satiny yellow-gold example has a strong strike, as usually seen, and impressive eye appeal. A rarity any finer, with just 39 such pieces known to PCGS (2/09).(#9164)

3407 **1915 MS63 PCGS.** Dusky yellow-gold shadings overall with occasional abrasions accounting for the grade. Softly lustrous and appealing, an interesting Select example.(#9167)

Attractive 1915 Saint-Gaudens Twenty, MS64

3408 **1915 MS64 PCGS.** This is a bright, satiny example with yellow-gold coloration and faint hints of pale green color in the fields. Boldly struck with generally excellent design definition, excluding a bit of softness on Liberty's torch hand. This issue is readily available at the current grade level, but Gems are scarce and considerably more expensive.(#9167)

Fully Struck Gem 1915 Saint-Gaudens Twenty

3409 **1915 MS65 PCGS.** Incredibly vibrant for this condition rarity, there are only a few surface marks to keep this remarkable '15-P Saint-Gaudens from an even higher rating. A well-preserved survivor, this coin is sharply struck in all but one or two isolated areas. The variegated yellow-gold and green-gold color is quite pleasing, as are the lustrous, satiny-textured surfaces. Conditionally rare, and an issue that is seldom offered at the Gem level. Only one piece has been certified above MS65 between both of the major grading services. Population: 32 in 65, 0 finer (2/09).
Ex: Phillip H. Morse Collection of Saint-Gaudens Coinage (Heritage, 11/2005), lot 6629.(#9167)

Elusive 1916-S Double Eagle, MS66

3410 **1916-S MS66 PCGS.** A rich, frosty glow encompasses the orange-gold surfaces of this beautiful Premium Gem. A few tiny marks are noted on the obverse, but they are not inconsistent with the MS66 grade assessment. This San Francisco Mint issue was very scarce until 1983, when a hoard of 4,000 pieces was discovered in South America. None are graded any finer by PCGS (2/09). (#9169)

Radiant 1916-S Double Eagle, MS66

3411 **1916-S MS66 PCGS.** The 1915-S and 1916-S double eagles are among the most common in Gem and higher levels among the mintmarked Saint-Gaudens issues from the teens, although bagmarks or lack of eye appeal keep many examples from those lofty levels. The present example has no such drawbacks, however. Radiant cartwheel luster flashes forth from deep orange-gold-colored surfaces. The few minor abrasions noted are consistent with the Premium Gem grade level. Among the finest certified at PCGS.(#9169)

Bright 1920 Double Eagle, MS64

3412 **1920 MS64 NGC. CAC.** Bright luster invigorates the yellow-gold surfaces of this near-Gem. A solid strike translates into crisp definition on the devices, including the panes on the Capitol building, Liberty's fingers and toes, and the eagle's plumage. A few minute marks preclude a Gem grade. Elusive any finer. (#9170)

Gorgeous Near-Gem 1920 Saint-Gaudens Twenty

3413 **1920 MS64 NGC.** This is a gorgeous near-Gem example, with intense coruscating luster and deep rose-gold and lime coloration. Excellent striking definition is found on all of the design elements. A handful of small abrasions on each side prevent an even finer grade. This issue is relatively common through the MS64 grade level, but suddenly becomes extremely rare as a Gem.(#9170)

3414 **1922 MS64 PCGS.** Strongly struck with attractive luster. This piece is generally yellow-gold, though small dots of alloy are present at the lower reverse margins.(#9173)

Beautiful MS65 1922 Twenty

3415 **1922 MS65 PCGS. CAC.** A beautiful coin with sumptuous luster and lovely honey-gold toning across both sides. Nicely preserved overall with just one noticeable mark in the right obverse field, below Liberty's elbow. This issue is surprisingly easy to obtain at the MS65 grade level, but in MS66 it suddenly becomes exceedingly scarce.(#9173)

Lovely Gem 1922 Double Eagle

3416 **1922 MS65 PCGS.** Though this post-World War I issue is available in grades up to and including Gem, availability falls off a cliff immediately after; PCGS has certified just seven finer examples (2/09). This impressively lustrous yellow-gold example is solidly struck and carefully preserved.(#9173)

Handsome Gem 1922 Twenty Dollar

3417 **1922 MS65 PCGS.** The 1922 begins a run of available Philadelphia dates that continues through 1928. Other issues from the decade are rarities, with the exception of the 1923-D. Most 1922 twenties are bagmarked, however, which makes the present smooth and lustrous Gem highly attractive by comparison. PCGS has graded only seven pieces finer (2/09).(#9173)

Scarce 1922-S Double Eagle MS62

3418 **1922-S MS62 NGC.** Like all San Francisco issues after the 1916-S, the 1922-S is very scarce since most examples never left Treasury vaults. Those coins were swept up in Roosevelt's 1933 gold recall, and were eventually melted into gold bricks stored at Fort Knox. A couple of 1922-S bags escaped to foreign vault holdings, where they bided time until their repatriation by knowledgeable gold dealers. Most pieces displayed bagmarks, as does the present coin, although the dazzling luster and bold strike ensure the eye appeal. (#9174)

Lustrous 1922-S Double Eagle, MS64

3419 **1922-S MS64 PCGS. CAC.** This issue suffered extensive melting in the 1930s. Most survivors, as evident from PCGS/NGC population figures, are in the lower Mint State or circulated grades. This near-Gem specimen displays pleasing luster and orange-gold coloration, along with well struck motifs. Minimally marked surfaces reveal some light copper spots. PCGS has graded only 12 coins finer, and NGC 14 pieces higher (2/09).(#9174)

Popular MS64 1922-S Double Eagle

3420 **1922-S MS64 PCGS.** With just 12 finer examples graded by PCGS (2/09), the MS64 coin offered here is among the best within the grasp of most Saint-Gaudens double eagle collectors. Strongly lustrous and well-defined with a primarily wheat-gold obverse and deeper sun-yellow shadings on the reverse.(#9174)

3421 **1923 MS64 PCGS.** Subtle peach tints as found on the obverse are all but invisible on the pale yellow-gold reverse. An appealing near-Gem that is well-defined and desirable.(#9175)

Marvelous 1923-D Twenty Dollar, MS66

3422 **1923-D MS66 NGC. CAC.** Beautiful peach-gold patina with greenish-yellow accents endows the radiantly lustrous surfaces of this Premium Gem. A well executed strike delivers crisp definition to the design elements, including Liberty's face, fingers, and toes, the panes on the Capitol building, and the eagle's plumage. A few trivial marks do not negate the appeal of this marvelous specimen, as is evident from the CAC sticker. This is a great coin for a high grade type set.(#9176)

3423 **1923-D MS66 PCGS.** Strong luster and excellent surface preservation are the prime attributes of this Premium Gem. Elegant lavender accents grace the otherwise orange-gold surfaces. (#9176)

3424 **1924 MS66 PCGS.** Bright and attractive yellow-gold luster. This Premium Gem is clearly superior to the mass of MS65 examples and represents an opportunity as such. PCGS has graded 80 finer pieces (2/09).(#9177)

3425 **1924-D AU58 PCGS.** Wheat-gold patina runs over each side of this near-Mint State example that retains a considerable amount of luster. The design elements are well defined, except for weakness on the tops of UNITE. Quite clean for a coin that has seen some circulation.(#9178)

Near-Gem 1924-D Double Eagle

3426 **1924-D—Planchet Flaw, Missing D Due to Lamination—MS64 PCGS. CAC.** A well struck and satiny sun-gold near-Gem that has unexpectedly few marks. The PCGS-mentioned planchet flaw (or strike through, mint-made in either case) is quite small but is located at the exact site of the Denver mintmark, which is not readily evident. The 1924-D has a mintage of over 3 million pieces, and could have been obtained for face value from the Treasury prior to the great 1933 gold recall. But most 1924-D twenties never left Federal vaults, and were eventually melted. PCGS has certified a mere 10 pieces finer (2/09).(#9178)

Elusive Near-Gem 1924-S Saint-Gaudens Twenty

3427 **1924-S MS64 NGC.** This is one of the issues that was virtually wiped out by Roosevelt's 1933 gold recall, and the subsequent mass meltings. Fewer than 1,000 pieces have been certified by NGC and PCGS, despite the substantial mintage of 2.9 million pieces. The obverse of this near-Gem exhibits fine-grain textures reminiscent of matte proofs, while the reverse is bright and satiny. A well struck piece with mild surface marks.(#9179)

Important 1925-D Double Eagle, MS64

3428 **1925-D MS64 PCGS. CAC.** The 1925-D twenty is one of several rare branch mint issues of the decade from an originally high mintage, in this case nearly three million coins. Dave Bowers writes in A Guide Book of Double Eagle Gold Coins: "The 1925-D is another entry in the enticing lineup of later-date Saint-Gaudens mintmarks that once were rare, but today are less so, although it remains very elusive. Most are in lower Mint State ranges and probably came from French banks in recent decades." He continues to suggest that between 550 and 880 examples of this date survive in all grades, including both certified and noncertified coins.

This near-Gem is highly lustrous with rich orange-gold surfaces, splashed with pink and bright orange toning. The surfaces have tiny abrasions on each side that are entirely consistent with the grade. PCGS has only certified six finer examples (2/09).(#9181)

3429 **1925-S—Improperly Cleaned—NCS. XF Details.** Light but distinct wear is noted largely on the high points. While a typical example would have luster in the protected areas, this coin shows overall yellow-gold brightness from a past cleaning.(#9182)

Well Struck 1925-S Double Eagle, MS60 Details

3430 **1925-S—Damaged—ICG. MS60 Details.** The 1925-S is a rarely encountered mintmarked issue from this difficult decade. If one factors out the damage, the orange-gold surfaces are actually much finer than the details grade. The mint luster is frosted and bright and the definition on the devices is almost fully brought up. But there are several small digs on the obverse that appear to be intentional damage, netting an otherwise very pleasing coin down to an MS60 Details grade.(#9182)

Crisply Impressed 1925-S Double Eagle, MS62

3431 **1925-S MS62 PCGS.** Most of the large mintage of 1925-S double eagles of nearly 4 million pieces was melted in the 1930s. PCGS/NGC data indicate that certified Mint State examples are primarily in the MS60 to MS63 range. The yellow-gold surfaces of this MS62 coin display soft luster and well impressed devices. Both sides reveal minute grade-defining marks.(#9182)

3432 **1926 MS66 NGC.** A warmly lustrous Premium Gem that shows pink overtones to otherwise wheat-gold surfaces. Strongly struck and minimally marked, an attractive survivor from this interesting later Philadelphia double eagle issue. A rarity any finer, with just eight such pieces known to NGC (2/09).(#9183)

Desirable MS62 1926-D Double Eagle

3433 **1926-D MS62 PCGS.** Like its much rarer D-mint counterpart from the following year, the 1926-D double eagle was heavily melted. As described by Garrett and Guth: "The few that did survive were either found overseas or were held back by a handful of wealthy collectors able to keep them through the turmoil of the ensuing few decades."

The present example is strongly appealing for the grade, with lustrous wheat-gold surfaces showing hints of orange. The devices are well struck. Though abrasions below Liberty's flowing hair, at her midsection, and near the olive branch combine to preclude Select status, this remains an important survivor. PCGS has graded 72 finer examples (2/09).(#9184)

Lovely MS64 1926-S Twenty

3434 **1926-S MS64 PCGS.** A near-Gem survivor from a heavily melted San Francisco issue, this coin is near the top of the grading curve, with just 29 finer pieces known to PCGS (2/09). The obverse is butter-yellow with strong orange overtones, while the reverse appears more fully orange-gold. Minimally marked and gorgeous. (#9185)

Appealing MS64 1926-S Twenty

3435 **1926-S MS64 PCGS. CAC.** Rich yellow-orange color with strong, slightly satiny luster. Aside from a few small marks and wispy abrasions, the surfaces of this near-Gem are largely untouched. Though the 1926-S is not so great a melt rarity as certain surrounding issues, there is little doubt that it is far less available than its mintage of over 2 million pieces would suggest. PCGS has graded 29 finer examples (2/09).(#9185)

Elusive 1926-S Twenty, MS64

3436 **1926-S MS64 PCGS. CAC.** An important rarity in the series, despite a mintage in excess of 2 million pieces, few examples of this issue survived the massive gold melts of the 1930s. The same can be said of most mintmarked issues of the 1920s, nearly all that are more plentiful in Mint State than they are in circulated grades. This gorgeous near-Gem is highly lustrous with brilliant light gold surfaces and peripheral lemon-yellow toning. The few surface marks on each side are entirely consistent with the grade. PCGS has only certified 29 finer examples of this issue (2/09).(#9185)

Scarce 1926-S Double Eagle MS64

3437 **1926-S MS64 PCGS.** For most collectors, even those that are quite advanced, the MS64 grade level provides an ideal compromise between grade and price. Although more than 2 million of these coins were originally struck, few were actually distributed at the time of issue, with the majority of pieces melted a few years later. Delightful orange toning is evident at the centers, especially on the obverse, with fully lustrous yellow-gold surfaces. This piece is sharply struck with only a few scattered bagmarks.(#9185)

Interesting AU55 Details 1927-S Twenty

3438 **1927-S—Cleaned—ICG. AU55 Details.** The yellow-orange surfaces are subdued with faint hairlines from a past cleaning. Despite this flaw, the present coin offers significant eye appeal, with few abrasions and only a touch of rub on the high points. An affordable alternative for the budget-conscious Saint-Gaudens double eagle collector.(#9188)

3439 **1928 MS66 NGC.** Strongly lustrous and impressively satiny with a blend of copper-gold and sun-yellow on each side. Smooth and appealing, a delightful Premium Gem.(#9189)

Vibrant 1928 Double Eagle, MS67

3440 **1928 MS67 PCGS.** Both sides of this Superb Gem are awash with vibrant luster, and each is bathed with wonderful orange-gold, mint-green, and lilac patina. A well executed strike leaves exquisite definition on the design elements. Nicely preserved throughout. Housed in a green label holder. Population: 65 in 67, 0 finer (2/09).(#9189)

Rare 1929 Saint-Gaudens Twenty MS62

3441 **1929 MS62 PCGS. CAC.** The 1922 to 1928 Philadelphia issues are common, but the distribution was different for the 1929. Practically the entire mintage remained in Treasury storage, and only a couple hundred pieces managed to escape the furnace. Those coins are subject to enormous demand, since the Saint-Gaudens type is widely collected despite its formidable cost of entry. The median certified grade is MS64, and such pieces cost about twice that of an MS62. The present piece is comparatively affordable, yet has full luster and sharpness. Distributed small marks, mostly confined to the obverse, correspond to the grade.(#9190)

3442 1929 MS64 PCGS. CAC. The later date Saint-Gaudens double eagles, beginning with the 1929, have always been considered key-date rarities in the series. The explanation for this rarity lies in low distribution rather than low mintage. The 1929 twenty had a substantial production figure of 1.8 million pieces, typical of Philadelphia issues of the era. The vast majority of these coins was stored in Mint or Treasury vaults, with only a few examples released into circulation or saved by collectors. Some examples were used in international trade and remained hidden in European holdings for decades, but most of the large mintage was melted after the great recall of the mid-1930s.

The actual rarity of the 1929 double eagle has become a subject of controversy in recent years. The issue is generally acknowledged to be the most available of the later date twenties, but estimates of the surviving population vary widely among the experts. Walter Breen ventured a lower boundary figure of 60 pieces, but with more than 300 specimens currently certified, that total is clearly too low. Q. David Bowers is at the other end of the spectrum, with an upper boundary of 1,250-1,750 pieces. Once again, population data casts grave doubt upon this estimate. A hoard of 40 pieces was discovered in England in 1984 and Jeff Garrett uncovered a mini-hoard of 10 pieces in the early 1990s. All things considered, a surviving population of 300-400 examples in all grades seems reasonable.

The present coin is a particularly attractive specimen, as attested by the CAC endorsement. The surfaces are richly toned, with luxuriant mint luster. Lovely shades of pale lilac highlight the obverse center, with deep rose-gold color predominating on the rest of the coin. A sharp strike enhances the considerable visual appeal. Population: 99 in 64, 27 finer (2/09). *From The Burning Tree Colletion.*(#9190)

Choice AU A. Bechtler Dollar
Plain Edge, 27G, 21C, K-24

3443 (1842-52) A. Bechtler Dollar, 27G. 21C., Plain Edge AU55
NGC. K-24, R.3. This Bechtler gold type coin has smooth green-
gold surfaces aside from a few faint marks near the prominent 1.
The legends glimmer with luster. A minor mark near the O in
GOLD causes a slight wave. Listed on page 359 of the 2009 *Guide
Book*.(#10040)

Bechtler family

3444 **1860 Clark, Gruber & Co. Quarter Eagle MS65 NGC.** K-1, R.4. The territory (later state) of Colorado has seen its fate closely intertwined with gold and silver throughout its recent history. Pioneers traveling to Deseret, Oregon, or Gold Rush California had to avoid the Continental Divide that bisects the state, with more than 500 mountain peaks each rising above 4,000 meters (13,123 feet), instead taking a northern route, following the North Platte and Sweetwater rivers through Wyoming. Colorado saw its own influx of fortune-seekers beginning in July 1858, when the glittering metal was discovered in western Kansas along the South Platte River, precipitating the Pike's Peak Gold Rush. Although the alluvial gold deposits in the rivers and streams rapidly played out, the miners found far more productive deposits of gold, silver, and other minerals in the bedrock of the mountains nearby. A major strike of silver near Leadville in 1878 led to a silver rush, and the Sherman Silver Purchase Act of 1890 and its 1893 repeal respectively invigorated and enervated the state's economy.

Even a successful American opera in the standard repertory tells of the rise and fall of Colorado gold and silver mining. *The Ballad of Baby Doe* by composer Douglas Moore tells the story of Elizabeth "Baby" Doe Tabor and her lifelong love for silver king Horace Tabor, owner of the Matchless Mine. The work includes a scene depicting presidential candidate William Jennings Bryan making his famous "Cross of Gold" speech decrying the gold standard, and Baby Doe's lovely aria "Gold is a fine thing for those who admire it / Gold is like the sun / But I am a child of the moon, and silver / Silver is the metal of the moon." The opera premiered in 1956 at the Central City (Colorado) Opera. Today place names such as Leadville, Golden, La Plata, Gypsum, Silverton, Silver Plume, and Coal Creek bear mute testimony to Colorado's mineral riches.

The 1860 Clark, Gruber quarter eagle, produced during the Pike's Peak Gold Rush, greatly resembles the federal-style issue of the same era, except that CLARK & CO. substitutes for LIBERTY on the coronet. The date features a big, round 0 that more resembles an O, and the denomination on the reverse also shows a majuscule D of impressive proportions. The reverse legend reads PIKE'S PEAK GOLD.

This is a remarkable Clark, Gruber quarter eagle. The surfaces have a pronounced greenish-yellow color and bright, softly frosted mint luster. The centers of each side are a bit softly defined, but this is not visually distracting. There also are no obvious or distracting abrasions present. In MS65 this piece is one of only two so graded at NGC, with none finer (2/09). The highest pieces at PCGS are five MS63 coins. Listed on page 375 of the 2009 *Guide Book*.(#10135)

3445 1861 Clark, Gruber & Co. PCGS Genuine. In-house graded: Holed, plugged, resurfaced, lacquer. XF Details. K-5a, R.4. Well detailed with worn, but unabraded surfaces. Greenish color with traces of reddish copper alloy near the margins. Listed on page 376 of the 2009 Guide Book.(#10139)

Historic 1861 Clark, Gruber Five Dollar, K-6, VG10

3446 1861 Clark, Gruber & Co. Five Dollar VG10 NGC. K-6, R.4. If only this coin could talk! A well circulated but nonetheless pleasing example of this popular Territorial gold issue. The pleasing pale-olive surfaces show a few marks on Liberty's neck and one above the eagle's left (facing) wing—all perfectly acceptable at this stage of circulation. Listed on page 375 of the 2009 Guide Book. (#10140)

3447 (1850) Dubosq & Co. Ten Dollar Uniface Reverse White Metal Splasher MS62 NGC. K-4a, R.8. 0.8 gm. Any Dubosq & Co. territorial piece is very rare, due to the March 26, 1851 assay report of Augustus Humbert. This report, published in the *Pacific News* two days later, revealed that many private gold coins contained less gold bullion than their face value indicated. According to the *Alta California*, the reputable firm of Dubosq & Co struck $150,000 face in gold during the first quarter of 1851 from 1850-dated dies. If this report is accurate, nearly all must have been melted shortly thereafter, as they were refused in commerce except at a drastic discount.

The present piece is a white metal splasher, presumably struck to test the $10 reverse die. It is unencapsulated, but an NGC photo certificate accompanies the lot. The piece is out of round and has a ragged lower edge, which prevents a complete impression of the lower left reverse. The strike is very sharp where the flan allows. The reverse die was later used by Wass Molitor & Co. to strike 1852-dated ten dollar gold pieces.

Ex: Franklinton Collection, Part Two (Stack's, 1/2008), lot 1158.

AU Details K-6 Reeded Edge 887 Thous. 1851 Humbert Fifty

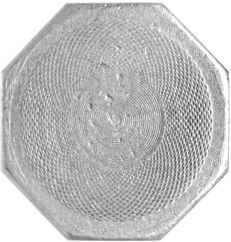

3448 1851 Humbert Fifty Dollar, 887 Thous.—Damaged—NCS. AU Details. K-6, R.4. A dozen or so tiny digs on the reverse and a mark beneath the obverse right ribbon end are designated as damage by NGC, although most surviving Humbert slugs have problems of one kind or another. Gold Rush participants cared little about preserving such historic pieces, which were contemporarily prized solely for their generous bullion content. This example was perhaps lightly cleaned at one time but retains most of its initial detail, with wear generally limited to the eagle's leg and arrows. Listed on page 362 of the 2009 Guide Book.(#10214)

Desirable AU Details 1853 Assay Office Twenty 900 Thous., K-18

3449 1853 Assay Office Twenty Dollar, 900 Thous.—Rim Filed, Improperly Cleaned—NCS. AU Details. K-18, R.2. This Territorial piece sustained little wear in its frontier days, though it does show a handful of small digs for its trouble. The yellow-gold surfaces are bright from a past cleaning, and the left obverse rim shows evidence of filing. Still, a readily collectible example of this popular issue. Listed on page 364 of the 2009 Guide Book. (#10013)

Popular 1853 U.S. Assay Office
Twenty, K-18, MS63

3450 **1853 Assay Office Twenty Dollar, 900 Thous. MS63 PCGS. CAC.** K-18, R.2. The 1853 Assay Office twenty ranks among the most plentiful of all California gold coins. It is generally classified under the category of Private or Territorial Gold, although it is strictly a Federally authorized coinage issued by and for the United States government. By all rights, it should be considered part of the regular issue double eagle series. It is the only California gold issue that bears the legend UNITED STATES OF AMERICA. Congress appointed Augustus Humbert to the position of assayer, and he operated the California facility.

This frosty and highly lustrous piece has brilliant green-gold surfaces and bold aesthetic appeal. Both sides are exceptional in quality with only a few surface marks that are consistent with the grade. Listed on page 364 of the 2009 Guide Book. Population: 30 in 63, 22 finer (2/09).(#10013)

Desirable 1855 Kellogg & Co. Twenty Dollar
'Long Arrows' Reverse, K-3, AU Details

3451 **1855 Kellogg & Co. Twenty Dollar—Repaired, Improperly Cleaned—NCS. AU Details.** K-3, R.4. The Long Arrows reverse is diagnostic for the variety. This yellow-orange example has glossy luster and numerous hairlines, suggestive of a past cleaning, and both sides show suggestions of repair at the periphery, with Liberty's hair detail jarringly sharp. Still, a readily collectible example of this important territorial gold issue. Listed on page 372 of the 2009 Guide Book.(#10225)

1849 Moffat & Company Five Dollar
K-4a, R.4, AU53

3452 **1849 Moffat & Co. Five Dollar AU53 NGC.** K-4a, R.4. This later die state is attributed by the thick die break over E in ONE and DO in DOLLAR, on the lower reverse. Bright yellow-gold surfaces show on both sides of this AU53 Moffat piece. Nicely defined, save for softness on Liberty's hair curls and the eagle's claws. Distributed ticks are scattered over both faces.(#10240)

Landmark 1849 Norris, Gregg, & Norris Five Dollar, Reeded Edge, K-4, AU55

3453 1849 Norris, Gregg, & Norris Five Dollar R.E. AU55 NGC. Period, K-4, R.4. The Norris, Gregg, & Norris gold coins were the first private gold pieces of California, produced shortly after gold was discovered at Sutter's Mill. In fact, a May 31, 1849, newspaper account of the five dollar Norris, Gregg, & Norris pieces was the earliest printed record of any California gold coins. Examples are known with a plain or reeded edge, and with or without a period after ALLOY. This example has a reeded edge and a weak but visible period.

Only a trace of wear is evident on the green-gold surfaces of this attractive and lustrous gold piece. Both sides are lightly abraded, typical of the early California private gold coins. Listed on page 360 of the 2009 *Guide Book*.(#10282)

Famous 1855 Wass Molitor Fifty, K-9

3454 1855 Wass Molitor Fifty Dollar PCGS Genuine. In-house graded XF details, cleaned, re-engraved, damaged. K-9, R.5. Both fields have been extensively smoothed, and much of the design is re-engraved, such as DOLLARS, the wreath, and Liberty's hair. While this hefty Wass Molitor fifty dollar piece will never make the Condition Census, it is true that most survivors also have various problems, and any example of this well known issue is subject to considerable demand from pioneer gold collectors.(#10363)

CALIFORNIA FRACTIONAL GOLD

3455 1853 Liberty Octagonal 25 Cents, BG-102, Low R.4, MS65 PCGS. Typically struck for this crudely designed octagonal quarter variety. Well preserved, however, and the single finest-graded example at PCGS. NGC has seen just two Gems, and none any finer (1/09).(#10371)

3456 1856 Liberty Octagonal 25 Cents, BG-111, R.3, MS65 NGC. Butter-yellow surfaces offer a considerable gleam. Well-defined and attractive, an appealing example of this well-established octagonal quarter variant.(#10380)

3457 1853 Liberty Round 25 Cents, BG-215, Low R.7—Holed—NCS. Unc Details. An extremely rare variety that Heritage has offered at auction only twice before. Luminous butter-yellow surfaces show no trace of wear, though a hole is noted just off the tip of Liberty's coronet.(#10400)

3458 1855 Liberty Round 25 Cents, BG-226A, R.5, MS64 NGC. Eight pearls on coronet, the main difference between the BG-226A and the BG-227 designation it might have received prior to the second edition of Breen-Gillio (the latter variant has nine pearls). Copper-gold surfaces have considerable radiance. For the variety, Census: 1 in 64, 0 finer (1/09).(#10417)

Charming 1853 Peacock Gold 50 Cent, BG-302, MS65

3459 1853 Peacock Reverse 50 Cents, BG-302, Low R.4, MS65 NGC. The charming 'Peacock' reverse subtype of this octagonal fifty cent. From late state dies with a small obverse cud at 3 o'clock. Yellow-gold surfaces display frosty luster, along with well struck design elements. The 'Peacock' is actually an eagle with glory rays behind it and a tail below the arrow. Census: 2 in 65, 0 finer (2/09). (#10422)

Elusive 1853 Gold 50 Cent, BG-302, MS64 Prooflike Peacock Reverse Design

3460 **1853 Peacock Reverse 50 Cents, BG-302, Low R.4, MS64 Prooflike NGC.** The bright yellow-gold surfaces of this near-Gem display occasional whispers of apricot, especially on the obverse. The central devices are well struck, and are highlighted against the reflective prooflike fields. A few minor handling marks are visible over each side. NGC has certified 16 submissions of this variety but the present piece is the only one with a Prooflike designation. (#710422)

Popular 1854 Gold 50 Cent, BG-436, MS61 Humbert "Slug" Reverse Style

3461 **1854 Liberty Round 50 Cents, BG-436, R.6, MS61 PCGS.** The popular type with the Humbert/Assay Office eagle motif on the reverse. Die State II with "period" die defect after date. The die crack beneath the chin is unrecorded in Breen-Gillio. Rich apricot and yellow-gold patina bathes luminous surfaces, and the design elements display excellent design detail. Population: 3 in 61, 5 finer (2/09).(#10472)

Desirable 1854 Large Eagle Dollar, BG-504, AU58

3462 **1854 Large Eagle Octagonal 1 Dollar, BG-504, Low R.5, AU58 NGC.** This lovely canary-gold borderline Mint State octagonal dollar is boldly struck and has unabraded fields, although the field near Liberty's forehead is slightly granular. The reverse motif, which emulates the contemporary U.S. Assay Office ingots, adds to the desirability of this scarce variety. Census: 3 in 58, 0 finer (2/09).(#10481)

Rare 1854 Liberty Gold Dollar, BG-507, AU58

3463 **1854 Liberty Octagonal 1 Dollar, BG-507, High R.6, AU58 PCGS.** A rarely encountered Frontier and Deviercy Period One octagonal dollar variety. This momentarily circulated example has lilac and olive-gold toning. The obverse border shows thin marks at 3, 4, and 5 o'clock. A good strike despite some weakness on the date and the lower portion of the beaded circle. Population: 3 in 58, 1 finer (2/09).(#10484)

3464 **1853 Liberty Octagonal 1 Dollar, BG-518, R.5, MS63 NGC.** Brassy-gold luster exudes from both sides of this octagonal dollar, each of which exhibits well struck design elements. Several cracks show on the reverse.(#10495)

Later State 1853 BG-518 Gold Dollar, MS64

3465 **1853 Liberty Octagonal 1 Dollar, BG-518, R.5, MS64 PCGS.** Die State II, with a die crack from the left corner of the bust to the rim, and numerous radial cracks originate at the center of the reverse. The letters DERI at the lower reverse refer to the minter, M. Deriberpie. Strongly lustrous and carefully preserved with a typical strike and lovely yellow-gold color. Population: 3 in 64, 0 finer (2/09).(#10495)

3466 **1853 Liberty Octagonal 1 Dollar, BG-530, R.2, MS63 NGC.** Well struck with lovely green-gold color and semiprooflike fields. A few wispy field marks keep it from an even higher grade. Census: 5 in 63, 2 finer (1/09).(#10507)

3467 **1853 Liberty Octagonal 1 Dollar, BG-531, R.4, MS62 NGC.** Well-defined with bright yellow-gold surfaces that are slightly pale. Though a number of wispy flaws affect the obverse fields, the reverse is comparatively well-preserved.(#10508)

Gorgeous 1870 Liberty 25 Cent
BG-757, MS64 Deep Prooflike

3468 **1870 Liberty Octagonal 25 Cents, BG-757, R.6, MS64 Deep Prooflike NGC.** Over the years, NGC has only certified six examples of the BG-757 variety, including two prooflike pieces and one deep prooflike example—the present specimen. It is a lovely green-gold example with excellent contrast. A splash of rose toning on the reverse adds to its overall eye appeal and desirability. (#710584)

3469 **1870 Goofy Head Octagonal 25 Cents, BG-789, R.4, MS66 NGC.** Well struck and free of any post-striking impairments, with just a slight degree of milkiness over the greenish-gold surfaces. The single finest-graded example of this scarce octagonal quarter dollar variety. Census: 1 in 66, 0 finer (2/09).(#10616)

3470 **1873 Indian Octagonal 25 Cents, BG-794, High R.5, MS64 PCGS.** An appealing near-Gem, bright yellow-gold with considerable mirrors. Impressively preserved for this rare variant. Population: 15 in 64, 1 finer (1/09).(#10621)

3471 **1876 Indian Octagonal 25 Cents, BG-799C, High R.4, MS65 PCGS.** Impressively reflective and well struck for the issue, though the flan shows a distinct curve. Housed in a green label holder. This Gem is tied for finest graded by NGC or PCGS (1/09). (#10629)

3472 **1859 Liberty Round 25 Cents, BG-801, R.3, MS65 PCGS.** Deep yellow-gold luster with hints of orange gracing the obverse. Well-defined and pleasingly preserved, a great coin housed in a green label holder. Population: 12 in 65, 0 finer (1/09).(#10662)

3473 **1870 Liberty Round 25 Cents, BG-808, R.3, MS65 PCGS.** A reflective honey-gold Gem that has hints of peach toning on the center of the portrait. Virtually flawless from a technical perspective, since no abrasions are detected. Certified in an old green label holder.(#10669)

3474 **1870 Liberty Round 25 Cents, BG-832, Low R.6, MS64 PCGS.** A beautiful yellow-gold near-Gem whose surfaces appear exemplary except for faint marks near the R in DOLLAR. This rare variety round quarter is certified in a green label holder. Population: 1 in 64, 1 finer (2/09).(#10693)

3475 **1871 Liberty Round 25 Cents, BG-840, Low R.4, MS65 Deep Prooflike NGC.** Profoundly reflective with pale yellow-gold surfaces that reflect the high polish of the devices. The strike is crisp for the issue.

3476 **1876 Indian Round 25 Cents, BG-849, High R.5, MS64 PCGS.** A bright green-gold example with prooflike fields and minimal surface disturbances. Some of the design elements are softly struck, as usual, including 1 and 76 in the date, and the A in DOLLAR. Population: 5 in 64, 0 finer (2/09).(#10710)

3477 **1874 Indian Round 25 Cents, BG-875, High R.4, MS66 NGC.** Misattributed by NGC as BG-876. The prooflike surfaces are highly attractive, and exhibit lovely green-gold and orange coloration. Impeccably preserved on both sides. If reattributed as BG-875, this would be the single finest-graded example at NGC.(#10736)

3478 **1874 Indian Round 25 Cents, BG-875, High R.4, MS65 Prooflike NGC.** Significantly reflective despite the inherently uneven texture of the obverse. Crisply struck and gleaming, a pleasing example of this elusive issue.(#710736)

3479 **1875 Indian Round 25 Cents, BG-878, R.3, MS65 Deep Prooflike NGC.** BG-878, R.3. Die State II. An impressive example with deeply mirrored fields set against frosty devices. This issue is highly elusive with Deep Prooflike surfaces.(#10739)

3480 **1876 Indian Round 25 Cents, BG-882, R.7, MS65 Prooflike NGC.** Well struck with glassy, highly reflective fields and impressively preserved surfaces. A rare die variety, and tied with one other piece as the finest-graded Prooflike example at NGC, as of (2/09).(#710743)

3481 **1872 Liberty Octagonal 50 Cents, BG-914, R.4, MS64 Prooflike NGC.** Pale green-gold fields are profoundly reflective. A well-defined example that is minimally marked and highly desirable. (#710772)

3482 **1870 Liberty Octagonal 50 Cents, BG-922, R.3, MS65 Prooflike NGC.** A gorgeous piece with astonishing reflectivity in the fields and deep green-gold toning. The single finest-graded example of this scarcer variety graded by NGC. Census: 1 in 65 Cameo, 0 finer (2/09).(#710780)

3483 **1872 Indian Octagonal 50 Cents, BG-939, Low R.5, MS64 PCGS.** Profoundly mirrored with few marks, an appealing example of this popular octagonal half. Solid striking definition complements the luster. Population: 14 in 64, 1 finer (1/09).(#10797)

3484 **1876 Indian Octagonal 50 Cents, BG-949, R.4, MS65 Prooflike NGC.** An amazingly fine example of this scarce variety, with sea-green color in the watery fields, and bright, frosted golden devices. Crisply struck and well preserved. Census: 3 in 65 Prooflike, 0 finer (2/09).(#710807)

3485 **1868 Indian Octagonal 50 Cents, BG-960A, High R.6, MS64 PCGS.** CAL. is all but effaced on this variant of the also rare BG-960. First published in the March 1884 *Coin Collector's Journal*. The design elements are sharply defined, save for CAL. Green-gold surfaces display smooth reflective fields. Population: 1 in 64, 1 finer (2/09).(#10829)

3486 **1871 Liberty Round 50 Cents, BG-1011, R.2, MS66 NGC.** Strong, swirling luster is the hallmark of this green-gold Premium Gem. Well-defined with smooth and carefully preserved surfaces. Census: 5 in 66, 0 finer (1/09).(#10840)

Scarce 1860/56 Overdate Gold 50 Cent, BG-1014, MS65

3487 **1860/56 Liberty Round 50 Cents, BG-1014, High R.4, MS65 PCGS.** Struck by Robert B. Gray & Co., described by Breen-Gillio as "successors to Antoine Louis Nouizillet." The dies for Nouizillet's Period One BG-434 were re-used and overdated for the Period Two BG-1014 issue. This yellow-gold piece is well struck and nearly devoid of contact. The reverse has a network of fine die cracks. One of two Gems graded by PCGS, with none finer (2/09). (#10843)

3488 **1871 Liberty Round 50 Cents, BG-1045, R.5, MS64 NGC.** Gleaming yellow-gold surfaces show hints of orange. A well struck example that offers high preservation for this rare variant. (#10874)

3489 **1875 Indian Round 50 Cents, BG-1056, High R.4, MS65 Deep Prooflike NGC.** A network of fine die cracks traverses the reverse of this formidably mirrored Gem. The devices are frosty and display deep cameo contrast. Outstanding eye appeal for this popular Indian 50 cent variety.(#710885)

Remarkable Prooflike Premium Gem
1872 Octagonal Dollar, BG-1119

3490 **1872 Indian Octagonal 1 Dollar, BG-1119, High R.5, MS66 Prooflike NGC.** BG-1119, High R.5. This issue is distinguished from the similar BG-1120 variety by having a berry beneath the G in GOLD, along the upper right reverse periphery. This remarkable example is well struck and exhibits deeply reflective fields and sharply frosted devices, creating noteworthy cameo contrast on each side. Thick rim cuds are evident on the reverse near 10 and 2 o'clock, respectively. Surface distractions are minimal. Census: 2 in 66 Prooflike, 0 finer (2/09).(#10930)

3491 **1875 Indian Octagonal 1 Dollar, BG-1127, R.4, MS64 NGC.** A beautifully satiny, mattelike example with olive-khaki and gold toning. Boldly struck, save for LA in DOLLAR, and free of distracting marks.(#10938)

Impressive 1871 BG-1204 Gold Dollar
MS64 Deep Prooflike

3492 **1871 Liberty Round 1 Dollar, BG-1204, High R.5, MS64 Deep Prooflike NGC. CAC.** NGC has only certified three examples of BG-1204, one each in MS62PL, MS63PL, and the current MS64 DPL (2/09). Peach-gold surfaces exhibit fairly well struck design features, except for Liberty's crown and forehead curls, and the bow above the knot. Deeply mirrored fields highlight the motifs, enhancing the coin's eye appeal. The center of the reverse shows a few shallow roller marks that were not struck out of the coin at the time of production. A few minor handling marks do not disturb the overall pleasing appearance of this high grade piece. (#710949)

1870 'Goofy Head' Round Dollar
BG-1205, AU58

3493 **1870 Goofy Head Round 1 Dollar, BG-1205, High R.4, AU58 NGC.** One of the only eight varieties of Period Two Round gold dollars, here in a nice near-Mint State condition. The "Goofy Head" appellation, of course, comes from the somewhat androgynous, lantern-jawed representation of Liberty. Only lightly circulated. A small scrape appears in the obverse field behind the head. Census: 3 in 58, 5 finer (2/09).(#10950)

3494 **1872 Indian Round 1 Dollar, BG-1207, R.4, AU58 PCGS.** The flashy fields retain nearly all of their initial luster, but the Indian's cheek and hair has a hint of wear. The design elements are quite well brought up, except for minor weakness in the reverse center. A few minor circulation marks do not detract. Only eight Period Two round dollar varieties were struck. Population: 11 in 58, 57 finer (2/09).(#10952)

End of Session 4

Heritage Auction Galleries Staff

Steve Ivy - Co-Chairman and CEO

Steve Ivy began collecting and studying rare coins in his youth, and as a teenager in 1963 began advertising coins for sale in national publications. Seven years later, at the age of twenty, he opened Steve Ivy Rare Coins in downtown Dallas, and in 1976, Steve Ivy Numismatic Auctions was incorporated. Steve managed the business as well as serving as chief numismatist, buying and selling hundreds of millions of dollars of coins during the 1970s and early 1980s. In early 1983, James Halperin became a full partner, and the name of the corporation was changed to Heritage Rare Coin Galleries. Steve's primary responsibilities now include management of the marketing and selling efforts of the company, the formation of corporate policy for long-term growth, and corporate relations with financial institutions. He remains intimately involved in numismatics, attending all major national shows. Steve engages in daily discourse with industry leaders on all aspects of the rare coin/currency business, and his views on grading, market trends and hobby developments are respected throughout the industry. He serves on the Board of Directors of the Professional Numismatists Guild (and was immediate past president), is the current Chairman of The Industry Council for Tangible Assets, and is a member of most leading numismatic organizations. Steve's keen appreciation of history is reflected in his active participation in other organizations, including past or present board positions on the Texas Historical Foundation and the Dallas Historical Society (where he also served as Exhibits Chairman). Steve is an avid collector of Texas books, manuscripts, and national currency, and he owns one of the largest and finest collections in private hands. He is also a past Board Chair of Dallas Challenge, and is currently the Finance Chair of the Phoenix House of Texas.

James Halperin - Co-Chairman

Jim Halperin and the traders under his supervision have transacted billions of dollars in rare coin business, and have outsold all other numismatic firms every year for over two decades. Born in Boston in 1952, Jim attended Middlesex School in Concord from 1966 to 1970. At the age of 15, he formed a part-time rare coin business after discovering that he had a knack (along with a nearly photographic memory) for coins. Jim scored a perfect 800 on his math SATs and received early acceptance to Harvard College, but after attending three semesters, he took a permanent leave of absence to pursue his full-time numismatic career. In 1975, Jim personally supervised the protocols for the first mainframe computer system in the numismatic business, which would catapult New England Rare Coin Galleries to the top of the industry in less than four years. In 1983, Jim's business merged with that of his friend and former archrival Steve Ivy. Their partnership has become the world's largest and most successful numismatic company, as well as the third-largest auctioneer in America. Jim remains arguably the best "eye" in the coin business today (he won the professional division of the PCGS World Series of Grading). In the mid-1980s, he authored "How to Grade U.S. Coins" (now posted on the web at www.CoinGrading.com), a highly-acclaimed text upon which the NGC and PCGS grading standards would ultimately be based. Jim is a bit of a Renaissance man, as a well-known futurist, an active collector of EC comics and early 20th-century American art (visit www.jhalpe.com), venture capital investor, philanthropist (he endows a multimillion-dollar health education foundation), and part-time novelist. His first fictional novel, "The Truth Machine," was published in 1996 and became an international science fiction bestseller, and was optioned for movie development by Warner Brothers. Jim's second novel, "The First Immortal," was published in early 1998 and immediately optioned as a Hallmark Hall of Fame television miniseries.

Greg Rohan - President

At the age of eight, Greg Rohan started collecting coins as well as buying them for resale to his schoolmates. By 1971, at the age of 10, he was already buying and selling coins from a dealer's table at trade shows in his hometown of Seattle. His business grew rapidly, and by 1985 he had offices in both Seattle and Minneapolis. He joined Heritage in 1987 as Executive Vice-President and Manager of the firm's rare coin business. Today, as an owner and as President of Heritage, his responsibilities include overseeing the firm's private client group and working with top collectors in every field in which Heritage is active. Greg has been involved with many of the rarest items and most important collections handled by the firm, including the purchase and/or sale of the Ed Trompeter Collection (the world's largest numismatic purchase according to the Guinness Book of World Records), the legendary 1894 San Francisco Dime, the 1838 New Orleans Half Dollar, and the 1804 Silver Dollar. During his career, Greg has handled more than $1 billion of rare coins, collectibles and art, and provided expert consultation concerning the authenticity and grade condition of coins for the Professional Coin Grading Service (PCGS). He has provided expert testimony for the United States Attorneys in San Francisco, Dallas, and Philadelphia, and for the Federal Trade Commission (FTC). He has worked with collectors, consignors, and their advisors regarding significant collections of books, manuscripts, comics, currency, jewelry, vintage movie posters, sports and entertainment memorabilia, decorative arts, and fine art. Additionally, Greg is a Sage Society member of the American Numismatic Society, and a member/life member of the PNG, ANA, and most other leading numismatic organizations. Greg is also Chapter Chairman for North Texas of the Young Presidents' Organization (YPO), and is an active supporter of the arts. Greg co-authored "The Collectors Estate Handbook," winner of the NLG's Robert Friedberg Award for numismatic book of the year. Mr. Rohan currently serves on the seven-person Advisory Board to the Federal Reserve Bank of Dallas, in his second appointed term.

Paul Minshull - Chief Operating Officer

As Chief Operating Officer, Paul Minshull's managerial responsibilities include integrating sales, personnel, inventory, security and MIS for Heritage. His major accomplishments include overseeing the hardware migration from mainframe to PC, the software migration of all inventory and sales systems, and implementation of a major Internet presence. Heritage's successful employee-suggestion program has generated 200 or more ideas each month since 1995, and has helped increase employee productivity, expand business, and improve employee retention. Paul oversees the company's highly-regarded IT department, and has been the driving force behind Heritage's Web development, now a significant portion of Heritage's future plans. As the only numismatic auction house that combines traditional floor bidding with active Internet bidding, the totally interactive system has catapulted Heritage to the top rare coin Web site (according to Forbes Magazine's "Best of the Web"). Paul came to Heritage in 1984. Since 1987, he has been a general partner in Heritage Capital Properties, Sales Manager, Vice President of Operations, and Chief Operating Officer for all Heritage companies and affiliates since 1996.

Todd Imhof - Vice President
Todd Imhof did not start collecting coins in his teens, unlike most professional numismatists. Shortly after graduating college, Todd declined an offer from a prestigious Wall Street bank to join a former high school classmate in his small rare coin firm in the Seattle area. In the mid-1980s, the rare coin industry was rapidly changing, with the advent of third-party grading and growing computer technologies; as a newcomer, Todd more easily embraced these new dynamics. In 1991, he co-founded Pinnacle Rarities, a firm specialized in servicing the savviest and most prominent collectors in numismatics. At 25, he was accepted into the PNG, and currently serves on its Consumer Protection Committee and its Legislation/Taxation Issues Committee. In 1992, he was invited to join the Board of Directors for the Industry Council for Tangible Assets, later serving as its Chairman (2002-2005).

Leo Frese - Vice President
Leo has been involved in numismatics for nearly 40 years, a professional numismatist since 1971, and has been with Heritage for more than 20 years. He literally worked his way up the Heritage "ladder," working with Bob Merrill for nearly 15 years, then becoming Director of Consignments. Leo has been actively involved in assisting clients sell nearly $500,000,000 in numismatic material. Leo was recently accepted as a member of PNG, is a life member of the ANA, and holds membership in FUN, CSNS, and other numismatic organizations.

Jim Stoutjesdyk - Vice President
Jim Stoutjesdyk was named Vice President of Heritage Rare Coin Galleries in 2004. He was named ANA's Outstanding Young Numismatist of the Year in 1987. A University of Michigan graduate, he was first employed by Superior Galleries, eventually becoming their Director of Collector Sales. Since joining Heritage in 1993, Jim has served in many capacities. Jim's duties now include buying and selling, pricing all new purchases, assisting with auction estimates and reserves, and overseeing the daily operations of the rare coin department.

Norma L. Gonzalez - VP of Auction Operations
Norma Gonzalez joined the U.S. Navy in August of 1993 and received her Bachelor's Degree in Resource Management. She joined Heritage in 1998 and was promoted to Vice President in 2003. She currently manages the operations departments, including Coins, Currency, World & Ancient Coins, Sportscards & Memorabilia, Comics, Movie Posters, Pop Culture and Political Memorabilia.

Debbie Rexing - VP - Marketing
Debbie's marketing credentials include degrees in Business Administration in Marketing and Human Resource Management from The Ohio State University, as well as sales and brand development experience for General Foods and Proctor & Gamble. After joining Heritage in 2001, Debbie became an integral part of the marketing teams involved with Heritage's most exciting and successful specialties, including U.S. Coins, World Coins, Currency, Music & Entertainment, Vintage Movie Posters, Americana, and U.S. Tangibles Inc. Her varied responsibilities included cross-functional coordination of photography, auction logistics, and marketing.

Ron Brackemyre - Vice President
Ron Brackemyre began his career at Heritage Auction Galleries in 1998 as the Manager of the Shipping Department, and was promoted to Consignment Operations Manager for Numismatics in 2004. He is responsible for the security of all of Heritage's coin and currency consignments, both at the Dallas world headquarters and at shows. His department also coordinates the photography, scanning, and cataloging of coins for upcoming auctions; coordination of auction planning; security and transportation logistics, and lot-view and auction prep.

Marti Korver - Manager - Credit/Collections
Marti Korver was recruited out of the banking profession by Jim Ruddy, and she worked with Paul Rynearson, Karl Stephens, and Judy Cahn on ancients and world coins at Bowers & Ruddy Galleries, in Hollywood, CA. She migrated into the coin auction business, and represented bidders as agent at B&R auctions for 10 years. She also worked as a research assistant for Q. David Bowers for several years.

Coin Department Specialists

David Mayfield - Vice President, Numismatics
David Mayfield has been collecting and trading rare coins and currency for over 35 years. A chance encounter with his father's coin collection at the age of nine led to his lifetime interest. David has been buying and selling at coin shows since the age of 10. He became a full time coin and currency dealer in the mid-1980s. David's main collecting interest is in all things Texas, specializing in currency and documents from the Republic of Texas.

Jim Jelinski - Consignment Director
Jim Jelinski has been involved in numismatics for more than five decades as a collector, dealer and educator. He started as Buyer for Paramount International Coin Corporation in 1972, opened Essex Numismatic Properties in 1975 in New Hampshire and has held numerous executive positions at M.B. Simmons & Associates of Narberth, Pennsylvania He works at Heritage as a Senior Numismatist and Consignment Coordinator.

Bob Marino - Consignment Director & Senior Numismatist
Bob Marino joined Heritage in 1999, managing and developing Internet coin sales, and building Heritage's client base through eBay and other Internet auction Web sites. He has successfully concluded more than 40,000 transactions on eBay. He is now a Consignment Director, assisting consignors in placing their coins and collectibles in the best of the many Heritage venues. .

Sam Foose - Consignment Director and Auctioneer
Sam Foose joined Heritage Numismatic Auctions, Inc., in 1993 as an Auction Coordinator. He rose to Assistant Auction Director in 1998, and began calling auctions. After a stint serving as a Senior Manager and Consignment Director in other collectible fields, he returned to Heritage in 2002 as a Consignment Director to help Heritage's expansion into other collectibles fields. Besides calling auctions as one of Heritage's primary auctioneers, he travels the nation assisting clients who wish to liquidate their collections of coins, paper money, decorative arts, and sports collectibles.

David Lindvall - Consignment Director
David Lindvall's career in numismatics started in 1973 at International Coin of Minneapolis. He joined the Heritage Wholesale Division in 1988, ultimately rising to become Manager. David joined Heritage's Consignment Director team, where he brings his lifetime of numismatic experience to benefit Heritage clients. David is a Life Member of the American Numismatic Association, and it seems at times that he has spent his entire life traveling to coin shows across America.

Katherine Kurachek - Consignment Director
Katherine Kurachek graduated from the University of Mississippi in 1993 as an art major. She came to Heritage in January 2003, working alongside Leo Frese for several years, learning the numismatic wholesale trade. Katherine frequently travels to coin shows to represent Heritage and service her dealer accounts along with her wide ranging duties as Consignment Director.

Shaunda Fry - Consignment Director
Shaunda Fry ran her own textile company for 22 years before meeting Leo Frese while co-coordinating a local school auction. She followed his suggestion to add auctioneering to her list of talents. After training, she worked part-time at Heritage's auctions and began to call, and auction excitement inspired a career change. She is now a Consignment Director, and travels to shows on the "Wholesale Dealers Team." Outside of work you might see Shaunda bungee jumping, singing karaoke, baking, reading, or jumping out of airplanes; if you see her inside the plane, chances are that she will be calling an auction or gathering consignments.

Mike Sadler - Consignment Director
Mike Sadler joined the Heritage team in September 2003. He attended the United States Air Force Academy, flew jets for the military and is a longtime pilot with American Airlines. Before coming to Heritage, his unlimited access to air travel enabled Mike to attend coin shows around the nation, and to build a world class collection that was auctioned by Heritage in 2004. He is known for his tremendous knowledge of rare coins, making him a trusted colleague to many of today's most active collectors.

Cataloged by: Mark Van Winkle, Chief Cataloger
Mark Borckardt, Senior Numismatist; Jon Amato, John Beety, George Huber, Brian Koller, John Salyer, David Stone
Edited by: Mark Van Winkle, John Beety, George Huber, Stewart Huckaby
Operations Support by: Cristina Gonzales, Miguel Reynaga Sr., Edna Lopez, Alma Villa, Maria Flores, Celeste Robertson, Manuela Bueno, Cristina Ibarra, Maria Jimenez
Catalog and Internet Imaging by: Travis Awalt, Joel Gonzalez, Colleen McInerney, Tony Webb, Jason Young
Production and Design by: Carl Watson, Matt Pegues, Mary Hermann, Mark Masat, Debbie Rexing

Doug Nyholm - Consignment Director
Doug Nyholm is a lifelong collector with an expertise in all U.S. coins and varieties, as well as a sub-specialty in U.S. Federal Currency and obsoletes. He is a noted numismatic writer and, in 2004, wrote and published *The History of Mormon Currency* and has authored many articles on Kirtland currency, scrip and related Utah items. He is currently writing several additional books including one on Utah National Banknotes. Doug was the President of the Utah Numismatic Society for 2006-07. His current collecting interests include Capped Bust & Seated half dollars, U.S. Type, and Mormon coins & currency.

Jason Friedman - Consignment Director
Jason's interest in rare coins, which began at 12 and expanded into his own numismatic business, allowed him to pay for most of his college tuition at the University of North Texas, from which he graduated in 2005. He joined Heritage soon after. He is a member of the American Numismatic Association (ANA) and Florida United Numismatists (FUN).

Dennis Nowicki - Consignment Director
Dennis Nowicki began his numismatic career as the Auction Manager for Bowers and Ruddy Galleries/American Auction Association in the mid-1970s. In the 1990s, he joined Heritage as webmaster/designer, garnering the NLG's Outstanding Web Site award. Dennis later designed and supported Web sites for several numismatic firms and worked cataloging lots, as well. He recently returned to Heritage as a Consignment Director and cataloger for the US and World coin departments.

Mark Van Winkle - Chief Cataloger
Mark has worked for Heritage, and Steve Ivy, since 1979. He has been Chief Cataloger since 1990, and has handled some of the premier numismatic rarities sold at public auction. Mark was editor of Legacy magazine, won the 1989 NLG award for Best U.S. Commercial Magazine, and has won numerous awards for his writing, including the 1990 NLG award for Best Article for his *Interview With John Ford*, the 1996 NLG Best Numismatic Article for *Changing Concepts of Liberty*. He has published extensively and written articles for *Coin World*, *Numismatic News* and has contributed to editions of the *Red Book*, *United States Patterns and Related Issues*, and *The Guide Book of Double Eagle Gold Coins*.

Mark Borckardt - Senior Cataloger
Mark started attending coin shows and conventions as a dealer in 1970, and has been a full-time professional numismatist since 1980. He received the Early American Coppers Literary Award, and the Numismatic Literary Guild's Book of the Year Award, for the *Encyclopedia of Early United States Cents, 1793-1814*, published in 2000. He serves as a contributor to *A Guide Book of United States Coins,* and has contributed to many references, including the Harry W. Bass, Jr. Sylloge, and the *Encyclopedia of Silver Dollars and Trade Dollars of the United States*. Most recently, he was Senior Numismatist with Bowers and Merena Galleries. Mark is a life member of the A. N. A., and an active member of numerous organizations.

Brian Koller - Cataloger & Catalog Production Manager
Brian Koller has been a Heritage cataloger since 2001, before that working as a telecom software engineer for 16 years. He is a graduate of Iowa State University with a Bachelor's degree in Computer Engineering, and is an avid collector of U.S. gold coins. His attention to detail ensures that every catalog, printed and on-line, is as error free as technology and human activity allows. In addition to his coin cataloging duties, he also helps with consignor promises and client service issues.

John Salyer - Cataloger
John Salyer has been a numismatist and coin cataloger with Heritage since 2002. He graduated from the University of Texas with a bachelor's degree in English. Prior to his numismatic employment, he worked primarily within the federal government and for several major airlines.

Dr. Jon Amato - Cataloger
Jon Amato has been with Heritage since 2004. He earned his Ph. D. from the University of Toronto, and was previously a Program Manager in the NY State Dept. of Economic Development, and an Adjunct Professor at the State University of New York at Albany. He is currently writing a monograph on the draped bust, small eagle half dollars of 1796-1797. He has published numerous articles in prestigious numismatic publications and belongs to many numismatic organizations, including the ANA, ANS, John Reich Collectors Society, and the Liberty Seated Collectors Club, and has made several presentations at ANA Numismatic Theaters.

John Dale Beety - Cataloger
John Dale Beety accepted a position with Heritage as a cataloger immediately after graduation from Rose-Hulman Institute of Technology, after serving an internship at Heritage during the summer of 2004. He grew up in Logansport, Indiana, a small town associated with several numismatic luminaries. Highlights as a Young Numismatist include attending Pittman III, four ANA Summer Seminars, and placing third in the 2001 World Series of Numismatics with Eric Li Cheung.

Auctioneer and Auction:

1. This Auction is presented by Heritage Auction Galleries, a d/b/a/ of Heritage Auctions, Inc., or its affiliates Heritage Numismatic Auctions, Inc., or Heritage Vintage Sports Auctions, Inc., or Currency Auctions of America, Inc., as identified with the applicable licensing information on the title page of the catalog or on the HA.com Internet site (the "Auctioneer"). The Auction is conducted under these Terms and Conditions of Auction and applicable state and local law. Announcements and corrections from the podium and those made through the Terms and Conditions of Auctions appearing on the Internet at HA.com supersede those in the printed catalog.

Buyer's Premium:

2. On bids placed through Auctioneer, a Buyer's Premium of fifteen percent (15%) will be added to the successful hammer price bid on lots in Coin and Currency auctions, or nineteen and one-half percent (19.5%) on lots in all other auctions. There is a minimum Buyer's Premium of $9.00 per lot. In Gallery Auctions (sealed bid auctions of mostly bulk numismatic material), the Buyer's Premium is 19.5%.

Auction Venues:

3. The following Auctions are conducted solely on the Internet: Heritage Weekly Internet Auctions (Coin, Currency, Comics, and Vintage Movie Poster); Heritage Monthly Internet Auctions (Sports, and Stamps). Signature® Auctions and Grand Format Auctions accept bids from the Internet, telephone, fax, or mail first, followed by a floor bidding session; Heritage Live and real-time telephone bidding are available to registered clients during these auctions.

Bidders:

4. Any person participating or registering for the Auction agrees to be bound by and accepts these Terms and Conditions of Auction ("Bidder(s)").
5. All Bidders must meet Auctioneer's qualifications to bid. Any Bidder who is not a client in good standing of the Auctioneer may be disqualified at Auctioneer's sole option and will not be awarded lots. Such determination may be made by Auctioneer in its sole and unlimited discretion, at any time prior to, during, or even after the close of the Auction. Auctioneer reserves the right to exclude any person from the auction.
6. If an entity places a bid, then the person executing the bid on behalf of the entity agrees to personally guarantee payment for any successful bid.

Credit:

7. Bidders who have not established credit with the Auctioneer must either furnish satisfactory credit information (including two collectibles-related business references) well in advance of the Auction or supply valid credit card information. Bids placed through our Interactive Internet program will only be accepted from pre-registered Bidders; Bidders who are not members of HA.com or affiliates should pre-register at least 48 hours before the start of the first session (exclusive of holidays or weekends) to allow adequate time to contact references. Credit may be granted at the discretion of Auctioneer. Additionally Bidders who have not previously established credit or who wish to bid in excess of their established credit history may be required to provide their social security number or the last four digits thereof to us so a credit check may be performed prior to Auctioneer's acceptance of a bid.

Bidding Options:

8. Bids in Signature® Auctions or Grand Format Auctions may be placed as set forth in the printed catalog section entitled "Choose your bidding method." For auctions held solely on the Internet, see the alternatives on HA.com. Review at HA.com/common/howtobid.php.
9. Presentment of Bids: Non-Internet bids (including but not limited to podium, fax, phone and mail bids) are treated similar to floor bids in that they must be on-increment or at a half increment (called a cut bid). Any podium, fax, phone, or mail bids that do not conform to a full or half increment will be rounded up or down to the nearest full or half increment and this revised amount will be considered your high bid.
10. Auctioneer's Execution of Certain Bids. Auctioneer cannot be responsible for your errors in bidding, so carefully check that every bid is entered correctly. When identical mail or FAX bids are submitted, preference is given to the first received. To ensure the greatest accuracy, your written bids should be entered on the standard printed bid sheet and be received at Auctioneer's place of business at least two business days before the Auction start. Auctioneer is not responsible for executing mail bids or FAX bids received on or after the day the first lot is sold, nor Internet bids submitted after the published closing time; nor is Auctioneer responsible for proper execution of bids submitted by telephone, mail, FAX, e-mail, Internet, or in person once the Auction begins. Internet bids may not be withdrawn until your written request is received and acknowledged by Auctioneer (FAX: 214-4438425); such requests must state the reason, and may constitute grounds for withdrawal of bidding privileges. Lots won by mail Bidders will not be delivered at the Auction unless prearranged.
11. Caveat as to Bid Increments. Bid increments (over the current bid level) determine the lowest amount you may bid on a particular lot. Bids greater than one increment over the current bid can be any whole dollar amount. It is possible under several circumstances for winning bids to be between increments, sometimes only $1 above the previous increment. Please see: "How can I lose by less than an increment?" on our website. Bids will be accepted in whole dollar amounts only. No "buy" or "unlimited" bids will be accepted.

The following chart governs current bidding increments.

Current Bid	Bid Increment	Current Bid	Bid Increment
<$10	$1	$20,000 - $29,999	$2,000
$10 - $29	$2	$30,000 - $49,999	$2,500
$30 - $49	$3	$50,000 - $99,999	$5,000
$50 - $99	$5	$100,000 - $199,999	$10,000
$100 - $199	$10	$200,000 - $299,999	$20,000
$200 - $299	$20	$300,000 - $499,999	$25,000
$300 - $499	$25	$500,000 - $999,999	$50,000
$500 - $999	$50	$1,000,000 - $1,999,999	$100,000
$1,000 - $1,999	$100	$2,000,000 - $2,999,999	$200,000
$2,000 - $2,999	$200	$3,000,000 - $4,999,999	$250,000
$3,000 - $4,999	$250	$5,000,000 - $9,999,999	$500,000
$5,000 - $9,999	$500	>$10,000,000	$1,000,000
$10,000 - $19,999	$1,000		

12. If Auctioneer calls for a full increment, a bidder may request Auctioneer to accept a bid at half of the increment ("Cut Bid") only once per lot. After offering a Cut Bid, bidders may continue to participate only at full increments. Off-increment bids may be accepted by the Auctioneer at Signature® Auctions and Grand Format Auctions. If the Auctioneer solicits bids other than the expected increment, these bids will not be considered Cut Bids.

Conducting the Auction:

13. Notice of the consignor's liberty to place bids on his lots in the Auction is hereby made in accordance with Article 2 of the Texas Business and Commercial Code. A "Minimum Bid" is an amount below which the lot will not sell. THE CONSIGNOR OF PROPERTY MAY PLACE WRITTEN "Minimum Bids" ON HIS LOTS IN ADVANCE OF THE AUCTION; ON SUCH LOTS, IF THE HAMMER PRICE DOES NOT MEET THE "Minimum Bid", THE CONSIGNOR MAY PAY A REDUCED COMMISSION ON THOSE LOTS. "Minimum Bids" are generally posted online several days prior to the Auction closing. For any successful bid placed by a consignor on his Property on the Auction floor, or by any means during the live session, or after the "Minimum Bid" for an Auction have been posted, we will require the consignor to pay full Buyer's Premium and Seller's Commissions on such lot.
14. The highest qualified Bidder recognized by the Auctioneer shall be the buyer. In the event of any dispute between any Bidders at an Auction, Auctioneer may at his sole discretion reoffer the lot. Auctioneer's decision and declaration of the winning Bidder shall be final and binding upon all Bidders. Bids properly offered, whether by floor Bidder or other means of bidding, may on occasion be missed or go unrecognized; in such cases, the Auctioneer may declare the recognized bid accepted as the winning bid, regardless of whether a competing bid may have been higher.
15. Auctioneer reserves the right to refuse to honor any bid or to limit the amount of any bid, in its sole discretion. A bid is considered not made in "Good Faith" when made by an insolvent or irresponsible person, a person under the age of eighteen, or is not supported by satisfactory credit, collectibles references, or otherwise. Regardless of the disclosure of his identity, any bid by a consignor or his agent on a lot consigned by him is deemed to be made in "Good Faith." Any person apparently appearing on the OFAC list is not eligible to bid.
16. Nominal Bids. The Auctioneer in its sole discretion may reject nominal bids, small opening bids, or very nominal advances. If a lot bearing estimates fails to open for 40–60% of the low estimate, the Auctioneer may pass the item or may place a protective bid on behalf of the consignor.
17. Lots bearing bidding estimates shall open at Auctioneer's discretion (approximately 50% of the low estimate). In the event that no bid meets or exceeds that opening amount, the lot shall pass as unsold.
18. All items are to be purchased per lot as numerically indicated and no lots will be broken. Auctioneer reserves the right to withdraw, prior to the close, any lots from the Auction.
19. Auctioneer reserves the right to rescind the sale in the event of nonpayment, breach of a warranty, disputed ownership, auctioneer's clerical error or omission in exercising bids and reserves, or for any other reason and in Auctioneer's sole discretion. In cases of nonpayment, Auctioneer's election to void a sale does not relieve the Bidder from their obligation to pay Auctioneer its fees (seller's and buyer's premium) and any other damages or expenses pertaining to the lot.
20. Auctioneer occasionally experiences Internet and/or Server service outages, and Auctioneer periodically schedules system downtime for maintenance and other purposes, during which Bidders cannot participate or place bids. If such outages occur, we may at our discretion extend bidding for the Auction. Bidders unable to place their Bids through the Internet are directed to contact Client Services at 1-800-872-6467.
21. The Auctioneer or its affiliates may consign items to be sold in the Auction, and may bid on those lots or any other lots. Auctioneer or affiliates expressly reserve the right to modify any such bids at any time prior to the hammer based upon data made known to the Auctioneer or its affiliates. The Auctioneer may extend advances, guarantees, or loans to certain consignors, and may extend financing or other credits at varying rates to certain Bidders in the auction.
22. The Auctioneer has the right to sell certain unsold items after the close of the Auction. Such lots shall be considered sold during the Auction and all these Terms and Conditions shall apply to such sales including but not limited to the Buyer's Premium, return rights, and disclaimers.

Payment:

23. All sales are strictly for cash in United States dollars (including U.S. currency, bank wire, cashier checks, travelers checks, eChecks, and bank money orders, all subject to reporting requirements). All are subject to clearing and funds being received In Auctioneer's account before delivery of the purchases. Auctioneer reserves the right to determine if a check constitutes "good funds" when drawn on a U.S. bank for ten days, and thirty days when drawn on an international bank. Credit Card (Visa or Master Card only) and PayPal payments may be accepted up to $10,000 from non-dealers at the sole discretion of the Auctioneer, subject to the following limitations: a) sales are only to the cardholder, b) purchases are shipped to the cardholder's registered and verified address, c) Auctioneer may pre-approve the cardholder's credit line, d) a credit card transaction may not be used in conjunction with any other financing or extended terms offered by the Auctioneer, and must transact immediately upon invoice presentation, e) rights of return are governed by these Terms and Conditions, which supersede those conditions promulgated by the card issuer, f) floor Bidders must present their card.
24. Payment is due upon closing of the Auction session, or upon presentment of an invoice. Auctioneer reserves the right to void an invoice if payment in full is not received within 7 days after the close of the Auction. In cases of nonpayment, Auctioneer's election to void a sale does not relieve the Bidder from their obligation to pay Auctioneer its fees (seller's and buyer's premium) on the lot and any other damages pertaining to the lot.
25. Lots delivered in the States of Texas, California, or other states where the Auction may be held, are subject to all applicable state and local taxes, unless appropriate permits are on file with Auctioneer. Bidder agrees to pay Auctioneer the actual amount of tax due in the event that sales tax is not properly collected due to: 1) an expired, inaccurate, inappropriate tax certificate or declaration, 2) an incorrect interpretation of the applicable statute, 3) or any other reason. The appropriate form or certificate must be on file at and verified by Auctioneer five days prior to Auction or tax must be paid; only if such form or certificate is received by Auctioneer within 4 days after the Auction can a refund of tax paid be made. Lots from different Auctions may not be aggregated for sales tax purposes.
26. In the event that a Bidder's payment is dishonored upon presentment(s), Bidder shall pay the maximum statutory processing fee set by applicable state law. If you attempt to pay via eCheck and your financial institution denies this transfer from your bank account, or the payment cannot be completed using the selected funding source, you agree to complete payment using your credit card on file.
27. If any Auction invoice submitted by Auctioneer is not paid in full when due, the unpaid balance will bear interest at the highest rate permitted by law from the date of invoice until paid. If the Auctioneer refers any invoice to an attorney for collection, the buyer agrees to pay attorney's fees, court costs, and other collection costs incurred by Auctioneer. If Auctioneer assigns collection to its in-house legal staff, such attorney's time expended on the matter shall be compensated at a rate comparable to the hourly rate of independent attorneys.

28. In the event a successful Bidder fails to pay any amounts due, Auctioneer reserves the right to sell the lot(s) securing the invoice to any underbidders in the Auction that the lot(s) appeared, or at subsequent private or public sale, or relist the lot(s) in a future auction conducted by Auctioneer. A defaulting Bidder agrees to pay for the reasonable costs of resale (including a 10% seller's commission, if consigned to an auction conducted by Auctioneer). The defaulting Bidder is liable to pay any difference between his total original invoice for the lot(s), plus any applicable interest, and the net proceeds for the lot(s) if sold at private sale or the subsequent hammer price of the lot(s) less the 10% seller's commissions, if sold at an Auctioneer's auction
29. Auctioneer reserves the right to require payment in full in good funds before delivery of the merchandise.
30. Auctioneer shall have a lien against the merchandise purchased by the buyer to secure payment of the Auction invoice. Auctioneer is further granted a lien and the right to retain possession of any other property of the buyer then held by the Auctioneer or its affiliates to secure payment of any Auction invoice or any other amounts due the Auctioneer or affiliates from the buyer. With respect to these lien rights, Auctioneer shall have all the rights of a secured creditor under Article 9 of the Texas Uniform Commercial Code, including but not limited to the right of sale. In addition, with respect to payment of the Auction invoice(s), the buyer waives any and all rights of offset he might otherwise have against the Auctioneer and the consignor of the merchandise included on the invoice. If a Bidder owes Auctioneer or its affiliates on any account, Auctioneer and its affiliates shall have the right to offset such unpaid account by any credit balance due Bidder, and it may secure by possessory lien any unpaid amount by any of the Bidder's property in their possession.
31. Title shall not pass to the successful Bidder until all invoices are paid in full. It is the responsibility of the buyer to provide adequate insurance coverage for the items once they have been delivered to a common carrier or third-party shipper.

Delivery; Shipping; and Handling Charges:

32. Buyer is liable for shipping and handling. Please refer to Auctioneer's website www.HA.com/common/shipping.php for the latest charges or call Auctioneer. Auctioneer is unable to combine purchases from other auctions or affiliates into one package for shipping purposes. Lots won will be shipped in a commercially reasonable time after payment in good funds for the merchandise and the shipping fees is received or credit extended, except when third-party shipment occurs.
33. Successful international Bidders shall provide written shipping instructions, including specified customs declarations, to the Auctioneer for any lots to be delivered outside of the United States. NOTE: Declaration value shall be the item'(s) hammer price together with its buyer's premium and Auctioneer shall use the correct harmonized code for the lot. Domestic Buyers on lots designated for third-party shipment must designate the common carrier, accept risk of loss, and prepay shipping costs.
34. All shipping charges will be borne by the successful Bidder. Any risk of loss during shipment will be borne by the buyer following Auctioneer's delivery to the designated common carrier or third-party shipper, regardless of domestic or foreign shipment.
35. Due to the nature of some items sold, it shall be the responsibility for the successful bidder to arrange pick-up and shipping through third-parties; as to such items Auctioneer shall have no liability. Failure to pick-up or arrange shipping in a timely fashion (within ten days) shall subject Lots to storage and moving charges, including a $100 administration fee plus $10 daily storage for larger items and $5.00 daily for smaller items (storage fee per item) after 35 days. In the event the Lot is not removed within ninety days, the Lot may be offered for sale to recover any past due storage or moving fees, including a 10% Seller's Commission.
36. The laws of various countries regulate the import or export of certain plant and animal properties, including (but not limited to) items made of (or including) ivory, whalebone, turtleshell, coral, crocodile, or other wildlife. Transport of such lots may require special licenses for export, import, or both. Bidder is responsible for: 1) obtaining all information on such restricted items for both export and import; 2) obtaining all such licenses and/or permits. Delay or failure to obtain any such license or permit does not relieve the buyer of timely compliance with standard payment terms. For further information, please contact Bill Taylor at 800-872-6467 ext. 1280.
37. Any request for shipping verification for undelivered packages must be made within 30 days of shipment by Auctioneer.

Cataloging, Warranties and Disclaimers:

38. NO WARRANTY, WHETHER EXPRESSED OR IMPLIED, IS MADE WITH RESPECT TO ANY DESCRIPTION CONTAINED IN THIS AUCTION OR ANY SECOND OPINE. Any description of the items or second opine contained in this Auction is for the sole purpose of identifying the items for those Bidders who do not have the opportunity to view the lots prior to bidding, and no description of items has been made part of the basis of the bargain or has created any express warranty that the goods would conform to any description made by Auctioneer. Color variations can be expected in any electronic or printed imaging, and are not grounds for the return of any lot.
39. Auctioneer is selling only such right or title to the items being sold as Auctioneer may have by virtue of consignment agreements on the date of auction and disclaims any warranty of title to the Property. Auctioneer disclaims any warranty of merchantability or fitness for any particular purposes. All images, descriptions, sales data, and archival records are the exclusive property of Auctioneer, and may be used by Auctioneer for advertising, promotion, archival records, and any other uses deemed appropriate.
40. Translations of foreign language documents may be provided as a convenience to interested parties. Auctioneer makes no representation as to the accuracy of those translations and will not be held responsible for errors in bidding arising from inaccuracies in translation.
41. Auctioneer disclaims all liability for damages, consequential or otherwise, arising out of or in connection with the sale of any Property by Auctioneer to Bidder. No third party may rely on any benefit of these Terms and Conditions and any rights, if any, established hereunder are personal to the Bidder and may not be assigned. Any statement made by the Auctioneer is an opinion and does not constitute a warranty or representation. No employee of Auctioneer may alter these Terms and Conditions, and, unless signed by a principal of Auctioneer, any such alteration is null and void.
42. Auctioneer shall not be liable for breakage of glass or damage to frames (patent or latent); such defects, in any event, shall not be a basis for any claim for return or reduction in purchase price.

Release:

43. In consideration of participation in the Auction and the placing of a bid, Bidder expressly releases Auctioneer, its officers, directors and employees, its affiliates, and its outside experts that provide second opines, from any and all claims, cause of action, chose of action, whether at law or equity or any arbitration or mediation rights existing under the rules of any professional society or affiliation based upon the assigned description, or a derivative theory, breach of warranty express or implied, representation or other matter set forth within these Terms and Conditions of Auction or otherwise. In the event of a claim, Bidder agrees that such rights and privileges conferred therein are strictly construed as specifically declared herein; e.g., authenticity, typographical error, etc. and are the exclusive remedy. Bidder, by non-compliance to these express terms of a granted remedy, shall waive any claim against Auctioneer.
44. Notice: Some Property sold by Auctioneer are inherently dangerous e.g. firearms, cannons, and small items that may be swallowed or ingested or may have latent defects all of which may cause harm to a person. Purchaser accepts all risk of loss or damage from its purchase of these items and Auctioneer disclaims any liability whether under contract or tort for damages and losses, direct or inconsequential, and expressly disclaims any warranty as to safety or usage of any lot sold.

Dispute Resolution and Arbitration Provision:

45. By placing a bid or otherwise participating in the auction, Bidder accepts these Terms and Conditions of Auction, and specifically agrees to the alternative dispute resolution provided herein. Arbitration replaces the right to go to court, including the right to a jury trial.
46. Auctioneer in no event shall be responsible for consequential damages, incidental damages, compensatory damages, or any other damages arising or claimed to be arising from the auction of any lot. In the event that Auctioneer cannot deliver the lot or subsequently it is established that the lot lacks title, or other transfer or condition issue is claimed, In such cases the sole remedy shall be limited to rescission of sale and refund of the amount paid by Bidder; in no case shall Auctioneer's maximum liability exceed the high bid on that lot, which bid shall be deemed for all purposes the value of the lot. After one year has elapsed, Auctioneer's maximum liability shall be limited to any commissions and fees Auctioneer earned on that lot.
47. In the event of an attribution error, Auctioneer may at its sole discretion, correct the error on the Internet, or, if discovered at a later date, to refund the buyer's purchase price without further obligation.
48. Arbitration Clause: All controversies or claims under this Agreement or arising from or pertaining to: this Agreement or related documents, or to the Properties consigned hereunder, or the enforcement or interpretation hereof of this or any related agreements, or damage to Properties, payment, or any other matter, or because of an alleged breach, default or misrepresentation under the provisions hereof or otherwise, that cannot be settled amicably within one (1) month from the date of notification of either party to the other of such dispute or question, which notice shall specify the details of such dispute or question, shall be settled by final and binding arbitration by one arbitrator appointed by the American Arbitration Association ("AAA"). The arbitration shall be conducted in Dallas, Dallas County, Texas in accordance with the then existing Commercial Arbitration Rules of the AAA. The arbitration shall be brought within two (2) years of the alleged breach, default or misrepresentation or the claim is waived. The prevailing party (a party that is awarded substantial and material relief on its claim or defense) may be awarded its reasonable attorney's fees and costs. Judgment upon the award rendered by the arbitrator may be entered in any court having jurisdiction thereof; provided, however, that the law applicable to any controversy shall be the law of the State of Texas, regardless of its or any other jurisdiction's choice of law principles and under the provisions of the Federal Arbitration Act.
49. No claims of any kind can be considered after the settlements have been made with the consignors. Any dispute after the settlement date is strictly between the Bidder and consignor without involvement or responsibility of the Auctioneer.
50. In consideration of their participation in or application for the Auction, a person or entity (whether the successful Bidder, a Bidder, a purchaser and/or other Auction participant or registrant) agrees that all disputes in any way relating to, arising under, connected with, or incidental to these Terms and Conditions and purchases, or default in payment thereof, shall be arbitrated pursuant to the arbitration provision. In the event that any matter including actions to compel arbitration, construe the agreement, actions in aid or arbitration or otherwise needs to be litigated, such litigation shall be exclusively in the Courts of the State of Texas, in Dallas County, Texas, and if necessary the corresponding appellate courts. For such actions, the successful Bidder, purchaser, or Auction participant also expressly submits himself to the personal jurisdiction of the State of Texas.
51. These Terms & Conditions provide specific remedies for occurrences in the auction and delivery process. Where such remedies are afforded, they shall be interpreted strictly. Bidder agrees that any claim shall utilize such remedies; Bidder making a claim in excess of those remedies provided in these Terms and Conditions agrees that in no case whatsoever shall Auctioneer's maximum liability exceed the high bid on that lot, which bid shall be deemed for all purposes the value of the lot.

Miscellaneous:

52. Agreements between Bidders and consignors to effectuate a non-sale of an item at Auction, inhibit bidding on a consigned item to enter into a private sale agreement for said item, or to utilize the Auctioneer's Auction to obtain sales for non-selling consigned items subsequent to the Auction, are strictly prohibited. If a subsequent sale of a previously consigned item occurs in violation of this provision, Auctioneer reserves the right to charge Bidder the applicable Buyer's Premium and consignor a Seller's Commission as determined for each auction venue and by the terms of the seller's agreement.
53. Acceptance of these Terms and Conditions qualifies Bidder as a client who has consented to be contacted by Heritage in the future. In conformity with "do-not-call" regulations promulgated by the Federal or State regulatory agencies, participation by the Bidder is affirmative consent to being contacted at the phone number shown in his application and this consent shall remain in effect until it is revoked in writing. Heritage may from time to time contact Bidder concerning sale, purchase, and auction opportunities available through Heritage and its affiliates and subsidiaries.
54. Rules of Construction: Auctioneer presents properties in a number of collectible fields, and as such, specific venues have promulgated supplemental Terms and Conditions. Nothing herein shall be construed to waive the general Terms and Conditions of Auction by these additional rules and shall be construed to give force and effect to the rules in their entirety.

State Notices:

Notice as to an Auction in California. Auctioneer has in compliance with Title 2.95 of the California Civil Code as amended October 11, 1993 Sec. 1812.600, posted with the California Secretary of State its bonds for it and its employees, and the auction is being conducted in compliance with Sec. 2338 of the Commercial Code and Sec. 535 of the Penal Code.

Notice as to an Auction in New York City. These Terms and Conditions are designed to conform to the applicable sections of the New York City Department of Consumer Affairs Rules and Regulations as Amended. This is a Public Auction Sale conducted by Auctioneer. The New York City licensed Auctioneers are Kathleen Guzman, No.0762165, and Samuel W. Foose, No.0952360, who will conduct the Auction on behalf of Heritage Auctions, Inc. ("Auctioneer"). All lots are subject to: the consignor's right to bid thereon in accord with these Terms and Conditions of Auction, consignor's option to receive advances on their consignments, and Auctioneer, in its sole discretion, may offer limited extended financing to registered bidders, in accord with Auctioneer's internal credit standards. A registered bidder may inquire whether a lot is subject to an advance or reserve. Auctioneer has made advances to various consignors in this sale.

Notice as to an Auction in Texas. In compliance with TDLR rule 67.100(c)(1), notice is hereby provided that this auction is covered by a Recovery Fund administered by the Texas Department of Licensing and Regulation, P.O. Box 12157, Austin, Texas 78711 (512) 463-6599. Any complaints may be directed to the same address.

Rev. 11_18_08

Additional Terms & Conditions:
COINS & CURRENCY

COINS and CURRENCY TERM A: Signature® Auctions are not on approval. No certified material may be returned because of possible differences of opinion with respect to the grade offered by any third-party organization, dealer, or service. No guarantee of grade is offered for uncertified Property sold and subsequently submitted to a third-party grading service. There are absolutely no exceptions to this policy. Under extremely limited circumstances, (e.g. gross cataloging error) a purchaser, who did not bid from the floor, may request Auctioneer to evaluate voiding a sale: such request must be made in writing detailing the alleged gross error; submission of the lot to the Auctioneer must be pre-approved by the Auctioneer; and bidder must notify Ron Brackemyre (1-800-8726467 Ext. 1312) in writing of such request within three (3) days of the non-floor bidder's receipt of the lot. Any lot that is to be evaluated must be in our offices within 30 days after Auction. Grading or method of manufacture do not qualify for this evaluation process nor do such complaints constitute a basis to challenge the authenticity of a lot. AFTER THAT 30-DAY PERIOD, NO LOTS MAY BE RETURNED FOR REASONS OTHER THAN AUTHENTICITY. Lots returned must be housed intact in their original holder. No lots purchased by floor Bidders may be returned (including those Bidders acting as agents for others) except for authenticity. Late remittance for purchases may be considered just cause to revoke all return privileges.

COINS and CURRENCY TERM B: Auctions conducted solely on the Internet THREE (3) DAY RETURN POLICY: Certified Coin and Uncertified and Certified Currency lots paid for within seven days of the Auction closing are sold with a three (3) day return privilege. You may return lots under the following conditions: Within three days of receipt of the lot, you must first notify Auctioneer by contacting Client Service by phone (1-800-872-6467) or e-mail (Bid@HA.com), and immediately ship the lot(s) fully insured to the attention of Returns, Heritage, 3500 Maple Avenue, 17th Floor, Dallas TX 75219-3941. Lots must be housed intact in their original holder and condition. You are responsible for the insured, safe delivery of any lots. A non-negotiable return fee of 5% of the purchase price ($10 per lot minimum) will be deducted from the refund for each returned lot or billed directly. Postage and handling fees are not refunded. After the three-day period (from receipt), no items may be returned for any reason. Late remittance for purchases revokes these Return privileges.

COINS and CURRENCY TERM C: Bidders who have inspected the lots prior to any Auction, or attended the Auction, or bid through an Agent, will not be granted any return privileges, except for reasons of authenticity.

COINS and CURRENCY TERM D: Coins sold referencing a third-party grading service are sold "as is" without any express or implied warranty, except for a guarantee by Auctioneer that they are genuine. Certain warranties may be available from the grading services and the Bidder is referred to them for further details: Numismatic Guaranty Corporation (NGC), P.O. Box 4776, Sarasota, FL 34230; Professional Coin Grading Service (PCGS), PO Box 9458, Newport Beach, CA 92658; ANACS, 6555 S. Kenton St. Ste. 303, Englewood, CO 80111; and Independent Coin Grading Co. (ICG), 7901 East Belleview Ave., Suite 50, Englewood, CO 80111.

COINS and CURRENCY TERM E: Notes sold referencing a third-party grading service are sold "as is" without any express or implied warranty, except for guarantee by Auctioneer that they are genuine. Grading, condition or other attributes of any lot may have a material effect on its value, and the opinion of others, including third-party grading services such as PCGS Currency, PMG, and CGA may differ with that of Auctioneer. Auctioneer shall not be bound by any prior or subsequent opinion, determination, or certification by any grading service. Bidder specifically waives any claim to right of return of any item because of the opinion, determination, or certification, or lack thereof, by any grading service. Certain warranties may be available from the grading services and the Bidder is referred to them for further details: Paper Money Guaranty (PMG), PO Box 4711, Sarasota FL 34230; PCGS Currency, PO Box 9458, Newport Beach, CA 92658; Currency Grading & Authentication (CGA), PO Box 418, Three Bridges, NJ 08887. Third party graded notes are not returnable for any reason whatsoever.

COINS and CURRENCY TERM F: Since we cannot examine encapsulated coins or notes, they are sold "as is" without our grading opinion, and may not be returned for any reason. Auctioneer shall not be liable for any patent or latent defect or controversy pertaining to or arising from any encapsulated collectible. In any such instance, purchaser's remedy, if any, shall be solely against the service certifying the collectible.

COINS and CURRENCY TERM G: Due to changing grading standards over time, differing interpretations, and to possible mishandling of items by subsequent owners, Auctioneer reserves the right to grade items differently than shown on certificates from any grading service that accompany the items. Auctioneer also reserves the right to grade items differently than the grades shown in the prior catalog should such items be reconsigned to any future auction.

COINS and CURRENCY TERM H: Although consensus grading is employed by most grading services, it should be noted as aforesaid that grading is not an exact science. In fact, it is entirely possible that if a lot is broken out of a plastic holder and resubmitted to another grading service or even to the same service, the lot could come back with a different grade assigned.

COINS and CURRENCY TERM I: Certification does not guarantee protection against the normal risks associated with potentially volatile markets. The degree of liquidity for certified coins and collectibles will vary according to general market conditions and the particular lot involved. For some lots there may be no active market at all at certain points in time.

COINS and CURRENCY TERM J: All non-certified coins and currency are guaranteed genuine, but are not guaranteed as to grade, since grading is a matter of opinion, an art and not a science, and therefore the opinion rendered by the Auctioneer or any third party grading service may not agree with the opinion of others (including trained experts), and the same expert may not grade the same item with the same grade at two different times. Auctioneer has graded the non-certified numismatic items, in the Auctioneer's opinion, to their current interpretation of the American Numismatic Association's standards as of the date the catalog was prepared. There is no guarantee or warranty implied or expressed that the grading standards utilized by the Auctioneer will meet the standards of any grading service at any time in the future.

COINS and CURRENCY TERM K: Storage of purchased coins and currency: Purchasers are advised that certain types of plastic may react with a coin's metal or transfer plasticizer to notes and may cause damage. Caution should be used to avoid storage in materials that are not inert.

COINS and CURRENCY TERM L: Storage of purchased coins and currency: Purchasers are advised that certain types of plastic may react with a coin's metal or transfer plasticizer to notes and may cause damage. Caution should be used to avoid storage in materials that are not inert.

COINS and CURRENCY TERM M: NOTE: Purchasers of rare coins or currency through Heritage have available the option of arbitration by the Professional Numismatists Guild (PNG); if an election is not made within ten (10) days of an unresolved dispute, Auctioneer may elect either PNG or A.A.A. Arbitration.

COINS and CURRENCY TERM N: For more information regarding Canadian lots attributed to the Charlton reference guides, please contact: Charlton International, PO Box 820, Station Willowdale B, North York, Ontario M2K 2R1 Canada.

WIRING INSTRUCTIONS:
Bank Information: JP Morgan Chase Bank, N.A., 270 Park Avenue, New York, NY 10017
Account Name: HERITAGE NUMISMATIC AUCTIONS MASTER ACCOUNT
ABA Number: 021000021
Account Number: 1884827674
Swift Code: CHASUS33

Your five most effective bidding techniques:

1 Interactive Internet™ Proxy Bidding
(leave your maximum Bid at HA.com before the auction starts)

Heritage's exclusive Interactive Internet™ system is fun and easy! Before you start, you must register online at HA.com and obtain your Username and Password.

1. Login to the HA.com website, using your Username and Password.

2. Chose the specialty you're interested in at the top of the homepage (i.e. coins, currency, comics, movie posters, fine art, etc.).

3. Search or browse for the lots that interest you. Every auction has search features and a 'drop-down' menu list.

4. Select a lot by clicking on the link or the photo icon. Read the description, and view the full-color photography. Note that clicking on the image will enlarge the photo with amazing detail.

5. View the current opening bid. Below the lot description, note the historic pricing information to help you establish price levels. Clicking on a link will take you directly to our Permanent Auction Archives for more information and images.

6. If the current price is within your range, Bid! At the top of the lot page is a box containing the Current Bid and an entry box for your "Secret Maximum Bid" – the maximum amount you are willing to pay for the item before the Buyer's Premium is added. Click the button marked "Place Bid" (if you are not logged in, a login box will open first so you can enter your username (or e-mail address) and password.

7. After you are satisfied that all the information is correct, confirm your "Secret Maximum Bid" by clicking on the "Confirm Absentee Bid" button. You will receive immediate notification letting you know if you are now the top bidder, or if another bidder had previously bid higher than your amount. If you bid your maximum amount and someone has already bid higher, you will immediately know so you can concentrate on other lots.

8. Before the auction, if another bidder surpasses your "Secret Maximum Bid", you will be notified automatically by e-mail containing a link to review the lot and possibly bid higher.

9. Interactive Internet™ bidding closes at 10 P.M. Central Time the night before the session is offered in a floor event. Interactive Internet™ bidding closes two hours before live sessions where there is no floor bidding.

10. The Interactive Internet™ system generally opens the lot at the next increment above the second highest bid. As the high bidder, your "Secret Maximum Bid" will compete for you during the floor auction. Of course, it is possible in a Signature® or Grand Format live auction that you may be outbid on the floor or by a Heritage Live bidder after Internet bidding closes. Bid early, as the earliest bird wins in the event of a tie bid. For more information about bidding and bid increments, please see the section labeled "Bidding Increments" elsewhere in this catalog.

11. After the auction, you will be notified of your success. It's that easy!

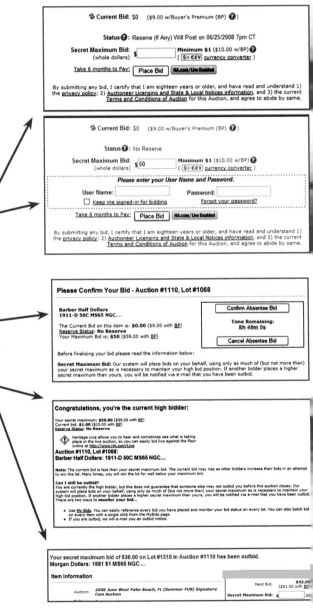

② HERITAGE Live!™ Bidding
(participate in the Live auction via the Internet)

1. Look on each auction's homepage to verify whether that auction is "HA.com/Live Enabled." All Signature® and Grand Format auctions use the HERITAGE Live!™ system, and many feature live audio and/or video. Determine your lots of interest and maximum bids.

2. Note on the auction's homepage the session dates and times (and especially time zones!) so you can plan your participation. You actually have two methods of using HERITAGE Live!™: a) you can leave a proxy bid through this system, much like the Interactive Internet™ (we recommend you do this before the session starts), or b) you can sit in front of your computer much as the audience is sitting in the auction room during the actual auction.

3. Login at HA.com/Live.

4. Until you become experienced (and this happens quickly!) you will want to login well before your lot comes up so you can watch the activity on other lots. It is as intuitive as participating in a live auction.

5. When your lot hits the auction block, you can continue to bid live against the floor and other live bidders by simply clicking the "Bid" button; the amount you are bidding is clearly displayed on the console.

③ Mail Bidding
(deposit your maximum Bid with the U.S.P.S. well before the auction starts)

Mail bidding at auction is fun and easy, but by eliminating the interactivity of our online systems, some of your bids may be outbid before you lick the stamp, and you will have no idea of your overall chances until the auction is over!

1. Look through the printed catalog, and determine your lots of interest.

2. Research their market value by checking price lists and other price guidelines.

3. Fill out your bid sheet, entering your maximum bid on each lot. Bid using whole dollar amounts only. Verify your bids, because you are responsible for any errors you make! Please consult the Bidding Increments chart in the Terms & Conditions.

4. Please fill out your bid sheet completely! We also need: a) Your name and complete address for mailing invoices and lots; b) Your telephone number if any problems or changes arise; c) Your references; if you have not established credit with Heritage, you must send a 25% deposit, or list dealers with whom you have credit established; d) Total your bid sheet; add up all bids and list that total in the box; e) Sign your bid sheet, thereby agreeing to abide by the Terms & Conditions of Auction printed in the catalog.

5. Mail early, because preference is given to the first bid received in case of a tie.

6. When bidding by mail, you frequently purchase items at less than your maximum bid. Bidding generally opens at the next published increment above the second highest mail or Internet bid previously received; if additional floor, phone, or HERITAGE Live!™ bids are made, we act as your agent, bidding in increments over any additional bid until you win the lot or are outbid. For example, if you submitted a bid of $750, and the second highest bid was $375, bidding would start at $400; if no other bids were placed, you would purchase the lot for $400.

7. You can also Fax your Bid Sheet if time is short. Use our exclusive Fax Hotline: 214-443-8425.

④ Telephone Bidding (when you are traveling, or do not have access to HERITAGE Live!™)

1. To participate in an auction by telephone, you must make preliminary arrangements with Client Services (Toll Free 866-835-3243) at least three days before the auction.

2. We strongly recommend that you place preliminary bids by mail or Internet if you intend to participate by telephone. On many occasions, this dual approach has reduced disappointments due to telephone (cell) problems, unexpected travel, late night sessions, and time zone differences. Keep a list of your preliminary bids, and we will help you avoid bidding against yourself.

⑤ Attend in Person (whenever possible)

Auctions are fun, and we encourage you to attend as many as possible – although our HERITAGE Live!™ system brings all of the action right to your computer screen. Auction dates and session times are printed on the title page of each catalog, and appear on the homepage of each auction at HA.com. Join us if you can!

Take 4 Months to Pay...

Heritage will Finance Your Purchase

We're collectors too, and we understand that on occasion there is more to buy than there is cash. Consider Heritage's Extended Payment Plan [EPP] for your purchases totaling $2,500 or more.

Extended Payment Plan [EPP] Conditions

- Minimum invoice total is $2,500.
- Minimum Down Payment is 25% of the total invoice.
- A signed and returned EPP Agreement is required.
- The EPP is subject to a 3% *fully refundable* Set-up Fee (based on the total invoice amount) payable as part of the first monthly payment.
- The 3% Set-up Fee is refundable provided all monthly payments are made by eCheck, bank draft, personal check drawn on good funds, or cash; and if all such payments are made according to the EPP schedule.
- Monthly payments can be automatically processed with an eCheck, Visa, or MasterCard.
- You may take up to four equal monthly payments to pay the balance.
- Interest is calculated at only 1% per month on the unpaid balance.
- Your EPP must be kept current or additional interest may apply.
- There is no penalty for paying off early.
- Shipment will be made when final payment is received.
- All traditional auction and sales policies still apply.

There is no return privilege once you have confirmed your sale, and penalties can be incurred on cancelled invoices. To avoid additional fees, you must make your down payment within 14 days of the auction. All material purchased under the EPP will be physically secured by Heritage until paid in full.

To exercise the EPP option, please notify **Eric Thomas** at **214.409.1241** or email at **EricT@HA.com** upon receipt of your invoice.

We appreciate your business and wish you good luck with your bidding.

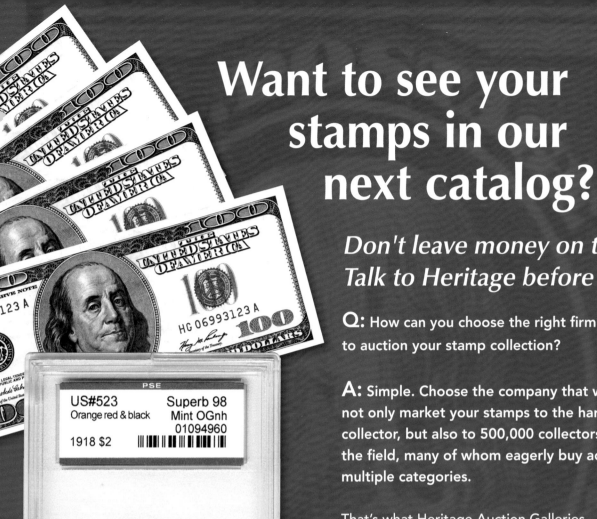

LONG BEACH
COIN, STAMP & COLLECTIBLES EXPO
Held at the Long Beach Convention Center

FUTURE SHOW DATES
May 28-30, 2009
Sept 10-12, 2009

Official Auctioneer

The World's #1 Numismatic Auctioneer
HERITAGE **HA.com**
Auction Galleries

Onsite Grading

Fun for the entire FAMILY! $$Multi-Million Dollar Exhibits$$! *Daily Gold Prize Drawings!*

Santa Clara
Coin, Stamp & Collectibles Expo
Held at the Santa Clara Convention Center

FUTURE SHOW DATES
April 2-5, 2009
November 19-22, 2009

Bring your Collectibles to our Expos for competitive offers from *America's Top Buyers.*

**FREE
Kids
Treasure Hunt**

www.exposunlimited.com

**FREE
Educational
Seminars**

www.longbeachexpo.com

EXPOS
UNLIMITED

www.santaclaraexpo.com

**A Division of Collectors Universe, Inc. Nasdaq; CLCT
8 West Figueroa Street Santa Barbara, CA 93101
Ph (805)962-9939 Fx (805)963-0827
Email: warreckert@collectors.com**